RAND ARROYO CENTER and
NATIONAL DEFENSE RESEARCH INSTITUTE

T0289423

The Deployment Life Study

Longitudinal Analysis of Military Families Across the Deployment Cycle

Sarah O. Meadows, Terri Tanielian, Benjamin R. Karney, editors

Prepared for the United States Army and the Office of the Secretary of Defense

For more information on this publication, visit www.rand.org/t/rr1388

Library of Congress Cataloging-in-Publication Data is available for this publication.

ISBN: 978-0-8330-9475-9

Published by the RAND Corporation, Santa Monica, Calif.

© Copyright 2016 RAND Corporation

RAND® is a registered trademark.

Support RAND
Make a tax-deductible charitable contribution at
www.rand.org/giving/contribute

www.rand.org

The Deployment Life Study Team

Principal Investigators
Terri L. Tanielian
Benjamin R. Karney
Sarah O. Meadows

Project Director
Karen Yuhas

Co-Investigators
Lynsay Ayer
Anita Chandra
Esther M. Friedman
Beth Ann Griffin
Lisa H. Jaycox
Rajeev Ramchand
Terry L. Schell
Thomas E. Trail
Wendy M. Troxel

**Survey Data Collection, Management,
and Programming Support**
Robin Beckman
Bernadette Benjamin
Josephine Levy
Adrian Montero
Julie Newell

Administrative Support
Donna White

Preface

In 2009, the RAND Corporation launched the Deployment Life Study, a longitudinal study of military families to examine family readiness. *Family readiness* has been referred to as the state of being prepared to effectively navigate the challenges of daily living experienced in the unique context of military service. The study surveyed families at frequent intervals throughout a complete deployment cycle—that is, before a service member deploys (sometimes months before), during the actual deployment, and after the service member returns (possibly a year or more after she or he has redeployed). It assessed outcomes over time, including the following:

- the quality of marital and parental relationships
- the psychological, behavioral, and physical health of family members
- child and teen well-being (e.g., emotional, behavioral, social, and academic)
- military integration (e.g., attitudes toward military service, retention intentions).

The Deployment Life Study used a single design and the same survey instruments to study military family members in the Army, Navy, Air Force, and Marine Corps (modified only slightly to make them service- and component-appropriate), thus allowing for potential comparisons across services and components (active, reserve, and guard).

Broadly, the Deployment Life Study is designed to address several policy questions. First, how are deployments associated with family well-being and overall functioning? Second, what family- and individual-level factors can account for both positive and negative adaptation to deployment (i.e., what constitutes family readiness)? And third, what policies and programs can DoD develop to help families navigate the stress associated with deployment?

This culminating report briefly reviews the study design and data collection procedures,[1] then addresses the policy questions posed by the study by presenting results from analyses of the longitudinal data collected from some 2,700 military families.

This research was jointly sponsored by the Office of the Surgeon General, U.S. Army, and by the Defense Centers of Excellence for Psychological Health and Traumatic Brain Injury. The work was conducted jointly within the RAND Arroyo Center's Army Personnel, Training, and Health Program and the Forces and Resources Policy Center of the RAND National Defense Research Institute. RAND Arroyo Center, part of the RAND Corporation, is a federally funded research and development center sponsored by the United States Army. The RAND National Defense Research Institute is a federally funded research and development

---

[1] For more detail on the study design, see, T. Tanielian, B. R. Karney, A. Chandra, and S. O. Meadows, *The Deployment Life Study: Methodological Overview and Baseline Sample Description*, Santa Monica, Calif.: RAND Corporation, RR-209-A/OSD, 2014.

center sponsored by the Office of the Secretary of Defense, the Joint Staff, the Unified Combatant Commands, the Navy, the Marine Corps, the defense agencies, and the defense Intelligence Community.

The Army Project Unique Identification Code (PUIC) for the project that produced this document is DASGP09144.

For more information on the RAND Forces and Resources Policy Center, see www.rand.org/nsrd/ndri/centers/frp or contact the director (contact information is provided on the web page).

Contents

Figures

Tables

Summary

Armed conflict between nations and groups usually requires those who fight to leave behind their families and loved ones. From the Greeks mounting their siege of Troy to the "Greatest Generation" preparing to enter World War II, the three phases of the deployment cycle—preparation, separation, and reintegration—have been a regular part of military life throughout the ages. Although many service members anticipate deployments, eager for the opportunity to defend their country and utilize their training, few look forward to time spent separated from spouses and children. Indeed, the separations required by deployments have long been described as one of the most stressful aspects of being a military family.

How are military families affected by the challenges of deployment? To what extent are service members and their loved ones able to maintain their individual health and interpersonal relationships in the face of lengthy separations? To what extent does the well-being of service members and their families change across the phases of the deployment cycle? The Deployment Life Study was designed to address these questions. The broad goal of the study was to gather data to evaluate the effects of deployment on service members, spouses, and their children. In particular, this study sought to identify which families are best able to withstand the strains of deployment and the kinds of coping strategies that characterize these families, and which families are most vulnerable to the negative consequences of deployment so that those families might be targeted for extra support.

The Deployment Life Study examined these issues by interviewing married service members, their spouses, and (when available) one child, multiple times across a three-year period, and across all phases of a deployment cycle. At baseline, the study recruited 2,724 Army, Air Force, Navy, and Marine Corps families. The sampling frame was restricted to cohabiting, married service members who were deemed eligible for deployment (by their respective services) within six to 12 months of the baseline survey. In each family, a service member, his or her spouse, and a child between the ages of 11 and 17 (if there was one in the household) each provided information independently. Interviewers obtained consent from each participating family member and conducted the baseline interviews by phone. Every four months thereafter, respondents logged into the study website and completed a follow-up survey online. Data collection included a total of nine waves spanning the entire deployment cycle, including periods of predeployment, deployment, and postdeployment. Each interview included instruments measuring a wide range of variables relevant to understanding how the social, economic, and psychological well-being of military families change across the deployment cycle. As a consequence of this breadth, the Deployment Life Study data set can serve as a resource for researchers from multiple disciplines and, more importantly, provide robust data with which to assess the association between deployment and military family health and well-being.

The data accumulated through these efforts are suitable for addressing a wide range of questions about the health and well-being of military families, but the following questions were priorities that guided the design of the study:

- *Controlling for initial conditions and functioning, how is deployment related to military family outcomes?* This study evaluated the association between deployment and a range of outcomes, including those relevant to the functioning of the entire family unit and outcomes relevant to understanding the well-being of each individual family member.
- *Across the phases of the deployment cycle—preparation, separation, and reintegration—how do the outcomes of military families change or remain stable over time?* This study is the first of which we are aware to describe changes before, during, and after deployment on a wide range of outcomes for multiple family members at once.
- *Across families that experience deployment, what accounts for variability in families' postdeployment outcomes? Of the factors accounting for such variability, which are the most important?* The implications of deployment are likely to vary significantly across families, and even across individuals within families. The Deployment Life Study assessed and analyzed the individual and family traits, resources, and circumstances that account for which families thrive after a deployment and which families suffer.

As described in this report, analyses focused on identifying the characteristics of more (or less) successful families over time, where success is defined in terms of a range of important outcomes that were measured at every assessment, including:

- quality of marital and parental relationships
- psychological, behavioral, and physical health of family members
- child and teen well-being (e.g., emotional, behavioral, social, and academic)
- military integration (e.g., attitudes toward military service, retention intentions).

Strengths of the Deployment Life Study

The Deployment Life Study has several unique characteristics that allow it to address issues that no other study to date can address as effectively.

Anchoring on Deployment

The primary rationale for conducting longitudinal research on military families is that longitudinal designs allow for estimates of changes in family outcomes after a deployment, controlling for preexisting differences between families prior to deployment. The greatest benefits of this design, therefore, arise from the power to observe families before and after a deployment cycle, and compare them with matched families that did not experience a deployment during the same period. The Deployment Life Study was designed to take advantage of the power of such analyses. Whereas the other ongoing longitudinal studies sampled from the general military population (some of whom may already be deployed and others of whom may never deploy over the course of a study), the Deployment Life Study sampled exclusively from the population of married service members eligible for deployment within the next six to 12 months. Moreover, to be eligible for the study, the service member could not be deployed at baseline.

Thus, baseline assessment of the Deployment Life sample was a true baseline for a sample highly likely to experience a deployment over the course of the study.

Repeated Assessments over Three Years

Military families may cope in different ways across different stages of the deployment cycle (i.e., functioning at predeployment may not be the same as functioning during deployment or postdeployment). Moreover, the consequences of deployments may evolve or fade as families adjust and restore their predeployment equilibrium. Even longitudinal studies risk missing or mischaracterizing these effects if the interval between assessments is too long or the duration of the entire study is too short. The Deployment Life Study was designed to produce higher-resolution descriptions of the deployment cycle than has been available in other studies by assessing families every four months over three years (nine assessments total). Because all families were recruited prior to a deployment, not only did this design allow for assessments of family functioning at each stage of the deployment cycle; in most cases, it allowed for *multiple* assessments at each stage, including multiple assessments shortly after a deployment. Thus, the Deployment Life Study is able to describe how families change within each stage of the cycle, how long changes associated with deployment last, and what characteristics of families prior to deployment predict a family's postdeployment return to equilibrium.

Data from Multiple Family Members

The vast majority of existing research on military families assesses family functioning exclusively through the reports of a single family member, usually the service member or the spouse. There are several reasons that reliance on the reports of a single family member offer only a limited window into family functioning across a deployment cycle. First, service members and spouses may use different resources to cope with deployment. Second, coping strategies that are effective for one member of a family may not be effective for another. Third, to the extent that mental health is an outcome of major importance and the rates of mental health problems in this population are relatively high, the perceptions of any single family member may be distorted in ways that are impossible to estimate. Fourth, to the extent that one family member is asked to describe outcomes for another family member (e.g., parents reporting on their children, service members reporting on their spouses), associations among responses can be inflated by shared method variance. The Deployment Life Study avoided these problems by obtaining responses from service members, their spouses, and one child between the ages of 11 and 17, if available.

The Historical Context of the Deployment Life Study—A Caveat

Interpretations of the results reported in this report must keep in mind the specific period in which this sample was assembled and the data were gathered. Support for this study was motivated by the severe increase in the pace of deployments for service members in the middle to later part of the 2000s. By the time this study was commissioned and data collection began, however, the period of peak deployments for the U.S. military had passed. The surge in Iraq, for example, took place in 2007–2008 and was followed by a gradual reduction in troop strength through the formal end of operations there in December 2011. Deployments to Afghanistan peaked in 2010, and have been declining ever since. Initial recruitment of the initial sample for the Deployment Life Study began in March 2011 and ended in August 2012 for the Army, Air Force, and Marine Corps sample, and began in November 2012 and ended in February 2013 for the Navy sample. The subsequent three years of longitudinal data collection ended for all samples by the summer of 2015. Thus, although the Deployment Life Study took place following a period of frequent and lengthy deployments for the U.S. military, those deployments were becoming less frequent during the data collection phase of the study.

This historical context has several important implications for understanding the Deployment Life Study data. First, by the time recruitment for the Deployment Life Study began, most married service members eligible for the study *had already been deployed* at least once before to support the current conflicts. As such, the consequences of deployment may have already been felt for most of the population from which the study sampled. This means that the military families vulnerable to experiencing the worst consequences from deployments may have left the population (either through separation from the military or through divorce) before the study began. By studying couples who remained married and serving in the military during this period, the Deployment Life Study was able to examine a sample of military families that had already endured and survived the worst of the recent operations. As a consequence, although the results reported here can be generalized to the current married population of the military (i.e., a population that has survived prior, and sometimes multiple, deployments), these results may not generalize to populations that have yet to be deployed and may underestimate the negative effects of deployment for the population of first-time deployers.

Second, during the period of the Deployment Life Study, deployments were, on average, shorter across all services and arguably less dangerous (because the combat zones were less volatile) than they had been earlier in the decade. During the period of data collection, the number and rates of injury and death among American troops were much lower than in prior years, and certainly significantly less than during the peak of combat operations.[1] Thus, the effects of deployment reported here may not reflect the effects experienced during the period of greatest demand on the military in the early to mid-2000s.

Summary of Findings

This report presents detailed findings across a number of important domains. Here, we summarize high-level findings across the major outcomes of interest.

Marital Relationships

We examined marital satisfaction, positive and negative affect, and psychological and physical aggression as reported by service members and spouses. Key findings include:

- Across the entire deployment cycle, couples, on average, become significantly less satisfied with their marriages and engage in less psychological and physical aggression than they reported prior to the deployment.

---

[1]   H. Fischer, *A Guide to U.S. Military Casualty Statistics: Operation Freedom's Sentinel, Operation Inherent Resolve, Operation New Dawn, Operation Iraqi Freedom, and Operation Enduring Freedom*, Washington, D.C.: Congressional Research Service, 2015.

- These changes in marital outcomes across the deployment cycle do not significantly differ from the changes experienced during the same period by matched couples that did not deploy.
- For spouses, more frequent communication with the service member during deployment predicts greater marital satisfaction postdeployment, controlling for baseline characteristics of the couple.
- Service members' exposure to physical (e.g., being injured) and psychological (e.g., seeing injured noncombatants) trauma during deployment predicts spouses' reports of *higher* levels of psychological and physical aggression postdeployment, while service members' exposure to combat trauma (e.g., engaging in hand-to-hand combat or experiencing explosions) during deployment predicts *lower* levels of psychological aggression from both the service member and the spouse postdeployment, as reported by the spouse.
- For spouses, separating from the military during the postdeployment period is associated with lower marital satisfaction, and lower positive affect and higher negative affect after communicating with the service member, during the postdeployment period.

Family Relationships

We examined the family environment, satisfaction with parenting, and financial distress as reported by service members and spouses. Key findings include:

- Family outcomes change over the deployment cycle, but these changes occur primarily during the deployment itself and are not always the same for all family members.
- Service members report *better* family environments during deployments than before or after deployments, possibly because they are removed from the day-to-day challenges associated with family life. Spouses, in contrast, report no significant changes in family environment across the deployment cycle.
- Service members' and spouses' reports of parenting satisfaction both change over a deployment cycle, but service members report *higher* parenting satisfaction during the deployment while spouses report *declines* in parenting satisfaction over the entire deployment cycle.
- Financial distress, as felt by both service members and spouses, declined during deployment.
- Service members who report engaging in more predeployment preparation activities report higher satisfaction with parenting postdeployment. Similarly, spouses who report more preparation activities and greater satisfaction with the frequency of communication with the service member during deployment reported higher parenting satisfaction postdeployment.
- The negative psychological consequences of deployment, including psychological trauma and stress reported by the service member, are associated with increased risk for negative family outcomes for both service members and spouses postdeployment.

Psychological and Behavioral Health

We examined several psychological and behavioral health outcomes, including posttraumatic stress disorder (PTSD), depression, binge drinking, and the perceived need for counseling or therapy as reported by service members and spouses. Key findings include:

- We found no overall significant effect of deployment on persistent psychological or behavioral health outcomes for service members or spouses. This is consistent with the fact that we studied an experienced military population, serving during a period of the conflict with comparatively low levels of reported deployment trauma.
- However, the deployed service members who experience deployment trauma during the study did show a persistent increase in depression, PTSD, and anxiety symptoms relative to their predeployment levels. When the service member experienced physical trauma (i.e., injury) during the study deployment, their spouses also showed persistent increases in those symptoms, as well as in binge drinking.
- Mean levels of psychological symptoms showed substantial variation across the deployment cycle. During the deployment period, service members showed heightened depressive symptoms; spouses showed elevated depression, PTSD and anxiety symptoms. In contrast, service members showed significantly less binge drinking during deployments, perhaps because of limited access to alcohol.
- Those deployed members who subsequently separated or retired from the military showed increased levels of psychological symptoms. It may be that these symptoms facilitated the separation (for example, the service member no longer met retention standards), or that separation caused the increase in these symptoms (for example, as an individual experiences a loss of purpose, social support, or income). Regardless of the mechanism, this finding suggests that the period just after separation is one of increased risk and that addressing psychological problems in the critical window around the time of separation may be important for avoiding the longer-term difficulties.

Child and Teen Well-Being

We examined the emotional, behavioral, social, and academic functioning of children (as reported by spouses) and teens, across some 40 outcomes as reported by spouses (for children) and teens. Key findings include:

- Based on trajectory models of outcomes over the deployment cycle, most outcomes did not change over the course of a deployment cycle. Those that did change might reflect maturational changes among children and teens, rather than changes related to deployment. The passage of time, which underlies the trajectory models, also captures the natural process of aging through different developmental periods, which may also influence how children and teens adapt to a parental deployment. There were a few significant exceptions, however:
  - Three child outcomes (reported by spouses) showed significant changes over the deployment cycle: total difficulties (and more specifically, emotional problems), as well as depression screener scores. Spouses reported elevated symptoms in their children during deployment.
  - Two self-reported teen outcomes showed significant changes across the deployment cycle. Teen reports of drug use were very low before and during deployment (hovering around "never"), but increased afterward (to just slightly more than "never" on average). In addition, teens reported higher-quality relationships with their parents who deployed before and during deployment, with lower quality upon return.
- We generally found no significant effect of deployment on child and teen outcomes, which is consistent with the fact that we studied a relatively experienced population, serv-

ing during a period of the conflict with comparatively low levels of reported deployment trauma. However, there were some notable exceptions.

- Spouses in families that experienced a study deployment reported elevated child difficulties at the end of the study (specifically, emotional conduct and peer problems), as well as a higher need for child mental health services, as compared with spouses in matched families that did not experience a study deployment. Interestingly, this was only found for spouse concerns about their children younger than age 11 following a study deployment; there was no such evidence of an effect for spouse concerns on teens or in teen self-reports.

- We also examined three sets of risk and resilience factors within families that experienced a study deployment.

  - The first set included parent deployment factors (e.g., deployment trauma, length of deployment, and separation from the military). Spouses reported that, the longer the study deployment, the more emotional problems and depressive symptoms children had. For teens, these factors were not related to spouse report of teen outcomes or for most of the teen self-reported outcomes. However, there were two exceptions: parental experience of trauma during the study deployment was associated with teen reports of their functioning and family relationships. The pattern of findings indicates that combat traumas were related to poorer functioning and relationships, whereas psychological traumas (in the absence of injury or combat trauma) were related to better functioning and relationships.

The second set of factors examined several measures of child or teen adjustment during the study deployment. When the same informant reported on adjustment and outcomes, there were many significant associations and many trends. That is, when teens self-reported on both adjustment during deployment and postdeployment outcomes, many significant associations were observed. The same was true when parents reported on both teen adjustment during deployment and teen outcomes during postdeployment. However, when informants were mixed—for example, when we examined parent report of teen adjustment during deployment and teen self-report on postdeployment outcomes, these associations were less robust. Thus, perceptions of problems during deployment are highly related to perceptions of problems postdeployment, especially when these perceptions are reported from the same informant. Finally, we examined three types of social support for teens. Socialization with other military children during deployment was strongly protective and associated with more positive outcomes at the end of the study.

Military Integration

Finally, we examined the military satisfaction, military commitment, retention intentions, and teen military career aspirations as reported by service members, spouses, and teens in active component, nondivorced families. Key findings include:

- Across the phases of the deployment cycle, measures of military integration varied more for service members than for spouses and teens. In fact, teen trajectories revealed no evidence of change over time. When there were changes in aspects of military integration during deployment, family members appeared to adapt well and return to predeployment levels of the outcome in the postdeployment period.

- Any communication with other military families during deployment was associated with higher service member retention intentions and greater spouse and teen military commitment postdeployment.
- Trauma experienced during the study deployment, especially physical and psychological trauma, was associated with decreased military satisfaction among service members postdeployment, as well as decreased retention intentions by service members themselves and by teens of service members postdeployment.
- Experiences of nondeployed families may also be stressful, which may minimize the gap between deployed and nondeployed families. For example, among nondeployed families, relocation was related to decreased military satisfaction, commitment, and retention intentions among service members.

Common Themes

Although each of the analyses described in this report focused on a separate set of outcomes, several common themes emerged.

First, and most notably, the most-significant changes experienced by military families across the deployment cycle occur during the deployment itself. With respect to many of the outcomes examined in this study, the participants' status during the study deployment was significantly different from their status reported before and after the deployment. The dominant pattern over the deployment cycle was one of change or adaptation during the deployment period followed by a return to near predeployment levels of functioning.

Second, significant variation exists across family members with respect to how they experience deployment. For example, while service members rated the family environment higher and reported higher parenting satisfaction during deployment, spouses showed little change in these outcomes across the deployment cycle. It is plausible that service members are spared from day-to-day difficulties that families experience during their absences, although we have no direct evidence from our study to support this hypothesis. Given the physical absence of a service member during deployment, some of the differences we observed across family members (e.g., declines in binge drinking, as well as psychological and physical aggression) were expected. However, absence may not fully explain all the variations in outcomes across service members, spouses, children, and teens. For children and teens in particular, it may be important to ask them directly about how well they are coping with a deployment, as we found that for some outcomes (e.g., total difficulties and anxiety) parent and teen reports about teen well-being had little association with one another.

Third, the analyses reported here revealed a set of risk and readiness factors that appear to be associated reliably with multiple domains of postdeployment outcomes. With respect to factors associated with more successful adaptation to deployment, we find across several outcomes that families who engaged in predeployment readiness activities experienced more favorable outcomes postdeployment than families that did not. Given the correlational design of this study, it is not possible to know whether these activities protect or enhance family functioning across the deployment experience or whether the most-resilient families are the ones most likely to engage in these activities. Across a number of outcomes, we also found that more frequent communication and higher satisfaction with the amount of communication with the service member during deployment was associated with more-favorable outcomes postdeployment.

Here, too, it is not possible to know whether communication plays a causal role in effective coping or if the most-resilient families were the ones taking the time to communicate with each other regularly. Until further research attempts to tease apart these alternatives, the fact that these associations emerge even after controlling for family characteristics at baseline is consistent with the view that more frequent communication during deployment has incremental benefits for families after the deployment.

Finally, with respect to risk factors, we identified the experience of traumatic events during the deployment as a risk factor for worse outcomes postdeployment. These findings join an emerging body of research suggesting that it may be the traumatic experience that service members are exposed to during deployment, rather than separation from family, that carries any negative effects associated with the deployment experience. Indeed, in most analyses, the length of the deployment itself showed little association with the postdeployment status of service members, spouses, or children—even when we did not control for deployment trauma.

However, the relationship between deployment experiences and postdeployment outcomes was far more complex than the current literature suggests. The measure of deployment experiences used in the study was designed to assess psychological trauma, and it included a range of descriptively different experiences that were all hypothesized to be psychologically traumatic and all shown to be associated with posttraumatic psychopathology.[2] As expected, we found evidence that the members' physical trauma, combat trauma, and psychological trauma (i.e., witnessing trauma or vicarious exposure to trauma) were each positively associated with postdeployment symptoms of PTSD and depression. However, these different types of service member experiences did not have homogeneous effects when looking at other service member outcomes, or when looking at outcomes for spouses or children/teens. This may suggest that the deployment experiences may have direct effects on the family that are not mediated through service member psychopathology. For example, being directly engaged in violence against the enemy during deployment may affect a service member's interactions with his or her family even in the absence of PTSD or depression. This intriguing finding deserves further exploration to see if parental deployment experiences may promote different mindsets, behaviors, and interactional styles with family members postdeployment. Unfortunately, this study (along with most others designed to look at the effects of deployment) has focused narrowly on assessing deployment events hypothesized to be traumatic, and most prior studies analyze these experiences as functionally interchangeable. New theory, measures, and analyses may be needed to better understand which deployment experiences have persistent effects on service members and their families, as well as how those effects are produced. Viewing all deployment events through the narrow lens of psychological trauma may lead us to miss, or misrepresent, the long-term effects of deployment.

Study Limitations

Despite the strengths of the Deployment Life Study, it is also limited in several ways that constrain the conclusions that these results can support. First, the baseline sample consisted of a

---

2   T. L. Schell and G. N. Marshall, "Survey of Individuals Previously Deployed for OEF/OIF," in T. L. Tanielian and L. H. Jaycox, eds., *Invisible Wounds of War: Psychological and Cognitive Injuries, Their Consequences, and Services to Assist Recovery*, Santa Monica, Calif.: RAND Corporation, MG-720-CCF, 2008, pp. 87–115.

selective sample of older, more-experienced family members who not only have remained in the military but also stayed married long enough to be included in our sample. This selectivity may have increased our odds of finding resilient families. We cannot speculate about what the results would look like for first-time deployers or newlyweds, given our sample. Nor can we speak to what deployment looks like for other types of families that were not part of our sample, including single-parent households or unmarried service members without dependents.

Second, some families that participated in the baseline assessment dropped out during the course of the study, which could have biased estimates. However, it is not entirely clear which direction the bias is in. Most likely, these families are worse on our outcomes, which would upwardly bias our estimates.

Third, our analyses include a large number of statistical tests and thus the results presented in this report should be viewed in terms of patterns, rather than select, individually significant associations.

Fourth, as with any survey that attempts to measure phenomena that cannot be observed directly, measurement error is a potential problem. To the extent possible, our surveys used well-validated measures that have been used in other studies of both civilian and service members and their families.

Fifth, self-report data, even if they are collected outside of direct human contact (i.e., over the phone) may be subject to social response bias. That is, service members, spouses, and teens may have overestimated the positive aspects of their lives and underestimated the negative aspects.

Finally, although we have done a significant amount of work to minimize bias from observed differences between the deployed and nondeployed samples in our doubly robust analyses, a limitation of doubly robust methods is that they cannot guard against bias from unobserved factors whose effect on an outcome is not captured via the included confounders.

Taken together, these potential limitations should not overshadow the uniqueness of the Deployment Life Study or the contribution it makes to understanding the consequences of deployment for military families. Rather, they should be viewed as a caution for how broadly the results apply to the overall population of military families.

Policy Implications

Our findings have a number of implications for programs and policies aimed at improving the well-being and quality of life of service members, spouses, and their children across the deployment cycle.

Programs, services, and policies should target families that experience deployment trauma, especially during the postdeployment phase. To the extent that traumatic experiences during deployment are associated with a host of negative consequences in the postdeployment period, these experiences, when documented during deployments, can be used to target families for extra support upon the return of the service member. Programs that target families based on documented experiences, regardless of self-reported symptoms, might help mitigate problems before they metastasize, or at least before they have time to affect multiple family members. The challenge for providing the programs, services, and supports to these families, of course, is identifying families *before* problems occur.

Addressing psychological problems around the time of separation may be important for avoiding the longer-term impairments caused by these problems, such as increased morbidity, homelessness, unemployment, or substance use among veterans. Our results indicate that service members who have separated from service postdeployment have significantly elevated psychological symptoms. Regardless of whether psychological problems predate separation, the separation period appears to be a high-risk period for individuals who leave the military.

Attention to the challenges associated with deployment should not detract from supporting services that address other challenges of military life. Although they are perhaps the most salient stressor in the lives of military families, deployments are far from the only challenges that military families face. The fact that characteristics of military families measured prior to the deployment accounted for outcomes after the deployment highlights the importance of programs that support families in other ways—e.g., by reducing financial stress or addressing mental health issues.

Programs that facilitate communication both between and within military families during a deployment may promote not only greater military integration, but also better outcomes across the domains highlighted in this report. Family connectedness to the military is higher when families engage with other military families. In addition, interacting with other military children was protective among teens in our study, across a number of outcomes. These relationships with peers are likely to help family members share important emotional, instrumental, and informational resources that can be used to cope with a deployment and to develop strong ties within the military community. Similarly, communication among family members, and satisfaction with that communication, were associated with improved marital and parenting relationships. Despite the fact that this study was not designed to evaluate family support programs, our results show that targeted efforts, such as those surrounding communication during deployment, could have great promise as family support programs. The true impact of these programs, however, has yet to be seen.

Support to improve relationships between service members, spouses, and their teen children during the postdeployment reintegration period may improve family functioning. Our results indicated that both postdeployment family cohesion and the quality of the relationship with the nondeployed parent were worse among deployed versus nondeployed teens, and that relationship quality with the service member declined during the deployment period. Programs should focus on preventing declines in relationship quality and family cohesion after the service member returns, as opposed to waiting for families to seek help as relationships disintegrate.

Future Research on Military Families

Our findings also highlight several areas where changes to research strategies could result in improved data—in terms of both timeliness and quality—for making policy decisions. *Future work on military families should explore ways in which data can be collected from multiple family members at the same time.* Across the analyses presented in this report, results based on spouses' data were more-frequently significant than results based on data from service members. Spouses' reports may be more sensitive to conditions within the family, and so may be promising sources of data on military families when data from service members are unavailable. For some outcomes, such as the family environment and anxiety, family members' (i.e., service members and spouses) reports of outcomes differed during the same period of the deployment cycle. Collecting data from multiple members of the same families can capture these differences and help tailor support for individual family members based on their relation to the service member (e.g., spouse, child, teen).

As funding resources become scarcer, future work on military families should prioritize longitudinal studies. Many existing studies of military families rely on retrospective or cross-sectional reports. Unfortunately, this means that much of the existing body of work on the impact of deployment on families does not allow for anchoring of family function prior to the deployment, potentially leading to an exaggeration of any deployment effect. Longitudinal study designs offer the most methodologically robust way to assess the impact of deployment on families. Without following the same families over time, we would not have been able to observe changes in the functioning of family members (and families) during the deployment period, and we would not have been able to report that those changes do not usually lead to sustained problems in the postdeployment period.

Procedures for collecting real-time data from military families should be explored. Throughout the report, we have been sensitive to the unique historical climate in which the data collection for the Deployment Life Study took place. Had we conducted the same study in 2006 or 2007, when deployments to Iraq and Afghanistan were longer and more frequent, our results may have painted a different picture of how well military families adapt to deployment. Longitudinal data have a lot to offer researchers, but they are time-consuming to collect, and results are often not known for several months or even years after the respondents have provided their data. Having a real-time source of data—one that is capable of tracking changes in the historical, political, and social climates—would provide a huge benefit to researchers and policymakers who seek to help families navigate the stress associated with military life. There is no single type of real-time data that would be able to address all the relevant research and policy questions that may be asked. The costs and benefits associated with different types of data should also be considered when deciding what type of real-time data collection methods to invest in. Some combination of administrative data for service members (e.g., medical records, personnel data) as well as ongoing data from a representative panel of military family members could prove to be a very useful, cost-effective solution.

Develop new theories, measures, and analyses of deployment experiences that can account for apparent complexities in the relationships between deployment and postdeployment outcomes. The complex pattern of findings relating service member deployment experiences and the outcomes across the family deserves further study. It is possible, for instance, that the experience of combat during deployment produces a set of psychological and behavioral factors that make reintegration with the family more difficult. On the other hand, witnessing of wartime traumas without being in combat or being personally injured may produce a very different set of psychological and behavioral reactions that make service members more eager or able to engage with their families. Further research is needed to investigate the persistent effects of deployment, both good and bad. The existing theory (focused almost exclusively on factors leading to posttraumatic psychopathology), the existing measures (focused on traumatic events and often geared toward the experiences of infantry), and the standard analyses (focused on using these measures as forming a homogeneous scale with consistent effects) may obscure the full effects of deployment on members and their families. Such research is necessary to develop policies or interventions that can effectively minimize the harm—and maximize the benefits—of military deployments.

Examine the intersections and relative timing of military and family events. Contemporary service members are more likely than previous generations to have families. When examining outcomes, including those detailed in this report, it is worthwhile for future research to examine interactions between the relative timing of military (e.g., deployment, promotion, relocation) and family (e.g., birth of a child) events. Such research would facilitate a deeper understanding of when families might be most vulnerable or resilient in the face of deployment.

Conclusion

Across all of our analyses, comparisons between families that experienced a deployment and matched families that did not experience a deployment revealed few significant differences in outcomes that occurred after a service member returned from a deployment. Yet, the Deployment Life Study data revealed that life during the deployment itself was stressful in a number of ways, albeit differently for different family members. Given the unquestionable stresses of the deployment period and the well-established negative associations between stress and family outcomes among civilians, it is remarkable that most families are able to adjust. On one hand, this apparent resilience might reveal the noteworthy success of the support programs currently in place for military families. On the other hand, the findings presented here may reflect the natural ability of many military families to thrive, even in the face of severe challenges. In reality, both stories are probably true—existing programs help military families cope, and families have natural coping abilities. However, it is important to remember that not all military families are the same. While the sample of families in the Deployment Life Study is generally more experienced, with both deployments and military life in general, some are not. Likewise, for some families, military life is a struggle. What we can learn from these more-experienced, resilient families can then be used to help those who may be less successful at adapting and adjusting to the unique demands associated with military life.

Finally, we would be remiss if we did not acknowledge the tremendous amount of data that the Deployment Life Study collected and the analyses yet to come. It is our hope that future exploration of these data will allow us to make even finer-grained recommendations about how to create and promote readiness and resilience among all military families.

Acknowledgments

The study team is grateful for the support, oversight, and guidance of our past and current project monitors from the Department of Defense:[3] COL (Ret.) Paul Cordts, COL (Ret.) Elspeth Cameron Ritchie, CAPT Edward Simmer, COL Rebecca Porter, Col Christopher Robinson, CAPT Wanda Finch, CAPT Janet Hawkins, and LTC Christopher Ivany. We are also grateful for the assistance of CAPT Paul Hammer and CDR Kathleen Watkins for their assistance in securing access to data and facilitating regulatory approvals.

Through the peer-review process, we gained constructive and helpful comments and suggestions from James Hosek (RAND Corporation), Paul Bliese (University of South Carolina, Darla Moore School of Business), Jennifer Lundquist (University of Massachusetts-Amherst), Abigail Gewirtz (University of Minnesota), and Mady Segal (University of Maryland). We thank them for their time and help in improving the report. We also thank our former and current program management team at RAND, including Sue Hosek, Beth Asch, Margaret Harrell, Kristie Gore, John Winkler, and Michael Hansen, for their continued support and guidance throughout the study. We also are grateful for the editorial assistance of Arwen Bicknell as well as Donna White and Christopher Dirks for helping to format the document.

Finally, we want to thank the many military families who have participated in the Deployment Life Study. We hope that, in some way, our work will lead to improvements in programs and policies that support their health, happiness, and well-being.

---

[3] Ranks and affiliations are current as of July 2015.

Abbreviations

ASMD	absolute standard mean difference
AVF	all-volunteer force
CES	Combat Experiences Scale
DMDC	Defense Manpower Data Center
DoD	U.S. Department of Defense
FES	Family Environment Scale
FMIM	Family Military Integration Model
GBM	Generalized Boosted Models
IOM	Institute of Medicine
MHAT	Mental Health Advisory Team
OCONUS	outside the continental United States
OIF/OEF/OND	Operation Iraqi Freedom/Operation Enduring Freedom/Operation New Dawn
PANAS	Positive and Negative Affect Schedule
PCL	PTSD Check List
PedsQL	Pediatric Quality of Life Inventory
PHQ	Patient Health Questionnaire
PHQ-A	Patient Health Questionnaire for Adolescents
POA	power of attorney
PSID	Panel Study of Income Dynamic
PTSD	posttraumatic stress disorder
RQ	research question

SCARED	Screen for Child Anxiety Related Emotional Disorders
SD	standard deviation
SDQ	Strengths and Difficulties Questionnaire
SE	standard error
SMD	standardized mean difference
STARRS	Army Study to Assess Risk and Resilience in Servicemembers
TBI	traumatic brain injury
TWANG	Toolkit for Weighting and Analysis of Nonequivalent Groups

CHAPTER ONE

Introduction

Benjamin R. Karney, Sarah O. Meadows, and Terri Tanielian

> What a cruel thing is war: to separate and destroy families and friends, and mar the purest
> joys and happiness God has granted us in this world.
> —*Robert E. Lee, from a letter to his wife, December 25, 1862*

Armed conflict between nations and groups usually requires those who fight to leave behind their families and loved ones. From the Greeks mounting their siege of Troy to the "Greatest Generation" preparing to enter World War II, the three phases of the deployment cycle—preparation, separation, and reintegration—have been a regular part of military life throughout the ages. Although many service members anticipate deployments, eager for the opportunity to defend their country and utilize their training (Hosek, Kavanagh, and Miller, 2006), few look forward to time spent away from spouses and children. Indeed, the separations required by deployments have long been described as one of the most stressful aspects of being a military family (Rosen and Durand, 2000).

In the years since the terrorist attacks of September 11, 2001, those stresses increased markedly. That year, the United States embarked upon Operation Enduring Freedom (OEF) in Afghanistan, and two years later initiated Operation Iraqi Freedom (OIF; later renamed Operation New Dawn [OND]) in Iraq. To date, nearly 2.8 million service members have been deployed in these military actions, a level of deployments unmatched since the Vietnam War. Moreover, deployments to these fields of combat have been longer and more frequent, with shorter intervals at home, than deployments in previous conflicts over the past several decades (Belasco, 2007; Bruner, 2006; Serafino, 2003). Due in part to advances in field medicine, fatality rates have been lower than they might have been, but the latest figures indicate that more than 50,000 service members have been wounded in combat and more than 1,600 have lost limbs (Fischer, 2015). Rates of "invisible wounds" have been much higher, with nearly 500,000 service members returning home with posttraumatic stress disorder (PTSD) or varying degrees of traumatic brain injury (Fischer, 2015). In light of the well-documented reluctance of service members to report their symptoms (Tanielian and Jaycox, 2008) and seek help, these are undoubtedly underestimates of the true prevalence of war-related injuries.

Service members are not the only ones shouldering the burden. Since the birth of the All-Volunteer Force (AVF) in 1973, the U.S. armed forces has been described as a "military of families" (Hosek, Asch, et al., 2002). Indeed, the majority of service members are married (Karney and Crown, 2007), and nearly 50 percent have dependent children living at home (Clever and Segal, 2013). When a service member is deployed, these family members must adjust their lives, taking on new roles and responsibilities, and must adjust again when the service member returns. Many in military families take pride in serving their country by supporting their service members. Nevertheless, in survey after survey, the challenges associated with preparing for deployments, being separated from the service member, and reintegrating after deployments are rated as the most challenging aspects of military life (Blue Star Families, 2012; Knobloch and Theiss, 2012; Newby et al., 2005).

How do the challenges of deployment affect military families? To what extent are service members and their loved ones able to maintain their individual health and interpersonal relationships in the face of lengthy separations? To what extent does the well-being of service members and their families change across the phases of the deployment cycle? To what extent do the stresses associated with deployments have lasting effects on military families, and what might those effects be? For a military obligated to provide services for more people out of uniform than in uniform (Clever and Segal, 2013), these are crucial questions. Since the birth of the AVF, the military has recognized that it needs to support military families, and has devoted increasing resources toward doing so (Rostker, 2006). Toward this end, every service of the military has developed family resource centers (O'Keefe, Eyre, and Smith, 1984; Rubin and Harvie, 2012) and several programs address the challenges faced by families experiencing deployment in particular (e.g., the Yellow Ribbon Reintegration Program). Budgets for programs to support the health and well-being of service members and their families have never been higher. Nevertheless, in an environment of limited resources, the efficient allocation of these resources will depend on an accurate understanding of how military families are affected by the demands that military service makes on them.

In recent years, the need for a more precise understanding of the ways that deployments affect military families has begun to be recognized. For example, at least five congressional hearings (convened by the Senate Armed Services Committee, House Armed Services Committee, or the House Committee on Veterans' Affairs) and more than 60 pieces of legislation have addressed the effects of deployment on military families. In 2009, the Institute of Medicine (IOM) was asked by Congress (Public Law 110-181, 2008) to undertake a review of the empirical evidence on the physical, mental health, and other readjustment needs of military families containing a member who had been deployed to OIF or OEF. Among the major findings of the report was documentation of the relative paucity of data adequate to support evidence-based policy on most issues of concern to OIF and OEF populations. Because the unique effects of deployment on family functioning have yet to be documented rigorously, the characteristics of families that are more or less successful at maintaining their functions across a deployment cycle are unknown as well. In response to their concerns, the IOM committee made several recommendations, including funding research on military families and deployments that addresses methodological and substantive gaps in the existing literature and that assesses effects of deployment across multiple domains (e.g., social and economic effects). Heeding this call, Congress has requested and required longitudinal studies of the effects of deployment on service members and veterans (see U.S. House of Representatives, 2009; U.S. Senate, 2009) and separate longitudinal studies of the effects of deployment on children of military personnel and families (see Institute of Medicine, 2010, as one example).

The Deployment Life Study was designed to respond to these calls. The broad goal of the study was to gather data to evaluate the effects of deployment on service members, spouses, and their children. Which families are best able to withstand the strains of deployment, and what kinds of coping strategies characterize these families? Which families are most vulnerable to the negative consequences of deployment, and how might those families be targeted for extra support? The Deployment Life Study examined these questions by interviewing married service members, their spouses, and (when available) one child, at nine assessment points spread across a three-year period, and across all phases of a deployment cycle.[1] Each interview included instruments measuring a wide range of variables relevant to understanding how the social, economic, and psychological well-being of military families change across the deployment cycle. As a consequence of this breadth, the Deployment Life Study data set should be a resource for researchers from multiple disciplines and, most importantly, provides robust data with which to assess the association between deployment and military family health and well-being.

The specific aim of this report is to document the initial results of the Deployment Life Study with respect to understanding the impact of deployments on marital relationships, family relationships, psychological and behavioral health, child and teen well-being, and military integration among families in the military. Toward that end, the rest of this introductory chapter is organized as follows. First, we briefly comment on the methodological limitations of prior research on deployment and military families, explaining why, despite considerable attention from scholars over the past decade, new data on the effects of deployment are still sorely needed. Second, we highlight the unique strengths of the Deployment Life Study, especially in the context of other longitudinal studies of military families that have been initiated in recent years. Third, we describe the conceptual framework that guided the design of the Deployment Life Study. Fourth, we describe the historical context in which these data were collected, and explain how that context constrains the conclusions that can be drawn from the results described in the rest of this report. Finally, we offer a brief overview of the remaining chapters of this report.

The Limits of Existing Research on Deployment Effects

Given the high pace of deployments over the past decade and a half, and the explicit calls for data to illuminate the effects of deployment on military families, there is already a burgeoning research literature exploring and documenting those effects (see Tanielian et al., 2014, for a review). Generally, the results of existing research suggest that those consequences are negative on many, but not all, outcomes that can be measured. Before accepting this conclusion, however, several limitations of the existing literature must be taken into account.

First, the existing research on deployment effects relies almost exclusively on retrospective designs. That is, researchers have typically collected samples of military families and compared current outcomes in families that did or did not experience a prior deployment. This is a reasonable strategy for comparing the two groups, but it cannot distinguish between the consequences of deployment and problems that may have existed prior to deployment. Retrospective designs also offer no ability to describe how families may change across the deployment cycle, or the possibility of recovery over time after deployments. Further, retrospective designs may suffer from recall bias, which could systematically bias estimates (Loughran, 2002). As a consequence, retrospective designs run the risk of exaggerating deployment effects and their duration.

---

[1] This study operationalized "families" as married couples with or without children. We did so in part because of the sponsors' interest in this particular definition. Obviously, "family" can mean many things to different people.

Second, although the main effects of deployment have been mostly negative, this does not mean that most military families experience negative effects of deployment. Even if a particular negative outcome is more prevalent among families experiencing deployments than among other families, most military families may nevertheless avoid these negative consequences, and some may even thrive. Understanding the sources of variability in responses to deployment is crucial if military leaders are to tailor programs and allocate resources toward families that might need the resources most. Doing so requires research that emphasizes the qualities of families prior to deployment that account for their well-being after deployment.

Third, although research to date has examined service members, spouses, and children, no large-scale studies have examined multiple respondents in the same families. As a result, the accumulated research offers no way of determining whether deployments have independent or different effects on each family member.

Fourth, although deployments are likely to affect a wide range of family outcomes, existing research has generally focused on a single domain at a time. The results of such research offer no way of evaluating which domains are affected more or less than any others. Understanding how military families react to deployment requires research that assesses the health, well-being, and characteristics of all members of military families, as well as relationships between spouses and their children, circumstances outside the family, and the varying demands of military service and other life stressors.

Strengths of the Deployment Life Study

In light of the pressing need for data to inform policies to improve readiness in families facing deployments, and in light of the limitations of existing research on the effects of deployment, research is sorely needed that describes the association between deployment and multiple dimensions of family well-being and examines how characteristics of families prior to deployment account for variability in their responses to the experience. To meet this need, the RAND Corporation conducted the Deployment Life Study, a multiyear longitudinal study to identify the effects of deployment and describe how military families change or remain stable across each phase of the deployment cycle. At baseline, the study recruited 2,724 Army, Air Force, Navy, and Marine Corps families. The sampling frame was restricted to married service members who were eligible for deployment within the next six to 12 months. In each family, a service member, his or her spouse, and a child between the ages of 11 and 17 (if there was one in the household) each provided information independently. Interviewers obtained consent from each participating family member and conducted the baseline interviews by phone. Every four months thereafter, respondents logged into the study website and completed a follow-up survey online. Data collection included a total of nine waves spanning the entire deployment cycle, including periods of predeployment, deployment, and postdeployment.

The data accumulated through these efforts are suitable for addressing a wide range of questions about the health and well-being of military families, but the following questions were priorities that guided the design of the study:

- *Controlling for initial conditions and functioning, how is deployment related to military family outcomes?* This study evaluated the association between deployment and a range of outcomes, including those relevant to the functioning of the entire family unit and outcomes relevant to understanding the well-being of each individual family member.

- *Across the phases of the deployment cycle—preparation, separation, and reintegration—how do the outcomes of military families change or remain stable over time?* This study is the first of which we are aware to describe changes before, during, and after deployment on a wide range of outcomes for multiple family members at once.
- *Across families that experience deployment, what accounts for variability in families' postdeployment outcomes? Of the factors accounting for such variability, which are the most important?* The implications of deployment are likely to vary significantly across families, and even across individuals within families. The Deployment Life Study assessed and analyzed the individual and family traits, resources, and circumstances that account for which families thrive after a deployment and which families suffer.

As described in the rest of this report, analyses focused on identifying the characteristics of more (or less) successful families over time, where success is defined in terms of a range of important outcomes that were measured at every assessment, including:

- the quality of marital and parental relationships
- the psychological, behavioral, and physical health of family members
- child outcomes (e.g., emotional, behavioral, social, and academic functioning)
- military integration (e.g., attitudes toward military service, retention intentions).

The Deployment Life Study is not the only project that has responded to the call for longitudinal research on military families. To facilitate comparisons between this and other prominent longitudinal studies that have also been examining this population, details about the designs of each study are presented side by side in Table 1.1. As the table reveals, the Deployment Life Study has the smallest sample of the five major studies of military families currently ongoing—but, as the table also reveals, the Deployment Life Study has several unique characteristics that will allow it to address issues that no other study can address as effectively.

Anchoring on Deployment

The primary rationale for conducting longitudinal research on military families is that longitudinal designs allow for estimates of changes in family outcomes after a deployment, controlling for preexisting differences between families prior to deployment. The greatest benefits of this design, therefore, arise from the power to observe families before and after a deployment cycle, and compare them with matched families that did not experience a deployment during the same period. The Deployment Life Study was designed to take advantage of the power of such analyses. Whereas the other ongoing longitudinal studies sampled from the general military population (some of whom may already be deployed and others of whom may never deploy over the course a study), the Deployment Life Study sampled exclusively from the population of married service members eligible for deployment within the next six to 12 months. Moreover, to be eligible for the study, the service member could not be deployed at baseline. Thus, baseline assessment of the Deployment Life Study sample was a true baseline for a sample highly likely to experience a deployment over the course of the study.

Repeated Assessments over Three Years

Military families may cope in different ways across different stages of the deployment cycle (i.e., functioning at predeployment may not be the same as functioning during deployment or postdeployment). Moreover, the consequences of deployments may evolve or fade as families adjust and restore their predeployment equilibrium. Even longitudinal studies risk missing or mischaracterizing these effects if the interval between assessments is too long or the duration of the entire study is too short. The Deployment Life Study was designed to produce higher-resolution descriptions of the deployment cycle than has been available in other studies by assessing families every four months over three years (nine assessments total). Because all families were recruited prior to a deployment, this design allowed not only for assessments of family functioning at each stage of the deployment cycle, but also for *multiple* assessments at each stage, in most cases, including multiple assessments shortly after a deployment. Thus, the Deployment Life Study is able to describe how families change within each stage of the cycle, how long changes associated with deployment last, and what characteristics of families prior to deployment predict a family's postdeployment return to equilibrium.

Data from Multiple Family Members

The vast majority of existing research on military families and three of the five ongoing longitudinal studies described in Table 1.1 assess family functioning exclusively through the reports of a single family member, usually the service member or the spouse. There are several reasons that reliance on the reports of a single family member offers only a limited window into family functioning across a deployment cycle. First, service members and spouses may use different resources to cope with deployment. Second, coping strategies that are effective for one member of a family may not be effective for another. Third, to the extent that mental health is an outcome of major importance and the rates of mental health problems in this population are relatively high, the perceptions of any single family member may be distorted in ways that are impossible to estimate. Fourth, to the extent that one family member is asked to describe outcomes for another family member (e.g., parents reporting on their children, service members reporting on their spouses), associations among responses can be inflated by shared method variance. The Deployment Life Study avoided these problems by obtaining responses from service members, their spouses, and one child between the ages of 11 and 17, if available.

The Conceptual Framework

In the interest of supporting a comprehensive understanding of the association between deployment and the health and well-being of military families, the Deployment Life Study included assessments of a wide range of variables. Selection of those variables required a conceptual framework to suggest which ones, out of the countless constructs that could have been assessed, warranted inclusion within the limited claims we could make on the time of participating families. Thus, a preliminary step in the design of the Deployment Life Study was to identify a conceptual model that accounts for well-being in military families across the deployment cycle, and so could offer direction for selecting constructs and forming initial hypotheses.

There were not many models to choose from. Despite the substantial resources that have been directed toward supporting military families since the birth of the All-Volunteer Force, these programs have been characterized as "largely reactive, developed primarily in response

Table 1.1
Comparing Deployment Life and Other Studies of Military Families

Study Name	Sample Size	Population and Sampling Method	Service	Component	Number of Waves	Interval Between Waves	Constructs Assessed
Deployment Life Study	2,724	Stratified random sample of deployable married service members, spouses, and one child	Army, Navy,[a] Air Force, Marine Corps	Active, guard, reserve	9 over 3 years	4 months	Psychological, behavioral, and physical health of family members; Marital and parental relationships; Military integration; Child well-being; Financial well-being
Military Family Life Project	28,552	Random sample of spouses of service members	Army, Navy, Air Force, Marine Corps	Active	4 over 2 years	6 months	Health and well-being; Financial well-being; Military life; Deployment history; Child outcomes; Reunion and reunification
Millennium Cohort Study and Millennium Cohort Family Study	100,000 service members and 10,000 couples	Random sample of service members and spouses	Army, Navy, Air Force, Marine Corps	Active, guard, reserve	7 over 21 years	3 years	Physical and functional status; Psychosocial assessment; Medical conditions; Self-reported symptoms; PTSD; Alcohol and tobacco use; Alternative medicine use; Life events; Occupational exposure
Army Study to Assess Risk and Resilience in Servicemembers (STARRS)	1.6 million, archival data	Convenience sample of service members[b]	Army	Active	5-year data-collection period	Not applicable; there are several data-collection efforts within Army STARRS, so no waves.	Stress; Deployment experiences; Exposure to trauma; Family and personal history; Coping; Personality and temperament; Social networks and support
Blue Star Families 2015 Military Family Lifestyle Survey	6,291	Convenience sample of service members, their spouses, and their parents	Army, Navy, Air Force, Marine Corps	Active, guard, reserve, veterans	6 to date, but not longitudinal with same sample	1 year	Pay, benefits, and changes to retirement; Family well-being; Satisfaction with military; Deployment and wellness; Financial security/readiness; Military/civilian connectedness; Spouse employment; Transition

[a] Because of the time line required to secure the Navy sample, this enrollment started one year later than those for the other services.
[b] Note that the Army STARRS study does not collect information from other family members.

to specific problems and their symptoms" (Bowen and Orthner, 1989, p. 180), rather than grounded in a priori theories of how military families function. Bowen and Orthner describe the standards that a comprehensive theory must meet (1989, p. 180):

> There is a critical need for an explicit model of work-family linkages in the military (replete with underlying assumptions and operational outcome statements) that not only identifies the factors that promote level of adaptation to the multiplicity of organizational and family demands faced by service members and their families, but also specifies the direct and indirect impact that military policies, practices, and programs have on the ability of service members and their families to successfully respond to these demands. This model must reflect the dynamic and interactive quality of work and family life across the work and family life cycles. In addition, it must respect the tremendous age, ethnic, and cultural diversity found among families in the military services today by accounting for personal system-level influences, including the values, needs, and expectations of service members and their families toward both work and family life. Finally, for purposes of clinical and community intervention, the model must be practice based—capable of guiding the development, implementation, and evaluation of policies, programs, and practices in support of families.

Acknowledging this this call to arms, Karney and Crown (2007) published an integrative framework to account for success and failure in military marriages. Although goals of the Deployment Life Study extend beyond marital outcomes to include child outcomes, parenting outcomes, and the physical and mental health of each family member, the Karney and Crown framework provided a starting point for identifying general categories of constructs to account for the outcomes of interest in the Deployment Life Study. With the goal of understanding how families experience deployments, the framework divides those general categories roughly into four domains: preexisting conditions, deployment experiences, short-term outcomes, and long-term outcomes.

Preexisting Conditions

No family goes into a deployment as a blank slate. Rather, even before entering the predeployment phase, each military family possesses a unique set of traits, personal histories, capabilities, vulnerabilities, and resources that are likely to play a role in how family members function across the deployment experience. Among the major categories of preexisting conditions are the following:

- *Enduring traits.* These are the relatively stable qualities of each family member, including demographic characteristics, personality, prior psychopathology, and personal history. Some qualities of family members, such as having more education, a stable childhood environment, and lack of personality problems or psychopathology (e.g., depression, anxiety), should contribute to effective adaptation across a deployment. Other qualities, such as a history of depression or substance abuse, should be associated with less-effective coping and poorer postdeployment outcomes.
- *Relationship resources.* These are attributes of the relationships among family members, including the duration of the marriage, the presence or absence of children, the number of children, and the quality of the relationships among all family members. Families with

more relationship resources, such as a longer and higher-quality marriage, should endure the experience of deployment more successfully than families with fewer resources.

- *Nonmilitary circumstances.* Each family lives in its own ecological niche, characterized by specific neighborhoods, social networks, levels of chronic stress, and availability of social support. Some niches, presumably those with more-abundant sources of support and lower levels of chronic stress, should promote more-resilient military families; other niches, presumably those with fewer sources of support and more sources of stress, should predict families being more vulnerable to experiencing problems when confronted with the additional stresses of a deployment.

- *Prior military experiences.* Because this is a model to account for a family's experiences across a deployment, it makes sense to highlight preexisting conditions relating specifically to a family's experiences in the military prior to a deployment. Families differ by the rank and branch of the service member. Some families face deployment for the first time, whereas others have already experienced multiple deployments. Some families have long histories in the military and may come from military families, whereas others are new to the military and to the expectations of the institution. Families with deeper ties to the military and longer histories in the military may cope more effectively with the strains of deployment than families for whom those strains are new or unexpected.

Experiences During Deployment

It would be a mistake to use the word *deployment* and assume that the experience is the same for every service member who is deployed. On the contrary, the aftermath of deployments for military families is likely to depend on what happens during the deployment, and those experiences are likely to vary widely across families. Some relevant categories of deployment experiences are:

- *Deployment characteristics.* Across service members, deployments may differ in length, time since the last deployment, and likelihood of exposure to combat. Some service members are deployed with their own units, and some are deployed with unfamiliar units. Some service members confront traumatic experiences or injuries during deployments, whereas others return unscathed. Some service members and their families feel more prepared or ready for an upcoming deployment than others. Almost all of these sources of variability in deployment characteristics lie outside service members' control, but each could predict the nature of the aftermath of deployments for service members and their families.

- *Adaptive processes.* This construct refers to all of the ways in which family members interact, cope with stress, support each other, communicate, and resolve problems. Of particular interest are adaptive processes directly related to deployment, such as making efforts to communicate with the deployed service member, or moving to be closer to extended family while the service member is away. Adaptive processes, unlike deployment characteristics, are largely within the control of military families, and so should be facilitated or constrained by their preexisting conditions and should, in turn, directly account for immediate and long-term outcomes, such that more-effective adaptive processes should allow military families to endure or even thrive across the deployment cycle, whereas less effective adaptive processes should predict negative changes.

Immediate Outcomes

Some of the potential outcomes of the deployment experience may be evident immediately or soon after the deployment ends. We identified the following categories of immediate outcomes:

- *Emergent traits.* Family members may emerge from the experience of deployment irrevocably altered in ways that affect their subsequent functioning. Service members may return from a deployment with permanent physical or emotional injuries; they may return having grown or matured. In either case, they possess different capacities than they did prior to the deployment. The family members who remain at home may be similarly altered in positive or negative ways (e.g., by additional education, noteworthy employment experiences, or new problems with substance abuse or the law).
- *Relationship quality.* The quality of the relationships among and between family members may be highly sensitive to the experience of deployment. Families in which these relationships were strong prior to the deployment and that adapt effectively during deployment should experience the least change across deployment and may even use the experience to draw closer. Families with problematic relationships prior to deployment and those without the skills or resources to adapt effectively during deployment may experience declines in the quality of their relationships across the deployment cycle. Either way, the postdeployment relationships will play a role in determining the long-term consequences for the family.

Long-Term Outcomes

The ultimate question that the Deployment Life Study is designed to address is how the experience of deployment affects the long-term well-being of military families. By closely examining those families that are successful, it is possible to start to paint a picture of what characteristics, qualities, and resources are related to family readiness. The dimensions of long-term well-being of greatest concern are *marital and family relationships, military integration, child well-being, and psychological and behavioral health of all family members.*

All of these constructs can be assembled into the framework presented in Figure 1.1.[2] The general shape of the figure is derived from the Karney and Crown (2007) model of military marriages, but it has been adapted to encompass the broader range of outcomes of interest in the Deployment Life Study.

The model suggests multiple pathways by which the experience of deployment may interact with preexisting conditions of military families to account for their immediate and long-term outcomes after a deployment. First, the model suggests that all of the preexisting conditions of a family affect that family's outcomes through their direct effects on the quality of the family's adaptive processes during deployment. Adaptive processes, from this perspective, are the "skills and tools" that have been the defining features of family readiness. Placing these skills in a developmental context, the model describes the ability to adapt effectively as partially mediating the effects that a family's preexisting conditions can have on their postdeployment outcomes. For example, families should adapt more effectively to the extent that family members have enduring traits that provide strength, such as strong values, a commitment to marriage and the family unit, higher levels of education, or a history of mental health. Second, the model highlights the fact that the deployment itself is an exogenous variable that has direct

---

[2]   Although the model is depicted here in a structural equation framework, we do not analyze it as such in this report (more detailed methods are available in Chapter Two). Future work, however, should consider using such an approach.

Figure 1.1
Conceptual Model of Military Family Health and Well-Being for the Deployment Life Study

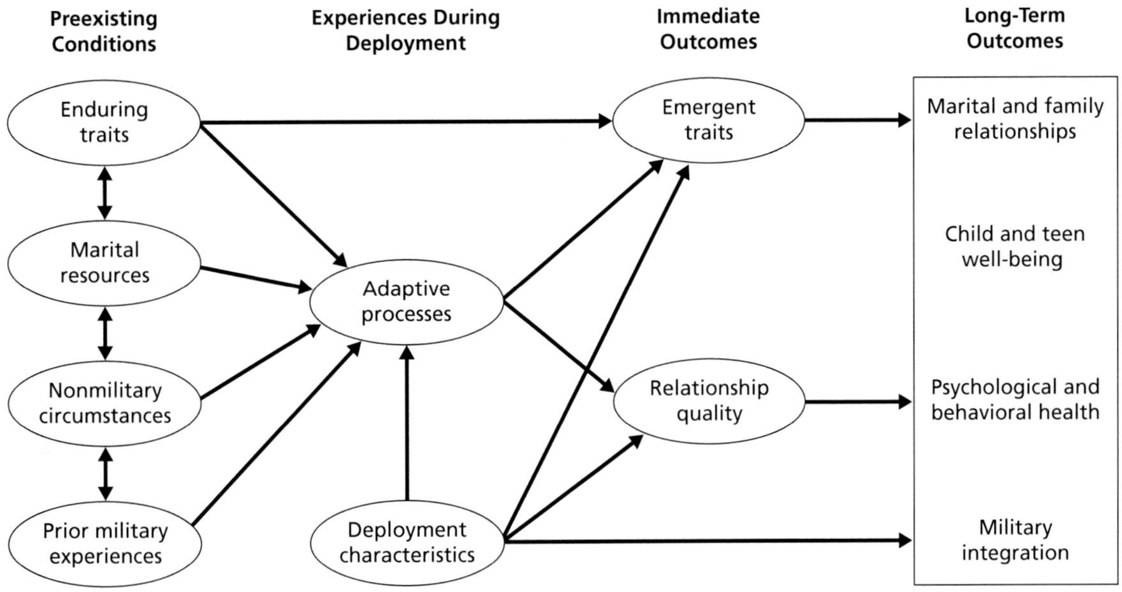

effects on outcomes, as well as interactions with adaptive processes to affect a family's outcomes. The longer the deployment, for example, the greater demands the experience makes on a family's capacity to adapt effectively. Third, the model recognizes that military service can be a life-altering experience for each member of the family, leading to emergent traits that can be positive (e.g., personal growth) or negative (e.g., cognitive deficits resulting from traumatic brain injury). This impact can be experienced at both individual and family levels because such events can disrupt how the family functions as a whole. Finally, the model recognizes that the consequences of deployment for families may evolve over time, such that the immediate impact can differ from the long-term impact.

The Historical Context of the Deployment Life Study—A Caveat

Interpretations of the results described in the rest of this report must factor in the specific period in which this sample was assembled and the data were provided. Support for this study was motivated by the severe increase in the pace of deployments for service members in the middle to later part of the 2000s. By the time data collection began for this study, however, the period of peak deployments for the U.S. military had passed. The surge in Iraq, for example, took place in 2007–2008 and was followed by a gradual reduction in troop strength through the formal end of operations there in December 2011. Deployments to Afghanistan peaked in 2010, and have been declining ever since. Initial recruitment of the initial sample for the Deployment Life Study began in March 2011 and ended in August 2012 for the Army, Air Force, and Marine Corps sample; for the Navy sample, it began in November 2012 and ended in February 2013. The subsequent three years of longitudinal data collection ended for all samples by the summer of 2015. Thus, although the Deployment Life Study took place following a period of frequent and lengthy deployments for the U.S. military, those deployments were becoming less frequent during the data collection phase of the study.

This historical context has several important implications for understanding the Deployment Life Study data. First, by the time recruitment for the Deployment Life Study began, most married service members eligible for the study *had already been through at least one deployment*. The consequences of deployment had already been felt for most of the population from which the study sampled. This means that the military families vulnerable to experiencing the most-negative consequences from deployments may have left the population (either through separation from the military or through divorce) before the study began. By studying couples who remained married and serving in the military during this period, the Deployment Life Study was able to examine a sample of military families that had already endured and survived the worst of the recent operations. As a consequence, although the results reported here can be generalized to the current married population of the military (i.e., a population that has survived prior, and sometimes multiple, deployments), these results may not generalize to populations that have yet to be deployed and may underestimate the negative effects of deployment for the population of first-time deployers.

Second, during the period of the Deployment Life Study, deployments were shorter and arguably less dangerous (because the combat zones were less volatile) than they had been earlier in the decade. During the period of data collection, the number and rates of injury and death among American troops were much lower than in prior years, and certainly significantly less than during the peak of combat operations (Fischer, 2015). Thus, the effects of deployment reported here may not reflect the effects experienced during the period of greatest demand on the military.

Organization of This Report

The rest of this report is organized as follows. Chapter Two describes in detail the methods and procedures of the Deployment Life Study. In particular, this chapter outlines the analytic strategies employed in each of the subsequent chapters. Chapters Three through Seven each present the results of these analyses with respect to a different set of outcomes. Chapter Three explores the marital relationship, including marital satisfaction, interpartner conflict, and divorce intentions. Chapter Four explores the quality of the family environment, including parenting satisfaction and financial distress. Chapter Five examines the psychological and behavioral health of service members and spouses. Chapter Six explores child well-being, including both parent and teen reports. Chapter Seven assesses military integration, including satisfaction with the military and retention intentions. Finally, Chapter Eight offers general conclusions, policy implications, and recommendations for future research.

One final note: The report is designed such that each substantive chapter (Chapters Three through Six) can be read independently. Thus, each chapter briefly describes the methods used in the analysis (which themselves are described in detail in Chapter Two). Because these short descriptions of the methods are the same across chapters, readers of the full report can skip these sections in subsequent chapters. Similarly, many of the strengths and weaknesses of the study are discussed across chapters, and these sections may also be skipped in subsequent substantive chapters.

References

Belasco, A., *The Cost of Iraq, Afghanistan, and Other Global War on Terror Operations Since 9/11*, Washington, D.C.: Congressional Research Service, 2007.

Blue Star Families, *2012 Military Family Lifestyle Survey: Comprehensive Report-Sharing the Pride of Service*, Washington, D.C.: Blue Star Families, 2012.

Bowen, G. L., and D. K. Orthner, "Postscript: Toward Further Research," in G. L. Bowen and D. K. Orthner, eds., *The Organization Family: Work and Family Linkages in the U.S. Military*, New York: Praeger, 1989, pp. 179–188.

Bruner, E. F., *Military Forces: What Is the Appropriate Size for the United States?* Washington, D.C.: Congressional Research Service, 2006.

Clever, M., and D. R. Segal, "The Demographics of Military Children and Families," *The Future of Children*, Vol. 23, No. 2, 2013, pp. 13–39.

Fischer, H., *A Guide to U.S. Military Casualty Statistics: Operation Freedom's Sentinel, Operation Inherent Resolve, Operation New Dawn, Operation Iraqi Freedom, and Operation Enduring Freedom*, Washington, D.C.: Congressional Research Service, 2015.

Hosek, J., B. J. Asch, C. C. Fair, C. Martin, and M. Mattock, *Married to the Military: The Employment and Earnings of Military Wives Compared with Those of Civilian Wives*, Santa Monica, Calif.: RAND Corporation, MR-1565-OSD, 2002. As of November 10, 2015:
http://www.rand.org/pubs/monograph_reports/MR1565.html

Hosek, J., J. Kavanagh, and L. Miller, *How Deployments Affect Service Members*, Santa Monica, Calif.: RAND Corporation, MG-432-RC, 2006. As of November 10, 2015:
http://www.rand.org/pubs/monographs/MG432.html

Institute of Medicine, *Returning Home from Iraq and Afghanistan: Preliminary Assessment of Readjustment Needs of Veterans, Service Members, and Their Families*, Washington, D.C.: National Academies Press, 2010.

Karney, B. R., and J. S. Crown, *Families Under Stress: An Assessment of Data, Theory, and Research on Marriage and Divorce in the Military*, Santa Monica, Calif.: RAND Corporation, MG-599-OSD, 2007. As of November 10, 2015:
http://www.rand.org/pubs/monographs/MG599.html

Knobloch, L. K., and J. A. Theiss, "Experiences of U.S. Military Couples During the Post-Deployment Transition: Applying the Relational Turbulence Model," *Journal of Social and Personal Relationships*, Vol. 29, No. 4, 2012, pp. 1–28.

Loughran, D. S., *Wage Growth in the Civilian Careers of Military Retirees*, Santa Monica, Calif.: RAND Corporation, MR-1363-OSD, 2002. As of November 10, 2015:
http://www.rand.org/pubs/monograph_reports/MR1363.html

Newby, J. H., J. E. McCarroll, R. J. Ursano, Z. Z. Fan, J. Shigemura, and Y. Tucker-Harris, "Positive and Negative Consequences of a Military Deployment," *Military Medicine*, Vol. 170, 2005, pp. 815–819.

O'Keefe, R. A., M. C. Eyre, and D. L. Smith, "Military Family Service Centers," in F. W. Kaslow and R. I. Ridenour, eds., *The Military Family*, New York: Guilford, 1984, pp. 254–268.

Public Law 110-181, Section 1661, Study on Physical and Mental Health and Other Readjustment Needs of Members and Former Members of the Armed Forces Who Deployed in Operation Iraqi Freedom and Operation Enduring Freedom and Their Families, January 28, 2008. As of November 11, 2015:
http://www.gpo.gov/fdsys/pkg/PLAW-110publ181/html/PLAW-110publ181.htm

Rosen, L. N., and D. B. Durand, "Coping with the Unique Demands of Military Family Life," in J. A. Martin, L. N. Rosen, and L. R. Sparachino, eds., *The Military Family: A Practice Guide for Human Service Providers*, Westport, Conn.: Praeger, 2000, pp. 55–72.

Rostker, B. D., *I Want You: The Evolution of the All-Volunteer Force*, Santa Monica, Calif.: RAND Corporation, MG-265-RC, 2006. As of November 10, 2015:
http://www.rand.org/pubs/monographs/MG265.html

Rubin, A., and H. Harvie, "A Brief History of Social Work with the Military and Veterans," in A. Rubin, E. L. Weiss, and J. E. Coll. eds., *Handbook of Military Social Work*, Hoboken, N.J.: John Wiley & Sons, 2012, pp. 3–20.

Serafino, N. M., *Peacekeeping: Issues of U.S. Military Involvement*, Washington, D.C.: Congressional Research Service, Issue Brief 94040g, updated February 7, 2003.

Tanielian, T., and L. H. Jaycox, eds., *Invisible Wounds of War: Psychological and Cognitive Injuries, Their Consequences, and Services to Assist Recovery*, Santa Monica, Calif.: RAND Corporation, MG-720-CCF, 2008. As of November 10, 2015:
http://www.rand.org/pubs/monographs/MG720.html

Tanielian, T., B. R. Karney, A. Chandra, and S. O. Meadows, *The Deployment Life Study: Methodological Overview and Baseline Sample Description*, Santa Monica, Calif.: RAND Corporation, RR-209-A/OSD, 2014. As of November 10, 2015:
http://www.rand.org/pubs/research_reports/RR209.html

U.S. House of Representatives, Heroes at Home Act of 2009, H.R. 667, 111th Congress, referred to the Committee on Armed Services Subcommittee on Military Personnel on February 6, 2009.

U.S. Senate, Servicemembers Mental Health Care Commission Act, S. 1429, 111th Congress, hearings held in the Committee on Veterans' Affairs on October 21, 2009.

CHAPTER TWO

Data and Methods

Beth Ann Griffin, Terry L. Schell, Esther M. Friedman, Sarah O. Meadows, and Robin L. Beckman

All methods, procedures, and instruments used in the study were approved by the RAND Human Subject Protection Committee. The survey instruments are licensed by the U.S. Department of Defense (DoD) Washington Headquarters Services in December 2010 (Record Control Schedule HA [TRA] 2423). In addition, the study was granted a certificate of confidentiality from the National Institute of Mental Health (CC-MH-10-55).

Basic Study Design

This longitudinal study of military families was designed to examine military *family readiness* and included surveys of families at frequent intervals throughout a complete deployment cycle—that is, before a service member deployed (sometimes months before), during the actual deployment, and after the service member returned (possibly a year or more after she or he had redeployed). Outcomes of interest including the following:

- quality of marital and parental relationships
- psychological, behavioral, and physical health of family members
- child outcomes (e.g., emotional, behavioral, social, and academic functioning)
- military integration (e.g., attitudes toward military service, retention intentions).

The Deployment Life Study uses a single design and the same survey instruments (modified only slightly to make them service- and component-appropriate) to assess service members and their families, thus allowing for potential comparisons across services and components (active, reserve, and guard). At baseline, the study focused on enrolling married service members who were likely to deploy in the subsequent six- to 12-month period so as to maximize the ability to observe changes across the deployment cycle. Dual military families were included, but small sample sizes precluded separate analyses of just these families. Full details describing the design and baseline sample can be found in a separate report (see Tanielian et al., 2014).

The longitudinal study design used for the Deployment Life Study includes nine individual assessments with the service member, his or her spouse, and a teen between the ages of 11 and 17 (if available) over a three-year period.[1] Service members and spouses answered questions about themselves as well as about their family members and family relationships.

---

[1]   Due to delayed entry into the field for the Navy sample, those families were eligible only for seven waves of data collection. This allowed us to end data collection at roughly the same time for all families in the study.

Spouses reported on a specific (random) child between the ages of 3 and 18 in the household (if relevant). If that child was age 11 or older, he or she was then also invited to participate as a separate respondent and to complete his or her own surveys. We refer to these respondents as "teens."[2] In this manner, assessments were conducted every four months during this period (see Figure 2.1).

The unit of recruitment (and subsequent analysis) for the study is the household, defined as the service member, spouse, and teen, if available.[3] Initial recruitment and the administration of the baseline assessment described in this report began in March 2011 and ended in August 2012 for the Army, Air Force, and Marine Corps sample, and began in November 2012 and ended in February 2013 for the Navy sample. Because not every household began the baseline survey at the same time, the enrollment period was considered rolling, with subsequent surveys anchored to a household's baseline completion. For example, if a household enrolled in March 2011, the first follow-up survey was in July 2011 (i.e., four months after baseline). However, if a household enrolled in December 2011, its first follow-up was in April 2012.

The total baseline sample included 2,724 households: In 2,236 of these, a service member and spouse completed surveys; in the remaining 488, a service member, spouse, and teen completed surveys. Table 2.1 presents the final baseline sample, broken down by service and component. Please note that this table is *unweighted*.

Survey Administration

Baseline: Wave 1

Rolling enrollment meant that baseline assessments of service members, spouses, and teens occurred between March 31, 2011, and August 31, 2012, via computer-assisted telephone interview, with a limited number of potential participants completing the baseline survey via

Figure 2.1
Deployment Life Study Time Line

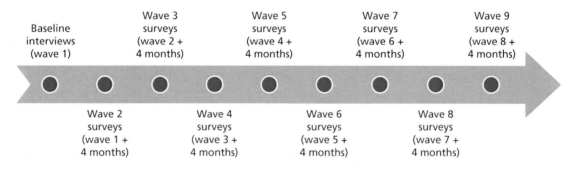

NOTE: Spaces between dots indicate four-month intervals.
RAND *RR1388-2.1*

---

[2]   In an earlier description of the study we referred to these as "study children" (see Tanielian et al., 2014).

[3]   If an eligible teen is not available or if an eligible teen is available but does not participate in the survey, then the service member and spouse are considered a household. Detailed information about the sampling strategy, recruitment, incentives, and response rates at baseline can be found in Tanielian et al. (2014).

Table 2.1
Final Deployment Life Baseline Sample by Service and Component (Raw Sample Sizes [Ns] and Unweighted Percentages)

Service and Component	Deployment Life Family[a] (n=2,724)	
	Raw N	Unweighted Percentage
Air Force	298	10.9
Active	254	9.3
Guard	32	1.2
Reserve	12	0.4
Army	1,426	52.3
Active	773	28.4
Guard	591	21.7
Reserve	62	2.3
Navy	873	32.0
Active	866	31.8
Reserve	7	0.3
Marine Corps	127	4.7
Active	110	4.0
Reserve	17	0.6

[a] Families are allocated to service and component based on service member self-report in the baseline survey.

the Internet. Not including the initial eligibility screening and consent (described in Tanielian et al., 2014), median completion time for baseline interviews was approximately 48 minutes for each adult and 26 minutes for each teen. Full copies of the baseline survey instruments can be found in Tanielian et al. (2014).

Follow-Up Surveys: Waves 2 Through 7/9
The longitudinal design was constructed to allow for, on average, one to three additional follow-up assessments prior to an expected deployment, approximately one to three assessments during deployment (depending on length of deployment), and approximately one to four assessments postdeployment (depending on timing of redeployment, or when the service member returned home). Because deployment characteristics vary by service, the number of survey waves completed before, during, and after deployment differed across families.

Households received invitations to complete follow-up surveys (i.e., waves 2 through 7/9) via email, as well as postal mail, approximately four months after the previous wave. Similar to the baseline, follow-up surveys remained open for eight weeks. However, the eight-week time frame for completion of follow-up waves did not begin when the first household member completed his or her survey; rather, it started on the date that the household was eligible to complete the follow-up (i.e., four months after the household completed the baseline interview and thus was "officially" enrolled).

According to this timing system, participants who completed the survey near the end of the eight-week window still received the next invitation four months from the previous invitation. Thus, it was possible that a household could complete consecutive waves anywhere between two months and six months after the previous wave. The RAND Survey Research Group provided reminder phone calls to households that had not yet completed a survey during the eight-week window. During these calls, which occurred four weeks after the first household member completed his or her survey, the research group offered the participant an opportunity to complete the survey via telephone. The vast majority of follow-up surveys, however, were completed via the Internet (96 percent), with roughly 4 percent of all service member, spouse, and teen follow-up surveys taking place through the research group phone center. Median completion time for follow-up interviews was approximately 37 minutes for each adult and 24 minutes for each teen.

The following guidelines were used for ongoing participation in the Deployment Life Study:

- If a respondent—or all the participating family members—missed or skipped a survey, the household was still considered enrolled unless it specifically requested to be removed from the study.
- If one adult wanted to drop out of the survey but the second adult wished to remain, both were allowed to take their desired actions.
- A teen could not remain in the study unless at least one adult respondent in his or her household remained enrolled.
- If a marriage dissolved, both adults could continue to participate in the study and complete a truncated version of the instruments.

In each follow-up interview, each respondent was asked whether the service member was preparing for deployment, deployed, or recently returned from deployment. A module of survey questions specific to that aspect of deployment was added to that survey wave for each family member.

Completion Rates and Attrition

One of the benefits of a multirespondent longitudinal design is that not every respondent has to complete every available survey in order for his or her data to be used. For example, if a service member was deployed and unable to complete a survey, his or her spouse and/or teen could complete their own surveys, allowing the analyses to include that household. Thus, at a minimum, knowing how a household functioned across the deployment cycle required only one member of the household to respond. Obviously, the preferred scenario was for all eligible members of a household to complete all available surveys. Figure 2.2 graphically depicts the percentage of service members, spouses, and teens who completed each wave of data collection (i.e., baseline through Wave 7 for Navy households and Wave 9 for Army, Air Force, and Marine Corps households). The figure also shows the percentage of households where all eligible members complete a survey (by wave) and where at least one member competes a survey (again, by wave).

As shown in Figure 2.2, individual completion rates fell somewhere between those completion rates for households where at least one member completed a survey (roughly 80 percent to 85 percent) and households where all eligible members completed a survey (roughly 55 percent to 60 percent). Spouses were more likely to complete surveys, followed by teens, and then service members. This may be due to the fact that many of the service members in the sample deployed during the study period, often making it much more difficult for them to find the resources (e.g., time, a computer, Internet) necessary to complete a survey either in the lead up to or during a deployment.

Figure 2.2
Completion Percentages by Respondent, Household, and Wave

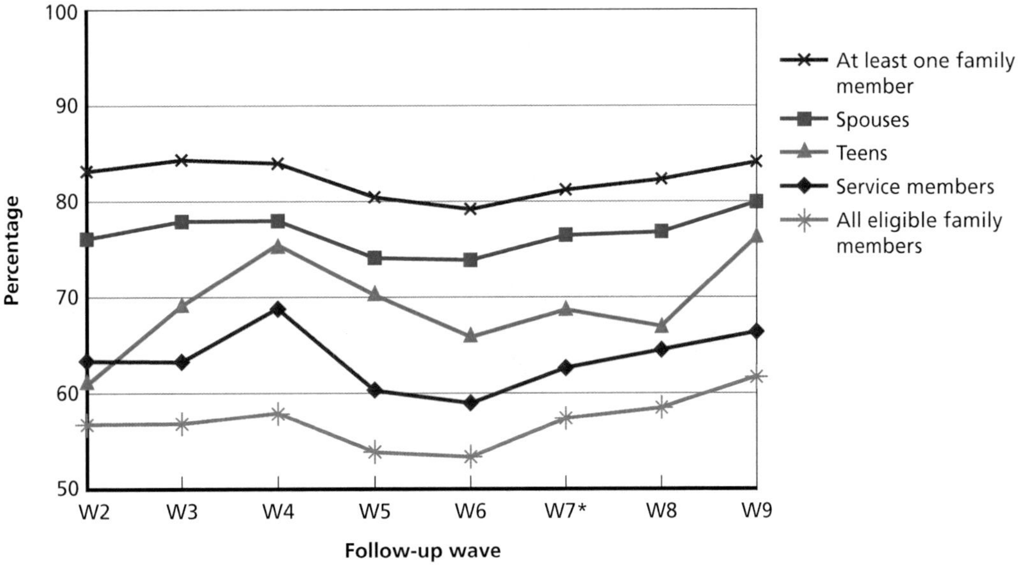

*By design, the Navy subsample completed only seven waves.
RAND RR1388-2.2

Figure 2.2 also shows that completion rates varied over time. Survey fatigue was the most likely reason for the drop in completion rates seen around follow-up waves 5 and 6. However, completion rates trended upward after that, suggesting that our incentive structure, which included bonuses for completing a certain number of surveys during the second half of the study, may have played a role in improving responses.

Although it was important for at least one member of the household to complete a survey, consistently completing surveys across time was also important. That is, we wanted the same respondent to complete surveys over time in order to track their health and well-being, and to detect changes that occurred every four months. Thus, it is important to understand how many surveys each respondent contributed to the overall longitudinal data collection. To a certain extent, this can be thought of as an indicator of attrition, or ebb and flow into and out of the survey. Figures 2.3, 2.4, and 2.5 show the total number of surveys completed by service members, spouses, and teens, respectively.

Darker shades represent completing more surveys. Each bar sums to 100 percent of the sample, for each service and component. For example, in Figure 2.3, the first bar indicates that, among active component soldiers enrolled in the study, 7 percent completed only one survey (presumably the baseline survey), 8 percent completed two surveys, 7 percent completed three surveys, 9 percent completed four surveys, 11 percent completed five surveys, 10 percent completed six surveys, 12 percent completed seven surveys, 13 completed eight surveys, and 20 percent completed all nine surveys. With three exceptions, among all respondents—service members, spouses, and teens—across all services and branches, the greatest percentages of completions are in the darker bars.[4] Said another way, the majority of all respondents com-

---

[4] Those exceptions are service members in the Navy and Marine Corps Reserve and study children in the Marine Corps Reserve.

Figure 2.3
Number of Completed Surveys, Service Members by Service and Component

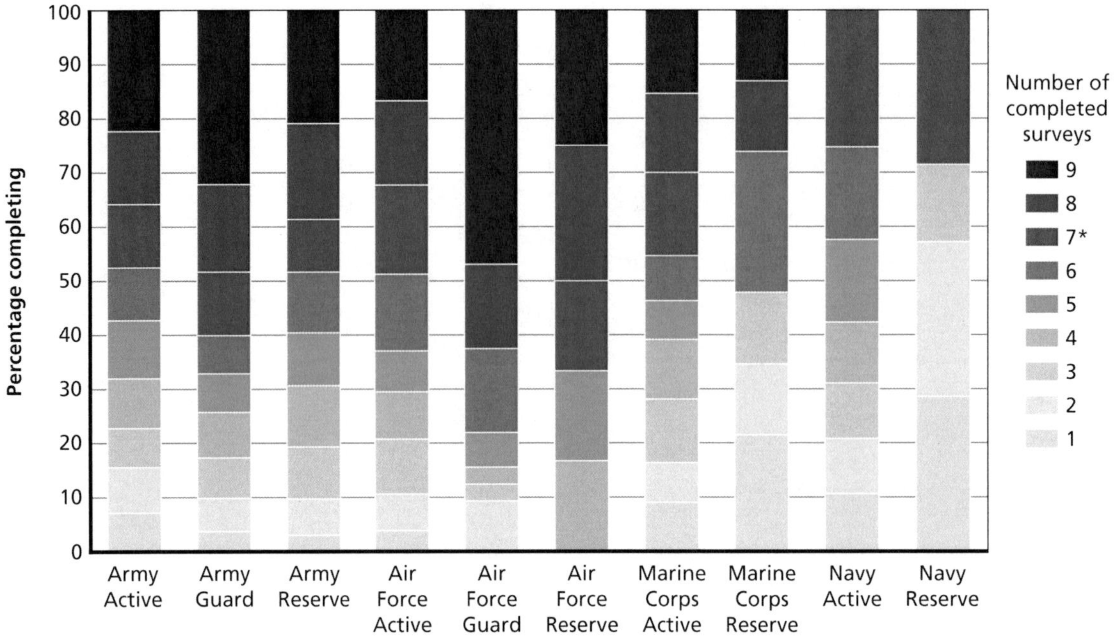

*By design, the Navy subsample completed only seven waves.

RAND *RR1388-2.3*

Figure 2.4
Number of Completed Surveys, Spouses by Service and Component

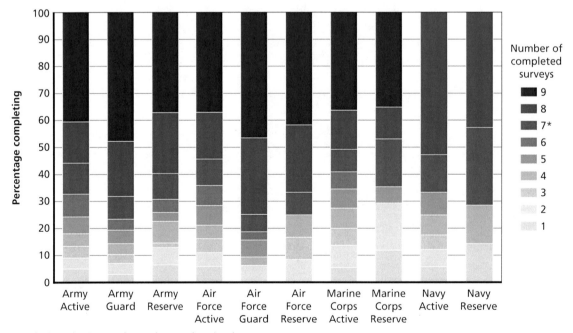

*By design, the Navy subsample completed only seven waves.

RAND *RR1388-2.4*

Figure 2.5
Number of Completed Surveys, Teens by Service and Component

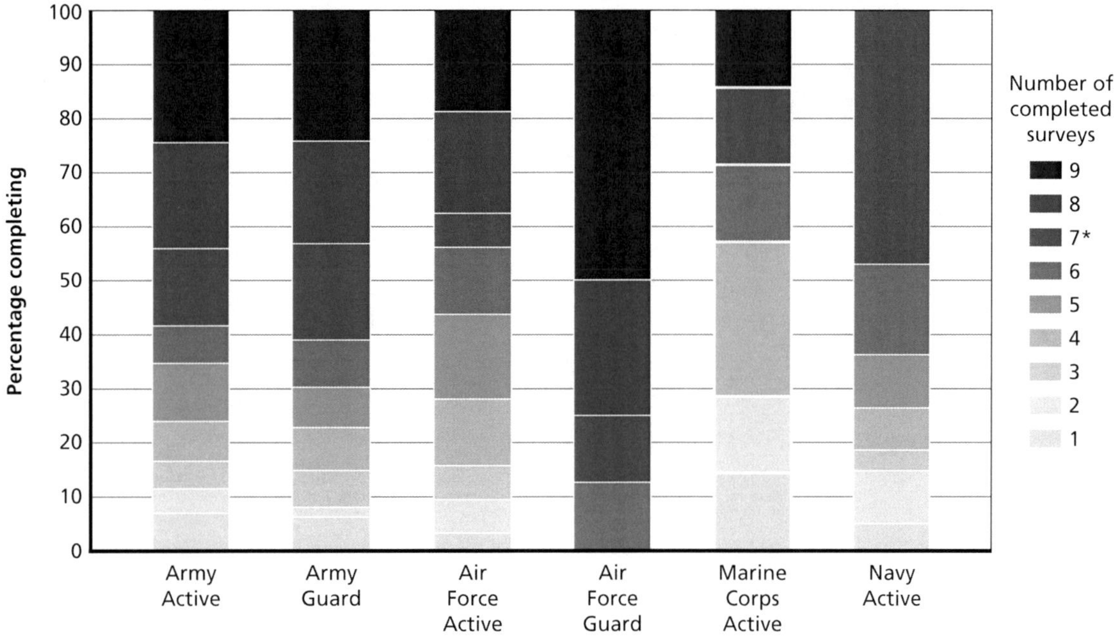

*By design, the Navy subsample completed only seven waves.
NOTE: Army, Air Force, Marine Corps, and Navy Reserve are not shown due to small sample sizes.
RAND RR1388-2.5

pleted at least half of the surveys for which they were eligible (i.e., nine for Army, Air Force, and Marine Corps families, and seven for Navy families).

There are several implications of these completion and attrition rates for the analyses. First, there are sufficient data to examine trajectories of key outcomes over the deployment cycle, and this is true for each individual member of the household (i.e., service members, spouses, and teens). Second, analyses of within-person changes at a more micro level (i.e., every few months versus annually) are also possible. Third, analyses within certain subgroups in the data cannot be supported, due to insufficient sample sizes. For example, reserve and guard component data, particularly the Navy and Marine Corps Reserve, are too small to analyze separately. The next section reviews the content of the follow-up surveys, paying special attention to measures that are repeated over time and those that are in the predeployment, deployment, and postdeployment modules.

Survey Content

Baseline Survey

The baseline survey was designed to assess four domains related to military family health and well-being across the deployment cycle:[5] preexisting conditions, experiences during deploy-

---

[5] Baseline surveys for service members, spouses, and teens can be found in Tanielian et al. (2014). This report also discusses the theoretical model and measure used in construction of the surveys in greater detail.

ment, immediate outcomes, and long-term outcomes. These domains, and related constructs, are depicted in Figure 1.1. As noted in Chapter One, the model suggests multiple pathways by which the experience of deployment may interact with preexisting conditions of military families to account for their immediate and long-term outcomes after a deployment. First, the model suggests that all of the preexisting conditions of a family affect that family's outcomes through their direct effects on the quality of the family's adaptive processes during deployment. Second, the model highlights the fact that the deployment itself is an exogenous variable that has direct effects on outcomes, as well as interactions with adaptive processes to affect a family's outcomes. Third, the model recognizes that military service can be a life-altering experience for each member of the family, leading to emergent traits that can be positive or negative. This impact can be experienced at both individual and family levels because such events can disrupt how the family functions as a whole. Finally, the model recognizes that the consequences of deployment for families may evolve over time, such that the immediate impact can differ from the long-term impact.

The baseline survey collected information from service members, spouses, and teens related to:

- *enduring traits*, or the relatively stable qualities of each family member (e.g., demographic characteristics, childhood experiences)
- *marital resources*, including the attributes of the relationships among service members and spouses (e.g., duration of marriage, presence of children)
- *nonmilitary circumstances*, or each family's own ecological niche (e.g., financial distress, social networks)
- *prior military experiences*, including prior experience with deployment (e.g., years of service, prior deployment history)
- *adaptive processes*, or all the ways in which family members interact, cope with stress, support each other, communicate, and resolve problems (e.g., communication, coping)
- *characteristics of a current deployment* (e.g., length of deployment, trauma exposure)
- *emergent traits*, or how family members emerge from the experience of deployment (e.g., physical injury, additional education)
- *relationship quality* among and between family members (e.g., marital satisfaction, family cohesion).

The ultimate question that the Deployment Life Study was designed to address is how the experience of deployment affects the long-term well-being of military families. By closely examining those families that are successful, it is possible to start to paint a picture of what characteristics, qualities, and resources are related to family readiness. The dimensions of long-term well-being of greatest concern are marital and family relationships, the psychological and behavioral health of family members, child and teen well-being, and military integration. The baseline survey provided a predeployment anchor for these outcomes; however, these same outcomes were assessed at every wave to enable examination of a trajectory of well-being over the deployment cycle. We discuss specific measures within these categories of outcomes.

Follow-Up Surveys

Follow-up surveys contained a number of items about individual and family health, well-being, and functioning. Many, if not most, of those items were repeated at every wave, again allowing for assessment of microchanges. However, because the study was interested in family readiness—what makes some families better able to adapt to stress and strain experienced during a deployment—follow-up surveys also included three special modules depending on whether the respondent reported the service member was preparing for a deployment, was currently deployed, or had returned from a deployment in the past year.

Information About Children and Teens

In the baseline survey, spouses provided a roster of all persons living in the household, including both adults and children. A random child (based on the first letter of the first name) was chosen to be the focus of this study. If the selected child was younger than age 11 (which we refer to as a "child"), the spouse was asked questions about the child on the baseline survey and all subsequent surveys. If the selected child was 11 or older (a "teen"), the spouse was also asked questions about the teen *and* he or she was invited to complete his or her own survey. Thus, information on teens in this study comes from two sources in most cases: the teen survey and the spouse survey. In some cases, the teen did not agree to participate; in those instances, information about the teen comes only from the spouse.

Deployment Modules

Predeployment

The predeployment phase of the deployment cycle is the time in which service members and their families are informed of an impending deployment and prepare for it. The characteristics and activities of families during this period can set the stage for how well, or how poorly, the family will adapt during a deployment. The predeployment module focused on a number of family readiness activities (see Troxel et al., forthcoming).

Readiness. Readiness is a key construct among military families. Whether a service member, spouse, or child feels prepared for a deployment may be a protective factor in helping adapt to additional stresses and strains associated with deployment. In contrast, families that do not feel prepared for such a tumultuous period may be at a disadvantage when it comes to coping with a deployment. The predeployment module included two types of readiness: family and child. In total, the survey included 14 items from the Deployment Risk and Resilience Inventory (King et al., 2006). These items are also used in the Defense Manpower Data Center's (DMDC's) Status of Forces Survey (DMDC, 2012).

- *Family and marital readiness.* Family readiness included five items asked of both service members and spouses. The first three items asked whether the family had money for food, rent, and other living expenses during the deployment; whether the family had developed a financial emergency plan; and whether the service member or spouse had life insurance. The next two items referred specifically to the couple and asked whether the service member or spouse had talked to his or her spouse about how the upcoming deployment may affect the marriage and whether either party had talked with a professional (e.g., counselor) about it.
- *Child readiness.* Parents—both service members and spouses—received four items about how well the child or children (regardless of age) in the household had been prepared for an upcoming deployment. Items asked about whether the service member or spouse had talked with a professional about how the deployment might affect the children, talked

directly with the children about what to expect during the deployment, connected the children with a support group (e.g., Operation Purple Camp), and connected with other military children in the community.

During Deployment

Experiences during a deployment could have a direct or indirect impact on individual and family functioning, in both the short and long term. Direct effects include consequences that can be attributed to experiences during deployment (e.g., physical and emotional injuries). The indirect effects include consequences that are mediated by adaptive or maladaptive processes within the family (e.g., the stress of deployment can lead to emotional distance between spouses, which, in turn, can lead to marital distress or divorce). The deployment module measured both sets of consequences, which allowed us to tease apart the degree to which family members' own actions may have buffered, or exacerbated, the effects that deployment experiences had on their outcomes.

At each wave for which a service member reported that she or he was currently deployed, the Deployment Life Study asked a series of items about what life was like for both the service member and his or her family. These measures will be described more thoroughly in the substantive chapters that follow, so they are only briefly mentioned here. For service members, items in the deployment module focused on information about the length of the current deployment, communication with his or her family, and general military-related stressors. For spouses, items in the deployment module covered communication with the service member, problems the family may have been experiencing during the deployment, sources of support, and how children were coping with deployment. For teens, items in the deployment module examined communication with both parents (including the service member who was deployed), general items rating how the family was doing during the deployment, experiences the teen had during deployment, and sources of support.

Key Outcome Domains

Five key outcome domains were identified for further exploration in this final report: marital outcomes, family outcomes, psychological and behavioral health outcomes, child and teen well-being, and military integration outcomes. Survey items used to measure key outcomes within each domain are briefly reviewed in the following sections. All the constructs have high reliability and validity (see Tanielian et al., 2014, for a review). Note that the discussion here is not exhaustive; additional variables of interest will be discussed, as relevant, in subsequent substantive chapters.

Marital Outcomes

The quality of the relationships among family members, especially spouses, was one of the central outcomes of interest in the Deployment Life Study. The longitudinal design of the study allows for analyses of change in the quality of these relationships, controlling for the quality of those relationships prior to the deployment. There are three key constructs in this domain:

- *Marital satisfaction* surveys were administered to both service members and spouses at every wave, measured with a series of items adapted from a set used previously in the Florida Family Formation Survey (Rauer et al., 2008). These surveys assessed relationship satisfaction in nine areas, including satisfaction with time spent together, communication, and trust.

- Service members and spouses reported on their *affective responses to interactions* with each other. To measure these responses, eight items were adapted from the Positive and Negative Affect Schedule (PANAS) short form, a frequently used measure of positive and negative affect (Watson, Clark, and Tellegen, 1988; Thompson and Cavallaro, 2007). Both partners were asked to report on their experienced affect after typical interactions with each other.
- *Intimate-partner violence* was measured using three items each from the physical-assault and psychological-aggression subscales from the Conflict Tactics Scale 2 (Straus et al., 1996). For each of these items, service members and spouses reported the frequency with which they or their partners demonstrated aggressive behaviors (e.g., insulting or swearing at partner, pushing or shoving partner).

Family Outcomes

Similar to marital outcomes, family outcomes were also of central importance to the Deployment Life Study. There are three key constructs in this domain, as well:

- For military couples who were also parents, *parenting satisfaction* was assessed via a six-item measure asking service members and spouses to rate their level of agreement with statements about parenting (e.g., "Being a parent is harder than I thought it would be"). This measure was adapted from a nine-item measure of parental aggravation developed for the Child Development Supplement of the Panel Study of Income Dynamics (Abidin, 1995; see also Hofferth et al., 1997; Panel Study of Income Dynamics, undated).
- Service members and spouses rated the *quality of family environment* using a six-item measure of family environment that assesses how the family functions as a unit. These items were selected from the cohesion and conflict subscales of the Family Environment Scale (Moos and Moos, 1994) and asked respondents to rate how well statements described their families (e.g., "We fight a lot in our family").
- Both service members and spouses rated the *family's financial health* via four items adapted from Gutman and Eccles (1999). These items assessed whether the family could make ends meet, whether there had been enough money to pay bills, whether there was any money left over at the end of the month, and the level of worry caused by the family's financial situation.

Psychological and Behavioral Health Outcomes

The largest domain evaluated in the Deployment Life Study concerns the psychological and behavioral health of adults (i.e., service members and spouses). There are four key constructs in this domain:

- The eight-item Patient Health Questionnaire (PHQ8) is a brief assessment of the severity of *depression symptoms*, based on the *Diagnostic and Statistical Manual of Mental Disorders*, fourth edition criteria for depressive disorders and was used with both service members and spouses (American Psychiatric Association, 1994; Kroenke, Spitzer, and Williams, 2001; Kroenke, Strine, et al., 2009).
- *Anxiety* among service members and spouses was measured using the anxiety subscale of the Mental Health Inventory 18 (Sherbourne et al., 1992). This subscale is seen as an assessment of general anxiety.

- The Posttraumatic Stress Disorder (PTSD) Checklist (PCL) (Weathers, Huska, and Keane, 1991) is used to assess *PTSD symptoms* among service members. Respondents indicated how much they had been bothered by 17 different symptoms in the past 30 days. Only service members who indicated that they had, in fact, experienced a traumatic event received the full PCL. The PCL has been used in prior work on military populations (see Bliese et al., 2007; Hoge, Castro, et al., 2004; Hoge, Terhakopian, et al., 2007; Tanielian and Jaycox, 2008); the version used in the Deployment Life Study was the specific PCL. Probable diagnoses of PTSD were derived using guidelines offered by Weathers, Litz, and colleagues (1993).
  - The survey also assesses *PTSD symptoms among spouses* using the Primary Care PTSD Screen (Prins et al., 2004).[6] This measure used a screen item to "cue" respondents to traumatic events and then asked whether four specific symptoms have occurred in the past 30 days.
- Use of *alcohol* may also represent a maladaptive response to a deployment experience. Service members who may not have used or abused these substances before a deployment may change their habits upon return. We used three items to assess the frequency and amount of alcohol consumption by service members and spouses. These items included the number of days the respondent had consumed alcohol in the past 30 days, the average number of drinks consumed on those days, and the number of days the respondent binge-drank (five or more drinks for men, four or more drinks for women) in the past 30 days. All items came from the 2007 National Survey on Drug Use and Health (U.S. Department of Health and Human Services, 2008).

Child and Teen Well-Being

The potential impact that deployment can have on children (regardless of age) is assessed across several important domains, including psychological and behavioral health outcomes, social relationships, and academic engagement. We include a broad array of measures, including four key constructs:

- The Strengths and Difficulties Questionnaire (SDQ), asked of spouses (for all ages) and teens, is a 25-item assessment *of overall child well-being and functioning* in five areas: emotional problems (e.g., "You have many fears"), conduct problems (e.g., "You fight a lot"), hyperactivity (e.g., "You get easily distracted"), peer relationships (e.g., "You have at least one good friend"), and prosocial behavior (e.g., "You try to be nice to other people") (Goodman, 1997, 2001). The SDQ has been used to screen for child psychiatric disorders (Goodman et al., 2000), and is completed by both spouses and the children.
- *Anxiety* was assessed using the five-item Screen for Child Anxiety Related Emotional Disorders (SCARED) (Birmaher, Brent, et al., 1999; Birmaher, Khetarpal, et al., 1997), which was asked of spouses (for all ages) and teens. The items include a single measure for five underlying factors: panic, generalized anxiety, separation anxiety, social phobia, and school phobia. Both study children and spouses received the SCARED.

---

[6] This measure is not directly comparable to the Primary Care Checklist–Military Version (PCL-M) used in service members.

- A modified version of the Patient Health Questionnaire for Adolescents (Version 3.6.05; American Academy of Pediatrics, 2010) was used to assess the presence of eight depressive symptoms, rated in terms of their frequency in the prior two weeks. This measure was completed by spouses for all ages, and by teen via self-report.
- A seven-item *academic engagement* scale developed by Rosenthal and Feldman (1991) asked teens how frequently they did their homework, prepared for class, and engaged in other similar activities.

Military Integration Outcomes

Military integration refers to the degree of assimilation and bonding one has with the military. It is operationalized as individuals' military satisfaction, commitment, retention intentions, and children's interest in joining the military. From the perspective of DoD, retention is a key long-term outcome. The all-volunteer force is dependent on service members choosing to remain in their military careers beyond their required terms of service. A family's experience with deployment very likely affects this decision. There are four key constructs in this domain:

- *Satisfaction with the military way of life* was assessed using a single item from the DMDC Status of Forces Survey (Defense Manpower Data Center, 2012) and asked of both service members and spouses.
- A single item drawn from the DMDC survey assessed *retention intentions* from the perspective of different family members. For this report, we used a single item per active-duty respondent: the service member's preference for remaining in the military, the spouse's preference for the service member remaining in the military, and the teen's preference for the service member remaining in the military.
- A scale of three items, also taken from the Status of Forces Survey, assessed service member, spouse, and teen *commitment to the military*.
- A single item, created specifically for the Deployment Life Study, asked the teen whether she or he planned to have a *career in the military*.

Measuring Deployment Trauma

Given the novel way in which this study addressed trauma experienced during deployment, this section briefly describes the related measures used in Chapters Three through Eight. It is important to recognize that the Deployment Life Study included two different measures of deployment trauma, measured at different points in the survey and referring to different periods of the service members military career. At baseline, all service members were asked if they had ever experienced any one of 15 possible experiences. Taken from the Hoge Experiences Scale (Hoge et al., 2004), service members selected a yes/no response indicating whether they had experienced the following events:

- being ambushed or attacked
- participating in demining operations
- seeing ill or injured women or children whom you were unable to help
- receiving small arms fire
- shooting or directing fire at the enemy

- receiving incoming artillery, rocket, or mortar fire
- seeing dead bodies or human remains
- engaging in hand-to-hand combat
- being directly responsible for the death of an enemy combatant or noncombatant
- handling uncovered human remains
- clearing or searching homes or buildings
- had a close call, were hot or hit but protective gear saved you
- knowing someone who was killed or injured
- being wounded or injured
- had a buddy shot or hit who was near service member.

Positive responses ("yes") were summed to create an index of baseline trauma exposure, ranging from 0 to 15.

During follow-up waves of the study, deployment trauma exposure was linked to the current, or study, deployment. This measure of deployment trauma exposure was taken from the *Invisible Wounds* study (see Tanielian and Jaycox, 2008, p. 91). Service members were asked if, during their most recent deployment (experienced while the study was taking place), they experienced any of a set of 11 events. A sum score of all positive ("yes") responses was created for each service member. In addition, in order to assess different types of trauma, we also included three additional dichotomous measures indicating whether the service member experienced any combat trauma, physical trauma, or psychological trauma during the study deployment. The 11 events, grouped by type of trauma, are as follows:

- combat
  - engaging in hand-to-hand combat
  - being physically knocked over by an explosion
  - being responsible for the death of a civilian
- psychological
  - witnessing an accident which resulted in serious injury or death
  - having a friend who was seriously wounded or killed
  - smelling decomposing bodies
  - seeing dead or seriously injured noncombatants (e.g., women, children, elderly)
  - witnessing brutality toward detainees or prisoners
- physical
  - being wounded or injured requiring hospitalization
  - being wounded or injured but not requiring hospitalization
  - having a bump or blow to the head from any accident or injury.

Overview of Methods

Analytic Weights

The weights used in the analysis of longitudinal data from the Deployment Life Study are designed to address several possible problems with the representativeness of the analytic sample.[7] Sources of these threats to representativeness include: (a) differing sampling probabilities across military services; (b) differences in characteristics between the baseline sample and the sample frames provided by the military services due to nonresponse at baseline; (c) differences in characteristics between the respondents who were successfully followed to the later waves of the study relative to the full respondent sample at baseline; and (d) differences in the characteristics of the follow-up respondents relative to the inferential populations of interest, populations that are defined based on factors that were not known at the time of sampling. (For this last type of sample representativeness, we want to address differences between the longitudinal respondents who deployed during the three-year study and the full population of married U.S. service members who deployed during that same period, as well any differences between the longitudinal respondents who did *not* deploy during the study period and the full population of married U.S. service members who did *not* deploy during this period.) The final weights were derived through a multiple-step process that relied on both model-based inverse probability weights and poststratification weights to either population or sample distributions.

The baseline sample weights are described in Tanielian et al. (2014), and were designed to address issues (a) and (b) above, related to the sample design and baseline nonresponse. Weights for the longitudinal analyses build on those baseline weights to address issues (c) and (d) above (i.e., longitudinal attrition and the representativeness to sample relative to the final inferential populations). The weight components are described in the following section.

The Deployment Life Study faced a number of challenges in enrolling a representative sample of military families and retaining families over time. First, when recruiting study participants, stratified random samples were drawn from the population-based files sent by each service branch. These samples resulted in a pool of recruited participants that were representative of the service members included in the sampling files on a number of key characteristics (e.g., officer versus enlisted status, gender, number of previous deployments, number of dependents [Army only], component, occupation code [Air Force only]). However, the actual participants who enrolled and completed a baseline survey differed from the original sample on a number of factors (e.g., we had a disproportionately high number of officers enroll in our study for each service, so our sample of respondents had a higher percentage of officers than the sample files; see Tanielian et al. [2014]). In light of these shifts, sampling weights were created using model-based inverse probability weights that aimed to make our enrolled sample representative of the original sampling files provided by each service. While those weights balance the respondent sample within each service to the sample files from each service, the sample files were not generated the same way across services and components. To merge these into an aggregate sample that was more representative of the armed forces during a similar time period, the sample was poststratified so that the aggregate respondent sample was distributed across services and components in a way that matched the actual distribution of married personnel between 2012 and 2013 according to the DoD Contingency Tracking File.

Additionally, the study experienced attrition rates that ranged from 31.1 percent to 41.0 percent for service members, 20.1 percent to 26.1 percent for spouses, and 23.6 percent to 39.1 percent for teens at each wave of the study relative to the full sample enrolled at baseline (see Figure 2.2). This attrition can cause "sample drift" such that the sample available for longitudinal analyses is no longer representative of either the baseline sample or the full sampled

---

[7]   Note that weights discussed here may differ from those used in the baseline report (see Tanielian et al., 2014).

population (e.g., those lost to follow-up may be worse in terms of outcomes than those who stayed enrolled). In order to minimize bias from longitudinal attrition, we computed attrition weights for those respondents who continued responding into the later waves of the study—in other words, those who had responded to at least one of the final three waves and would be used in the primary longitudinal models (waves 7, 8, and 9 for the Army, Air Force and Marine Corps; waves 5, 6, and 7 for the Navy). Those weights made the follow-up sample representative of the full sample of baseline respondents on a number of important factors assessed at baseline, including measures of all study outcomes.

Attrition weights were estimated using Generalized Boosted Models (GBM) via the Toolkit for Weighting and Analysis of Nonequivalent Groups (TWANG) package in R (Ridgeway et al., 2014). GBM is a flexible, nonparametric estimation method that has been shown to outperform logistic regression for a variety of purposes (Lee, Lessler, and Stuart, 2010; McCaffrey, Ridgeway, and Morral, 2004). This method is particularly useful when one has a large number of baseline covariates to include in a model of the dichotomous indicator for attrition. Our attrition weights controlled for between 49 and 63 baseline characteristics, depending on the respondent (service member, spouse, or teen). These included factors that might be associated with either the likelihood of deployment or the ultimate outcomes of interest in the study. Those baseline characteristics included: sociodemographic characteristics (e.g., gender, age, minority status, length of marriage, presence of children younger than age 18 in the home), military characteristics (e.g., pay grade, number of previous combat deployments, service branch, component, previous trauma/combat exposure), and baseline measures of key outcomes included in this report (see Appendix Tables 2A.1, 2A.2, and 2A.3). The attrition weights were combined with the baseline sample weights already discussed. Attrition weights were estimated separately for each of the three types of respondents (service member, spouse, and teen). The success of the attrition weights can be assessed by measuring how similar our attrition weighted longitudinal respondent sample is to the entire weighted sample of baseline respondents. Table 2.A1 contains the standardized mean differences (SMD) between the follow-up respondent sample and the full baseline respondent sample for each covariate. The SMD for the *k-th* covariate equals

$$\frac{\overline{X}_{k,1} - \overline{X}_{k,0}}{\widehat{\sigma}_{x_{k,1}}}$$

where $\overline{X}_{k,j}$ denotes the mean of the *k-th* covariate at baseline for the full sample *(j=1)* and for the subset that continued to respond in the latter portion of study *(j=0)*, and $\widehat{\sigma}_{X_{k,1}}$ denotes the estimated standard deviation of the *k-th* covariate among the original baseline sample. The SMD provides an assessment of the size of the imbalance both before and after attrition weighting that is less affected by sample size than tests of statistical significance. We utilize this effect size measure rather than relying on significance tests because we wanted to ensure that our sample of responders looked representative of the original cohorts without depending on significance tests that can be sensitive to sample sizes (e.g., for a study with a large sample size, all differences, even small ones, might be considered significant when in fact the differences are not notable—or, for a small study, no significant differences might be found when in fact differences between groups are large). We interpret values between −0.20 and 0.20 as generally indicative of descriptively small differences between the follow-up sample and the original baseline sample. As shown in Appendix Tables 2A.1, 2A.2, and 2A.3, our sample of responders were actually quite representative of the original baseline sample, even prior to the use of our attrition weights. Nonetheless, our attrition weights do a good job at improving the balance between our respondent sample and the original baseline sample in the Deployment Life Study.

Finally, the study was designed to allow statistical inference for two specific populations: (1) the population of married service members who deployed during the study period and (2) the population of all married service members during the study period. Because the characteristics of those populations were not knowable at the time of sampling, it is possible that the resulting sample, even with baseline sampling weights and longitudinal attrition weights, is not representative of these populations. To better ensure that the analytic sample is representative of the inferential populations, we weighted the service member and spouse follow-up respondent samples to the characteristics of the populations of interests. Specifically, the sample of longitudinal service member respondents who deployed during the study was weighted to be representative of the population of married service members who deployed in 2012 and 2013. Similarly, the sample of longitudinal service member respondents who did not deploy during the study period was weighted to be representative of the married service members who did not deploy in either 2012 or 2013. These weights were derived separately for both service members and their spouses, although the characteristics on which spouses are being matched to the population are defined by the service members (e.g., service member pay grade), so that the weighted spouses are a sample whose service members are representative of the service member deployed/nondeployed population. Summary characteristics for the target populations were obtained from personnel data provided by the DMDC.

Appendix Tables 2.A4, 2.A5, 2.A6, and 2.A7 compare the characteristics of the Deployment Life Study longitudinal sample and the target populations. A number of significant differences are noted. First, among those service members experiencing a deployment, our attrition-weighted study samples in the Army, Air Force, and Marine Corps were younger on average than those service members in 2012 and 2013; in the Navy, they were slightly older. Our attrition-weighted samples also had fewer minorities and prior combat deployments than the target populations of interest. Moreover, the Army, Air Force, and Navy had attrition-weighted study samples with a greater percentage of senior enlisted service members than the target populations, while the Marine Corps had a disproportionately high number of officers enrolled in the deployed sample relative to the target population (70 percent versus 18 percent. This imbalance goes back to the original sampling file provided by the Marine Corps, which contained a substantially larger proportion of officers than is representative). Among those service members who did not experience a study deployment, various differences can be noted, often in the opposite direction than was observed with the deployed sample.

Weights to align the longitudinal respondent sample with the inferential populations were estimated using a raking procedure, which iteratively adjusts the weights so the weighted marginal distribution of the analytic sample matches the marginal distribution of the target population on each characteristic included (Bacharach, 1965). Estimation took place in the R statistical package using the *rake* command. These raked weights were also computed separately for the spouse and service member respondents. For each type of respondent, the weights were estimated within eight poststratification cells (the four services crossed with deployment status). After estimating the weights within each of these eight subsamples, aggregate poststratification weights were computed across the services; this maintained the proportionate representation of the services in the personnel data and across the deployed and nondeployed samples, which maintained their proportionate representation in the overall target population of married service members in the military in 2012 and 2013. Variables included in the weights were generally consistent across the services. All weights attempted to match on age, gender, percentage minority, whether the service member had ever been deployed previously, and pay grade. The pay grade classification differed slightly across branch, with the Army, Navy, and Air Force using up to five categories (E1–E3, E4–E9, O1–O3, O4–O6, and WO1–WO5) and the Marine Corps using two categories (E1–E9, and O1–O6 and WO1–WO5 combined). Additionally, the Army and Air Force were also matched on component—active, reserve, and guard. Thus, the poststratification weights make the follow-up sample of service members representative of the married service members in the military between 2012 and 2013 on these characteristics, while the follow-up sample of spouses of service members are also weighted to have service members who are representative of married service members in the military between 2012 and 2013. Similarly, the sample of respondents who experienced a deployment during our study is representative of the married service members who deployed between 2012 and 2013 on these characteristics. Poststratification weights were not computed for the teens because we did not have population data from DMDC about the distribution of service member characteristics for those who had children eligible to be respondents in the study.

Appendix 2A Tables 2A.4 through 2A.7 show how well the poststratification weights align the sample with the target population within each service. As shown, the weights make the analytic sample look very similar, and in most cases even identical, to the target population for the characteristics upon which it was matched. However, there are several factors where we could not align our sample with the target population. First, the study sample had very few Navy and Marine Corps reservists; thus, we were unable to make those services representative on component. Second, no junior enlisted Marine Corps service members participated in the survey. Thus, the poststratification weights cannot make the Marine Corps look representative of the target population on the five-category version of pay grade. However, we were able to adjust the representation of officers successfully with the poststratification weights so that the proportion of officers in the sample is in line with the target population. Unfortunately, given the small sample size of Marine Corps service members, we were unable to obtain perfect balance for the deployed cohort on other measures. For example, for the Marine Corps service member and spouse deployed samples, the samples still had a lower percentage of minorities (18 percent in the weighted sample and 30 percent in the target population) and a younger mean age (29.1 years for both service members and spouses in the weighted sample) than the target population (31.0 years for spouses and 31.3 years for service members).

In the analyses described in the various chapters, the baseline sample weights, attrition weights, and poststratification weights have been combined into one analytic weight. The baseline sample weight components are constant for all respondents within a household, because they are based on service members' characteristics available in the sample files or personnel records. The attrition component of the weight (and the poststratification weights that build upon them) differs across members within a household; thus, the final analytic weights are not identical across service member, spouse, or teen within a given household.

Imputation of Item Missing Data at Baseline

The Deployment Life Study was designed to follow service members and their families over the course of a deployment cycle to document changes that occurred within the studied period. Thus, most of the statistical analyses involve the use of respondents' baseline characteristics to identify change or to control for prestudy differences across various subsamples. In general, such analyses require data to be provided on all included baseline measures.

All study respondents completed the baseline assessment but may have skipped some items. In general, the absence of items is extremely low (less than 1 percent) for the majority of measures. However, when 20 or more baseline measures are included as covariates within a statistical model, minor absences on each variable may accumulate, resulting in the loss of a nontrivial amount of the overall data. For example, the study would lose the use of nine waves of outcome assessments because a respondent failed to provide their age at baseline. Such a loss could make the analytic sample less representative of the intended population, and would reduce statistical power and precision.

To avoid these problems, items and scales missing at baseline were imputed. These imputations were conducted using Stata 14's *mi impute* command. The imputed values were constructed as regression model–predicted values plus a single value drawn at random from that model's error distribution. These model-based imputations were conditioned on all of the available variables at baseline.

Describing Family Trajectories through a Deployment Cycle

Overview

The goals of the trajectory analyses were to examine whether outcomes of interest changed over the course of a deployment cycle (i.e., predeployment, during deployment, and postdeployment) for both service members and their families. Unlike the analyses to assess the persistent effects of deployment described later, these analyses are descriptive in nature and are included to provide a picture of trends in the outcomes during the three phases of a deployment. All analyses were limited to the subsample of families where the service member experienced at least one deployment during the period of observation, and the respondent completed at least one of the latter waves of data collections so that these trajectories could be observed within individuals.

Standard methods for trajectory modeling (e.g., multilevel growth models or growth mixture models) cannot be easily applied to the data from the Deployment Life Study. This is because we were interested in trajectories with respect to two specific events: (1) deployment to Operation Iraqi Freedom/Operation Enduring Freedom/Operation New Dawn (OIF/OEF/OND) and (2) return from a deployment to OIF/OEF/OND. Neither of these events was aligned within the time the nine waves of survey data were collected.[8] It is not informative to simply plot the mean of each outcome across survey waves because each wave contained a mix of service members who were about to deploy, were currently deployed, and had just returned from deployment. Even within individual families assessed at a particular wave, statuses may have been affected by the service members' prior deployments, as well as by the preparations for, and anticipation of, their next deployments.

---

[8]   Note that the Navy sample only has seven waves of data by design.

Our selected approach to producing trajectories needed to account for the complex nature of this time series data, allowing for: the simultaneous estimation of effects on each family member from service members' prior and upcoming deployments; a range of time intervals between the baseline wave and study deployment; deployments with varying durations; and a range of intervals assessed after deployment. For this reason, we used a multilevel model that was customized for these data. In general, these regression models included random intercepts for individuals, as well as time-varying trajectory factors, which capture the stage in the deployment cycle. These factors index each wave for each respondent with respect to the last deployment event (i.e., time since last deployment or return from deployment) as well as the next deployment event (i.e., time until the next deployment or return from deployment). These trajectory factors are used to predict each study outcome across the nine (or seven in the case of Navy participants) assessment waves of the study. Similar to other trajectory models that are based on blending multiple, correlated trajectory factors (e.g., those that include age, and age-squared), the resulting aggregate trajectory from these separate factors cannot be easily interpreted from the model coefficients themselves. However, the model can be used to estimate a predicted average trajectory for any specific deployment cycle. We note that our key control covariates (e.g., gender, service, etc.) were also included in our models as fixed effects; random slopes were not used for these measures in light of concerns about stability of the outcome models.

In addition to producing a description of the average values on an outcome over a typical deployment cycle, this model is also used to make population inference about the characteristics of the trajectory over the deployment cycle. Specifically, for each outcome measure within each respondent type, we assessed if the trajectory varied significantly with respect to the deployment cycle. This was done as two related tests:

1. Did the overall trajectory differ significantly from a flat line (i.e., no changes in average values over the deployment cycle)?
2. Did the overall trend differ significantly from a straight line (i.e., a constant change over time unrelated to the phase of, or timing within, the deployment cycle)?

The average trajectory before, during, and after a deployment can be graphed and described. In the event that there is evidence that the mean level of the outcome varied as a function of the deployment cycle for that respondent type, these trajectory graphs can be used to describe the pattern of change in an outcome over the course of a typical deployment cycle.

In addition to describing the average trajectory for a given type of respondent, the model is also used to investigate dyadic effects within the marriage. Specifically, for each outcome measured on both service members and their spouses, we tested a third hypothesis:

3. Are there significant differences between the trajectories of service members and their spouses over the course of the deployment cycle?

Data and Measures

For these trajectory analyses, we constructed a data set with information on families that experience a deployment at some point during the study. This includes outcomes measured for each respondent type (i.e., service member, spouse, or teen) at each completed wave, from baseline through Wave 7/9. To be included in the trajectory analyses, respondents needed to have a follow-up analytic weight, which required that they complete the baseline assessment and at least one of the final three waves of the study.

The data set links those outcomes within respondent type to a range of covariates. These are primarily factors assessed at baseline that were treated as time-invariant covariates (i.e., a constant value held by an individual used to predict the outcome across all waves of data). These covariates were selected to be relatively consistent across chapters and include the key factors that are seen as conferring risk or resilience across the full range of outcomes studied. Covariates generally included age, gender, presence of a child(ren) younger than age six in the household, length of marriage, minority status, service member pay grade (collapsed to four categories in these models), service member branch, service member component (active versus reserve), service member's number of prior combat deployments, whether the service member had any prior combat deployments, service member experience of combat trauma at baseline, spouse educational attainment (four categories), and spouse employment status (four categories). However, because the baseline assessment was completed primarily over the phone and later waves were completed mostly on the web, the mode of administration at each wave was also included as a time-varying covariate. Although most covariates are specific to the respondent whose outcome is being analyzed, spouse, child, and teen analyses also include many service member characteristics, specifically those relating to military characteristics and deployment experiences (e.g., branch of service, rank, years of service, number of combat deployments, prior combat trauma experience). A slightly reduced set of covariates was included in the child and teen models due to smaller sample sizes.

There are some differences in covariate selection, as well as in the analytic sample, across chapters and respondent type (e.g., family outcomes were not assessed on respondents without children). Each chapter discusses the analytic sample used and provides a list of the covariates used in those analyses, along with their mean values at baseline within that analytic sample (see Chapters Three through Seven).

The primary purpose of these analyses is to describe the average trajectory of these outcomes over the course of a deployment cycle for all respondent types in the family. Thus, the analytic data set contains several deployment cycle trajectory factors that have been derived from deployment dates reported by the service member, and when possible, augmented by spouse report. Deployment factors are derived from the deployment history survey modules that capture the date and duration of all prebaseline deployments and any new study deployments.[9] The start and end dates of each deployment are compared with the interview dates to derive two time measures: *months until the start of a study deployment and months since the end of a deployment.* These measures position every survey with respect to the service member's last deployment event (either a deployment or a return from a deployment) as well as his or her next deployment event (either a deployment or a return from a deployment). They are continuous, time-varying (available in each wave we observe a family member), and range from negative to positive values, depending on whether the service member was predeployment, deployed, or postdeployment.[10] Using this information, we can capture a variety of different deployment

---

[9] Service members may have had more than one deployment during the study period, in which case information on multiple deployments is coded separately.

[10] During a deployment, both values are negative because the reference *deployment event* is the start of a current deployment and the *months until deployment start* measure counts down to that event and then past it into negative values. Similarly,

patterns (e.g., someone currently deployed; someone with a past deployment and upcoming deployment; someone who recently completed a deployment).

The goal of the trajectory model is to use a very flexible functional form (i.e., nonlinear) that describes how the time course of each outcome looks relative to the deployment cycle. Thus, these two deployment timing variables are decomposed into a larger number of trajectory factors to be included in the regression models. The resulting model allows for discontinuities—an immediate "jump" up or down at the time of deployment or return from deployment—as well as more gradual changes that occur during the predeployment, deployment, or postdeployment phases of the cycle. To capture all of these possible forms of the trajectory, the two time measures—*months until the start of a study deployment* and *months since the end of a deployment*—are recoded into five linear splines and three step functions for use in the trajectory models (described below). Rather than examining the outcomes as a linear function of each piece, this technique was used to allow both slopes and intercepts to vary, depending on whether they were capturing the time period before, during, or after a study deployment.

Linear splines for *months until the start of a study deployment* included knots at zero months and eight months, thus defining three periods with linear trajectories in each: (1) more than eight months prior to deployment, (2) between eight months prior to deployment and the deployment, and (3) the period during deployment. Linear splines for *months from the end of a deployment* also included knots at zero months and eight months, thus defining three periods with linear trajectories in each: (1) during the deployment, (2) between return from deployment and eight months after return, and (3) more than eight months after return. By design, this yields six linear time slopes; however, only five slopes were actually included in the model because the two separate slopes for the deployment period were highly collinear.[11]

We placed knots at eight months for two separate reasons. First, the three-year study collected most of the survey data in the period eight months prior to the study deployment and eight months after the study deployment, which ensures that the slopes in those periods can be estimated with sufficient precision. For example, the median time until study deployment at the baseline wave (among those who deployed) was approximately eight months. Second, the survey waves occurred every four months, and each slope estimated over a period of eight months typically contains two assessments per respondent. Thus, individual slopes over an eight-month period can be estimated within respondents rather than across respondents. In short, the temporal resolution built into the longitudinal study design was not ideal for estimating nonlinear effects occurring within an eight-month period.[12] In addition to the five splines, we also included variables that allow for stepped changes in the outcome trajectory at the time of deployment or return from deployment. Thus, the resulting trajectory model has the following conceptual form over a specific deployment cycle:

---

during deployment, the reference *return from deployment event* is in the future, and the *months until deployment end* measure counts up from negative months to get to zero at the time of return.

[11] The two slopes during deployment were not both useful for prediction, thus the *time since end of deployment* spline that captures change during the deployment was not entered in the final model.

[12] For many of the studied outcomes, the temporal resolution of the study is also limited by the time frame used in the assessment instrument. Thus, if family communication is assessed with questions about behaviors that have occurred over the prior four months, it is difficult to construct fine grained temporal analyses either within or across subjects because the temporal effects have been smoothed within the instrument itself. This smoothing may introduce a slight bias toward zero in the step functions estimated within the model (i.e., the sharp transitions at deployment and return from deployment).

1. a linear slope for the period more than eight months prior to a study deployment
2. a linear slope from eight months before a study deployment to the date of a study deployment
3. a step up or down on the date of a study deployment
4. a linear slope during a study deployment
5. a step up or down on the end date of a study deployment
6. a linear slope from the end of a study deployment for eight months
7. a linear slope beyond eight months after the end of a study deployment.

Estimation of Trajectory Models

Using Stata 14, we estimated multilevel models with random intercepts. In models including a single respondent type (service member, spouse, or teen), these are two-level models that account for clustering within individuals over waves; when modeling marital dyads (service members and their spouses together) these are three-level models that account for the nesting of individuals within households. Standard errors within these models are estimated using robust methods that account for variance inflation due to the use of analytic weights, described above. Separate models are run for each outcome. Models were linear, logistic, or Poisson regression depending on the measurement properties of the outcome. All models include effects for key covariates (described earlier). In addition, dyadic models allow all covariates to interact with respondent type; i.e., the effect of each covariate was not assumed to be equal for service members and spouses.

As described above, all models include trajectory factors based on piecewise linear splines calculated using the *mkspline* function with five slopes capturing the distinct phases of the deployment cycle, as well as the two-step functions for transitions associated with deployment events.[13] In dyadic models, all of these deployment trajectory factors are allowed to interact with respondent type. As noted earlier, the individual parameters from the models are not tested or interpreted separately, due to the high correlation among them. Instead, joint Wald tests are used to assess three statistical hypotheses:[14]

1. Does the overall trajectory differ significantly from a flat line (i.e., no changes in average values over the deployment cycle)? This is tested using a joint Wald test in which all trajectory factors are tested against a null hypothesis that the parameters=0.
2. Does the overall trend differ significantly from a straight line (i.e., a constant change over time that is unrelated to the phase of, or timing within, the deployment cycle)? This is tested using a slightly different base model that includes a linear change over time unrelated to deployment. We then perform a joint Wald test against a null hypothesis that all trajectory factors=0.

---

[13] In addition to these seven trajectory parameters, there is an additional variable that indicates when *months from the end of deployment* is undefined/missing. This occurs before the study deployment for members who had not had a prior deployment. No slope related to *months from the end of deployment* is included in the model for that subgroup, but a constant is included. This yields a total of eight degrees of freedom across the deployment cycle trajectory factors.

[14] In some cases, additional post-hoc tests are performed to follow up on evidence of a significant relationship between a given outcome and the phases of the deployment cycle (e.g., a test of whether the mean level of the outcome is the same while the service member is deployed compared with when he/she is not deployed).

3. Are there significant differences between the trajectories of service members and their spouses over the course of the deployment cycle? This is tested within a longitudinal dyadic (three-level) model. A joint Wald test is performed testing against a null hypothesis that all interactions between respondent type (service member versus spouse) and the trajectory factors=0.

Predicted Average Trajectories

Because several correlated parameters are used to model outcome trajectories throughout the deployment cycle, the model parameters themselves are not easily interpretable as descriptions of the trajectories. To convert these parameters into a useful description, we use the model to derive a predicted average trajectory within our sample for a specific, hypothetical deployment cycle. Predictions were estimated using the *predict* command with the margins option in Stata, which integrates over the random intercepts. Beginning with Stata 14, the *margins* command also appropriately handles retransformation of nonlinear outcomes (in addition to linear outcomes) by integrating over the random intercepts. The particular deployment cycle selected was designed to be relatively typical of the deployment cycles observed over the course of the study. The cycle covers a two-year period beginning eight months before a study deployment (i.e., predeployment), then covering a deployment lasting eight months (the median length of a study deployment in the sample), and ending with a period eight months after deployment (i.e., postdeployment).

Model-predicted estimates of the average value of each outcome are produced over this particular hypothetical deployment cycle, and are presented graphically (Figure 2.6). The model-predicted values have been produced at the average level of all covariates (or the mode

Figure 2.6
Sample Predicted Average Trajectory of Outcome Y

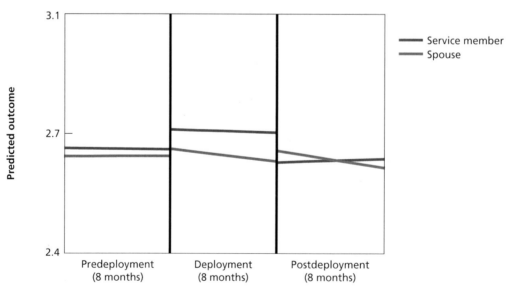

for categorical covariates).[15] The resulting average-predicted trajectories are presented separately for each respondent type. However, whenever the same outcome was assessed for both service members and spouses, their trajectories are presented on the same graph, and are taken from the three-level model that included both respondents. See Figure 2.6 as an example.

The x-axis in the figure represents time—with vertical black lines demarking the three phases of the deployment cycle. The y-axis depicts the predicted average outcome. The y-axis for all outcomes has been scaled to allow comparisons of effect sizes across graphs. This axis is centered on the mean value and presents a range representing plus or minus one standard deviation from the mean.[16]

In general, these plots serve as descriptive tools to understand how service members and their families changed over the course of a deployment cycle. However, they should only be interpreted as showing variation related to the deployment cycle when both of the gateway tests (i.e., statistical hypotheses 1 and 2, listed earlier) show significant association with the deployment cycle. Similarly, any apparent differences in the shapes of the trajectories for service members versus spouses should not be interpreted unless the joint test (i.e., hypothesis 3 above) indicated that the trajectories are significantly different from one another. In the event that one of the gateway tests suggested that the mean level varies over time in association with the deployment cycle, post-hoc tests were performed in order to aid in interpretation. Specifically, the mean level during the deployment was compared with the mean level when not deployed for each trajectory. This was conducted within a model that contains no other deployment cycle factors.[17]

The trajectory models provide a detailed picture of outcome trajectories during the study deployment cycle; however, it is important to note that these analyses are descriptive and cannot be used to infer a causal relationship between deployment and any given outcome. Thus, we next review models that are intended to examine the causal association between deployment and key outcomes.

Estimating the Persistent Effects of Deployment on the Family

While the trajectory models detailed above provide a description of how outcomes change over the course of a deployment cycle, they do not estimate the longer-term "causal impact" that a deployment might have on a family. For example, changes observed over time within families that include a deployed service member might have occurred even if the service member had not deployed—deployment is only one of many possible reasons for changes within a family. To address this issue, we performed a series of analyses designed to estimate how the outcomes for a family—months or years after a deployment has ended—were different than if the service member had not been deployed. Specifically, these analyses identified the effect of deployment

---

[15] The predicted values are based on a hypothetical deployment cycle in which the prior deployment ended 32 months prior to the start of the study deployment. This is the mean "dwell time" value within the subsample that had a prior deployment.

[16] Standard deviation is calculated within wave and within respondent type (service member versus spouse) and averaged across the 18 respondent type x wave values.

[17] Readers might reasonably expect to see a separate comparison of the predeployment mean levels with postdeployment levels. We have opted to avoid making this post-hoc comparison because it could easily be misinterpreted as the causal effect of deployment on the deployed. In the next section, we outline a more rigorous method for estimating this particular causal effect and would encourage the reader to view the trajectories as descriptive models of variation over time, rather than as causal models.

on a given outcome by investigating the changes that occurred between the beginning and the end of this three-year study, comparing those who deployed within that studied period with those who did not deploy.

This longitudinal study provides a good design for estimating causal effects (i.e., a design in which the outcomes are measured both before and after service members' deployments, and over the same time period for service members who did and did not deploy). However, it is still an observational design and the analyses could not proceed as though service members had been randomly assigned to deployments. Confounding variables still existed that were associated with both experiencing a deployment and the change in outcomes over time; such variables could threaten the validity of the estimated effect of deployment. For this reason, our analyses employed both propensity and covariate adjustment methods to minimize the risk of such confounds across the broad range of participant characteristics and outcomes assessed in the study. One way to eliminate such confounds was to ensure that the deployed and non-deployed subsamples were well matched on all of their predeployment characteristics. Appendix Tables 2A.1, 2A.2, and 2A.3 highlight how families deployed during the study differed from families not deployed during the study at baseline. As shown, families that did not experience a deployment during the study were significantly different on a number of baseline characteristics, necessitating the use of weights to balance the deployed and nondeployed samples.

In light of these differences, we estimated *propensity score weights* that balanced our nondeployed sample to match the deployed sample with respect to between 49 and 63 baseline measures, depending on the respondent (i.e., service member, spouse, or teen). The propensity score (i.e., the conditional probability of being deployed given a set of baseline/pretreatment factors) can be used to weight data so that deployment effects are estimated by comparing individuals with similar baseline characteristics, thus mimicking the randomization process of a randomized trial (Rosenbaum and Rubin, 1983). The use of propensity scores to control for pretreatment/baseline imbalances on observed variables in nonrandomized or observational studies examining causal effects has become widespread over the past decade.

A common alternative method to eliminate confounds when drawing causal inference from observational data is to include possible confounds as covariates within the statistical model in which the causal effect is estimated. Unfortunately, when such models are used alone, one cannot guarantee the sample of service members with and without a deployment will be well matched on the characteristics controlled for in the model and lingering bias may exist on the estimated impact of the deployment indicator in such a model. However, when multivariate regression models are combined with propensity score methods so that the deployed and nondeployed subsamples are balanced on the full range of baseline characteristics within that same regression model, it is feasible to obtain more-robust estimates of the impact of deployment on outcomes than either method alone might yield. Estimating treatment effects through such models is one type of "doubly robust" estimation, which combines a model for the outcome with propensity weighting to obtain an estimator that yields consistent estimates of the effect of deployment, as long as either the model for the outcome or the propensity score is correct (but not necessarily both) (Kang and Schafer, 2007). Doubly robust estimation can also be more efficient than the simple propensity score–weighted estimator when some of the covariates are strong predictors of the outcome (Neugebauer and van der Laan, 2007). In the following sections, we discuss the methods used to derived propensity weights and specify the models in which the deployment effects are estimated.

Similar to the attrition component of the longitudinal sample weight, the propensity score weights were estimated using the TWANG package in R (Ridgeway et al., 2014), which is based on GBM, a flexible, nonparametric estimation method that has been shown to outperform logistic regression for propensity score estimation (Lee, Lessler, and Stuart, 2010; McCaffrey, Ridgeway, and Morral, 2004). Baseline factors were selected when we thought they may be associated with either (a) outcomes assessed near the end of the study or (b) the likelihood of being deployed within the study period. These factors include sociodemographic characteristics (e.g., gender, age, minority status, length of marriage, presence of children younger than age 18 in the home), military characteristics of the service member (e.g., pay grade, number of previous combat deployments, service, component, previous trauma/combat exposure), and the baseline measures of all key outcomes used within the various chapters. Propensity score weights were estimated separately for service member, spouse, and teen respondents, so that the set of factors on which we attempt to balance the subsamples could be tailored to each respondent type. (See Appendix 2A Tables 2A.1, 2A.2, and 2A.3 for a list of included variables for each respondent type.) The propensity models were run using the follow-up sample analytic weights (discussed earlier) and the resulting propensity weights were combined with those analytic weights in the subsequent regression models in order to ensure the results are generalizable to married, deployed service members in the military between 2012 and 2013.

Performance of the propensity score weights was assessed by examining the absolute standardized mean difference (ASMD) for each baseline covariate before and after weighting. The ASMD for the *k-th* covariate equals

$$\frac{\left| \bar{X}_{k,1} - \bar{X}_{k,0} \right|}{\hat{\sigma}_{X_{k,1}}}$$

where $\bar{X}_{k,j}$ denotes the mean of the *k-th* covariate for the deployed *(j=1)* and the nondeployed *(j=0)* groups and $\hat{\sigma}_{X_{k,1}}$ denotes the estimated standard deviation of the *k-th* covariate in the deployed group. A value of 0 represents no difference in means, whereas a value of 1 represents one standard deviation difference between the exposed and unexposed groups. We considered balance successful if all ASMDs were under 0.20. Each of the substantive chapters provides figures that show the change in ASMD before and after propensity score weighting for each analysis performed, highlighting how well each set of propensity score weights did at balancing the deployed and nondeployed groups on their baseline characteristics.

After deriving the propensity score weights, doubly robust regression models were used to estimate the effects of the study deployment. These models predicted the key study outcome measures across the last three waves of data in the study (waves 7, 8, and 9 for the Army, Air Force, and Marine Corps; and waves 5, 6, and 7 for the Navy) for both the deployed and nondeployed groups.[18] Because each respondent could have up to three outcome assessments included in these models, random intercepts for each individual were estimated to account for

---

[18] We note that outcomes were set to missing whenever a service member was actively deployed at an assessment wave so that all outcomes for the deployed subsample occur postdeployment. Rates of actively deployed service members ranged from 1 percent to 2 percent at each of the last three follow-up waves in the study. Thus, the rate is low enough that these observations can be treated as missing for the deployed service members without creating an imbalance across the deployed and nondeployed subsamples. Expanding the outcome period beyond these three waves would result in a large number of observations within the deployed group falling within the deployment period.

the nonindependence of outcomes measured within an individual. We elected to include three waves of outcome data within the model to increase statistical power to detect the effects of deployments that occurred between the baseline wave and these later waves of the study. Separate models were run for each outcome variable of interest, within each type of respondent. Depending on the measurement properties for a given outcome, a linear, logistic, or Poisson regression was used. Models were run within Stata 14 with standard errors that account for variance inflation due to survey weights and controlled for time-varying measures of survey mode.

Each regression model included as a predictor a dichotomous indicator of deployment (service member deployed between baseline and follow-up versus no deployment). They also included the baseline value of the particular outcome being modeled, so that the estimated effect of deployment can be interpreted as a type of longitudinal change (i.e., residualized change) between the baseline and late assessment waves. Several additional covariates assessed at baseline were also included in these models. The inclusion of such covariates in propensity-weighted models can improve the validity of causal conclusions when the propensity weights do not achieve complete balance (i.e., it provides doubly robust properties), and can increase statistical power when they are good predictors of the outcome. However, we did not include all of the variables used in propensity weights in every regression model; the inclusion of a large number of highly associated predictors may cause estimation problems in these models. Instead, we include a smaller set of baseline characteristics that were thought to capture the most-important characteristics of the individuals or families. These are the same set of covariates that were selected for use in the trajectory models discussed earlier. While the statistical significance of the deployment effect is estimated directly within the regression model, that model coefficient is not always a useful indicator of the effect size (particularly when looking across models using different link functions). To improve the interpretability of effects, we present these results as covariate-adjusted means, with standard errors, on the outcome variable for the deployed and the nondeployed subgroups. These were estimated by using the *margins* command in Stata 14, which calculates predicted means for the deployed and nondeployed groups from predictions of the doubly robust regression model at fixed values for the deployment indicator (first assuming everyone in the data set was deployed and then assuming everyone in the data set was not deployed) and averaging (or integrating) over the remaining covariates and the random effects. Beginning with Stata 14, when implementing predictions for nonlinear outcomes, the *margins* command integrates over the random effects. This allows for a direct comparison of the adjusted predicted mean outcomes for the two deployment groups (i.e., deployment versus no deployment during the study), rather than a focus on the regression coefficient of the deployment indicator.

This analytic framework is designed to estimate the persistent effects of deployment across a range of outcomes for each member of the family. Within the individual chapters of this report, the specific findings from these analyses will be discussed and interpreted in light of the broader literature and the limitations of the data. This will generally include: (1) outlining specific research questions and hypotheses for the results, (2) reviewing the theory that guided the selection of variables in the propensity weighting or covariate adjustment (including identifying any key variables from the literature that were not included), (3) discussing the extent to which balance was achieved on the available variables, (4) interpreting practical and statistical significance of the effects of deployment on subsequent outcomes, and (5) discussing those findings in light of any limitations related to the study design or data quality.

Identifying Predictors of Postdeployment Outcomes for Service Members and Their Families

Regardless of the study's findings on persistent effects of deployment on service members or their families, it may be useful to identify risk factors that are predictive of better or worse outcomes following deployments (i.e., risk and resilience factors). To gain a better understanding of which factors predict whether families do well or poorly after experiencing a deployment (i.e., what factors are associated with readiness and resilience), we implemented a series of additional multivariate regression models within the deployed subsample. These are based on the longitudinal (i.e., pre–post deployment) regression models used when comparing respondents who deployed with those who did not deploy. They predict the same outcomes and include a random intercept to control for clustering within individuals, given possible repeated measures during the postdeployment period. However, because these models are run solely on the deployed subsample, they include no propensity weights. Instead, these models utilize the study analytic weights for each respondent. Each of these models include, as a predictor, the baseline assessment of the outcome being predicted, as well as the same set of baseline covariates used in the propensity score models described earlier.

In addition to these baseline predictors, each model contains one additional variable of interest that was hypothesized to be associated with change in outcome from predeployment to postdeployment. In most cases, these hypothesized risk and resilience factors are experiences that are tied to the study deployments (e.g. deployment trauma, length of deployment, communication frequency during deployment) and that were assessed in the survey waves after baseline. These model coefficients indicate the extent to which the given factor can serve as a measure of risk or resilience with respect to the postdeployment well-being of service members and their families. Readers are cautioned to avoid assuming that these conditional associations represent causal effects of the studied risk or resilience factor on the outcome. For example, the fact that separation from service is associated with mental health problems assessed at follow-up while controlling for all baseline factors does not imply that separation caused the mental health problems. The model coefficient may reflect the causal effect of the modeled outcome on the risk or resilience factor. Further investigation of the causal direction of such effects (e.g., through dynamic modeling across our nine waves of data) is beyond the scope of the current report.

Interpretation of Multiple Tests

Across the different respondent types, the different outcome measures, and the different types of statistical hypotheses, the current report contains many inferential statistical tests. The large number of these tests complicates the interpretation of statistical significance, and might lead the reader to overestimate the probability that the effect would replicate in subsequent research. Even when the null hypothesis is true, the null hypothesis will be incorrectly rejected for one in 20 statistical tests at a $p<0.05$ level of significance. Such spurious effects are particularly likely when interpreting a small set of "significant" effects that have been culled from a large number of nonsignificant findings.

Several corrections exist that are designed to adjust for situations in which multiple inferential tests are performed. However, we have not applied these corrections within the report for three reasons: (a) these corrections increase the risk of type II errors (i.e., failure to reject null hypotheses that are actually false); (b) the corrections are based on defining families of repeated tests, which is highly subjective within the context of this report; and (c) the corrections assume that tests are independent, which is substantially untrue when repeating tests across highly correlated outcomes or across individuals within a household.

Rather than apply a predetermined correction to the p-values we present, we suggest that readers interpret the overall patterns of significant results—looking for multiple significant effects across measures, statistical tests, or respondents—that tell a coherent theoretical story, rather than focusing on the statistical significance of individual effects. Similarly, we suggest that readers treat individual p-values between 0.01 and 0.05 as "trends" rather than genuinely significant effects. (This is functionally equivalent to conducting a Bonferroni or Šidák correction for a family of five independent tests.) This will substantially decrease the likelihood that the reader will interpret findings as meaningful when they are unlikely to replicate in subsequent studies. Finally, the patterns of significant effects should be interpreted with respect to the actual effect sizes to ensure that the interpreted findings are both statistically and practically significant.

Presentation of Results

In the following chapters, we present the results of the three analyses outlined above: trajectory models of key outcomes over the deployment cycle, doubly robust propensity score weighting models comparing family members who do and do not experience a study deployment, and random intercept regression models of risk and resilience factors that may be associated with outcomes postdeployment. Each chapter begins with a review of the relevant literature, then reviews the research questions, data, and methods as they relate to each outcome area, and finally presents the results. Chapter Three examines outcomes related to marriage and couples in the Deployment Life Study. Chapter Four examines family-level outcomes, from the perspective of service members and spouses. Chapter Five examines psychological and behavioral outcomes among service members and spouses. Chapter Six examines child outcomes, including both teens (i.e., those children who complete their own surveys and for whom spouses also provide information) and younger children (i.e., those children for whom only spouses provide data). Chapter Seven examines military integration from the perspective of all three household members for whom we have data. Finally, Chapter Eight summarizes all of the findings and discusses relevant policy implications. A final set of appendixes to the report provides means of key outcomes for service members and spouses by wave and by study deployment status (Appendix A1), by wave and by gender (Appendix A2), by wave and by component (i.e., active versus reserve/guard; Appendix A3), by wave and by service branch (i.e., Army, Air Force, Navy, Marine Corps; Appendix A4), and a final table presents means for teens by wave (Appendix A5).

Appendix 2A: Tables

The following tables provide means of key outcomes for service members and spouses by wave and by gender.

Table 2A.1
Balance Table for Nonresponse: Service Members

	Baseline Sample (n=2,724)	Responders:[a] Sample Weight Only	Responders: Sample and Attrition Weights	Sample Weight vs. Baseline Sample	Attrition and Sample Weights vs. Baseline Sample
	Mean (SD)	Mean	Mean	SMD	SMD
SERVICE MEMBER VARIABLES					
Female	0.09 (0.29)	0.09	0.09	0.01	0.01
Age	34.13 (8.18)	34.70	34.35	-0.07	-0.03
Minority Race/Ethnicity	0.26 (0.44)	0.26	0.26	0.00	-0.02
Minority Race/Ethnicity, Missing	0.01 (0.09)	0.01	0.01	-0.01	0.00
Children Younger Than Age 6	0.42 (0.49)	0.41	0.43	0.01	-0.03
Pay Grade: Junior Enlisted	0.05 (0.21)	0.04	0.04	0.01	0.00
Pay Grade: Junior Officer	0.09 (0.29)	0.10	0.09	-0.03	-0.01
Pay Grade: Mid and Senior Enlisted	0.75 (0.43)	0.72	0.74	0.06	0.02
Pay Grade: Mid and Senior Officer	0.09 (0.29)	0.11	0.10	-0.07	-0.03
Pay Grade: Warrant Officer	0.02 (0.14)	0.02	0.02	-0.01	0.00
Pay Grade, Missing	0.00 (0.06)	0.00	0.00	0.02	0.02
Length of Marriage (Months)	105.17 (86.39)	109.64	106.54	-0.05	-0.02
Length of Marriage, Missing	0.00 (0.06)	0.00	0.00	0.00	0.02
Parents in the Military	0.00 (0.03)	0.00	0.00	-0.03	-0.03
Parents in the Military, Missing	3.95 (0.49)	3.97	3.96	-0.05	-0.01
Total Number of Prior Deployments	1.67 (1.28)	1.73	1.72	-0.04	-0.04
Total Number of Prior Deployments, Missing	0.01 (0.10)	0.00	0.01	0.08	0.05
Army	0.49 (0.50)	0.49	0.49	-0.01	-0.01
Air Force	0.17 (0.38)	0.15	0.17	0.05	0.00
Navy	0.25 (0.44)	0.28	0.26	-0.06	-0.01
Marine Corps	0.09 (0.29)	0.08	0.08	0.03	0.05
Reserve Component	0.33 (0.47)	0.34	0.33	-0.01	0.01
Hoge Combat Experiences Scale	4.03 (4.15)	3.97	4.00	0.02	0.01
Hoge Combat Experiences Scale, Missing	0.00 (0.04)	0.00	0.00	0.00	0.00

Table 2A.1—Continued

	Baseline Sample (n=2,724)	Responders:[a] Sample Weight Only	Responders: Sample and Attrition Weights	Sample Weight vs. Baseline Sample	Attrition and Sample Weights vs. Baseline Sample
	Mean (SD)	Mean	Mean	SMD	SMD
Deployment Trauma Exposure	1.89 (2.43)	1.85	1.91	0.02	–0.01
Deployment Trauma Exposure, Missing	0.08 (0.28)	0.02	0.06	0.23	0.09
Marital Satisfaction Scale	3.95 (0.49)	3.97	3.96	–0.05	–0.01
PANAS: Positive	4.16 (0.66)	4.18	4.16	–0.03	–0.01
PANAS: Positive, Missing	0.00 (0.05)	0.00	0.00	0.04	0.04
PANAS: Negative	1.99 (0.56)	1.97	1.98	0.04	0.02
PANAS: Negative, Missing	0.00 (0.05)	0.00	0.00	0.04	0.04
Conflict Tactics Scale: Prevalence of Physical Aggression Toward Partner	0.02 (0.13)	0.01	0.02	0.03	0.02
Conflict Tactics Scale: Prevalence of Physical Aggression Toward Partner, Missing	0.00 (0.05)	0.00	0.00	0.02	0.02
Conflict Tactics Scale: Chronicity of Psychological Aggression Toward Partner	0.68 (0.88)	0.64	0.66	0.04	0.03
Conflict Tactics Scale: Chronicity of Psychological Aggression Toward Partner, Missing	0.00 (0.04)	0.00	0.00	0.05	0.05
Conflict Tactics Scale: Prevalence of Physical Aggression Toward You	0.05 (0.23)	0.05	0.05	0.01	0.00
Conflict Tactics Scale: Prevalence of Physical Aggression Toward You, Missing	0.00 (0.04)	0.00	0.00	0.05	0.05
Conflict Tactics Scale: Chronicity of Psychological Aggression Toward You	0.79 (1.03)	0.74	0.76	0.05	0.03
Conflict Tactics Scale: Chronicity of Psychological Aggression Toward You, Missing	0.00 (0.04)	0.00	0.00	0.05	0.05
Depression (PHQ)	2.79 (3.61)	2.52	2.71	0.07	0.02
Depression (PHQ), Missing	0.00 (0.03)	0.00	0.00	0.04	0.04
Anxiety	2.07 (1.00)	1.99	2.04	0.08	0.04
Anxiety, Missing	0.00 (0.01)	0.00	0.00	0.00	0.00

Table 2A.1—Continued

	Baseline Sample (n=2,724)	Responders:[a] Sample Weight Only	Responders: Sample and Attrition Weights	Sample Weight vs. Baseline Sample	Attrition and Sample Weights vs. Baseline Sample
	Mean (SD)	Mean	Mean	SMD	SMD
PTSD	5.48 (9.65)	4.88	5.23	0.06	0.03
PTSD, Missing	0.02 (0.13)	0.02	0.02	-0.03	-0.01
Traumatic Brain Injury (TBI)	0.12 (0.32)	0.12	0.12	0.00	-0.01
TBI, Missing	0.00 (0.02)	0.00	0.00	0.00	0.00
Binge Drinking	0.24 (0.43)	0.23	0.24	0.03	0.01
Binge Drinking, Missing	0.03 (0.16)	0.02	0.02	0.02	0.01
Problematic Substance Use Scale	0.17 (0.59)	0.16	0.16	0.02	0.01
Medication for Mental Health Problem	0.05 (0.21)	0.04	0.05	0.02	0.00
Medication for Mental Health Problem, Missing	0.00 (0.04)	0.00	0.00	-0.03	-0.03
Received Mental Health Care	0.15 (0.35)	0.13	0.14	0.05	0.03
Received Mental Health Care, Missing	0.00 (0.02)	0.00	0.00	-0.05	-0.05
Financial Distress Scale	1.94 (0.71)	1.88	1.92	0.09	0.04
Financial Distress Scale, Missing	0.00 (0.01)	0.00	0.00	0.00	0.00
Family Environment Scale	2.80 (0.26)	2.81	2.80	-0.04	-0.01
Family Environment Scale, Missing	0.39 (0.49)	0.41	0.40	-0.05	-0.02
Parenting Stress Scale	3.34 (0.40)	3.36	3.35	-0.04	-0.02
Parenting Stress Scale, Missing	0.39 (0.49)	0.41	0.40	-0.05	-0.02
Military Commitment	4.38 (0.68)	4.39	4.37	0.00	0.02
Job Satisfaction	3.91 (1.03)	3.95	3.91	-0.04	0.00
Job Satisfaction, Missing	0.00 (0.04)	0.00	0.00	0.00	0.00
Retention Intentions	4.01 (1.38)	4.03	4.03	-0.01	-0.01
Retention Intentions, Missing	0.34 (0.47)	0.34	0.33	-0.01	0.02

Table 2A.1—Continued

	Baseline Sample (n=2,724)	Responders:[a] Sample Weight Only	Responders: Sample and Attrition Weights	Sample Weight vs. Baseline Sample	Attrition and Sample Weights vs. Baseline Sample
	Mean (SD)	Mean	Mean	SMD	SMD
SPOUSE VARIABLES					
Marital Satisfaction Scale	3.85 (0.59)	3.88	3.87	-0.06	-0.04
PANAS: Positive	4.10 (0.73)	4.14	4.13	-0.05	-0.04
PANAS: Positive, Missing	0.00 (002)	0.00	0.00	0.00	0.00
PANAS: Negative	2.14 (0.65)	2.11	2.12	0.04	0.02
PANAS: Negative, Missing	0.00 (0.02)	0.00	0.00	0.00	0.00
Conflict Tactics Scale: Prevalence of Physical Aggression Toward Partner	0.04 (0.20)	0.04	0.05	0.00	-0.01
Conflict Tactics Scale: Prevalence of Physical Aggression Toward Partner, Missing	0.00 (0.02)	0.00	0.00	0.04	0.04
Conflict Tactics Scale: Chronicity of Psychological Aggression Toward Partner	0.76 (0.93)	0.71	0.73	0.05	0.03
Conflict Tactics Scale: Prevalence of Physical Aggression Toward You	0.03 (0.16)	0.02	0.02	0.06	0.03
Conflict Tactics Scale: Prevalence of Physical Aggression Toward You, Missing	0.00 (0.02)	0.00	0.00	0.00	0.00
Conflict Tactics Scale: Chronicity of Psychological Aggression Toward You	0.72 (0.97)	0.65	0.67	0.07	0.05
Depression (PHQ)	3.28 (4.01)	3.13	3.19	0.04	0.02
Depression (PHQ), Missing	0.00 (0.04)	0.00	0.00	-0.03	-0.03
Anxiety	2.15 (1.00)	2.10	2.11	0.05	0.03
Anxiety, Missing	0.00 (0.03)	0.00	0.00	0.00	0.00
PTSD	0.49 (1.00)	0.46	0.48	0.03	0.01
PTSD, Missing	0.00 (0.05)	0.00	0.00	0.00	0.00
Binge Drinking	0.12 (0.33)	0.12	0.13	0.00	0.00
Binge Drinking, Missing	0.02 (0.13)	0.02	0.02	-0.02	-0.02
Problematic Substance Use Scale	0.08 (0.46)	0.06	0.06	0.05	0.04
Problematic Substance Use Scale, Missing	0.01 (0.10)	0.01	0.01	0.00	0.01

Table 2A.1—Continued

	Baseline Sample (n=2,724)	Responders:[a] Sample Weight Only	Responders: Sample and Attrition Weights	Sample Weight vs. Baseline Sample	Attrition and Sample Weights vs. Baseline Sample
	Mean (SD)	Mean	Mean	SMD	SMD
Medication for Mental Health Problem	0.14 (0.35)	0.14	0.14	0.01	0.02
Medication for Mental Health Problem, Missing	0.00 (0.06)	0.00	0.00	0.00	0.00
Received Mental Health Care	0.15 (0.36)	0.14	0.15	0.03	0.02
Received Mental Health Care, Missing	0.00 (0.06)	0.01	0.00	−0.02	0.00
Financial Distress Scale	2.00 (0.76)	1.91	1.96	0.12	0.06
Family Environment Scale	2.79 (0.28)	2.81	2.80	−0.05	−0.04
Family Environment Scale, Missing	0.38 (0.49)	0.40	0.39	−0.04	−0.01
Parenting Stress Scale	3.25 (0.39)	3.26	3.24	−0.01	0.03
Parenting Stress Scale, Missing	0.38 (0.49)	0.40	0.39	−0.05	−0.01
Military Commitment	4.44 (0.63)	4.45	4.45	−0.02	−0.01
Military Commitment, Missing	0.00 (0.02)	0.00	0.00	0.00	0.00
Satisfaction as Military Spouse	4.06 (1.00)	4.10	4.07	−0.04	−0.01
Satisfaction as Military Spouse, Missing	0.00 (0.03)	0.00	0.00	0.00	0.00
Retention Intentions	4.02 (1.28)	4.07	4.06	−0.03	−0.03
Retention Intentions, Missing	0.01 (0.11)	0.02	0.01	−0.03	−0.02

Table 2A.1—Continued

TEEN VARIABLES	Baseline Sample (n=2,724) Mean (SD)	Responders:[a] Sample Weight Only Mean	Responders: Sample and Attrition Weights Mean	Sample Weight vs. Baseline Sample SMD	Attrition and Sample Weights vs. Baseline Sample SMD
SDQ: Total	7.80 (5.31)	7.62	7.75	0.03	0.01
SDQ: Total, Missing	0.51 (0.50)	0.52	0.51	−0.03	−0.01
SDQ Subscale: Emotional Problems	1.56 (1.78)	1.57	1.60	−0.01	−0.03
SDQ Subscale: Emotional Problems, Missing	0.50 (0.50)	0.52	0.51	−0.03	−0.01
SDQ Subscale: Conduct Problems	1.11 (1.43)	1.03	1.06	0.05	0.03
SDQ Subscale: Conduct Problems, Missing	0.50 (0.50)	0.52	0.51	−0.04	−0.01
SDQ Subscale: Hyperactivity	3.43 (2.45)	3.35	3.40	0.03	0.01
SDQ Subscale: Hyperactivity, Missing	0.50 (0.50)	0.52	0.51	−0.03	−0.01
SDQ Subscale: Peer Relationships	1.70 (1.72)	1.65	1.68	0.03	0.01
SDQ Subscale: Peer Relationships, Missing	0.50 (0.50)	0.51	0.50	−0.03	−0.01
SDQ Subscale: Prosocial Behavior	8.47 (1.64)	8.53	8.53	−0.04	−0.04
SDQ Subscale: Prosocial Behavior, Missing	0.50 (0.50)	0.52	0.51	−0.03	−0.01
Depression Symptoms	0.95 (1.76)	0.94	0.97	0.01	−0.01
Depression Symptoms, Missing	0.50 (0.50)	0.51	0.50	−0.02	0.00
Anxiety (SCARED)	1.48 (1.68)	1.47	1.47	0.00	0.00
Anxiety (SCARED), Missing	0.50 (0.50)	0.51	0.50	−0.03	−0.01

[a] "Responders" refers to service members who have valid data in at least one of the final three waves of the study (Waves 7, 8, and 9 for the Army, Air Force, Marine Corps sample; Waves 5, 6, and 7 for the Navy sample).

NOTE: SD=standard deviation.

Table 2A.2
Balance Table for Nonresponse: Spouses

	Baseline Sample (n=2,724)	Responders:[a] Sample Weight Only	Responders: Sample and Attrition Weights	Sample Weight vs. Baseline Sample	Attrition and Sample Weights vs. Baseline Sample
	Mean (SD)	Mean	Mean	SMD	SMD
SERVICE MEMBER VARIABLES					
Pay Grade: Junior Enlisted	0.05 (0.21)	0.04	0.04	0.02	0.02
Pay Grade: Junior Officer	0.09 (0.29)	0.09	0.09	0.00	0.01
Pay Grade: Mid and Senior Enlisted	0.75 (0.43)	0.75	0.75	0.00	0.00
Pay Grade: Mid and Senior Officer	0.09 (0.29)	0.10	0.10	-0.02	-0.01
Pay Grade: Warrant Officer	0.02 (0.14)	0.02	0.02	0.00	0.00
Pay Grade: Missing	0.00 (0.06)	0.00	0.00	0.02	0.02
Length of Marriage (Months)	105.17 (86.39)	108.17	106.79	-0.03	-0.02
Length of Marriage: Missing	0.00 (0.06)	0.00	0.00	0.02	0.02
Total Number of Prior Deployments	1.67 (1.28)	1.69	1.68	-0.01	-0.01
Total Number of Prior Deployments: Missing	0.01 (0.10)	0.01	0.01	0.04	0.01
Army	0.49 (0.50)	0.49	0.49	-0.02	-0.01
Air Force	0.17 (0.38)	0.17	0.18	0.01	-0.01
Navy	0.25 (0.44)	0.25	0.25	0.00	0.01
Marine Corps	0.09 (0.29)	0.09	0.09	0.02	0.02
Reserve Component	0.33 (0.47)	0.33	0.33	0.00	0.01
Hoge Combat Experiences Scale	4.03 (4.15)	4.08	4.08	-0.01	-0.01
Hoge Combat Experiences Scale, Missing	0.00 (0.04)	0.00	0.00	0.00	0.00
Deployment Trauma Exposure	1.89 (2.43)	1.91	1.90	-0.01	-0.01
Deployment Trauma Exposure, Missing	0.08 (0.28)	0.05	0.07	0.12	0.05
Marital Satisfaction Scale	3.95 (0.49)	3.98	3.97	-0.05	-0.04
PANAS: Positive	4.16 (0.66)	4.18	4.17	-0.02	-0.01
PANAS: Positive, Missing	0.00 (0.05)	0.00	0.00	0.02	0.02
PANAS: Negative	1.99 (0.56)	1.97	1.98	0.04	0.03
PANAS: Negative, Missing	0.00 (0.05)	0.00	0.00	0.02	0.02

Table 2A.2—Continued

	Baseline Sample (n=2,724)	Responders:[a] Sample Weight Only	Responders: Sample and Attrition Weights	Sample Weight vs. Baseline Sample	Attrition and Sample Weights vs. Baseline Sample
	Mean (SD)	Mean	Mean	SMD	SMD
Conflict Tactics Scale: Prevalence of Physical Aggression Toward Partner	0.02 (0.13)	0.02	0.02	0.02	0.02
Conflict Tactics Scale: Prevalence of Physical Aggression Toward Partner, Missing	0.00 (0.05)	0.00	0.00	0.02	0.02
Conflict Tactics Scale: Chronicity of Psychological Aggression Toward Partner	0.68 (0.88)	0.64	0.66	0.05	0.02
Conflict Tactics Scale: Chronicity of Psychological Aggression Toward Partner, Missing	0.00 (0.04)	0.00	0.00	0.05	0.05
Conflict Tactics Scale: Prevalence of Physical Aggression Toward You	0.05 (0.23)	0.05	0.05	0.02	0.00
Conflict Tactics Scale: Prevalence of Physical Aggression Toward You, Missing	0.00 (0.04)	0.00	0.00	0.05	0.05
Conflict Tactics Scale: Chronicity of Psychological Aggression Toward You	0.79 (1.03)	0.74	0.77	0.05	0.03
Conflict Tactics Scale: Chronicity of Psychological Aggression Toward Partner, Missing	0.00 (0.04)	0.00	0.00	0.05	0.05
Depression (PHQ)	2.79 (3.61)	2.63	2.68	0.05	0.03
Depression (PHQ), Missing	0.00 (0.03)	0.00	0.00	0.00	0.00
Anxiety	2.07 (1.00)	2.04	2.06	0.03	0.02
Anxiety, Missing	0.00 (0.01)	0.00	0.00	0.00	0.00
PTSD	5.48 (9.65)	5.35	5.39	0.01	0.01
PTSD, Missing	0.02 (0.13)	0.02	0.02	-0.02	-0.02
TBI	0.12 (0.32)	0.12	0.12	-0.01	-0.01
TBI, Missing	0.00 (0.02)	0.00	0.00	0.00	0.00
Binge Drinking	0.24 (0.43)	0.23	0.23	0.02	0.02
Binge Drinking, Missing	0.03 (0.16)	0.02	0.02	0.03	0.03
Problematic Substance Use Scale	0.17 (0.59)	0.16	0.17	0.01	0.01

Table 2A.2—Continued

	Baseline Sample (n=2,724)	Responders:[a] Sample Weight Only	Responders: Sample and Attrition Weights	Sample Weight vs. Baseline Sample	Attrition and Sample Weights vs. Baseline Sample
	Mean (SD)	Mean	Mean	SMD	SMD
Medication for Mental Health Problem	0.05 (0.21)	0.05	0.05	0.00	0.00
Medication for Mental Health Problem, Missing	0.00 (0.04)	0.00	0.00	0.00	0.00
Received Mental Health Care	0.15 (0.35)	0.13	0.13	0.04	0.03
Received Mental Health Care, Missing	0.00 (0.02)	0.00	0.00	0.00	0.00
Financial Distress Scale	1.94 (0.71)	1.91	1.92	0.05	0.04
Financial Distress Scale, Missing	0.00 (0.01)	0.00	0.00	0.00	0.00
Family Environment Scale	2.80 (0.26)	2.81	2.80	-0.03	-0.01
Family Environment Scale, Missing	0.39 (0.49)	0.40	0.40	-0.02	-0.02
Parenting Stress Scale	3.34 (0.04)	3.36	3.35	-0.04	-0.03
Parenting Stress Scale, Missing	0.39 (0.49)	0.40	0.40	-0.02	-0.02
Military Commitment	4.38 (0.68)	4.38	4.37	0.00	0.02
Job Satisfaction	3.91 (1.03)	3.94	3.93	-0.03	-0.01
Job Satisfaction, Missing	0.00 (0.04)	0.00	0.00	0.00	0.00
Retention Intentions	4.01 (1.38)	4.01	4.00	0.00	0.01
Retention Intentions, Missing	0.34 (0.47)	0.34	0.33	0.01	0.01
SPOUSE VARIABLES					
Female	0.91 (0.29)	0.92	0.92	-0.02	-0.03
Age	33.44 (8.50)	33.72	33.60	-0.03	-0.02
Age, Missing	0.00 (0.02)	0.00	0.00	0.00	0.00
Minority Race/Ethnicity	0.27 (0.44)	0.26	0.27	0.00	0.00
Minority Race/Ethnicity, Missing	0.00 (0.04)	0.00	0.00	0.02	0.02
Children Younger Than Age 6	0.42 (0.49)	0.41	0.41	0.02	0.01
Education: Less than High School	0.02 (0.14)	0.02	0.02	0.02	0.02
Education: High School	0.18 (0.39)	0.18	0.18	0.02	0.01
Education: Some College	0.28 (0.45)	0.27	0.27	0.01	0.01

Table 2A.2—Continued

	Baseline Sample (n=2,724)	Responders:[a] Sample Weight Only	Responders: Sample and Attrition Weights	Sample Weight vs. Baseline Sample	Attrition and Sample Weights vs. Baseline Sample
	Mean (SD)	Mean	Mean	SMD	SMD
Education: Associate/Vocational/Technical Degree	0.19 (0.39)	0.18	0.19	0.01	0.00
Education: Bachelor's Degree	0.26 (0.44)	0.27	0.26	-0.03	-0.02
Education: Graduate or Professional Degree	0.08 (0.27)	0.08	0.08	-0.01	0.00
Education, Missing	0.00 (0.04)	0.00	0.00	0.03	0.03
Employment: Outside or Inside Home	0.42 (0.49)	0.43	0.43	-0.03	-0.02
Employment: Homemaker	0.32 (0.47)	0.31	0.32	0.00	0.00
Employment: Student	0.07 (0.26)	0.07	0.07	0.00	0.00
Employment: Not Employed	0.14 (0.35)	0.13	0.13	0.02	0.02
Employment, Missing	0.05 (0.22)	0.05	0.05	0.03	0.02
Parent in the Military	0.44 (0.50)	0.45	0.45	-0.02	-0.02
Parent in the Military, Missing	0.01 (0.07)	0.01	0.01	0.00	0.00
Marital Satisfaction Scale	3.85 (0.59)	3.87	3.86	-0.04	-0.03
PANAS: Positive	4.10 (0.73)	4.13	4.12	-0.03	-0.02
PANAS: Positive Missing	0.00 (0.02)	0.00	0.00	0.00	0.00
PANAS: Negative	2.14 (0.65)	2.12	2.13	0.02	0.01
PANAS: Negative Missing	0.00 (0.02)	0.00	0.00	0.00	0.00
Conflict Tactics Scale: Prevalence of Physical Aggression Toward Partner	0.04 (0.20)	0.05	0.05	-0.01	-0.02
Conflict Tactics Scale: Prevalence of Physical Aggression Toward Partner, Missing	0.00 (0.02)	0.00	0.00	0.04	0.00
Conflict Tactics Scale: Chronicity of Psychological Aggression Toward Partner	0.76 (0.93)	0.72	0.74	0.04	0.02
Conflict Tactics Scale: Prevalence of Physical Aggression Toward You	0.03 (0.16)	0.03	0.03	0.01	-0.01
Conflict Tactics Scale: Prevalence of Physical Aggression Toward You, Missing	0.00 (0.02)	0.00	0.00	0.00	0.00

Table 2A.2—Continued

	Baseline Sample (n=2,724)	Responders:[a] Sample Weight Only	Responders: Sample and Attrition Weights	Sample Weight vs. Baseline Sample	Attrition and Sample Weights vs. Baseline Sample
	Mean (SD)	Mean	Mean	SMD	SMD
Conflict Tactics Scale: Chronicity of Psychological Aggression Toward You	0.72 (0.97)	0.67	0.68	0.05	0.03
Depression (PHQ)	3.28 (4.01)	3.15	3.20	0.03	0.02
Depression (PHQ), Missing	0.00 (0.04)	0.00	0.00	0.00	0.00
Anxiety	2.15 (1.00)	2.13	2.14	0.02	0.01
Anxiety, Missing	0.00 (0.03)	0.00	0.00	0.03	0.03
PTSD	0.49 (1.00)	0.45	0.47	0.04	0.03
PTSD, Missing	0.00 (0.05)	0.00	0.00	0.00	0.02
Binge Drinking	0.12 (0.33)	0.12	0.12	0.02	0.02
Binge Drinking, Missing	0.02 (0.13)	0.02	0.02	0.01	0.01
Problematic Substance Use Scale	0.08 (0.46)	0.06	0.07	0.03	0.03
Problematic Substance Use Scale, Missing	0.01 (0.10)	0.01	0.01	0.02	0.02
Medication for Mental Health Problem	0.14 (0.35)	0.14	0.14	0.01	0.01
Medication for Mental Health Problem, Missing	0.00 (0.06)	0.00	0.00	0.00	0.00
Received Mental Health Care	0.15 (0.36)	0.14	0.15	0.03	0.02
Received Mental Health Care, Missing	0.00 (0.06)	0.00	0.00	0.00	0.00
Financial Distress Scale	2.00 (0.76)	1.97	1.98	0.05	0.03
Family Environment Scale	2.79 (0.28)	2.80	2.80	-0.03	-0.02
Family Environment Scale, Missing	0.38 (0.49)	0.39	0.39	-0.02	-0.02
Parenting Stress Scale	3.25 (0.39)	3.25	3.25	-0.01	0.01
Parenting Stress Scale, Missing	0.38 (0.49)	0.39	0.39	-0.02	-0.02
Military Commitment	4.44 (0.63)	4.46	4.45	-0.02	-0.01
Military Commitment, Missing	0.00 (0.02)	0.00	0.00	0.00	0.00
Satisfaction as Military Spouse	4.06 (1.00)	4.10	4.08	-0.04	-0.02
Satisfaction as Military Spouse, Missing	0.00 (0.03)	0.00	0.00	0.00	0.00
Retention Intentions	4.02 (1.28)	4.06	4.04	-0.03	-0.02
Retention Intentions, Missing	0.01 (0.11)	0.01	0.01	-0.02	-0.02

Table 2A.2—Continued

	Baseline Sample (n=2,724)	Responders:[a] Sample Weight Only	Responders: Sample and Attrition Weights	Sample Weight vs. Baseline Sample	Attrition and Sample Weights vs. Baseline Sample
	Mean (SD)	Mean	Mean	SMD	SMD
TEEN VARIABLES					
SDQ: Total	7.80 (5.31)	7.77	7.81	0.00	0.00
SDQ: Total, Missing	0.51 (0.50)	0.51	0.51	-0.01	-0.01
SDQ Subscale: Emotional Problems	1.56 (1.78)	1.60	1.60	-0.02	-0.02
SDQ Subscale: Emotional Problems, Missing	0.50 (0.50)	0.51	0.51	-0.01	-0.01
SDQ Subscale: Conduct Problems	1.11 (1.43)	1.06	1.08	0.03	0.02
SDQ Subscale: Conduct Problems, Missing	0.50 (0.50)	0.51	0.51	-0.01	-0.01
SDQ Subscale: Hyperactivity	3.43 (2.45)	3.37	3.39	0.02	0.01
SDQ Subscale: Hyperactivity, Missing	0.50 (0.50)	0.51	0.51	-0.01	-0.01
SDQ Subscale: Peer Relationships	1.70 (1.72)	1.74	1.74	-0.02	-0.02
SDQ Subscale: Peer Relationships, Missing	0.50 (0.50)	0.50	0.50	-0.01	-0.01
SDQ Subscale: Prosocial Behavior	8.47 (1.64)	8.50	8.49	-0.02	-0.01
SDQ Subscale: Prosocial Behavior, Missing	0.50 (0.50)	0.51	0.51	-0.01	-0.01
Depression Symptoms	0.95 (1.76)	0.92	0.93	0.02	0.01
Depression Symptoms, Missing	0.50 (0.50)	0.50	0.50	0.00	0.00
Anxiety (SCARED)	1.48 (1.68)	1.49	1.49	-0.01	-0.01
Anxiety (SCARED), Missing	0.50 0.50)	0.50	0.50	-0.01	-0.01

[a] Refers to spouses who have valid data in at least one of the final three waves of the study (Waves 7, 8, and 9 for the Army, Air Force, Marine Corps sample; Waves 5, 6, and 7 for the Navy sample).

Table 2A.3
Balance Table for Nonresponse: Teens

	Baseline Sample (n=2,724)	Responders:[a] Sample Weight Only	Responders: Sample and Attrition Weights	Sample Weight vs. Baseline Sample	Attrition and Sample Weights vs. Baseline Sample
	Mean (SD)	Mean	Mean	SMD	SMD
SERVICE MEMBER VARIABLES					
Pay Grade: Junior Enlisted	0.01 (0.09)	0.01	0.01	0.02	0.02
Pay Grade: Junior Officer	0.05 (0.22)	0.05	0.05	0.00	0.00
Pay Grade: Mid and Senior Enlisted	0.74 (0.44)	0.74	0.74	0.01	0.01
Pay Grade: Mid and Senior Officer	0.17 (0.38)	0.18	0.18	-0.02	-0.02
Pay Grade: Warrant Officer	0.03 (0.16)	0.02	0.02	0.02	0.02
Pay Grade: Missing	0.00 (0.02)	0.00	0.00	0.04	0.04
Total Number of Prior Deployments	1.74 (1.18)	1.75	1.75	0.00	-0.01
Total Number of Prior Deployments: Missing	0.02 (0.15)	0.02	0.02	0.04	0.03
Army	0.53 (0.50)	0.50	0.51	0.05	0.03
Air Force	0.19 (0.39)	0.20	0.20	-0.03	-0.03
Navy	0.25 (0.43)	0.28	0.27	-0.06	-0.03
Marine Corps	0.03 (0.18)	0.02	0.02	0.06	0.06
Reserve Component	0.46 (0.50)	0.49	0.48	-0.06	-0.04
Hoge Combat Experiences Scale	4.26 (3.85)	4.15	4.21	0.03	0.01
Deployment Trauma Exposure	1.89 (2.27)	1.85	1.90	0.02	-0.01
Deployment Trauma Exposure, Missing	0.09 (0.28)	0.06	0.06	0.11	0.08
Marital Satisfaction Scale	3.97 (0.46)	3.97	3.97	0.00	0.00
Depression (PHQ)	2.86 (3.53)	2.87	2.87	0.00	0.00
Anxiety	2.01 (1.02)	1.99	1.99	0.02	0.02
PTSD	7.29 (11.11)	7.29	7.29	0.00	0.00
PTSD, Missing	0.05 (0.21)	0.05	0.05	-0.02	-0.01
TBI	0.12 (0.33)	0.13	0.13	-0.02	-0.02
TBI, Missing	0.00 (0.03)	0.00	0.00	0.00	0.00

Table 2A.3—Continued

	Baseline Sample (n=2,724)	Responders:[a] Sample Weight Only	Responders: Sample and Attrition Weights	Sample Weight vs. Baseline Sample	Attrition and Sample Weights vs. Baseline Sample
	Mean (SD)	Mean	Mean	SMD	SMD
Binge Drinking	0.16 (0.37)	0.14	0.14	0.04	0.04
Binge Drinking, Missing	0.02 (0.15)	0.03	0.03	-0.03	-0.03
SPOUSE VARIABLES					
Education: Less than High School	0.02 (0.15)	0.01	0.01	0.06	0.05
Education: High School	0.17 (0.37)	0.17	0.17	0.00	0.00
Education: Some College	0.25 (0.43)	0.24	0.24	0.02	0.03
Education: Associate/Vocational/Technical Degree	0.24 (0.43)	0.25	0.25	-0.04	-0.03
Education: Bachelor's Degree	0.25 (0.43)	0.26	0.26	-0.03	-0.03
Education: Graduate or Professional Degree	0.08 (0.27)	0.07	0.07	0.03	0.02
Employment: Outside or Inside Home	0.45 (0.50)	0.48	0.47	-0.05	-0.04
Employment: Homemaker	0.36 (0.48)	0.35	0.36	0.02	0.01
Employment: Student	0.05 (0.22)	0.05	0.05	0.00	0.00
Employment: Not Employed	0.13 (0.34)	0.11	0.12	0.04	0.04
Employment, Missing	0.01 (0.10)	0.01	0.01	0.02	0.02
Marital Satisfaction Scale	3.76 (0.61)	3.80	3.79	-0.05	-0.04
Depression (PHQ)	3.13 (4.14)	2.93	2.96	0.05	0.04
Anxiety	2.01 (0.90)	1.96	1.98	0.05	0.04
PTSD	0.36 (0.89)	0.32	0.33	0.05	0.03
Binge Drinking	0.05 (0.23)	0.04	0.04	0.07	0.05
Binge Drinking, Missing	0.05 (0.21)	0.05	0.05	-0.03	-0.02

Table 2A.3—Continued

	Baseline Sample (n=2,724)	Responders:[a] Sample Weight Only	Responders: Sample and Attrition Weights	Sample Weight vs. Baseline Sample	Attrition and Sample Weights vs. Baseline Sample
	Mean (SD)	Mean	Mean	SMD	SMD
TEEN VARIABLES					
Age	13.70 (1.85)	13.71	13.70	0.00	0.00
Age, Missing	0.00 (0.02)	0.00	0.00	0.04	0.04
Female	0.51 (0.50)	0.50	0.50	0.01	0.02
Family Environment Scale	2.71 (0.31)	2.72	2.72	-0.02	-0.01
Family Environment Scale, Missing	0.00 (0.06)	0.00	0.00	0.03	0.03
PANAS: Positive	4.14 (0.61)	4.15	4.14	-0.01	0.00
PANAS: Positive, Missing	0.00 (0.06)	0.00	0.00	0.03	0.03
PANAS: Negative	1.95 (0.56)	1.94	1.95	0.01	0.01
PANAS: Negative, Missing	0.00 (0.06)	0.00	0.00	0.03	0.03
Life Satisfaction	4.51 (0.79)	4.51	4.51	0.00	0.01
Life Satisfaction, Missing	0.06 (0.24)	0.07	0.06	-0.03	-0.01
Self-Rated Health	4.06 (0.90)	4.06	4.04	0.00	0.02
Self-Rated Health, Missing	0.01 (0.09)	0.00	0.00	0.05	0.05
PedsQL	4.27 (0.71)	4.32	4.30	-0.07	-0.05
PedsQL, Missing	0.14 (0.34)	0.15	0.14	-0.03	-0.01
Depressive Symptoms	2.24 (2.64)	2.18	2.19	0.02	0.02
Depressive Symptoms, Missing	0.01 (0.07)	0.00	0.00	0.11	0.11
Anxiety (SCARED)	1.33 (1.48)	1.33	1.33	0.00	0.00
Anxiety (SCARED), Missing	0.01 (0.07)	0.00	0.00	0.04	0.04
SDQ Subscale: Emotional Problems	1.90 (2.00)	1.87	1.87	0.02	0.02
SDQ Subscale: Emotional Problems, Missing	0.01 (0.07)	0.00	0.00	0.04	0.04
SDQ Subscale: Conduct Problems	1.36 (1.41)	1.33	1.35	0.02	0.01
SDQ Subscale: Conduct Problems, Missing	0.01 (0.07)	0.00	0.00	0.04	0.04
SDQ Subscale: Hyperactivity	3.26 (2.14)	3.21	3.22	0.02	0.02
SDQ Subscale: Hyperactivity, Missing	0.01 (0.08)	0.00	0.00	0.04	0.04

Table 2A.3—Continued

	Baseline Sample (n=2,724)	Responders: Sample Weight Only[a]	Responders: Sample and Attrition Weights	Sample Weight vs. Baseline Sample	Attrition and Sample Weights vs. Baseline Sample
	Mean (SD)	Mean	Mean	SMD	SMD
SDQ Subscale: Peer Relationships	1.87 (1.56)	1.86	1.86	0.01	0.00
SDQ Subscale: Peer Relationships, Missing	0.01 (0.07)	0.00	0.00	0.04	0.04
SDQ Subscale: Prosocial Behavior	8.49 (1.51)	8.46	8.46	0.02	0.02
SDQ Subscale: Prosocial Behavior, Missing	0.01 (0.8)	0.00	0.00	0.04	0.04
SDQ: Total	8.39 (5.43)	8.27	8.30	0.02	0.02
SDQ: Total, Missing	0.01 (0.08)	0.00	0.00	0.04	0.04
Behavior Problems Scale: Physical Aggression	1.17 (0.33)	1.18	1.18	-0.02	-0.03
Behavior Problems Scale: Physical Aggression, Missing	0.15 (0.36)	0.15	0.16	0.00	-0.01
Behavior Problems Scale: Nonphysical Aggression	1.40 (0.86)	1.42	1.42	-0.02	-0.02
Behavior Problems Scale: Nonphysical Aggression, Missing	0.16 (0.36)	0.16	0.16	-0.01	-0.01
Behavior Problems Scale: Relational Aggression	1.11 (0.35)	1.12	1.12	-0.03	-0.03
Behavior Problems Scale: Relational Aggression, Missing	0.15 (0.36)	0.16	0.16	0.00	-0.01
Behavior Problems Scale: Drug Use	1.06 (0.24)	1.06	1.06	0.01	0.00
Behavior Problems Scale: Drug Use, Missing	0.15 (0.36)	0.15	0.16	0.00	-0.01
Medication for Mental Health Problem	0.09 (0.29)	0.08	0.09	0.03	0.02
Medication for Mental Health Problem, Missing	0.02 (0.14)	0.02	0.02	0.01	0.01
Received Mental Health Care	0.10 (0.30)	0.09	0.09	0.03	0.02
Received Mental Health Care, Missing	0.01 (0.08)	0.00	0.00	0.04	0.04
Academic Engagement Scale	2.03 (0.55)	2.02	2.02	0.02	0.01
Academic Engagement Scale, Missing	0.14 (0.35)	0.13	0.13	0.04	0.04
Wants Career in Military	0.27 (0.45)	0.27	0.27	0.01	0.01
Wants Career in Military, Missing	0.24 (0.43)	0.25	0.24	-0.02	-0.01

Table 2A.3—Continued

	Baseline Sample (n=2,724) Mean (SD)	Responders:[a] Sample Weight Only Mean	Responders: Sample and Attrition Weights Mean	Sample Weight vs. Baseline Sample SMD	Attrition and Sample Weights vs. Baseline Sample SMD
Retention Intentions	3.94 (1.17)	3.94	3.93	0.00	0.01
Retention Intentions, Missing	0.03 (0.16)	0.02	0.02	0.01	0.01
Military Commitment	4.19 (0.67)	4.20	4.20	-0.01	-0.01
Military Commitment, Missing	0.01 (0.07)	0.00	0.00	0.04	0.04
Socialize with Military Kids	0.69 (0.45)	0.68	0.69	0.02	0.01
Socialize with Military Kids, Missing	0.01 (0.11)	0.01	0.01	0.02	0.01
Relationship Quality with Service Member	4.18 (0.56)	4.18	4.18	0.00	0.01
Relationship Quality with Service Member, Missing	0.00 (0.06)	0.00	0.00	0.03	0.03
Relationship Quality with Spouse	4.16 t(0.69)	4.16	4.15	0.00	0.00
Relationship Quality with Spouse, Missing	0.00 (0.06)	0.00	0.00	0.03	0.03
Emotional Support: Enough People to Count On	0.89 (0.31)	0.90	0.90	-0.02	-0.02
Emotional Support: Not Enough People to Count On	0.08 (0.28)	0.09	0.09	0.00	0.00
Emotional Support: No One to Count On	0.01 (0.11)	0.01	0.01	0.02	0.01
Emotional Support: Missing	0.01 (0.10)	0.01	0.01	0.05	0.04

[a] Refers to teens who have valid data in at least one of the final three waves of the study (Waves 7, 8, and 9 for the Army, Air Force, Marine Corps sample; Waves 5, 6, and 7 for the Navy sample).

Table 2A.4
Impact of Poststratification Weights: Army

	Sample: Nonresponse Weighted Mean[a]	Sample: Nonresponse and Poststratification Weighted Mean[a]	Target Population Mean[b]
DEPLOYED SAMPLE: SERVICE MEMBERS			
Female	0.08	0.07	0.07
Age	34.08	32.37	32.60
Minority Race/Ethnicity	0.27	0.35	0.34
Pay Grade: Junior Enlisted	0.07	0.05	0.05
Pay Grade: Junior Officer	0.10	0.10	0.10
Pay Grade: Mid and Senior Enlisted	0.74	0.71	0.71
Pay Grade: Mid and Senior Officer	0.05	0.09	0.09
Pay Grade: Warrant Officer	0.03	0.05	0.05
Ever Deployed	0.78	0.91	0.91
Component: Active	0.62	0.77	0.77
Component: National Guard	0.20	0.16	0.16
Component: Reserve	0.18	0.07	0.07
DEPLOYED SAMPLE: SPOUSES			
Female	0.08	0.07	0.07
Age	34.17	32.30	32.60
Minority Race/Ethnicity	0.26	0.35	0.34
Pay Grade: Junior Enlisted	0.06	0.05	0.05
Pay Grade: Junior Officer	0.09	0.10	0.10
Pay Grade: Mid and Senior Enlisted	0.76	0.71	0.71
Pay Grade: Mid and Senior Officer	0.06	0.09	0.09
Pay Grade: Warrant Officer	0.03	0.05	0.05
Ever Deployed	0.80	0.91	0.91
Component: Active	0.61	0.77	0.77
Component: National Guard	0.19	0.16	0.16
Component: Reserve	0.20	0.07	0.07
NONDEPLOYED SAMPLE: SERVICE MEMBERS			
Female	0.10	0.13	0.13
Age	36.44	35.46	35.60
Minority Race/Ethnicity	0.26	0.35	0.36
Pay Grade: Junior Enlisted	0.02	0.05	0.05
Pay Grade: Junior Officer	0.08	0.08	0.08
Pay Grade: Mid and Senior Enlisted	0.79	0.75	0.75
Pay Grade: Mid and Senior Officer	0.09	0.09	0.09
Pay Grade: Warrant Officer	0.03	0.03	0.03
Ever Deployed	0.82	0.72	0.72
Component: Active	0.51	0.47	0.47
Component: National Guard	0.36	0.32	0.32
Component: Reserve	0.13	0.21	0.21
NONDEPLOYED SAMPLE: SPOUSES			
Female	0.09	0.13	0.13
Age	36.24	35.57	35.60
Minority Race/Ethnicity	0.25	0.35	0.36
Pay Grade: Junior Enlisted	0.02	0.05	0.05
Pay Grade: Junior Officer	0.08	0.08	0.08
Pay Grade: Mid and Senior Enlisted	0.78	0.75	0.75
Pay Grade: Mid and Senior Officer	0.09	0.09	0.09
Pay Grade: Warrant Officer	0.02	0.03	0.03
Ever Deployed	0.81	0.72	0.72
Component: Active	0.52	0.47	0.47
Component: National Guard	0.36	0.32	0.32
Component: Reserve	0.12	0.21	0.21

[a] From Deployment Life Study data.

[b] From sampling file provided by DMDC and each service.

Table 2A.5
Impact of Poststratification Weights: Air Force

	Sample: Nonresponse Weighted Mean[a]	Sample: Nonresponse and Poststratification Weighted Mean[a]	Target Population Mean[b]
DEPLOYED SAMPLE: SERVICE MEMBERS			
Female	0.08	0.11	0.11
Age	34.20	33.84	33.40
Minority Race/Ethnicity	0.22	0.23	0.23
Pay Grade: Junior Enlisted	0.06	0.04	0.03
Pay Grade: Junior Officer	0.09	0.12	0.12
Pay Grade: Mid and Senior Enlisted	0.76	0.70	0.70
Pay Grade: Mid and Senior Officer	0.09	0.15	0.15
Ever Deployed	0.00	0.00	0.00
Component: Active	0.87	0.90	0.90
Component: Air Guard	0.71	0.77	0.77
Component: Reserve	0.11	0.15	0.15
DEPLOYED SAMPLE: SPOUSES			
Female	0.10	0.11	0.11
Age	34.09	33.83	33.40
Minority Race/Ethnicity	0.22	0.23	0.23
Pay Grade: Junior Enlisted	0.07	0.04	0.03
Pay Grade: Junior Officer	0.09	0.12	0.12
Pay Grade: Mid and Senior Enlisted	0.80	0.70	0.70
Pay Grade: Mid and Senior Officer	0.05	0.15	0.15
Ever Deployed	0.00	0.00	0.00
Component: Active	0.92	0.90	0.90
Component: Air Guard	0.76	0.77	0.77
Component: Reserve	0.14	0.15	0.15
NONDEPLOYED SAMPLE: SERVICE MEMBERS			
Female	0.14	0.18	0.18
Age	36.88	36.17	36.30
Minority Race/Ethnicity	0.23	0.25	0.25
Pay Grade: Junior Enlisted	0.04	0.02	0.02
Pay Grade: Junior Officer	0.09	0.09	0.09
Pay Grade: Mid and Senior Enlisted	0.62	0.73	0.73
Pay Grade: Mid and Senior Officer	0.26	0.16	0.16
Ever Deployed	0.00	0.00	0.00
Component: Active	0.97	0.60	0.60
Component: Air Guard	0.58	0.58	0.57
Component: Reserve	0.22	0.23	0.23
NONDEPLOYED SAMPLE: SPOUSES			
Female	0.13	0.18	0.18
Age	37.23	36.16	36.30
Minority Race/Ethnicity	0.21	0.25	0.25
Pay Grade: Junior Enlisted	0.02	0.02	0.02
Pay Grade: Junior Officer	0.07	0.09	0.09
Pay Grade: Mid and Senior Enlisted	0.66	0.73	0.73
Pay Grade: Mid and Senior Officer	0.25	0.16	0.16
Ever Deployed	0.00	0.00	0.00
Component: Active	0.95	0.60	0.60
Component: Air Guard	0.58	0.57	0.57
Component: Reserve	0.22	0.23	0.23

[a] From Deployment Life Study data.

[b] From sampling file provided by DMDC and each service.

Table 2A.6
Impact of Poststratification Weights: Navy

	Sample: Nonresponse Weighted Mean[a]	Sample: Nonresponse and Poststratification Weighted Mean[a]	Target Population Mean[b]
DEPLOYED SAMPLE: SERVICE MEMBERS			
Female	0.08	0.09	0.09
Age	30.84	32.89	32.90
Minority Race/Ethnicity	0.36	0.45	0.45
Pay Grade: Junior Enlisted	0.01	0.07	0.07
Pay Grade: Junior Officer	0.07	0.10	0.10
Pay Grade: Mid and Senior Enlisted	0.87	0.71	0.72
Pay Grade: Mid and Senior Officer	0.04	0.11	0.11
Pay Grade: Warrant Officer	0.01	0.01	0.01
Ever Deployed	0.70	0.92	0.92
Component: Active	1.00	1.00	0.92
Component: Reserve	0.00	0.00	0.09
DEPLOYED SAMPLE: SPOUSES			
Female	0.05	0.09	0.09
Age	31.11	32.92	32.90
Minority Race/Ethnicity	0.35	0.45	0.45
Pay Grade: Junior Enlisted	0.02	0.07	0.07
Pay Grade: Junior Officer	0.08	0.10	0.10
Pay Grade: Mid and Senior Enlisted	0.85	0.71	0.72
Pay Grade: Mid and Senior Officer	0.05	0.11	0.11
Pay Grade: Warrant Officer	0.01	0.01	0.01
Ever Deployed	0.67	0.92	0.92
Component: Active	1.00	1.00	0.92
Component: Reserve	0.00	0.00	0.09
NONDEPLOYED SAMPLE: SERVICE MEMBERS			
Female	0.07	0.14	0.14
Age	31.24	34.26	35.00
Minority Race/Ethnicity	0.29	0.43	0.44
Pay Grade: Junior Enlisted	0.05	0.04	0.04
Pay Grade: Junior Officer	0.06	0.09	0.09
Pay Grade: Mid and Senior Enlisted	0.85	0.71	0.71
Pay Grade: Mid and Senior Officer	0.04	0.16	0.16
Pay Grade: Warrant Officer	0.00	0.01	0.01
Ever Deployed	0.70	0.72	0.72
Component: Active	0.92	0.97	0.75
Component: Reserve	0.08	0.03	0.25
NONDEPLOYED SAMPLE: SPOUSES			
Female	0.06	0.14	0.14
Age	31.23	34.94	35.00
Minority Race/Ethnicity	0.24	0.43	0.44
Pay Grade: Junior Enlisted	0.04	0.04	0.04
Pay Grade: Junior Officer	0.05	0.09	0.09
Pay Grade: Mid and Senior Enlisted	0.88	0.71	0.71
Pay Grade: Mid and Senior Officer	0.03	0.16	0.16
Pay Grade: Warrant Officer	0.00	0.01	0.01
Ever Deployed	0.72	0.72	0.72
Component: Active	0.83	0.94	0.75
Component: Reserve	0.17	0.06	0.25

[a] From Deployment Life Study data.

[b] From sampling file provided by DMDC and each service. The address files provided by the Navy did not include reserve component members.

Table 2A.7
Impact of Poststratification Weights: Marine Corps

	Sample: Nonresponse Weighted Mean[a]	Sample: Nonresponse and Poststratification Weighted Mean[a]	Target Population Mean[b]
DEPLOYED SAMPLE: SERVICE MEMBERS			
Female	0.06	0.04	0.03
Age	33.62	31.31	29.10
Minority Race/Ethnicity	0.14	0.18	0.30
Pay Grade: Officer	0.70	0.18	0.18
Ever Deployed	0.94	0.96	0.93
Component: Active	1.00	1.00	0.96
Component: Reserve	0.00	0.00	0.04
DEPLOYED SAMPLE: SPOUSES			
Female	0.05	0.04	0.03
Age	32.89	30.96	29.10
Minority Race/Ethnicity	0.12	0.18	0.30
Pay Grade: Officer	0.64	0.18	0.18
Ever Deployed	0.92	0.96	0.93
Component: Active	0.96	0.94	0.96
Component: Reserve	0.04	0.06	0.04
NONDEPLOYED SAMPLE: SERVICE MEMBERS			
Female	0.03	0.06	0.07
Age	29.29	30.76	30.70
Minority Race/Ethnicity	0.27	0.32	0.32
Pay Grade: Officer	0.23	0.15	0.15
Ever Deployed	0.95	0.75	0.75
Component: Active	0.87	0.80	0.82
Component: Reserve	0.14	0.20	0.19
NONDEPLOYED SAMPLE: SPOUSES			
Female	0.05	0.06	0.07
Age	29.88	30.41	30.70
Minority Race/Ethnicity	0.27	0.32	0.32
Pay Grade: Officer	0.22	0.15	0.15
Ever Deployed	0.94	0.75	0.75
Component: Active	0.86	0.81	0.82
Component: Reserve	0.14	0.19	0.19

[a] From Deployment Life Study data.

[b] From sampling file provided by DMDC and each service. The Marine Corps did not provide a breakdown of pay grade by seniority.

References

Abidin, R. R., *Parenting Stress Index*, 3rd ed., Odessa, Fla.: Psychological Assessment Resources, 1995.

American Academy of Pediatrics, *Addressing Mental Health Concerns in Primary Care: A Clinician's Toolkit*, Washington, D.C., 2010.

American Psychiatric Association, *Diagnostic and Statistical Manual of Mental Disorders*, 4th ed., Washington, D.C.: American Psychiatric Association, 1994.

Bacharach, M., "Estimating Nonnegative Matrices from Marginal Data," *International Economic Review*, Vol. 6, No. 3, 1965, pp. 294–310.

Birmaher, B., D. A. Brent, L. Chiappetta, J. Bridge, S. Monga, and M. Baugher, "Psychometric Properties of the Screen for Child Anxiety Related Emotional Disorders (SCARED): A Replication Study," *Journal of the American Academy of Child and Adolescent Psychiatry*, Vol. 38, No. 10, October 1999, pp. 1230–1236.

Birmaher, B., S. Khetarpal, D. Brent, M. Cully, L. Balach, J. Kaufman, and S. M. Neer, "The Screen for Child Anxiety Related Emotional Disorders (SCARED): Scale Construction and Psychometric Characteristics," *Journal of the American Academy of Child and Adolescent Psychiatry*, Vol. 36, No. 4, April 1997, pp. 545–553.

Bliese, P. D., K. M. Wright, A. B. Adler, J. L. Thomas, and C. W. Hoge, "Timing of Postcombat Mental Health Assessments," *Psychological Services*, Vol. 4, No. 3, August 2007, pp. 141–148.

Defense Manpower Data Center, *February 2012 Status of Forces Survey of Active Duty Members*, Alexandria, Va., 2012.

DMDC—*See* Defense Manpower Data Center.

Goodman, R., "The Strengths and Difficulties Questionnaire: A Research Note," *Journal of Child Psychology and Psychiatry*, Vol. 38, No. 5, 1997, pp. 581–586.

———, "Psychometric Properties of the Strengths and Difficulties Questionnaire," *Journal of the American Academy of Child and Adolescent Psychiatry*, Vol. 40, No. 11, November 2001, pp. 1337–1345.

Goodman, R., T. Ford, H. Simmons, R. Gatward, and H. Meltzer, "Using the Strengths and Difficulties Questionnaire (SDQ) to Screen for Child Psychiatric Disorders in a Community Sample," *British Journal of Psychiatry*, Vol. 177, December 2000, pp. 534–539.

Gutman, L. M., and J. S. Eccles, "Financial Strain, Parenting Behaviors, and Adolescents' Achievement: Testing Model Equivalence Between African American and European American Single- and Two-Parent Families," *Child Development*, Vol. 70, No. 6, November–December 1999, pp. 1464–1476.

Hofferth, S., P. E. Davis-Kean, J. Davis, and J. Finkelstein, *The Child Development Supplement to the Panel Study of Income Dynamics: 1997 User Guide*, Ann Arbor, Mich.: Survey Research Center, Institute for Social Research, University of Michigan, 1997. As of February 13, 2013: https://psidonline.isr.umich.edu/CDS/cdsi_userGD.pdf

Hoge, C. W., C. A. Castro, S. C. Messer, D. McGurk, D. I. Cotting, and R. L. Koffman, "Combat Duty in Iraq and Afghanistan, Mental Health Problems, and Barriers to Care," *New England Journal of Medicine*, Vol. 351, July 1, 2004, pp. 13–22.

Hoge, C. W., A. Terhakopian, C. A. Castro, S. C. Messer, and C. C. Engel, "Association of Posttraumatic Stress Disorder with Somatic Symptoms, Health Care Visits, and Absenteeism Among Iraq War Veterans," *American Journal of Psychiatry*, Vol. 164, No. 1, 2007, pp. 150–153.

Kang, J. D. Y., and J. L. Schafer, "Demystifying Double Robustness: A Comparison of Alternative Strategies for Estimating a Population Mean from Incomplete Data," *Statistical Science*, Vol. 22, No. 4, 2007, pp. 523–539.

King, L. A., D. W. King, D. S. Vogt, J. Knight, and R. E. Samper, "Deployment Risk and Resilience Inventory: A Collection of Measures for Studying Deployment-Related Experiences of Military Personnel and Veterans," *Military Psychology*, Vol. 18, No. 2, 2006, pp. 89–120.

Kroenke, K., R. L. Spitzer, and J. B. Williams, "The PHQ-9: Validity of a Brief Depression Severity Measure," *Journal of General Internal Medicine*, Vol. 16, No. 9, September 2001, pp. 606–613.

Kroenke, K., T. W. Strine, R. L. Spitzer, J. B. Williams, J. T. Berry, and A. H. Mokdad, "The PHQ-8 as a Measure of Current Depression in the General Population," *Journal of Affective Disorders*, Vol. 114, Nos. 1–3, April 2009, pp. 163–173.

Lee, B. K., J. Lessler, and E. A. Stuart, "Improving Propensity Score Weighting Using Machine Learning," *Statistics in Medicine*, Vol. 29, 2010, pp. 337–346.

McCaffrey, D. F., G. Ridgeway, and A. R. Morral, "Propensity Score Estimation with Boosted Regression for Evaluating Causal Effects in Observational Studies," *Psychological Methods*, Vol. 9, 2004, pp. 403–425.

Moos, R. H., and B. S. Moos, *Family Environment Scale Manual*, Menlo Park, Calif.: Consulting Psychologists Press, 1994.

Neugebauer, R., and M. van der Laan, "Why Prefer Double Robust Estimators in Causal Inference?" *Journal of Statistical Planning and Inference*, Vol. 129, 2005, pp. 405–426.

Panel Study of Income Dynamics, home page, undated. As of January 7, 2013:
http://psidonline.isr.umich.edu

Prins, A., P. Ouimette, R. Kimerling, R. P. Camerond, D. S. Hugelshofer, J. Shaw-Hegwer, A. Thrailkill, F. D. Gusman, and J. I. Sheikh, "The Primary Care PTSD Screen (PC-PTSD): Development and Operating Characteristics," *International Journal of Psychiatry in Clinical Practice*, Vol. 9, No. 1, January 1, 2004, pp. 9–14.

Rauer, A. J., B. R. Karney, C. W. Garvan, and W. Hou, "Relationship Risks in Context: A Cumulative Risk Approach to Understanding Relationship Satisfaction," *Journal of Marriage and Family*, Vol. 70, No. 5, December 2008, pp. 1122–1135.

Ridgeway, G., D. McCaffrey, A. Morral, L. Burgette, and B. A. Griffin, *Toolkit for Weighting and Analysis of Nonequivalent Groups: A Tutorial for the Twang Package*, Santa Monica, Calif.: RAND Corporation, TL-136/1-NIDA, 2014. As of November 10, 2015:
http://www.rand.org/pubs/tools/TL136z1.html

Rosenbaum, P. R., and D. B. Rubin, "The Central Role of the Propensity Score in Observational Studies for Causal Effects," *Biometrika*, Vol. 70, 1983, pp. 41–55.

Rosenthal, Doreen A., and S. Shirley Feldman, "The Influence of Perceived Family and Personal Factors on Self-Reported School Performance of Chinese and Western High School Students," *Journal of Research on Adolescence*, Vol. 1, No. 2, 1991, pp. 135–154.

Sherbourne, C. D., R. D. Hays, L. Ordway, M. R. DiMatteo, and R. L. Kravitz, "Antecedents of Adherence to Medical Recommendations: Results from the Medical Outcomes Study," *Journal of Behavioral Medicine*, Vol. 15, No. 5, October 1992, pp. 447–468.

Straus, M. A., S. L. Hamby, S. Boney-McCoy, and D. B. Sugarman, "The Revised Conflict Tactics Scales (CTS2): Development and Preliminary Psychometric Data," *Journal of Family Issues*, Vol. 17, No. 3, May 1996, pp. 283–316.

Tanielian, T., and L. H. Jaycox, eds., *Invisible Wounds of War: Psychological and Cognitive Injuries, Their Consequences, and Services to Assist Recovery*, Santa Monica, Calif.: RAND Corporation, MG-720-CCF, 2008. As of February 14, 2013:
http://www.rand.org/pubs/monographs/MG720.html

Tanielian, T., B. R. Karney, A. Chandra, and S. O. Meadows, *The Deployment Life Study: Methodological Overview and Baseline Sample Description*, Santa Monica, Calif.: RAND Corporation, RR-209-A/OSD, 2014. As of November 10, 2015:
http://www.rand.org/pubs/research_reports/RR209.html

Thompson, B. M., and L. Cavallaro, "Gender, Work-Based Support and Family Outcomes," *Stress and Health*, Vol. 23, No. 2, April 2007, pp. 73–85.

Troxel, W. M., T. E. Trail, L. Jaycox, and A. Chandra, *Preparing for Deployment: Examining Family and Individual-Level Factors*, Santa Monica, Calif.: RAND Corporation, forthcoming.

U.S. Department of Health and Human Services, Substance Abuse and Mental Health Services Administration, Office of Applied Studies, *National Survey on Drug Use and Health*, 2007, Ann Arbor, Mich.: Inter-University Consortium for Political and Social Research, released December 1, 2008, updated January 4, 2013. As of February 27, 2013:
http://dx.doi.org/10.3886/ICPSR23782.v3

Watson, D., L. A. Clark, and A. Tellegen, "Development and Validation of Brief Measures of Positive and Negative Affect: The PANAS Scales," *Journal of Personality and Social Psychology*, Vol. 54, No. 6, June 1988, pp. 1063–1070.

Weathers, F. W., J. A. Huska, and T. M. Keane, *The PTSD Checklist Military Version (PCLM)*, Boston, Mass.: National Center for PTSD, 1991.

Weathers, F. W., B. T. Litz, D. S. Herman, J. A. Huska, and T. M. Keane, "The PTSD Checklist (PCL): Reliability, Validity, and Diagnostic Utility," paper presented at the annual meeting of the International Society for Traumatic Stress Studies, San Antonio, Texas, October 1993. As of February 14, 2013:
http://www.pdhealth.mil/library/downloads/pcl_sychometrics.doc

CHAPTER THREE

Marital Outcomes

Benjamin R. Karney, Thomas E. Trail, Beth Ann Griffin, Esther Friedman, and Robin L. Beckman

In 2005, headlines in news outlets around the country announced a troubling finding: Divorce rates appeared to have spiked in the active duty Army (e.g., McIntyre, 2005; Zoroya, 2005). Concern about the suffering of military couples sparked a search for causes, and it was not hard to identify one. Since the terrorist attacks of 2001 and the subsequent military actions in Iraq and Afghanistan, rates of deployment had been higher and durations of deployments had been longer than at any time since the dawn of the all-volunteer military (Hosek and Martorell, 2009). Deployments had long been described as one of the most stressful and demanding elements of military service (Rosen and Durand, 2000). To the extent that the recent period had been characterized by especially demanding deployments, it made sense to many that rising divorce rates in the military signaled the power of deployments to break apart marriages that would otherwise have thrived.

In the intervening decade, the media has continued to report on the damaging stresses that burden military marriages (e.g., Alvarez, 2007; Kaufman, 2008). In survey after survey, service members and their spouses continue to emphasize the stresses associated with deployments—and reintegration in particular (Blue Star Families, 2012; Knobloch and Theiss, 2012; Newby et al., 2005). The Pentagon has responded, investing substantial resources in programs designed to strengthen and support military families facing deployment (Rostker, 2006; Rubin and Harvie, 2012).

Despite the widespread assumption that deployments harm military marriages, empirical evidence of such harm remains limited. The 2005 spike in Army divorce rates, for example, turned out to be an anomaly. In fact, during the period where deployments were longest, most frequent, and most dangerous, divorce rates across the military rose only slightly (Karney and Crown, 2007) and remained lower than the divorce rates for comparable civilians during the same period (Karney, Loughran, and Pollard, 2012). Research that directly examines links between divorce and deployments has been inconsistent, with some studies finding that the experience of deployment predicts an increased risk of divorce (Negrusa, Negrusa, and Hosek, 2014) and others reporting negligible or even beneficial effects (Karney and Crown, 2010).

One reason that evidence of the harmful effects of deployment on marriage has been limited may be that most of the existing research has focused on divorce, a weak indicator of how spouses experience their relationship. As decades of research has established (Levinger, 1976; Lewis and Spanier, 1982), spouses may elect to maintain or dissolve their marriages for many reasons that are independent of the quality of their relationship. Within the military, for example, marriage entitles service members and their spouses to concrete benefits (including housing allowances, health benefits, and separation pay) that are terminated if the marriage ends

(Lundquist and Xu, 2014). The threatened loss of these resources may prevent some couples from ending their marriages regardless of their experience of the relationship itself.

A more direct indicator of the health of military marriages is spouses' reports of their marital satisfaction. Among civilians, spouses' evaluations of their relationships are powerfully associated with their own physical and mental health, as well as the health of their children (Robles et al., 2014). When spouses feel close and perceive that their communication with each other is effective, they recover more quickly from stress (Cranford, 2004), experience more-effective immune response to illness (Kiecolt-Glaser et al., 1993), and are less likely to experience depression and other psychopathology (Whisman, 2001). In contrast, marital conflict and aggression predict higher levels of individual distress (Arriaga and Schkeryantz, 2015), less effective parenting (Sturge-Apple, Davies, and Cummings, 2006), and ultimately higher rates of divorce (Rogge and Bradbury, 1999).

Current policy and conventional wisdom assume that the stresses associated with deployment and reintegration create distress, negativity, and conflict in marriages that otherwise would have been satisfying, but support for this view requires data that directly assess spouses' reports of the emotional climate of their marriage across the deployment cycle. To date, such data have been unavailable. The goal of this report is to bridge this gap in the literature by analyzing data from the Deployment Life Study, a multiwave longitudinal study of military families assessed before, during, and after a deployment. Toward this goal, the rest of the introduction to this chapter is organized into the following sections. First, we briefly review theory relevant to understanding the potential effects of a deployment on marital satisfaction and related outcomes. Second, we review the existing research on the associations between experiences of deployment and the quality of relationships among military couples, highlighting the methodological limitations of that research. Third, we introduce the Deployment Life Study, explaining how the new data set overcomes the limitations of prior research on these issues and allows us to address new questions about the impact of deployment on military marriages.

Theoretical Perspectives on the Effects of Deployment on Military Marriages

Most existing scholarship on the impact of deployment on military marriages has been informed by Family Stress Process theories, especially as articulated in Rubin Hill's (1949) ABC-X model (see also Karney and Crown, 2007; McCubbin and Patterson, 1983). According to these perspectives, stressors are events that make demands on a couple's resources. The severity of those stressors (A) (e.g., deployment, trauma exposure during deployment, duration of deployment), the level of resources available to the couple (B), and the couple's interpretation of the event (C) combine to determine the couple's response to the stressor (X), particularly whether that response brings the couple closer together or pushes them apart.

Family Stress Process models highlight several reasons to expect that the average effects of deployment on marital relationships should be negative. First, because deployments and reintegration are undeniably stressful, they present an opportunity for unsuccessful coping that is avoided by couples that do not experience a deployment. For the same reason that people who drive experience more car accidents than those who do not drive, couples experiencing deployment have more opportunities to experience negative stress than couples that do not. Moreover, the more stressful the deployment (e.g., longer periods of separation, less time at home between deployments, greater exposure to combat), the greater the drain on a couple's resources and the more negative the impact on the marriage is expected to be. Indeed, prior analyses suggest that exposure to combat during deployments accounts for a significant portion of the associations between deployments and marital outcomes (Karney and Trail, forthcoming).

Second, in addition to presenting couples with stress, deployments reduce the resources that couples have available to respond to stress. One resource substantially curtailed by deployment is the amount of time that couples have to communicate. While separated during a deployment, spouses have fewer opportunities to share feelings, support each other, and negotiate differences, compared with couples that are not separated by deployment. A second resource diminished by deployment is mental health. As many researchers have observed with concern (e.g., Hoge, Auchterlonie, and Milliken, 2006; Ramchand et al., 2010), rates of mental health difficulties, especially depression, anxiety, and posttraumatic stress disorder (PTSD), have been strikingly high among service members returning from deployment to Iraq and Afghanistan. Service members who return from deployment suffering from such problems make for poorer relationship partners (Ahmadi et al., 2006; Meis et al., 2010; Renshaw and Campbell, 2011) and are less equipped to handle the other challenges related to deployment and reintegration. To the extent that the communication and mental health deficits that may result from deployment are lasting, they could contribute to negative effects of deployment that persist even after the deployment has ended.

Although Family Stress Process models have most often been used as a framework to understand the negative effects of stress on marriages, the same models also suggest how couples may prove resilient or even thrive in the face of stress. According to these models, couples that do possess sufficient resources may be able to cope effectively, even with relatively severe stressors. Couples in stronger or longer relationships prior to a deployment, for example, may have well-established coping skills that carry them successfully through the deployment cycle with their relationship intact. Couples that maintain more frequent and more satisfying communication during a deployment may have an easier time reintegrating after the deployment than couples that do not communicate as well or as frequently while separated. Effective coping across a deployment cycle should contribute to a couple's confidence in the ability of the relationship to withstand future challenges, and so can maintain, rather than detract from, a couple's satisfaction with and commitment to the relationship.

Prior Research on the Effects of Deployment on Marital Satisfaction

During the most active years of the conflicts in Afghanistan and Iraq, divorce rates within the military did not change substantially (Karney and Crown, 2007) but marital satisfaction declined significantly (Riviere et al., 2012), suggesting that the high pace of deployments during that period may well have harmed the relationships of military couples. Yet the few studies that have directly examined associations between the experience of deployment and marital satisfaction have struggled to pin down an effect.

Most of the limited prior research on deployments and marital satisfaction has consisted of retrospective studies; i.e., they have compared current marital satisfaction within couples that have or have not experienced a prior deployment. For example, in a sample of 434 Army husbands and civilian wives who were enrolled in a marriage education program provided by the military, Allen and colleagues (2010) found no differences in marital satisfaction between couples that had experienced a deployment in the past year and those that had not. Surveys of larger samples, however, revealed significant differences between these groups, with couples that have experienced deployment reporting lower marital satisfaction (Keeling et al., 2015; McLeland, Sutton, and Schumm, 2008).

Drawing upon the baseline sample of the Deployment Life Study, Karney and Trail (forthcoming) conducted analyses that might explain the discrepancy in the prior studies. At baseline, couples in the Deployment Life Study who had experienced a deployment also reported significantly lower marital satisfaction than couples that had never experienced deployment (controlling for age, rank, and other differences between the two groups). Among those that had experienced a deployment, however, there were no significant differences in marital satisfaction among couples that had experienced more or fewer deployments. The one prior study that failed to find associations between deployment and marital satisfaction (Allen et al., 2010) asked only about "deployment in the past year" and so may well have been comparing two groups that both had histories of prior deployment at different times in the past. Together, the prior retrospective studies that asked about lifetime history of deployment suggest that initial deployments may harm military marriages, but that marriages surviving this initial shock may prove resilient to the stresses of future deployments.

As suggestive as these results may be, there are serious limits to the conclusions that retrospective studies of deployment can support. Although a retrospective analysis can reveal differences between couples with and without a history of deployment, it cannot distinguish between the consequences of deployment and problems that may have existed prior to deployment because such designs lack data on the characteristics of the couple prior to deployment. For the same reasons, retrospective designs offer no way of describing whether or how couples may change across the deployment cycle, and no way of assessing the possibility of recovery over time after deployments. Retrospective designs also exclude couples that have left the population (through either divorce or separation from the military) as a result of their deployment experiences, leading to underestimates of possible deployment effects. Finally, data obtained through retrospective designs may suffer from recall biases (see Loughran, 2002), such that couples that have been deployed may respond differently to questions about how their relationships have changed regardless of how those relationships may have actually changed.

Longitudinal research is a superior alternative for estimating and describing the effects of deployment on marriages, for several reasons. First, collecting multiple waves of data from the same couples over the course of a deployment cycle allows for rich descriptions of how marital relationships may change in the periods before, during, and after a deployment. Second, the availability of data from couples before deployments allows for analyses that separate the effects of predeployment characteristics of the marriage from the effects of experiences during deployment on postdeployment outcomes.

To date, very few longitudinal studies have examined how experiences during deployments affect marital satisfaction. One of these (Andres, 2014) reported data from 153 female spouses of Dutch military personnel who had been contacted before, during, and after their partner's deployment. Results indicated that marital satisfaction declined significantly from the predeployment to the postdeployment period, and that the strongest predictor of postdeployment satisfaction was predeployment satisfaction. That is, even though spouses in this sample had experienced their partner's deployment, their marital satisfaction was nonetheless relatively stable. A second longitudinal study (Cigrang et al., 2014) examined 76 partnered service members who provided data before, during, and after a deployment. These analyses also revealed significant increases in marital distress from predeployment to postdeployment.

Further analyses of this sample (Balderrama-Durbin et al., 2015) found that characteristics of the marriage prior to deployment were the strongest predictors of the quality of the relationship after the deployment.

Despite the consistent picture that emerges from these studies, the longitudinal research to date also has been limited in ways that prevent strong conclusions. First, despite the availability of data from before, during, and after the deployment, no prior studies have offered descriptive data on how military marriages change throughout, and especially during, the deployment cycle. Instead, the existing research has simply compared the predeployment and postdeployment periods. This is an improvement over retrospective designs, but it also represents a missed opportunity to address whether military marriages undergo no changes at all across a deployment cycle, or whether marriages do change during deployment but then recover after the service member returns home. Second, the existing studies have all addressed samples consisting exclusively of service members or spouses that have experienced deployments. Without a well-matched comparison group that did not experience a deployment, the existing research has been unable to determine whether observed changes are due to something about the deployment experience itself, or whether the observed changes reflect the established finding that marital satisfaction tends to decline over time (Karney and Bradbury, 1995; Karney and Bradbury, 1997). Third, the existing longitudinal research has all been conducted on small, unrepresentative samples. It remains unclear how well the results of published analyses generalize across services, ranks, and components. Finally, despite their interest in military couples, prior studies have all examined data from either service members or their spouses, but never both members of the same couple.

The Deployment Life Study

In light of the continuing concerns for the well-being of military marriages experiencing the stress of repeated deployments, policymakers and program developers hoping to support service members and their spouses require accurate data on how marriages change over the course of a deployment and whether the experience of deployment harms couples that might otherwise have thrived. Existing studies have circled these issues, but the methodological limitations of those studies have left the central questions unanswered. To fill this gap in the existing literature and strengthen the empirical foundation of family support programs in the military, the current analyses drew upon the multiwave longitudinal data available in the Deployment Life Study, a nine-wave study of service members and their spouses before, during, and after a combat deployment.

The Deployment Life Study is an ideal data set in which to address these issues, for several reasons. First, the study solicited data from couples in which the service member was deemed eligible to be deployed in the next six to 12 months. Thus, the complete longitudinal data set contains couples that experienced deployment, as well as couples from the same population that were eligible but did not actually deploy, allowing an unprecedented comparison between the two groups. Second, the study collected multiple waves of data at each phase of the deployment cycle, allowing for estimates of change not only across each phase but within each phase as well. Third, the Deployment Life Study sample is large and has been weighted to be representative of the entire population of married service members who experienced a deployment during the survey field period.

Research Questions and Hypotheses

The analyses described in this report drew upon these data to address the following research questions and hypotheses.

- **Research Question (RQ) 1**: How do service members' and spouses' perceptions of their marriages change over the course of a typical deployment cycle, i.e., predeployment, during deployment, and postdeployment?
  - **RQ1a:** Do the trajectories of marital outcomes vary significantly over the deployment cycle?
    ◦ **Hypothesis:** We expect that marital outcomes will vary across the deployment cycle. This could be due to deployment factors or to broader changes over time consistent with a general decline in marital satisfaction over time.
  - **RQ1b:** Are the trajectories of marital outcomes significantly different from a constant time trend?
    ◦ **Hypothesis:** We hypothesize that changes will not be well explained by a constant time trend (for example, by a steady decline in marital satisfaction over time) but will be tied to the specific phases of the deployment cycle.
  - **RQ1c:** Do service members and their spouses experience the same changes in their perceptions of the marriage across the deployment cycle?
    ◦ **Hypothesis:** Given their different experiences during deployment, we expected that the trajectories of service members' and spouses' views of the marriage would change in significantly different ways across the deployment cycle.
- **RQ2:** How does deployment affect postdeployment marital outcomes? By comparing outcomes between couples where a service member experienced a study deployment and matched couples where the service member did not deploy during the study, we can estimate the incremental effect of deployments, controlling for characteristics of the couple prior to deployment.
  - ◦ **Hypothesis:** Given retrospective data revealing lower marital satisfaction among couples that have experienced a deployment compared with couples that have not, we predicted that both partners in couples that experienced a deployment would have worse perceptions of their marriage than matched couples that did not experience a deployment over the same period.
- **RQ3:** To what extent do characteristics of the couple prior to deployment (age, marital duration, initial marital quality) and experiences during deployment (combat exposure, length of time away, frequency of communication) account for spouses' perceptions of their marriage postdeployment?
  - ◦ **Hypothesis:** Given the general stability of military marriages revealed by prior longitudinal studies of couples facing deployments, we predicted that predeployment characteristics would account for significant variance in postdeployment marital outcomes for this sample. Nevertheless, given prior research on the effects of combat exposure and lengthy separations, we predicted that aspects of the deployment experience itself would also account for significant variance in postdeployment marital outcomes, even after controlling for the effects of predeployment marital characteristics.

Method

Sample

The data described here were drawn from all nine assessment waves of the Deployment Life Study, a longitudinal survey of the deployable, married population of the military, their spouses, and their children, stratified by service. (See Tanielian et al., 2014, for additional details).[1] Married service members and their spouses were randomly sampled within service components. Sampled couples were invited to participate in the survey, and only those couples where both the service members and spouses completed the baseline survey were included in the study. A total of 2,724 service members and their families were sampled.

Measures

Marital Outcomes

To ensure that any effects of deployment observed here were not unique to a single aspect of spouses' evaluations of their relationships, couples in the Deployment Life Study were asked to evaluate three different aspects of their feelings about their relationships: their satisfaction with the marriage, their experienced affect after communicating with each other, and the frequency of enacted and received psychological and physical aggression. Each of these constructs was assessed through self-reports from each partner on the following instruments, administered at every wave of assessment.

Marital Satisfaction. Marital satisfaction was assessed using nine items adapted from the Florida Formation Survey (Rauer et al., 2008). Five of the items assessed participants' satisfaction with the amount of time the couple spent together, their sexual relations, the amount of support provided by the spouse, the spouse's contribution to household chores, and general satisfaction with the marriage, all rated on a 5-point scale. The other four items asked participants to assess how much they felt they could share their thoughts and dreams with their spouse, how much they trusted their spouse, how well the couple communicated during disagreements, and how well their partner understood their hopes and dreams, all rated on a 4-point scale. We summed and then calculated a mean of all items to form separate relationship satisfaction scales for service members and spouses. Previous research using this instrument has shown it to be sensitive to indicators of stress and marital functioning (e.g., Rauer et al., 2008).

Positive and Negative Affect Following Communication. We used the Positive and Negative Affect Scale (Thompson, 2007; Watson, Clark, and Tellegen, 1988) to assess the level of positive and negative affect that service members and spouses experienced after communicating with each other. Respondents were provided with a list of eight emotions (four positive and four negative) that were taken from the short form of the Positive and Negative Affect Schedule (PANAS), and asked about "how you feel when you communicate with [SPOUSE name]." Respondents then rated how often they felt each emotion "after talking with [SPOUSE name]" on a five-point scale: *never, rarely, sometimes, often, or all the time.* The four negative emotional items were summed and the mean of those items indicated negative affect following communication scale, and the four positive emotional items were summed and the mean of those items indicated positive affect following communication scale.

Intimate Partner Violence. We assessed the level of physical and psychological aggression in the relationship using the Conflict Tactics Scale 2 (Straus et al., 1996). This scale has been

---

[1]   The Navy sample only has seven total waves of data. See Chapter Two for more details on the study design and sample.

widely used to measure intimate partner violence. Three items from the *physical aggression* subscale (e.g., pushing or shoving) and three items from the *psychological aggression* subscale (e.g., insulting or swearing at) assessed physical and psychological aggression, respectively. Each item was asked twice, once for one's own behavior (e.g., "You insulted or swore at your partner"), and once for one's partner's behavior (e.g., "Your partner insulted or swore at you"). Respondents indicated how often each behavior had occurred in the past four months using a three-point scale (*never, once, or two or more times*). For psychological aggression, responses were summed to form two continuous scales—own psychological aggression and partner's psychological aggression—where higher numbers indicate more aggression. Reports of physical aggression were less prevalent, so those responses were collapsed into a dichotomous response: 1 if any physical aggression had occurred in the past four months and 0 if none had occurred. Indicators for own physical aggression and partner's physical aggression were calculated separately.

Characteristics of the Deployment

Trauma Exposure. Three dichotomous variables assessed whether the service member experienced any physical trauma (e.g., received an injury requiring hospitalization), psychological trauma (e.g., having a friend who was seriously wounded or killed), or combat trauma (e.g., engaging in hand-to-hand combat) during a study deployment (see Chapter Two of this report for more details). These measures were drawn from 11 items described by Tanielian and Jaycox (2008, p. 91) and are cumulative across the study deployment. Thus, if a service member indicated "yes" to any items in the three categories she or he received a score of 1.

Length of the Study Deployment. We assessed the length of the service member's study deployment in months.

Frequency of Communication. At each assessment occurring when the service member was deployed, we assessed communication frequency between service members and their spouses/families by asking service members to indicate, "How often do you talk or communicate with your family at home during this deployment?" Spouses were asked to report the frequency of communication with the service member in a parallel question. Responses ranged from "never" (0) to "every day" (7). Since very few respondents indicated that they "never" communicated with their spouse/family, responses were recoded into a four-category variable that included communication every day, at least once a week, at least once a month, and less than once a month (including never). If multiple assessments were obtained during one study deployment, we took the average across all assessments.

Satisfaction with Frequency of Communication. During assessments occurring when the service member was deployed, we asked service members and spouses to rate their satisfaction with the frequency of communication with each other during the study deployment. Responses ranged from 1 for "very unsatisfied" to 4 for "very satisfied." If multiple assessments were obtained during one study deployment, we took the average across all assessments.

Separation from Military Service. For all couples experiencing a deployment, we created a dummy variable to indicate subsequent separation from military service. When service members reported their current military status as "separated from the military" or "retired" at any time during Wave 2 through Wave 9, they were defined as separated.

Control Variables

Our models include a number of control variables that may be associated with marital outcomes. Table 3.1 presents means, percentages, and standard errors (SEs) for all the control variables at baseline for the overall sample of service members and spouses (i.e., the deployed and nondeployed sample combined), as well as the sample used in the analyses contained in this chapter. Means are reported separately for service members and spouses who do and do not experience a study deployment. All means are weighted and baseline data are imputed, as detailed in Chapter Two.

The control variables mainly consist of demographic characteristics of the service member and spouse—such as respondent's age, gender, and minority status—and household characteristics, such as length of marriage and whether the household includes a young child (i.e., a child younger than age six in the household).

For both service members and spouses, we also include whether the service member (or in the case of spouses, the corresponding service member) had any prior deployment (defined as any deployment of 30 days or more outside the continental United States, the number of prior combat deployments experienced by the service member (including all deployments as part of Operation Iraqi Freedom, Operation Enduring Freedom, and Operation New Dawn), the service member's branch of service (i.e., Army, Air Force, Navy, Marine Corps), the service member's reserve component (including the National Guard and Air Guard) status, and the service member's pay grade (capturing both enlisted and officer status, as well as rank). Finally, to capture each spouse's socioeconomic status, models include information on spouse educational attainment and employment status.

In addition, we include two historical measures of deployment experiences and combat trauma exposure that occurred prior to the baseline survey. The first is an 11-item checklist of possible traumatic experiences during deployment and has been used in prior work by Tanielian and Jaycox (2008).[2] It includes items such as, "During any prior deployment, did you witness an accident which resulted in serious injury in death?" Endorsed items are summed to create an index score. The second is a modified version of the Hoge et al. (2004) Combat Experiences Scale (CES), which measures combat trauma exposure. The original CES contains 18 items that assess the occurrence of different potentially traumatic events in combat (e.g., being attached or ambushed, participating in demining operations.) Three items were eliminated to minimize the sensitivity of the questions and the time it takes to complete the measure (see Tanielian and Jaycox, 2008). Endorsed items are summed to create an index score.

Results

Descriptive Information and Preliminary Analyses

Descriptive information about the demographic characteristics of the analytic sample—for the sample overall, and then broken down by whether the service member was deployed during the study period—is presented in Table 3.1. As the table reveals, service members who did or did not deploy during the study period were significantly different from each other on several demographic characteristics assessed at baseline. For example, among those couples experiencing a deployment, both service members and spouses were significantly younger, and the service member was more likely to have experienced prior combat deployments and less likely to be in the reserve component, compared with couples that did not experience deployment

---

[2] This measure is referred to as "deployment trauma" and not "combat trauma" because it does not differentiate trauma experienced while in an engagement with an enemy.

during the study period. Table 3.2 displays descriptive information for marital outcomes at baseline, again broken down by whether the service member experienced a deployment during the study period. This table also reveals significant differences in the marriages of couples that did and did not experience a deployment during the study period. At baseline, service members and spouses who would go on to experience a deployment each reported significantly higher marital satisfaction, less positive and more negative affect after communication, and lower levels of their own psychological aggression, compared with service members and spouses who did not experience a deployment. To account for these predeployment differences, we controlled for baseline descriptive measures and predeployment characteristics of the marriage in all subsequent analyses. Because service members and spouses who experience a study deployment differ in numerous ways from those who do not, we also employ propensity score methods to match service members (and their families) who deploy with those who do not in the results, which examine the impact of deployment on postdeployment outcomes.

To evaluate the shared variance among the self-reported marital characteristics assessed in the Deployment Life Study, Table 3.3 presents the correlation between all of the marital outcomes for each member of the couple, with the correlation between service member and spouse measures on the diagonal, within-spouse correlations below the diagonal, and within-service member correlations above the diagonal. All correlations were statistically significant and in the expected direction.

Research Question 1: Trajectories of Marital Outcomes Across the Deployment Cycle

The first goal of these analyses was to describe how service members' and spouses' evaluations of their marriages change across each phase of a deployment cycle. Toward this end, we graphed the trajectories of each marital outcome across the deployment cycle for service members and spouses. Trajectories were plotted for service members and spouses separately, although they were estimated from joint random effects models fit to both the service member and spouse data with random effects for both the household and the respondent type. All models control for respondent gender, age, racial/ethnic minority status, length of marriage, spouse education, spouse employment status, having children younger than age six in the household, rank and officer/enlisted status, number of prior combat deployments, years of service, branch and component of service, and the Hoge CES at baseline. Survey mode (phone or web) is included as a time-varying covariate at each wave. Predicted values for each outcome are plotted for an eight-month period immediately prior to a deployment, eight months during a deployment, and eight months postdeployment. (As noted in Chapter Two, these are the average periods that our sample of deployed families spent in each phase of deployment.) Outcomes for service members and spouses were centered on the group mean for each group and graphed between one standard deviation above and below the mean on the y-axis, so lines hovering near the mean are evidence of changes that are very small in size.

Figure 3.1 presents trajectories for marital satisfaction. In this figure, and all subsequent figures, the blue lines represent the trajectories for service members and the green lines represent the trajectories for spouses. To evaluate the trajectories in this figure, we first tested whether there was significant variation in the mean level of service members' and spouses' marital satisfaction scores across the deployment cycle (Research Question 1A). Joint Wald tests of all trajectory parameters revealed significant variation in marital satisfaction for both service members ($\chi 2(8)=17.89$, $p=0.02$) and spouses ($\chi 2(8)=84.61$, $p<0.001$).

Table 3.1
Means and Standard Errors of Descriptive Information for Service Members and Spouses at Baseline

Variable (Range)	Overall Sample		Service Members			Spouses		
	Service Members (n=2,146)	Spouses (n=2,321)	Study Deployment (n=902)	No Study Deployment (n=1,244)	p-value	Study Deployment (n=958)	No Study Deployment (n=1,363)	p-value
Age (20–56)	34.54 (0.41)	33.87 (0.45)	32.72 (0.39)	35.05 (0.52)	<0.01	32.2 (0.43)	34.34 (0.56)	<0.01
Length of Marriage, in Months (0–432)	106.88 (4.43)	105.93 (4.41)	96.84 (4.17)	109.71 (5.57)	0.06	94.81 (4.18)	109.06 (5.49)	0.04
Number of Prior Combat Deployments (0–5)	1.52 (0.08)	1.47 (0.07)	2.02 (0.09)	1.38 (0.09)	<0.01	1.99 (0.07)	1.33 (0.09)	<0.01
Prior Combat Trauma Exposure (0–10)	1.86 (0.16)	1.95 (0.13)	2.25 (0.18)	1.72 (0.2)	0.05	2.36 (0.20)	1.79 (0.16)	0.02
CES (0–15)	3.97 (0.2)	3.86 (0.20)	4.61(0.33)	3.79 (0.24)	0.04	4.66 (0.29)	3.63 (0.23)	0.01
Percent Male	87.57 (2.21)	12.46 (2.34)	92.23 (1.39)	86.26 (2.8)	0.03	7.77 (1.44)	13.78 (2.95)	0.04
Percent Nonwhite	32.48 (2.68)	29.42 (2.48)	32.03 (2.57)	32.61 (3.36)	0.89	28.61 (2.50)	29.65 (3.10)	0.79
Percent with Children Younger Than Age 6	46.15 (2.98)	43.98 (2.70)	51.12 (2.99)	44.75 (3.74)	0.19	47.69 (2.77)	42.93 (3.35)	0.27
Percent with Parent in the Military	52.06 (2.91)	48.97 (2.82)	52.81 (2.95)	51.85 (3.64)	0.84	40.27 (2.75)	51.42 (3.45)	0.01
Percent with Any Prior Deployment	74.09 (3.42)	74.08 (3.41)	91.47 (1.28)	69.2 (4.17)	<0.01	91.47 (1.29)	69.17 (4.13)	<0.01
Percent Reserve Component	34.1 (2.85)	34.53 (3.08)	15.96 (2.20)	39.21 (3.57)	<0.01	16.48 (2.21)	39.62 (3.73)	<0.01
Branch Of Service (%)								
Army	48.91 (2.92)	48.91 (2.77)	45.71 (2.88)	49.81 (3.67)	0.74	45.71 (2.65)	49.81 (3.49)	0.67
Air Force	17.04 (1.28)	17.05 (1.27)	19.98 (1.83)	16.22 (1.52)		19.99 (1.8)	16.22 (1.51)	
Navy	25.26 (3.49)	25.26 (3.45)	24.39 (2.61)	25.51 (4.4)		24.39 (2.58)	25.51 (4.35)	
Marine Corps	8.78 (1.63)	8.78 (1.39)	9.92 (3.66)	8.46 (1.81)		9.92 (3.01)	8.46 (1.56)	
Pay Grade (%)								
E1 to E3	4.07 (0.90)	4.52 (0.89)	4.51 (1.24)	3.95 (1.10)	0.18	4.51 (1.34)	4.52 (1.08)	0.55
E4 to E9	72.53 (2.30)	72.83 (2.17)	68.85 (2.74)	73.57 (2.82)		71.09 (2.28)	73.32 (2.70)	
O1 to O3	8.94 (1.36)	8.8 (1.25)	10.6 (1.30)	8.47 (1.70)		10.58 (1.27)	8.3 (1.56)	
O4 +	11.2(1.59)	11.31 (1.57)	10.18 (1.43)	11.49 (1.99)		10.18 (1.41)	11.63 (1.97)	
Warrant Officer	3.25 (0.71)	2.53 (0.43)	5.86 (2.16)	2.52 (0.66)		3.63 (0.79)	2.23 (0.50)	

Table 3.1—Continued

	Overall Sample		Service Members			Spouses		
Variable (Range)	Service Members (n=2,146)	Spouses (n=2,321)	Study Deployment (n=902)	No Study Deployment (n=1,244)	p-value	Study Deployment (n=958)	No Study Deployment (n=1,363)	p-value
Spouse Education								
Less than High School	1.21 (0.44)	1.27 (0.30)	0.66 (0.25)	1.37 (0.56)	0.82	0.74 (0.26)	1.42 (0.38)	0.93
High School	18.82 (2.69)	17.96 (2.26)	18.84 (2.04)	18.82 (3.40)		18.28 (1.87)	17.87 (2.85)	
Some College	28.57 (2.98)	26.20 (2.16)	30.04 (3.34)	28.16 (3.70)		27.69 (2.52)	25.78 (2.66)	
Associate/Vocational/Technical Degree	16.76 (1.92)	17.98 (2.00)	16.74 (2.09)	16.76 (2.39)		18.01 (2.56)	17.97 (2.46)	
Bachelor's Degree	28.24 (2.35)	26.64 (2.14)	25.80 (2.23)	28.93 (2.95)		27.07 (2.28)	26.52 (2.66)	
Graduate Degree	6.40 (0.70)	9.96 (2.85)	7.93 (1.27)	5.96 (0.80)		8.22 (1.51)	10.45 (3.62)	
Spouse Employment								
Military Spouse	6.79 (1.99)	7.22 (2.14)	**5.65 (1.19)**	**7.11 (2.53)**	0.01	**4.64 (0.97)**	**7.95 (2.72)**	0.02
Employed	41.61 (2.97)	41.44 (2.87)	**31.81 (2.60)**	44.38 (3.70)		33.46 (2.55)	43.70 (3.57)	
Homemaker	32.24 (2.67)	31.36 (2.30)	**40.64 (3.17)**	29.88 (3.27)		39.10 (2.69)	29.18 (2.80)	
Student	8.18 (1.35)	7.76 (1.22)	**7.39 (1.16)**	8.41 (1.70)		7.69 (1.16)	7.78 (1.53)	
Unemployed	11.17 (1.26)	12.21 (1.35)	14.51 (1.77)	10.23 (1.52)		15.1 (2.38)	11.40 (1.57)	

NOTES: SEs are in parentheses. Results are weighted. Missing data are imputed. P-values are for results of a weighted t-test of differences between the study deployment and no study deployment groups. Bold indicates difference between study deployment and no study deployment groups is statistically significant at the $p<0.05$ level.

Table 3.2
Means and Standard Errors of Marital Outcomes at Baseline

Variable (Range)	Overall Sample		Service Members			Spouses		
	Service Members (n=2,146)	Spouses (n=2,321)	Study Deployment (n=902)	No Study Deployment (n=1,244)	p-value	Study Deployment (n=958)	No Study Deployment (n=1,363)	p-value
Marital Satisfaction (1.63–4.63)	3.92 (0.03)	3.76 (0.05)	4.01 (0.03)	3.90 (0.04)	0.01	3.95 (0.03)	3.70 (0.06)	<0.01
Positive Affect Following Communication (1–5)	2.04 (0.04)	2.22 (0.05)	1.92 (0.03)	2.07 (0.05)	<0.01	2.07 (0.03)	2.27 (0.07)	0.01
Negative Affect Following Communication (1–5)	4.13 (0.04)	4.01 (0.07)	4.24 (0.04)	4.10 (0.05)	0.03	4.19 (0.03)	3.95 (0.09)	0.01
Partner Psychological Aggression (0–6)	0.74 (0.06)	0.77 (0.04)	0.62 (0.04)	0.77 (0.07)	0.08	0.71 (0.04)	0.78 (0.06)	0.36
Own Psychological Aggression (0–6)	0.84 (0.06)	0.81 (0.06)	0.67 (0.05)	0.89 (0.07)	0.01	0.60 (0.04)	0.87 (0.08)	<0.01
Partner Physical Aggression (%)	1.80 (0.44)	5.93 (1.16)	1.39 (0.48)	1.91 (0.55)	0.48	5.63 (1.65)	6.02 (1.41)	0.86
Own Physical Aggression (%)	5.17 (0.89)	4.09 (1.27)	4.52 (0.89)	5.36 (1.11)	0.56	1.80 (0.66)	4.74 (1.61)	0.09

NOTES: SEs are in parentheses. Results are weighted. Missing data are imputed. P-values are for results of a weighted t-test of differences between the study deployment and no study deployment groups. Bold indicates difference between study deployment and no study deployment groups is statistically significant at the p<0.05 level.

Table 3.3
Correlation Between Marital Outcomes at Baseline

	Outcomes						
	Marital Satisfaction	Positive Affect Following Communication	Negative Affect Following Communication	Partner Psychological Aggression	Own Psychological Aggression	Partner Physical Aggression	Own Physical Aggression
Marital Satisfaction	0.47	0.71	−0.64	−0.22	−0.33	−0.08	−0.15
Positive Affect Following Communication	0.71	0.40	−0.64	−0.15	−0.28	−0.05	−0.15
Negative Affect Following Communication	−0.70	−0.64	0.38	0.29	0.35	0.06	0.11
Partner Psychological Aggression	−0.32	−0.25	0.30	0.37	0.74	0.35	0.21
Own Psychological Aggression	−0.47	−0.47	0.44	0.63	0.47	0.21	0.30
Partner Physical Aggression	−0.19	−0.07	0.15	0.23	0.23	0.31	0.49
Own Physical Aggression	−0.15	−0.11	0.13	0.22	0.41	0.42	0.25

NOTES: SEs are in parentheses. Results are weighted. Missing data are imputed. P-values are for results of a weighted t-test of differences between the study deployment and no study deployment groups. Bold indicates difference between study deployment and no study deployment groups is statistically significant at the p<0.05 level.

Figure 3.1
Trajectory Model for Marital Satisfaction for Service Members and Spouses

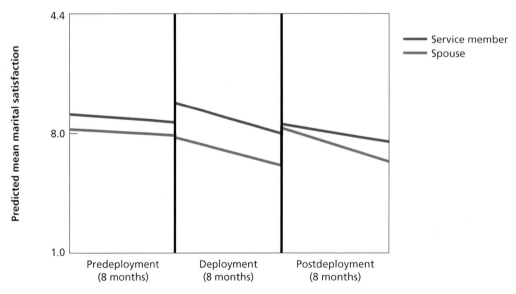

NOTES: Service member and spouse trajectories show significant variation over the deployment cycle (service member: $p=0.02$; spouse: $p<0.001$). The spouse trajectory is significantly different from a constant trend over time ($p<0.001$), but the service member trajectory is not ($p=0.73$). The service member trajectory is significantly different from the spouse trajectory ($p=0.001$).
RAND RR1388-3.1

We next examined whether the overall trends in marital satisfaction for service members and spouses were significantly different from a constant trend over time (Research Question 1B). This test analyzed whether any variation that occurred over time could be attributed to a constant time trend that is unrelated to the specific timing of the study deployment (i.e., predeployment, during deployment, and postdeployment). Analysis revealed that, for service members, the trajectory of marital satisfaction across the deployment cycle did not differ significantly from a straight line ($X2(8)=5.21$, $p=0.73$). Correspondingly, Figure 3.1 shows a constant decline in marital satisfaction for service members, but no significant evidence that this change is related to the deployment cycle. In contrast, we had significant evidence that spouses' marital satisfaction was not well described as a constant time trend, but was related to the timing on the study deployment ($X2(8)=48.67$, $p<0.001$). Figure 3.1 suggests that spouses' satisfaction declined during deployment, jumped immediately postdeployment, then declined to baseline levels over the postdeployment period. A post-hoc test comparing mean spouse marital satisfaction during deployment to the pre- and postdeployment phases was not significant ($X2(1)=2.80$, $p=0.09$), indicating that, although the trend for spouses' marital satisfaction changed across phases of the deployment cycle, levels of spouses' marital satisfaction were not significantly different during the deployment than when not deployed.

We also analyzed whether the overall trajectories of service members and their spouses over the course of the deployment cycle significantly differed from one another (Research Question 1C). Analysis of differences between service members and spouses revealed that their slopes and trajectories differed significantly across the deployment cycle ($X2(8)=25.51$, $p=0.001$). Thus, although both spouse and service member marital satisfaction declined over time, spouses showed a significantly different pattern that, as described above, varied across the deployment cycle.

Figure 3.2 presents trajectories for reports of feeling positive affect following communication with the partner across the deployment cycle. There was significant variation in this outcome across the deployment cycle for service members ($X2(8)=58.41$, $p<0.001$) and for spouses ($X2(8)=64.83$, $p<0.001$). Both of these trajectories were significantly different than a constant time-trend ($X2(8)=21.20$, $p=0.007$, for service members; $X2(8)=31.41$, $p<0.001$, for spouses). Post-hoc tests revealed that mean positive affect following communication was significantly higher during the deployment than when not deployed for service members ($X2(1)=26.95$, $p<0.001$) and spouses ($X2(1)=35.75$, $p<0.001$). The slopes and trajectories of service members and spouses did not differ from each other significantly across the deployment cycle ($X2(8)=9.10$, $p=0.33$).

Figure 3.3 presents trajectories for reports of feeling negative affect following communication with the partner. Analysis of these trajectories revealed little variation across the deployment cycle. While the trajectory for service members showed significant variation over time ($X2(8)=15.88$, $p=0.04$), this variation was not significantly different than a constant trend over time ($X2(8)=12.74$, $p=0.12$) and thus not associated with the deployment cycle. Neither of these tests was significant for spouses ($X2(8)=11.18$, $p=0.19$, and $X2(8)=8.40$, $p=0.40$, respectively). Moreover, the trajectories of service members and spouses only differed from each other marginally across the deployment cycle ($X2(8)=15.65$, $p=0.05$). Overall, there is only limited evidence of significant changes in negative affect during the deployment cycle for service members and spouses.

Figure 3.4 presents trajectories for ratings of partners' psychological aggression across the deployment cycle; i.e., service members' and spouses' ratings of each other's psychologi-

Figure 3.2
Trajectory Model for Positive Affect Following Communication for Service Members and Spouses

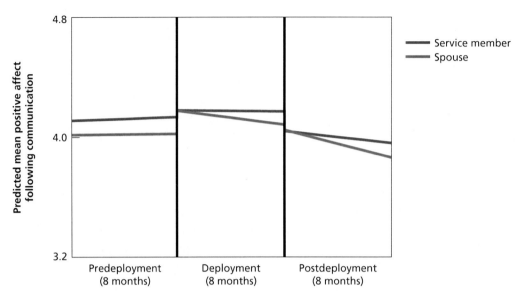

NOTES: Service member ($p<0.001$) and spouse ($p<0.001$) trajectories show significant variation over the deployment cycle. Both service member ($p=0.007$) and spouse ($p<0.001$) trajectories are significantly different from a constant trend over time. The service member trajectory was not significantly different from the spouse trajectory ($p=0.33$).
RAND *RR1388-3.2*

Figure 3.3
Trajectory Model for Negative Affect Following Communication for Service Members and Spouses

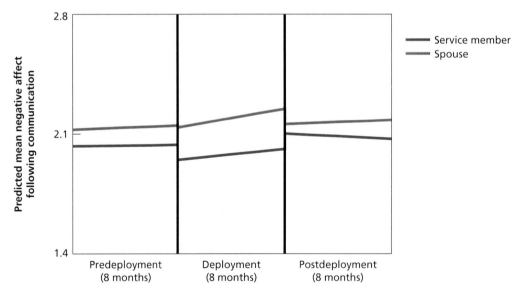

NOTES: The service member trajectory ($p=0.04$) shows significant variation over the deployment cycle; the spouse trajectory does not ($p=0.19$). Neither the service member nor spouse trajectories were significantly different from constant trend over time (service member: $p=0.12$; spouse: $p=0.40$). The service member trajectory is significantly different from the spouse trajectory ($p=0.05$).
RAND *RR1388-3.3*

Figure 3.4
Trajectory Model for Partner's Psychological Aggression for Service Members and Spouses

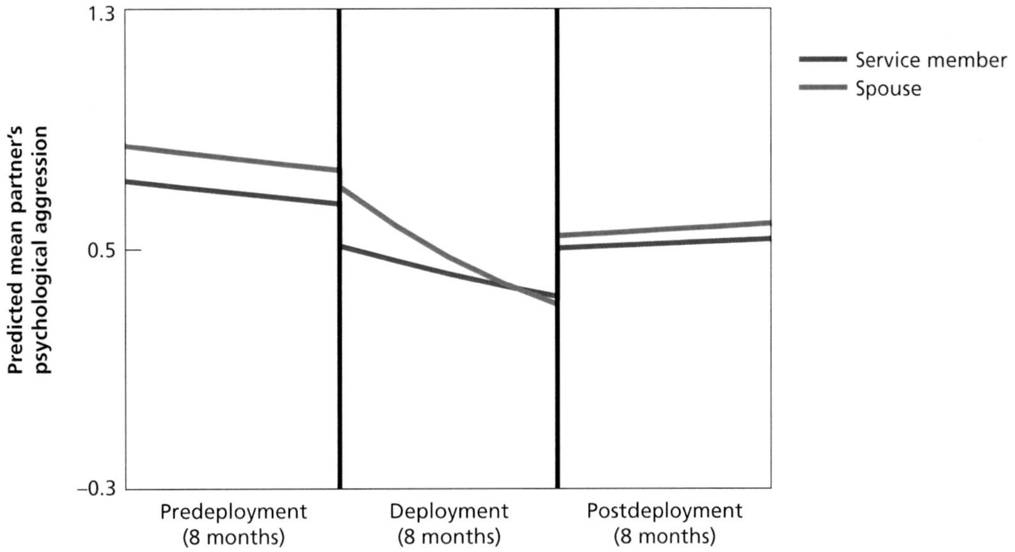

NOTES: Service member (*p*<0.001) and spouse (*p*<0.001) trajectories show significant variation over the deployment cycle. Both service member (*p*<0.001) and spouse (*p*<0.001) trajectories are significantly different from a constant trend over time. The service member trajectory is not significantly different from the spouse trajectory (*p*=0.61).
RAND RR1388-3.4

cal aggression at each assessment. Analyses revealed that reports of psychological aggression varied throughout the deployment cycle for service members and spouses. Specifically, there was significant variation in trajectories for service members ($\chi 2(8)=52.42$, $p<0.001$) and spouses ($\chi 2(8)=72.19$, $p<0.001$), and this variation across the trajectory was significantly different than a constant time trend for both ($\chi 2(8)=46.16$, $p<0.001$, for service members; ($\chi 2(8)=57.79$, $p<0.001$, for spouses). Post-hoc tests revealed that mean partner psychological aggression was significantly lower during the deployment phase than when not deployed for service members ($\chi 2(1)=22.85$, $p<0.001$), and for spouses ($\chi 2(1)=20.33$, $p<0.001$). These patterns did not differ significantly between service members and spouses across the deployment cycle ($\chi 2(8)=6.31$, $p=0.61$).

Figure 3.5 presents trajectories for ratings of one's own psychological aggression toward a partner across the deployment cycle. The mean trajectories showed significant variation over the deployment cycle ($\chi 2(8)=49.19$, $p<0.001$, for service members and $\chi 2(8)=46.10$, $p<0.001$, for spouses) and were significantly different from a constant trend over time ($\chi 2(8)=47.73$, $p<0.001$, for service members and $\chi 2(8)=43.68$, $p<0.001$, for spouses). Post-hoc tests revealed significantly lower psychological aggression during the deployment period than during the pre-and postdeployment period for service members ($\chi 2(1)=31.44$, $p<0.001$) and spouses ($\chi 2(1)=16.60$, $p<0.001$). These patterns did not differ significantly for service members and spouses ($\chi 2(8)=4.32$, $p=0.83$).

Figure 3.6 presents trajectories for ratings of partner physical aggression across the deployment cycle; i.e., service members' and spouses' ratings of each other's physical aggression at each assessment. Because partner physical aggression, as opposed to psychological aggression, was very rarely reported in this sample, we treated these reports as a binary outcome, col-

Figure 3.5
Trajectory Model for One's Own Psychological Aggression Toward One's Spouse for Service Members and Spouses

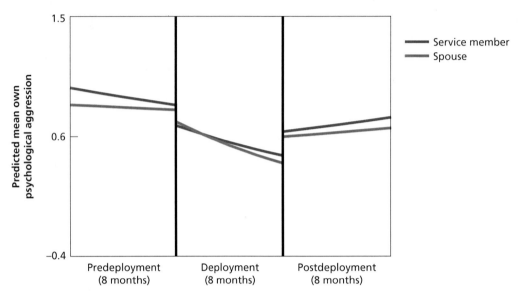

NOTES: Service member ($p<0.001$) and spouse ($p<0.001$) trajectories show significant variation over the deployment cycle. Both service member ($p<0.001$) and spouse ($p<0.001$) trajectories are significantly different from a constant trend over time. The service member trajectory is not significantly different from the spouse trajectory ($p=0.83$).

RAND *RR1388-3.5*

Figure 3.6
Trajectory Model for Partner's Physical Aggression (Yes/No) for Service Members and Spouses

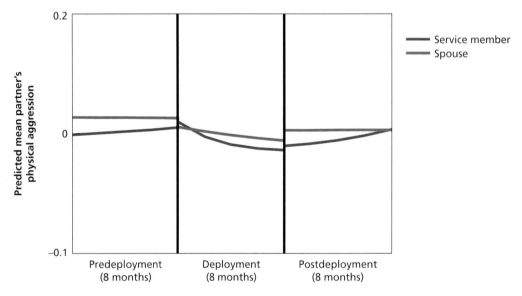

NOTES: The service member trajectory ($p=0.003$) shows significant variation over the deployment cycle; the spouse trajectory ($p=0.25$) does not. The service member trajectory ($p=0.004$) differs significantly from a constant trend over time; the spouse trajectory does not ($p=0.32$). The service member trajectory is significantly different from the spouse trajectory ($p=0.03$).

RAND *RR1388-3.6*

lapsing responses into "any" partner physical aggression and "no" partner physical aggression reported during each assessment period. These reports showed evidence of significant variation across the deployment cycle for service members ($\chi 2(8)=23.65$, $p=0.003$) but not spouses ($\chi 2(8)=10.27$, $p=0.25$). The trajectory for service members was also significantly different from a constant trend over time ($\chi 2(8)=22.38$, $p=0.004$). Similar tests revealed no significant changes for spouses ($\chi 2(8)=9.23$, $p=0.32$). Although service members showed significant variation across the deployment cycle, a test for whether rates of partner aggression was higher or lower during the deployment than when not deployed was not significant ($\chi 2(1)=1.97$, $p=0.16$). The direct test of the difference in the trajectories of service members and spouses was significant ($\chi 2(8)=17.37$, $p=0.03$).

Figure 3.7 presents trajectories for ratings of own physical aggression across the deployment cycle, i.e., service members' and spouses' ratings of their own physical aggression at each assessment. As with partner physical aggression, one's own physical aggression was very rarely reported in this sample. We treated these reports as a binary outcome, collapsing responses into "any" physical aggression and "no" physical aggression reported during each assessment period. As the figure reveals, these reports varied significantly across deployment cycles for service members ($\chi 2(8)=27.26$, $p<0.001$) and for spouses ($\chi 2(8)=22.52$, $p=0.004$). Moreover, the change in mean levels of physical aggression was significantly different than a constant trend over time for service members ($\chi 2(8)=26.71$, $p<0.001$) and for spouses ($\chi 2(8)=21.40$, $p=0.006$). A post-hoc test revealed that, for service members, self-reports of own physical aggression were significantly lower during deployment than in the pre- and post-deployment phases ($\chi 2(1)=6.12$, $p=0.01$). This post-hoc test was not significant for spouses

Figure 3.7
Trajectory Model for Own Physical Aggression (Yes/No) for Service Members and Spouses

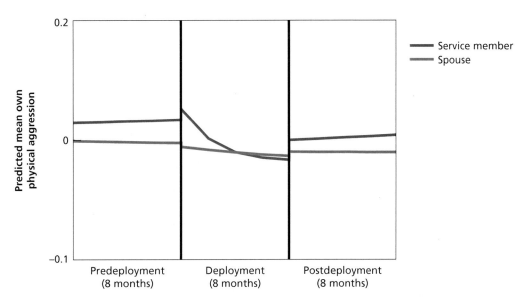

NOTES: Service member ($p<0.001$) and spouse ($p=0.004$) trajectories show significant variation over the deployment cycle. Service member ($p<0.001$) and spouse ($p = 0.006$) trajectories differ significantly from a constant trend over time. The service member trajectory is not significantly different from the spouse trajectory ($p=0.42$).
RAND RR1388-3.7

(χ 2(1)=0.44, p=0.51). The direct test of the difference in the trajectories of service members and spouses was also not significant (χ 2(8)=8.12, p=0.42).

Research Question 2: Impact of Deployment

The fact that some marital outcomes changed significantly across phases of the deployment cycle does not necessarily indicate that deployment causes lasting changes in couples' perceptions of their marriage. To evaluate the causal impact of the deployment on marital outcomes postdeployment, we used a doubly robust matched comparison approach to compare the postdeployment outcomes of service members and spouses who experienced a study deployment to matched couples that were not deployed during the study period (for details on these analyses, see Chapter Two; for details on the propensity score weighting for this analysis, see Appendix 3A). Results of this analysis that included respondent level random effects are presented in Table 3.4. As the table reveals, despite the fact that several of these variables changed significantly over the course of the deployment cycle, service members and spouses who experienced a study deployment did not significantly differ from those who did not experience a study deployment on any of the measures by the last phases of the study, once between-group differences in baseline characteristics were taken into account.

All models control for respondent gender, age, racial/ethnic minority status, having children younger than age six in the household, rank and officer/enlisted status, number of prior combat deployments, years of service, branch and component of service, the Hoge CES, prior combat trauma, survey mode at baseline (phone or web), and the outcome in question at baseline. Models for spouse outcomes additionally controlled for spouse education and employment status.

Research Question 3: Accounting for Postdeployment Marital Outcomes

Although marital outcomes among the deployed couples did not differ from marital outcomes among the nondeployed couples by the end of the study period, there was still considerable variance in the outcomes of the deployed couples. In our last set of analyses, we examined how characteristics of the deployment accounted for those outcomes, controlling for differences among the deployed couples at baseline.

Table 3.4
Predicted Mean Marital Outcomes for Service Members and Spouses With and Without a Study Deployment

	Service Members		Spouses	
	Study Deployment (n=902)	No Study Deployment (n=1,244)	Study Deployment (n=958)	No Study Deployment (n=1,363)
Marital Satisfaction	3.75 (0.03)	3.69 (0.03)	3.62 (0.03)	3.64 (0.02)
Positive Affect Following Communication	3.95 (0.03)	3.88 (0.04)	3.83 (0.03)	3.85 (0.03)
Negative Affect Following Communication	2.08 (0.03)	2.12 (0.03)	2.21 (0.03)	2.18 (0.03)
Partner Psychological Aggression	0.59 (0.04)	0.67 (0.04)	0.58 (0.04)	0.63 (0.04)
Own Psychological Aggression	0.81 (0.06)	0.86 (0.07)	0.57 (0.04)	0.59 (0.03)
Partner Physical Aggression	0.03 (0.01)	0.03 (0.01)	0.04 (0.01)	0.03 (0.00)
Own Physical Aggression	0.05 (0.01)	0.08 (0.01)	0.02 (0.01)	0.03 (0.01)

Descriptive statistics for the deployment experience variables we focused on in these analyses are shown in Table 3.5. As the table demonstrates, service members' and spouses' average descriptions of deployment characteristics were very similar on all of the characteristics measured. On average, both partners reported communicating with each other between once a month and once a week during the deployment, and reported being between "satisfied" and "very satisfied" with that level of contact. The average deployment in this study was eight months long. Finally, 7 percent of couples experiencing a deployment subsequently separated or retired from the military.

Considering these characteristics of the deployment experience, the final set of analyses examined associations between deployment characteristics and postdeployment marital outcomes using random effects regression models, adjusted for repeated measures within each respondent (i.e., allowing for a random effect for each respondent) and controlling for respondent gender, age, racial/ethnic minority status, length of marriage, having children younger than age six in the household, rank and officer/enlisted status, number of prior combat deployments experienced by the service member, years of service, branch and component of service, combat exposure at baseline assessed with the Hoge CES, a missing indicator for the deployment experience variable, and the baseline measure of the marital outcome being modeled. Models for spouse outcomes additionally controlled for spouse education and employment status.

Controlling for those baseline characteristics of couples, we examined whether specific characteristics of the study deployment accounted for additional variance in couples' evaluations of their marriages postdeployment. Results for service members are shown in Table 3.6 and results for spouses are shown in Table 3.7. Before reviewing the results of this analysis, it is worth noting the number of statistical tests that were conducted: 35 for service members and 35 for spouses. For any given outcome, the more statistical tests that are performed, the more likely it is that at least some of the tests will be statistically significant by chance. Thus, in discussing the results, we focus on patterns of statistical significance that emerge across mul-

Table 3.5
Means, Percentages, and Standard Errors of Readiness and Resilience Factors
(Study Deployment Sample Only)

	Service Members (n=902)	Spouses (n=958)
Frequency of Communication During Study Deployment[a]	2.44 (0.04)	2.38 (0.04)
Satisfaction with Frequency of Communication During Study Deployment[b]	3.45 (0.05)	3.29 (0.06)
Trauma Exposure During Study Deployment		
Physical (%)	21.15 (2.26)	20.88 (2.60)
Psychological (%)	33.43 (2.50)	36.88 (3.17)
Combat (%)	6.57 (1.17)	6.54 (1.25)
Length of Study Deployment[c]	8.01 (0.15)	8.04 (0.14)
Rate of separation from the military	0.07 (0.01)	0.07 (0.01)

NOTE: SEs are in parentheses.
[a] Range: 0 (less than once a month) to 4 (every day).
[b] Range: 1 to 4.
[c] In months.

Table 3.6
Regression Coefficients (and p-values) for Service Member Reports of Experiences During Deployment (n=902)

		Outcomes					
	Marital Satisfaction	Positive Affect Following Communication	Negative Affect Following Communication	Partner Psychological Aggression	Own Psychological Aggression	Partner Physical Aggression	Own Physical Aggression
Frequency of Communication During Study Deployment[a]	0.08 (p=0.12)	0.11 (p=0.08)	−0.06 (p=0.41)	0.07 (p=0.63)	0.19 (p=0.18)	−0.01 (p=0.99)	0.01 (p=0.37)
Satisfaction with Frequency of Communication During Study Deployment[b]	0.05 (p=0.16)	0.05 (p=0.53)	−0.02 (p=0.71)	−0.05 (p=0.65)	−0.07 (p=0.47)	**−0.60* (p=0.04)**	0.00 (p=1.00)
Trauma Exposure During Study Deployment (%)							
Physical	0.00	−0.07	0.06	−0.13	−0.37	**−0.99**	−0.03
Psychological	0.00	−0.05	0.05	−0.03	0.30	**−0.83**	0.01
Combat	0.01	−0.02	0.04	−0.18	−0.22	**−1.31**	0.00
Joint p-value	p=0.95	p=0.56	p=0.60	p=0.60	p=0.12	**p=0.03***	p=0.34
Length of Study Deployment[c]	0.00 (p=0.84)	0.00 (p=0.84)	−0.01 (p=0.54)	0.00 (p=0.94)	0.00 (p=1.00)	0.02 (p=0.86)	0.00 (p=0.34)
Separation from Military	−0.10 (p=0.28)	**−0.20* (p=0.03)**	0.21 (p=0.10)	1.03 (p=0.22)	0.04 (p=0.31)	0.11 (p=0.73)	−0.02 (p=0.95)

NOTES: Significant coefficients are shown in bold. Models controlled for respondent gender, age, racial/ethnic minority status, length of marriage, having children younger than age six in the household, rank and officer/enlisted status, number of prior combat deployments, years of service, branch and component of service, baseline combat exposure from the Hoge CES, a missing indicator for the deployment experience variable, and the baseline measure of the key outcome being modeled. For deployment trauma, a joint F-test p-value is presented; for individual coefficients, significance is shown only when the joint test has a p-value<0.05.

* $p<0.05$

[a] Range: 0 (less than once a month) to 4 (every day).

[b] Range: 1 to 4.

[c] In months.

tiple predictors and outcomes, and do not devote much space to reviewing isolated statistically significant results.

As Table 3.6 reveals, only three of the 35 associations tested for service members reached statistical significance, and these three were isolated associations, did not form a pattern, and were only significant at the $p<0.05$ level. Thus, for service members, the deployment characteristics assessed here generally did not account for significant variance in postdeployment outcomes once baseline characteristics of the couple, prior deployment history, and predeployment levels of those outcomes were controlled.

Table 3.7, in contrast, tells a different story. For spouses, ten of the 35 tests reached statistical significance; these were generally larger effects, and several meaningful patterns emerged. First, spouses' ratings of the frequency of their communication with the service member during the deployment and their ratings of satisfaction with that frequency each independently accounted for postdeployment marital satisfaction and positive affect after communication with the service member, even after baseline characteristics of the couple, prior deployment history, and baseline levels of these outcomes were taken into account. The more that couples were able to communicate while deployed and the more satisfied spouses were with the frequency of their communication while deployed, the more satisfied spouses were after the deployment, and the more positively they felt after communicating with the returned service member.

Table 3.7 also reveals a robust association between the service member's experience of trauma during the deployment and the spouse's perceptions of psychological and physical aggression after the deployment. As noted in Chapter Two, the test of this association first examined the joint effect of physical, psychological, and combat trauma experienced by service members during deployment. Where the joint effect of trauma was significant, we then examined the specific effects of type of trauma. For spouses, the physical, psychological, and combat trauma experienced by service members during deployment were jointly associated with spouses' postdeployment reports of partner psychological aggression, own psychological aggression, and partner physical aggression. Delving into the specific effects of the different types of trauma revealed that each had different types of associations with postdeployment marital outcomes. The service member's experience of psychological trauma during the deployment (e.g., having a friend who was seriously wounded or killed) was significantly associated with higher levels of own and partner psychological aggression and higher levels of partner physical aggression, as reported by the spouse. The service member's experience of physical trauma (e.g., being injured) was similarly associated with the spouse reporting higher levels of physical aggression from the service member in the postdeployment period. In contrast, the service member's experience of combat exposure (e.g., engaging in hand-to-hand combat with the enemy) was significantly associated with *lower* levels of partner and own psychological aggression, as reported by the spouse. Additionally, there was some marginal evidence that the service member's experience of any type of trauma (physical, psychological, or combat) during the deployment was significantly associated with *lower* levels of their own psychological aggression postdeployment.

Third, separation from the military after a deployment was associated with spouses' lower marital satisfaction, and their less positive affect and more negative affect after communicating with the service member during the postdeployment period, even after controlling for baseline characteristics of the couple, prior deployment history, and predeployment levels of these outcomes.

Table 3.7
Regression Coefficients (and p-values) for Spouse Reports of Experiences During Deployment (n=958)

				Outcomes			
	Marital Satisfaction	Positive Affect Following Communication	Negative Affect Following Communication	Partner Psychological Aggression	Own Psychological Aggression	Partner Physical Aggression	Own Physical Aggression
Frequency of Communication During Study Deployment[a]	**0.16* (p=0.03)**	**0.21** (p<0.01)**	−0.07 (p=0.26)	−0.04 (p=0.75)	−0.09 (p=0.60)	0.54 (p=0.20)	0.03 (p=0.09)
Satisfaction with Frequency of Communication During Study Deployment[b]	**0.10* (p=0.03)**	**0.14** (p<0.01)**	−0.07 (p=0.06)	−0.05 (p=0.58)	−0.04 (p=0.76)	−0.36 (p=0.14)	0.01 (p=0.20)
Trauma Exposure During Study Deployment (%)							
Physical	−0.08	−0.04	0.03	−0.13	0.27	**1.15***	0.04
Psychological	−0.10	−0.19	0.13	**0.46****	**0.56*****	**0.85***	0.00
Combat	0.06	0.20	−0.16	**−1.02****	**−0.91*****	−1.04	−0.02
Joint p-value	(p=0.34)	(p<0.13)	(p=0.18)	**(p<0.01)**	**(p<0.01)**	**(p<0.01)**	(p=0.45)
Length of Study Deployment[c]	0.01 (p=0.61)	−0.01 (p=0.39)	0.00 (p=0.66)	0.03 (p=0.23)	0.04 (p=0.21)	−0.05 (p=0.54)	0.00 (p=0.34)
Separation from the Military	**−0.35* (p=0.01)**	**−0.37** (p=0.00)**	**0.26* (p=0.02)**	0.33 (p=0.68)	0.00 (p=0.88)	−0.10 (p=0.61)	0.21 (p=0.42)

NOTES: Significant coefficients are shown in bold. Models controlled for respondent gender, age, racial/ethnic minority status, length of marriage, spouse education, spouse employment status, having children younger than age six in the household, rank and officer/enlisted status, number of prior combat deployments, years of service, branch and component of service, baseline combat exposure from the Hoge CES, a missing indicator for the deployment experience variable, and the baseline measure of the key outcome being modeled. For deployment trauma, a joint F-test p-value is presented; for individual coefficients, significance is shown only when the joint test has a p-value<0.05. * p<0.05; ** p<0.01; *** p<0.001.

[a] Range: 0 (less than once a month) to 4 (every day).

[b] Range: 1 to 4.

[c] In months.

Discussion

Rationale

Although deployments have been a fact of military life for as long as there have been wars on foreign soil, the recent conflicts in Iraq and Afghanistan made demands on service members and their families that exceeded anything military families had experienced in the several decades prior to 2001. Service members and spouses have described the stresses of deployments in survey after survey, but the direct effects of deployments on military marriages remained surprisingly hard to pin down, and rich descriptive data on how marriages change over the course of the deployment cycle has been lacking. The goal of the analyses described here was to fill these gaps in the existing literature on the effects of deployment, by drawing upon data from the Deployment Life Study, a nine-wave longitudinal study of married service members and their spouses assessed at each stage of a deployment cycle.

Summary of Results

What happens to military marriages as couples prepare for, endure, and then reintegrate after a deployment? This was our first research question, and over the single deployment addressed in these analyses we observed different patterns of change at different stages of the deployment cycle. During the predeployment period, we observed relatively flat trajectories on most of the marital outcomes we assessed, indicating little change in the marriage as couples prepared for a deployment. During the deployment period, however, we did observe changes. For service members, self-reported marital satisfaction declined over the observation period, but for spouses, the decline during the deployment separation period was especially pronounced compared with the nondeployed period, even though positive affect was significantly higher during the deployment for both spouses. Rates of reported psychological and physical aggression enacted by the self and received from the partner all dropped sharply upon deployment and then declined further during deployment (with the exception of spouse report of partner's physical aggression, which was not associated with the deployment itself). The actual drop in aggression at the time of deployment is likely more abrupt than shown; because these outcomes are measured over a four-month period, even an immediate change at the time of deployment may take a few months to fully appear in the data. This drop was not a surprise: Couples who are separated in space and communicating less frequently have fewer opportunities to engage in aggressive or hostile behaviors than when they are living together. The return of the service member generally corresponded to an abrupt return to near baseline levels on most marital outcomes. For example, marital satisfaction, which declined on average during the entire deployment cycle, jumped to higher than baseline levels when the service member returned before declining gradually across the postdeployment months. Levels of positive and negative affect reported after the deployment generally corresponded to the levels that service members and spouses had reported prior to the deployment. All measures of psychological and physical aggression also jumped abruptly upon the service member's return, as couples were able to resume patterns of behavior that had been disrupted by the deployment. Yet, in the months after the service member's return, aggressive behaviors of all types generally declined or maintained slightly lower than their predeployment levels. Thus, by the end of the study period, couples that experienced a deployment were on average less satisfied with their marriages, experienced similar levels of positive and negative affect after communicating with each other, and engaged in less psychological and physical aggression than they reported prior to the deployment. Significant differences between service members' and spouses' trajectories were rare—again, not surprisingly, as both partners were reporting on the same relationship.

These patterns are consistent with two prior longitudinal studies of married service members over the course of a deployment, both of which also reported significant declines in marital satisfaction from predeployment to postdeployment (Andres, 2014; Cigrang et al., 2014). By themselves, however, these analyses are not sufficient evidence to conclude that the experience of deployment caused these changes, as many longitudinal studies have observed similar changes over time, even for couples that do not experience deployments. In fact, declines in satisfaction over time are one of the most reliable findings in longitudinal research on marriage (Karney and Bradbury, 1995; VanLaningham, Johnson, and Amato, 2001). Longitudinal studies of civilian couples also regularly observe declines in aggressive behavior over time (Lawrence and Bradbury, 2007; O'Leary et al., 1989). Thus, these descriptive data raise the question: How do the changes experienced by couples going through deployment compare with the changes experienced by matched couples that did not deploy over the same period of time?

This was our second research question, and the results were unambiguous. Despite significant changes across phases of the deployment cycle among the couples where the service member deployed, the overall patterns of change from predeployment to postdeployment did not differ significantly from the changes experienced by nondeployed couples assessed over the same period. This conclusion held true for service members and for spouses on every one of the marital outcomes assessed in this study. In other words, although couples changed significantly during the transition into and out of deployment, by the end of the deployment cycle, we found no evidence that the marriages of couples that deployed were any different from what they would have been had they not deployed.

Despite the lack of average differences between couples that did and did not deploy during the study period, there was still considerable variability in postdeployment marital outcomes among the couples that deployed. Controlling for initial differences among those couples, what aspects of the deployment experience accounted for better or worse postdeployment outcomes? This was our third research question, and the answer depended on whom we asked. Service members' reports of their marriages postdeployment did not appear sensitive to the characteristics of the deployment, in that very few of the possible associations we tested were significant in the service members' data after predeployment characteristics of the couple were taken into account. Spouses' reports, in contrast, were far more sensitive, and their postdeployment evaluations of their marriages were associated with characteristics of the service member's deployment in three general ways. First, we found robust associations between communication during deployment and marital satisfaction postdeployment. Specifically, spouses who reported more-frequent communication with the service member during the deployment, and more satisfaction with the frequency of their communication, reported higher marital satisfaction and greater positive feelings about communication with the service member postdeployment. From the perspective of Family Stress Process models, partners' abilities to communicate effectively can be considered a resource that can promote effective coping with stress. Indeed, research on the reintegration process has identified open communication between partners as an important correlate of successful reintegration (Knobloch and Theiss, 2012), and have noted that ineffective communication and difficulties with disclosure are associated with greater distress during this period (Balderrama-Durbin et al., 2015). The current findings are consistent with this perspective. Maintaining regular communication with the service member may allow spouses to preserve closeness while separated, easing the way for both partners to resume the relationship once the service member returns. A question for future research is whether these benefits accrue to all couples separated by deployment. It seems likely that couples with generally satisfying relationships and stable situations at home might benefit from regular contact during deployment, but for couples in distressed relationships or facing challenges at home (e.g., financial strain, health problems), more communication might raise difficult issues that partners who are separated are in a poor position to resolve.

Second, spouses' data revealed links between the service member's exposure to trauma during deployment and both partners' aggressive behaviors postdeployment. The existing literature on traumatic experiences and interpersonal difficulties is vast. Traumatic brain injuries (TBIs) have been consistently linked to increases in interpersonal aggression (Dyer et al., 2006; Kim, 2002), as has PTSD (for meta-analyses, see Lambert et al., 2012; Taft et al., 2011). What these results add to this literature is the possibility that different types of traumatic experience have different effects on aggressive behaviors. According to spouses' reports of their own and their partner's psychological and physical aggression, the service member's exposure to physical and psychological trauma predicted higher levels of psychological aggression in both partners and higher levels of physical aggression in the service member, even after predeployment levels of these behaviors and baseline characteristics of the couple were controlled. Yet combat trauma during deployment predicted significantly lower levels of psychological aggression in both partners. These results await replication, but to the extent that the same patterns emerge in independent data sets, they should motivate future research to determine what it is about different types of traumatic experiences that predict higher or lower levels of aggression. In light of the consistent findings that PTSD symptoms are associated with higher levels of aggression, it may be that some forms of trauma exposure are more likely to lead to PTSD symptoms than others.

Third, spouses' data revealed significant associations between separation from the military and feelings about the marriage postdeployment. Specifically, among couples that separated from the military or retired after a deployment, spouses reported lower marital satisfaction, as well as less positive and more negative feelings about communicating with the service member. This analysis cannot be called prediction: All of the separations observed in the deployed couples necessarily took place during the postdeployment period, so these analyses were not able to determine whether the declines in feelings about the marriage preceded or followed the separation. Nevertheless, the association between separation and more-vulnerable marriages is consistent with analyses highlighting all of the ways that the concrete benefits associated with military service (e.g., guaranteed employment, housing supplements, health care) may prop up marriages that might otherwise fail (Karney and Crown, 2007; Lundquist, 2006). After separating from the military and experiencing the loss of those benefits, previously hidden vulnerabilities in the relationship may be revealed.

Among the deployment characteristics that we analyzed, the length of study deployment was not associated with postdeployment marital outcomes for either partner on any of the variables we assessed. This contrasts other research that has found significant negative associations between length of time deployed and risk of divorce (Negrusa, Negrusa, and Hosek, 2014). One difference between prior analyses and the current one is that we controlled for prior combat trauma exposure in addition to prior history of deployment. To the extent that exposure to trauma during combat accounts for the effects of deployment length on deployment outcomes that could account for the difference between the two sets of results.

Strengths and Limitations

Several unique strengths in the methods and design of the Deployment Life Study enhance our confidence in the results reported here. First, these data come from a large sample weighted to be representative of a deployed married population of the military, the precise population to which we would like to generalize. Second, the Deployment Life Study included data from multiple family members, including both partners in each couple, and thus do not depend on the perspective of a single observer. Third, the patterns of results emphasized in this discussion replicated across multiple related predictors and multiple related outcomes, reducing the likelihood that they arise due to idiosyncrasies in specific measures or instruments. Fourth, these data come from a multiwave longitudinal study that, in most cases, provided multiple assessments from couples during each stage of the deployment cycle. This level of detail offered what we believe to be an unprecedented description of how military couples' marriages change across the deployment cycle.

Yet, despite these strengths, the conclusions that can be drawn from these results are limited by the historical context in which the data were collected. At the time of that the initial sample was being recruited, the United States was reducing the number of troops deployed to Iraq and Afghanistan after nearly a decade of conflicts in both countries. As a consequence of the high pace of deployments during that decade, most of the population from which the current sample was drawn had already experienced, and survived, a prior deployment or multiple deployments by the time they began their participation in this study. The result is a sample composed predominately of well-established veterans of war and separation. Although these couples are indeed representative of the military after more than a decade of war, they may not be representative of the couples most vulnerable to negative consequences after a deployment. Therefore, these results may underestimate the negative effects of deployment on couples that had already left the military (through either retirement or separation) before the study began, or who were not well represented in this sample, i.e., younger couples, married more recently, without children, who had not experienced prior deployments. Moreover, just as the population had changed by the time the study began, the nature of deployments had changed as well. As operations in Iraq and Afghanistan were winding down, deployments to those fields of combat became shorter and less dangerous than they had been in the earlier part of the decade, resulting in far lower casualty rates during the study period than had been the case in the years prior to the study period (Fischer, 2015).

Implications for Policy

The deployment cycle observed in this study took place in the years after the Department of Defense had invested unprecedented levels of funding in programs and policies to support military families (Rostker, 2006; Rubin and Harvie, 2012). One hypothesized explanation for the general pattern of resilience observed here might be taken as evidence that this investment paid off, although it is important to remember that this study is unable to identify which families used such programs (rendering us unable to account for self-selection into program utilization), nor can it say anything about program effectiveness. When civilian marriages face separations and stresses comparable to the stress of a deployment, the implications are generally negative for dyadic interactions and marital relationships (Karney and Neff, 2013). The fact that military couples are emerging from these stresses looking similar to couples that did not experience them suggests that they had access to resources, either personal (e.g., a strong commitment to the institution of marriage, a stronger relationship prior to the deployment) or structural (e.g., a supportive network of military families, the availability of family support centers, longer time since relocation prior to deployment), that helped them cope effectively with demands that would have damaged marriages that lacked these resources. One task for future research is to identify the specific resources that make the largest difference in the lives of military families.

In advance of that future research, the results from the Deployment Life Study presented here highlight at least two ways that the allocation of resources for programs to support military families could be refined. First, these results draw attention to the importance of communication during deployment in easing the successful reintegration of the service member after the deployment. Due to advances in communication technology, the contemporary armed forces are already more connected to their families back home than any military force in the history of warfare (Carter and Renshaw, 2015). At least from the perspective of spouses, the ability to connect appears to make a difference to marital outcomes. The military's policies around communication during deployment are therefore worth examining further, to determine the modes and amount of communication that best facilitate optimal outcomes for military couples. The initial picture from these data is simply "more is better," but this is a picture that is likely to develop more nuance with more-detailed data.

Second, although these data presented little evidence of lasting marital changes associated with deployments, these results point out that military couples also need support for reasons independent of deployments. Even before they are deployed, some military marriages may be vulnerable to marital distress or dissolution due to experiences of PTSD, younger age at marriage, or financial stress. Prior analyses of the baseline data of the Deployment Life Study sample revealed that these sources of vulnerability tend to cluster together, such that families characterized by one source of vulnerability are often characterized by others as well (Trail et al., 2015). Deployments are such salient sources of stress in the lives of military couples that they can draw disproportionate levels of attention from policymakers and program developers. These data indicate that resources should still be invested in services to address the other difficult issues that military couples face, especially for couples that have already proven their ability to survive deployments.

Conclusions

Throughout the past 15 years of war, service members and their spouses have described deployments as one of the most stressful aspects of military life. Indeed, these analyses confirm that when married service members are deployed, their marriages change significantly. Marital satisfaction declines, negative feelings increase, and aggressive behaviors decline as partners separated by thousands of miles have fewer opportunities to engage in any behaviors at all. Yet, in the midst of all of this stress and change, the take-away message of these analyses is this: For the most part, military marriages change back when the deployment is over. These data therefore speak most eloquently of the strength and resilience of military marriages. After long hours, extended separations, undeniable hazards, and limited opportunities to communicate, service members and their spouses appear able to return their relationships to the trajectories they were on prior to their deployments. It remains for future research to identify the personal and structural sources of this resilience, so that we may identify the most-effective programs to support military families, and improve our ability to direct extra support to those who are most vulnerable.

Appendix 3A: Balance Tables and Plots

Tables 3A.1 and 3A.2 present balance statistics for service members and spouses, respectively. Each table compares standardized mean differences (SMDs) across a number of key study variables for service members and spouses who did and did not experience a study deployment. SMDs are presented before and after applying propensity score weights. Generally, SMDs between −0.20 and 0.20 indicate good balance across groups.

Figures 3A.1 and 3A.2 present the balance plots for service members and spouses, respectively, who did and did not experience a study deployment. Each dot on the plot represents a variable in Tables 3A.1 and 3A.2. The left side of each plot depicts absolute standard mean differences (ASMDs) before applying propensity score weights, while the right side of each plot depicts ASMDs after applying the propensity score weights. As can be seen in both figures, once the weights are applied, ASMDs between service members and spouses who do and do not experience a study deployment fall below the cutoff of 0.20 ASMDs.

Table 3A.1
Weighted Balance Table: Service Members (Study Deployment Versus No Study Deployment)

	Unweighted					Weighted				
	Study Deployment		No Study Deployment			Study Deployment		No Study Deployment		
	Mean	SD	Mean	SD	SMD	Mean	SD	Mean	SD	SMD
SERVICE MEMBER VARIABLES										
Female	0.08	0.27	0.14	0.34	-0.22	0.08	0.27	0.09	0.28	-0.04
Age	32.72	7.13	35.05	8.08	-0.33	32.72	7.13	33.38	7.53	-0.09
Minority Race/Ethnicity	0.32	0.47	0.33	0.47	-0.01	0.32	0.47	0.31	0.46	0.02
Children Younger Than Age 6	0.51	0.50	0.45	0.50	0.13	0.51	0.50	0.48	0.50	0.06
Pay Grade: Junior Enlisted	0.05	0.21	0.04	0.20	0.03	0.05	0.21	0.03	0.18	0.06
Pay Grade: Junior Officer	0.11	0.31	0.09	0.28	0.07	0.11	0.31	0.10	0.30	0.02
Pay Grade: Mid and Senior Enlisted	0.69	0.46	0.74	0.44	-0.10	0.69	0.46	0.73	0.45	-0.09
Pay Grade: Mid and Senior Officer	0.10	0.30	0.12	0.32	-0.04	0.10	0.30	0.11	0.31	-0.02
Pay Grade: Warrant Officer	0.06	0.24	0.03	0.16	0.14	0.06	0.24	0.03	0.17	0.13
Length of Marriage (Months)	96.86	77.86	109.80	84.90	-0.17	96.86	77.86	96.49	77.17	0.01
Parents in the Military	0.53	0.50	0.52	0.50	0.02	0.53	0.50	0.50	0.50	0.06
Total Number of Prior Deployments	2.02	1.32	1.38	1.27	0.49	2.02	1.32	1.85	1.26	0.13
Years of Service	12.07	7.41	13.83	8.54	-0.24	12.07	7.41	12.53	7.71	-0.06
Army	0.46	0.50	0.50	0.50	-0.08	0.46	0.50	0.48	0.50	-0.05
Air Force	0.24	0.43	0.26	0.44	-0.03	0.24	0.43	0.19	0.40	0.12
Navy	0.20	0.40	0.16	0.37	0.09	0.20	0.40	0.25	0.43	-0.13
Marine Corps	0.10	0.30	0.09	0.28	0.05	0.10	0.30	0.07	0.26	0.09
Reserve Component	0.16	0.37	0.39	0.49	-0.64	0.16	0.37	0.21	0.40	-0.12
Hoge Combat Experiences Scale	4.61	4.40	3.79	3.98	0.19	4.61	4.40	4.21	4.09	0.09
Deployment Trauma Exposure	2.13	2.38	1.67	2.43	0.19	2.13	2.38	1.96	2.47	0.07
Marital Satisfaction Scale	4.01	0.44	3.90	0.51	4.01	4.01	0.44	4.00	0.46	0.03
PANAS: Positive	4.24	0.62	4.10	0.67	4.24	4.24	0.62	4.21	0.62	0.06
PANAS: Negative	1.92	0.51	2.07	0.60	1.92	1.92	0.51	1.97	0.55	-0.11

Table 3A.1—Continued

	Unweighted					Weighted				
	Study Deployment		No Study Deployment		SMD	Study Deployment		No Study Deployment		SMD
	Mean	SD	Mean	SD		Mean	SD	Mean	SD	
Conflict Tactics Scale: Prevalence of Physical Aggression Toward Partner	0.01	0.12	0.02	0.14	0.01	0.01	0.12	0.02	0.13	−0.04
Conflict Tactics Scale: Chronicity of Psychological Aggression Toward Partner	0.63	0.86	0.77	0.91	0.63	0.63	0.86	0.68	0.87	−0.07
Conflict Tactics Scale: Prevalence of Physical Aggression Toward You	0.05	0.21	0.05	0.23	0.05	0.05	0.21	0.05	0.22	−0.03
Conflict Tactics Scale: Chronicity of Psychological Aggression Toward You	0.67	0.98	0.89	1.04	0.67	0.67	0.98	0.75	1.01	−0.08
Depression (Patient Health Questionnaire [PHQ])	2.39	3.06	3.11	3.90	−0.24	2.39	3.06	2.52	3.32	−0.04
Anxiety	2.02	0.98	2.13	1.02	−0.11	2.02	0.98	2.06	0.98	−0.04
PTSD	21.33	8.00	22.69	10.21	−0.17	21.33	8.00	21.82	8.96	−0.06
TBI	0.11	0.32	0.13	0.33	−0.04	0.11	0.32	0.12	0.32	0.00
Binge Drinking	0.25	0.43	0.24	0.43	0.02	0.25	0.43	0.26	0.44	−0.02
Problematic Substance Use Scale	0.14	0.49	0.17	0.62	−0.06	0.14	0.49	0.15	0.55	−0.01
Medication for Mental Health Problem	0.03	0.17	0.06	0.23	−0.17	0.03	0.17	0.04	0.19	−0.06
Received Mental Health Care	0.07	0.26	0.18	0.39	−0.42	0.07	0.26	0.11	0.31	−0.13
Military Commitment	4.43	0.63	4.38	0.69	0.09	1.78	0.64	1.82	0.67	−0.07
Job Satisfaction	3.98	0.95	3.85	1.03	0.14	2.81	0.23	2.80	0.26	0.02
Retention Intentions	4.21	1.23	4.12	1.37	0.08	0.24	0.43	0.25	0.44	−0.03
Retention Intentions, Missing	0.16	0.37	0.39	0.49	−0.52	3.36	0.37	3.34	0.39	0.03
SPOUSE VARIABLES										
Marital Satisfaction Scale	3.98	0.51	3.77	0.61	0.42	3.98	0.51	3.92	0.54	0.12
PANAS: Positive	4.25	0.66	4.06	0.76	0.28	4.25	0.66	4.21	0.67	0.06
PANAS: Negative	2.00	0.59	2.19	0.63	−0.32	2.00	0.59	2.06	0.61	−0.11
Conflict Tactics Scale: Prevalence of Physical Aggression Toward Partner	0.05	0.21	0.05	0.22	−0.04	0.05	0.21	0.05	0.22	−0.02

Table 3A.1—Continued

	Unweighted					Weighted				
	Study Deployment		No Study Deployment			Study Deployment		No Study Deployment		
	Mean	SD	Mean	SD	SMD	Mean	SD	Mean	SD	SMD
Conflict Tactics Scale: Chronicity of Psychological Aggression Toward Partner	0.71	0.88	0.78	0.96	-0.08	0.71	0.88	0.70	0.93	0.01
Conflict Tactics Scale: Prevalence of Physical Aggression Toward You	0.02	0.12	0.03	0.16	-0.08	0.02	0.12	0.02	0.15	-0.08
Conflict Tactics Scale: Chronicity of Psychological Aggression Toward You	0.59	0.84	0.78	0.97	-0.22	0.59	0.84	0.65	0.92	-0.06
Depression (PHQ)	2.75	3.64	3.08	3.81	-0.09	2.75	3.64	2.92	3.66	-0.05
Anxiety	2.05	0.93	2.07	0.95	-0.03	2.05	0.93	2.06	0.96	-0.01
PTSD	0.47	0.99	0.54	0.99	-0.07	0.47	0.99	0.47	0.97	0.01
Binge Drinking	0.15	0.35	0.11	0.32	0.10	0.15	0.35	0.12	0.33	0.07
Problematic Substance Use Scale	0.07	0.43	0.06	0.37	0.04	0.07	0.43	0.07	0.41	0.01
Medication for Mental Health Problem	0.12	0.33	0.12	0.32	0.01	0.12	0.33	0.13	0.34	-0.02
Received Mental Health Care	0.13	0.34	0.13	0.33	0.01	0.13	0.34	0.15	0.35	-0.04
Financial Distress Scale	1.85	0.68	2.02	0.75	-0.25	1.85	0.68	1.87	0.70	-0.03
Family Environment Scale	2.85	0.24	2.76	0.29	0.37	2.85	0.24	2.83	0.24	0.07
Family Environment Scale, Missing	0.24	0.43	0.26	0.44	-0.04	0.24	0.43	0.25	0.44	-0.03
Parenting Satisfaction	3.24	0.37	3.22	0.42	0.06	3.24	0.37	3.24	0.40	-0.01
Parenting Satisfaction, Missing	0.24	0.43	0.26	0.44	-0.04	0.24	0.43	0.25	0.44	-0.03
Military Commitment	4.51	0.58	4.36	0.70	0.26	4.51	0.58	4.46	0.61	0.08
Satisfaction as Military Spouse	4.13	1.01	3.84	1.15	0.28	4.13	1.01	4.12	0.99	0.02
Retention Intentions	4.14	1.16	3.91	1.32	0.20	4.14	1.16	4.06	1.27	0.07
TEEN VARIABLES										
Strengths and Difficulties Questionnaire (SDQ): Total	7.43	5.26	8.06	5.22	-0.12	7.43	5.26	7.75	5.47	-0.06
SDQ: Total, Missing	0.46	0.50	0.45	0.50	0.03	0.46	0.50	0.47	0.50	-0.01
SDQ Subscale: Emotional Problems	1.65	1.83	1.63	1.69	0.01	1.65	1.83	1.61	1.81	0.02
SDQ Subscale: Emotional Problems, Missing	0.47	0.50	0.45	0.50	0.04	0.47	0.50	0.47	0.50	0.00

Table 3A.1—Continued

	Unweighted					Weighted				
	Study Deployment		No Study Deployment		SMD	Study Deployment		No Study Deployment		SMD
	Mean	SD	Mean	SD		Mean	SD	Mean	SD	
SDQ Subscale: Conduct Problems	0.97	1.32	1.14	1.30	-0.13	0.97	1.32	1.03	1.36	-0.04
SDQ Subscale: Conduct Problems, Missing	0.47	0.50	0.45	0.50	0.04	0.47	0.50	0.47	0.50	0.00
SDQ Subscale: Hyperactivity	3.32	2.61	3.39	2.38	-0.03	3.32	2.61	3.47	2.57	-0.06
SDQ Subscale: Hyperactivity, Missing	0.49	0.50	0.45	0.50	0.09	0.49	0.50	0.47	0.50	0.05
SDQ Subscale: Peer Relationships	1.70	1.61	1.91	1.86	-0.13	1.70	1.61	1.64	1.66	0.03
SDQ Subscale: Peer Relationships, Missing	0.46	0.50	0.45	0.50	0.03	0.46	0.50	0.47	0.50	-0.01
SDQ Subscale: Prosocial Behavior	8.54	1.65	8.46	1.48	0.04	8.54	1.65	8.64	1.53	-0.06
SDQ Subscale: Prosocial Behavior, Missing	0.47	0.50	0.45	0.50	0.04	0.47	0.50	0.47	0.50	0.00
Depression Symptoms	1.01	1.85	1.10	1.81	-0.05	1.01	1.85	0.89	1.70	0.07
Depression Symptoms, Missing	0.47	0.50	0.45	0.50	0.04	0.47	0.50	0.47	0.50	0.01
Anxiety (Screen for Child Anxiety Related Emotional Disorders [SCARED])	1.66	1.95	1.34	1.45	0.16	1.66	1.95	1.50	1.73	0.08
Anxiety (SCARED), Missing	0.46	0.50	0.45	0.50	0.03	0.46	0.50	0.47	0.50	-0.01

NOTE: SD=standard deviation.

Table 3A.2
Weighted Balance Table: Spouses (Study Deployment Versus No Study Deployment)

	Unweighted					Weighted				
	Study Deployment		No Study Deployment			Study Deployment		No Study Deployment		
	Mean	SD	Mean	SD	SMD	Mean	SD	Mean	SD	SMD
SERVICE MEMBER VARIABLES										
Pay Grade: Junior Enlisted	0.05	0.21	0.05	0.21	0.00	0.05	0.21	0.03	0.17	0.07
Pay Grade: Junior Officer	0.11	0.31	0.08	0.28	0.07	0.11	0.31	0.10	0.31	0.01
Pay Grade: Mid and Senior Enlisted	0.71	0.45	0.73	0.44	-0.05	0.71	0.45	0.72	0.45	-0.03
Pay Grade: Mid and Senior Officer	0.10	0.30	0.12	0.32	-0.05	0.10	0.30	0.12	0.32	-0.05
Pay Grade: Warrant Officer	0.04	0.19	0.02	0.15	0.08	0.04	0.19	0.02	0.15	0.07
Length of Marriage (Months)	94.90	76.42	108.80	84.20	-0.18	94.90	76.42	98.65	78.27	-0.05
Total Number of Prior Deployments	1.99	1.23	1.33	1.23	0.54	1.99	1.23	1.84	1.21	0.13
Years of Service	11.84	7.24	14.00	8.96	-0.30	11.84	7.24	12.48	7.67	-0.09
Army	0.46	0.50	0.50	0.50	-0.08	0.46	0.50	0.49	0.50	-0.06
Air Force	0.24	0.43	0.26	0.44	-0.03	0.24	0.43	0.22	0.41	0.06
Navy	0.20	0.40	0.16	0.37	0.09	0.20	0.40	0.23	0.42	-0.08
Marine Corps	0.10	0.30	0.09	0.28	0.05	0.10	0.30	0.06	0.24	0.12
Reserve Component	0.17	0.37	0.40	0.49	-0.62	0.17	0.37	0.20	0.40	-0.09
Hoge Combat Experiences Scale	4.67	4.50	3.63	4.02	0.23	4.67	4.50	4.31	4.21	0.08
Deployment Trauma Exposure	2.24	2.50	1.69	2.41	0.22	2.24	2.50	2.03	2.46	0.08
Marital Satisfaction Scale	4.00	0.44	3.86	0.56	0.32	4.00	0.44	4.00	0.46	0.00
PANAS: Positive	4.24	0.61	4.05	0.76	0.32	4.24	0.61	4.19	0.62	0.09
PANAS: Negative	1.94	0.54	2.06	0.57	-0.21	1.94	0.54	1.96	0.53	-0.04
Conflict Tactics Scale: Prevalence of Physical Aggression Toward Partner	0.02	0.14	0.02	0.15	0.00	0.02	0.14	0.02	0.13	0.03
Conflict Tactics Scale: Chronicity of Psychological Aggression Toward Partner	0.65	0.87	0.75	0.92	-0.11	0.65	0.87	0.64	0.86	0.02
Conflict Tactics Scale: Prevalence of Physical Aggression Toward You	0.04	0.21	0.06	0.24	-0.07	0.04	0.21	0.05	0.22	-0.03
Conflict Tactics Scale: Chronicity of Psychological Aggression Toward You	0.69	0.98	0.91	1.10	-0.22	0.69	0.98	0.73	1.02	-0.03

Table 3A.2—Continued

| | Unweighted | | | | | Weighted | | | | |
| | Study Deployment | | No Study Deployment | | | Study Deployment | | No Study Deployment | | |
	Mean	SD	Mean	SD	SMD	Mean	SD	Mean	SD	SMD
Depression (PHQ)	2.41	3.17	2.96	3.73	-0.17	2.41	3.17	2.46	3.29	-0.02
Anxiety	2.01	1.01	2.14	0.98	-0.13	2.01	1.01	2.03	0.97	-0.02
PTSD	21.47	8.24	22.67	10.26	-0.15	21.47	8.24	21.61	8.66	-0.02
TBI	0.13	0.34	0.12	0.32	0.04	0.13	0.34	0.12	0.32	0.04
Binge Drinking	0.27	0.44	0.26	0.44	0.02	0.27	0.44	0.24	0.43	0.06
Problematic Substance Use Scale	0.20	0.64	0.21	0.63	-0.03	0.20	0.64	0.16	0.57	0.06
Medication for Mental Health Problem	0.04	0.20	0.06	0.25	-0.13	0.04	0.20	0.04	0.20	-0.01
Received Mental Health Care	0.08	0.27	0.18	0.38	-0.38	0.08	0.27	0.10	0.30	-0.09
Financial Distress Scale	1.82	0.66	2.03	0.76	-0.33	1.82	0.66	1.84	0.67	-0.03
Family Environment Scale	2.78	0.25	2.76	0.29	0.08	2.78	0.25	2.80	0.25	-0.08
Family Environment Scale, Missing	0.25	0.43	0.25	0.43	0.00	0.25	0.43	0.26	0.44	-0.03
Parenting Satisfaction	3.33	0.37	3.34	0.39	-0.03	3.33	0.37	3.33	0.38	-0.01
Parenting Satisfaction, Missing	0.25	0.43	0.25	0.43	0.01	0.25	0.43	0.26	0.44	-0.03
Military Commitment	4.44	0.61	4.33	0.67	0.18	4.44	0.61	4.38	0.64	0.09
Job Satisfaction	4.01	0.91	3.78	1.05	0.25	4.01	0.91	3.91	0.98	0.10
Retention Intentions	4.12	1.29	4.02	1.41	0.08	4.12	1.29	4.17	1.27	-0.04
Retention Intentions, Missing	0.17	0.37	0.40	0.49	-0.52	0.17	0.37	0.20	0.40	-0.07
SPOUSE VARIABLES										
Female	0.92	0.27	0.86	0.35	0.22	0.92	0.27	0.92	0.28	0.02
Age	32.21	7.63	34.35	8.49	-0.28	32.21	7.63	32.82	7.94	-0.08
Minority Race/Ethnicity	0.29	0.45	0.30	0.46	-0.02	0.29	0.45	0.29	0.45	0.00
Children Younger Than Age 6	0.48	0.50	0.43	0.50	0.09	0.48	0.50	0.47	0.50	0.02
Education: Less than High School	0.01	0.09	0.01	0.12	-0.08	0.01	0.09	0.02	0.13	-0.10
Education: High School	0.18	0.39	0.18	0.38	0.01	0.18	0.39	0.18	0.38	0.02
Education: Some College	0.28	0.45	0.26	0.44	0.04	0.28	0.45	0.27	0.44	0.01

Table 3A.2—Continued

	Unweighted					Weighted				
	Study Deployment		No Study Deployment			Study Deployment		No Study Deployment		
	Mean	SD	Mean	SD	SMD	Mean	SD	Mean	SD	SMD
Education: Associate/Vocational/Technical Degree	0.18	0.38	0.18	0.38	0.00	0.18	0.38	0.16	0.37	0.04
Education: Bachelor's Degree	0.27	0.44	0.27	0.44	0.01	0.27	0.44	0.29	0.45	-0.04
Education: Graduate or Professional Degree	0.08	0.28	0.11	0.31	-0.08	0.08	0.28	0.09	0.28	-0.02
Employment: Other	0.05	0.21	0.08	0.27	-0.16	0.05	0.21	0.06	0.23	-0.05
Employment: Employed	0.34	0.47	0.44	0.50	-0.22	0.34	0.47	0.37	0.48	-0.08
Employment: Homemaker	0.39	0.49	0.29	0.46	0.20	0.39	0.49	0.35	0.48	0.08
Employment: Student	0.08	0.27	0.08	0.27	0.00	0.08	0.27	0.08	0.27	-0.01
Employment: Not Employed	0.15	0.36	0.11	0.32	0.10	0.15	0.36	0.14	0.34	0.04
Marital Satisfaction Scale	3.95	0.52	3.70	0.65	0.46	3.95	0.52	3.91	0.53	0.06
PANAS: Positive	4.19	0.66	3.95	0.82	0.37	4.19	0.66	4.16	0.68	0.05
PANAS: Negative	2.07	0.60	2.27	0.68	-0.32	2.07	0.60	2.08	0.61	-0.01
Conflict Tactics Scale: Prevalence of Physical Aggression Toward Partner	0.06	0.23	0.06	0.24	-0.02	0.06	0.23	0.05	0.21	0.05
Conflict Tactics Scale: Chronicity of Psychological Aggression Toward Partner	0.72	0.89	0.78	0.96	-0.07	0.72	0.89	0.68	0.91	0.04
Conflict Tactics Scale: Prevalence of Physical Aggression Toward You	0.02	0.13	0.05	0.21	-0.22	0.02	0.13	0.03	0.16	-0.07
Conflict Tactics Scale: Chronicity of Psychological Aggression Toward You	0.60	0.88	0.87	1.06	-0.31	0.60	0.88	0.65	0.91	-0.06
Depression (PHQ)	2.84	3.62	3.25	3.70	-0.11	2.84	3.62	2.91	3.63	-0.02
Anxiety	2.08	0.92	2.18	0.99	-0.11	2.08	0.92	2.07	0.97	0.01
PTSD	0.48	0.99	0.49	0.98	-0.01	0.48	0.99	0.45	0.96	0.04
Binge Drinking	0.15	0.36	0.09	0.28	0.17	0.15	0.36	0.12	0.33	0.07
Problematic Substance Use Scale	0.10	0.55	0.05	0.36	0.09	0.10	0.55	0.07	0.44	0.06
Medication for Mental Health Problem	0.11	0.31	0.13	0.34	-0.07	0.11	0.31	0.14	0.34	-0.08
Received Mental Health Care	0.13	0.33	0.14	0.35	-0.04	0.13	0.33	0.14	0.35	-0.04
Financial Distress Scale	1.88	0.69	2.06	0.76	-0.27	1.88	0.69	1.89	0.70	-0.03

Table 3A.2—Continued

| | Unweighted | | | | | Weighted | | | | |
| | Study Deployment | | No Study Deployment | | | Study Deployment | | No Study Deployment | | |
	Mean	SD	Mean	SD	SMD	Mean	SD	Mean	SD	SMD
Family Environment Scale	2.82	0.26	2.73	0.33	0.35	2.82	0.26	2.82	0.26	0.00
Family Environment Scale, Missing	0.25	0.43	0.25	0.43	0.00	0.25	0.43	0.26	0.44	-0.03
Parenting Stress Scale	3.23	0.37	3.20	0.38	0.08	3.23	0.37	3.24	0.39	-0.03
Parenting Stress Scale, Missing	0.25	0.43	0.25	0.43	0.00	0.25	0.43	0.26	0.44	-0.03
Parent in the Military	0.40	0.49	0.51	0.50	-0.23	0.40	0.49	0.45	0.50	-0.10
Military Commitment	4.50	0.60	4.33	0.68	0.28	4.50	0.60	4.47	0.60	0.05
Satisfaction as Military Spouse	4.11	1.03	3.93	1.06	0.18	4.11	1.03	4.15	0.94	-0.04
Retention Intentions	4.16	1.12	3.94	1.32	0.20	4.16	1.12	4.11	1.22	0.05
TEEN VARIABLES										
SDQ: Total	7.33	5.09	8.04	5.20	-0.14	7.33	5.09	7.59	5.26	-0.05
SDQ: Total, Missing	0.49	0.50	0.46	0.50	0.04	0.49	0.50	0.48	0.50	0.01
SDQ Subscale: Emotional Problems	1.57	1.82	1.76	1.75	-0.11	1.57	1.82	1.61	1.76	-0.03
SDQ Subscale: Emotional Problems, Missing	0.49	0.50	0.47	0.50	0.06	0.49	0.50	0.48	0.50	0.03
SDQ Subscale: Conduct Problems	0.97	1.33	1.03	1.32	-0.05	0.97	1.33	0.99	1.35	-0.02
SDQ Subscale: Conduct Problems, Missing	0.49	0.50	0.47	0.50	0.06	0.49	0.50	0.48	0.50	0.03
SDQ Subscale: Hyperactivity	3.18	2.46	3.39	2.41	-0.08	3.18	2.46	3.39	2.51	-0.08
SDQ Subscale: Hyperactivity, Missing	0.49	0.50	0.46	0.50	0.06	0.49	0.50	0.48	0.50	0.03
SDQ Subscale: Peer Relationships	1.68	1.67	1.87	1.78	-0.11	1.68	1.67	1.60	1.64	0.05
SDQ Subscale: Peer Relationships, Missing	0.49	0.50	0.46	0.50	0.04	0.49	0.50	0.48	0.50	0.01
SDQ Subscale: Prosocial Behavior	8.53	1.65	8.35	1.51	0.11	8.53	1.65	8.60	1.57	-0.04
SDQ Subscale: Prosocial Behavior, Missing	0.49	0.50	0.47	0.50	0.06	0.49	0.50	0.48	0.50	0.03
Depression Symptoms	0.92	1.65	0.93	1.74	-0.01	0.92	1.65	0.80	1.62	0.07
Depression Symptoms, Missing	0.49	0.50	0.46	0.50	0.06	0.49	0.50	0.48	0.50	0.03
Anxiety (SCARED)	1.71	1.97	1.53	1.49	0.09	1.71	1.97	1.53	1.73	0.09
Anxiety (SCARED), Missing	0.49	0.50	0.47	0.50	0.04	0.49	0.50	0.48	0.50	0.01

Figure 3A.1
Balance Plot for Service Members

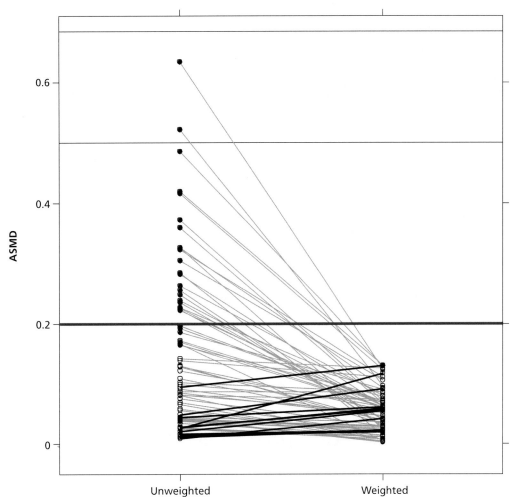

Figure 3A.2
Balance Plot for Spouses

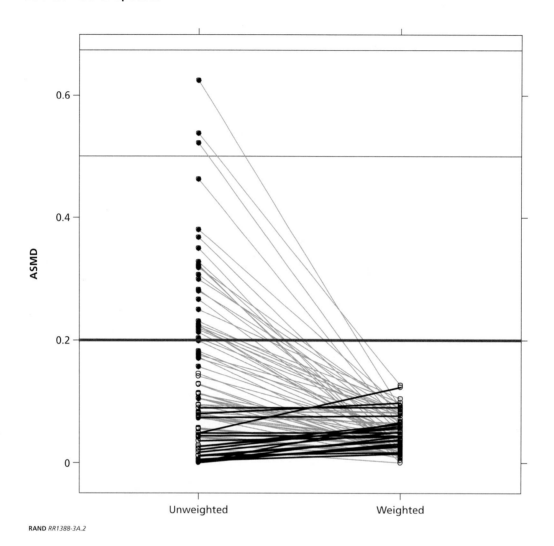

References

Ahmadi, K., A. Fathi-Ashtiani, A. Zareir, A. Arabnia, and M. Amiri, "Sexual Dysfunctions and Marital Adjustment in Veterans with PTSD," *Archives of Medical Science*, Vol. 2, No. 4, 2006, p. 280.

Allen, E. S., G. K. Rhoades, S. M. Stanley, and H. J. Markman, "Hitting Home: Relationships Between Recent Deployment, Posttraumatic Stress Symptoms, and Marital Functioning for Army Couples," *Journal of Family Psychology*, Vol. 24, No. 3, 2010, pp. 280–288.

Alvarez, L., "Long Iraq Tours Can Make Home a Trying Front," *New York Times*, February 23, 2007, p. A1.

Andres, M., "Distress, Support, and Relationship Satisfaction During Military-Induced Separations: A Longitudinal Study Among Spouses of Dutch Deployed Military Personnel," *Psychological Services*, Vol. 11, 2014, pp. 22–30.

Arriaga, X. B., and E. L. Schkeryantz, "Intimate Relationships and Personal Distress: The Invisible Harm of Psychological Aggression," *Personality and Social Psychology Bulletin*, Vol. 41, No. 10, 2015.

Balderrama-Durbin, C., J. A. Cigrang, L. J. Osborne, D. K. Snyder, G. W. Talcott, A. M. Slep, and S. Sonnek, "Coming Home: A Prospective Study of Family Reintegration Following Deployment to a War Zone," *Psychological Services*, Vol. 12, No. 3, 2015, pp. 213–221.

Blue Star Families, *2012 Military Family Lifestyle Survey: Comprehensive Report—Sharing the Pride of Service*, Washington, D.C., 2012.

Carter, S. P., and K. D. Renshaw, "Spousal Communication During Military Deployments: A Review," *Journal of Family Issues*, January 14, 2015.

Cigrang, J. A., G. W. Talcott, J. Tatum, M. Baker, D. Cassidy, S. Sonnek, and S. M. Slep, "Impact of Combat Deployment on Psychological and Relationship Health: A Longitudinal Study," *Journal of Trauma and Stress*, Vol. 27, No. 1, 2014, pp. 58–65.

Cranford, J. A., "Stress-Buffering or Stress-Exacerbation? Social Support and Social Undermining as Moderators of the Relationship Between Perceived Stress and Depressive Symptoms Among Married People," *Personal Relationships*, Vol. 11, 2004, pp. 23–40.

Dyer, K. F. W., R. Bell, J. McCann, and R. Rauch, "Aggression After Traumatic Brain Injury: Analysing Socially Desirable Responses and the Nature of Aggressive Traits," *Brain Injury*, Vol. 20, No. 11, 2006, pp. 1163–1173.

Fischer, H., *A Guide to U.S. Military Casualty Statistics: Operation Freedom's Sentinel, Operation Inherent Resolve, Operation New Dawn, Operation Iraqi Freedom, and Operation Enduring Freedom*, Washington, D.C.: Congressional Research Service, 2015.

Hill, R., *Families Under Stress*, New York: Harper & Row, 1949.

Hoge, C. W., J. L. Auchterlonie, and C. S. Milliken, "Mental Health Problems, Use of Mental Health Services, and Attrition from Military Service After Returning from Deployment to Iraq or Afghanistan," *Journal of the American Medical Association*, Vol. 295, 2006, pp. 1023–1032.

Hosek, J., and F. Martorell, *How Have Deployments During the War on Terrorism Affected Reenlistment?* Santa Monica, Calif.: RAND Corporation, MG-873-OSD, 2009. As of November 18, 2015: http://www.rand.org/pubs/monographs/MG873.html

Karney, B. R., and T. N. Bradbury, "The Longitudinal Course of Marital Quality and Stability: A Review of Theory, Methods, and Research," *Psychological Bulletin*, Vol. 118, No. 1, 1995, pp. 3–34.

———, "Neuroticism, Marital Interaction, and the Trajectory of Marital Satisfaction," *Journal of Personality and Social Psychology*, Vol. 72, No. 5, 1997, pp. 1075–1092.

Karney, B. R., and J. S. Crown, *Families Under Stress: An Assessment of Data, Theory, and Research on Marriage and Divorce in the Military*, Santa Monica, Calif.: RAND Corporation, MG–599-OSD, 2007. As of November 18, 2015: http://www.rand.org/pubs/monographs/MG599.html

—————, "Does Deployment Keep Military Marriages Together or Break Them Apart? Evidence from Afghanistan and Iraq," in S. M. Wadsworth and D. Riggs, eds., *Risk and Resilience in U.S. Military Families*, Berlin: Springer Science and Business Media, LLC, 2010.

Karney, B. R., D. S. Loughran, and M. S. Pollard, "Comparing Marital Status and Divorce Status in Civilian and Military Populations," *Journal of Family Issues,* Vol. 33, 2012, pp. 1572–1594.

Karney, B. R., and L. A. Neff, "Couples and Stress: How Demands Outside a Relationship Affect Intimacy Within the Relationship," in J. A. Simpson and L. Campbell, eds., *Handbook of Close Relationships*, Oxford: Oxford Press, 2013, pp. 664–684.

Karney, B. R., and T. E. Trail, "Associations Between Prior Deployments and Marital Satisfaction Among Army Couples," *Journal of Marriage and the Family*, forthcoming.

Kaufman, L., "After War, Love Can Be a Battlefield," *New York Times*, April 6, 2008.

Keeling, M., S. Wessely, C. Dandeker, N. Jones, and N. T. Fear, "Relationship Difficulties Among U.K. Military Personnel: Impact of Sociodemographic, Military, and Deployment-Related Factors," *Marriage & Family Review*, Vol. 51, No. 3, 2015, pp. 275–303.

Kiecolt-Glaser, J. K., W. B. Malarkey, M. Chee, and T. Newton, "Negative Behavior During Marital Conflict Is Associated with Immunological Down-Regulation," *Psychosomatic Medicine*, Vol. 55, No. 5, 1993, pp. 395–409.

Kim, E., "Agitation, Aggression, and Disinhibition Syndromes After Traumatic Brain Injury," *NeuroRehabilitation*, Vol. 17, No. 4, 2002, pp. 297–310.

Knobloch, L. K., and J. A. Theiss, "Experiences of U.S. Military Couples During the Post-Deployment Transition: Applying the Relational Turbulence Model," *Journal of Social and Personal Relationships*, 2012, pp. 1–28.

Lambert, J. E., R. Engh, A. Hasbun, and J. Holzer, "Impact of Posttraumatic Stress Disorder on the Relationship Quality and Psychological Distress of Intimate Partners: A Meta-Analytic Review," *Journal of Family Psychology*, Vol. 26, No. 5, 2012, pp. 729–737.

Lawrence, E., and T. N. Bradbury, "Trajectories of Change in Physical Aggression and Marital Satisfaction," *Journal of Family Psychology*, Vol. 21, No. 2, 2007, pp. 236–247.

Levinger, G., "A Social Psychological Perspective on Marital Dissolution," *Journal of Social Issues*, Vol. 32, 1976, pp. 21–47.

Lewis, R. A., and G. B. Spanier, "Marital Quality, Marital Stability, and Social Exchange," in F. I. Nye, ed., *Family Relationships: Rewards and Costs*, Beverly Hills, Calif: Sage, 1982, pp. 49–65.

Loughran, D. S., *Wage Growth in the Civilian Careers of Military Retirees*, Santa Monica, Calif.: RAND Corporation, MR-1363-OSD, 2002. As of November 18, 2015: http://www.rand.org/pubs/monograph_reports/MR1363.html

Lundquist, J. H., "The Black-White Gap in Marital Dissolution Among Young Adults: What Can a Counterfactual Scenario Tell Us?" *Social Problems*, Vol. 53, 2006, pp. 421–441.

Lundquist, J., and Z. Xu, "Reinstitutionalizing Families: Life Course Policy and Marriage in the Military," *Journal of Marriage and Family*, Vol. 76, No. 5, 2014, pp. 1063–1081.

McCubbin, H. I., and J. M. Patterson, "The Family Stress Process: The Double ABCX Model of Adjustment and Adaptation," *Marriage and Family Review*, Vol. 6, 1983, pp. 7–37.

McIntyre, J., "War Takes Toll on Military Marriages," CNN, June 8, 2005. As of November 20, 2015: http://www.cnn.com/2005/US/06/08/military.marriages/_

McLeland, K. C., G. W. Sutton, and W. R. Schumm, "Marital Satisfaction Before and After Deployments Associated with the Global War on Terror," *Psychological Reports*, Vol. 103, 2008, pp. 836–844.

Meis, L. A., R. A. Barry, S. M. Kehle, C. R. Erbes, and M. A. Polusny, "Relationship Adjustment, PTSD Symptoms, and Treatment Utilization Among Coupled National Guard Soldiers Deployed to Iraq," *Journal of Family Psychology*, Vol. 24, No. 5, 2010, pp. 560–567.

Negrusa, S., B. Negrusa, and J. Hosek, "Gone to War: Have Deployments Increased Divorces?" *Journal of Population Economics*, Vol. 27, 2014, pp. 473–496.

Newby, J. H., J. E. McCarroll, R. J. Ursano, Z. Z. Fan, J. Shigemura, and Y. Tucker-Harris, "Positive and Negative Consequences of a Military Deployment," *Military Medicine*, Vol. 170, 2005, pp. 815–819.

O'Leary, K. D., J. Barling, I Arias, A. Rosenbaum, J. Malone, and A. Tyree, "Prevalence and Stability of Physical Agression Between Spouses: A Longitudinal Analysis," *Journal of Consulting and Clinical Psychology*, Vol. 57, 1989, pp. 263–268.

Ramchand, R., T. L. Schell, B. R. Karney, K. C. Osilla, R. M. Burns, and L. B. Caldarone, "Disparate Prevalence Estimates of PTSD Among Service Members Who Served in Iraq and Afghanistan: Possible Explanations," *Journal of Traumatic Stress*, Vol. 23, No. 1, 2010, pp. 59–68.

Rauer, A. J., B. R. Karney, C. W. Garvan, and W. Hou, "Relationship Risks in Context: A Cumulative Risk Approach to Understanding Relationship Satisfaction," *Journal of Marriage and Family*, Vol. 70, No. 5, 2008, pp. 1122–1135.

Renshaw, K. D., and S. B. Campbell, "Combat Veterans' Symptoms of PTSD and Partners' Distress: The Role of Partners' Perceptions of Veterans' Deployment Experiences," *Journal of Family Psychology*, Vol. 25, No. 6, 2011, pp. 953–962.

Riviere, L. A., J. C. Merrill, J. L. Thomas, J. E. Wilk, and P. D. Bliese, "2003–2009 Marital Functioning Trends Among U.S. Enlisted Soldiers Following Combat Deployments," *Military Medicine*, Vol. 177, 2012, pp. 1169–1177.

Robles, T. F., R. B. Slatcher, J. M. Trombello, and M. M. McGinn, "Marital Quality and Health: A Meta-Analytic Review," *Psychological Bulletin*, Vol. 140, No. 1, 2014, pp. 140–187.

Rogge, R. D., and T. N. Bradbury, "Till Violence Does Us Part: The Differing Roles of Communication and Aggression in Predicting Adverse Marital Outcomes," *Journal of Consulting and Clinical Psychology*, Vol. 67, No. 3, 1999, pp. 340–351.

Rosen, L. N., and D. B. Durand, "Coping with the Unique Demands of Military Family Life," in J. A. Martin, L. N. Rosen, and L. R. Sparachino, eds., *The Military Family: A Practice Guide for Human Service Providers*, Westport, Conn.: Praeger, 2000, pp. 55–72.

Rostker, B. D., *I Want You! The Evolution of the All-Volunteer Force*, Santa Monica, Calif.: RAND Corporation, MG-265-RC, 2006. As of November 18, 2015:
http://www.rand.org/pubs/monographs/MG265.html

Rubin, A., and H. Harvie, "A Brief History of Social Work with the Military and Veterans," in A. Rubin, E. L. Weiss, and J. E. Coll, eds., *Handbook of Military Social Work*, Hoboken, N.J.: John Wiley & Sons, 2012, pp. 3–20.

Straus, M. A., S. L. Hamby, S. Boney-McCoy, and D. B. Sugarman, "The Revised Conflict Tactics Scales (CTS2) Development and Preliminary Psychometric Data," *Journal of Family Issues*, Vol. 17, No. 3, 1996, pp. 283–316.

Sturge-Apple, M. L., P. T. Davies, and E. M. Cummings, "Hostility and Withdrawal in Marital Conflict: Effects on Parental Emotional Unavailability and Inconsistent Discipline," *Journal of Family Psychology*, Vol. 20, No. 2, 2006, pp. 227–238.

Taft, C. T., L. E. Watkins, J. Stafford, A. E. Street, and C. M. Monson, "Posttraumatic Stress Disorder and Intimate Relationship Problems: A Meta-Analysis," *Journal of Consulting and Clinical Psychology*, Vol. 79, No. 1, 2011, pp. 22–33.

Tanielian, T., and L. H. Jaycox, eds., *Invisible Wounds of War: Psychological and Cognitive Injuries, Their Consequences, and Services to Assist Recovery*, Santa Monica, Calif.: RAND Corporation, MG-720-CCF, 2008. As of November 10, 2015:
http://www.rand.org/pubs/monographs/MG720.html

Tanielian, T., B. R. Karney, A. Chandra, and S. O. Meadows, *The Deployment Life Study: Methodological Overview and Baseline Sample Description*, Santa Monica, Calif.: RAND Corporation, RR-209-A/OSD, 2014. As of November 10, 2015:
http://www.rand.org/pubs/research_reports/RR209.html

Thompson, E. R., "Development and Validation of an Internationally Reliable Short-Form of the Positive and Negative Affect Schedule (PANAS)," *Journal of Cross-Cultural Psychology*, Vol. 38, No. 2, 2007, pp. 227–242.

Trail, T. E., S. O. Meadows, J. N. Miles, and B. R. Karney, "Patterns of Vulnerabilities and Resources in U.S. Military Families," *Journal of Family Issues*, June 30, 2015.

VanLaningham, J., D. R. Johnson, and P. Amato, "Marital Happiness, Marital Duration, and the U-Shaped Curve: Evidence from a Five-Wave Panel Study," *Social Forces*, Vol. 78, 2001, pp. 1313–1341.

Watson, D., L. A. Clark, and A. Tellegen, "Development and Validation of Brief Measures of Positive and Negative Affect: The PANAS Scales," *Journal of Personality and Social Psychology*, Vol. 54, 1988, pp. 1063–1070.

Whisman, M. A., "The Association Between Depression and Marital Dissatisfaction," in S. R. H. Beach, ed., *Marital and Family Processes in Depression: A Scientific Foundation for Clinical Practice*, Washington, D.C.: APA, 2001, pp. 49–65.

Zoroya, G., "Soldiers' Divorce Rates Up Sharply," *USA Today*, June 8, 2005, p. A1.

CHAPTER FOUR
Family Outcomes

Sarah O. Meadows, Esther M. Friedman, Beth Ann Griffin, Wendy M. Troxel, and Robin L. Beckman

Introduction

As the operational tempo of recent overseas conflicts has gradually declined, military stakeholders, researchers, policymakers, and families are in a position to reflect on the impact of war. Approximately two million service members have been deployed to Iraq or Afghanistan since 2001 (Institute of Medicine [IOM], 2010). Just over half were married and roughly 44 percent had at least one child (IOM, 2010). Some of those families were positively affected by the deployment experience, while others did not fare as well. What predicts which military families are able to do well and which are not? Are the same factors predictive of all family outcomes or are different factors predictive of different outcomes? Do different family members have different experiences? What does it mean for a family to be ready for a deployment? How can we translate those answers into policy? In this chapter, we address these questions by examining how family outcomes change over a deployment cycle, what the impact of deployment is on families that experience deployment compared with those that do not, and what risk and resilience factors, across a number of domains, may ameliorate (or exacerbate) the association between a deployment and family outcomes.

Surprisingly little information exists about changes in family functioning across the deployment cycle (especially during a deployment). Thus, there are significant knowledge gaps in what we know about risk or protective factors. Not only is there scant longitudinal research on family functioning across the deployment cycle, there are several notable limitations in the existing research that preclude definitive conclusions regarding the impact of deployment on family functioning. For instance, many studies collect retrospective information only after a deployment, or compare outcomes during deployment to those after deployment, ignoring the actual period where a service member is away from his or her family (Lester et al., 2010; Sheppard, Malatras, and Israel, 2010). Other studies compare families that experienced a deployment with other military families that did not experience a deployment, but do not ensure that those families are comparable on key demographic and military characteristics prior to deployment (Hoerster et al., 2012; Hoglund and Schwartz, 2014). Finally, few studies are able to compare self-reports from different members of the same families, typically relying only on service members or their spouses, but rarely including the perspectives of both. However, examining multiple perspectives within a military family is critical to obtain a comprehensive understanding of the impact of deployment on all members of the family and to inform policy that supports military families' readiness and resilience.

The analyses described in the chapter address the existing limitations in the literature in three ways. First, this study utilizes longitudinal data that capture changes within families in key constructs across the deployment cycle: predeployment, during deployment, and postdeployment. Second, this is the only study to use a matched comparison approach (i.e., matching families on key characteristics that may influence outcomes over and above a deployment) to compare families that do and do not deploy. Third, this is the only study to concurrently explore service member, spouse, and teen reports on the same family-level outcomes, thus providing the most comprehensive examination to date of the longitudinal impact of deployment on the family.

Background

There is no shortage of studies reporting that deployment has a negative impact on the health and well-being of members of military families, including service members, their spouses, and their children. A recent issue of *The Future of Children* (Cozza and Lerner, 2013) was devoted entirely to this topic. Deployment has been associated with mental and physical health problems among all family members; increased use of mental health services; substance use and abuse; suicide; lower marital satisfaction and marital dissolution; child maltreatment; and emotional, behavioral, and educational problems among children (see Creech, Hadley, and Borsari, 2014; Sheppard, Malatras, and Israel, 2010; Trautmann, Alhusen, and Gross, 2015; Wadsworth and Riggs, 2011).

Because of these findings, the Department of Defense (DoD) has invested millions of dollars in programs and policies that address family readiness, with the assumption that giving families both internal and external resources and other sources of support to prepare to address a deployment before it occurs will allow them to successfully adapt to stress when they experience it (Park, 2011; Saltzman et al., 2011). This focus on prevention is designed to circumvent problems before they occur. In 2012, DoD released Instruction 1342.22 (Under Secretary of Defense for Personnel and Readiness, 2012), which defined family readiness as "the state of being prepared to effectively navigate the challenges of daily living experienced in the unique context of military service." Further, it states that "ready" families are knowledgeable about the potential challenges they may face, equipped with the skills to competently function in the face of such challenges, aware of the supportive resources available to them, and make use of the skills and supports in managing such challenges. Thus, in theory, ready families should also be resilient families. However, this DoD instruction does not precisely describe what specific knowledge, skills, or supportive resources lead to family readiness.

Obviously, not all military families are negatively affected by deployment. And of those families that may be negatively affected in the short term while the deployment is happening, some may show evidence of resilience and, ultimately, recover. It is unclear what factors differentiate those families that ultimately recover after the initial stress of deployment recedes and which families maintain a negative risk trajectory in the postdeployment period. Family resilience models and theory can help frame our understanding of how and why some families fare well during this potentially difficult period, and others do not.

Family Resilience Models and Theory

Hill's (1949, 1958) ABC-X model of family stress, as mentioned briefly in Chapter Three, can be used to contextualize how families approach a deployment. In fact, Hill's original model was the product of his work with Army families. The goal of the model is to describe how families adapt and survive over a life course. Each letter in the model represents a different construct: A is the event, B represents family resources, C is the family's interpretation of the event, and X is the family's response, which may or may not result in a crisis (see Figure 4.1). If the response to the event is negative and results in a crisis, then a period of reorganization follows. The result of the reorganizations may be a stronger family unit—or, conversely, a weaker family unit.

According to the model, families experience "events" (A; deployment), which may be normative and developmental, exceptional and unexpected, or acute or chronic. When faced with such an event, the family marshals existing resources (B) to address those events and, in the process, makes decisions about how stressful the event is on some continuum (C). The result is a "response" (X). Depending on how the family views the event and what resources are used, there may be a period of lower functioning or "reorganization." Some families may return to pre-event levels of functioning, while others may enter the reorganization phase with lower functioning. This is especially likely when other stressors accumulate at the same time. Thus, the ABC-X model allows for some families to be strengthened by the fact that they survived a negative event (i.e., a crisis), which may help them face the next stressor more successfully. When the next event occurs, it may be viewed as less stressful, the period of reorganization may be shorter, or the decline in function may be less severe.

There are a number of theories of family resilience in the literature, but most build on Hill's original model (see Meadows et al., 2015, for a review of some of these models), and all recognize that there are individual or family-level differences in the degree to which a given stressor affects different families. These models all have a number of common themes. First, all are prevention-oriented and focus on family factors and processes that may prevent negative outcomes after experiencing stress. Second, all refer to what can be called family resilience factors—resources that families use to cope with stress. Meadows and colleagues (2015) reviewed the literature and identify the most commonly studied resilience factors, grouped into five domains:

1. family belief system
2. family organizational patterns
3. family support system
4. family communication/problem-solving
5. physical and psychological health of individual family members.

Figure 4.1
ABC-X Model of Family Stress

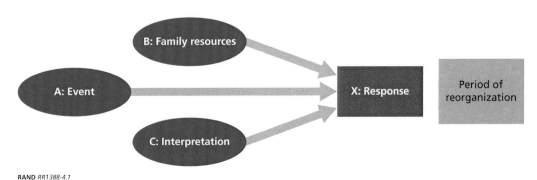

Specific factors within each of these domains are primary candidates for explaining family functioning differences across the deployment cycle.

Military Family Risk and Resilience Factors

As noted, the ABC-X model and derivative theories of family resilience all suggest that certain family resources are key to being a ready and resilient family in the face of stress. For the most part, these family factors can be thought of as protective, although some may actually put families at higher risk for negative outcomes. These risk factors may signal that a family has fewer available resources with which to address future stress, making them more vulnerable to negative outcomes (Trail et al., 2015).

For military families in particular, *participation in deployment preparation activities*, such as making financial preparations and talking to a spouse and children about an upcoming deployment, may provide a signal of who is more (or less) likely to navigate a deployment successfully (Troxel et al., forthcoming). Actual, active, problem-focused preparation, such as the activities mentioned above, may be more important than perceived readiness (Dimiceli, Steinhardt, and Smith, 2010). These types of activities, if done in the predeployment period, may help protect families during and after a deployment.

Existing studies also suggest that *frequency of communication during deployment* can help families feel more connected during deployment and is associated with positive mental, emotional, and behavioral health and relationship outcomes among service members, spouses, and children (Carter et al., 2011; Cigrang et al., 2014). However, the opposite has also been found—increased communication during deployment has also been associated with more emotional and behavioral problems among children (Houston et al., 2013), as well as higher levels of self-reported stress among adolescents (Wong and Gerras, 2010). In addition, increased communication with home, especially when there are problems there, may put service members at risk if their focus is shifted elsewhere (Durham, 2010). When expectations about communication, including frequency and mode (e.g., phone, email, video), are not met, both service members and family members can experience frustration, leading to further problems within the family unit (Greene et al., 2010). Further, how families communicate during a deployment also may have an impact on how well families reintegrate after deployment; the same communication style may be adaptive during deployment, but maladaptive during reintegration (Bowling and Sherman, 2004; Knobloch and Wilson, 2014). It should be noted that much of the literature on communication during deployment is cross-sectional, and cannot control for family's baseline functioning. Therefore, such evidence cannot rule out the possibility that families that have more problems already communicate more frequently.

A number of *deployment characteristics* may influence the degree to which a family is able to adapt to a deployment, primarily because they are associated with service member mental health and well-being. For example, longer deployments and those in which the service member has direct exposure to combat or noncombat traumatic events (e.g., seeing serious injuries, engaging in hand-to-hand combat, discharging a weapon) are associated with increased mental health problems, including posttraumatic stress disorder (PTSD), anxiety, and depression (Adler et al., 2005; Tanielian and Jaycox, 2008). These issues can reverberate throughout a family upon the service member's return, resulting in lower overall family functioning, especially between spouses (Allen et al., 2010; also see Chapter Three in this report). A service member's perception of how difficult or stressful his or her deployment was, as well as the perceived risk she or he faced during the deployment, can affect mental health and well-being (Lane et al., 2012; Solomon, 1993), potentially leading to problems during family reintegration.

We expect that the family risk and resilience factors reviewed here will help explain differences in family outcomes across military families that experience a deployment. Using family resilience models and theory as a guide, and focusing on key family risk and resilience factors identified in the existing literature on military families, this chapter addresses three main research questions (reviewed in the next section). In terms of the ABC-X model, *deployment* is the primary event (A), family resources include *deployment preparation activities* and *communication during deployment* (B), perception is a self-reported assessment of *deployment stress* (C), and the outcomes we focus on in this chapter are related to three components of family well-being—*the family environment, parenting satisfaction*, and *financial distress* (X). Notice that the ABC-X model implicitly depicts adaptation (or maladaptation) to stress as a process that occurs over time. For military families, this time element corresponds to the deployment cycle: predeployment, during deployment, and postdeployment.

Family Outcomes

As noted above, we have selected three outcomes to represent how well families are functioning—the family environment, parenting satisfaction, and financial distress. We selected these three outcomes for a number of reasons. First, each assesses a different aspect of family functioning. The family environment describes the relative levels of conflict and cohesion in the family. Parenting satisfaction reflects the ability of parents to manage the demands of parenting with the resources, both personal and social, available to them, and thus can be viewed as an indicator of how much satisfaction adults in the family derive from their parental roles. In some ways, parenting satisfaction can be thought of as the opposite of parenting stress. Finally, financial distress provides an indication of how individuals within a family perceive their family's financial health and can be seen as an indicator of underlying strain. Together, these measures of a family's affective health, role strain, and financial health provide a more well-rounded picture of family functioning than using any single measure alone (see Pritchett et al., 2011).

Second, these three measures represent some of the key elements of the psychological and financial capital that are associated with healthy child development (see Zubrick et al., 2000). Given that the task of raising children ultimately falls on families, we want to know if deployment has an impact on the resources that families can provide to children. If deployment does affect the availability of these resources, then we also want to know how to protect families from experiencing negative outcomes following a deployment.

And third, our survey instruments used the same items for each of the three outcomes for both service members and spouses. So, for example, while the experience of being a parent while deployed may be different for the service member who is not collocated with his or her child or children, we are able to compare service members and spouses using the exact same items. We note, however, that we do not include teen reports in this chapter; those are included in Chapter Six. As such, we rely on the adult members of families to provide information on family functioning.

Research Questions

- **Research Question (RQ) 1:** Do family outcomes of service members and their spouses, measured as family environment, parenting satisfaction, and financial distress, change over the course of a typical deployment cycle: predeployment, during deployment, and postdeployment?

- **RQ1a:** Is the trajectory significantly different from a flat line (i.e., zero slope or no change) over the deployment cycle?
  - ◦ **Hypothesis:** Trajectories will not be flat across the deployment cycle, as we expect changes in family outcomes to occur during the study deployment itself. Guided by the ABC-X model, as well as existing research, deployments should take a negative toll on family relationships, especially if the family's resources are not adequate enough to help the family adapt. We expect to see a decline in family and parenting outcomes; conversely, we expect that financial stress will likely be reduced during this period due to the greater income that comes with a deployment. The change in family functioning during deployment will shift the trajectory from a flat (zero slope) line across the entire deployment cycle, which is what this research question tests; it cannot tell us about the direction of the change however.
- **RQ1b:** Is the trajectory significantly different from a straight line, or constant time trend, over the deployment cycle?
  - ◦ **Hypothesis:** For the same reasons to those cited in hypothesis RQ1a, trajectories will not be constant across the deployment cycle; instead, we expect there to be periods of constant change within a given stage (predeployment, during deployment, and postdeployment) that vary between periods (e.g., a trajectory may decline immediately prior to a deployment and then improve/recover during the postdeployment period).
- **RQ1c:** Do service members and spouses have similar or divergent trajectories over a deployment?
  - ◦ **Hypothesis:** Trajectories between service members and spouses will differ significantly across the deployment cycle, especially during the study deployment, given their different family experiences during this time period. Service members are physically apart from the family while spouses take on a greater share of family responsibilities.
- **RQ2:** How does deployment affect postdeployment family outcomes? By comparing outcomes between families where a service member experienced a study deployment and matched families where the service member did not deploy during the study, we can estimate what a deployed service member or his or her spouse would be like had the service member not deployed.
  - **Hypothesis:** Based on family resilience theory, we expect most families to show limited to no impact on postdeployment family outcomes over the long term (i.e., to demonstrate resilience).
- **RQ3:** What risk and resilience factors predict differences in postdeployment family outcomes among deployed families? Risk and resilience factors fall into four categories: predeployment factors (i.e., preparation activities); during deployment factors (i.e., frequency and satisfaction with frequency of communication); deployment factors as experienced by the service member (i.e., combat exposure, duration, and military stress); and leaving the military during the study period.
  - **Hypothesis:** We expect that greater preparation activities in the predeployment phase and that more-frequent and better-quality communication during deployment would serve as protective factors in the postdeployment period (i.e., better outcomes). In con-

trast, we expect that some factors (e.g., negative experiences during the study deployment and mental health problems) will act as risk factors and be associated with worse family outcomes during the postdeployment period.

Method

Sample

Data for this chapter include all nine assessment waves of the Deployment Life Study. As described previously, the Deployment Life Study is a longitudinal survey of approximately 2,700 deployable, married, military families, including service members, their spouses, and (in some cases) a teen age 11 or older living in the household. (See Tanielian et al., 2014, for additional details.)[1] In total, 1,519 service members and 1,646 spouses compose the sample used in this chapter, which is restricted to couples with at least one child younger than age 18 and who remained married throughout the survey. Analysis of teens on the family environment measure is reported in Chapter Six.

Measures
Dependent Variables

The analysis focuses on three primary outcomes capturing different domains of family life: family environment, parenting satisfaction, and financial distress. *Quality of the family environment* is measured with the Family Environment Scale (FES) (Moos and Moos, 1994). At every assessment, service members and spouses receive a six-item measure of family environment that assesses how the family functions as a unit. These items were selected from the cohesion and conflict subscales of the FES and ask respondents to rate how well statements describe their families:

1. There is a feeling of togetherness in our family.
2. Family members often put each other down (reverse coded).
3. Family members really help and support one another.
4. We fight a lot in our family (reverse coded).
5. We really get along well with each other.
6. Family members sometimes get so angry they throw things (reverse coded).

The six items are averaged to create a single scale score for each respondent. Higher scores indicate a more-positive family environment (i.e., greater cohesion and lower conflict).

At every assessment, service members and spouses received a six-item measure of *satisfaction with parenting*. Each item asks the respondent to rate his or her level of agreement with statements about parenting:

1. Being a parent is harder than I thought it would be (reverse coded).
2. Being a parent is a source of joy and satisfaction in my life.
3. I feel trapped by my responsibilities as a parent (reverse coded).
4. I find that taking care of my child(ren) is much more work than pleasure (reverse coded).

---

[1] Recall that the Navy sample only has seven total waves of data. See Chapter Two for more details on the study design and sample.

This measure is adapted from a nine-item measure of parental aggravation (or stress) developed for the Child Development Supplement of the Panel Study of Income Dynamic (PSID) (Abidin, 1995; see also Hofferth et al., 1997; PSID, undated). The six items are averaged to create a single scale score for each respondent. Higher scores indicate greater satisfaction.

Service members and spouses are asked four items adapted from Gutman and Eccles's (1999) *financial distress* scale at baseline and again at every assessment. These items assess whether the family could make ends meet, whether there has been enough money to pay bills, whether there was any money left over at the end of the month, and the level of worry caused by the family's financial situation. The four items are averaged to create a single scale score for each respondent. Higher scores indicate more financial distress.

Table 4.1 shows the means and standard errors (SEs) for each outcome at baseline, as well as by whether the family experienced a study deployment. All means are weighted and baseline data are imputed, as detailed in Chapter Two. At baseline, service members and spouses report positive family environments, high levels of satisfaction with parenting, and moderate levels of financial distress. The only significant differences at baseline occur for financial distress, where those families that will eventually experience a study deployment report significantly higher financial distress than families that will not (service members: 1.80 versus 2.02, $p=0.01$; spouses: 1.90 versus 2.10, $p=0.00$).

Table 4.2 shows the correlations across outcomes for service members and spouses. The diagonal shows the correlation between service member and spouse reports of each of the three outcomes examined in this chapter. The FES is modestly, positively correlated at 0.47, as is the financial distress scale (0.61); however, the parenting satisfaction scale is much less positively correlated across partners at 0.18. We will explore why this might be the case. The areas above and below the diagonals show the correlations among the outcomes for service members and spouses, respectively. For both service members and spouses, the FES and parenting satisfaction scale are positively correlated such that higher scores on one are associated with high scores on the other. Financial distress, however, is negatively associated with the family environment and parenting satisfaction such that service members and spouses who report higher family financial distress also report lower-quality family environments and lower satisfaction with parenting.

Covariates

Our models include a number of covariates that may be associated with the family outcomes already described (Table. 4.3). The bulk of these covariates related to individual service member and spouse demographic and military characteristics. For example, we include respondent age, gender, minority status, whether the household includes a young child (i.e., having a child younger than age six in the household), and length of marriage. Additionally, to capture the socioeconomic status of spouses, models include information on spouse educational attainment and employment status.

For service members and spouses, we also include whether the service member (or in the case of spouses, the corresponding service member) had any prior deployment (defined as any deployment of 30 days or more outside the continental United States [OCONUS]), the number of prior combat deployments experienced by the service member (including all deployments as part of Operation Iraqi Freedom/Operation Enduring Freedom/Operation New Dawn [OIF/OEF/OND]), the service member's branch of service (i.e., Army, Air Force, Navy, Marine Corps), the service member's reserve component (including the National Guard

Table 4.1
Means and Standard Errors of Family Outcomes at Baseline

	Overall Sample		Service Members			Spouses		
	Service Members (n=1,519)	Spouses (n=1,646)	Study Deployment (n=647)	No Study Deployment (n=872)	p-value	Study Deployment (n=683)	No Study Deployment (n=963)	p-value
FES[a]	2.75 (0.03)	2.74 (0.04)	2.81 (0.01)	2.73 (0.04)	0.10	2.81 (0.02)	2.73 (0.05)	0.10
Satisfaction with Parenting[b]	3.34 (0.04)	3.20 (0.02)	3.36 (0.02)	3.34 (0.05)	0.77	3.23 (0.02)	3.20 (0.03)	0.32
Financial Distress Scale[c]	1.98 (0.05)	2.06 (0.04)	1.80 (0.05)	2.02 (0.06)	**0.01**	1.90 (0.03)	2.10 (0.05)	**0.00**

NOTES: SEs are in parentheses. Results are weighted. Missing data are imputed. Bold indicates a statistically significant difference between the study deployment and no study deployment groups based on a weighted t-test.

[a] Higher scores=more positive environment. Range: 1–3.

[b] Higher scores=more satisfaction. Range: 1–4.

[c] Higher scores=more distress. Range: 1–4.

Table 4.2
Correlation Between Family Outcomes At Baseline: Service Members and Spouses

	Family Environment Scale[a]	Parenting Satisfaction[b]	Financial Distress[c]
Family Environment Scale[a]	0.47	0.04	−0.15
Parenting Satisfaction[b]	0.36	0.18	−0.12
Financial Distress[c]	−0.29	−0.16	0.61

NOTES: Service Member N=1,519; Spouse N=1,646. Blue shading shows correlations among the outcomes among only service members. Green shading shows correlations among the outcomes among only spouses.
All correlations are significantly different from 0 at p<0.001 except parenting satisfaction and financial distress among service members.

[a] Higher scores=more positive environment. Range: 1–3.

[b] Higher scores=more satisfaction. Range: 1–4.

[c] Higher scores=more distress. Range: 1–4.

and Air Guard) status, and the service member's pay grade (capturing both enlisted and officer status, as well as rank).

In addition, we include two historical measures of deployment experiences and combat trauma exposure that occurred prior to the baseline survey. The first is an 11-item checklist of possible traumatic experiences during deployment and has been used in prior work by Tanielian and Jaycox (2008).[2] It includes items such as, "During any prior deployment, did you witness an accident that resulted in serious injury or death?" Endorsed items are summed to create an index score. The second is a modified version of the Hoge et al. (2004) Combat Experiences Scale (CES), which measures combat trauma exposure. The original CES contains 18 items that assess the occurrence of different potentially traumatic events in combat (e.g., being attached or ambushed, participating in demining operations). Three items were eliminated to minimize the sensitivity of the questions and the time it takes to complete the measure (see Tanielian and Jaycox, 2008). Endorsed items are summed to create an index score.

Table 4.3 presents means, percentages, and SEs for all the covariates at baseline for the overall sample of service members and spouses (i.e., the deployed and nondeployed sample combined), as well as the sample used in the analyses contained in this chapter. Means are reported separately for service members and spouses who do and do not experience a study deployment. Both service members and spouses are in their early to mid-30s; those who eventually experience a study deployment are younger than those who do not (service member: 32.94 versus 35.74, p=0.00; spouse: 32.59 versus 35.52, p=0.00). Correspondingly, service members and spouses who experience a study deployment have been married for fewer years than those who do not (service member: 8.5 years versus 10.1 years, p=0.02; spouse: 8.8 years versus 10.3 years, p=0.01). The vast majority of service members are male (approximately 90 percent), and spouses are female. Roughly one-third of service members and spouses are of minority racial/ethnicity (i.e., nonwhite) and although all service members and spouses in the sample have children, about two-thirds have a child younger than age six in the household.

Although spouses in the deployed and nondeployed groups did not differ significantly in the distribution of their educational attainment at baseline, with more than three-quarters having at least some college experience, there was a significant difference in the distribution of

---

[2] This measure is referred to as "deployment trauma" and not "combat trauma" because it does not differentiate trauma experienced while in an engagement with an enemy.

Table 4.3
Means, Percentages, and Standard Errors of Study Variables at Baseline

	Overall Sample		Service Members			Spouses		
	Service Members (n=1,519)	Spouses (n=1,646)	Study Deployment (n=647)	No Study Deployment (n=872)	p-value	Study Deployment (n=683)	No Study Deployment (n=963)	p-value
Age[a]	35.11 (0.44)	34.87 (0.51)	32.94 (0.44)	35.73 (0.54)	0.00	32.59 (0.44)	35.52 (0.60)	0.00
Length of Marriage[b]	116.78 (4.95)	119.18 (4.84)	102.59 (4.21)	120.88 (6.23)	0.02	105.06 (4.29)	128.18 (5.95)	0.01
Number of Prior Combat Deployments[c]	1.59 (0.10)	1.56 (0.10)	2.11 (0.12)	1.44 (0.11)	0.00	2.04 (0.09)	1.42 (0.11)	0.00
Deployment Trauma[d]	1.86 (0.16)	1.96 (0.13)	2.24 (0.18)	1.71 (0.20)	0.05	2.36 (0.20)	1.80 (0.16)	0.03
Combat Experiences Scale[e]	4.27 (0.26)	3.98 (0.26)	4.90 (0.43)	4.08 (0.30)	0.12	4.74 (0.37)	3.77 (0.31)	0.04
Male	89.77% (1.74)	9.51% (1.71)	93.99% (1.47)	88.55% (2.22)	0.04	6.66% (1.74)	10.32% (2.15)	0.19
Minority Race/Ethnicity	32.19% (2.99)	29.04% (2.66)	29.89% (3.02)	32.85% (3.77)	0.54	28.44% (3.12)	29.21% (3.30)	0.87
Children Younger Than Age 6 in Household	65.10% (3.14)	60.53% (3.65)	70.75% (2.81)	63.47% (4.00)	0.14	67.72% (2.98)	58.49% (4.54)	0.07
Any Prior Deployment[f]	77.25% (4.18)	76.44% (4.35)	92.39% (1.49)	72.90% (5.15)	0.00	92.85% (1.48)	71.78% (5.29)	0.00
Reserve Component	33.05% (3.51)	35.36% (3.95)	15.35% (2.27)	38.14% (4.41)	0.00	17.14% (2.64)	40.53% (4.74)	0.00
Branch Of Service								
Army	48.97% (3.59)	47.60% (3.35)	45.46% (0.98)	49.98% (4.52)	0.49	45.14% (3.19)	48.30% (4.24)	0.69
Air Force	19.16% (1.73)	19.21% (1.67)	21.07% (0.57)	18.61% (2.09)		22.90% (2.37)	18.17% (1.98)	
Navy	24.09% (4.32)	24.72% (4.42)	21.89% (0.57)	24.72% (5.46)		22.21% (3.02)	25.43% (5.57)	
Marine Corps	7.78% (1.84)	8.46% (1.67)	11.58% (1.24)	6.69% (1.82)		9.76% (3.85)	8.10% (1.83)	
Pay Grade								
E1 to E3	4.36% (1.20)	4.19% (1.10)	3.83% (1.45)	4.51% (1.49)	0.12	3.75% (1.71)	4.31% (1.32)	0.63
E4 to E9	73.07% (2.76)	73.41% (2.63)	70.84% (3.44)	73.71% (3.39)		73.64% (2.70)	73.34% (3.29)	
O1 to O3	6.75% (1.14)	6.77% (1.08)	8.40% (1.30)	6.28% (1.41)		8.55% (1.28)	6.27% (1.33)	
O4 +	12.76% (2.12)	13.08% (2.12)	10.62% (1.80)	13.37% (2.68)		10.70% (1.75)	13.76% (2.69)	
Warrant Officer	3.06% (0.84)	2.55% (0.51)	6.30% (2.97)	2.13% (0.60)		3.36% (0.88)	2.32% (0.60)	

Table 4.3—Continued

	Overall Sample		Service Members			Spouses		
	Service Members (n=1,519)	Spouses (n=1,646)	Study Deployment (n=647)	No Study Deployment (n=872)	p-value	Study Deployment (n=683)	No Study Deployment (n=963)	p-value
Spouse Education								
Less Than High School	0.87% (0.28)	1.16% (0.32)	0.76% (0.33)	0.90% (0.35)		0.75% (0.33)	1.27% (0.40)	
High School	18.18% (2.89)	17.11% (2.12)	19.83% (2.54)	17.70% (3.66)		20.45% (2.38)	16.17% (2.63)	
Some College	29.81% (3.91)	25.78% (2.67)	31.21% (4.39)	29.41% (4.89)		26.17% (2.92)	25.67% (3.32)	
Associate/Vocational/Technical Degree	18.33% (2.48)	18.46% (2.34)	16.21% (2.00)	18.94% (3.15)		17.70% (3.14)	18.67% (2.88)	
Bachelor's Degree	26.61% (2.70)	26.05% (2.57)	24.00% (2.62)	27.37% (3.42)		26.28% (2.80)	25.98% (3.20)	
Graduate Degree	6.20% (0.84)	11.44% (4.13)	7.99% (1.62)	5.69% (0.95)		8.65% (2.07)	12.24% (5.24)	
Spouse Employment Status								
Military Spouse	4.05% (0.86)	3.00% (0.58)	4.41% (1.22)	3.95% (1.05)	0.00	3.29% (0.92)	2.92% (0.70)	0.01
Employed (Full or Part Time)	39.98% (3.77)	41.47% (3.70)	27.02% (2.79)	43.71% (4.65)		29.82% (2.96)	44.77% (4.52)	
Homemaker	41.89% (3.52)	40.29% (3.17)	49.34% (3.80)	39.74% (4.36)		45.39% (3.32)	38.84% (3.92)	
Student	5.61% (0.97)	5.54% (0.85)	7.36% (1.36)	5.10% (1.18)		7.72% (1.39)	4.92% (1.00)	
Unemployed	8.48% (1.25)	9.70% (1.47)	11.87% (1.93)	7.50% (1.49)		13.78% (3.21)	8.55% (1.61)	

NOTES: SEs are in parentheses. Results are weighted. Missing data are imputed. Bold indicates a statistically significant difference between the study deployment and no study deployment groups.

[a] Service members and spouse range: 21–56.

[b] In months. Service member range: 0–432; spouse range: 3–528.

[c] Includes deployments as part of OIF, OEF, and OND. Service member range: 0–5.

[d] See Tanielian and Jaycox (2008, p. 91). These items are taken from the first follow-up survey (Wave 2). Service member range: 0–11.

[e] See Hoge et al. (2004). Service member range: 0–15.

[f] Includes all OCONUS deployments of 30 days or more.

employment status. In the deployed sample, a larger percentage of spouses report being home-makers (45 percent versus 39 percent, $p=0.00$); in the nondeployed sample, a larger percentage of spouses report being employed part or full time (45 percent versus 30 percent, $p=0.01$).

The majority of service members in the sample are in the active component, with roughly one-third in the reserve and guard. When we look across those who do and do not experience a study deployment, those with a study deployment had significantly fewer reserve and guard statuses than those without (15 percent versus 38 percent, $p=0.00$). The largest portion of service members comes from the Army (45 percent), followed by the Air Force and Navy (both 21 percent), and the Marine Corps (12 percent). Almost three-quarters of the sample of service members is in the midlevel to senior enlisted category (E4 to E9), followed by midlevel to senior officers (O4 and above), junior officers (O1 to O3), warrant officers, and junior enlisted (E1 to E3). No differences were found between the distributions of service members' branches and pay grades between those who experience a study deployment and those who do not.

At the time of the baseline survey, far more than two-thirds of service members had experienced at least one OCONUS deployment of at least 30 days, with an average of slightly more than one combat deployment. Service members who experienced a study deployment were more likely to have experienced prior deployments at baseline, with more than 90 percent of them experiencing any prior OCONUS deployment (versus 73 percent for those who do not experience a study deployment, $p=0.00$) and an average of 2.11 combat deployments (versus 1.44 for those who do not experience a study deployment, $p=0.00$).

Finally, given the prior experience with deployment in the sample, it is not surprising that service members also have experience with combat, and in some cases, related trauma. Average scores on the deployment trauma scale are roughly two out of 11, and 4 to 5 on the CES. Again, we see statistically significant differences across service members who do and do not have a study deployment, with higher deployment trauma exposure means among those who do have a study deployment (2.24 versus 1.71, $p=0.05$). This was not the case for the CES, however (4.90 versus 4.08, $p=0.12$). These descriptive results show that there are differences in how families that experience deployment compare with those that do not on baseline characteristics. Because service members and spouses who experience a study deployment differ in numerous ways from those who do not, we employ propensity score methods to match deploying service members (and their families) with those who do not deploy in the following results, which examine the impact of deployment on postdeployment outcomes.

Risk and Resilience Factors

As described in the Background section, we also hypothesized that a number of risk and resilience factors might mitigate (or exacerbate) how well families do after deployment. These factors are conceptualized broadly and include individual characteristics, characteristics of the deployment itself, and actions that families may take before and during a deployment. Specifically, we investigate deployment preparation activities during the predeployment phase; frequency and satisfaction with frequency of communication during the deployment; and combat exposure, duration, and military stress as they relate to the service member's deployment experience (Table 4.4). We also include an indicator for whether the service member leaves the military during the course of the study.

Deployment preparation activities is a count of activities that service members and spouses report engaging in prior to a deployment (see Troxel et al., forthcoming). The items come from the family, marital, and child readiness domains in the Deployment Risk and Resilience

Inventory (King et al., 2006), and are also used in the Defense Manpower Data Center's Status of Forces Survey. Those activities include: ensuring the family has money for basic necessities (e.g., rent, food, living expenses) to use during the deployment; developing an emergency financial plan; getting or increasing life insurance policies; talking to a spouse about how an upcoming deployment may affect the relationship; talking to a professional (e.g., counselor) about how the upcoming deployment may affect the relationship; talking to child(ren) about the upcoming deployment; connecting child(ren) with a deployment support group (e.g., guard youth programs, Operation Purple Camp); and facilitating a connection between child(ren) and other military children in the neighborhood. Spouses are also asked four items about legal preparedness, including: establishing a power of attorney (POA) to act on the service member's behalf, establishing a POA for someone else to act on the service member's behalf, signing an up-to-date will for the service member; and signing an up-to-date will for themselves. We use the count of activities reported in the assessment closest to the beginning of the study deployment. On average, service members engaged in almost five of the nine possible deployment preparation activities, while spouses engaged in almost six of the 13 possible activities.

Frequency of communication during the deployment is assessed via a single item that asks respondents how frequently they communicate with the other members of the family (either those who are at home or the member who deployed). Responses range from "never" (0) to "every day" (7); these responses were recoded into a four-category variable that included communication every day, at least once a week, at least once a month, and less than once a month (including never). Again, we use the mean score during the study deployment. On average, both service members and spouses report communicating with each other once per week. *Sat-*

Table 4.4
Means, Percentages, and Standard Errors of Risk and Resilience Factors
(Study Deployment Sample Only)

	Service Members (n=647)	Spouses (n=683)
Deployment Preparation Activities[a]	4.73 (0.14)	5.55 (0.17)
Frequency of Communication During Study Deployment[b]	2.39 (0.05)	2.37 (0.04)
Satisfaction with Frequency of Communication During Study Deployment[c]	3.43 (0.06)	3.29 (0.07)
Trauma Exposure During Study Deployment (%)		
Physical	23.22 (2.84)	23.10 (3.43)
Psychological	33.10 (2.86)	36.20 (3.87)
Combat	7.00 (1.38)	6.91 (1.54)
Length of Study Deployment[d]	8.00 (0.13)	8.00 (0.14)
Self-Rated Military Stress During Deployment[e]	3.66 (0.12)	3.64 (0.14)
Separation from the Military[f]	6.94 (1.64)	7.54 (2.41)

NOTE: SEs are in parentheses.

[a] Service member range: 0–9; spouse range: 0–13.

[b] Service member and spouse range: 0 (less than once a month) to 4 (every day).

[c] Service member and spouse range: 1 to 4.

[d] In months.

[e] Service member only; range 0–7.

[f] Includes retirement as well as separation (involuntary and voluntary).

isfaction with frequency of communication is assessed via a single item that asks respondents to rate their satisfaction with the frequency of communication with the service member or family, depending on the respondent, during the study deployment. Responses ranged from "very unsatisfied" (1) to "very satisfied" (4). We use the mean score during the study deployment. Service members and spouses report that they fall between being somewhat and very satisfied, on average, with the amount of communication they had with each other during the study deployment (service member=3.5; spouse=3.3).

We examine three conditions of the deployment itself from only the service member's perspective. First, to assess *trauma exposure* during the study deployment, we use three dichotomous variables to indicate whether the service member experienced any physical trauma (e.g., receiving an injury requiring hospitalization), psychological trauma (e.g., having a friend who was seriously wounded or killed), or combat trauma (e.g., engaging in hand-to-hand combat, firing on the enemy) during the deployment (see Chapter Two of this report for more details). These measures were created from 11 items taken from Tanielian and Jaycox (2008, p. 91) and are cumulative across the study deployment. Thus, if a service member indicates "yes" to any items in the three categories she or he receives a score of "1". During study deployments, 23 percent of the service members in the cohort for this chapter experienced physical trauma, 33 percent experienced psychological trauma, and 7 percent experienced combat trauma. Second, we measure the *length of the study deployment* in months. The average study deployment for service members in the cohort for this chapter was 8.0 months. And third, we assess the service members' *self-reported military stress* during the deployment. Six items, derived from the subscale on military tasks and demands in Zohar et al.'s (2004) Military Life Scale ask service members if they experienced a range of stressful experiences during their deployment (e.g., guard duty at night, work under pressure, physically demanding tasks). An additional item asks if the service member had been asked to do tasks that she or he did not feel well-trained to do. These items are summed and we use the mean score reported during the study deployment. The mean number of military stressors experienced by service members was just under four out of seven.

Finally, we examine whether a service member *separates from the military*, through either retirement or separation (voluntary or involuntary) at some point during the study. Service members are coded as retired/separated if they report leaving at any point between Wave 2 and Wave 9 of the study: 7 percent of service members reported leaving the military, 8 percent of spouses reported that their service member spouse left the military. (Note: Percentages are not of matched pairs; the service members responding are not necessarily married to the spouses in the same response group.)

Analysis Plan

The analysis plan is described in detail in Chapter Two so we only briefly outline it here. To address RQ1 (how family outcomes, measured as family environment, parenting satisfaction, and financial distress, change over the course of a typical deployment cycle), we use descriptive trajectories that depict the three outcomes of interest before, during, and after a study deployment. Predicted means are plotted in eight-month durations (predeployment, during deployment, and postdeployment) as this represents the "average" length of these periods in our data. Trajectories are plotted for service members and spouses separately, although they were estimated from joint random effects models fit to both the service member and spouse data with random effects for both the household and the respondent type. All models control for respondent gender, age, racial/ethnic minority status, length of marriage, spouse education, spouse employment status, having children younger than age six in the household, rank and officer/enlisted status, number of prior combat deployments, years of service, branch and component of service, and the Hoge CES at baseline. Survey mode (phone or web) is included as a time-varying covariate at each wave. Wald tests are used to determine the outcome of hypothesis tests. Results are presented graphically.

To address RQ2 (how deployment affects postdeployment family outcomes), we use doubly robust propensity score–matching models. These models match service members and spouses who experienced a study deployment to respondents who did not experience a study deployment across a number of demographic and military characteristics (see Appendix 4A), and are intended to address the causal impact of deployment on family outcomes. Predicted mean differences in outcomes are compared across the two groups, controlling for respondent gender, age, racial/ethnic minority status, length of marriage, spouse education, spouse employment status, having children younger than age six in the household, rank and officer/enlisted status, number of prior combat deployments, years of service, branch and component of service, the Hoge CES, survey mode at follow-up (phone or web), and the outcome in question at baseline (making the models "doubly robust"). Here, random effects models were fit separately to the service member and spouse data, which appropriately adjusted for repeated measures within each respondent using a random effect at the respondent level. These predicted means are reported later in this chapter. As noted in Chapter Two, all outcomes arise from the final three postdeployment assessments for each respondent, assuming the service member was not deployed at the time.

To address RQ3 (what risk and resilience factors predict differences in postdeployment family outcomes among deployed families), we used random effects regression models, adjusted for repeated measures within each respondent (i.e., allowing for a random effect for each respondent), to estimate the association between the risk and resilience factors already noted and outcomes among only those service members and spouses who have experienced a study deployment. We focus on factors that occur before deployment (i.e., deployment preparation activities) or during deployment (i.e., characteristics of the deployment itself, frequency and satisfaction with frequency of communication, and service member military stress). All outcomes come from the final three postdeployment assessments of the study for each respondent (thus necessitating a control for repeated measures). Each risk and resilience factor was added to the multivariate models, one at a time, in separate models. Models controlled for respondent gender, age, racial/ethnic minority status, length of marriage, spouse education, spouse employment status, having children younger than age six in the household, rank and officer/enlisted status, number of prior combat deployments, years of service, branch and component of service, the Hoge CES, and the baseline measure of the key outcome being modeled.

All analyses presented in this chapter use the poststratification weights described in Chapter Two.

Results

Research Question 1: Trajectories over the Deployment Cycle

RQ1 asks how family functioning changes over the deployment cycle. Figures 4.2, 4.3, and 4.4 present the results of the trajectory analysis for service members and spouses for the three family outcomes examined in this chapter: the family environment, parenting satisfaction, and financial distress. For each figure, we also test three global hypotheses: (1) whether the family outcome in question follows a flat line (i.e., no slope or trajectory) over the deployment cycle (RQ1a), (2) whether the trajectory is a constant line over the deployment cycle (RQ1b), and (3) whether the trajectories of different families are parallel to one another over the deployment cycle (RQ1c).

Each figure depicts trajectories of the outcome in question for an eight-month period immediately prior to a deployment, eight months during a deployment, and eight months after redeployment (or postdeployment) on the y-axis. As noted in Chapter Two, these are the average periods our sample of deployed families spent in each phase of deployment. On the x-axis, each outcome is centered on the group mean (i.e., service member or spouse), with one standard deviation above and below the mean shown in each.

Figure 4.2 shows the trajectory for the FES for service members and spouses. The blue lines represent the trajectories for service members and the green lines represent the trajectories for spouses. Based on statistical tests for service members, we can reject the null hypothesis that the trajectory is a flat line, with zero slope (χ^2, 8 df=25.57, p=0.001). As depicted by the blue line in the figure, service members rate the family environment better during the deployment phase than during either the pre- or postdeployment periods with reports on the family environment appearing to return to levels near where they were before the deployment once the service member returns. In contrast, for spouses, we cannot reject the null of a flat line (χ^2, 8 df=10.86, p=0.21). Thus, we have no evidence that spouses rate the family environment differently across the deployment cycle.

Figure 4.2
Family Environment Scale over the Deployment Cycle, Service Members and Spouses

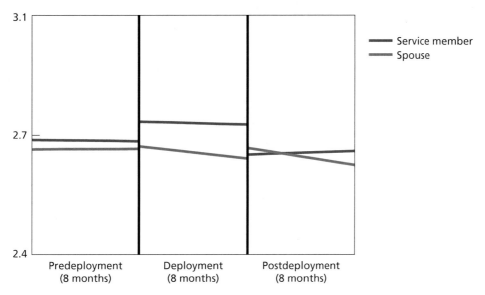

NOTES: RQ1a: Service member trajectories significantly different from no change over time (p=0.0011); spouse is not (p=0.2098).
RQ1b: Service member trajectories significantly different from constant trend over time (p=0.0068); spouse is not (p=0.5622).
RQ1c: Service member trajectory is significantly different from spouse trajectory (p=0.0306).
RAND RR1388-4.2

Another way to examine whether there is a statistically significant change in this outcome over the deployment cycle is to see if the trajectories are significantly different from a straight line. If deployment has a negative impact on family outcomes, but families improve postdeployment, then we might expect that the trajectory of family outcomes over the deployment cycle is not constant. That is, we might expect a fairly linear trajectory predeployment, a more-negative trajectory during deployment, and an improving trajectory postdeployment. For service members, we can reject the null hypothesis of a constant slope across the deployment cycle (χ^2, 8 df=21.14, p=0.01). Rather, ratings of the family environment actually appear to be more positive during the deployment period than before or after. Indeed, this is confirmed by post-hoc statistical tests that suggest that the mean family environment score for service members was significantly different during the deployment period than the other two nondeployment phases (χ^2, 1 df=20.97, p=0.00). For spouses, however, this is not the case. We cannot reject the null hypothesis of a straight line (χ^2, 8 df=6.76, p=0.56). Thus, we have no evidence that spouses' ratings of the family environment are substantially changed during the deployment cycle.

Finally, we examine whether trajectories of individual family members (i.e., service members and spouses) are parallel over the deployment cycle. Based on statistical tests, we can reject the null that service members' and spouses' trajectories are parallel (χ^2, 8 df=16.95, p=0.03). This is consistent with findings above about differences in the slope of the trajectory across the two groups. While service member's trajectories change over the deployment cycle; we have no evidence of such a change for spouses.

Figure 4.3
Parenting Satisfaction over the Deployment Cycle, Service Members, and Spouses

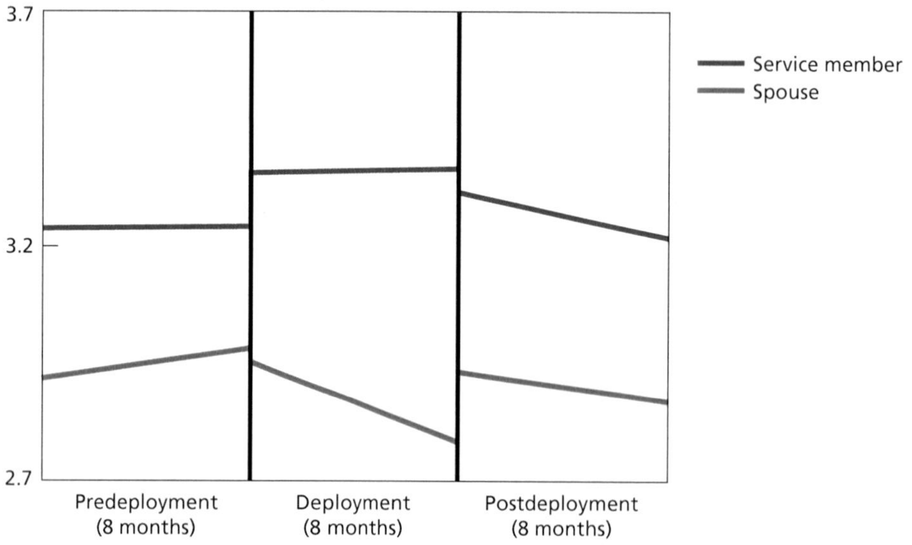

NOTES: RQ1a: Both service member and spouse trajectories significantly different than no change over time (p=0.0000 for both).
RQ1b: Both service member and spouse trajectories significantly different from a constant trend over time (p=0.0000 for both).
RQ1c: Service member trajectory significantly different from spouse trajectory (p=0.0000).
RAND RR1388-4.3

Figure 4.3 shows the trajectory for parenting satisfaction for service members and spouses. Based on statistical tests for service members, we can reject the null hypothesis that the trajectory is a flat line, with zero slope (χ^2, 8 df=45.06, p=0.00). A visual inspection of the plot suggests that service members are actually more satisfied with parenting during the deployment phase and that satisfaction with parenting appears to return to levels near where they were before the deployment once the service member returns. For spouses, we can also reject the null of a flat line (χ^2, 8 df=44.08, p=0.00), and the plot above suggests that satisfaction with parenting is lower during the deployment period than in the other time periods; however, the post-hoc tests in this case were nonsignificant (as described later in this chapter).

The results of the second test—whether trajectories are constant across time—are consistent with the prior test. Again, for service members we can reject the null hypothesis of a constant slope across the deployment cycle (χ^2, 8 df=43.98, p=0.00). Indeed, post-hoc tests confirm that mean parenting satisfaction is in fact different in the deployment phase relative to pre- and postdeployment among service members (χ^2, 1 df=27.07, p=0.00). Ratings of satisfaction with parenting actually appear to be *more* positive during the deployment period than before or after. For spouses, a different pattern emerges. Spouses' trajectories are also not constant over the deployment cycle (χ^2, 8 df=37.86, p=0.00), but they appear to have significantly *lower* satisfaction with parenting during the deployment phase than during nondeployment phases. However, for spouses, post-hoc tests suggest that the mean during the deployment period is only marginally different from the mean during the other nondeployment periods (χ^2, 1 df=2.84, p=0.09) but does not reach statistical significance at the p<0.05 level.

Perhaps not surprisingly, we can also reject the null that service members' and spouses' trajectories of parenting satisfaction are parallel across the deployment cycle (χ^2, 8 df=60.73, p=0.00). This is consistent with the fact that service members report an increase in parental satisfaction during deployment, whereas spouses report a decrease.

Figure 4.4 shows the trajectory for the financial distress scale for service members and spouses. For service members, we can reject the null hypothesis that the trajectory is a flat line, with zero slope (χ^2, 8 df=128.07, p=0.00). We can also reject the hypothesis of a straight line (χ^2, 8 df=131.46, p=0.00). Visually, the trajectories seem to suggest that at least some of this difference is due to lower financial distress during deployment. This hypothesis is confirmed by post-hoc tests that show that mean financial distress was significantly lower in the deployed period relative to pre- and postdeployment (χ^2, 1 df=50.38, p=0.00).

For spouses, we can also reject the null of a flat line (χ^2, 8 df=50.45, p=0.00) and straight line (χ^2, 8 df=53.48, p=0.00). Once again, post-hoc tests suggest that at least some of the change in trajectory is occurring during the deployment period, where spouses show lower financial stress than in other phases of the deployment cycle (χ^2, 1 df=13.80, p=0.00).

For financial distress, we cannot reject the null hypothesis that service members' and spouses' trajectories for financial distress across the deployment cycle are parallel (χ^2, 8 df=13.38, p=0.10). In fact, the lines in Figure 4.4 appear parallel, suggesting no evidence that the experience of service members and spouses are dissimilar across the deployment cycle. This is consistent with the fact that both service members and spouses report a decrease in perceived financial distress through a deployment, but increasing distress postdeployment.

Research Question 2: Impact of Deployment

RQ2 asks how, if at all, deployment affects postdeployment family outcomes using a doubly robust matched comparison approach. Table 4.5 presents the predicted means for each of the

Figure 4.4
Financial Distress Scale over the Deployment Cycle, Service Members and Spouses

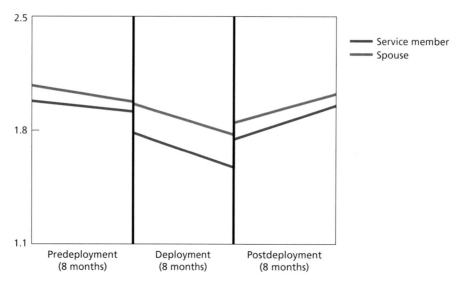

NOTES: RQ1a: Both service member and spouse trajectories significantly different than no change over time (p=0.0000 for both).
RQ1b: Both service member and spouse trajectories significantly different from a constant trend over time (p=0.0000 for both).
RQ1c: Service member trajectory is not significantly different from spouse trajectory (p=0.0995).
RAND RR1388-4.4

Table 4.5
Predicted Mean Differences (with Standard Errors) of Family Outcomes by Study Deployment Status

	Service Members		Spouses	
	Study Deployment (n=647)	No Study Deployment (n=872)	Has Study Deployment (n=683)	No Study Deployment (n=963)
FES	2.74 (0.01)	2.72 (0.01)	2.72 (0.02)	2.73 (0.01)
Satisfaction with Parenting	3.23 (0.02)	3.26 (0.02)	3.07 (0.02)	3.12 (0.02)
Financial Distress Scale	1.85 (0.03)	1.88 (0.03)	1.90 (0.03)	1.91 (0.03)

NOTES: SEs are in parentheses. Models control for respondent gender, age, racial/ethnic minority status, having children younger than age six in the household, rank and officer/enlisted status, number of prior combat deployments, years of service, branch and component of service, the Hoge CES, prior deployment trauma, survey mode at follow-up (phone or web), and the outcome in question at baseline. Models for spouse outcomes additionally controlled for spouse education and employment status.

three family outcomes we examined—the family environment, parenting satisfaction, and financial distress—among service members and spouses who did and did not experience a study deployment. As can be seen in the table, there is no evidence that the predicted post-deployment means differ across the study deployers and nondeployers. The deployments that we observed among our sample of military families do not appear to have negatively affected family functioning during the postdeployment period. These findings are generally consistent with the trajectory analyses reported for RQ1. While trajectories of the family environment, parenting satisfaction, and financial stress may be different during the deployment period (compared with the predeployment period, postdeployment period, or both), especially for service members, overall trajectories across the entire deployment cycle are generally unchanged, suggesting that most families are, in fact, resilient in the face of a deployment. Next, we turn to an examination of risk and resilience that may contribute to family resilience, or lack of it, in the face of a deployment.

Research Question 3: Risk and Resilience Factors

RQ3 examines a set of risk and resilience factors that may be associated with postdeployment family outcomes among deployed families. Those risk and resilience factors fall into four categories: predeployment factors (i.e., preparation activities); deployment factors (i.e., frequency and satisfaction with frequency of communication); deployment factors as experienced by the service member (i.e., combat exposure, duration, and military stress), and separation from the military during the study. Table 4.6 presents the results (i.e., regression coefficients and p-values) of a series of multivariate models, run separately for each family outcome and for service members and spouses. Each regression includes a series of controls (noted in the table), an indicator for whether the risk or resilience factor was missing during the predeployment or deployment period, the baseline value of the outcome, and a random intercept to control for clustering within respondents. Note that these models do not include the propensity weights used in the analysis of RQ2 because the analysis is limited to families that experienced a study deployment. Thus, we can interpret the coefficients in Table 4.6 as indication of whether certain predeployment or deployment experiences are associated with risk or resilience postdeployment.

Of the factors examined in Table 4.7, six show a significant association with postdeployment family functioning, as we will describe. This is important to consider in the context of the number of statistical tests that were conducted. For any given outcome, the more statistical tests that are performed, the more likely it is that at least some of the tests will be statistically significant by chance. Thus, in discussing the results, we focus on patterns of statistical significance that emerge across multiple predictors and outcomes, and do not devote much space to reviewing isolated statistically significant results.

First, service members and spouses who report engaging in more predeployment preparation activities report better family environments (service member β=0.02, p=0.03), and higher satisfaction with parenting (service member β=0.04, p=0.01) than service members who did fewer of those activities. Spouses who engaged in more readiness activities reported higher satisfaction with parenting (β=0.02, p=0.02). Second, spouses who were more satisfied with the frequency of communication with the service member during deployment also reported greater satisfaction with parenting (β=0.08, p 0.03).

Third, in terms of deployment characteristics, somewhat surprisingly, spouses whose service member partner experienced any combat trauma during the deployment reported higher

Table 4.6
Regression Coefficients and p-values for Risk and Resilience Factors
(Study Deployment Sample Only)

	Service Members (n=647)			Spouses (n=681)		
	Family Environment	Parenting Satisfaction	Financial Stress	Family Environment	Parenting Satisfaction	Financial Stress
Deployment Preparation Activities[a]	0.02*	0.04***	0.03	0.00	0.02*	−0.01
p-value	(0.03)	(0.01)	(0.05)	(0.67)	(0.02)	(0.59)
Frequency of Communication During Study Deployment[b]	0.01	0.07	−0.07	0.03	0.08	−0.02
p-value	(0.69)	(0.29)	(0.21)	(0.22)	(0.07)	(0.78)
Satisfaction with Frequency of Communication During Study Deployment[c]	0.00	−0.03	−0.04	0.03	0.08*	−0.07
p-value	(0.98)	(0.49)	(0.38)	(0.14)	(0.03)	(0.05)
Trauma Exposure During Study Deployment (%)						
Physical	0.04	−0.06	0.04	0.05	0.00	0.10
Psychological	−0.04	−0.02	−0.08	−0.05	−0.17**	−0.08
Combat	−0.11	0.09	0.13	0.06	0.21*	0.12
Joint p-value	(0.13)	(0.81)	(0.55)	(0.37)	(0.01)	(0.31)
Length of Study Deployment[d]	0.00	0.00	−0.02*	0.01	0.00	0.00
p-value	(0.69)	(0.87)	(0.04)	(0.25)	(0.81)	(0.88)
Self-Rated Military Stress During Deployment[e]	−0.02*	−0.04*	0.04*	−0.01	−0.04*	0.03
p-value	(0.03)	(0.02)	(0.03)	(0.19)	(0.01)	(0.09)
Separation[f]	−0.03	−0.26*	0.49**	−0.09	−0.28**	0.27
p-value	(0.60)	(0.01)	(0.00)	(0.08)	(0.00)	(0.09)

NOTES: Models controlled for respondent gender, age, racial/ethnic minority status, length of marriage, having children younger than age six in the household, rank and officer/enlisted status, number of prior combat deployments, years of service, branch and component of service, baseline combat exposure from the Hoge CES, a missing indicator for the risk/resilience factor, and the baseline measure of the key outcome being modeled. Models for spouse outcomes additionally controlled for spouse education and employment status. For deployment trauma, a joint F-test p-value is presented; for individual coefficients, significance is shown only when the joint test has a p-value<0.05. * p<0.05; ** p<0.01; *** p<0.001.

[a] Service member range: 0–9; spouse range: 0–13.

[b] Service member and spouse range: 0 (less than once a month) to 4 (every day).

[c] Service member and spouse range: 1 to 4.

[d] In months.

[e] Service member only; range 0–7.

[f] Includes retirement as well as separation (involuntary and voluntary).

satisfaction with parenting during the postdeployment period (β=0.21, p=0.01). In contrast, spouses whose service member partner experienced any psychological trauma during the study deployment reported lower parenting satisfaction (r=−0.17, p=0.01). Similarly, service members who experienced more military stress during the study deployment reported a worse family environment (β=−0.02, p=0.03) and lower parenting satisfaction during the postdeployment period (β=−0.04, p=0.02). Spouses whose service member partner experienced more military stress during the study deployment also reported lower parenting satisfaction during the postdeployment period (β=−0.04, p=0.01). Taken together, the results suggest that negative psychological sequelae of deployments (i.e., psychological trauma or stress) are risk factors for poorer outcomes for service members and spouses postdeployment; however, combat exposure was unexpectedly associated with higher parenting satisfaction among spouses. Fifth, the longer the study deployment, the lower the financial stress reported by the service member (β=−0.02, p=0.04), likely because longer combat deployments result in more combat/hazard duty pay.

Finally, service members who leave the military during the course of the study, through either separation or retirement, reported lower parenting satisfaction (β=−0.26, p=0.01) and higher financial distress (β=0.49, p=0.00); spouses whose partners left the military also reported lower satisfaction with parenting (β=−0.28, p=0.00). The results should be interpreted with caution, however, because it is not clear if leaving the military causes these negative outcomes or if the reverse is true—low satisfaction with parenting and financial distress cause individuals to leave the military. And again, due to the large number of statistical tests performed, all the results presented above should be viewed as patterns, rather than isolated findings.

Discussion

Our study expands on past work by using newly collected longitudinal data tracking families over the deployment cycle, information on multiple family members, and advanced statistical methods to account for differences between those who deploy and those who do not, rendering this sample representative of married and deployed service members during 2012. It is important to keep in mind the historical context in which these data were collected—the drawdown was in full effect and deployments were shorter and were characterized as lower risk compared with earlier in OIF/OEF/OND. While other work has shown the adverse consequences experienced by families during deployment, our study is the first to observe families over the entire deployment cycle and shows that, on average, families are resilient and tend to bounce back from this experience in the postdeployment phase. Our findings also provide evidence that the experience of deployment is not uniformly associated with negative changes. For instance, the trajectory models showed that financial distress actually decreased during the deployment phase. This finding is consistent with the fact that families are provided extra compensation while service members are deployed.

We also show that it is important to examine multiple family members as the experience of deployment is sometimes quite different for service members and spouses. For instance, service members show significant change in their reports of family environments over the deployment cycles, while there is no evidence of such change among spouses. In this case, service members reported better family environments while deployed, possibly because they are removed from the day-to-day arguments and challenges associated with family life and/or more appreciative of the family while separated from them. In contrast, spouses' family environment trajectories were not significantly different from a flat line over the deployment cycle, suggesting relative stability in this construct among spouses. Service members and spouses also showed divergent trajectories in terms of parenting satisfaction over the course of deployment. Specifically, while both show significant changes in outcomes over the course of a deployment cycle, service members report higher parenting satisfaction during deployment, while spouses report lower parenting satisfaction over the entire deployment cycle. This finding suggests that parenting stress is eased for service members while away on deployment but spouses, who are left at home to take on additional responsibilities as single parents, have more parenting demands and stress. Again, these findings appear to be mitigated during the postdeployment period, once service members return home and things have time to return to normal. Overall, these findings are consistent with the ABC-X model theory of family resilience, which suggests that when faced with a stressor (in this case, deployment) families may experience an initial adjustment period wherein functioning declines from a baseline, prestress state; however, over time, most families show a correction pattern, in which their functioning returns to prestressor levels.

Furthermore, while families appear to be quite resilient, our overall findings show that some families are better able than others to "bounce back" after a deployment. Identifying such factors that are linked to better family outcomes is critical to inform policy aimed at promoting military family health and readiness, and for mitigating risk among families in the postdeployment period. In particular, we found that spouses and service members who report engaging in more predeployment preparation activities report better family environments (significant only for service members) and higher satisfaction with parenting. Similarly, spouses who report more preparation activities and greater satisfaction with the frequency of communication with the service member during deployment reported higher parenting satisfaction during the postdeployment period. These findings are consistent with prior work demonstrating that active strategies to manage stressful experiences, including preparing for the event, are associated with resilience (Compas et al., 2012; Palmer, 2008). For instance, in a prior study of military wives facing spousal deployment, engagement in financial and legal planning, problem-solving, and seeking social support was associated with lower levels of self-reported physical health symptoms and depressive symptoms (Dimiceli, Steinhardt, and Smith, 2010). However, these findings are also consistent with an alternative explanation, namely those families who are already high-functioning (e.g., highly organized, psychologically healthy, happily married, etc.) are more likely to engage in preparation activities.

Regarding deployment characteristics, overall findings suggest that the negative psychological consequences of deployment, including psychological trauma and stress reported by the service member, is associated with increased risk for negative outcomes for both service members and spouses during the postdeployment period. Again, these findings are consistent with the ABC-X model as well as contemporary theories of stress more generally, which suggest that it is the interpretation of the stressful event or the experience of distress that differentiates those who experience a stressor but ultimately "bounce back" from those who continue to show persistent, negative consequences (Hill, 1949, 1958). In contrast to these findings, and somewhat surprisingly, exposure to combat trauma among service members was associated with higher parenting satisfaction among spouses. As mentioned in Chapter Two, given the overall number of statistical tests, it is important not to overinterpret single significant results, but rather to examine the overall pattern of results, as such findings may not replicate in future research.

Finally, and consistent with the notion that experiencing deployment is not uniformly associated with negative consequences for families, service members with longer study deployment reported lower financial stress. These findings are consistent with the fact that longer combat deployments result in more combat/hazard duty pay. We come back to a discussion of these results in the context of all the chapters of this report in Chapter Seven.

Strengths and Limitations

These findings should be interpreted within the context of the study's strengths and limitations. In particular, this study provides a unique opportunity to longitudinally examine the impact of deployment on various indicators of family functioning in a representative sample of service members and spouses. The multi-informant perspective from both service members and spouses is also a notable strength, as our findings demonstrated that spouses' and service members' trajectories of functioning across the deployment cycle differed. Identifying such divergent discrepancies has important policy implications because it suggests that targeted efforts to support family resilience across the deployment cycle may need to be tailored, to some extent, to the unique experiences of spouses versus service members. Finally, no study to date has employed such advanced statistical techniques to be able to more directly examine the causal impact of deployment on families functioning in a representative sample of service members and spouses across all service branches and components. Further, this is the first study to date that has followed the same families through predeployment, during deployment, and postdeployment.

Several methodological and design limitations should also be taken into consideration. First, the use of survey methodology for all study constructs introduces several biases inherent to self-reports, such as forgetfulness or social desirability biases (i.e., trying to present oneself in a more positive light, or under- or overreporting of symptoms of psychological stress or distress). Second, selective attrition, both among families that experienced a study deployment and those that did not, could have affected our results, especially if those families that left the survey are worse off on the outcomes examined in this chapter. Third, that same sort of selectivity potentially affected the beginning of our survey: Clearly, we had a predominantly experienced sample of military families in our study (i.e., most had experienced a deployment before). These experiences no doubt were associated with how families addressed the study deployment that we observed. We did not have a large enough sample of first-time deployers to examine them separately, but future work should seek to address how those families adapt to their first deployment experience. These strengths and limitations will be further discussed in Chapter Eight.

Policy Implications

What do the results of this chapter imply for family readiness and resilience programs and policies? The past 13 years of protracted combat deployments have exacted an unprecedented toll on U.S. military members and their families (Chandra et al., 2010; Hosek, Kavanagh, and Miller, 2006; Lester et al., 2010; Werber et al., 2008). The stress of extended and often repeated deployments in threatening environments is a unique source of stress for families. However, the extant research on the impact of deployments on military families' functioning has a number of methodological limitations that preclude definitive conclusions regarding whether deployments increase risk for maladjustment or poor functioning in the postdeployment period, or which families are more or less likely to demonstrate resilience in the postdeployment period.

Providing data to answer these questions is critical to support DoD efforts to provide programs and resources for military families.

The findings of this report highlight several issues that are germane to family readiness and resilience policies. Perhaps one of the most striking findings of this research is the overall resilience of military families. This is not to say that deployments are a benign experience for military families, nor that *all* families demonstrate resilience in the face of deployments. But overall, there were few differences over the medium to long term in family outcomes in families that experienced a deployment compared with a matched group that did not experience a deployment. The lack of statistically significant differences between the deployers and nondeployers may suggest that nondeployers experience stressors of their own, suggesting that nondeployment-related factors are also important to consider among military families. Thus, policymakers and program leaders should not undervalue support provided to military families as they prepare for deployments, as well as when facing the day-to-day stressors of military life, such as frequent relocations (see Chapter Seven of this report). Whether existing programs and policies are adequate, or whether new programs are required, is an open question and beyond the scope of the current analyses.

Our findings also highlight that military spouses and service members, even within the same family, may have different experiences and needs across the deployment cycle, and especially during the deployment period itself. Therefore, tailored programs are needed to address the specific needs of spouses, service members, and their children. Support *during the deployment itself* may have the largest impact on long-term outcomes of military families, especially if that support is designed to meet the needs of specific family members.

Finally, findings suggest that while deployments themselves may not be uniformly associated with negative consequences for families after a service member's return, the negative psychological sequelae of war may have downstream consequences for service members and their spouses. Thus, continued efforts to identify and treat mental health problems among service members in the acute phase, before they become chronic and debilitating and have negative postdeployment consequences for the family, is also critical. Toward that end, programs to reduce stigma associated with mental health issues in service members are also critical.

There are several areas of research that are still needed to better inform policy initiatives to support military families. For example, research on the availability and effectiveness of resources to help families respond to extended and multiple deployments, reunion, and death or injury is needed. Research is also needed on the optimal timing of providing education and support to families of deployed members, as there have been no systematic investigations in this area. Finally, there is an urgent need for evaluating whether dissemination of education and other support materials for families is reaching the families most in need across the armed forces.

Integrative Implications of Chapters Three and Four

We opted to separate the analyses of couple outcomes (i.e., married service members and their spouses; discussed in Chapter Three) from family outcomes, which we have examined in this chapter. To some degree, this distinction is artificial—certainly couple functioning can affect family functioning and vice versa. If a marriage is in crisis, the family will likely respond in many ways that could be reflected in the family measures examined here. One's rating of the family environment, for instance, should be closely related to such factors as marital quality, positive and negative affect, and interpartner violence. We can also learn more about family processes by identifying where marital and family outcomes diverge. Taken together, Chapters Three and Four provide a rich picture of family life and highlight a number of important implications for policy.

In particular, although marital outcomes suffer during the deployment phase for both spouses, the family experience is different for service members and their spouses. More specifically, service members and spouses respond remarkably similarly to the deployment when it comes to factors related to their marriage (with a couple of exceptions where only one member of the couple shows a statistically different change). Marital satisfaction declined during the separation, for instance, and both partners reported more positive affect during the deployment itself. Rates of reported psychological and physical aggression enacted by the self and received from the partner also dropped sharply during deployment. When it comes to broader family outcomes, however, service members and spouses generally both show changes during the deployment cycle, but these are not as uniform within couples as for the marital outcomes. For instance, service members report better family environments during deployments than before or after deployments while spouses, in contrast, report no significant changes in family environment across the deployment cycle. Service members also report higher parenting satisfaction during the deployment while spouses report declines in parenting satisfaction over the entire deployment cycle. These differences may be explained by the fact that service members are removed from the day-to-day challenges associated with family life and that spouses likely have greater parenting challenges while serving as single periods during the deployment period. The stress to marriage, on the other hand, is more comparable within couples. Recognizing that deployments have different implications for the spouse and service members' family roles and responsibilities is critically important, and may inform postdeployment reintegration programs. For instance, postdeployment programs that encourage and provide guidance on how to effectively communicate about the unique challenges and stressors experienced by both the service member and spouse during deployment may help bridge these divergent experiences and foster empathy within couples. In addition, during deployments, programs could provide support to address the increased burden for managing daily household responsibilities among spouses, and to increase communication between marital partners.

Another important finding across these chapters is that both marriage and family return to normal levels after the stress of the deployment period subsides. This is consistent with Hills' ABC-X theory and is a common theme throughout this report. Furthermore, these results are consistent with data attesting to the resilience of military families. As we note in both chapters, however, the overall resilience demonstrated by military couples and families should not be interpreted as evidence that family readiness programs are not needed. Rather, given the substantial investment in family readiness programs over the past decade, the current findings provide suggestive support for the effectiveness of these programs in supporting family resiliency, although we did not directly examine this possibility. Indeed, true program effectiveness evaluations of family support programs are sorely needed. On the other hand, results from the propensity score analyses that showed few differences in marital or family functioning outcomes among deployers to nondeployers might suggest a need for targeted programs to address the "everyday" stressors of military life, including long work schedules, separations due to training responsibilities, frequent residential moves, or child care issues. Indeed, the protracted nature of overseas combat operations since 2001 has considerably raised the public and DoD awareness of the importance of considering the readiness and resilience of military families. However, particularly in light of the drawdown of operations in Iraq and Afghanistan, these findings highlight the importance of continuing to invest in the needs of military families, and to provide support and programs that address the numerous nondeployment related stressors that are also an endemic part of military family life.

Finally, synthesizing the evidence from Chapters Three and Four, it is clear that while most military couples and families are resilient in the face of deployments and return to baseline levels of functioning in the postdeployment period, there are certain "high-risk" groups, based on exposure to different types of combat trauma or mental health, that may increase vulnerability to adverse postdeployment outcomes for not only the service member but also the family. Thus, at the level of both the couple and the family, it is critical that programs target these vulnerable populations.

In summary, the combined results of Chapters Three and Four provide arguably the most comprehensive evaluation to date of the impact of deployment on marital and family functioning in military families. Collectively, these findings highlight the overall resilience of military families, and suggest an ongoing need to consider the multitude of stressors experienced by military families, risk and vulnerability factors, and opportunities for both evidence-based prevention and intervention programs to support family readiness and resilience.

Appendix 4A: Balance Tables and Plots

Tables 4A.1 and 4A.2 present balance statistics for service members and spouses, respectively. Each table compares standardized mean differences (SMDs) across a number of key study variables for service members and spouses who did and did not experience a study deployment. SMDs are presented before and after applying propensity score weights. Generally, SMDs between −0.20 and 0.20 indicate good balance across groups.

Figures 4A.1 and 4A.2 present the balance plots for service members and spouses, respectively, who did and did not experience a study deployment. Each dot on the plot represents a variable in Tables 4A.1 and 4A.2. The left side of each plot depicts absolute standard mean differences (ASMDs) before applying propensity score weights, while the right side of each plot depicts ASMDs after applying the propensity score weights. As can be seen in both figures, once the weights are applied, ASMDs between service members and spouses who did and did not experience a study deployment fall below the cutoff of 0.20 ASMDs.

Table 4A.1
Weighted Balance Table: Service Members (Study Deployment Versus No Study Deployment)

	Unweighted					Weighted				
	Study Deployment		No Study Deployment		SMD	Study Deployment		No Study Deployment		SMD
	Mean	SD	Mean	SD		Mean	SD	Mean	SD	
SERVICE MEMBER VARIABLES										
Female	0.06	0.24	0.12	0.32	−0.23	0.06	0.24	0.08	0.28	−0.10
Age	32.94	6.53	35.73	6.93	−0.43	32.94	6.53	33.88	6.71	−0.10
Minority Race/Ethnicity	0.30	0.46	0.33	0.47	−0.06	0.30	0.46	0.29	0.45	−0.15
Children Younger Than Age 6	0.71	0.46	0.64	0.48	0.16	0.71	0.46	0.68	0.47	0.02
Pay Grade: Junior Enlisted	0.04	0.19	0.05	0.21	−0.04	0.04	0.19	0.03	0.17	0.07
Pay Grade: Junior Officer	0.08	0.28	0.06	0.24	0.08	0.08	0.28	0.09	0.29	0.04
Pay Grade: Mid and Senior Enlisted	0.71	0.45	0.74	0.44	−0.06	0.71	0.45	0.72	0.45	−0.03
Pay Grade: Mid and Senior Officer	0.11	0.31	0.13	0.34	−0.09	0.11	0.31	0.13	0.34	−0.03
Pay Grade: Warrant Officer	0.06	0.24	0.02	0.14	0.17	0.06	0.24	0.03	0.17	−0.07
Length of Marriage (Months)	102.65	70.57	120.88	76.45	−0.26	102.65	70.57	92.78	71.50	0.14
Parents in the Military	0.51	0.50	0.55	0.50	−0.08	0.51	0.50	0.51	0.50	0.01
Total Number of Prior Deployments	2.11	1.36	1.44	1.23	0.49	2.11	1.36	1.93	1.26	0.13
Years of Service	12.32	7.06	14.45	7.80	−0.30	12.32	7.06	12.89	7.12	−0.08
Army	0.46	0.50	0.50	0.50	−0.09	0.46	0.50	0.49	0.50	−0.06
Air Force	0.21	0.41	0.19	0.39	0.06	0.21	0.41	0.27	0.44	−0.15
Navy	0.22	0.41	0.25	0.43	−0.07	0.22	0.41	0.18	0.38	0.10
Marine Corps	0.12	0.32	0.07	0.25	0.15	0.12	0.32	0.07	0.25	0.15
Reserve Component	0.15	0.36	0.38	0.49	−0.63	0.15	0.36	0.20	0.40	−0.14
Hoge Combat Experiences Scale	4.90	4.56	4.08	4.04	0.18	4.90	4.56	4.46	4.14	0.10
Deployment Trauma Exposure	2.29	2.50	1.86	2.53	0.17	2.29	2.50	2.13	2.52	0.06
Marital Satisfaction Scale	4.01	0.44	3.89	0.51	0.26	4.01	0.44	3.98	0.45	0.07
Positive and Negative Affect Schedule (PANAS): Positive	4.23	0.63	4.12	0.69	0.18	4.23	0.63	4.18	0.61	0.08
PANAS: Negative	1.94	0.52	2.06	0.63	−0.23	1.94	0.52	1.98	0.55	−0.07

Table 4A.1—Continued

	Unweighted					Weighted				
	Study Deployment		No Study Deployment		SMD	Study Deployment		No Study Deployment		SMD
	Mean	SD	Mean	SD		Mean	SD	Mean	SD	
Conflict Tactics Scale: Prevalence of Physical Aggression Toward Partner	0.01	0.11	0.02	0.14	-0.10	0.01	0.11	0.02	0.14	-0.08
Conflict Tactics Scale: Chronicity of Psychological Aggression Toward Partner	0.64	0.85	0.74	0.91	-0.11	0.64	0.85	0.66	0.87	-0.02
Conflict Tactics Scale: Prevalence of Physical Aggression Toward You	0.04	0.20	0.04	0.20	-0.02	0.04	0.20	0.05	0.21	-0.03
Conflict Tactics Scale: Chronicity of Psychological Aggression Toward You	0.70	1.01	0.84	1.05	-0.14	0.70	1.01	0.74	1.00	-0.04
Depression (Patient Health Questionnaire [PHQ])	2.43	3.09	3.21	3.91	-0.25	2.43	3.09	2.53	3.31	-0.03
Anxiety	2.03	1.00	2.11	1.04	-0.08	2.03	1.00	2.08	0.98	-0.05
PTSD	21.62	8.27	23.24	10.62	-0.20	21.62	8.27	21.91	8.97	-0.04
Traumatic Brain Injury (TBI)	0.11	0.31	0.13	0.34	-0.08	0.11	0.31	0.13	0.34	-0.09
Binge Drinking	0.26	0.44	0.25	0.44	0.01	0.26	0.44	0.27	0.44	-0.02
Problematic Substance Use Scale	0.14	0.49	0.16	0.61	-0.04	0.14	0.49	0.13	0.55	0.01
Medication for Mental Health Problem	0.04	0.19	0.07	0.26	-0.17	0.04	0.19	0.05	0.21	-0.04
Received Mental Health Care	0.08	0.27	0.20	0.40	-0.46	0.08	0.27	0.12	0.32	-0.14
Financial Distress Scale	1.80	0.62	2.03	0.77	-0.36	1.80	0.62	1.86	0.66	-0.09
Family Environment Scale	2.81	0.23	2.74	0.32	0.31	2.81	0.23	2.81	0.26	-0.01
Parenting Satisfaction	3.36	0.37	3.34	0.43	0.04	3.36	0.37	3.34	0.39	0.05
Military Commitment	4.48	0.60	4.39	0.68	0.15	4.48	0.60	4.40	0.63	0.13
Job Satisfaction	4.01	0.94	3.86	1.04	0.16	4.01	0.94	3.87	1.00	0.15
Retention Intentions	4.27	1.16	4.16	1.32	0.10	4.27	1.16	4.22	1.22	0.04
SPOUSE VARIABLES										
Marital Satisfaction Scale	3.97	0.52	3.77	0.63	0.38	3.97	0.52	3.89	0.52	0.14
PANAS: Positive	4.21	0.67	4.10	0.77	0.16	4.21	0.67	4.19	0.66	0.03
PANAS: Negative	2.02	0.59	2.16	0.62	-0.24	2.02	0.59	2.07	0.60	-0.09

Table 4A.1—Continued

	Unweighted					Weighted				
	Study Deployment		No Study Deployment			Study Deployment		No Study Deployment		
	Mean	SD	Mean	SD	SMD	Mean	SD	Mean	SD	SMD
Conflict Tactics Scale: Prevalence of Physical Aggression Toward Partner	0.04	0.20	0.03	0.17	0.05	0.04	0.20	0.04	0.19	0.03
Conflict Tactics Scale: Chronicity of Psychological Aggression Toward Partner	0.71	0.87	0.76	0.97	-0.06	0.71	0.87	0.71	0.91	0.01
Conflict Tactics Scale: Prevalence of Physical Aggression Toward You	0.02	0.14	0.02	0.15	-0.03	0.02	0.14	0.02	0.13	0.01
Conflict Tactics Scale: Chronicity of Psychological Aggression Toward You	0.60	0.82	0.74	0.98	-0.16	0.60	0.82	0.64	0.91	-0.04
Depression (PHQ)	2.56	3.54	2.82	3.46	-0.07	2.56	3.54	2.71	3.36	-0.04
Anxiety	2.02	0.92	1.99	0.88	0.03	2.02	0.92	2.02	0.94	0.00
PTSD	0.44	0.95	0.56	1.00	-0.12	0.44	0.95	0.44	0.95	0.00
Binge Drinking	0.11	0.31	0.10	0.30	0.04	0.11	0.31	0.12	0.33	-0.03
Problematic Substance Use Scale	0.04	0.28	0.05	0.39	-0.05	0.04	0.28	0.06	0.42	-0.08
Medication for Mental Health Problem	0.11	0.32	0.11	0.31	0.02	0.11	0.32	0.14	0.35	-0.10
Received Mental Health Care	0.11	0.32	0.12	0.33	-0.04	0.11	0.32	0.14	0.35	-0.09
Financial Distress Scale	1.88	0.64	2.09	0.77	-0.33	1.88	0.64	1.93	0.69	-0.07
Family Environment Scale	2.85	0.24	2.77	0.29	0.35	2.85	0.24	2.83	0.24	0.07
Parenting Stress Scale	3.24	0.36	3.22	0.42	0.06	3.24	0.36	3.25	0.40	-0.03
Military Commitment	4.52	0.55	4.45	0.64	0.13	4.52	0.55	4.51	0.56	0.03
Satisfaction as Military Spouse	4.11	0.98	3.80	1.14	0.31	4.11	0.98	4.13	0.95	-0.02
Retention Intentions	4.20	1.12	4.00	1.29	0.17	4.20	1.12	4.10	1.24	0.09
TEEN VARIABLES										
Strengths and Difficulties Questionnaire (SDQ): Total	7.34	5.19	7.98	5.13	-0.12	7.34	5.19	7.51	5.23	-0.03
SDQ Subscale: Emotional Problems	1.64	1.81	1.62	1.68	0.01	1.64	1.81	1.55	1.75	0.05
SDQ Subscale: Conduct Problems	0.97	1.31	1.12	1.27	-0.11	0.97	1.31	0.96	1.30	0.00
SDQ Subscale: Hyperactivity	3.26	2.60	3.39	2.39	-0.05	3.26	2.60	3.38	2.57	-0.05

Table 4A.1—Continued

	Unweighted					Weighted				
	Study Deployment		No Study Deployment			Study Deployment		No Study Deployment		
	Mean	SD	Mean	SD	SMD	Mean	SD	Mean	SD	SMD
SDQ Subscale: Peer Relationships	1.69	1.60	1.86	1.80	-0.10	1.69	1.60	1.63	1.61	0.04
SDQ Subscale: Prosocial Behavior	8.56	1.63	8.48	1.46	0.04	8.56	1.63	8.66	1.52	-0.07
Depression Symptoms	1.01	1.82	1.07	1.70	-0.03	1.01	1.82	0.85	1.61	0.09
Anxiety (Screen for Child Anxiety Related Emotional Disorders [SCARED])	1.67	1.97	1.31	1.42	0.18	1.67	1.97	1.46	1.70	0.11

NOTE: SD=standard deviation.

Table 4A.2
Weighted Balance Table: Spouses (Study Deployment Versus No Study Deployment)

	Unweighted					Weighted				
	Study Deployment		No Study Deployment			Study Deployment		No Study Deployment		
	Mean	SD	Mean	SD	SMD	Mean	SD	Mean	SD	SMD
SERVICE MEMBER VARIABLES										
Pay Grade: Junior Enlisted	0.04	0.19	0.04	0.20	-0.03	0.04	0.19	0.03	0.16	0.07
Pay Grade: Junior Officer	0.09	0.28	0.06	0.24	0.08	0.09	0.28	0.09	0.29	-0.02
Pay Grade: Mid and Senior Enlisted	0.74	0.44	0.73	0.44	0.01	0.74	0.44	0.73	0.44	0.01
Pay Grade: Mid and Senior Officer	0.11	0.31	0.14	0.34	-0.10	0.11	0.31	0.13	0.34	-0.07
Pay Grade: Warrant Officer	0.03	0.18	0.02	0.15	0.06	0.03	0.18	0.02	0.15	0.06
Length of Marriage (Months)	104.65	69.21	122.63	76.18	-0.26	104.65	69.21	107.25	70.21	-0.04
Total Number of Prior Deployments	2.04	1.24	1.42	1.24	0.50	2.04	1.24	1.87	1.19	0.13
Years of Service	12.39	6.91	15.07	8.41	-0.39	12.39	6.91	13.05	7.19	-0.10
Army	0.45	0.50	0.48	0.50	-0.06	0.45	0.50	0.48	0.50	-0.05
Air Force	0.23	0.42	0.18	0.39	0.11	0.23	0.42	0.25	0.44	-0.06
Navy	0.22	0.42	0.25	0.44	-0.08	0.22	0.42	0.20	0.40	0.05
Marine Corps	0.10	0.30	0.08	0.27	0.06	0.10	0.30	0.07	0.25	0.11
Reserve Component	0.17	0.38	0.41	0.49	-0.62	0.17	0.38	0.21	0.41	-0.10
Hoge CES	4.74	4.56	3.77	4.11	0.21	4.74	4.56	4.43	4.24	0.07
Deployment Trauma Exposure	2.31	2.55	1.85	2.52	0.18	2.31	2.55	2.21	2.56	0.04
Marital Satisfaction Scale	3.98	0.45	3.84	0.59	0.30	3.98	0.45	3.98	0.47	0.00
PANAS: Positive	4.20	0.63	4.01	0.80	0.30	4.20	0.63	4.16	0.63	0.07
PANAS: Negative	1.98	0.56	2.05	0.58	-0.12	1.98	0.56	1.98	0.53	0.01
Conflict Tactics Scale: Prevalence of Physical Aggression Toward Partner	0.02	0.13	0.03	0.16	-0.06	0.02	0.13	0.02	0.14	-0.02
Conflict Tactics Scale: Chronicity of Psychological Aggression Toward Partner	0.69	0.88	0.71	0.91	-0.02	0.69	0.88	0.64	0.85	0.05
Conflict Tactics Scale: Prevalence of Physical Aggression Toward You	0.05	0.21	0.05	0.22	-0.01	0.05	0.21	0.05	0.22	-0.03
Conflict Tactics Scale: Chronicity of Psychological Aggression Toward You	0.73	1.01	0.83	1.01	-0.09	0.73	1.01	0.74	1.00	-0.01

Table 4A.2—Continued

| | Unweighted | | | | | Weighted | | | | |
| | Study Deployment | | No Study Deployment | | SMD | Study Deployment | | No Study Deployment | | SMD |
	Mean	SD	Mean	SD		Mean	SD	Mean	SD	
Depression (PHQ)	2.54	3.25	2.97	3.85	-0.13	2.54	3.25	2.50	3.33	0.01
Anxiety	2.04	1.03	2.12	1.01	-0.08	2.04	1.03	2.03	0.97	0.01
PTSD	21.77	8.40	23.24	10.78	-0.18	21.77	8.40	22.04	9.27	-0.03
TBI	0.13	0.34	0.13	0.33	0.02	0.13	0.34	0.14	0.35	-0.02
Binge Drinking	0.26	0.44	0.27	0.45	-0.03	0.26	0.44	0.24	0.43	0.04
Problematic Substance Use Scale	0.22	0.70	0.20	0.62	0.02	0.22	0.70	0.15	0.57	0.10
Medication for Mental Health Problem	0.03	0.17	0.08	0.27	-0.29	0.03	0.17	0.05	0.21	-0.10
Received Mental Health Care	0.08	0.27	0.20	0.40	-0.42	0.08	0.27	0.12	0.32	-0.13
Financial Distress Scale	1.84	0.62	2.05	0.76	-0.34	1.84	0.62	1.87	0.67	-0.06
Family Environment Scale	2.78	0.25	2.77	0.29	0.03	2.78	0.25	2.80	0.26	-0.08
Parenting Satisfaction	3.33	0.38	3.34	0.40	-0.04	3.33	0.38	3.33	0.39	0.00
Military Commitment	4.46	0.59	4.34	0.67	0.20	4.46	0.59	4.40	0.63	0.11
Job Satisfaction	4.00	0.90	3.80	1.03	0.22	4.00	0.90	3.90	0.98	0.10
Retention Intentions	4.23	1.16	4.01	1.41	0.19	4.23	1.16	4.23	1.22	0.00
SPOUSE VARIABLES										
Female	0.93	0.25	0.90	0.30	0.15	0.93	0.25	0.93	0.26	0.03
Age	32.58	6.67	35.52	7.44	-0.44	32.58	6.67	33.16	6.94	-0.09
Minority Race/Ethnicity	0.29	0.45	0.29	0.46	-0.02	0.29	0.45	0.30	0.46	-0.02
Children Younger Than Age 6	0.68	0.47	0.59	0.49	0.20	0.68	0.47	0.67	0.47	0.02
Education: Less than High School	0.01	0.09	0.01	0.11	-0.06	0.01	0.09	0.02	0.13	-0.11
Education: High School	0.21	0.40	0.16	0.37	0.11	0.21	0.40	0.18	0.39	0.06
Education: Some College	0.26	0.44	0.26	0.44	0.01	0.26	0.44	0.28	0.45	-0.03
Education: Associate/Vocational/ Technical Degree	0.18	0.38	0.19	0.39	-0.03	0.18	0.38	0.17	0.38	0.02
Education: Bachelor's Degree	0.26	0.44	0.26	0.44	0.00	0.26	0.44	0.27	0.45	-0.03
Education: Graduate or Professional Degree	0.09	0.28	0.12	0.33	-0.13	0.09	0.28	0.08	0.28	0.01

Table 4A.2—Continued

| | Unweighted | | | | | Weighted | | | | |
| | Study Deployment | | No Study Deployment | | | Study Deployment | | No Study Deployment | | |
	Mean	SD	Mean	SD	SMD	Mean	SD	Mean	SD	SMD
Employment: Other	0.03	0.18	0.03	0.17	0.02	0.03	0.18	0.03	0.18	0.01
Employment: Employed	0.30	0.46	0.45	0.50	-0.33	0.30	0.46	0.33	0.47	-0.06
Employment: Homemaker	0.45	0.50	0.39	0.49	0.13	0.45	0.50	0.47	0.50	-0.02
Employment: Student	0.08	0.27	0.05	0.22	0.11	0.08	0.27	0.07	0.25	0.04
Employment: Not Employed	0.14	0.35	0.09	0.28	0.15	0.14	0.35	0.11	0.31	0.08
Marital Satisfaction Scale	3.90	0.55	3.68	0.69	0.39	3.90	0.55	3.88	0.54	0.04
PANAS: Positive	4.13	0.69	3.93	0.88	0.29	4.13	0.69	4.13	0.69	0.00
PANAS: Negative	2.12	0.61	2.28	0.71	-0.27	2.12	0.61	2.10	0.61	0.04
Conflict Tactics Scale: Prevalence of Physical Aggression Toward Partner	0.05	0.21	0.04	0.21	0.02	0.05	0.21	0.03	0.17	0.08
Conflict Tactics Scale: Chronicity of Psychological Aggression Toward Partner	0.72	0.90	0.76	0.94	-0.04	0.72	0.90	0.66	0.89	0.07
Conflict Tactics Scale: Prevalence of Physical Aggression Toward You	0.02	0.15	0.03	0.18	-0.08	0.02	0.15	0.02	0.14	0.02
Conflict Tactics Scale: Chronicity of Psychological Aggression Toward You	0.62	0.90	0.84	1.05	-0.23	0.62	0.90	0.63	0.91	-0.01
Depression (PHQ)	2.67	3.71	3.02	3.51	-0.09	2.67	3.71	2.79	3.55	-0.03
Anxiety	2.07	0.92	2.07	0.89	0.01	2.07	0.92	2.05	0.95	0.03
PTSD	0.47	0.98	0.51	1.00	-0.04	0.47	0.98	0.45	0.96	0.02
Binge Drinking	0.12	0.32	0.08	0.27	0.13	0.12	0.32	0.10	0.30	0.07
Problematic Substance Use Scale	0.08	0.49	0.05	0.38	0.05	0.08	0.49	0.06	0.40	0.03
Medication for Mental Health Problem	0.10	0.31	0.12	0.33	-0.06	0.10	0.31	0.14	0.34	-0.11
Received Mental Health Care	0.11	0.31	0.14	0.34	-0.10	0.11	0.31	0.15	0.35	-0.13
Financial Distress Scale	1.90	0.65	2.10	0.77	-0.30	1.90	0.65	1.95	0.70	-0.07
Family Environment Scale	2.81	0.26	2.73	0.34	0.32	2.81	0.26	2.81	0.26	-0.01
Parenting Stress Scale	3.23	0.38	3.20	0.39	0.09	3.23	0.38	3.24	0.39	-0.02
Parent in the Military	0.40	0.49	0.52	0.50	-0.26	0.40	0.49	0.45	0.50	-0.11

Table 4A.2—Continued

| | Unweighted | | | | | Weighted | | | | |
| | Study Deployment | | No Study Deployment | | | Study Deployment | | No Study Deployment | | |
	Mean	SD	Mean	SD	SMD	Mean	SD	Mean	SD	SMD
Military Commitment	4.53	0.56	4.37	0.66	0.27	4.53	0.56	4.47	0.58	0.10
Satisfaction as Military Spouse	4.08	1.06	3.88	1.06	0.19	4.08	1.06	4.11	0.96	-0.03
Retention Intentions	4.20	1.10	3.97	1.32	0.21	4.20	1.10	4.09	1.23	0.10
TEEN VARIABLES										
SDQ: Total	7.26	5.06	7.90	5.09	-0.13	7.26	5.06	7.45	5.11	-0.04
SDQ Subscale: Emotional Problems	1.58	1.82	1.73	1.69	-0.09	1.58	1.82	1.56	1.70	0.01
SDQ Subscale: Conduct Problems	0.99	1.35	1.01	1.29	-0.02	0.99	1.35	0.99	1.31	0.00
SDQ Subscale: Hyperactivity	3.10	2.43	3.34	2.40	-0.10	3.10	2.43	3.34	2.51	-0.10
SDQ Subscale: Peer Relationships	1.68	1.65	1.82	1.75	-0.09	1.68	1.65	1.56	1.59	0.07
SDQ Subscale: Prosocial Behavior	8.52	1.64	8.38	1.49	0.08	8.52	1.64	8.59	1.55	-0.04
Depression Symptoms	0.93	1.66	0.94	1.74	0.00	0.93	1.66	0.81	1.61	0.07
Anxiety (SCARED)	1.73	2.00	1.51	1.47	0.11	1.73	2.00	1.49	1.65	0.12

Figure 4A.1
Balance Plot for Service Members

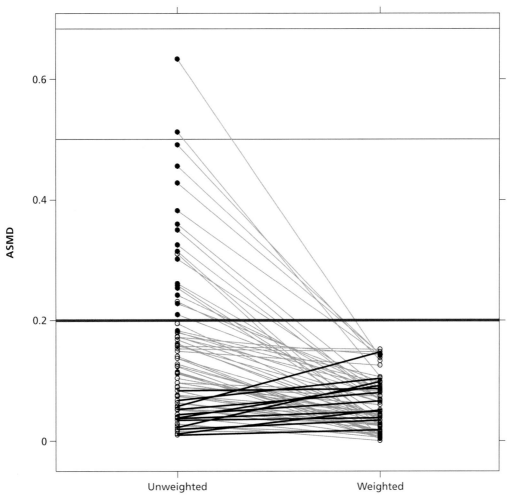

Figure 4A.2
Balance Plot for Spouses

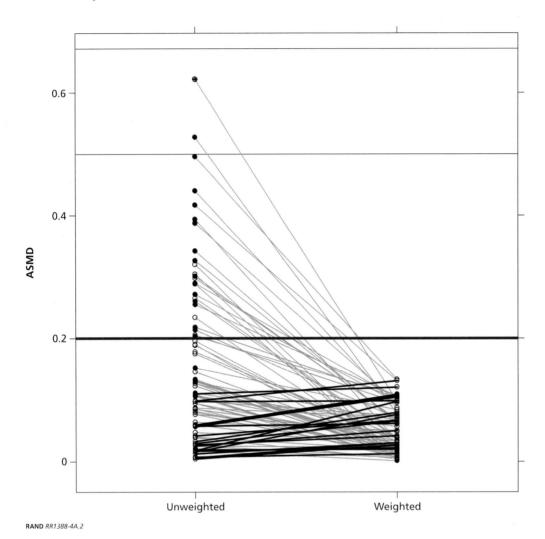

References

Abidin, R. R., *Parenting Stress Index*, 3rd ed., Odessa, Fla.: Psychological Assessment Resources, 1995.

Adler, A. B., A. H. Huffman, P. D. Bliese, and C. A. Castro, "The Impact of Deployment Length and Experience on the Well-Being of Male and Female Soldiers," *Journal of Occupational Health Psychology*, Vol. 20, 2005, pp. 121–137.

Allen, E. S., G. K. Rhoades, S. M. Stanley, and H. J. Markman, "Hitting Home: Relationships Between Recent Deployment, Posttraumatic Stress Symptoms, and Marital Functioning for Army Couples," *Journal of Family Psychology*, Vol. 24, 2010, pp. 280–288.

Bowling, U. B., and M. D. Sherman, "Welcoming Them Home: Supporting Service Members and Their Families in Navigating the Tasks of Reintegration," *Professional Psychology: Research and Practice,* Vol. 39, 2008, pp. 451–458.

Carter, S., B. Loew, E. Allen, S. Stanley, G. Rhoades, and H. Markman, "Relationship Between Soldiers' PTSD Symptoms and Spousal Communication During Deployment," *Journal of Traumatic Stress,* Vol. 24, 2011, pp. 352–355.

Chandra, A., S. Lara-Cinisomo, L. H. Jaycox, T. Tanielian, R. M. Burns, T. Ruder, and B. Han, "Children on the Homefront: The Experience of Children from Military Families," *Pediatrics*, Vol. 125, No. 1, 2010, pp. 16–25.

Cigrang, J. A., G. W. Talcott, J. Tatum, M. Baker, D. Cassidy, S. Sonnek, D. G. Snyder, C. Balderrama-Durbin, R. E. Heyman, and A. M. Smith Slep, "Intimate Partner Communication from the War Zone: A Prospective Study of Relationship Functioning, Communication Frequency, and Combat Effectiveness," *Journal of Marital and Family Therapy*, Vol. 40, 2014, pp. 332–343.

Compas, B. E., S.S. Jaser, M.J. Dunn, and E.M. Rodriguez, "Coping with Chronic Illness in Childhood and Adolescence," *Annual Review of Clinical Psychology*, 2012, pp. 455–480.

Cozza, S. J., and R. M. Lerner, "Military Children and Families: Introducing the Issues," *The Future of Children*, Vol. 23, 2013, pp. 3–11.

Creech, S. K., W. Hadley, and B. Borsari, "The Impact of Military Deployment and Reintegration on Children and Parenting: A Systematic Review," *Professional Psychological: Research and Practice*, Vol. 45, 2014, pp. 452–464.

Dimiceli, E. E., M. A. Steinhardt, and S. E. Smith, "Stressful Experiences, Coping Strategies, and Predictors of Health-Related Outcomes Among Wives of Deployed Military Servicemen," *Armed Forces & Society*, Vol. 36, 2010, pp. 351–373.

Durham, S. W., "In Their Own Words: Staying Connected in a Combat Environment," *Military Medicine*, Vol. 175, 2010, pp. 554–559.

Greene, T., J. Buckman, C. Dandeker, and N. Greenberg, "How Communication with Families Can Both Help and Hinder Service Members' Mental Health and Occupational Effectiveness on Deployment," *Military Medicine*, Vol. 175, No. 10, 2010, pp. 745–749.

Gutman, L. M., and J. S. Eccles, "Financial Strain, Parenting Behaviors, and Adolescents' Achievement: Testing Model Equivalence Between African American and European American Single- and Two-Parent Families," *Child Development,* Vol. 70, No. 6, November-December 1999, pp. 1464–1476.

Hill, R., *Families Under Stress: Adjustment to the Crises of War Separation and Reunion*, New York: Harper & Brothers. 1949.

———, "Generic Features of Families Under Stress," *Social Casework,* Vol. 39, 1958, pp. 139–150.

Hoerster, K. D., K. Lehavot, T. Simpson, M. McFall, G. Reiber, and K. M. Nelson, "Health and Health Behavior Differences: U.S. Military, Veteran and Civilian Men," *American Journal of Preventive Medicine*, Vol. 43, 2012, pp. 483–489.

Hofferth, S., P. E. Davis-Kean, J. Davis, and J. Finkelstein, *The Child Development Supplement to the Panel Study of Income Dynamics: 1997 User Guide*, Ann Arbor, Mich.: Survey Research Center, Institute for Social Research, University of Michigan, 1997. As of September 26, 2015:
https://psidonline.isr.umich.edu/CDS/cdsi_userGD.pdf

Hoge, C. W., C. A. Castro, S. C. Messer, D. McGurk, D. I. Cotting, and R. L. Koffman, "Combat Duty in Iraq and Afghanistan, Mental Health Problems, and Barriers to Care," *New England Journal of Medicine,* Vol. 351, July 1, 2004, pp. 13–22.

Hoglund, M. W., and R. M. Schwartz, "Mental Health in Deployed and Nondeployed Veteran Men and Women in Comparison with Their Civilian Counterparts," *Military Medicine,* Vol. 179, 2014, pp. 19–25.

Hosek, J., J. Kavanagh, and L. L. Miller, *Deployment, Stress, and Intention to Stay in the Military,* Santa Monica, Calif.: RAND Corporation, RB-9150-RC, 2006. As of November 20, 2015:
http://www.rand.org/pubs/research_briefs/RB9150.html

Houston, J. B., B. Pfefferbaum, M. D. Sherman, A. G. Melson, and W. Brand, "Family Communication Across the Military Deployment Experience: Child and Spouse Report of Communication Frequency and Quality and Associated Emotions, Behaviors, and Reactions," *Journal of Loss and Trauma*, Vol. 18, 2013, pp. 103–119. As of September 2015:
http://www.rand.org/pubs/monographs/MG720.html

Institute of Medicine, *Returning Home from Iraq and Afghanistan: Preliminary Assessment of Readjustment Needs of Veterans, Service Members, and Their Families,* Washington, D.C.: The National Academies Press, 2010.

IOM—*See* Institute of Medicine.

King, L. A., D. W. King, D. S. Vogt, J. Knight, and R. E. Samper, "Deployment Risk and Resilience Inventory: A Collection of Measures for Studying Deployment-Related Experiences of Military Personnel and Veterans," *Military Psychology*, Vol. 18. No. 2, 2006, pp. 89–120.

Knobloch, L. K., and S. R. Wilson, "Communication in Military Families Across the Deployment Cycle," in L. H. Turner and R. West, eds., *Handbook of Family Communication*, Thousand Oaks, Calif.: Sage, 2014, pp. 370–385.

Lane, M., L. L. Hourani, R. M. Bray, and J. Williams, "Prevalence of Perceived Stress and Mental Health Indicators Among Reserve-Component and Active-Duty Military Personnel," *American Journal of Public Health*, Vol. 102, 2012, pp. 1213–1220.

Lester, P., K. Peterson, J. Reeves, L. Knauss, D. Glover, C. Mogil, N. Duan, W. Saltzman, R. Pynoos, K. Wilt, and W. Beardslee, "The Long War and Parental Combat Deployment: Effects on Military Children and At-Home Spouses," *Journal of the American Academy of Child and Adolescent Psychiatry*, Vol. 49, 2010, pp. 310–320.

Meadows, S. O., M. Beckett, K. Bowling, D. Golinelli, M. P. Fisher, L. T. Martin, L. S. Meredith, and K. C. Chan Osilla, *Family Resilience in the Military: Definitions, Models, and Policies,* Santa Monica: Calif.: RAND Corporation, RR-470-OSD, 2015. As of September 26, 2015:
http://www.rand.org/pubs/research_reports/RR470.html

Moos, R. H., and B. S. Moos, *Family Environment Scale Manual,* Menlo Park, Calif.: Consulting Psychologists Press, 1994.

Palmer, C., "A Theory of Risk and Resilience: Factors in Military Families," *Military Psychology*, Vol. 20, 2008, pp. 205–217.

Panel Study of Income Dynamics, home page, undated. As of September 26, 2015:
http://psidonline.isr.umich.edu

Park, N., "Military Children and Families: Strengths and Challenges During Peace and War," *American Psychologist*, Vol. 66, 2011, pp. 65–72.

Pritchett, R., J. Kemp, P. Wilson, H. Minnis, G. Bryce, and C. Gillbert, "Quick, Simple Measures of Family Relationships for Use in Clinical Practice and Research: A Systematic Overview," *Family Practice*, Vol. 28, 2011, pp. 172–187.

PSID—*See* Panel Study of Income Dynamics.

Saltzman, W. R., P. Lester, W. R. Beardslee, C. M. Layne, K. Woodward, and W. P. Nash, "Mechanisms of Risk and Resilience in Military Families: Theoretical and Empirical Basis of a Family-Focused Resilience Enhancement Program," *Clinical Child and Family Psychological Review*, Vol. 14, 2011, pp. 213–230.

Sheppard, S. C., J. W. Malatras, and A. C. Israel, "The Impact of Deployment of U.S. Military Families," *American Psychologist*, Vol. 65, 2010, pp. 599–609.

Solomon, Z., *Combat Stress Reaction: The Enduring Toll of War*, New York: Springer, 1993.

Tanielian, T., and L. H. Jaycox, eds., *Invisible Wounds of War: Psychological and Cognitive Injuries, Their Consequences, and Services to Assist Recovery*, Santa Monica, Calif.: RAND Corporation, MG-720-CCF, 2008. As of September 26, 2015:
http://www.rand.org/pubs/monographs/MG720.html

Tanielian, T., B. R. Karney, A. Chandra, S. O. Meadows, and the Deployment Life Study Team, *The Deployment Life Study Methodological Overview and Baseline Sample Description*, Santa Monica, Calif.: RAND Corporation, RR-209-OSD/A, 2014. As of September 26, 2015:
http://www.rand.org/pubs/research_reports/RR209.html

Trail, T. E., S. O. Meadows, J. N. Miles, and B. R. Karney, "Patterns of Vulnerability and Resources in U.S. Military Families," *Journal of Family Issues*, June 30, 2015, pp. 1–22.

Trautmann, J., J. Alhusen, and D. Gross, "Impact of Deployment on Military Families with Young Children: A Systematic Review," *Nursing Outlook*, June 12, 2015, pp. 1–24.

Troxel, W. M., T. E. Trail, L. Jaycox, and A. Chandra, "Preparing for Deployment: Examining Family and Individual-Level Factors," *Military Psychology*, forthcoming.

Under Secretary of Defense for Personnel and Readiness, *Military Family Readiness*, Washington, D.C., Department of Defense Instruction 1342.22, July 3, 2012. As of September 26, 2015:
http://www.dtic.mil/whs/directives/corres/pdf/134222p.pdf

Wadsworth, S. M. D., and D. Riggs, eds., *Risk and Resilience in U.S. Military Families*, New York: Springer, 2011.

Werber, L., M. C. Harrell, D. M. Varda, K. C. Hall, M. K. Beckett, and S. Howard, *Deployment Experiences of Guard and Reserve Families*, Santa Monica, Calif.: RAND Corporation, MG-645-OSD, 2008. As of November 20, 2015:
http://www.rand.org/pubs/monographs/MG645.html

Wong, L., and S. Gerras, *The Effects of Multiple Deployments on Army Adolescents*, Carlisle, Pa.: Strategic Studies Institute, United States Army War College, 2010.

Zohar, A. H., G. Shen, A. Dycian, D. Pauls, A. Apter, R. King, D. Cohen, and S. Kron, "The Military Life Scale: A Measure of Perceived Stress and Support in the Israeli Defense Force," *Israel Journal of Psychiatry and Related Sciences*, Vol. 41, No. 1, 2004, pp. 33–44.

Zubrick, S. R., A. A. Williams, S. R. Silburn, and G. Vimpani, *Indicators of Social and Family Functioning*, Canberra, Australia: Department of Family and Community Services, 2000.

CHAPTER FIVE

Psychological and Behavioral Health of Service Members and Their Spouses

Rajeev Ramchand, Terry L. Schell, Terri Tanielian, Beth Ann Griffin, Esther M. Friedman, Robin Beckman, and Christine Vaughan

Introduction

The toll of war on the psychological and behavioral health of deployed service members has been a longstanding public health concern. In fact, throughout the history of warfare, concerns have been raised about the persistent emotional and behavioral effects that war has on the warrior. Over history, this toll has been documented in many ways (storytelling, in historical accounts of war casualties), and referred to with different labels (war neuroses, battle fatigue, etc.). The issue increased significantly as an area of scientific scholarship after the Vietnam War, particularly after 1980 when the American Psychiatric Association incorporated posttraumatic stress disorder (PTSD) into the Diagnostic and Statistical Manual, due in large part to the influx of Vietnam veterans presenting with a particular pattern of symptoms that did not directly correspond to other common diagnoses (Fisher and Schell, 2013). Since then, estimates have been produced on the prevalence of PTSD among American troops who served in Vietnam (Dohrenwend et al., 2006) and the first Gulf War (Kang et al., 2003). More recently, the scholarship expanded greatly, with studies estimating the prevalence of risk factors for, and consequences of, psychological and behavioral health outcomes of U.S. service members supporting Operation Iraqi Freedom/Operation Enduring Freedom/Operation New Dawn (OIF/OEF/OND) (see Ramchand, Karney, et al., 2008; Ramchand, Rudavsky, et al., 2015; Ramchand, Schell, et al., 2010; Sundin, Fear, et al., 2010).

Although the scientific literature on this generation of veterans is quite large, it has several notable omissions: The studies that have included current service members are often not representative of the deployed force; the studies are almost exclusively cross-sectional in their design; and the studies lack comparison groups of nondeployed service members who are well matched to the deployed group. The lack of either longitudinal samples or carefully constructed comparison groups limits the ability of this literature to address the full range of research hypotheses, including documenting the time course of symptoms or the factors associated with risk and resilience. In addition, the literature has been focused primarily on the warrior's psychological health, although there is increased recognition that war can produce indirect harm on the warriors' families.

In this chapter, we add to this literature by examining: (1) the changes over time in the psychological and behavioral health of those who experienced a deployment relative to similar individuals who did not; (2) how symptoms of these health outcomes vary across the predeployment, deployment, and postdeployment phases of the deployment cycle; and (3) potential risk and resilience factors that predict postdeployment psychological and behavioral health outcomes. For all three of these analyses, the current study looks at both married service members and their spouses, a group that has received little research attention in the past.

In contrast to the marital, family, child, and military career outcomes that are the focus of Chapters Three, Four, Six, and Seven (respectively), a significant body of research has been devoted to the psychological and behavioral health of service members. This literature allows us to have relatively specific hypotheses about how these outcomes are related to the deployment cycle and various risk and resilience factors. However, the design of the current study is unique within the existing literature, and will address several significant gaps. First and foremost, it offers a three-year, longitudinal design with up to nine assessments during a deployment cycle. Second, it tracks outcomes for those who deployed, as well as for those who did not. Third, the study population is unique—a representative sample of married, deployable service members during the latter stages of these conflicts (i.e., 2011–2013). We anticipate that the studied population is at reduced risk for psychological and behavioral problems relative to the overall population of those who have served in these conflicts. As a married sample, they tend to be older, higher ranking, and have better social support than the broader population. Similarly, they deployed during a more stable and less threatening security climate overseas (Ramchand, Rudavsky, et al., 2015) and with greater experience from prior deployments relative to those who deployed earlier in the conflicts.

A number of review articles have summarized findings from the literature on the mental, emotional, and behavioral health conditions among service members who have deployed, mostly to Iraq and/or Afghanistan, since 2001. We summarize key findings relevant to the current analysis below.

Deployment Trauma

Exposure to deployment trauma is the strongest predictor of psychological and behavioral health outcomes among service members. Regardless of how often or how long a person deploys, exposure to deployment trauma, typically due to direct combat or related injuries, is consistently associated with adverse psychological and behavioral health outcomes. Reviews confirm that trauma/combat exposure is the strongest predictor of PTSD among military personnel deployed to Iraq and Afghanistan (Kok et al., 2012; Ramchand, Rudavsky, et al., 2015; Ramchand, Schell, et al., 2010). Deployment trauma exposure also has been associated with depression (Baker et al., 2009; Heron et al., 2013; Jacobson et al., 2012; Luxton, Skopp, and Maguen, 2010; Maguen, Ren, et al., 2010; Mayo et al., 2013; Schell and Tanielian, 2011) and substance misuse (Sundin, Herrell, et al., 2014) among previously deployed troops. In studies that have examined whether deployment increases the risk of PTSD and depression relative to service members who have not deployed, relationships are attenuated once controlling for deployment trauma exposure (Jones et al., 2013; Vanderploeg et al., 2012). Because service members in our sample deployed at a time when the security climate was relatively stable and in which most service members would not be regularly exposed to direct combat, we hypothesize that the effect of deployment on psychological and behavioral health outcomes will be small.

Deployments and Psychological and Behavioral Health

There is no significant relationship between length of deployments and psychological and behavioral health independent of deployment trauma. All else being equal, a longer deployment increases the probability that a given service member will be exposed to a traumatic experience on that deployment, which puts him or her at increased risk for psychological and behavioral health problems. Thus, although there has been some evidence to suggest that longer deployments have a bivariate association with PTSD (Adler et al., 2005; Allison-Aipa et al., 2010; Armed Forces Health Surveillance Center, 2012; Escolas et al., 2013; Macera et al., 2013; MacGregor et al., 2013; Shen, Arkes, and Williams, 2012), depression (Adler et al., 2005; Allison-Aipa et al., 2010; Shen, Arkes, and Williams, 2012), and substance misuse (Allison-Aipa et al., 2010; Mustillo et al., 2015; Rona et al., 2007; Shen, Arkes, and Williams, 2012; Spera et al., 2011; Wittchen et al., 2013), only two of the studies that showed an association between deployment length and behavioral health outcomes controlled for combat-related traumatic events (Mustillo et al., 2015; Spera et al., 2011). In contrast, several studies that do adjust for combat exposure find no evidence of an association between deployment length and PTSD, depression, and substance misuse (Gehrman et al., 2013; Grieger et al., 2006; Mustillo et al., 2015; Schell and Marshall, 2008; Schultz, Glickman, and Eisen, 2014; Seelig et al., 2012; Wood et al., 2012).

Symptoms over a Deployment Cycle

The course of psychological and behavioral health symptoms over a deployment cycle are largely unknown. Very few studies have examined trajectories of psychological or behavioral health symptoms over the course of a deployment cycle. The Mental Health Advisory Team (MHAT) series of studies has looked cross-sectionally at symptoms during the deployment itself, but has not included pre- or postdeployment assessments. The MHAT-V, an in-theater study of OIF soldiers deployed during September and October 2007, found that inhalant use, positive screens for PTSD, and alcohol use were greatest at roughly eight to nine months, ten months, and 11 months into the deployment period, respectively (U.S. Department of the Army, Office of the Surgeon General, 2008). The successive MHAT (MHAT-VI-OIF) suggested that symptoms of acute stress, the precursor to PTSD, and depression were greatest at approximately the midpoint of the deployment period (U.S. Department of the Army, Office of the Surgeon General, 2009). Similarly, a growth curve analysis of monthly changes in soldiers' PTSD and depressive symptoms during a deployment to Iraq found that symptoms were most severe roughly eight months into a 16-month deployment (i.e., roughly halfway through the deployment); however, symptoms declined to their baseline levels or lower by the end of the deployment (Telch et al., 2012). In contrast, there have been some longitudinal studies of symptoms following deployment. A longitudinal study of a brigade combat team immediately upon returning from deployment and four months later found a marked increase in PTSD symptoms over time (Bliese et al., 2007), resulting in the Department of Defense (DoD)–wide requirement that service members complete a postdeployment health reassessment six months after returning from deployment, screening data that went on to inform subsequent longitudinal studies of postdeployment symptoms (e.g., Milliken, Auchterlonie, and Hoge, 2007). Both longitudinal and cross-sectional studies (e.g., Sharkey and Rennix, 2011; Thomas et al., 2010) have continued to show stable or slightly increasing symptoms in the period from three to 12 months postdeployment. However, there are concerns that the measurement environment shifts during this period, which may make these assessments difficult to compare. (For a discussion of these limitations, see Milliken, Auchterlonie, and Hoge, 2007.)

Differential Exposure to Trauma

Service members have differential risk of psychological and behavioral health outcomes based on their demographic (i.e., age, gender) and military-specific characteristics (i.e., service branch, rank) that may partially be explained by differential exposure to deployment trauma. Unmarried or separated service members and veterans who have deployed have been found to be at higher risk of developing PTSD, depression, and substance misuse than those who are married (Booth-Kewley et al., 2010; Iversen et al., 2009; Maguen, Cohen, et al., 2012; Pietrzak et al., 2009). Similarly, younger age groups, particularly men, have been identified at increased risk for PTSD (Maguen, Cohen, et al., 2012; Maguen, Ren, et al., 2010; Seal et al., 2009). These trends are important to consider when we examine psychological and behavioral health outcomes of the Deployment Life sample—which is, by definition, married and also older than the general force. Other demographic trends from the literature suggest that, consistent with civilian populations, women who have deployed are at increased risk for depression (Carter-Visscher et al., 2010; Elbogen et al., 2013; Haskell et al., 2010; Kehle et al., 2011; Luxton, Skopp, and Maguen, 2010; Maguen, Cohen, et al., 2012; Maguen, Madden, et al., 2014; Maguen, Ren, et al., 2010; Seal et al., 2009), while men are at increased risk for substance misuse (Elbogen et al., 2013; Iversen et al., 2009; Maguen, Cohen, et al., 2012; Maguen, Madden, et al., 2014; Maguen, Ren, et al., 2010; Seal et al., 2009). There is conflicting evidence about whether military PTSD is more common in men (Cohen, Brown, et al., 2010; Haskell et al., 2010; Heron et al., 2013; Iversen et al., 2009; Maguen, Madden, et al., 2014; Maguen, Ren, et al., 2010) or women (Kehle et al., 2011; LeardMann et al., 2009; Luxton, Skopp, and Maguen, 2010), although studies that control for exposure to trauma generally find an elevated risk of PTSD in women (Luxton, Skopp, and Maguen, 2010; Schell and Marshall, 2008).

In general, military characteristics, such as service branch, rank, or military occupation, are weakly linked to PTSD once studies account for differential exposure to trauma across these groups (Ramchand, Rudavsky, et al., 2015). Thus, combat exposure may explain the Army's higher prevalence rates of PTSD (Armed Forces Health Surveillance Center, 2012; Baker et al., 2009; Cohen, Gima, et al., 2010; LeardMann et al., 2009; Maguen, Cohen, et al., 2012; Seal et al., 2009) and depression (Maguen, Cohen, et al., 2012), as well as higher rates of PTSD in the Marine Corps (Armed Forces Health Surveillance Center, 2012; Baker et al., 2009; Cohen, Gima, et al., 2010) or higher rates of PTSD and depression among enlisted personnel and those of lower rank (Cohen, Gima, et al., 2010; Goodwin et al., 2012; Hickling et al., 2011; LeardMann et al., 2009; Maguen, Ren, et al., 2010; Mayo et al., 2013; Seal et al., 2009).

In addition, predeployment factors, including perceptions of being prepared for deployment (Carter-Visscher et al., 2010; Mulligan et al., 2010; Shea et al., 2013), have been found to be related to mental health problems. We return to these constructs in Research Question (RQ) 3, when we examine factors that predict psychological and behavioral health outcomes postdeployment.

Mental Health Services

Mental health services are underutilized among those in need. In general, fewer than half of those who have deployed and report symptoms indicating that they could benefit from mental health services actually receive such care (Gorman et al., 2011; Pietrzak et al., 2009; Schell and Tanielian, 2011). There is some evidence that greater symptom severity increases treatment-seeking (Balderrama-Durbin et al., 2013; Cohen, Gima, et al., 2010; Elbogen et al., 2013; Possemato et al., 2010; Whealin et al., 2014). Some of the more commonly endorsed reasons about why those who might benefit from treatment don't get it are: difficulty scheduling an appointment or getting time off, stigma, and treatment costs (Elbogen et al., 2013; Elnitsky et al., 2013; Schell and

Tanielian, 2011). Although we do not study treatment utilization in this set of analyses, we do measure service members' and spouses' self-reported perceived need for mental health treatment.

Health of Military Spouses

The psychological and behavioral health of military spouses is adversely affected by deployment, particularly those of longer durations. The number of research studies on the psychological and behavioral health of military spouses pales in comparison to that of service members, although some reviews exist (de Burgh et al., 2011; Levy and Sidel, 2009; Yambo and Johnson, 2014). This limited group of studies suggests that there are adverse effects of deployment on military spouses. We identified only one study that examined symptoms prior to deployment, finding elevated rates in spouses relative to service members (Erbes et al., 2012). In the post-deployment period, one comprehensive study showed that military spouses who experienced a deployment exhibited elevated rates of many mental health diagnoses, and those with lengths of deployment longer than 11 months were even more likely to have such diagnoses (Mansfield et al., 2010). Other research similarly confirms that length of deployment may increase spouse distress (Rodriguez and Margolin, 2015). One study suggests that it may be not only duration of deployment, but extended deployments that exacerbate psychological and behavioral health symptoms (SteelFisher, Zaslavsky, and Blendon, 2008) while another finds increased symptomatology in the postdeployment period when spouses perceive that their service members have such symptoms but do not report having them (Renshaw, Rodrigues, and Jones, 2008). On the other hand, spouses are more likely to seek care and are less concerned about stigma associated with accessing mental health care than their spouses (Eaton et al., 2008; Gorman et al., 2011; Renshaw, Rodrigues, and Jones, 2008).

Research Questions

To examine the impact of deployment on the psychological and behavioral health of service members and their spouses, we pose three research questions in the current analyses:

- **RQ1:** How does deployment affect postdeployment psychological and behavioral health outcomes? These effects are estimated by documenting the changes over the course of the three-year study in the psychological and behavioral health of those who deployed relative to matched individuals who did not deploy.
  - ◦ **Hypothesis:** We expect deployment to be positively related to mental and behavioral health problems; however, because of the relatively secure climate in Afghanistan during the period of study, as well as the risk characteristics of the sample itself (i.e., married, older, higher rank, multiple prior deployments), we expect the effect to be small.
- **RQ2:** How do psychological and behavioral health outcomes change, on average, over the predeployment, deployment, and postdeployment phases of the deployment cycle?
  - – **RQ2a:** Does the overall trajectory differ significantly from a flat line (i.e., no changes in average values over the studied deployment cycle)?
  - – **RQ2b:** Does the overall trend differ significantly from a straight line (i.e., a constant change over time that is unrelated to the phase of, or timing within, the deployment cycle)?

- **RQ2c:** Are there significant differences between the trajectories of service members and their spouses over the course of the deployment cycle (i.e., are they parallel)?
  - ◦ **Hypothesis:** Due to the lack of longitudinal studies of symptoms over the deployment cycle, we do not have *a priori* hypotheses for the shapes of these trajectories.
- **RQ3:** What potential risk and resilience factors assessed between the baseline and follow-up periods predict change in psychological and behavioral outcomes over this period among service members and spouses who experienced a deployment?
  - ◦ **Hypotheses:** We hypothesize that deployment trauma—specifically, experiencing physical trauma—will be predictive of changes in PTSD and depression symptoms from the baseline to postdeployment period. Similarly, we expect that predeployment readiness will be associated with lower levels of symptoms in these same domains.

Analytic Sample

Data for this chapter include up to nine assessment waves of the Deployment Life Study. As described previously, the Deployment Life Study is a longitudinal survey of 2,724 deployable, married, military families, including service members, their spouses, and in some cases a teen living in the household (see Chapter Two, as well as Tanielian, Karney, et al., 2014, for additional details of the baseline sample). In total, 2,146 service members and 2,323 spouses with longitudinal follow-up data compose the sample used in this chapter. This includes service members and their spouses regardless of whether they had a child or whether they remained married during the course of the study.

Outcome Measures

We have assessed five outcomes to represent the psychological and behavioral health of each service member and spouse: depression symptoms, PTSD symptoms, anxiety symptoms, binge drinking, and perceived need for mental health treatment. These are discussed in Chapter Two, and we review them briefly here:

Symptoms of Major Depression. Depression is a mood disorder that is marked by feelings of sadness or a general loss of interest. In this study, we ask about symptoms over the past two weeks using the eight-item version of the Patient Health Questionnaire (PHQ)-8. The total scale value ranges from 0 to 24; scores less than four indicate no or minimal depression; scores between 4 and 14 indicate minor to mildly severe depression; scores between 15 and 19 indicate moderately severe depression, and those 20 and above indicate severe depression.

Symptoms of PTSD. PTSD is diagnosable based on symptoms that persist for at least 30 days after an individual traumatic experience. For service members, we measure PTSD symptoms over the past 30 days using the PTSD Check List. The scale ranges from 17 to 85, with higher scores indicating greater PTSD symptoms; thresholds of total scores of 50 and above and of 44 and above have both been used to identify cases of PTSD (Brewin, 2005), although scores as low as 30 may also efficiently identify clinical cases (Bliese et al., 2008). For spouses, we use the Primary Care PTSD screen, which is only four items and thus ranges in score from zero to four; patients are typically referred for further evaluation in clinical settings if they score three or four, although answering "yes" to two of the four questions may also efficiently identify clinical cases (Bliese et al., 2008).

Generalized Anxiety. Generalized anxiety is marked by excessive and exaggerated anxiety and worry about commonplace events with no obvious rationale. We measure anxiety over the past four weeks using four items from the anxiety subscale from the Mental Health Inventory 18. Each item used a six-point response scale from "none of the time" to "all of the time." A mean across the four items was computed (ranging 1–6) with higher scores indicating greater anxiety.

Binge Drinking. Male respondents were asked about the number of days in the past month they drank five or more drinks on one occasion, while females were asked about the number of days in the past month they drank four or more drinks on one occasion. We present the proportion that meet the criteria for any days of drinking more than five/four drinks.

Perceived Need for Mental Health Treatment. Perceived need for treatment comes from one survey item in which both service members and spouses were asked, "In the past four months, did you have a need for counseling or therapy for personal or emotional problems from a mental health specialist, such as a psychiatrist, psychologist, social worker, or family counselor in a mental health clinic or office, whether or not you actually received any counseling?" We present the proportion that endorsed this item.

Sample Characteristics

Table 5.1 shows descriptive statistics for each outcome at baseline, stratified by whether the family experienced a deployment during the studied period. At baseline, it is worth noting the relatively low levels of depressive, PTSD, and anxiety symptoms among both service members and spouses. However, there were substantial differences at baseline between those who would go on to deploy within the next three years, and those who would not. In general, those who subsequently deployed were healthier than those who did not, with lower depression symptoms and less than half the rate of members who perceived a need for mental health treatment. These two findings provide a clear indication that deployment is not randomly assigned to service members and reiterates the importance of using the propensity score approach we apply for RQ1, presented below. On the other hand, the data reveal that spouses of a service member who subsequently deployed have higher prevalence of binge drinking at baseline than those whose service members did not subsequently deploy (15 percent versus 9 percent, $p=0.01$).

Table 5.2 displays the correlation between outcomes assessed at baseline for service members and spouses. The diagonal shows the correlation between service member and spouse reports of each of the five outcomes examined in this chapter. As expected, the mental, emotional, and behavioral health outcomes are not strongly correlated across partners. However, symptoms of depression, PTSD, and anxiety are highly correlated between the service member and the spouse.

Table 5.3 provides additional information on key covariates assessed at baseline for both service members and spouses. As with Table 5.1, these characteristics are stratified by whether the service member subsequently deployed in the study period. Service members who subsequently deployed were substantially different from those who did not on a range of key measures at baseline. Those with a study deployment tended to be younger, yet they had experienced more deployments prior to baseline and had more prior deployment trauma. They were also more likely to be male and in the active component.

Table 5.1
Psychological and Behavioral Health Outcomes at Baseline

	Overall Sample		Service Members			Spouses		
	Service Members (n=2,146)	Spouses (n=2,321)	Study Deployment (n=902)	No Study Deployment (n=1,244)	p-value	Study Deployment (n=958)	No Study Deployment (n=1,363)	p-value
Average Depression Symptoms[a]	2.95 (0.16)	3.16 (0.15)	**2.39 (0.16)**	**3.11 (0.21)**	**0.01**	2.84 (0.17)	3.25 (0.19)	0.10
Average PTSD Symptoms[b]	22.39 (0.43)	0.49 (0.04)	**21.33 (0.41)**	**22.69 (0.55)**	**0.05**	0.48 (0.05)	0.49 (0.05)	0.87
Average Anxiety Symptoms[c]	2.10 (0.05)	2.16 (0.04)	2.02 (0.05)	2.13 (0.06)	0.20	2.08 (0.04)	2.18 (0.05)	0.15
Percentage Binge Drinking	24.17 (2.75)	10.13 (1.05)	24.71 (2.65)	24.02 (3.45)	0.87	**14.85 (1.78)**	**8.80 (1.21)**	**0.01**
Percentage Perceiving Need for Treatment	15.96 (1.74)	13.53 (1.27)	**7.39 (1.18)**	**18.37 (2.24)**	**0.00**	12.60 (1.44)	13.79 (1.58)	0.58

NOTES: Bold indicates a statistically significant difference between the Study Deployment and No Study Deployment Groups based on a weighted t-test. Standard errors (SEs) of the estimates are in parentheses.

[a] Higher scores=more depressive symptoms. Range: 0–24.

[b] Higher scores=more PTSD symptoms. Range: 17–85 for service member, 0–4 for spouse.

[c] Higher scores=more anxiety. Mean subscale score range: 1–6.

Table 5.2
Correlation Between Outcomes at Baseline: Service Members and Spouses

	Depression Symptoms	PTSD Symptoms	Anxiety Symptoms	Binge Drinking	Perceived Need for Treatment
Depression Symptoms	0.18	0.63	0.70	0.05	0.49
PTSD Symptoms	0.40	0.13	0.53	0.07	0.48
Anxiety Symptoms	0.64	0.38	0.14	0.13	0.37
Binge Drinking	0.05	0.09	0.09	0.22	0.04
Perceived Need for Treatment	0.40	0.31	0.40	0.10	0.20

NOTES: Correlations between outcomes among service members are shaded in blue in the upper-right triangle of the matrix; correlations between outcomes among spouses are coded in green in the lower-left triangle of the matrix. The diagonal contains correlations between service members and spouses for each measure at baseline. All correlations are statistically significant at p<0.05, except for the r=0.04 correlation between binge drinking and perceived need for treatment for the service member.

RQ1: How Does Deployment Affect Service Member and Spouse Postdeployment Outcomes?

Analysis

As discussed in Chapter Two, we use propensity score weighting to estimate the causal effect of deployment on psychological and behavioral health outcomes. Thus, participants who experienced a study deployment are compared with those who did not have a study deployment but have been weighted to match the deployed sample on all baseline characteristics. The change in each outcome from baseline to the latter waves of the study is assessed within regression models that control for a range of baseline covariates and random effects for each respondent that appropriately adjusted for the correlation between the repeated measures within each respondent. The covariates include: respondent gender, age, racial/ethnic minority status, length of marriage, having children younger than age six in the household, having a parent in the military, rank and officer/enlisted status, number of prior combat deployments, years of service, branch and component of service, prior deployment trauma, prior combat trauma, survey mode at follow-up (phone or web), and the baseline measure of outcome in question. For models of spouse outcomes, we additionally controlled for spouse educational attainment and employment status. As shown in Tables 5.1 and 5.3, before applying propensity score weights, service members who subsequently experienced a deployment were significantly different from those who did not on their baseline characteristics. Without propensity weighting or covariate adjustments, comparisons between these two groups would be difficult to interpret due to these differences. The service members who subsequently deployed were, paradoxically, both more combat experienced and in better mental health at baseline than service members who did not deploy. As shown in Appendix Table 5A.1, applying the propensity score weights attenuated these differences, resulting in a more apples-to-apples comparison between those who experienced a study deployment and those who did not.

Results

Predicted means were estimated using outcome data from the final three postdeployment assessments. Table 5.4 presents the predicted means for each of the five mental, emotional, and behavioral health outcomes among service members and spouses who did and did not experience a study deployment. None of the predicted means differ significantly across those who did experi-

Table 5.3
Means, Percentages, and Standard Errors of Study Variables at Baseline

	Overall Sample		Service Members			Spouses		
	Service Members (n=2,146)	Spouses (n=2,323)	Study Deployment (n=904)	No Study Deployment (n=1244)	p-value	Study Deployment (n=960)	No Study Deployment (n=1363)	p-value
MEANS								
Age[a]	34.54 (0.41)	33.88 (0.45)	32.73 (0.39)	35.05 (0.52)	0.00	32.21 (0.43)	34.35 (0.56)	0.00
Length of Marriage[b]	106.94 (4.42)	105.99 (4.41)	96.82 (4.17)	109.79 (5.56)	0.06	94.93 (4.16)	109.11 (5.49)	0.04
Number of Prior Combat Deployments[c]	1.52 (0.08)	1.47 (0.07)	2.02 (0.09)	1.38 (0.09)	0.00	1.99 (0.07)	1.33 (0.09)	0.00
Deployment Trauma[d]	1.86 (0.16)	1.96 (0.13)	2.24 (0.18)	1.71 (0.20)	0.05	2.36 (0.20)	1.80 (0.16)	0.03
Combat Experiences Scale (CES)[e]	3.97 (0.20)	3.86 (0.20)	4.61 (0.33)	3.79 (0.24)	0.04	4.67 (0.29)	3.63 (0.23)	0.01
Percentages								
Male	87.58 (2.22)	12.46 (2.33)	92.24 (1.38)	86.26 (2.80)	0.03	7.76 (1.44)	13.78 (2.94)	0.04
Minority Race/Ethnicity	32.47 (2.68)	29.4 (2.47)	31.99 (2.56)	32.61 (3.36)	0.88	28.58 (2.50)	29.63 (3.09)	0.79
Children Younger Than Age 6 in Household	46.16 (2.98)	44.11 (2.70)	51.24 (2.99)	44.73 (3.74)	0.18	47.81 (2.77)	43.06 (3.35)	0.27
Parent in the Military	51.99 (2.91)	48.95 (2.82)	52.76 (2.95)	51.77 (3.65)	0.83	40.31 (2.74)	51.39 (3.45)	0.01
Any Prior Deployment[f]	74.09 (3.42)	74.08 (3.41)	91.48 (1.28)	69.2 (4.17)	0.00	91.48 (1.29)	69.17 (4.13)	0.00
Reserve Component	34.10 (2.85)	34.56 (3.08)	15.98 (2.20)	39.21 (3.57)	0.00	16.52 (2.21)	39.64 (3.73)	0.00
Branch Of Service								
Army	48.91 (2.92)	48.91 (2.76)	45.7 (2.87)	49.81 (3.67)	0.73	45.7 (2.64)	49.81 (3.49)	0.67
Air Force	17.06 (1.28)	17.06 (1.27)	20.04 (1.82)	16.22 (1.53)		20.04 (1.79)	16.22 (1.51)	
Navy	25.26 (3.49)	25.26 (3.45)	24.36 (2.61)	25.51 (4.40)		24.36 (2.58)	25.51 (4.35)	
Marine Corps	8.78 (1.63)	8.78 (1.39)	9.91 (3.66)	8.46 (1.81)		9.91 (3.010)	8.46 (1.56)	
Pay Grade								
E1 to E3	4.07 (0.90)	4.52 (0.89)	4.50 (1.24)	3.95 (1.10)	0.18	4.51 (1.34)	4.53 (1.08)	0.54
E4 to E9	72.53 (2.30)	72.83 (2.17)	68.85 (2.73)	73.56 (2.82)		71.09 (2.28)	73.33 (2.70)	
O1 to O3	8.94 (1.36)	8.81 (1.25)	10.63 (1.30)	8.47 (1.70)		10.61 (1.27)	8.30 (1.56)	
O4 +	11.20 (1.58)	11.31 (1.57)	10.16 (1.43)	11.49 (1.99)		10.18 (1.41)	11.63 (1.97)	
Warrant Officer	3.26 (0.71)	2.52 (0.43)	5.86 (2.17)	2.52 (0.66)		3.62 (0.79)	2.21 (0.50)	

Table 5.3—Continued

	Overall Sample		Service Members			Spouses		
	Service Members (n=2,146)	Spouses (n=2,323)	Study Deployment (n=904)	No Study Deployment (n=1244)	p-value	Study Deployment (n=960)	No Study Deployment (n=1363)	p-value
Spouse Education								
Less Than High School	1.21 (0.44)	1.27 (0.30)	0.66 (0.25)	1.37 (0.56)	0.82	0.74 (0.26)	1.42 (0.38)	0.93
High School	18.82 (2.69)	17.96 (2.26)	18.84 (2.04)	18.82 (3.40)		18.28 (1.87)	17.87 (2.85)	
Some College	28.57 (2.98)	26.20 (2.16)	30.04 (3.34)	28.16 (3.70)		27.69 (2.52)	25.78 (2.66)	
Associate/Vocational/Technical Degree	16.76 (1.92)	17.98 (2.00)	16.74 (2.09)	16.76 (2.39)		18.01 (2.56)	17.97 (2.46)	
Bachelor's Degree	28.24 (2.35)	26.64 (2.14)	25.80 (2.23)	28.93 (2.95)		27.07 (2.28)	26.52 (2.66)	
Graduate Degree	6.40 (0.70)	9.96 (2.85)	7.93 (1.27)	5.96 (0.80)		8.22 (1.51)	10.45 (3.62)	
Spouse Employment Status								
Military Spouse	6.79 (1.99)	7.22 (2.14)	**5.65 (1.19)**	**7.11 (2.53)**	0.01	**4.64 (0.97)**	**7.95 (2.72)**	0.02
Employed (Full or Part Time)	41.61 (2.97)	41.44 (2.87)	**31.81 (2.60)**	44.38 (3.70)		**33.46 (2.55)**	**43.70 (3.57)**	
Homemaker	32.24 (2.67)	31.36 (2.30)	**40.64 (3.17)**	29.88 (3.27)		**39.10 (2.69)**	**29.18 (2.80)**	
Student	8.18 (1.35)	7.76 (1.22)	7.39 (1.16)	8.41 (1.70)		**7.69 (1.16)**	**7.78 (1.53)**	
Unemployed	11.17 (1.26)	12.21 (1.35)	**14.51 (1.77)**	10.23 (1.52)		**15.1 (2.38)**	**11.40 (1.57)**	

NOTES: Bold indicates a statistically significant difference between the Study Deployment and No Study Deployment Groups.

[a] Service member and spouse range: 19–65.

[b] In months. Service member range: 0–528; spouse range: 0–474.

[c] Includes deployments as part of OIF/OEF/OND. Service member range: 0–5.

[d] See Tanielian and Jaycox (2008, p. 91). These items are taken from the first follow-up survey (Wave 2). Service member range: 0–11.

[e] See Hoge et al. (2004). Service member range: 0–15.

[f] Includes all deployments of 30 days or more outside the continental United States.

ence a deployment during the study from those who did not. These results differ somewhat from other studies in this area, which have typically found an increase in mental or behavioral health problems following deployment. However, they are consistent with our earlier observations that (a) this older, married, and experienced population is at relatively low risk for problems caused by one additional deployment and (b) the deployment environment during the period being studied involved less trauma or combat exposure than at earlier points in the war.

RQ2: How Do Psychological and Behavioral Health Outcomes Change over the Phases of the Deployment Cycle?

Analysis

The descriptive trajectories we use depict psychological and behavioral health outcomes before, during, and after a study deployment. They derive from random effects regression models that predict each outcome from a range of trajectory factors tied to the specific phase of the deployment cycle in which they were measured. These models were jointly fitted to spouse and service member data allowing for random effects at the household and respondent type level. In addition, the regression models control for respondent gender, age, racial/ethnic minority status, length of marriage, having children younger than age six in the household, spouse educational attainment, spouse employment status, rank and officer/enlisted status, number of prior combat deployments, years of service, branch and component of service, and prior deployment trauma at baseline. Survey mode (phone or web) is included as a time-varying covariate at each wave. The results from the regression models are used to derive a predicted average trajectory within our sample for a specific, hypothetical deployment cycle. The particular deployment cycle selected was designed to be relatively typical of the deployment cycles observed over the course of the study. This covers a 24-month period, including eight months before and eight months after a deployment of an eight-month duration. We also test three hypotheses about

Table 5.4
Predicted Mean Differences of Outcomes by Study Deployment Status

	Service Members		Spouses	
	Study Deployment (n=907)	No Study Deployment (n=1244)	Study Deployment (n=960)	No Study Deployment (n=1363)
Average Depression Symptoms[a]	3.71 (0.19)	4.19 (0.18)	3.80 (0.14)	3.74 (0.12)
Average PTSD Symptoms[b]	23.10 (0.39)	23.77 (0.45)	0.35 (0.03)	0.39 (0.03)
Average Anxiety Symptoms[c]	2.16 (0.05)	2.28 (0.04)	2.34 (0.04)	2.28 (0.04)
Percentage Binge Drinking	0.27 (0.02)	0.28 (0.01)	0.18 (0.01)	0.17 (0.01)
Percentage Perceiving Need for Treatment	0.14 (0.01)	0.15 (0.01)	0.19 (0.01)	0.21 (0.01)

NOTES: None of the differences between deployed and nondeployed were statistically significant at the p<0.05 level. Estimate SEs are included in parentheses. Models control for respondent gender, age, racial/ethnic minority status, having children younger than age six in the household, rank and officer/enlisted status, number of prior combat deployments, years of service, branch and component of service, prior deployment trauma, prior combat trauma, survey mode at baseline (phone or web), and the outcome in question at baseline. Models for spouse outcomes additionally controlled for spouse education and employment status.

[a] Higher scores=more depressive symptoms. Range: 0–24.

[b] Higher scores=more PTSD symptoms. Range: 17–85 for service member, 0–4 for spouse.

[c] Higher scores=more anxiety. Mean subscale score range: 1–6.

the trajectory factors within the model, specifically: RQ2a (whether the overall trajectory differs significantly from a flat line), RQ2b (whether the overall trend differs significantly from a constant change over time that is unrelated to the phase of the deployment cycle), and RQ2c (whether there are significant differences between the trajectories of service members and their spouses over the course of the deployment cycle). Our hypothesis for RQ2c was not tested for PTSD because service members and spouses were administered different PTSD scales.

Results

Binge Drinking. We begin with binge drinking because it is the outcome for which we have the most pronounced and interpretable effect. Neither tests for RQ2a nor RQ2b were significant for spouses; however, both were significant for service members. Binge drinking for service members varied dramatically as a function of the deployment cycle. The trajectories for service members and spouses were not parallel. Figure 5.1 shows the trends graphically. As can be seen, the percentage of service members who report binge drinking when deployed is very low: most likely a reflection that alcohol is generally not available on the installations to which service members are deployed. However, upon returning from deployment, the proportion of binge drinking returns to levels similar to those prior to deploying.

　　Depression Symptoms. Service members and spouses have changes in depressive symptoms associated with the deployment cycle. The pattern of these changes across the deployment cycle differs for service members and their spouses. The average predicted trajectory across a typical deployment cycle is shown in Figure 5.2. For both service members and spouses, depression symptoms are slightly higher when the service member is deployed than when they are not deployed

Figure 5.1
Predicted Average Trajectories of Binge Drinking Across a Deployment Cycle

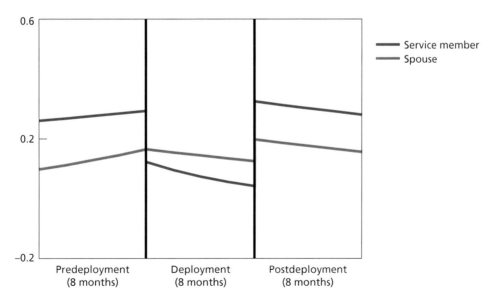

NOTES: The service member trajectory shows significant variation over the deployment cycle ($p<0.001$), the spouse trajectory does not ($p=0.104$). The service member trajectory is significantly different from a constant trend over time ($p<0.001$), the spouse trajectory is not ($p=0.097$). The service member trajectory is significantly different from the spouse trajectory ($p<0.001$).
RAND *RR1388-5.1*

Figure 5.2
Predicted Average Trajectories of Depression Symptoms Across a Deployment Cycle

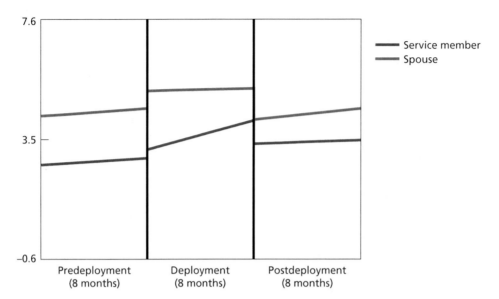

NOTES: Both trajectories show significant variation over the deployment cycle (service member: $p=0.001$; spouse: $p<0.001$). Both trajectories are significantly different from a constant trend over time (service member: $p=0.001$; spouse: $p<0.001$). The service member trajectory is significantly different from the spouse trajectory ($p=0.030$).
RAND RR1388-5.2

(p's<0.01). In both cases, however, symptoms after the deployment return to levels near where they were before the deployment. (It is worth noting that spouses have, on average, higher predicted depression symptoms than service members. This is largely due to the well-known gender difference in depression combined with the fact that a substantial majority of spouses are female.)

PTSD Symptoms. Although there is evidence that PTSD symptoms among service members change significantly over time, there is no significant evidence that these changes are tied to the deployment cycle, as opposed to a constant trend over time. The trajectories for service members can be seen in Figure 5.3. In contrast, there is evidence that PTSD symptoms among spouses change over time and that these changes are associated with the deployment cycle. Figure 5.4 shows the trajectory for spouses. This shows that spouses have slightly elevated PTSD symptoms while the members are deployed relative to when they are home ($p=0.020$), although these represent relatively small changes.

Anxiety Symptoms. There is no significant evidence that service member anxiety changes over the deployment cycle; however, there is evidence that spouse anxiety symptoms change over time, and for spouses, such changes are associated with the deployment cycle. In addition, there is evidence that the two trajectories differ from each other. As shown in Figure 5.5, spouse anxiety symptoms are substantially elevated during the period their service member is deployed.

Perceived Need for Treatment. Finally, there is evidence that service members' perceived need for treatment changes over time, although there was no significant evidence that this change is related to the deployment cycle rather than being a simple linear trend over time (Figure 5.6). There is no significant evidence that need perceived by spouses changed over the deployment cycle. However, there is evidence that the trajectories of spouses and service members differ from each other, with the largest gap between spouse and service member occurring during the deployment period.

Figure 5.3
Predicted Average Trajectory of Service Member PTSD Symptoms Across a Deployment Cycle

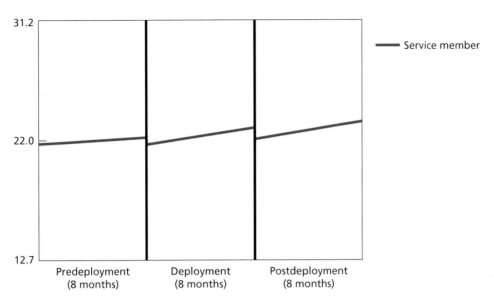

NOTES: This trajectory shows significant variation over the deployment cycle ($p<0.001$), but it is not significantly different from a constant trend over time ($p=0.113$).
RAND RR1388-5.3

Figure 5.4
Predicted Average Trajectory of Spouse PTSD Symptoms Across a Deployment Cycle

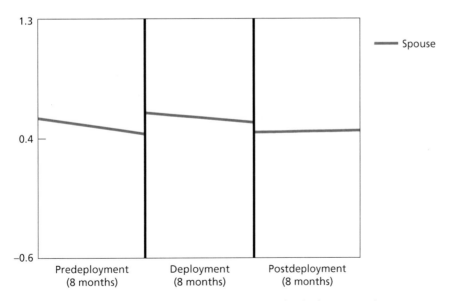

NOTES: This trajectory shows significant variation over the deployment cycle ($p=0.016$), and is significantly different from a constant trend over time ($p=0.043$).
RAND RR1388-5.4

Figure 5.5
Predicted Average Trajectories of Anxiety Symptoms Across a Deployment Cycle

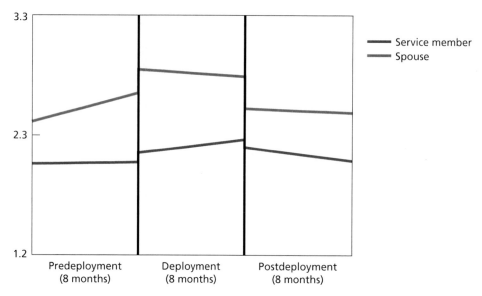

NOTES: The service member trajectory shows no significant variation over the deployment cycle ($p=0.056$); the spouse trajectory shows significant variation over the deployment cycle ($p<0.001$). Both trajectories are significantly different from a constant trend over time (service member: $p=0.047$; spouse: $p<0.001$). The service member trajectory is significantly different from the spouse trajectory ($p=0.001$).
RAND *RR1388-5.5*

Figure 5.6
Predicted Average Trajectories of Perceived Need for Treatment Across a Deployment Cycle

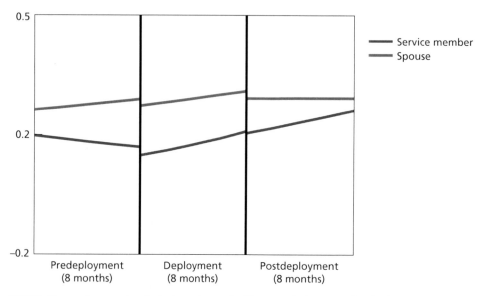

NOTES: The service member trajectory shows significant variation over the deployment cycle ($p<0.001$); the spouse trajectory does not ($p=0.138$). Neither trajectory is significantly different from a constant trend over time (service member: $p=0.284$; spouse: $p=0.140$). The service member trajectory is significantly different from the spouse trajectory ($p<0.001$).
RAND *RR1388-5.6*

RQ3: What Potential Risk and Resilience Factors Predict Change in Psychological and Behavioral Outcomes Among Service Members and Spouses Who Experienced a Deployment?

Analysis

As discussed in Chapter Two, we use random effects regression models, adjusted for repeated measures within each respondent (i.e., allowing for a random effect for each respondent), to estimate the association between the risk and resilience factors already noted and outcomes among only those service members and spouses who have experienced a study deployment. For each outcome, we start with a base model that predicts outcomes from the final three waves of data postdeployment from the baseline (predeployment) value on that outcome, as well as a range of covariates. Additionally, we investigate in a series of separate models the role of five potential risk and resilience factors that were assessed between the baseline and follow-up waves, and that may explain changes that were observed over this period.

Potential Risk and Resilience Factors

We were specifically interested in five predictors. Descriptive statistics of these constructs at baseline are presented in Table 5.5.

Traumatic Events. Deployment trauma is the most significant predictor of mental, emotional, and behavioral health symptoms following deployment (Kok et al., 2012; Ramchand, Rudavsky, et al., 2015; Ramchand, Schell, et al., 2010). Because the various types of trauma may not have the same relationships with outcomes, the 11 traumatic deployment experiences that were assessed have been broken down into conceptually meaningful groups (see Chapter Two in this report). Any physical trauma assesses if the member was injured during the deployment, or received a blow to the head. Any combat trauma assesses whether the member directly engaged the enemy (e.g., hand-to-hand combat or experiencing explosions). Any psychological trauma assesses if the member had experiences that have been shown to be traumatic, but that do not fall into the other categories. These include having friends who are seriously injured or killed, smelling decomposing bodies, or seeing dead or injured noncombatants. These three variables are assessed with respect to the study deployment both during and after each study deployment, and the maximum value across waves is taken as the value of the measure for that service member. These three variables are included simultaneously in the model and tested jointly for statistical significance on three degrees of freedom.

Table 5.5
Means or Percentages of Risk and Resilience Factors

	Service Members (n=907)	Spouses (n=960)
Percentage Any Combat Trauma	6.57 (1.17)	6.54 (1.25)
Percentage Any Psychological Trauma	21.15 (2.26)	20.88 (2.60)
Percentage Any Physical Trauma	33.43 (2.50)	36.88 (3.17)
Average Total Study Deployment Time (Months)	8.01 (0.15)	8.04 (0.14)
Average Deployment Preparation	4.36 (0.11)	5.23 (0.13)
Percentage Probable Traumatic Brain Injury (TBI)	11.21 (0.02)	11.64 (1.95)
Percentage Separated/Retired	6.87 (1.29)	7.08 (1.73)

NOTE: SEs are in parentheses.

Total Number of Months Deployed. As discussed in the introduction to this chapter, there is little evidence to suggest that the length of deployment independently predicts psychological and behavioral health outcomes for service members, and some preliminary evidence that it may predict outcomes for spouses. To investigate this relationship, we added to the base regression model a measure of the number of months the service member was deployed during the study.

Deployment Preparation. Participants reported on the number of deployment preparation activities they performed in advance of the study deployment and we investigated if these preparations were associated with subsequent psychological and behavioral health outcomes for the service member or the spouse (Carter-Visscher et al., 2010; Mulligan et al., 2010; Shea et al., 2013). In the current analyses, we assess *deployment preparation* as a count of several specific deployment preparation activities that service members and spouses engaged in prior to a deployment (see Troxel et al., forthcoming). The items come from the family, marital, and child readiness domains in the Deployment Risk and Resilience Inventory (King et al., 2006). Those activities include: ensuring the family has money for basic necessities; developing an emergency financial plan; getting or increasing life insurance policies; talking to a spouse about how an upcoming deployment may affect the relationship; talking to a professional about how the upcoming deployment may affect the relationship; talking to child(ren) about the upcoming deployment; connecting child(ren) with a deployment support group (e.g., guard youth programs, Operation Purple Camp); and facilitating a connection between child(ren) and other military children in the neighborhood. Spouses are asked four additional items about legal preparedness, including: establishing a power of attorney (POA) to act on the service member's behalf, establishing a POA for someone else to act on the service member's behalf, signing an up-to-date will for the service member; and signing an up-to-date will for the spouse. In the analyses, we use the count of activities reported in the assessment closest to the beginning of the study deployment.

Probable TBI. Probable TBI is defined as having experienced an injury that resulted in losing consciousness, memory loss, being dazed or confused, or "seeing stars" (Schwab et al., 2007). We used four items adapted from the Brief Traumatic Brain Injury Screen (Schwab et al., 2007) to assess whether service members (not spouses) experienced a probable TBI. These items were asked at all survey waves to assess possible TBI since the last assessment. Service members were defined as having a probable TBI if during ANY of their assessments they reported being hit or experiencing an injury that resulted in any alteration in consciousness (e.g., being dazed or confused, not remembering the injury, or losing consciousness).

Separation from Military Service. There is some evidence to suggest that mental health symptoms increase among those who leave the service. Most significantly, the risk of suicide is elevated after service members separate from military service (Reger et al., 2015). In these analyses, if a service member reported their current military status as "separated from the military" or "retired" at any time during Waves 2 through 9, they were defined as separated.

Results

As shown in Table 5.6, there was no evidence that deployment preparation was associated with any of the five psychological and behavioral health outcomes for service members, nor was there any evidence for total months deployed. As hypothesized, exposure to deployment trauma was highly significantly related to postdeployment PTSD, depression, and anxiety symptoms among service members. Similarly, having had a probable TBI increased risk for postdeployment PTSD, depression, and anxiety symptoms, as did separating from service.

Table 5.6
Multivariate Regression Coefficients of Risk and Resilience Factors on Service Member Postdeployment Psychological and Behavioral Health Outcomes

	Depression Symptoms	PTSD Symptoms	Anxiety Symptoms	Binge Drinking	Perceived Need for Treatment
Any Combat Trauma	1.35	**4.69***	**0.41**	0.68	0.09
Any Psychological Trauma	0.83	**2.68***	**0.11**	0.81	0.05
Any Physical Trauma	**1.54***	**3.69****	**0.23**	−0.53	0.05
Joint p-value	*p<0.001*	*p<0.001*	*p=0.005*	*p=0.10*	*p=0.064*
Total Study Deployment Time (Months)	0.03 p=0.65	0.06 p=0.67	−0.01 p=0.42	0.12 p=0.06	0.00 p=0.51
Deployment Preparation	0.05 p=0.71	−0.05 p=0.85	0.01 p=0.78	−0.11 p=0.31	−0.01 p=0.41
Probable TBI	**1.90 p<0.001**	**5.08 p<0.001**	**0.52 p<0.001**	−0.59 p=0.18	0.58 p=0.37
Separation/Retirement	**3.64 p<0.001**	**8.21 p<0.001**	**0.75 p<0.001**	−0.19 p=0.82	0.20 p=0.09

NOTE: Models predict postdeployment outcomes assessed in the final year of the study and control for covariates assessed at baseline, including respondent gender, age, racial/ethnic minority status, having children younger than age six in the household, rank and officer/enlisted status, number of prior combat deployments, years of service, branch and component of service, prior deployment trauma, and the outcome in question at baseline. Bold indicates a statistically significant difference between the Study Deployment and No Study Deployment Groups based on a weighted t-test. * p<0.05 and ** p<0.01 when comparing means of study deployment versus no study deployment groups.

Table 5.7
Multivariate Regression Coefficients of Risk and Resilience Factors on Spouse Postdeployment Psychological and Behavioral Health Outcomes

	Depression Symptoms	PTSD Symptoms	Anxiety Symptoms	Binge Drinking	Perceived Need for Treatment
Any Combat Trauma	0.80	0.27	0.10	−0.05	−0.01
Any Psychological Trauma	−0.59	**−0.19***	−0.18	**−1.33****	−0.05
Any Physical Trauma	**0.91***	**0.16***	**0.28****	**0.98***	0.07
Joint p-value	*p=0.011*	*p=0.007*	*p=0.006*	*p=0.006*	*p=0.104*
Total Study Deployment Time (Months)	0.00 p=0.97	0.01 p=0.29	0.01 p=0.36	**0.16 p=0.02**	0.01 p=0.90
Deployment Preparation	−0.01 p=0.88	0.00 p=0.77	−0.01 p=0.34	−0.07 p=0.42	−0.01 p=0.25
Probable TBI	0.58 p=0.25	−0.03 p=0.72	0.13 p=0.32	−0.76 p=0.21	−0.03 p=0.49
Separation/Retirement	0.20 p=0.70	−0.03 p=0.77	0.00 p=1.00	0.12 p=0.87	−0.05 p=0.33

NOTE: Models predict postdeployment outcomes assessed in the final year of the study and control for covariates assessed at baseline, including respondent gender, age, racial/ethnic minority status, having children younger than age six in the household, spouse education, spouse employment status, rank and officer/enlisted status, number of prior combat deployments, years of service, branch and component of service, prior deployment trauma, and the outcome in question at baseline. Bold indicates a statistically significant difference between the Study Deployment and No Study Deployment Groups based on a weighted t-test.
* p<0.05 and ** p<0.01 when comparing means of study deployment versus no study deployment groups.

There was no significant evidence that any of the investigated risk and resilience factors were associated with changes in binge drinking or a perceived need for mental health services over the three-year study period.

In general, there were fewer associations between predictors and spouse outcomes (see Table 5.7). There was some evidence that a service member's deployment trauma was associated with mental health outcomes for the spouses, but the effects were generally weaker than for service members and in a mixed direction. Exposure to psychological trauma was uniquely associated with better outcomes for the spouse, including significantly reduced PTSD symptoms and binge drinking. In contrast, physical trauma showed a unique and harmful effect on all types of mental health symptoms, as well as binge drinking, showing an increase in these problems at follow-up controlling for baseline symptoms and drinking. The only significant nontrauma predictor was the length of the deployment on spouses' binge drinking, with longer deployments associated with slightly increased rates of postdeployment binge drinking. However, this effect is not highly significant and should be interpreted with caution, given the large number of inferential tests performed.

Discussion

Using advanced approaches to estimate causal effects with longitudinal data, we found no significant causal effect of deployment on psychological or behavioral health outcomes. While this effect may appear somewhat unusual given the large body of research showing harmful effects of combat deployment, it is consistent with the fact that this is a relatively low-risk population, serving during a period of the conflict with comparatively low levels of deployment trauma. In short, the married population being studied is higher-ranking, older, and has had more prestudy combat experience than the full population of service members who have deployed for these conflicts. One should expect that the effect of one additional deployment in this population would be small, particularly because that deployment occurred during the late period of the war, when the rates of casualties were low and the coalition forces largely had moved from combat to training missions. In this context, the lack of significant persistent effects of deployment on either the service members or their spouses should not be seen as contradicting prior research.

Consistent with this interpretation, the minority of study participants who did experience deployment trauma during the study showed worse postdeployment psychological and behavioral health outcomes. In particular, those service members showed a persistent increase in their depression, PTSD, and anxiety symptoms relative to predeployment levels. Similarly, when service members experienced physical trauma (i.e., injury) during the study deployment, their spouses also showed persistent increases in those symptoms, as well as in binge drinking.

However, our results extend past research, particularly with respect to RQ2, in which we examine average trajectories of psychological and behavioral health symptoms across a deployment cycle. These trajectories show substantial variability in these outcomes across the deployment cycle. For service members, perhaps the most important finding is that depressive symptoms are heightened during a deployment and appear to be highest toward the end of a deployment, a finding consistent with the MHAT studies (U.S. Department of the Army, Office of the Surgeon General, 2008; U.S. Department of the Army, Office of the Surgeon General, 2009). While service member depression symptoms were high during the deployment, binge drinking occurred at dramatically lower levels, which is likely attributable to the reduced availability of alcohol in theater. In contrast, service member PTSD symptoms, anxiety symptoms, and perceived need for mental health treatment were relatively stable across the phases of the deployment cycle. The trajectories across the deployment cycle often were significantly different for spouses relative to their service members. Spouses showed elevated depression, PTSD, and anxiety symptoms during the deployment period, which generally returned to baseline levels following service members' return from deployment. Unlike binge drinking among service members, binge drinking among spouses did not differ across the phases of the deployment cycle.

The research also investigated some risk and resilience factors that may explain the changes in psychological and behavioral health over the course of the three-year study. Service members who experienced a probable TBI during the study period showed substantially higher levels of persistent psychological symptoms. Similarly, those members who separated or retired from the military also showed higher levels of these symptoms. In contrast, neither service member TBI nor military separation was associated with the subsequent psychological and behavioral health outcomes for spouses.

Strengths and Limitations

These findings should be interpreted within the context of the study's strengths and limitations. In particular, this study provides a unique opportunity to longitudinally examine the impact of deployment on various indicators of psychological and behavioral health in a representative sample of married service members and their spouses. The study is also unique within the literature in that it followed the same families before, during, and after deployment. Prior studies have not been able to employ advanced statistical techniques to estimate the causal impact of deployment on psychological and behavioral health. The multi-informant perspective from both service members and spouses is also a notable strength. Identifying differences in the trajectories and risk factors for service members and spouses has important policy implications.

Several methodological and design limitations should also be taken into consideration. First, the use of survey methodology for all study constructs introduces several biases inherent to self-reports, such as forgetfulness or social desirability biases. Second, selective attrition and nonresponse may reduce the representativeness of the sample, although nonresponse and attrition weights minimize these biases to the extent that we have data on who was lost from the respondent sample. Finally, the study was conducted in the late stages of the current conflict and may not be generalizable to future conflicts or deployments earlier in this conflict. Specifically, the population sampled included a large number of service members on their second or third deployment, the deployments are shorter than at some points earlier in the conflict, and the study deployments are known to have included substantially less trauma than deployments earlier in the conflict. These strengths and limitations will be further discussed in Chapter Eight.

Policy Implications

We draw from these findings four policy implications:

1. **High-quality mental health services during deployments are needed for both service members and their spouses.** While much attention has been focused on identifying and supporting service members with psychological and behavioral health problems after their deployments, our study findings suggest that these problems likely peak during the deployment itself. Thus, ensuring adequate prevention, identification, and intervention strategies during deployment is critical for improving service member and spousal

well-being. However, attempts to provide improved psychological support during the deployment need to be designed in a way that acknowledges that the perceived need for mental health treatment does not spike during deployment. Traditional approaches in which mental health professionals wait for clients to realize they have a diagnosable mental health problem and then request assistance may not work well. Indeed, anxiety and depression symptoms during a combat deployment (or a spouse's combat deployment) may be seen by service members and their spouses as an entirely normal reaction to the situation—not evidence of a psychiatric disorder requiring treatment. Nevertheless, such symptoms may cause substantial functional impairment or degrade their quality of life. In this situation, programs that provide treatment focused on coping and management strategies may be more useful than a medical model approach focused on treatment of diagnosable disorders. For example, programs that address specific problems by teaching cognitive-behavioral skills to improve relaxation or sleep, or to reduce rumination, may be more useful than standard mental health treatment protocols and delivery systems designed to treat diagnosable disorders.

2. **Service members who experience deployment trauma should receive targeted psychological support, as should their spouses.** Our study confirms that service members who experience a deployment trauma have increased psychological problems following the deployment. When those deployment experiences include physical injury, similar psychological and behavioral problems occur among spouses. While much attention has been given to the sophistication of the military and veteran health treatment of physical injuries, such as burns and amputations, there have been very few studies that have examined how well these programs integrate psychological and behavioral health support into their treatment plans, or if those issues are deferred to postacute settings and left to the service member to access and navigate. We know that for those experiencing physical trauma, the road to recovery can be long and mental health problems can complicate recovery.

   Spouses to those who have experienced physical trauma are also at increased risk of similar outcomes. This is consistent with research examining post–9/11 military and veteran caregivers, many of whom are spouses caring for a service member or veteran with a combination of physical and mental health symptoms. Prior RAND work identified several recommendations for improving the care offered to military caregivers, including promoting the use of social support, expanding respite services, and evaluating programs to ensure evidence of effectiveness (Ramchand, Tanielian et al., 2014). Findings from the current study provide evidence that such programs would address a significant need in this population.

3. **Military separation or retirement is a critical time for addressing psychological and behavioral health problems, and assistance making this transition may be critical for long-term well-being.** Our results suggest that service members who have separated from service postdeployment have significantly elevated psychological symptoms. It may be that these symptoms facilitated the separation (for example, the service member no longer met retention standards), or that separation caused the increase in these symptoms (for example, as an individual experiences a loss of purpose, social support, or income). Regardless of the mechanism, this finding is similar to other research (e.g., Schell and Marshall, 2008) suggesting that the time just after separation is a period of increased risk. Addressing psychological problems in the critical window around the time of separation

may be important for avoiding the longer-term impairments caused by these problems, such as homelessness, unemployment, or substance abuse among veterans.

Efforts to improve well-being during this transition are complicated by the fact that service members are transitioning between health service systems. Some improvements may be facilitated by making sure that those separating from the military are aware of the services and benefits available to them to address mental health issues. However, other reforms may require more fundamental changes in how DoD, the Veterans Health Administration, and civilian health systems cooperate. Several efforts have been made over the past few years to increase support during the transition process, including assistance finding postservice employment and registering for the Veterans Affairs health care system. However, additional efforts may be needed to help them navigate and identify appropriate sources of mental health care when needed, apply for additional financial benefits, or get connected with veteran communities of support.

4. **Longitudinal data should be collected throughout the course of future military operations.** By collecting detailed longitudinal data from service members and their spouses, we were able to apply advanced modeling techniques to estimate the causal effects of deployment, describe the course of symptoms over a deployment cycle, and identify prospective predictors of psychological and behavioral health outcomes in the postdeployment period. While this study can provide information that will guide programs and policies to improve the well-being of military service members and their families, this guidance is substantially limited by the fact that it is the only study of its kind. We studied only married service members who deployed to a conflict more than a decade after the war began. Because of the lack of similar studies on other populations or other periods of the war, we do not know how well these results would generalize to the conditions of future conflicts. To improve decisionmaking and policy for DoD and the military services, it would be helpful if this type of longitudinal data collection were initiated at the beginning of future conflicts. Given the complexity of designing such a study, getting the required funding and regulatory approvals, and generating the appropriate sample, it may be important to prepare for such a study even before the next conflict begins.

Appendix 5A: Balance Tables and Plots

Tables 5A.1 and 5A.2 present balance statistics for service members and spouses, respectively. Each table compares standardized mean differences (SMDs) across a number of key study variables for service members who did and did not experience a study deployment. SMDs are presented before and after applying propensity score weights. Generally, SMDs under 0.20 (or above −0.20) indicate good balance across groups.

Figures 5A.1 and 5A.2 present the balance plots for service members and spouses, respectively, who did and did not experience a study deployment. Each dot on the plot represents a variable in Tables 5A.1 and 5A.2. The left side of each plot depicts absolute standard mean differences (ASMDs) before applying propensity score weights, while the right side of each plot depicts ASMDs after applying the propensity score weights. As can be seen in both figures, once the weights are applied, ASMDs between service members and spouses who did and did not experience a study deployment fall below the cutoff of 0.20 ASMDs.

Table 5A.1
Weighted Balance Table: Service Members (Study Deployment Versus No Study Deployment)

	Unweighted					Weighted				
	Study Deployment		No Study Deployment			Study Deployment		No Study Deployment		
	Mean	SD	Mean	SD	SMD	Mean	SD	Mean	SD	SMD
SERVICE MEMBER VARIABLES										
Female	0.08	0.27	0.14	0.34	-0.22	0.08	0.27	0.09	0.28	-0.04
Age	32.72	7.13	35.05	8.08	-0.33	32.72	7.13	33.38	7.53	-0.09
Minority Race/Ethnicity	0.32	0.47	0.33	0.47	-0.01	0.32	0.47	0.31	0.46	0.02
Children Younger Than Age 6	0.51	0.50	0.45	0.50	0.13	0.51	0.50	0.48	0.50	0.06
Pay Grade: Junior Officer	0.05	0.21	0.04	0.20	0.03	0.05	0.21	0.03	0.18	0.06
Pay Grade: Junior Officer	0.11	0.31	0.09	0.28	0.07	0.11	0.31	0.10	0.30	0.02
Pay Grade: Mid and Senior Enlisted	0.69	0.46	0.74	0.44	-0.10	0.69	0.46	0.73	0.45	-0.09
Pay Grade: Mid and Senior Officer	0.10	0.30	0.12	0.32	-0.04	0.10	0.30	0.11	0.31	-0.02
Pay Grade: Warrant Officer	0.06	0.24	0.03	0.16	0.14	0.06	0.24	0.03	0.17	0.13
Length of Marriage (Months)	96.86	77.86	109.80	84.90	-0.17	96.86	77.86	96.49	77.17	0.01
Parents in the Military	0.53	0.50	0.52	0.50	0.02	0.53	0.50	0.50	0.50	0.06
Total Number of Prior Deployments	2.02	1.32	1.38	1.27	0.49	2.02	1.32	1.85	1.26	0.13
Years of Service	12.07	7.41	13.83	8.54	-0.24	12.07	7.41	12.53	7.71	-0.06
Army	0.46	0.50	0.50	0.50	-0.08	0.46	0.50	0.48	0.50	-0.05
Air Force	0.24	0.43	0.26	0.44	-0.03	0.24	0.43	0.19	0.40	0.12
Navy	0.20	0.40	0.16	0.37	0.09	0.20	0.40	0.25	0.43	-0.13
Marine Corps	0.10	0.30	0.09	0.28	0.05	0.10	0.30	0.07	0.26	0.09
Reserve Component	0.16	0.37	0.39	0.49	-0.64	0.16	0.37	0.21	0.40	-0.12
CES	4.61	4.40	3.79	3.98	0.19	4.61	4.40	4.21	4.09	0.09
Deployment Trauma Exposure	2.13	2.38	1.67	2.43	0.19	2.13	2.38	1.96	2.47	0.07
Marital Satisfaction Scale	4.01	0.44	3.90	0.51	4.01	4.01	0.44	4.00	0.46	0.03
Positive and Negative Affect Schedule (PANAS): Positive	4.24	0.62	4.10	0.67	4.24	4.24	0.62	4.21	0.62	0.06
PANAS: Negative	1.92	0.51	2.07	0.60	1.92	1.92	0.51	1.97	0.55	-0.11

Table 5A.1—Continued

	Unweighted					Weighted				
	Study Deployment		No Study Deployment			Study Deployment		No Study Deployment		
	Mean	SD	Mean	SD	SMD	Mean	SD	Mean	SD	SMD
Conflict Tactics Scale: Prevalence of Physical Aggression Toward Partner	0.01	0.12	0.02	0.14	0.01	0.01	0.12	0.02	0.13	-0.04
Conflict Tactics Scale: Chronicity of Psychological Aggression Toward Partner	0.63	0.86	0.77	0.91	0.63	0.63	0.86	0.68	0.87	-0.07
Conflict Tactics Scale: Prevalence of Physical Aggression Toward You	0.05	0.21	0.05	0.23	0.05	0.05	0.21	0.05	0.22	-0.03
Conflict Tactics Scale: Chronicity of Psychological Aggression Toward You	0.67	0.98	0.89	1.04	0.67	0.67	0.98	0.75	1.01	-0.08
Depression (PHQ)	2.39	3.05	3.11	3.89	-0.23	2.39	3.05	2.51	3.32	-0.04
Anxiety	2.02	0.98	2.13	1.02	-0.11	2.02	0.98	2.06	0.98	-0.04
PTSD	21.33	8.00	22.69	10.21	-0.17	21.33	8.00	21.82	8.96	-0.06
TBI	0.11	0.32	0.13	0.33	-0.04	0.11	0.32	0.12	0.32	0.00
Binge Drinking	0.25	0.43	0.24	0.43	0.02	0.25	0.43	0.26	0.44	-0.02
Problematic Substance Use Scale	0.14	0.49	0.17	0.62	-0.06	0.14	0.49	0.15	0.55	-0.01
Medication for Mental Health Problem	0.03	0.17	0.06	0.23	-0.17	0.03	0.17	0.04	0.19	-0.06
Received Mental Health Care	0.07	0.26	0.18	0.39	-0.42	0.07	0.26	0.11	0.31	-0.13
Military Commitment	4.43	0.63	4.38	0.69	0.09	4.43	0.63	4.38	0.66	0.09
Job Satisfaction	3.98	0.95	3.85	1.03	0.14	3.98	0.95	3.88	1.00	0.11
Retention Intentions	4.21	1.23	4.12	1.37	0.08	4.21	1.23	4.17	1.27	0.03
Retention Intentions, Missing	0.16	0.37	0.39	0.49	-0.52	0.16	0.37	0.20	0.40	-0.10
SPOUSE VARIABLES										
Marital Satisfaction Scale	3.98	0.51	3.77	0.61	0.42	3.98	0.51	3.92	0.54	0.12
PANAS: Positive	4.25	0.66	4.06	0.76	0.28	4.25	0.66	4.21	0.67	0.06
PANAS: Negative	2.00	0.59	2.19	0.63	-0.32	2.00	0.59	2.06	0.61	-0.11
Conflict Tactics Scale: Prevalence of Physical Aggression Toward Partner	0.05	0.21	0.05	0.22	-0.04	0.05	0.21	0.05	0.22	-0.02
Conflict Tactics Scale: Chronicity of Psychological Aggression Toward Partner	0.71	0.88	0.78	0.96	-0.08	0.71	0.88	0.70	0.93	0.01

Table 5A.1—Continued

	Unweighted					Weighted				
	Study Deployment		No Study Deployment			Study Deployment		No Study Deployment		
	Mean	SD	Mean	SD	SMD	Mean	SD	Mean	SD	SMD
Conflict Tactics Scale: Prevalence of Physical Aggression Toward You	0.02	0.12	0.03	0.16	-0.08	0.02	0.12	0.02	0.15	-0.08
Conflict Tactics Scale: Chronicity of Psychological Aggression Toward You	0.59	0.84	0.78	0.97	-0.22	0.59	0.84	0.65	0.92	-0.06
Depression (PHQ)	2.76	3.65	3.09	3.82	-0.09	2.76	3.65	2.92	3.67	-0.05
Anxiety	2.05	0.93	2.07	0.95	-0.03	2.05	0.93	2.06	0.96	-0.01
PTSD	0.47	0.99	0.54	0.99	-0.07	0.47	0.99	0.47	0.97	0.01
Binge Drinking	0.15	0.35	0.11	0.32	0.10	0.15	0.35	0.12	0.33	0.07
Problematic Substance Use Scale	0.07	0.43	0.06	0.37	0.04	0.07	0.43	0.07	0.41	0.01
Medication for Mental Health Problem	0.12	0.33	0.12	0.32	0.01	0.12	0.33	0.13	0.34	-0.02
Received Mental Health Care	0.13	0.34	0.13	0.33	0.01	0.13	0.34	0.15	0.35	-0.04
Financial Distress Scale	1.85	0.68	2.02	0.75	-0.25	1.85	0.68	1.87	0.70	-0.03
Family Environment Scale	2.85	0.24	2.76	0.29	0.37	2.85	0.24	2.83	0.24	0.07
Family Environment Scale, Missing	0.24	0.43	0.26	0.44	-0.04	0.24	0.43	0.25	0.44	-0.03
Parenting Satisfaction	3.24	0.37	3.22	0.42	0.06	3.24	0.37	3.24	0.40	-0.01
Parenting Satisfaction, Missing	0.24	0.43	0.26	0.44	-0.04	0.24	0.43	0.25	0.44	-0.03
Military Commitment	4.51	0.58	4.36	0.70	0.26	4.51	0.58	4.46	0.61	0.08
Satisfaction as Military Spouse	4.13	1.01	3.84	1.15	0.28	4.13	1.01	4.12	0.99	0.02
Retention Intentions	4.14	1.16	3.91	1.32	0.20	4.14	1.16	4.06	1.27	0.07
TEEN VARIABLES										
Strengths and Difficulties Questionnaire (SDQ): Total	7.43	5.26	8.06	5.22	-0.12	7.43	5.26	7.75	5.47	-0.06
SDQ: Total, Missing	0.46	0.50	0.45	0.50	0.03	0.46	0.50	0.47	0.50	-0.01
SDQ Subscale: Emotional Problems	1.65	1.83	1.63	1.69	0.01	1.65	1.83	1.61	1.81	0.02
SDQ Subscale: Emotional Problems, Missing	0.47	0.50	0.45	0.50	0.04	0.47	0.50	0.47	0.50	0.00
SDQ Subscale: Conduct Problems	0.97	1.32	1.14	1.30	-0.13	0.97	1.32	1.03	1.36	-0.04
SDQ Subscale: Conduct Problems, Missing	0.47	0.50	0.45	0.50	0.04	0.47	0.50	0.47	0.50	0.00

Table 5A.1—Continued

	Unweighted					Weighted				
	Study Deployment		No Study Deployment			Study Deployment		No Study Deployment		
	Mean	SD	Mean	SD	SMD	Mean	SD	Mean	SD	SMD
SDQ Subscale: Hyperactivity	3.32	2.61	3.39	2.38	-0.03	3.32	2.61	3.47	2.57	-0.06
SDQ Subscale: Hyperactivity, Missing	0.49	0.50	0.45	0.50	0.09	0.49	0.50	0.47	0.50	0.05
SDQ Subscale: Peer Relationships	1.70	1.61	1.91	1.86	-0.13	1.70	1.61	1.64	1.66	0.03
SDQ Subscale: Peer Relationships, Missing	0.46	0.50	0.45	0.50	0.03	0.46	0.50	0.47	0.50	-0.01
SDQ Subscale: Prosocial Behavior	8.54	1.65	8.46	1.48	0.04	8.54	1.65	8.64	1.53	-0.06
SDQ Subscale: Prosocial Behavior, Missing	0.47	0.50	0.45	0.50	0.04	0.47	0.50	0.47	0.50	0.00
Depression Symptoms	1.01	1.85	1.10	1.81	-0.05	1.01	1.85	0.89	1.70	0.07
Depression Symptoms, Missing	0.47	0.50	0.45	0.50	0.04	0.47	0.50	0.47	0.50	0.01
Anxiety (Screen for Child Anxiety Related Emotional Disorders [SCARED])	1.66	1.95	1.34	1.45	0.16	1.66	1.95	1.50	1.73	0.08
Anxiety (SCARED), Missing	0.46	0.50	0.45	0.50	0.03	0.46	0.50	0.47	0.50	-0.01

NOTE: SD=standard deviation.

Table 5A.2
Weighted Balance Table: Spouses (Study Deployment Versus No Study Deployment)

	Unweighted			Weighted		
	Study Deployment (Mean, SD)	No Study Deployment (Mean, SD)	SMD	Study Deployment (Mean, SD)	No Study Deployment (Mean, SD)	SMD
SERVICE MEMBER VARIABLES						
Pay Grade: Junior Enlisted	0.05	0.03 0.17	0.07	0.05 0.21	0.05 0.21	0.00
Pay Grade: Junior Officer	0.11 0.31	0.10 0.31	0.01	0.11 0.31	0.08 0.28	0.07
Pay Grade: Mid and Senior Enlisted	0.71 0.45	0.72 0.45	−0.03	0.71 0.45	0.73 0.44	−0.05
Pay Grade: Mid and Senior Officer	0.10 0.30	0.12 0.32	−0.05	0.10 0.30	0.12 0.32	−0.05
Pay Grade: Warrant Officer	0.04 0.19	0.02 0.15	0.07	0.04 0.19	0.02 0.15	0.08
Length of Marriage (Months)	94.90 76.42	98.65 78.27	−0.05	94.90 76.42	108.80 84.20	−0.18
Total Number of Prior Deployments	1.99 1.23	1.84 1.21	0.13	1.99 1.23	1.33 1.23	0.54
Years of Service	11.84 7.24	12.48 7.67	−0.09	11.84 7.24	14.00 8.96	−0.30
Army	0.46 0.50	0.49 0.50	−0.06	0.46 0.50	0.50 0.50	−0.08
Air Force	0.24 0.43	0.22 0.41	0.06	0.24 0.43	0.26 0.44	−0.03
Navy	0.20 0.40	0.23 0.42	−0.08	0.20 0.40	0.16 0.37	0.09
Marine Corps	0.10 0.30	0.06 0.24	0.12	0.10 0.30	0.09 0.28	0.05
Reserve Component	0.17 0.37	0.20 0.40	−0.09	0.17 0.37	0.40 0.49	−0.62
CES	4.67 4.50	4.31 4.21	0.08	4.67 4.50	3.63 4.02	0.23
Deployment Trauma Exposure	2.24 2.50	2.03 2.46	0.08	2.24 2.50	1.69 2.41	0.22
Marital Satisfaction Scale	4.00 0.44	4.00 0.46	0.00	4.00 0.44	3.86 0.56	0.32
PANAS: Positive	4.19 0.61	4.19 0.62	0.09	4.24 0.61	4.05 0.76	0.32
PANAS: Negative	1.94 0.54	1.96 0.53	−0.04	1.94 0.54	2.06 0.57	−0.21
Conflict Tactics Scale: Prevalence of Physical Aggression Toward Partner	0.02 0.14	0.02 0.13	0.03	0.02 0.14	0.02 0.15	0.00
Conflict Tactics Scale: Chronicity of Psychological Aggression Toward Partner	0.65 0.87	0.64 0.86	0.02	0.65 0.87	0.75 0.92	−0.11
Conflict Tactics Scale: Prevalence of Physical Aggression Toward You	0.04 0.21	0.05 0.22	−0.03	0.04 0.21	0.06 0.24	−0.07
Conflict Tactics Scale: Chronicity of Psychological Aggression Toward You	0.69 0.98	0.73 1.02	−0.03	0.69 0.98	0.91 1.10	−0.22

Table 5A.2—Continued

	Unweighted			Weighted		
	Study Deployment (Mean, SD)	No Study Deployment (Mean, SD)	SMD	Study Deployment (Mean, SD)	No Study Deployment (Mean, SD)	SMD
Depression (PHQ)	2.41, 3.17	2.46, 3.29	-0.02	2.41, 3.17	2.96, 3.73	-0.17
Anxiety	2.01, 1.01	2.03, 0.97	-0.02	2.01, 1.01	2.14, 0.98	-0.13
PTSD	21.47, 8.24	21.61, 8.66	-0.02	21.47, 8.24	22.67, 10.26	-0.15
TBI	0.13, 0.34	0.12, 0.32	0.04	0.13, 0.34	0.12, 0.32	0.04
Binge Drinking	0.27, 0.44	0.24, 0.43	0.06	0.27, 0.44	0.26, 0.44	0.02
Problematic Substance Use Scale	0.20, 0.64	0.16, 0.57	0.06	0.20, 0.64	0.21, 0.63	-0.03
Medication for Mental Health Problem	0.04, 0.20	0.04, 0.20	-0.01	0.04, 0.20	0.06, 0.25	-0.13
Received Mental Health Care	0.08, 0.27	0.10, 0.30	-0.09	0.08, 0.27	0.18, 0.38	-0.38
Financial Distress Scale	1.82, 0.66	1.84, 0.67	-0.03	1.82, 0.66	2.03, 0.76	-0.33
Family Environment Scale	2.78, 0.25	2.80, 0.25	-0.08	2.78, 0.25	2.76, 0.29	0.08
Family Environment Scale, Missing	0.25, 0.43	0.26, 0.44	-0.03	0.25, 0.43	0.25, 0.43	0.00
Parenting Satisfaction	3.33, 0.37	3.33, 0.38	-0.01	3.33, 0.37	3.34, 0.39	-0.03
Parenting Satisfaction, Missing	0.25, 0.43	0.26, 0.44	-0.03	0.25, 0.43	0.25, 0.43	0.01
Military Commitment	4.44, 0.61	4.38, 0.64	0.09	4.44, 0.61	4.33, 0.67	0.18
Job Satisfaction	4.01, 0.91	3.91, 0.98	0.10	4.01, 0.91	3.78, 1.05	0.25
Retention Intentions	4.12, 1.29	4.17, 1.27	-0.04	4.12, 1.29	4.02, 1.41	0.08
Retention Intentions, Missing	0.17, 0.37	0.20, 0.40	-0.07	0.17, 0.37	0.40, 0.49	-0.52
SPOUSE VARIABLES						
Female	0.92, 0.27	0.92, 0.28	0.02	0.92, 0.27	0.86, 0.35	0.22
Age	32.21, 7.63	32.82, 7.94	-0.08	32.21, 7.63	34.35, 8.49	-0.28
Minority Race/Ethnicity	0.29, 0.45	0.29, 0.45	0.00	0.29, 0.45	0.30, 0.46	-0.02
Children Younger Than Age 6	0.48, 0.50	0.47, 0.50	0.02	0.48, 0.50	0.43, 0.50	0.09
Education: Less than High School	0.01, 0.09	0.02, 0.13	-0.10	0.01, 0.09	0.01, 0.12	-0.08
Education: High School	0.18, 0.39	0.18, 0.38	0.02	0.18, 0.39	0.18, 0.38	0.01
Education: Some College	0.28, 0.45	0.27, 0.44	0.01	0.28, 0.45	0.26, 0.44	0.04
Education: Associate/Vocational/Technical Degree	0.18, 0.38	0.16, 0.37	0.04	0.18, 0.38	0.18, 0.38	0.00

Table 5A.2—Continued

	Unweighted			Weighted		
	Study Deployment (Mean, SD)	No Study Deployment (Mean, SD)	SMD	Study Deployment (Mean, SD)	No Study Deployment (Mean, SD)	SMD
Education: Bachelor's Degree	0.27, 0.44	0.29, 0.45	-0.04	0.27, 0.44	0.27, 0.44	0.01
Education: Graduate or Professional Degree	0.08, 0.28	0.09, 0.28	-0.02	0.08, 0.28	0.11, 0.31	-0.08
Employment: Other	0.05, 0.21	0.06, 0.23	-0.05	0.05, 0.21	0.08, 0.27	-0.16
Employment: Employed	0.34, 0.47	0.37, 0.48	-0.08	0.34, 0.47	0.44, 0.50	-0.22
Employment: Homemaker	0.39, 0.49	0.35, 0.48	0.08	0.39, 0.49	0.29, 0.46	0.20
Employment: Student	0.08, 0.27	0.08, 0.27	-0.01	0.08, 0.27	0.08, 0.27	0.00
Employment: Not Employed	0.15, 0.36	0.14, 0.34	0.04	0.15, 0.36	0.11, 0.32	0.10
Marital Satisfaction Scale	3.95, 0.52	3.91, 0.53	0.06	3.95, 0.52	3.70, 0.65	0.46
PANAS: Positive	4.19, 0.66	4.16, 0.68	0.05	4.19, 0.66	3.95, 0.82	0.37
PANAS: Negative	2.07, 0.60	2.08, 0.61	-0.01	2.07, 0.60	2.27, 0.68	-0.32
Conflict Tactics Scale: Prevalence of Physical Aggression Toward Partner	0.06, 0.23	0.05, 0.21	0.05	0.06, 0.23	0.06, 0.24	-0.02
Conflict Tactics Scale: Chronicity of Psychological Aggression Toward Partner	0.72, 0.89	0.68, 0.91	0.04	0.72, 0.89	0.78, 0.96	-0.07
Conflict Tactics Scale: Prevalence of Physical Aggression Toward You	0.02, 0.13	0.03, 0.16	-0.07	0.02, 0.13	0.05, 0.21	-0.22
Conflict Tactics Scale: Chronicity of Psychological Aggression Toward You	0.60, 0.88	0.65, 0.91	-0.06	0.60, 0.88	0.87, 1.06	-0.31
Depression (PHQ)	2.84, 3.62	2.91, 3.63	-0.02	2.84, 3.62	3.25, 3.70	-0.11
Anxiety	2.08, 0.92	2.07, 0.97	0.01	2.08, 0.92	2.18, 0.99	-0.11
PTSD	0.48, 0.99	0.45, 0.96	0.04	0.48, 0.99	0.49, 0.98	-0.01
Binge Drinking	0.15, 0.36	0.12, 0.33	0.07	0.15, 0.36	0.09, 0.28	0.17
Problematic Substance Use Scale	0.10, 0.55	0.07, 0.44	0.06	0.10, 0.55	0.05, 0.36	0.09
Medication for Mental Health Problem	0.11, 0.31	0.14, 0.34	-0.08	0.11, 0.31	0.13, 0.34	-0.07
Received Mental Health Care	0.13, 0.33	0.14, 0.35	-0.04	0.13, 0.33	0.14, 0.35	-0.04
Financial Distress Scale	1.88, 0.69	1.89, 0.70	-0.03	1.88, 0.69	2.06, 0.76	-0.27

Table 5A.2—Continued

	Unweighted			Weighted		
	Study Deployment (Mean, SD)	No Study Deployment (Mean, SD)	SMD	Study Deployment (Mean, SD)	No Study Deployment (Mean, SD)	SMD
Family Environment Scale	2.82 0.26	2.82 0.26	0.00	2.82 0.26	2.73 0.33	0.35
Family Environment Scale, Missing	0.25 0.43	0.26 0.44	-0.03	0.25 0.43	0.25 0.43	0.00
Parenting Satisfaction Scale	3.23 0.37	3.24 0.39	-0.03	3.23 0.37	3.20 0.38	0.08
Parenting Satisfaction Scale, Missing	0.25 0.43	0.26 0.44	-0.03	0.25 0.43	0.25 0.43	0.00
Parent in the Military	0.40 0.49	0.45 0.50	-0.10	0.40 0.49	0.51 0.50	-0.23
Military Commitment	4.50 0.60	4.47 0.60	0.05	4.50 0.60	4.33 0.68	0.28
Satisfaction as Military Spouse	4.11 1.03	4.15 0.94	-0.04	4.11 1.03	3.93 1.06	0.18
Retention Intentions	4.16 1.12	4.11 1.22	0.05	4.16 1.12	3.94 1.32	0.20
TEEN VARIABLES						
SDQ: Total	7.33 5.09	7.59 5.26	-0.05	7.33 5.09	8.04 5.20	-0.14
SDQ: Total, Missing	0.49 0.50	0.48 0.50	0.01	0.49 0.50	0.46 0.50	0.04
SDQ Subscale: Emotional Problems	1.57 1.82	1.61 1.76	-0.03	1.57 1.82	1.76 1.75	-0.11
SDQ Subscale: Emotional Problems, Missing	0.49 0.50	0.48 0.50	0.03	0.49 0.50	0.47 0.50	0.06
SDQ Subscale: Conduct Problems	0.97 1.33	0.99 1.35	-0.02	0.97 1.33	1.03 1.32	-0.05
SDQ Subscale: Conduct Problems, Missing	0.49 0.50	0.48 0.50	0.03	0.49 0.50	0.47 0.50	0.06
SDQ Subscale: Hyperactivity	3.18 2.46	3.39 2.51	-0.08	3.18 2.46	3.39 2.41	-0.08
SDQ Subscale: Hyperactivity, Missing	0.49 0.50	0.48 0.50	0.03	0.49 0.50	0.46 0.50	0.06
SDQ Subscale: Peer Relationships	1.68 1.67	1.60 1.64	0.05	1.68 1.67	1.87 1.78	-0.11
SDQ Subscale: Peer Relationships, Missing	0.49 0.50	0.48 0.50	0.01	0.49 0.50	0.46 0.50	0.04
SDQ Subscale: Prosocial Behavior	8.53 1.65	8.60 1.57	-0.04	8.53 1.65	8.35 1.51	0.11
SDQ Subscale: Prosocial Behavior, Missing	0.49 0.50	0.48 0.50	0.03	0.49 0.50	0.47 0.50	0.06
Depression Symptoms	0.92 1.65	0.80 1.62	0.07	0.92 1.65	0.93 1.74	-0.01
Depression Symptoms, Missing	0.49 0.50	0.48 0.50	0.03	0.49 0.50	0.46 0.50	0.06
Anxiety (SCARED)	1.71 1.97	1.53 1.73	0.09	1.71 1.97	1.49 1.53	0.09
Anxiety (SCARED), Missing	0.49 0.50	0.48 0.50	0.01	0.49 0.50	0.47 0.50	0.04

Figure 5A.1
Balance Plot for Service Members

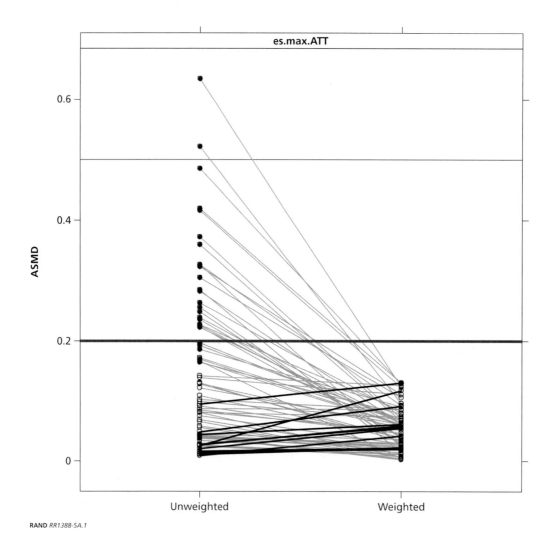

Figure 5A.2
Balance Plot for Spouses

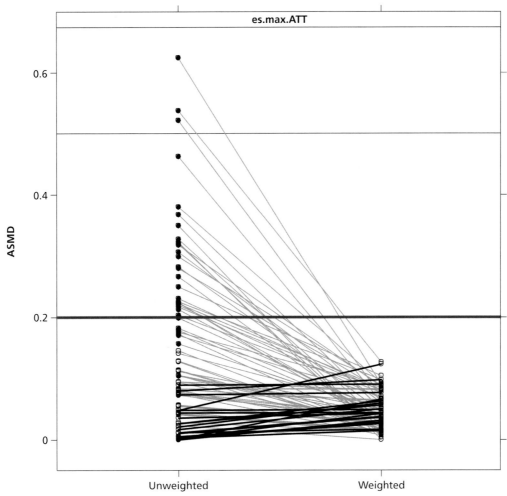

References

Adler, A. B., A. H. Huffman, P .D. Bliese, and C. A. Castro, "The Impact of Deployment Length and Experience on the Well-Being of Male and Female Soldiers," *Journal of Occupational Health Psychology*, Vol. 10, No. 2, April 2005, pp. 121–137.

Allison-Aipa, T. S., C. Ritter, P. Sikes, and S. Ball, "The Impact of Deployment on the Psychological Health Status, Level of Alcohol Consumption, and Use of Psychological Health Resources of Postdeployed U.S. Army Reserve Soldiers," *Military Medicine*, Vol. 175, No. 9, September 2010, pp. 630–637.

Armed Forces Health Surveillance Center, "Health of Women After Wartime Deployments: Correlates of Risk for Selected Medical Conditions Among Females After Initial and Repeat Deployments to Afghanistan and Iraq, Active Component, U.S. Armed Forces," *Medical Surveillance Monthly Report*, Vol. 19, No. 7, July 2012, pp. 2–10.

Baker, D. G., P. S. Heppner, N. Afari, S. E. Nunnink, M. T. Kilmer, A. N. Simmons, L. H. Harder, and B. Bosse, "Trauma Exposure, Branch of Service, and Physical Injury in Relation to Mental Health Among U.S. Veterans Returning from Iraq and Afghanistan," *Military Medicine*, Vol. 174, No. 8, August 2009, pp. 773–778.

Balderrama-Durbin, C., D. K. Snyder, J. A. Cigrang, G. W. Talcott, J. Tatum, M. T. Baker, D. Cassidy, S. Sonnek, R. E. Heyman, and A. M. S. Slep, "Disclosure in Intimate Relationships: Mediating the Impact of Partner Support on Posttraumatic Stress," *Journal of Family Psychology*, Vol. 27, No. 4, 2013, pp. 560–568.

Bliese, P. D., K. M. Wright, A. B. Adler, O. A. Cabrera, C. A. Castro, and C. W. Hoge, "Validating the Primary Care Posttraumatic Stress Disorder Screen and the Posttraumatic Stress Disorder Checklist with Soldiers Returning from Combat," *Journal of Consulting and Clinical Psychology*, Vol. 76, No. 2, 2008, pp. 272–281.

Bliese, P. D., K. M. Wright, A. B. Adler, J. L. Thomas, and C. M. Hoge, "Timing of Post-Combat Mental Health Assessments," *Psychological Services*, Vol. 4, No. 3, 2007, pp. 141–148.

Booth-Kewley, S., G. E. Larson, R. M. Highfill-McRoy, C. F. Garland, and T. A. Gaskin, "Correlates of Posttraumatic Stress Disorder Symptoms in Marines Back from War," *Journal of Traumatic Stress*, Vol. 23, No. 1, February 2010, pp. 69–77.

Brewin, C. R., "Systematic Review of Screening Instruments for Adults at Risk of PTSD," *Journal of Traumatic Stress*, Vol. 18, No. 1, February 2005, pp. 53–62.

Carter-Visscher, R. M., M. A. Polusny, M. Murdoch, P. D. Thuras, C. R. Erbes, and S. M. Kehle, "Predeployment Gender Differences in Stressors and Mental Health Among U.S. National Guard Troops Poised for Operation Iraqi Freedom Deployment," *Journal of Traumatic Stress*, Vol. 23, No. 1, February 2010, pp. 78–85.

Cohen, B. E., K. S. Gima, D. Bertenthal, S. Kim, C. R. Marmar, and K. H. Seal, "Mental Health Diagnoses and Utilization of VA Non-Mental Health Medical Services Among Returning Iraq and Afghanistan Veterans," *Journal of Generalized Internal Medicine*, Vol. 25, No. 1, January 2010, pp. 18–24.

Cohen, S. P., C. Brown, C. Kurihara, A. R. Plunkett, C. Nguyen, and S. A. Strassels, "Diagnoses and Factors Associated with Medical Evacuation and Return to Duty for Service Members Participating in Operation Iraqi Freedom or Operation Enduring Freedom: A Prospective Cohort Study," *Lancet*, Vol. 375, No. 9711, January 23, 2010, pp. 301–309.

de Burgh, H. T., C. J. White, N. T. Fear, and A. C. Iversen, "The Impact of Deployment to Iraq or Afghanistan on Partners and Wives of Military Personnel," *International Review of Psychiatry*, Vol. 23, No. 2, April 2011, pp. 192–200.

Dohrenwend, B. P., J. B. Turner, N. A. Turse, B. G. Adams, K. C. Koenen, and R. Marshall, "The Psychological Risks of Vietnam for U.S. Veterans: A Revisit with New Data and Methods," *Science*, Vol. 313, No. 5789, August 18, 2006, pp. 979–982.

Eaton, K. M., C. W. Hoge, S. C. Messer, A. A. Whitt, O. A. Cabrera, D. McGurk, A. Cox, and C. A. Castro, "Prevalence of Mental Health Problems, Treatment Need, and Barriers to Care Among Primary Care-Seeking Spouses of Military Service Members Involved in Iraq and Afghanistan Deployments," *Military Medicine*, Vol. 173, No. 11, November 2008, pp. 1051–1056.

Elbogen, E. B., H. R. Wagner, S. C. Johnson, P. M. Kinneer, H. K. Kang, J. J. Vasterling, C. Timko, and J. C. Beckham, "Are Iraq and Afghanistan Veterans Using Mental Health Services? New Data from a National Random-Sample Survey," *Psychiatric Services*, Vol. 64, No. 2, February 2013, pp. 134–141.

Elnitsky, C. A., P. L. Chapman, R. M. Thurman, B. L. Pitts, C. Figley, and B. Unwin, "Gender Differences in Combat Medic Mental Health Services Utilization, Barriers, and Stigma," *Military Medicine*, Vol. 178, No. 7, July 2013, pp. 775–784.

Erbes, C. R., L. A. Meis, M. A. Polusny, and P. A. Arbisi, "Psychiatric Distress Among Spouses of National Guard Soldiers Prior to Combat Deployment," *Mental Health Family Medicine*, Vol. 9, No. 3, September 2012, pp. 161–169.

Escolas, S. M., B. L. Pitts, M. A. Safer, and P. T. Bartone, "The Protective Value of Hardiness on Military Posttraumatic Stress Symptoms," *Military Psychology*, Vol. 25, No. 2, March 2013, pp. 116–123.

Fisher, M. P., and T. L. Schell, *The Role and Importance of the "D" in PTSD*, Santa Monica, Calif.: RAND Corporation, OP-389-OSD, 2013. As of November 20, 2015: http://www.rand.org/pubs/occasional_papers/OP389.html

Gehrman, P., A. D. Seelig, I. G. Jacobson, E. J. Boyko, T. I. Hooper, G. D. Gackstetter, C. S. Ulmer, and T. C. Smith, "Predeployment Sleep Duration and Insomnia Symptoms as Risk Factors for New-Onset Mental Health Disorders Following Military Deployment," *Sleep: Journal of Sleep and Sleep Disorders Research*, Vol. 36, No. 7, July 2013, pp. 1009–1018.

Goodwin, L., M. Jones, R. J. Rona, J. Sundin, S. C. Wessely, and N. T. Fear, "Prevalence of Delayed-Onset Posttraumatic Stress Disorder in Military Personnel: Is There Evidence for this Disorder? Results of a Prospective UK Cohort Study," *Journal of Nervous and Mental Disease*, Vol. 200, No. 5, May 2012, pp. 429–437.

Gorman, L. A., A. J. Blow, B. D. Ames, and P. L. Reed, "National Guard Families After Combat: Mental Health, Use of Mental Health Services, and Perceived Treatment Barriers," *Psychiatric Services*, Vol. 62, No. 1, January 2011, pp. 28–34.

Grieger, T. A., S. J. Cozza, R. J. Ursano, C. Hoge, P. E. Martinez, C. C. Engel, and H. J. Wain, "Posttraumatic Stress Disorder and Depression in Battle-Injured Soldiers," *American Journal of Psychiatry*, Vol. 163, No. 10, October 2006, pp. 1777–1783.

Haskell, S. G., K. S. Gordon, K. M. Mattocks, M. Duggal, J. Erdos, A. C. Justice, and C. A. Brandt, "Gender Differences in Rates of Depression, PTSD, Pain, Obesity, and Military Sexual Trauma Among Connecticut War Veterans of Iraq and Afghanistan," *Journal of Women's Health*, Vol. 19, No. 2, February 2010, pp. 267–271.

Heron, E. A., C. J. Bryan, C. A. Dougherty, and W. G. Chapman, "Military Mental Health: The Role of Daily Hassles While Deployed," *Journal of Nervous and Mental Disease*, Vol. 201, No. 12, December 2013, pp. 1035–1039.

Hickling, E. J., S. W. Gibbons, S. D. Barnett, and D. D. Watts, "The Psychological Impact of Deployment on OEF/OIF Healthcare Providers," *Journal of Traumatic Stress*, Vol. 24, No. 6, December 2011, pp. 726–734.

Hoge, C. W., C. A. Castro, S. C. Messer, D. McGurk, D. I. Cotting, and R. L. Koffman, "Combat Duty in Iraq and Afghanistan, Mental Health Problems, and Barriers to Care," *New England Journal of Medicine*, Vol. 351, July 1, 2004.

Iversen, A. C., L. Van Staden, J. G. Hacker Hughes, T. Browne, L. Hull, J. Hall, N. Greenberg, R. J. Rona, M. Hotopf, S. C. Wessely, and N. T. Fear, "The Prevalence of Common Mental Disorders and PTSD in the UK Military: Using Data from a Clinical Interview-Based Study," *BMC Psychiatry*, Vol. 9, October 30, 2009.

Jacobson, I. G., J. L. Horton, C. A. LeardMann, M. A. K. Ryan, E. J. Boyko, T. S. Wells, B. Smith, and T. C. Smith, "Posttraumatic Stress Disorder and Depression Among U.S. Military Health Care Professionals Deployed in Support of Operations in Iraq and Afghanistan," *Journal of Traumatic Stress*, Vol. 25, No. 6, December 2012, pp. 616–623.

Jones, M., J. Sundin, L. Goodwin, L. Hull, N. T. Fear, S. Wessely, and R. J. Rona, "What Explains Post-Traumatic Stress Disorder (PTSD) in UK Service Personnel: Deployment or Something Else?" *Psychological Medicine*, Vol. 43, No. 8, August 2013, pp. 1703–1712.

Kang, H. K., B. H. Natelson, C. M. Mahan, K. Y. Lee, and F. M. Murphy, "Post-Traumatic Stress Disorder and Chronic Fatigue Syndrome-Like Illness Among Gulf War Veterans: A Population-Based Survey of 30,000 Veterans," *American Journal of Epidemiology*, Vol. 157, No. 2, January 15, 2003, pp. 141–148.

Kehle, S. M., M. K. Reddy, A. G. Ferrier-Auerbach, C. R. Erbes, P. A. Arbisi, and M. A. Polusny, "Psychiatric Diagnoses, Comorbidity, and Functioning in National Guard Troops Deployed to Iraq," *Journal of Psychiatric Research*, Vol. 45, No. 1, January 2011, pp. 126–132.

King, L. A., D. W. King, D. S. Vogt, J. Knight, and R. E. Samper, "Deployment Risk and Resilience Inventory: A Collection of Measures for Studying Deployment-Related Experiences of Military Personnel and Veterans," *Military Psychology*, Vol. 18, No. 2, 2006, pp. 89–120.

Kok, B. C., R. K. Herrell, J. L. Thomas, and C. W. Hoge, "Posttraumatic Stress Disorder Associated with Combat Service in Iraq or Afghanistan: Reconciling Prevalence Differences Between Studies," *Journal of Nervous and Mental Disease*, Vol. 200, No. 5, May 2012, pp. 444–450.

LeardMann, C. A., T. C. Smith, B. Smith, T. S. Wells, M. A. K. Ryan, and Group Millennium Cohort Study, "Baseline Self Reported Functional Health and Vulnerability to Post-Traumatic Stress Disorder After Combat Deployment: Prospective U.S. Military Cohort Study," *British Medical Journal*, Vol. 338, April 16, 2009.

Levy, B. S., and V. W. Sidel, "Health Effects of Combat: A Life-Course Perspective," *Annual Review of Public Health*, Vol. 30, 2009, pp. 123–136.

Luxton, D. D., N. A. Skopp, and S. Maguen, "Gender Differences in Depression and PTSD Symptoms Following Combat Exposure," *Depression and Anxiety*, Vol. 27, No. 11, November 2010, pp. 1027–1033.

Macera, C. A., H. J. Aralis, M. J. Rauh, and A. J. MacGregor, "Do Sleep Problems Mediate the Relationship Between Traumatic Brain Injury and Development of Mental Health Symptoms After Deployment?" *Sleep*, Vol. 36, No. 1, January 2013, pp. 83–90.

MacGregor, A. J., A. L. Dougherty, J. J. Tang, and M. R. Galarneau, "Postconcussive Symptom Reporting Among U.S. Combat Veterans with Mild Traumatic Brain Injury from Operation Iraqi Freedom," *Journal of Head Trauma Rehabilitation*, Vol. 28, No. 1, 2013, pp. 59–67.

Maguen, S., B. E. Cohen, L. Ren, J. O. Bosch, R. E. Kimerling, and K. H. Seal, "Gender Differences in Military Sexual Trauma and Mental Health Diagnoses Among Iraq and Afghanistan Veterans with Posttraumatic Stress Disorder," *Women's Health Issues*, Vol. 22, No. 1, January 2012, pp. e61–e66.

Maguen, S., E. Madden, B. E. Cohen, D. Bertenthal, and K. H. Seal, "Association of Mental Health Problems with Gastrointestinal Disorders in Iraq and Afghanistan Veterans," *Depression and Anxiety*, Vol. 31, No. 2, February 2014, pp. 160–165.

Maguen, S., L. Ren, J. O. Bosch, C. R. Marmar, and K. H. Seal, "Gender Differences in Mental Health Diagnoses Among Iraq and Afghanistan Veterans Enrolled in Veterans Affairs Health Care," *American Journal of Public Health*, Vol. 100, No. 12, December 2010, pp. 2450–2456.

Mansfield, A. J., J. S. Kaufman, S. W. Marshall, B. N. Gaynes, J. P. Morrissey, and C. C. Engel, "Deployment and the Use of Mental Health Services Among U.S. Army Wives," *New England Journal of Medicine*, Vol. 362, No. 2, January 14, 2010, pp. 101–109.

Mayo, J. A., A. J. MacGregor, A. L. Dougherty, and M. R. Galarneau, "Role of Occupation on New-Onset Post-Traumatic Stress Disorder and Depression Among Deployed Military Personnel," *Military Medicine*, Vol. 178, No. 9, September 2013, pp. 945–950.

Milliken, C. S., J. L. Auchterlonie, and C. W. Hoge, "Longitudinal Assessment of Mental Health Problems Among Active and Reserve Component Soldiers Returning from the Iraq War," *Journal of the American Medical Association*, Vol. 298, No. 18, 2007, pp. 2141–2148.

Mulligan, K., N. Jones, C. Woodhead, M. Davies, S. C. Wessely, and N. Greenberg, "Mental Health of UK Military Personnel While on Deployment in Iraq," *British Journal of Psychiatry*, Vol. 197, No. 5, November 2010, pp. 405–410.

Mustillo, S. A., A. Kysar-Moon, S. R. Douglas, R. Hargraves, S. M. Wadsworth, M. Fraine, and N. L. Frazer, "Overview of Depression, Post-Traumatic Stress Disorder, and Alcohol Misuse Among Active Duty Service Members Returning from Iraq and Afghanistan, Self-Report and Diagnosis," *Military Medicine*, Vol. 180, No. 4, April 2015, pp. 419–427.

Pietrzak, R. H., M. B. Goldstein, J. C. Malley, D. C. Johnson, and S. M. Southwick, "Subsyndromal Posttraumatic Stress Disorder Is Associated with Health and Psychosocial Difficulties in Veterans of Operations Enduring Freedom and Iraqi Freedom," *Depression and Anxiety*, Vol. 26, No. 8, August 2009, pp. 739–744.

Possemato, K. A., M. Wade, J. Andersen, and P. C. Ouimette, "The Impact of PTSD, Depression, and Substance Use Disorders on Disease Burden and Health Care Utilization Among OEF/OIF Veterans," *Psychological Trauma: Theory, Research, Practice, and Policy*, Vol. 2, No. 3, September 2010, pp. 218–223.

Ramchand, R., B. R. Karney, K. C. Osilla, R. M. Burns, and L. B. Calderone, "Prevalence of PTSD, Depression, and TBI Among Returning Servicemembers," in T. L. Tanielian and L. H. Jaycox, eds., *Invisible Wounds of War: Psychological and Cognitive Injuries, Their Consequences, and Services to Assist Recovery*, Santa Monica, Calif.: RAND Corporation, MG-720-CCF, 2008, pp. 35–85. As of November 20, 2015: http://www.rand.org/pubs/monographs/MG720.html

Ramchand, R., R. Rudavsky, S. Grant, T. Tanielian, and L. Jaycox, "Prevalence of, Risk Factors for, and Consequences of Posttraumatic Stress Disorder and Other Mental Health Problems in Military Populations Deployed to Iraq and Afghanistan," *Current Psychiatry Reports*, Vol. 17, No. 5, May 2015, p. 37.

Ramchand, R., T. L. Schell, B. R. Karney, K. C. Osilla, R. M. Burns, and L. B. Caldarone, "Disparate Prevalence Estimates of PTSD Among Service Members Who Served in Iraq and Afghanistan: Possible Explanations," *Journal of Traumatic Stress*, Vol. 23, No. 1, February 2010, pp. 59–68.

Ramchand, R., T. Tanielian, M. P. Fisher, C. A. Vaughan, T. E. Trail, C. Batka, P. Voorhies, M. Robbins, E. Robinson, and B. Ghosh-Dastidar, *Hidden Heroes: America's Military Caregivers*, Santa Monica, Calif.: RAND Corporation, RR-499-TEDF, 2014. As of November 20, 2015: http://www.rand.org/pubs/research_reports/RR499.html

Reger, M. A., D. J. Smolenski, N. A. Skopp, M. J. Metzger-Abamukang, H. K. Kang, T. A. Bullman, S. Perdue, and G. A. Gahm, "Risk of Suicide Among U.S. Military Service Members Following Operation Enduring Freedom or Operation Iraqi Freedom Deployment and Separation from the U.S. Military," *Journal of the American Medical Association and Psychiatry*, Vol. 72, No. 6, June 2015, pp. 561–569.

Renshaw, K. D., C. S. Rodrigues, and D. H. Jones, "Psychological Symptoms and Marital Satisfaction in Spouses of Operation Iraqi Freedom Veterans: Relationships with Spouses' Perceptions of Veterans' Experiences and Symptoms," *Journal of Family Psychology*, Vol. 22, No. 4, August 2008, pp. 586–594.

Rodriguez, A. J., and G. Margolin, "Military Service Absences and Family Members' Mental Health: A Timeline Followback Assessment," *Journal of Family Psychology*, Vol. 29, No. 4, August 2015, pp. 642–648.

Rona, R. J., N. T. Fear, L. Hull, N. Greenberg, M. Earnshaw, M. Hotopf, and S. Wessely, "Mental Health Consequences of Overstretch in the UK Armed Forces: First Phase of a Cohort Study," *British Medical Journal*, Vol. 335, No. 7620, September 22, 2007, p. 603.

Schell, T. L., and G. N. Marshall, "Survey of Individuals Previously Deployed for OEF/OIF," in T. L. Tanielian and L. H. Jaycox, eds., *Invisible Wounds of War: Psychological and Cognitive Injuries, Their Consequences, and Services to Assist Recovery*, Santa Monica, Calif.: RAND Corporation, MG-720-CCF, 2008, pp. 87–115. As of November 20, 2015: http://www.rand.org/pubs/monographs/MG720.html

Schell, T. L., and T. L. Tanielian, *A Needs Assessment of New York State Veterans: Final Report to the New York State Health Foundation*, Santa Monica, Calif.: RAND Corporation, TR-920-NYSHF, 2011. As of September 30, 2015: http://www.rand.org/pubs/technical_reports/TR920

Schultz, M., M. E. Glickman, and S. V. Eisen, "Predictors of Decline in Overall Mental Health, PTSD and Alcohol Use in OEF/OIF Veterans," *Comprehensive Psychiatry*, Vol. 55, 2014, pp. 1654–1666.

Schwab, K. A., B. Ivins, G. Cramer, W. Johnson, M. Sluss-Tiller, K. Kiley, W. Lux, and D. Warden, "Screening for Traumatic Brain Injury in Troops Returning from Deployment in Afghanistan and Iraq: Initial Investigation of the Usefulness of a Short Screening Tool for Traumatic Brain Injury," *Journal of Head Trauma Rehabilitation*, Vol. 22, No. 6, 2007, pp. 377–389.

Seal, K. H., T. J. Metzler, K. S. Gima, D. Bertenthal, S. Maguen, and C. R. Marmar, "Trends and Risk Factors for Mental Health Diagnoses Among Iraq and Afghanistan Veterans Using Department of Veterans Affairs Health Care, 2002–2008," *American Journal of Public Health*, Vol. 99, No. 9, September 2009, pp. 1651–1658.

Seelig, A. D., I. G. Jacobson, B. Smith, T. I. Hooper, G. D. Gackstetter, M. A. Ryan, T. S. Wells, S. MacDermid Wadsworth, and T. C. Smith, "Prospective Evaluation of Mental Health and Deployment Experience Among Women in the U.S. Military," *American Journal of Epidemiology*, Vol. 176, No. 2, July 15, 2012, pp. 135–145.

Sharkey, J. M., and C. P. Rennix, "Assessment of Changes in Mental Health Conditions Among Sailors and Marines During Postdeployment Phase," *Military Medicine*, Vol. 176, No. 8, August 2011, pp. 915–921.

Shea, M. T., M. K. Reddy, A. R. Tyrka, and E. Sevin, "Risk Factors for Post-Deployment Posttraumatic Stress Disorder in National Guard/Reserve Service Members," *Psychiatry Research*, Vol. 210, No. 3, December 30, 2013, pp. 1042–1048.

Shen, Y., J. Arkes, and T. V. Williams, "Effects of Iraq/Afghanistan Deployments on Major Depression and Substance Use Disorder: Analysis of Active Duty Personnel in the U.S. Military," *American Journal of Public Health*, Vol. 102, Supplement 1, March 2012, pp. S80–S87.

Spera, C., R. K. Thomas, F. Barlas, R. Szoc, and M. H. Cambridge, "Relationship of Military Deployment Recency, Frequency, Duration, and Combat Exposure to Alcohol Use in the Air Force," *Journal of Studies of Alcohol and Drugs*, Vol. 72, No. 1, January 2011, pp. 5–14.

SteelFisher, G. K., A. M. Zaslavsky, and R. J. Blendon, "Health-Related Impact of Deployment Extensions on Spouses of Active Duty Army Personnel," *Military Medicine*, Vol. 173, No. 3, March 2008, pp. 221–229.

Sundin, J., N. T. Fear, A. Iversen, R. J. Rona, and S. Wessely, "PTSD After Deployment to Iraq: Conflicting Rates, Conflicting Claims," *Psychological Medicine*, Vol. 40, No. 3, March 2010, pp. 367–382.

Sundin, J., R. K. Herrell, C. W. Hoge, N. T. Fear, A. B. Adler, N. Greenberg, L. A. Riviere, J. L. Thomas, S. C. Wessely, and P. D. Bliese, "Mental Health Outcomes in U.S. and UK Military Personnel Returning from Iraq," *British Journal of Psychiatry*, Vol. 204, March 2014, pp. 200–207.

Tanielian, T., and L. H. Jaycox, eds., *Invisible Wounds of War: Psychological and Cognitive Injuries, Their Consequences, and Services to Assist Recovery*, Santa Monica, Calif.: RAND Corporation, MG-720-CCF, 2008. As of February 14, 2013:
http://www.rand.org/pubs/monographs/MG720.html

Tanielian, T., B. R. Karney, A. Chandra, S. O. Meadows, and the Deployment Life Study Team, *The Deployment Life Study Methodological Overview and Baseline Sample Description*, Santa Monica, Calif.: RAND Corporation, RR-209-OSD/A, 2014. As of September 26, 2015:
http://www.rand.org/pubs/research_reports/RR209.html

Telch, M. J., D. Rosenfield, H. J. Lee, and A. Pai, "Emotional Reactivity to a Single Inhalation of 35% Carbon Dioxide and Its Association with Later Symptoms of Posttraumatic Stress Disorder and Anxiety in Soldiers Deployed to Iraq," *Archives of General Psychiatry*, Vol. 69, No. 11, November 2012, pp. 1161–1168.

Thomas, J. L., J. E. Wilk, L. A. Riviere, D. M. McGurk, C. A. Castro, and C. W. Hoge, "Prevalence of Mental Health Problems and Functional Impairment Among Active Component and National Guard Soldiers 3 and 12 Months Following Combat in Iraq," *Archives of General Psychiatry*, Vol. 67, No. 6, June 2010, pp. 614–623.

Troxel, W. M., T. E. Trail, L. Jaycox, and A. Chandra, "Preparing for Deployment: Examining Family and Individual-Level Factors," *Military Psychology*, forthcoming.

U.S. Department of the Army, Office of the Surgeon General, *Mental Health Advisory Team (MHAT-V) Operation Iraqi Freedom 06-08 Report: Final Report*, Washington, D.C.: Office of the Surgeon, Multinational Force-Iraq and Office of the Surgeon General, U.S. Army Medical Command, 2008.

———, *Mental Health Advisory Team (MHAT) 6 Operation Enduring Freedom 2009 Afghanistan*, Washington, D.C.: Office of the Surgeon, Multinational Force-Iraq and Office of the Surgeon General, U.S. Army Medical Command, 2009.

Vanderploeg, R. D., H. G. Belanger, R. D. Horner, A. M. Spehar, G. Powell-Cope, S. L. Luther, and S. G. Scott, "Health Outcomes Associated with Military Deployment: Mild Traumatic Brain Injury, Blast, Trauma, and Combat Associations in the Florida National Guard," *Archives of Physical and Medical Rehabilitation*, Vol. 93, No. 11, November 2012, pp. 1887–1895.

Whealin, J. M., R. L. Stotzer, R. H. Pietrzak, D. S. Vogt, J. H. Shore, L. A. Morland, and S. M. Southwick, "Deployment-Related Sequelae and Treatment Utilization in Rural and Urban War Veterans in Hawaii," *Psychological Services*, Vol. 11, No. 1, February 2014, pp. 114–123.

Wittchen, H., S. Schönfeld, C. Kirschbaum, S. Trautmann, C. Thurau, J. Siegert, and M. Höfler, "Rates of Mental Disorders Among German Soldiers Deployed to Afghanistan: Increased Risk of PTSD or of Mental Disorders in General?" *Journal of Depression and Anxiety*, Vol. 2, No. 1, June 2013.

Wood, M. D., H. M. Foran, T. W. Britt, and K. M. Wright, "The Impact of Benefit Finding and Leadership on Combat-Related PTSD Symptoms," *Military Psychology*, Vol. 24, No. 6, 2012, pp. 529–541.

Yambo, T., and M. Johnson, "An Integrative Review of the Mental Health of Partners of Veterans with Combat-Related Posttraumatic Stress Disorder," *Journal of the American Psychiatric Nurses Association*, Vol. 20, No. 1, January–February 2014, pp. 31–41.

CHAPTER SIX
Child and Teen Outcomes

Lisa H. Jaycox, Thomas E. Trail, Lynsay Ayer, Beth Ann Griffin, Esther M. Friedman, and Robin L. Beckman

Introduction

Children in military families face unique stressors, including deployments. Throughout the deployment cycle, children endure periodic, extended separation from one of their parents, which could result in adverse child emotional, behavioral, and academic outcomes. Recent literature reviews have emphasized the importance of considering child adjustment throughout the deployment cycle (Sheppard, Malatras, and Israel, 2010; White et al., 2011). Sheppard and colleagues (2010) hypothesized that parental deployment poses psychosocial risk for children because of the deployment cycle's impact on the stability of the family environment. For instance, in the predeployment stage, a child may become anxious in anticipation of the parent's departure. During deployment, the child and other family members may take on new or additional roles and responsibilities, and routines may change. The child and family may eventually adjust to this new routine; however, when the deployed parent returns home, the family must help to reintegrate him or her, again adapting to different roles, responsibilities, and routines. Sheppard and colleagues (2010) proposed that this disruption of family routines and stability increases risk for negative child outcomes.

Child Outcomes

Previous literature, while limited, generally supports the hypothesis of Sheppard and his colleagues (2010) that the disruption of family routines and stability can lead to negative child outcomes in a range of areas. Children of deployed parents are more likely than those without deployed parents to experience internalizing and externalizing problems, such as anxiety, depression, and aggression, as well as attention and school problems (Aranda et al., 2011; Chandra, Lara-Cinisomo, et al., 2010; Chandra, Martin, et al., 2010; Chartrand et al., 2008; Lester et al., 2010; Trautmann, Alhusen, and Gross, 2015; White et al., 2011). For example, Chandra, Lara-Cinisomo and colleagues (2010) interviewed a sample of military children ages 11 to 17 and their caregivers and found that these youths had significant emotional problems compared with national samples. Another investigation that linked children's medical records to their parents' deployment records identified an 11-percent increase in pediatric visits, a 19-percent increase in behavioral disorders, and an 18-percent increase in stress disorders among youth with a deployed parent (Gorman, Eide, and Hisle-Gorman, 2010). Problems in school also have been linked to parental deployment. For example, Engel, Hyams, and Scott (2006) found significant decreases in test scores for children of deployed parents, with longer deployments associated with lower test scores. Chandra, Martin, and colleagues (2010) conducted focus groups with school personnel who reported that, for many children, parental deployment led to sadness and anger, resulting in classroom disruption and negative effects on peer relationships.

Limited research also suggests that parental deployment can result in increased family conflict and strained relationships between children and their parents (White et al., 2011). For example, Gibbs and colleagues (2007) found that rates of substantiated child maltreatment increased during deployment compared with nondeployment in the U.S. Army, and Gewirtz and colleagues (2010) found that parents with deployment-related PTSD experienced increased parenting challenges postdeployment.

There is some evidence for age differences in child outcomes as well. Specifically, research suggests that older children have more emotional and behavioral problems associated with parental deployment than younger children, perhaps because older youth are more aware of the danger their deployed parent could be facing (Chandra, Lara-Cinisomo, et al., 2010; Chartrand et al., 2008; Gorman et al., 2010; White et al., 2011). For example, Gorman and colleagues (2010) examined deployment and health records for more than 642,000 military children ages three to eight and noted that older youth showed larger increases in behavioral health visits than younger children did. Similarly, in a study of 1,507 military children ages 11 to 17 (Chandra, Lara-Cinisomo, et al., 2010), older youth reported higher levels of school, family, and peer-related difficulties with deployment.

Unfortunately, the existing literature consists primarily of retrospective and cross-sectional studies (Trautmann et al., 2015; White et al., 2011). For example, in a recent review of findings on the impact of deployment to Iraq or Afghanistan on military children, White and colleagues (2011) identified only two longitudinal studies (Barker and Berry, 2009; Barnes, Davis, and Treiber, 2007). Both of these studies reported increased psychological problems during deployment among youth with a deployed parent relative to national samples of youth with nondeployed parents. However, Barker and Berry (2009) and Barnes and colleagues (2007) used relatively small convenience samples (Ns=57 and 121, respectively) and did not follow families throughout the deployment cycle. Therefore, longer-term prospective research with larger samples is critical to improve understanding of how children adjust to parental deployment, and what parental, family, and child characteristics may pose risks for, or protect against, the potential negative impact of deployment on children.

Child Risk and Resilience Factors

Despite the aforementioned literature suggesting that parental deployment is associated with negative child outcomes, most military families and children are generally resilient (Sheppard et al., 2010). This can be ascribed partly to such distal influences as resources and systems supportive to military families in general—e.g., access to health care, employment, education, legal assistance, and other resources (Palmer, 2008). In this study, we examine more-proximal resilience factors that are likely to buffer youth more directly from any harmful effects of parental deployment. For example, there is strong evidence that social support from within and outside the home (e.g., from other military children) can buffer children from the negative mental health effects of such stressors as parental deployment (Repetti, Taylor, and Seeman, 2002). Other potential protective factors that have not yet been examined in relation to deployment and child outcomes include the child's level of communication with his or her deployed parent. For example, a child who has little communication with his or her deployed parent may worry frequently about the parent's well-being. Alternatively, increased communication could exacerbate the child's worry about his or her parent. Finally, adjustment during deployment could relate to a child's long-term outcomes. For instance, if a child is not doing well in school, or has trouble adjusting to a new routine without the deployed parent, he or she may develop more-serious problems with anxiety, depression, acting-out behavior, or academic difficulties. These potential risk factors have not been examined previously, to our knowledge, but will be tested as predictors of child outcomes in this study.

Research Questions

- **Research Question (RQ) 1:** How do child/teen outcomes change over the course of a typical deployment cycle: predeployment, during deployment, and postdeployment?
  - **RQ1a:** Is the trajectory significantly different from a flat line (i.e., no changes in average values) over the deployment cycle?
    - **Hypothesis:** We do not expect trajectories to be flat across the deployment cycle, as we expect changes in child/teen outcomes to occur during the study deployment itself.
  - **RQ1b:** Is the trajectory significantly different from a straight line (i.e., a constant change over time that is unrelated to the phase of, or timing within, the deployment cycle) over the deployment cycle?
    - **Hypothesis:** We do not expect trajectories to be linear across the deployment cycle; instead, we expect there to be change within a given stage of deployment that varies between periods (e.g., a trajectory may decline immediately prior to a deployment and then improve/recover during the postdeployment period).
- **RQ2:** How does deployment affect postdeployment child/teen outcomes? By comparing outcomes between families where a service member experienced a study deployment and matched families where the service member did not deploy, we can estimate what a child or teen of a deployed service member would look like had the service member not deployed.
  - **Hypothesis:** Based on resilience theory, we expect limited to no impact on postdeployment family outcomes. That is, we expect that the stress of deployment will, on average, create a short-term change in functioning that returns to baseline levels when the stress is removed.
- **RQ3:** What risk and resilience factors predict differences in postdeployment child/teen outcomes among deployed families? These factors fall into three categories: service member deployment variables (i.e., experience of trauma during deployment); social support for teens generally, with military children, and via communication with the service member during deployment; and child or teen functioning during deployment (i.e., adjustment and challenges).
  - **Hypotheses:**
    - The experience of deployment trauma by the service member during a study deployment will be related to worse child and teen outcomes at the end of the study. Longer study deployments and separation from the military could increase stress and also worsen outcomes for children and teens at the end of the study.
    - Functioning and challenges during the study deployment will be related to subsequent child and teen outcomes at the end of the study.
    - Social support for the teen at baseline and during a study deployment will improve teen outcomes at the end of the study.

Method

Data for this chapter includes all nine assessment waves of the Deployment Life Study. As described previously, the Deployment Life Study is a longitudinal survey of approximately 2,700 deployable, married, military families, including service members, their spouses, and children.[1] (For additional details, see Tanielian, Karney, et al., 2014.)

Child Sample

Children in this study were chosen at the spouse's baseline assessment. A single child was selected from the children between the ages of three and 17 living in the household more than half of the time, for which the spouse or service member had legal guardianship. If there was more than one child in the household that fit these criteria, then one child was randomly chosen to be the focus of the study.

The child sample is broken into two groups—*children* (younger than age 11) and *teens* (ages 11 and older). For children, data come from a single source: spouse report of child adjustment and behavior. For teens, data come from two sources: report by the spouse of the teen's adjustment and behavior, and the teen's own responses about his or her thoughts, feelings, and behaviors. However, not all teens agreed to participate, so data stemming from teen self-reports are available from a smaller number of households than data from the spouse report. In total, we have baseline information on 1,242 children in this study, including spouse reports on 690 children and on 552 teens. We also have self-reported data from 407 teens. We have both types of data (spouse and teen report) for 368 teens.

Measures
Dependent Measures (Child and Teen Outcomes)

As already described, data for children and teens come from different sources: the spouse report and the teen self-report. A list of outcome measures included in this chapter can be found in Table 6.1. Each measure is then described in detail.

Emotional and Behavioral Difficulties. Child and teen emotional and behavioral difficulties were measured by the Strengths and Difficulties Questionnaire (SDQ) (Goodman, 1997). The SDQ is a 25-item measure of child behavior over five areas: emotional problems, conduct problems, hyperactivity, peer relationships, and prosocial behavior. Spouses rated 25 statements of child behavior (e.g., "is often unhappy, depressed or tearful") and rated whether each statement was not true, somewhat true, or definitely true of the child's or teen's behavior in the past four months (coded 0, 1, and 2, respectively), and teens provided answers on the self-report version of the measure. Based on prior research (Goodman, 1997), we formed five subscales composed of five items each: *emotional problems, conduct problems, hyperactivity, peer problems, and prosocial behavior.* We summed items within each subscale, with higher values indicating greater difficulties/problems or more prosocial behavior. In addition, a *total difficulties* scale comprises all items except the prosocial behavior items.

Anxiety. We assessed child anxiety using the Screen for Child Anxiety Related Emotional Disorders (SCARED). The SCARED is a measure of the child's level of anxiety based on five underlying factors: panic, generalized anxiety, separation anxiety, social phobia, and school

---

[1]   Recall that the Navy sample only has seven total waves of data. See Chapter Two for more details on the study design and sample.

Table 6.1
Child and Teen Outcomes by Source

	Data on Children	Data on Teens	
	Spouse Report	Spouse Report	Teen Self-Report
SDQ Total Difficulties	X	X	X
SDQ Subscale: Emotional Problems	X	X	X
SDQ Subscale: Conduct Problems	X	X	X
SDQ Subscale: Hyperactivity	X	X	X
SDQ Subscale: Peer Problems	X	X	X
SDQ Subscale: Prosocial Behavior	X	X	X
Anxiety	X	X	X
Depressive Symptoms	X	X	X
Need for Mental Health Services	X	X	X
Pediatric Quality of Life	X	X	
Overall Health Functioning			X
Risky Behaviors			
Physical Aggression			X
Nonphysical Aggression			X
Relational Aggression			X
Drug Use			X
Life Satisfaction			X
Academic Disengagement			X
Family Cohesion			X
Relationship Quality with Service Member			X
Relationship Quality with Spouse			X

NOTES: *Child* or *children* refers to children younger than age 11 for whom we have spouse reports. *Teen* refers to children ages 11 and older for whom we have self-reports and/or spouse reports.

phobia (Birmaher et al., 1997). We used the five-item version of the SCARED, which contains a single item from each of the five factors (e.g., "gets really frightened for no reason at all") (Birmaher, Brent, et al., 1999). Spouses were asked "thinking about the last four months, how often have you seen the following behaviors in [child name]?" and rated whether each behavior occurred not at all, sometimes, or most of the time (coded 0, 1, and 2, respectively) over the stated period for children and teens; teens provided self-reports on this same measure. All five items were summed to form one scale measuring anxiety, with higher numbers indicating greater anxiety.

Depressive Symptoms. We assessed the severity of child and teen depressive symptoms using eight items from the Patient Health Questionnaire for Adolescents (PHQ-A) Version 3.6.05 (American Academy of Pediatrics, 2010), a clinical tool developed for pediatricians. Spouses completed these items in regard to children and teens, and teens also completed self-reports of these symptoms. Each item assessed whether the child or teen had the problem in the prior two weeks, and if so, whether it was a problem a few days (scored 1) or nearly every day (scored 2). Problems included little interest or pleasure in doing things; feeling down, depressed, irritable, or hopeless; and other depressive symptoms but did not include suicidal ideation. The eight items were summed such that scores could range from 0 to 16, with higher scores indicating more-depressive symptoms in the prior two weeks.

Need for Mental Health Services. We assessed the spouse's perception of the child's or teen's need for mental health services by asking "In the past four months, did [child name] have a need for counseling or therapy for personal or emotional problems from a mental (behavioral) health specialist like a psychiatrist, psychologist, social worker, or family counselor in a mental (behavioral) health clinic or office or at school?" Response options were yes (1) or no (0). Teens also completed this item as a self-report.

Pediatric Quality of Life Inventory (PedsQL). The PedsQL originally was designed to assess health-related quality of life for children with serious illnesses (Varni, Seid, and Rode, 1999). Items were adapted by Jaycox and colleagues (2009) to apply to all children, and specifically to assess family involvement. The four items measure how frequently a child had problems with different aspects of family life in the past four weeks (e.g., how often the child "had problems keeping up with responsibilities at home"). Items were rated on a five-point scale from *none of the time* (1) to *all of the time* (5), and scores on all four items were reverse-coded and averaged, with a higher score indicating greater quality of life. Spouses completed these items for children and teens.

Overall Health Functioning. Teens completed one item taken from the National Health Interview Study to measure overall health (Lorig et al., 1996). Teens rated "In general, how would you rate your physical health?" on a five-point scale from *poor* (1) to *excellent* (5).

Risky Behaviors. We assessed risky teen behaviors using a 15-item scale taken from the Problem Behavior Frequency Scale (Farrell et al., 2000) and used in previous studies of military children (e.g., RAND National Military Family Association study [Chandra et al., 2013]). The scale assesses the frequency of risky behaviors in five areas—physical aggression, nonphysical aggression, relational aggression, drug use, and delinquency. The scale contains three items addressing each area. The delinquency and drug use items were only administered to teens ages 15 or older. Items were rated on a six-point scale from *never* (1) to *20 or more times* (6). Delinquency items were rarely acknowledged, so that subscale was dropped from the analysis. Responses within the other risky-behavior subscales were averaged to form four indices: physical aggression, nonphysical aggression, relational aggression, and drug use (for older teens).

Life Satisfaction. Teen life satisfaction was assessed using one item completed by the teen from the Satisfaction with Life Scale (Diener et al., 1985): "Taking things altogether, how satisfied are you with your life right now?" Responses were rated on a five-point scale from *very dissatisfied* (1) to *very satisfied* (5).

Academic Disengagement. Seven items assessed the teen's disengagement with school and academics (Rosenthal and Feldman, 1991). These items ask teens how frequently they complete their homework, prepare for class, and engage in other similar activities, and were used in previous studies of military children (e.g., RAND National Military Family Association study [Chandra et al., 2013]). Responses were rated on a five-point scale from *none of the time* (0) to *all of the time* (4) and coded (or reverse-coded as necessary) so that higher scores indicate less academic engagement.

Family Environment—Conflict and Cohesion Scales. Conflict among family members was assessed using six items taken from the Conflict and Cohesion subscales of the Family Environment Scale (FES) (Moos and Moos, 1994). Respondents were asked to indicate whether they thought each item described their family using a three-point scale (*describes my family well, describes my family somewhat,* or *does not describe my family at all*). These items measure the degree of conflict within the family (e.g., "family members often put one another down") and the family's cohesiveness (e.g., "family members really help and support one another"). The conflict items were reverse-scored and combined with the cohesiveness items and then averaged to form a scale of family cohesion where higher values indicate more cohesion and less conflict. Spouses and service member data on this scale is presented in Chapter Four. In this chapter, we include the teen's perception of family conflict.

Relationship Quality with Parents. We assessed the teen's perception of relationship quality with the service member and spouse using the ten-item Parent-Child Communications scale (Loeber et al., 1998). Items ask about the quality of communication between the child and parent (e.g., "Do you talk about your problems with your mother/father?" "Do you think that you can tell your mother/father how you really feel about some things?"). Teens rated each parent separately using a five-point scale (*not at all* [1] to *almost always* [5]), and scores were averaged to provide an overall indicator of parent-child relationship quality and communication where higher scores indicate better-quality relationships.

Table 6.2 shows the means and standard errors (SEs) for each outcome at baseline for children, as well as whether the family experienced a study deployment. At baseline, children demonstrated relatively low average scores on Total SDQ and the SDQ problem subscales, with higher scores on the SDQ prosocial behavior subscale, suggesting that their levels of emotional and behavioral difficulties were not problematic. Levels of anxiety and depressive symptoms were also low, while pediatric quality of life was rated on the high end of the scale (4.39 out of 5), suggesting that children in the study were not experiencing a high level of emotional problems on average. In addition, only around 8 percent of children were identified as having a need for mental health services at baseline. We tested whether children who subsequently experienced a study deployment significantly differed on these measures from those who did not, and we found that both sets of children were rated similarly by their parents on mental health and need for mental health service dimensions at baseline.

Table 6.3 shows the same information for teens, including additional outcomes captured via teen self-report. At baseline, teen and parent reports indicate teens experienced relatively low levels of total difficulties, emotional problems, conduct problems, hyperactivity, and peer

Table 6.2
Outcomes for Children at Baseline and by Experience of Study Deployment

	Overall Sample (n=690)	Study Deployment (n=308)		No Study Deployment (n=382)		
		Mean (SE)	Range	Mean (SE)	Range	p-value
SDQ Total Difficulties	8.28 (0.34)	6.95 (0.71)	0–30	7.64 (0.47)	0–32	0.42
SDQ Subscale: Emotional Problems	1.78 (0.14)	1.65 (0.25)	0–10	1.66 (0.23)	0–9	0.97
SDQ Subscale: Conduct Problems	1.06 (0.07)	1.13 (0.24)	0–10	0.96 (0.18)	0–9	0.55
SDQ Subscale: Hyperactivity	3.84 (0.17)	2.44 (0.19)	0–10	2.86 (0.21)	0–10	0.14
SDQ Subscale: Peer Problems	1.59 (0.14)	1.72 (0.23)	0–8	2.16 (0.25)	0–8	0.19
SDQ Subscale: Prosocial Behavior	8.58 (0.11)	8.39 (0.23)	1–10	8.16 (0.21)	1–10	0.44
Anxiety	1.74 (0.11)	1.69 (0.30)	0–10	1.33 (0.26)	0–7	0.36
Depressive Symptoms	0.84 (0.10)	0.88 (0.11)	0–11	0.83 (0.13)	0–12	0.79
Need for Mental Health Services (%)	8.48 (2.14)	11.98 (2.86)		10.21 (2.63)		0.64
Pediatric Quality of Life	4.39 (0.05)	4.07 (0.10)	1.25–5	3.95 (0.18)	1–5	0.60

NOTE: Results are weighted. Missing data are imputed. P-values are for results of a weighted t-test of differences between the study deployment and no study deployment groups.

problems on the SDQ. Prosocial behavior and pediatric quality of life, on the other hand, were relatively high, and anxiety and depressive symptoms were low. These findings suggest that teens were generally doing well emotionally and behaviorally at baseline. The percentage of teens reported to be in need of mental health services ranged from 7 percent to 14 percent, indicating that regardless of the reporter and whether the child had a parent who deployed, most teens were viewed as not needing mental health services; this is consistent with the afore-mentioned reports of low levels of emotional and behavioral problems. Teens' self-reports on overall health functioning, life satisfaction, family cohesion, and quality of relationship with their parents were also consistent, with relatively high average scores in each of these areas. Teens reported relatively low levels of aggressive behavior, drug use, and academic disengage-ment, as well. Similar to the children, teens who subsequently experienced a study deployment and those who did not were rated similarly by their parents and by their self-report on almost all mental health and mental health service use dimensions at baseline. However, one signifi-cant difference was observed, in which teens who subsequently experienced a study deploy-ment reported a greater need for mental health services at baseline than those who did not.

We show the correlation between measures as reported by the spouse compared with the teen self-report in Table 6.4 (within families that completed both measures, n=368). The diagonal shows the correlation between the spouse and teen report on each of the outcomes for which we have reports from the two different sources. At baseline, spouse and teen showed some agreement on the scales of depression and need for mental health services, with correla-tions in the 0.35 to 0.45 range, but less agreement on total difficulties or anxiety (correlations in the 0.15 to 0.25 range). Correlations among the measures are generally low (below 0.30), indicating that these measures are tapping somewhat different underlying constructs, although all but two show significant associations with the others. The exceptions are that spouse report of total difficulties was uncorrelated with teen report of anxiety or teen report of need for mental health services.

Covariates/Controls

We included demographic and other covariates that might be associated with child outcomes in all our models. For all models, we included demographic variables: child age, child gender, whether the service member had a deployment prior to baseline (defined as any deployment of 30 days or more outside the continental United States [OCONUS]), service member pay grade (i.e., officer or enlisted and rank), and branch of service (i.e., Army, Air Force, Navy, Marine Corps). We also included a measure of service member combat trauma exposure prior to base-line, measured using 15 items taken from the Hoge et al. (2004) Combat Experiences Scale (CES), which measures combat trauma exposure. The original CES contains 18 items that assess the occurrence of different potentially traumatic events in combat (e.g., being attacked or ambushed, participating in demining operations.) Three items were eliminated to minimize the sensitivity of the questions and the time it takes to complete the measure (see Tanielian and Jaycox, 2008). Endorsed items are summed to create an index score. Each model also included the baseline version of the outcome as a covariate.

Table 6.5 presents means, percentages, and SEs for all of the control variables at baseline for the children (i.e., the deployed and nondeployed sample combined). Means are reported separately for children who do and do not experience a parental study deployment. Table 6.6 repeats this information for teens. All means are weighted and baseline data are imputed, as detailed in Chapter Two.

Table 6.3
Outcomes for Teens at Baseline and by Experience of Study Deployment

	Spouse Report						Teen Report					
	Overall	Study Deployment (n=219)		No Study Deployment (n=333)		p-value	Overall	Study Deployment (n=154)		No Study Deployment (n=253)		p-value
	n=552 Mean (SE)	Mean (SE)	Range	Mean (SE)	Range		n=407 Mean (SE)	Mean (SE)	Range	Mean (SE)	Range	
SDQ Total Difficulties	7.98 (0.31)	7.66 (0.33)	0–32	8.08 (0.39)	0–30	0.42	8.32 (0.54)	7.89 (0.61)	0–28	8.51 (0.73)	0–26	0.52
SDQ Subscale: Emotional Problems	1.90 (0.15)	1.61 (0.15)	0–9	1.99 (0.18)	0–10	0.11	1.87 (0.18)	1.81 (0.21)	0–9	1.90 (0.24)	0–10	0.79
SDQ Subscale: Conduct Problems	0.94 (0.11)	0.90 (0.07)	0–9	0.95 (0.14)	0–8	0.77	1.35 (0.13)	1.25 (0.13)	0–7	1.39 (0.18)	0–6	0.52
SDQ Subscale: Hyperactivity	3.54 (0.21)	3.49 (0.21)	0–10	3.55 (0.26)	0–10	0.86	3.23 (0.17)	3.05 (0.26)	0–9	3.31 (0.22)	0–9	0.44
SDQ Subscale: Peer Problems	1.61 (0.12)	1.67 (0.13)	0–8	1.59 (0.15)	0–8	0.69	1.86 (0.16)	1.78 (0.19)	0–7	1.90 (0.21)	0–8	0.66
SDQ Subscale: Prosocial Behavior	8.45 (0.16)	8.61 (0.12)	1–10	8.39 (0.20)	2.5–10	0.35	8.46 (0.16)	8.29 (0.21)	4–10	8.54 (0.22)	1.3–10	0.41
Anxiety	1.85 (0.14)	1.76 (0.14)	0–10	1.87 (0.17)	0–9	0.63	1.33 (0.14)	1.26 (0.12)	0–5	1.36 (0.19)	0–8	0.66
Depressive Symptoms	1.04 (0.21)	1.03 (0.17)	0–11	1.04 (0.25)	0–12	0.96	2.19 (0.21)	2.15 (0.22)	0–13	2.21 (0.29)	0–14.86	0.86
Need for Mental Health Services (%)	7.65 (1.91)	9.38 (2.01)		7.12 (2.39)		0.48	8.86 (1.74)	**14.12 (3.86)**		**6.47 (1.63)**		**0.03**
Pediatric Quality of Life	4.23 (0.14)	4.47 (0.05)	1–5	4.15 (0.18)	2–5	0.09						
Overall Health Functioning							4.05 (0.09)	4.04 (0.09)	1–5	4.05 (0.12)	(1–5)	0.93

204 The Deployment Life Study: Longitudinal Analysis of Military Families Across the Deployment Cycle

Table 6.3—Continued

	Spouse Report						Teen Report					
	Overall	Study Deployment (n=219)		No Study Deployment (n=333)			Overall	Study Deployment (n=154)		No Study Deployment (n=253)		
	n=552	Mean (SE)	Range	Mean (SE)	Range	p-value	n=407	Mean (SE)	Range	Mean (SE)	Range	p-value
Risky Behaviors												
Physical Aggression							1.18 (0.05)	1.14 (0.04)	(1–3.9)	1.20 (0.07)	(1–3.3)	0.48
Relational Aggression							1.12 (0.05)	1.08 (0.03)	(1–6)	1.14 (0.08)	(1–3)	0.41
Nonphysical Aggression							1.42 (0.16)	1.24 (0.07)	(1–6)	1.50 (0.22)	(1–5)	0.25
Drug Use							1.06 (0.02)	1.08 (0.03)	(1–2.7)	1.05 (0.02)	(1–2.7)	0.45
Life Satisfaction							4.49 (0.06)	4.52 (0.08)	(1–5)	4.47 (0.08)	(2–5)	0.62
Academic Disengagement							1.78 (0.09)	1.77 (0.12)	(0–3.3)	1.78 (0.11)	(0–3.3)	0.94
Family Cohesion							2.72 (0.03)	2.69 (0.03)	(1.5–3)	2.73 (0.04)	(1.7–3)	0.51
Relationship Quality with Service Member							4.15 (0.06)	4.23 (0.07)	(1.9–5)	4.12 (0.09)	(1.6–5)	0.29
Relationship Quality with Spouse							4.18 (0.06)	4.22 (0.05)	(2.7–5)	4.16 (0.08)	(1.7–5)	0.56

NOTE: Results are weighted. Missing data are imputed. P-values are for results of a weighted t-test of differences between the study deployment and no study deployment groups; statistically significant differences are shown in bold.

Table 6.4
Correlation Between Family Outcomes at Baseline: Spouse Versus Teen Report

		Teen Report			
		Total Difficulties	Anxiety	Depressive Symptoms	Need for Mental Health Services (%)
Spouse Report	Total Difficulties	0.24****	0.03	0.20***	0.10
	Anxiety	0.15**	0.16**	0.17**	0.14**
	Depressive Symptoms	0.25****	0.15**	0.36****	0.16**
	Need for Mental Health Services (%)	0.21****	0.11*	0.29****	0.46****

NOTE: *=p<0.05; **=p<0.01; ***=p<0.001; ****=p<0.0001.

Table 6.5
Means, Percentages, and Standard Errors of Study Variables at Baseline: Children (by Study Deployment Status)

	Overall Sample	Study Deployment (n=308)		No Study Deployment (n=382)		
	n=690	Mean (SE)	Range	Mean (SE)	Range	p-value
Age[a]	6.03 (0.20)	5.77 (0.19)	3–10	6.13 (0.27)	3–10	0.28
Male	53.93 (3.99)	46.66 (4.99)		56.59 (5.05)		0.16
Any Prior Deployment[b]	82.35 (4.01)	94.05 (1.64)		78.06 (5.26)		0.00
Combat Experiences Scale[c]	4.56 (0.36)	5.51 (0.60)	0–15	4.21 (0.42)	0–15	0.07
Branch of Service						
Army	46.79 (3.96)	44.69 (4.85)		47.56 (5.10)		0.69
Air Force	19.36 (2.08)	23.5 (3.15)		17.85 (2.55)		
Navy	19.52 (4.16)	15.58 (3.24)		20.96 (5.49)		
Marine Corps	14.33 (3.32)	16.22 (7.07)		13.63 (3.70)		
Pay Grade						
E1 to E3	3.19 (1.21)	1.82 (1.05)		3.69 (1.61)		0.42
E4 to E9	72.27 (3.95)	78.69 (3.23)		69.92 (5.18)		
O1 to O3	8.63 (2.33)	8.21 (1.98)		8.79 (3.10)		
O4 +	13.33 (3.56)	10.07 (2.16)		14.53 (4.75)		
Warrant Officer	2.57 (0.87)	1.20 (0.49)		3.08 (1.18)		

NOTES: Results are weighted. Missing data are imputed.

[a] Service member and spouse range: 21–56.

[b] Includes all OCONUS deployments of 30 days or more.

[c] See Hoge et al. (2004). Service member range: 0–15.

As can be seen in Tables 6.5 and 6.6, children and teens that have data from the spouse report and experienced a study deployment were generally similar to those who did not in terms of age, gender, service member parent rank, and branch of service. However, those who experienced a study deployment were more likely to have had their parent deploy prior to the beginning of the study than those who did not (94 percent versus 78 percent), and there was a nonsignificant trend such that those children (but not teens) who experienced a study deployment had service member parents with higher levels of combat experiences at baseline. Among those in the teen self-report sample, there were no apparent differences on these variables except with regard to the branch of service, with more Army and fewer Marine Corps families

Table 6.6
Means, Percentages, and Standard Errors of Study Variables at Baseline: Teens

	Spouse Report							Teen Self-Report						
	Overall		Study Deployment (n=219)		No Study Deployment (n=333)			Overall		Study Deployment (n=154)		No Study Deployment (n=253)		
	n=552		Mean (SE)	Range	Mean (SE)	Range	p-value	n=407		Mean (SE)	Range	Mean (SE)	Range	p-value
	Mean (SE)	Range						Mean (SE)	Range					
Age[a]	13.25 (0.30)	11–18	13.84 (0.25)	11–18	13.15 (0.33)	11–18	0.10	13.70 (0.16)	11–18	13.78 (0.21)	11–18	13.66 (0.21)	11–18	0.69
Male	37.62 (6.51)		46.63 (6.01)		36.06 (7.42)		0.25	50.01 (5.20)		50.52 (5.56)		49.78 (7.13)		0.94
Any Prior Deployment[b]	67.43 (9.48)		**91.1 (4.12)**		**63.35 (10.54)**		**0.00**	88.91 (2.38)		88.06 (4.71)		89.29 (2.69)		0.82
Combat Experiences Scale[c]	3.6 (0.52)	0–15	4.05 (0.47)	0–15	3.52 (0.59)	0–15	0.49	4.21 (0.34)	0–15	4.56 (0.49)	0–15	4.05 (0.42)	0–15	0.44
Branch of Service														
Army	46.49 (7.31)		43.71 (5.56)		46.98 (8.57)		0.94	51.01 (5.27)		**64.3 (5.92)**		**45.00 (6.59)**		**0.03**
Air Force	18.48 (3.41)		22.06 (3.81)		17.86 (3.87)			20.14 (5.86)		**8.57 (1.80)**		**25.37 (8.06)**		
Navy	32.45 (9.60)		30.76 (7.42)		32.74 (11.15)			26.75 (5.12)		**25.95 (6.22)**		**27.11 (6.89)**		
Marine Corps	2.57 (1.15)		3.47 (3.28)		2.42 (1.22)			2.11 (0.95)		**1.18 (1.17)**		**2.52 (1.29)**		
Pay Grade														
E1 to E3	1.76 (1.19)		0.83 (0.62)		1.91 (1.40)		0.28	0.67 (0.41)		0		0.97 (0.60)		N/A
E4 to E9	74.38 (5.02)		69.96 (4.76)		75.14 (5.76)			73.83 (4.40)		75.45 (3.91)		73.09 (6.14)		
O1 to O3	4.28 (1.30)		7.11 (1.93)		3.80 (1.46)			5.20 (1.10)		7.99 (2.29)		3.94 (1.15)		
O4 +	17.08 (4.22)		16.77 (3.88)		17.14 (4.90)			17.90 (4.31)		12.24 (2.87)		20.47 (6.06)		
Warrant Officer	2.5 (0.81)		5.34 (1.73)		2.02 (0.87)			2.40 (0.69)		4.31 (1.31)		1.53 (0.78)		

NOTES: Results are weighted. Missing data are imputed. There were no service members in pay grade E1 to E3 with teens who self-reported. Bold indicates a statistically significant difference between the study deployment and no study deployment groups based on a weighted t-test.

[a] Service members and spouse range: 21–56.

[b] Includes all OCONUS deployments of 30 days or more.

[c] See Hoge et al. (2004). Service member range: 0–15.

in the group of teens who experienced a study deployment. Because children and teens that experience a study deployment differ in some ways from those who do not, we employ propensity score methods to match those who deploy with those who do not in the following results, which examine the impact of a study deployment on postdeployment outcomes.

Risk and Resilience Factors

As described in the introduction to this chapter, we also hypothesized that a number of risk and resilience factors might mitigate (or exacerbate) how well families do after deployment. These factors are conceptualized into three categories: service member deployment and military variables that could have an impact on child functioning, child and teen adjustment during a study deployment; and teen social support before and during the deployment. Specifically, we investigate whether baseline social support for the child or teen might improve outcomes over time for those who experienced a study deployment. In terms of factors during deployment, we include the three aspects of the service member's experience: experience of combat trauma while deployed, the length of the study deployment(s), and whether the service member separated from the military at any time during the study. We examine four factors related to child and teen functioning during the study deployment: the spouse's report of adjustment during deployment and trouble in school, and teens' self-report of their own adjustment during deployment and the number of challenges they faced. We also examine the frequency of communication between the service member and teen during the study deployment. Each measure is listed in Table 6.7 and described in detail in the text.

Service Member Deployment and Military Measures

Deployment trauma exposure during the study deployment was assessed via 11 items taken from Tanielian and Jaycox (2008). Because the various types of trauma may not have the same relationships with outcomes, the 11 traumatic deployment experiences that were assessed have been broken down into conceptually meaningful groups: any physical trauma (e.g., received an injury requiring hospitalization or a blow to the head), any combat trauma (e.g., engaging in hand-to-hand combat or experiencing explosions), and psychological trauma that does not fall into the other categories (e.g., having friends who are seriously injured or killed, smelling decomposing bodies, or seeing dead or injured noncombatants) (see Chapter Two of this report for more details). These measures are cumulative across the study deployment. Thus, if a service member indicates "yes" to any items in the three categories, she or he receives a score of 1.

Length of study deployment was measured in months.

Separation from military. In these analyses, if service members reported their current military status as "separated from the military" or "retired" at any time during Wave 2 through 9, they were defined as separated.

Child and Teen Adjustment During Study Deployment Measures

Parent Concerns About Adjustment to the Study Deployment. On surveys completed while the service member was deployed, spouses were asked to rate child and teen adjustment to the study deployment along 11 dimensions (e.g., "feels lonely") which were developed for this study. Spouses rated whether each item was *not true* (1), *somewhat true* (2), or *definitely true* (3). We factor-analyzed these items and formed two variables based on the resultant factors. The first factor represented *negative adjustment to deployment,* and was composed of the items: *gets more easily upset or agitated, feels lonely, returns to behaviors he or she had previously outgrown, doesn't enjoy activities as much, isolates himself or herself more or prefers to spend more time alone,*

Table 6.7
Risk and Resilience Factors by Source

	Children	Teens	
	Spouse Report	Spouse Report	Teen Self-Report
Service Member Deployment and Military Variables			
Deployment Trauma Exposure	X	X	
Length of Study Deployment(s)	X	X	
Separation from Military	X	X	
Child/Teen Adjustment During Study Deployment			
Parent Concerns about Adjustment to Deployment			
Negative Adjustment to Deployment	X	X	
Positive Adjustment to Deployment	X	X	
Trouble with School	X	X	
Teen Adjustment to Deployment			X
Challenges During Deployment			X
Teen Social Support			
Baseline Social Support			X
Socialization with Military Children During Study Deployment			X
Frequency of Communication with Deployed Parent			X

NOTE: *Child* or *children* refers to children younger than age 11 for whom we have spouse reports. *Teen* refers to children ages 11 and older for whom we have self-reports and/or spouse reports.

and *feels worried about his or her military parent*. The second factor represented *positive adjustment to deployment*, and was composed of the items: *acts more mature, acts more independently, takes on more responsibilities or chores at home, and takes care of siblings more often*. Each scale was formed by taking the mean of these items. One item, *proud*, failed to successfully load onto either factor and was not included in either scale. If multiple assessments were obtained during a study deployment on these measures, we took the average across all assessments.

Trouble with School. Two items developed for child and teen trouble with school during the study deployment were rated by spouses in the first assessment following a deployment. The items, "had trouble with schoolwork when his or her parent was deployed" and "got into more trouble at school when his or her parent was deployed" were on a three point scale (*not at all*=1, *some of the time*=2, and *all of the time*=3). Values were coded so that higher values represent more trouble, and averaged.

Teen Adjustment Problems During the Study Deployment. We assessed teen adjustment to deployment along ten dimensions (e.g., "Having a parent deployed makes you . . . Feel lonely") that were developed for this study. Teens rated whether each item was *not true* (1), *somewhat true* (2), or *definitely true* (3). These items were very similar to those completed by the spouse. Although the factor analysis of spouses' ratings for children and teens resulted in two factors representing negative and positive adjustment, the factor analysis of teen ratings resulted in only one factor, with all items loading positively except *feel proud*, which did not successfully load onto the factor and was not included in the resulting index. The items that did load onto the factor were: *feel lonely, feel like you have more responsibilities or chores at home, find it hard to enjoy your usual activities or hobbies, rely on your friends more for help and support, worry about your (military parent), do more things on your own, have more trouble with schoolwork, get into more trouble at school,* and *worry about your (spouse parent).* We calculated the average of these items to form a scale of teen adjustment to deployment; in cases where more than one follow-up assessment was obtained during the study deployment, we took the average across all assessments to represent the average value of teen adjustment during the study deployment period.

Challenges During the Study Deployment. We assessed the challenges and difficulties that teens faced during the study deployment using ten items developed for this study. Teens were asked to indicate whether they had experienced the following difficulties during the current deployment: *missing classes at school because you don't feel like leaving home; missing classes at school because you don't like your school; missing after-school activities (such as school activities, sports) because you don't feel like participating; missing after-school activities (such as school activities, sports) because of transportation problems/issues; feeling misunderstood by people at school or in your community; having a hard time dealing with life without your [mother/father]; having more responsibilities with taking care of siblings; having more responsibilities at home either with chores or caring for pets; feeling like you have no one to talk to about how you are feeling, whether it be sadness or stress;* and *people just don't understand what life is like for you.* Responses were coded 1 for *yes* and 0 for *no* and summed to form an index of teen challenges during deployment. If multiple assessments were obtained during one study deployment, we took the average across all assessments.

Teen Social Support Measures

Low Baseline Social Support. We assessed the level of social support available to the teen using a one-item measure of expressive social support taken from the Fragile Families and Child Wellbeing study (Reichman et al., 2001)—"If you needed someone to listen to your problems if you were feeling low, are there . . . enough people you can count on, not enough people, or no one you can count on"—where a response of *enough people* was coded for 0 and *not enough* or *no one* were coded for 1, with higher scores indicating lower support.

Socialization with Children in Military Families During Deployment. A one-item *yes* (1)/*no* (0) measure of socializing with other military children was developed for this study: "Do you know, socialize, or communicate regularly with other kids from military families?"

Frequency of communication during the deployment is assessed via a single item that asks teens how frequently they communicate with the deployed parent. Responses range from *never* (0) to *every day* (7); these responses were recoded into a three-category variable that included less than weekly contact (1), at least weekly contact (2), and daily contact (3) such that higher scores indicate more-frequent communication.

For all of these items, if multiple assessments were obtained during one study deployment, we took the average across all assessments.

Risk and Resilience

Table 6.8 shows the risk and resilience factors for children and teens. In these samples, service members were deployed for an average of about eight months during the study period. They reported high rates of combat traumas during the study deployment (40 percent for children and 31 or 34 percent for the teen samples), with 5 percent to 9 percent reporting trauma

Table 6.8
Means, Percentages, and Standard Errors of Risk and Resilience Factors Among Children and Teens Who Experienced a Study Deployment

| | Children | | Teens | | | |
| | Parent Report Sample (n=307) | | Parent Report Sample (n=219) | | Teen Self-Report Sample (n=154) | |
	Mean	SE	Mean	SE	Mean	SE
Service Member Deployment and Military Measures						
Deployment Trauma Exposure[a]						
Combat	40.31	5.98	34.12	7.28	30.90	5.53
Physical	7.30	1.09	4.65	1.62	8.52	4.32
Psychological	15.84	2.99	26.40	8.03	22.05	5.93
Length of Study Deployment(s) (Months)[a]	7.78	0.20	8.23	0.28	8.21	0.23
Separation from Military[a]	3.40	1.09	12.75	6.63	9.03	2.69
Child/Teen Adjustment During Study Deployment						
Parent Concerns About Adjustment to Deployment[b]						
Negative Adjustment to Deployment[b]	1.84	0.04	1.76	0.06		
Positive Adjustment to Deployment[b]	1.87	0.05	2.01	0.08		
Trouble with School[b]	1.57	0.07	1.47	0.07		
Teen Adjustment to Deployment[c]					1.89	0.04
Challenges During Deployment[c]					2.79	0.27
Teen Social Support						
Low Baseline Social Support[c] (%)					11.95	3.54
Socialization with Military Children During Study Deployment[c]					0.55	0.06
Frequency of Communication with Deployed Parent[c]					1.94	0.09

NOTES: *Child* or *children* refers to children younger than age 11 for whom we have spouse reports. *Teen* refers to children ages 11 and older for whom we have self-reports and/or spouse reports.

[a] Risk and resilience factor reported by service member.

[b] Risk and resilience factor reported by spouse.

[c] Risk and resilience factor from teen self-report.

resulting in physical injury. Sixteen percent of parents of children, 26 percent of parents of teens, and 22 percent of teens themselves reported experiencing psychological trauma exposure only, without combat or injury. Three percent of service member parents of children reported separating from the military during the study, and 9 percent to 13 percent of teens and parents of teens reported military separation. These differences between children and teens likely reflect the ages of the parents and their stage in their military career, with parents of teens being older, less likely to experience combat, and more likely to separate from the military.

During study deployments, spouses reported that children's and teens' adjustments were, on average, between "not true" and "somewhat true" on both positive and negative aspects; teens themselves reported much the same on the similar self-report measure. Spouses reported low levels of trouble in school, with averages in the "not at all" to "some of the time" range. Teens reported that they experienced between two and three of the listed challenges (out of a possible ten) during deployment.

In terms of teen social support, at baseline, 12 percent of teens reported low social support, or that they did not have "enough" people that they could count on if they needed someone to listen when they were feeling low, and a little more than half the teens (55 percent) reported socializing with other military children during the study deployment. Teens reported communication with their deployed parent just under twice weekly on average.

Analysis Plan

The analysis plan is described in detail in Chapter Two, so we only briefly outline it here. To address RQ1 (how child/teen outcomes change over the course of a typical deployment cycle), we use descriptive trajectories that depict the three outcomes of interest before, during, and after a study deployment. Predicted means are plotted in eight-month durations (predeployment, during deployment, and postdeployment) as this represents the "average" length of these periods in our data. All models control for respondent gender, age, service member rank and officer/enlisted status, an indicator of whether the service member had prior combat deployments before the study, service branch, the Hoge CES at baseline, the outcome in question at baseline and a random effect for the individual child on whom repeated measures are being analyzed. Wald tests are used to determine the outcome of hypothesis tests. Results are presented graphically.

To address RQ2 (how deployment affects postdeployment child/teen outcomes), we use doubly robust propensity score–matching models. These models match children who experienced a study deployment to respondents who did not across a number of family demographic and military characteristics (see Appendix 6A), and are intended to address the causal impact of deployment on child outcomes in this study. Predicted mean differences in outcomes are compared across the two groups, controlling for child gender, age, service member rank and officer/enlisted status, history of prior combat deployments, branch and component of service, the Hoge CES, and the outcome in question at baseline (making the models doubly robust). Here, random effects models were fit that appropriately adjusted for repeated measures within each child respondent using a random effect at the respondent level. These predicted means are reported in this chapter. As noted in Chapter Two, all outcomes come from the final three postdeployment assessments for each respondent, assuming the service member was not deployed at the time.

To address RQ3 (what risk and resilience factors predict differences in postdeployment child/teen outcomes among deployed families), we used random effects regression models, adjusted for repeated measures within each respondent (i.e., allowing for random effects for each respondent), to estimate the association between the risk and resilience factors already noted and outcomes among only those children and teens who had experienced a study deployment. We focus on factors that fall into three categories: service member deployment and military variables that could have an impact on child functioning, child and teen functioning during deployment, and teen social support before and during the deployment. All outcomes come from the final three postdeployment assessments of the study for each respondent (thus necessitating a control for repeated measures). Each risk and resilience factor was added to the multivariate models one at a time, in separate models. Models controlled for respondent child gender, age, service member rank and officer/enlisted status, history of prior combat deployments, branch and component of service, the Hoge CES, and the baseline measure of the key outcome being modeled.

All analyses presented in this chapter use the spouse poststratification weights when analyzing data from spouse reports and the teen attrition weights when analyzing data from teen self-reports; both are described in detail in Chapter Two.

Results

Research Question 1: Trajectories over the Deployment Cycle

RQ1 asks how child and teen functioning changes over the deployment cycle. Figures of trajectories present the results of the trajectory analysis for the child and teen outcomes examined in this chapter. For each figure we also test two global hypotheses: (RQ1a) whether the child or teen outcome in question follows a flat line (i.e., no changes in average values) over the deployment cycle, and (RQ1b) whether the trajectory is a straight line (i.e., a constant change over time that is unrelated to the phase of, or timing within, the deployment cycle) over the deployment cycle.

Due to the number of variables tested and the possibility that child/teen outcomes would change over time even without a parent's deployment, we only interpret findings where the test for linear changes over time (i.e., RQ1a: the slope of the outcome across the deployment cycle), and the test of whether change over time covaried with deployment phases (RQ1b) were both significant. The combination of these two significant tests indicates not only that the slope of the outcome changed over time, but also that there was a change in outcomes that specifically occurred around the deployment cycle. Thus, we can have more confidence that the change over time in our trajectory models was associated with the deployment cycle rather than some other variable (e.g., maturation). We depict each outcome that satisfies this criterion in Figures 6.1–6.7 and interpret the trajectory across the deployment cycle. For comparison and to highlight that many of our tests did not find significant evidence of change over time, we also depict outcomes that are of particular interest but that did not meet this criterion.

Each figure depicts trajectories of the outcome in question for an eight-month period immediately prior to a deployment, eight months during a deployment, and eight months postdeployment on the x-axis. As noted in Chapter Two, these are the average periods our sample of deployed families spent in each phase of deployment. On the y-axis, each outcome is centered around the group mean, with one standard deviation above and below the mean shown in each figure.

Child Trajectory Results

As shown in Table 6.9, the child outcomes that had significant slope and change values were *total difficulties, emotional problems,* and *depressive symptoms.* We graph and interpret those results, as well as the result for *child need for mental health services* as a comparison.

The trajectory model for spouse report of child total difficulties scores is displayed in Figure 6.1. To evaluate the trajectory in this figure, we first tested whether the slope of the total difficulties score across the deployment cycle was statistically different from a flat line; i.e., whether there was any change at all in child total difficulties scores over time (RQ1a). Joint Wald tests of trajectory parameters revealed that the slope of child total difficulties scores significantly differed from zero across the deployment cycle (see Table 6.9). Examination of Figure 6.1 suggests that child total difficulties scores generally increased over time.

We next examined whether the overall trends in spouse report of child total difficulties scores were significantly different from a straight line across the deployment cycle (RQ1b). This test analyzed whether there were significant changes in child total difficulties that co-occur with predeployment, deployment, and/or postdeployment. If deployment is associated with increased child total difficulties scores, then we might expect a fairly linear trajectory predeployment, with a shift upward and a more positive trajectory during the deployment and postdeployment. Analysis revealed that the child total difficulties measure was not constant over time, but showed significant changes throughout deployment cycles (see Table 6.9). Figure 6.1 suggests that child total difficulties scores shifted upward from predeployment to deployment, with a slight shift upward from deployment to postdeployment. A post-hoc test comparing mean child total difficulties scores during deployment to the pre- and postdeployment phases was not significant ($\chi^2[1]=1.31$, $p=0.25$), indicating that, although the trend for child total difficulties changed over the deployment cycle, average child total difficulties scores during each phase were not significantly different overall.

Table 6.9
Significance Tests for Trajectories of Children with a Study Deployment

	Spouse Report			
	Any Change over Time		Constant Change over Time	
	Chi-square (df 8)		Chi-square (df 8)	
SDQ Total Difficulties	34.34	****	25.27	**
SDQ Subscale: Emotional Problems	43.60	****	38.38	***
SDQ Subscale: Conduct Problems	6.09		4.60	
SDQ Subscale: Hyperactivity	9.32		7.66	
SDQ Subscale: Peer Problems	21.30	**	12.70	
SDQ Subscale: Prosocial Behavior	9.10		9.11	
Anxiety	15.04		15.07	
Depressive Symptoms	21.11	**	24.08	**
PedsQL	21.67	**	14.40	
Need for Mental Health Services	22.27	**	10.72	

NOTE: We only interpret findings where both the test for any changes over time, and the test of whether change over time covaried with deployment phases were both significant (shown in bold). See Appendix 6B for graphs of the other trajectory models.

* p<0.05 ; **p<0.01; ***p<0.001; ****p<0.0001

Figure 6.1
Trajectory Model for Spouse Report of Child SDQ Total Difficulty Scores

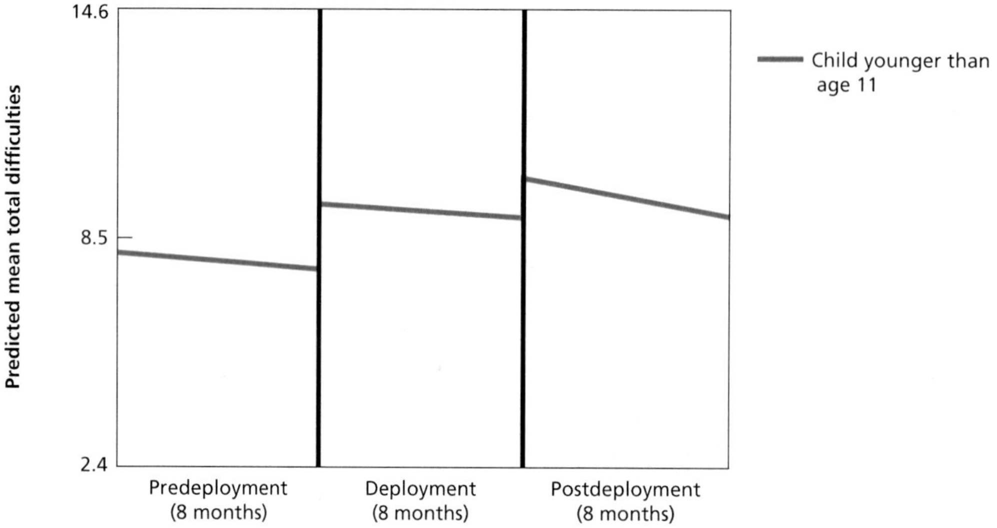

NOTE: The trajectory shows significant variation over the deployment cycle ($p<0.001$) and is significantly different from a constant trend over time ($p=0.001$).
RAND RR1388-6.1

The trajectory for spouse report of child emotional problems scores is displayed in Figure 6.2. The test of whether the slope of child emotional problems scores across the deployment cycle was statistically different from a flat line (RQ1a) was significant (see Table 6.9). Importantly, the test of whether the overall trends in child emotional problems scores were different from a straight line across the deployment cycle (RQ1b) was also significant (see Table 6.9), suggesting that the changes over time were not linear over the entire deployment cycle, but varied around the deployment cycle. Indeed, examination of Figure 6.2 suggests that child emotional problems scores shifted considerably upward from predeployment to deployment phases, with a continuing negative slope from deployment to postdeployment phases. A post-hoc test comparing mean child emotional problems scores during deployment to the pre- and postdeployment phases was significant ($\chi^2[1]=16.08$, $p<0.001$), suggesting that average child emotional problems scores were significantly different during deployment than predeployment and postdeployment phases. Thus, deployment was associated with a considerable increase in child emotional problems scores from predeployment levels.

The trajectory for spouse report of child depressive symptoms is displayed in Figure 6.3. The test of whether the slope of child depressive symptoms was different from a flat line (RQ1a) was significant (see Table 6.9). Examination of Figure 6.3 suggests that child depressive symptoms shifted upward from predeployment to deployment phases, with a descending slope during postdeployment. Importantly, the test of whether the overall trends in child depressive symptoms differed from a straight line across the deployment cycle (RQ1b) was also significant (see Table 6.9), suggesting that the changes over time were not linear, but varied around the deployment cycle. A post-hoc test comparing mean child depressive symptoms during deployment to the pre- and postdeployment phases was significant ($\chi^2[1]=3.90$, $p=0.048$), suggesting that average child depressive symptoms were significantly different during deployment than

Figure 6.2
Trajectory Model for Spouse Report of Child SDQ Emotional Problems Scores

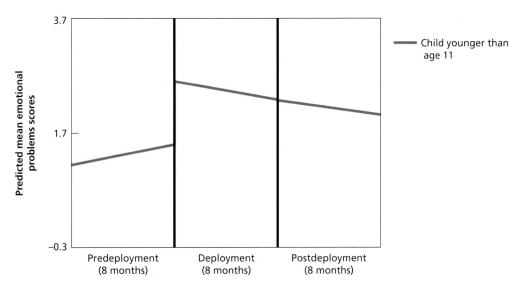

NOTE: The trajectory shows significant variation over the deployment cycle ($p<0.001$) and is significantly different from a constant trend over time ($p=0.001$).

RAND *RR1388-6.2*

Figure 6.3
Trajectory Model for Spouse Report of Child Depressive Symptoms

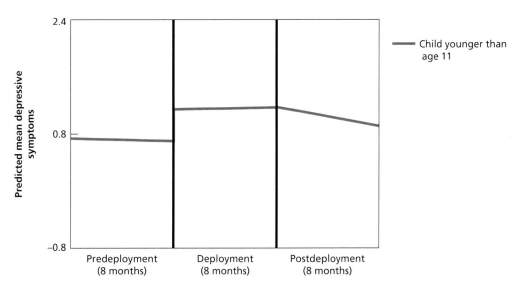

NOTE: The trajectory shows significant variation over the deployment cycle ($p=0.007$) and is significantly different from a constant trend over time ($p=0.002$).

RAND *RR1388-6.3*

predeployment and postdeployment phases. Thus, deployment was associated with a considerable increase in child depressive symptoms from pre- and postdeployment levels.

Although results for spouse report of child need for mental health services did not meet the criterion for interpretation, we graphed the trajectory of this outcome to use as a comparison (see Figure 6.4) and to highlight how results for our other nine child outcomes appeared. The test of whether the slope of child need for mental health services was different from a flat line (RQ1a) was significant, but the test of whether the overall trend differed from a straight line over the deployment cycle was not significant (see Table 6.9). Examination of Figure 6.4 suggests that child need for mental health services scores did not vary significantly with the deployment cycle (i.e., the positive slope did not change significantly in conjunction with the deployment cycle). Although there is evidence that child need for mental health services changed significantly over time, there is no significant evidence that these changes are tied to the deployment cycle as opposed to a constant trend over time.

Spouse Reports of Teens Trajectory Results

As shown in Table 6.10, none of the trajectory results for spouse reports of teen outcomes met the criteria for interpretation. That is, none of the outcomes had significant results for linear changes over time (i.e., RQ1a: the slope of the outcome across the deployment cycle), together with significant results for whether change over time covaried with deployment phases (RQ1b). Thus, we did not graph and interpret trajectories for spouse reports of teen outcomes.

Teen Self-Report Trajectory Results

For teen self-reports, drug use and relationship quality with the service member parent had significant slope and change values (see Table 6.10). We also graph teen self-reported anxi-

Figure 6.4
Trajectory Model for Spouse Report of Child Need for Mental Health Services

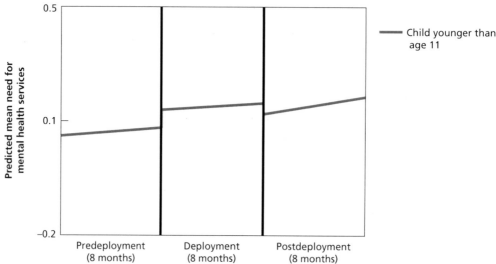

NOTE: The trajectory shows significant variation over the deployment cycle (p<0.001) but was not significantly different from a constant trend over time (p=0.23).
RAND RR1388-6.4

Table 6.10
Significance Tests for Trajectories of Teens with a Study Deployment

	Spouse Report			Teen Self-Report		
	Any Change over Time		Constant Change over Time	Any Change over Time		Constant Change over Time
	Chi-square (df 8)		Chi-square (df 8)	Chi-square (df 8)		Chi-square (df 8)
SDQ Total Difficulties	8.28		8.80	3.91		3.18
SDQ Subscale: Emotional Problems	13.85		13.93	2.78		1.26
SDQ Subscale: Conduct Problems	8.87		8.78	10.15		5.30
SDQ Subscale: Hyperactivity	32.82	***	11.67	11.44		13.51
SDQ Subscale: Peer Problems	18.24	*	8.00	8.42		11.67
SDQ Subscale: Prosocial Behavior	10.45		10.26	13.21		12.20
Anxiety	14.98		22.32 **	14.38		16.57 *
Depressive Symptoms	15.12		18.08 *	9.89		11.08
PedsQL	15.48		13.77			
Need for Mental Health Services	6.57		8.87	12.92		9.76
Overall Health Functioning				12.02		10.04
Risky Behaviors						
Physical Aggression				7.65		5.51
Nonphysical Aggression				9.08		8.01
Relational Aggression				5.14		4.48
Drug Use				22.31 **		15.92 *
Life Satisfaction				12.81		7.13
Academic Disengagement				8.14		8.38
Family Cohesion				9.13		6.09
Relationship Quality with Service Member				**24.92** **		**15.62** *
Relationship Quality with Spouse				15.57 *		10.49

NOTE: We only interpret findings where both the test for any changes over time, and the test of whether change over time covaried with deployment phases were both significant (shown in bold). See Appendix 6B for graphs of the other trajectory models.

*<0.05 ; **<0.01; ***<0.001; ****<0.0001.

ety (SCARED) as a comparison to highlight that for the vast majority of our teen self-reported outcomes we had no evidence of significant change over time.

The trajectory for teen self-reported drug use is displayed in Figure 6.5. The test of whether the slope was different from a flat line (RQ1a) was significant (see Table 6.10). Examination of Figure 6.5 suggests that teen drug use had a flat slope from predeployment to deployment phases, with a change upward at postdeployment. The test of whether the overall trends in teen drug use differed from a straight line across the deployment cycle (RQ1b) was also significant (see Table 6.10). Examination of Figure 6.5 suggests that teen self-reports of teen drug use shifted considerably upward from deployment to postdeployment phases. A post-hoc test comparing mean teen drug use during deployment to the pre- and postdeployment phases was

Figure 6.5
Trajectory Model for Teen Self-Reported Drug Use

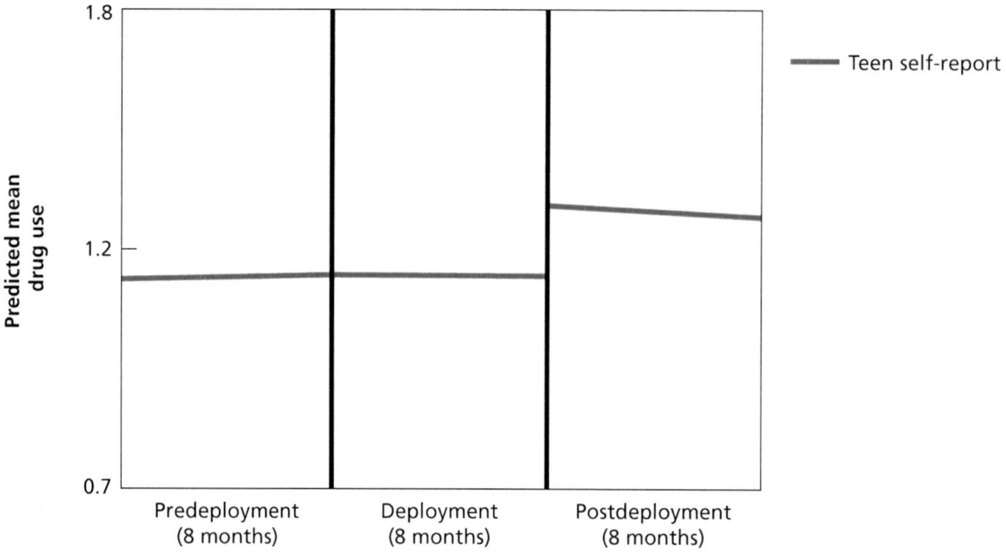

NOTE: The trajectory shows significant variation over the deployment cycle ($p=0.004$) and is significantly different from a constant trend over time ($p=0.044$).
RAND RR1388-6.5

significant ($\chi^2[1]=7.06$, $p=0.008$), suggesting that teen drug use significantly increased from deployment to postdeployment.

The trajectory for teen self-reported relationship quality with the service member is displayed in Figure 6.6. The test of whether the slope was different from a flat line (RQ1a) was significant (see Table 6.10). Examination of Figure 6.10 suggests that teen relationship quality with the service member was generally flat in the predeployment period, sloped upward during deployment, and then sloped more steeply downward postdeployment. The test of whether the overall trends in teen relationship quality with the service member differed from a straight line across the deployment cycle (RQ1b) was also significant (see Table 6.10), suggesting that the decrease over time was not just linear, but varied around the deployment cycle. A post-hoc test comparing mean teen relationship quality with the service member during deployment to the pre- and postdeployment phases was significant ($\chi^2[1]=17.61$, $p<0.001$), indicating that there was a significant mean difference in teen relationship quality with the service member across the deployment phases. Thus, teen relationship quality with the service member seemed to improve from predeployment to deployment, but decreased upon reintegration of the service member following deployment.

Although results for teen self-reported anxiety (SCARED) did not meet the criterion for interpretation, we graphed the trajectory of this outcome to use as a comparison to highlight that we had no evidence of significant change over time for the vast majority of our teen self-reported outcomes (Figure 6.7). The test of whether the slope of teen self-reported anxiety was different from a flat line (RQ1a) was not significant, but the test of whether the overall trend differed from a straight line over the deployment cycle was significant (see Table 6.10). Taken together, these results suggest we have very limited evidence of meaningful changes occurring over the deployment cycle with this outcome.

Figure 6.6
Trajectory Model for Teen Self-Reported Relationship Quality with Service Member

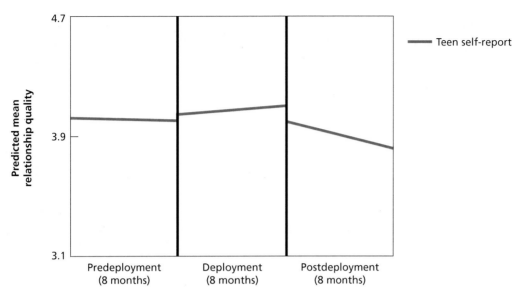

NOTE: The trajectory shows significant variation over the deployment cycle (p=0.002) and is significantly different from a constant trend over time (p=0.048).
RAND *RR1388-6.6*

Figure 6.7
Trajectory Model for Teen Self-Reported Anxiety (SCARED)

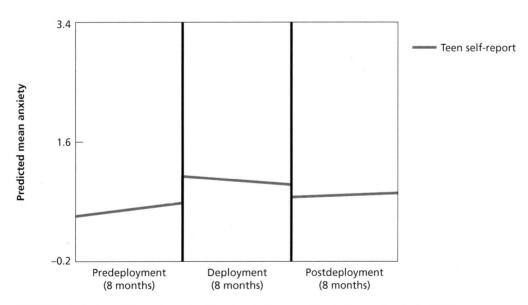

NOTE: The trajectory did not show significant variation over the deployment cycle (p=0.07); statistical tests show the teen trajectory was significantly different from a constant trend over time (p=0.04).
RAND *RR1388-6.7*

Research Question 2: Impact of Deployment

RQ2 asks how, if at all, deployment affects postdeployment child and teen outcomes using a doubly robust matched comparison approach. Tables 6.11 and 6.12 present the predicted means for each of the outcomes we examined among children and teens who did and did not experience a study deployment. As can be seen in Table 6.11, for children younger than age 11, spouses reported more total difficulties and also a trend for being more likely to indicate a need for mental health services at the final three waves of the study if the family experienced a deployment earlier in the study, as compared with spouses in families that did not experience a study deployment. Unpacking the total difficulties score into its components, spouses reported that children from families with a study deployment experienced more emotional problems, conduct problems, and peer problems, contributing to their overall assessment of more difficulties. On the other hand, no differences were observed in terms of spouse report of children's anxiety or depressive symptoms, prosocial behavior, or their overall quality of life.

In contrast to the measures for children younger than age 11, examination of outcomes for teens ages 11 and older (Table 6.12) showed no significant differences in spouses' perceptions of functioning during the last three waves of the study between those who experienced a study deployment and those who did not. Teens' self-report measures were also largely similar across the two groups, with only two trends reaching statistical significance. Teens who experienced a study deployment reported more family conflict and a poorer relationship with their nondeployed parent at the end of the study. However, due to the large number of outcomes tested and the marginal significance ($0.01 < p < 0.05$) observed, these findings are not conclusive and will need additional study.

Research Question 3: Risk and Resilience Factors

Next, we turn to an examination of risk and resilience factors that may contribute to the end-of-study outcomes for children and teens who experienced a study deployment. RQ3 examines three sets of risk and resilience factors that may be associated with postdeployment child and

Table 6.11
Predicted Means for Children With and Without a Study Deployment

	Spouse Report	
	Study Deployment	No Study Deployment
SDQ Total Difficulties	**8.74 (0.39)****	7.42 (0.28)
SDQ Subscale: Emotional Problems	**1.88 (0.12)***	1.54 (0.10)
SDQ Subscale: Conduct Problems	**1.22 (0.10)***	0.95 (0.07)
SDQ Subscale: Hyperactivity	3.66 (0.15)	3.33 (0.11)
SDQ Subscale: Peer Problems	**1.99 (0.13)***	1.62 (0.10)
SDQ Subscale: Prosocial Behavior	8.43 (0.11)	8.57 (0.09)
Anxiety (SCARED)	1.71 (0.12)	1.58 (0.10)
Depressive Symptoms	0.79 (0.08)	0.72 (0.08)
Need for Mental Health Services	**0.16 (0.03)***	0.10 (0.03)
PedsQL	4.31 (0.05)	4.39 (0.04)

NOTES: Models control for child age and gender, an indicator of whether the service member had a deployment prior to the start of the study; the service member's branch, pay grade, and baseline combat trauma scale; and the baseline measure of the outcome in question.

* p<0.05; ** p<0.01 when comparing means of study deployment versus no study deployment groups.

Table 6.12
Predicted Means for Teens With and Without a Study Deployment

	Spouse Report		Teen Self-Report	
	Study Deployment	No Study Deployment	Study Deployment	No Study Deployment
SDQ Total Difficulties	7.07 (0.25)	6.76 (0.34)	8.85 (0.34)	8.92 (0.48)
SDQ Subscale: Emotional Problems	1.43 (0.12)	1.40 (0.13)	2.48 (0.14)	2.30 (0.18)
SDQ Subscale: Conduct Problems	1.08 (0.09)	1.08 (0.10)	1.23 (0.09)	1.12 (0.10)
SDQ Subscale: Hyperactivity	2.35 (0.15)	2.34 (0.13)	2.92 (0.16)	3.26 (0.17)
SDQ Subscale: Peer Problems	2.22 (0.11)	1.93 (0.15)	2.24 (0.13)	2.21 (0.14)
SDQ Subscale: Prosocial Behavior	7.86 (0.15)	8.03 (0.17)	7.99 (0.16)	8.07 (0.15)
Anxiety (SCARED)	1.23 (0.14)	1.16 (0.13)	1.81 (0.15)	1.68 (0.14)
Depressive Symptoms	1.17 (0.21)	0.83 (0.12)	2.43 (0.22)	2.35 (0.26)
Need for Mental Health Services	0.14 (0.02)	0.14 (0.02)	0.12 (0.02)	0.17 (0.03)
PedsQL	3.95 (0.09)	3.95 (0.08)		
Overall Health Functioning			3.97 (0.08)	4.00 (0.06)
Risky Behavior				
Physical Aggression			1.12 (0.03)	1.14 (0.03)
Nonphysical Aggression			1.28 (0.06)	1.24 (0.04)
Relational Aggression			1.16 (0.04)	1.14 (0.03)
Drug Use			1.37 (0.06)	1.37 (0.06)
Life Satisfaction			4.07 (0.07)	4.24 (0.06)
Academic Disengagement			2.00 (0.04)	2.02 (0.04)
Family Cohesion			2.53 (0.03)*	2.62 (0.03)
Relationship Quality with Service Member			3.72 (0.06)	3.73 (0.08)
Relationship Quality with Spouse			3.77 (0.10)*	4.01 (0.07)

NOTES: *Teen* refers to children ages 11 and older for whom we have self-reports and/or spouse reports. Models control for teen age and gender; an indicator of whether the service member had a deployment prior to the start of the study; service member branch, pay grade, and baseline combat trauma scale; and the baseline measure of the outcome in question.

* $p<0.05$ when comparing means of study deployment versus no study deployment groups.

teen outcomes among deployed families. Those risk and resilience factors fall into three categories: service member deployment and military variables, child or teen functioning during deployment, and teen social support.

Tables 6.13 through 6.17 present the results (i.e., regression coefficients and p-values) of a series of multivariate models, run separately for each outcome. Each regression includes a series of controls (noted in the tables), an indicator for whether the risk or resilience factor was missing during the predeployment or deployment period, the baseline value of the outcome, as well as a random intercept to control for clustering within respondents. Note that these models do not include the propensity weights used in the analysis of RQ2 because the analysis is limited to families that experienced a study deployment. Thus, we can interpret the coefficients in each table as an indication of whether these risk and resilience factors are associated with outcomes at the end of the study. We conduct a large number of tests in this section; thus, there is a risk of significant findings by chance. As such, these analyses should be considered exploratory and in need of replication. We do not interpret findings at the level of $0.01<p<0.05$ significance, except for when they are very consistent, although those results can be reviewed in the tables.

Service Member Deployment and Military Risk Factors

Starting with children in Table 6.13, we find very little evidence of a relationship between service member deployment trauma, deployment length, or separation from the military during the study and the ten child outcomes as reported by the spouse during the last three waves of the study. Of the 30 regressions run, only two reached our threshold for interpretation. Specifically, longer deployment duration during the study was related to spouse reports of more emotional problems in children and more depressive symptoms (also noted was a trend for higher anxiety ratings). However, there was no evidence that deployment duration was related to any of the other outcomes, and we observed no significant relationships between service member deployment trauma and outcomes.

In Table 6.14 for teens, we examine more outcomes (ten spouse reports in the upper portion of the table, and 19 teen self-reports in the lower portion of the table) and therefore can examine the relationship among these variables in 87 regressions. Other than some trends at the $0.01 < p < 0.05$ level, we find only one significant association: service members' experiences with physical injury during deployment were associated with spouse report of higher teen depressive symptoms. In terms of teen self-report, we similarly find only a few significant relationships. There was no evidence of a significant association between length of deployment or separation from the military and teen outcomes. However, service members' experiences of deployment trauma was significantly associated with the teen's self-rating of behavioral problems (nonphysical aggression) during the last three waves of the study, with trends also for increased relational aggression and physical aggression. In addition, service member deployment trauma was related to the teen reports of the quality of the relationship with the service

Table 6.13
Relationships Between Service Member Deployment and Military Variables and Child Outcomes Among Children Who Experienced a Study Deployment (Regression Coefficients and p-values)

	Service Member Deployment Trauma Exposure				Duration of Deployment		Separation from the Military	
	Combat	Physical	Psychological	Joint p-value	Mean	p-value	Mean	p-value
SDQ Total Difficulties	−0.85	0.19	0.20	0.98	0.36	0.07	2.41	0.31
SDQ Subscale: Emotional Problems	−0.05	0.28	−0.20	0.86	**0.17**	**0.00**	−0.08	0.89
SDQ Subscale: Conduct Problems	−0.32	−0.18	0.11	0.70	0.03	0.58	1.04	0.22
SDQ Subscale: Hyperactivity	−0.28	0.20	0.27	0.82	0.07	0.40	1.69	0.15
SDQ Subscale: Peer Problems	0.04	0.05	0.05	0.99	0.07	0.18	−0.37	0.27
SDQ Subscale: Prosocial Behavior	0.15	−0.35	−0.23	0.58	−0.09	0.06	−0.39	0.44
Anxiety	−0.17	−0.17	−0.03	0.89	0.11	0.02	−0.65	0.20
Depressive Symptoms	0.28	−0.36	0.12	0.29	**0.11**	**0.01**	0.50	0.43
Need for Mental Health Services (%)	−0.64	−0.73	1.08	0.38	−0.01	0.94	0.75	0.48
PedsQL	0.05	−0.13	−0.10	0.67	−0.03	0.16	−0.05	0.81

NOTE: Significant associations p<0.01 shown in bold. Models control for study child age and gender; an indicator of whether the service member had a deployment prior to the start of the study; service member branch, pay grade, and baseline CES; and the baseline measure of the outcome in question.

Table 6.14
Relationships Between Service Member Deployment and Military Variables and Teen Outcomes Among Teens Who Experienced a Study Deployment (Regression Coefficients and p-values)

	Service Member Deployment Trauma Exposure				Duration of Deployment		Separation from the Military	
	Combat	Physical	Psychological	Joint p-value	Mean	p-value	Mean	p-value
Spouse Report								
SDQ Total Difficulties	0.96	−0.10	0.09	0.83	−0.03	0.76	0.92	0.19
SDQ Subscale: Emotional Problems	−0.03	0.41	−0.19	0.70	−0.05	0.26	0.95	0.02
SDQ Subscale: Conduct Problems	0.38	0.01	−0.04	0.75	0.04	0.20	−0.04	0.87
SDQ Subscale: Hyperactivity	−0.52	−0.23	−0.41	0.07	−0.01	0.82	−0.50	0.13
SDQ Subscale: Peer Problems	0.67	0.45	0.25	0.05	−0.02	0.67	0.42	0.18
SDQ Subscale: Prosocial Behavior	0.63	0.08	0.37	0.31	−0.04	0.45	0.34	0.43
Anxiety	0.01	0.55	−0.46	0.46	0.17	0.02	−0.10	0.75
Depressive Symptoms	−0.06	1.59***	−0.76*	0.00	−0.01	0.93	0.85	0.06
Pediatric Quality of Life	−0.39	0.08	0.49**	0.02	−0.07	0.02	0.68	0.04
Need for Mental Health Services (%)	0.72	2.08	−0.33	0.17	−0.18	0.27	2.43	0.03
Teen Self-Report								
SDQ Total Difficulties	2.05	0.15	−0.78	0.33	−0.05	0.72	0.74	0.63
SDQ Subscale: Emotional Problems	0.17	0.33	−0.39	0.76	−0.04	0.47	0.10	0.87
SDQ Subscale: Conduct Problems	0.64	−0.17	−0.29	0.25	0.05	0.25	0.08	0.83
SDQ Subscale: Hyperactivity	−0.25	0.13	−0.35	0.69	−0.01	0.82	0.36	0.50
SDQ Subscale: Peer Problems	1.05**	0.02	−0.07	0.03	−0.06	0.14	−0.15	0.67
SDQ Subscale: Prosocial Behavior	−0.15	0.20	0.42	0.57	0.00	0.99	−0.70	0.12
Anxiety	0.75	0.60	−0.70	0.19	−0.02	0.66	−0.33	0.63
Depressive Symptoms	2.18***	−0.85	−0.39	0.03	0.03	0.78	−0.09	0.91
Need for Mental Health Services (%)	−0.11	0.61	−1.46	0.50	0.07	0.57	0.48	0.70
Overall Health Functioning	−0.41	−0.09	0.35	0.09	0.03	0.16	−0.24	0.45
Risky Behaviors								
Physical Aggression	0.17*	0.06	−0.15*	0.02	0.00	0.89	0.10	0.45
Nonphysical Aggression	**0.48****	**−0.09**	**−0.15**	**0.01**	**−0.01**	**0.54**	**−0.21**	**0.10**
Relational Aggression	0.17	0.09	−0.16	0.04	0.00	0.87	−0.01	0.89
Drug Use	0.02	0.05	−0.33	0.06	−0.01	0.49	−0.02	0.87
Life Satisfaction	−0.44	0.11	0.29	0.11	−0.01	0.68	−0.26	0.39
Academic Disengagement	−0.05	0.15	−0.23*	0.03	0.01	0.71	0.22	0.24
Family Cohesion	**−0.27***	**0.15**	**0.19****	**0.00**	**0.00**	**0.89**	**−0.05**	**0.55**
Relationship Quality with Service Member	**−0.34***	**0.02**	**0.47*****	**0.00**	**0.03**	**0.14**	**−0.13**	**0.57**
Relationship Quality with Spouse	−0.98*	0.31	0.22	0.04	0.00	0.99	−0.29	0.36

NOTE: Significant associations p<0.01 shown in bold. Models control for study child age and gender; an indicator of whether the service member had a deployment prior to the start of the study; service member branch, pay grade, and baseline combat trauma scale; and the baseline measure of the outcome in question.

member and spouse and ratings of family cohesion, such that psychological trauma exposure (without combat exposure or injuries) was related to a better relationship with the service member and more cohesion at the end of the study, and that experience of combat trauma was associated with the opposite: less family cohesion (or more conflict) and a poorer relationship with the service member. Overall, the service members' study deployment traumas showed a consistent pattern in which combat exposure during deployment was related to teen ratings of worse adjustment and poorer family relationship, whereas the service members' experience of psychological traumas during deployment was related to better teen and family outcomes.

Child/Teen Adjustment During Deployment Factors

For children, we examined a set of three ratings of child adjustment during deployment in relation to the ten outcomes measured by spouse report during the last three waves of data collection (see Table 6.15). Not surprisingly, we found several relationships between these variables, as they are all measures of child functioning by the same reporters, just at different points in time and under different circumstances (during deployment or after return). Spouses' ratings of child positive adjustment during deployment (e.g., taking on more responsibilities at home) were related to end-of-study total difficulties being lower (specifically, less hyperactivity). Spouse reports of child negative adjustment during deployment (e.g., gets upset more easily) were related to reports of more emotional problems at the end of the study. Spouse reports of trouble at school during deployment were related to more total difficulties (specifically, emotional problems and conduct problems) as well as with lower overall quality of life and higher need for mental health services at the end of the study. Thus, it appears that spouses' concerns about child adjustment during deployment are related to several aspects of subsequent adjustment.

For teens, we examine five risk factors (three by spouse report and two by teen self-report) and their relationship with 19 teen outcomes and ten spouse-report outcomes (see Table 6.16). The spouse's reports of teen adjustment during deployment were related to many of their ratings of teen adjustment at the end of the study. Spouse reports of negative adjustment during deploy-

Table 6.15
Relationships Between Child Adjustment During Deployment and End-of-Study Outcomes Among Children Who Experienced a Study Deployment, Spouse Report (Regression Coefficients and p-values)

	Negative Adjustment		Positive Adjustment		Trouble with School	
	Mean	p-value	Mean	p-value	Mean	p-value
SDQ Total Difficulties	2.30*	0.03	−2.91**	0.00	1.89**	0.00
SDQ Subscale: Emotional Problems	**1.05****	**0.00**	−0.66*	0.01	**0.47****	**0.01**
SDQ Subscale: Conduct Problems	0.73*	0.02	−0.36	0.17	**0.64*****	**0.00**
SDQ Subscale: Hyperactivity	0.39	0.29	−1.29**	0.00	0.63*	0.01
SDQ Subscale: Peer Problems	0.69*	0.02	−0.56*	0.05	0.23	0.16
SDQ Subscale: Prosocial Behavior	−0.68*	0.05	0.33	0.21	−0.42*	0.02
Anxiety	0.54	0.06	−0.09	0.74	0.02	0.08
Depressive Symptoms	0.32	0.37	−0.30	0.21	0.34	0.05
Need for Mental Health Services (%)	1.96*	0.04	−1.25	0.06	**1.25*****	**0.00**
Pediatric Quality of Life	−0.15	0.71	0.28*	0.05	**−0.27*****	**0.00**

NOTE: Significant associations p<0.01 shown in bold. Models control for study child age and gender; an indicator of whether the service member had a deployment prior to the start of the study; service member branch, pay grade, baseline combat trauma scale; and the baseline measure of the outcome in question.

ment were related to SDQ total difficulties (specifically, emotional problems and hyperactivity), and trouble in school during deployment was related to SDQ total difficulties (specifically, hyperactivity). Spouse ratings of positive adjustment during deployment were related to lower reports of difficulties (specifically, hyperactivity), as well as higher scores on prosocial behavior. However, teen reports of their own adjustment during deployment were not associated with spouses' reports of end-of-study teen adjustment (except for a few trends at the p<0.05 level).

In terms of teen-reported outcomes, teens' ratings of their own adjustment and challenges during deployment were significantly associated with their later reports of their adjustment on several measures. Teen reports of adjustment difficulties during deployment were related to reporting more total difficulties (specifically, emotional problems), more physical aggression, higher academic disengagement, and a worse relationship with their nondeployed parent at the end of the study. Teens who reported a higher number of challenges during deployment also rated themselves as having more depressive symptoms, total difficulties (specifically, emotional and conduct, and peer problems), more nonphysical aggression, and a worse relationship with their nondeployed parent at the end of the study. In contrast, spouse reports of teen adjustment during deployment showed fewer associations with the teen self-report of functioning at the end of the study. Only two associations were significant, with spouse reports of negative adjustment related to higher teen reports of nonphysical aggression, and spouse reports of positive teen adjustment related to teen reports of prosocial behavior at the end of the study.

In summary, we found many associations between ratings of adjustment problems during deployment and subsequent outcomes for teens and children. This finding is expected inasmuch as they are all ratings of child or teen functioning. For teens, particularly strong associations were found when the same informant (spouse or teen) reported on each measure. There were far fewer associations when using two different informants. As noted in Table 6.3, correlations between informants for teens were only modest, indicating that they offer two different perspectives on teen functioning. Findings indicate that the perception of child or teen problems during deployment often persist after deployment ends.

Teen Social Support

We examined three measures of teen social support and their association with the ten outcomes reported by the spouse and 19 outcomes reported by the teen (see Table 6.17). We found no significant relationships between these three variables and the spouse reports of teen adjustment (other than some trends at the p<0.05 level). For teen outcomes, there was also no evidence that baseline social support and frequency of communication with the deployed parent was associated with teen outcomes. However, we found several significant associations between the teen's report of socialization with other military children during deployment and their self-reported outcomes at the end of the study. Specifically, socialization with other military children during deployment was related to lower levels of anxiety and depressive symptoms, total difficulties (specifically, peer problems), and need for mental health services, and with higher levels of life satisfaction and family cohesion at the end of the study.

Summary of Findings

Examination of the trajectories of outcomes among those who experienced a study deployment showed that only a few variables displayed both changes over time and a nonstraight

Table 6.16

Relationships Between Teen Adjustment During Deployment and End-of-Study Outcomes Among Teens Who Experienced a Study Deployment (Regression Coefficients and p-values)

	Spouse Report						Teen Report			
	Negative Adjustment		Positive Adjustment		Trouble with School		Adjustment during Deployment		Deployment Challenges	
	Mean	p-value	Mean	p-value	Mean	p-value	Mean	p-value	Mean	p-value
Spouse Report										
SDQ Total Difficulties	2.21***	0.00	−1.44*	0.01	1.56**	0.01	0.51	0.60	−0.03	0.89
SDQ Subscale: Emotional Problems	0.75**	0.00	−0.51*	0.01	0.62*	0.02	0.19	0.64	0.10	0.24
SDQ Subscale: Conduct Problems	0.60	0.05	−0.28	0.27	0.54*	0.01	0.60*	0.04	0.06	0.45
SDQ Subscale: Hyperactivity	0.72**	0.01	−0.91***	0.00	0.609**	0.00	0.30	0.52	−0.20*	0.05
SDQ Subscale: Peer Problems	0.51*	0.03	−0.14	0.47	0.19	0.37	0.27	0.35	−0.03	0.72
SDQ Subscale: Prosocial Behavior	−0.31	0.05	1.18***	0.00	−0.45	0.15	−0.78	0.09	−0.01	0.92
Anxiety	0.83	0.06	−0.57*	0.01	0.51	0.13	0.48	0.59	0.07	0.74
Depressive Symptoms	0.77*	0.02	−0.58*	0.03	0.34	0.17	1.28*	0.03	−0.12	0.35
Pediatric Quality of Life	−0.07	0.22	0.31	0.09	−0.60*	0.01	−0.57*	0.02	−0.01	0.92
Need for Mental Health Services (%)	2.06	0.07	−0.34	0.61	0.59	0.32	2.05	0.18	0.24	0.39
Teen Self-Report										
SDQ Total Difficulties	2.22*	0.04	−0.28	0.72	1.83*	0.04	3.02**	0.00	0.71***	0.00
SDQ Subscale: Emotional Problems	0.94*	0.01	−0.45	0.12	0.80*	0.04	1.18**	0.00	0.24**	0.01
SDQ Subscale: Conduct Problems	0.44	0.13	0.14	0.51	0.60	0.09	0.66*	0.05	0.18***	0.00
SDQ Subscale: Hyperactivity	0.07	0.88	−0.42	0.32	0.22	0.51	0.63	0.18	0.02	0.81
SDQ Subscale: Peer Problems	0.71	0.08	0.15	0.66	0.39	0.20	0.67	0.12	0.28***	0.00
SDQ Subscale: Prosocial Behavior	−0.22	0.60	0.89**	0.00	−0.48	0.13	0.02	0.96	0.06	0.55
Anxiety	0.15	0.75	0.04	0.75	0.35	0.48	0.90*	0.03	0.14	0.06
Depressive Symptoms	0.22	0.74	0.02	0.97	1.21*	0.04	0.53	0.47	0.39***	0.00
Need for Mental Health Services (%)	1.26	0.33	0.42	0.66	0.72	0.31	0.10	0.05	0.40*	0.02

Table 6.16—Continued

	Spouse Report						Teen Report			
	Negative Adjustment		Positive Adjustment		Trouble with School		Adjustment during Deployment		Deployment Challenges	
	Mean	p-value	Mean	p-value	Mean	p-value	Mean	p-value	Mean	p-value
Overall Health Functioning	−0.21	0.31	0.28	0.11	−0.45*	0.01	−0.25	0.27	−0.04	0.34
Risky Behaviors										
Physical Aggression	0.13*	0.03	−0.12*	0.05	−0.24	0.07	**0.25****	**0.01**	0.01	0.49
Nonphysical Aggression	**0.26****	**0.01**	0.07	0.49	0.19	0.09	0.28*	0.03	**0.08*****	**0.00**
Relational Aggression	0.11	0.10	−0.07	0.27	0.00	0.96	0.15	0.13	0.02	0.30
Drug Use	0.41*	0.04	−0.14	0.27	0.39*	0.04	0.13	0.61	0.03	0.62
Life Satisfaction	−0.21	0.46	0.28	0.86	−0.22	0.22	0.09	0.71	−0.08*	0.02
Academic Disengagement	0.21	0.06	−0.18	0.07	0.35*	0.01	**0.48****	**0.00**	0.03	0.38
Family Cohesion	−0.10	0.41	0.13	0.07	−0.14	0.12	−0.21	0.05	−0.05*	0.02
Relationship Quality with Service Member	0.16	0.50	−0.12	0.67	−0.24	0.08	0.16	0.43	0.01	0.69
Relationship Quality with Spouse	−0.41*	0.04	−0.14	0.67	−0.4	0.05	**−0.91*****	**0.00**	**−0.18****	**0.00**

NOTE: Significant associations p<0.01 shown in bold. Models control for study child age and gender; an indicator of whether the service member had a deployment prior to the start of the study; service member branch, pay grade, and baseline combat trauma scale; and the baseline measure of the outcome in question.

*<0.05 ; **<0.01; ***<0.001; ****<0.0001.

Table 6.17

Relationships Between Teen Social Support End-Of-Study Outcomes Among Teens Who Experienced a Study Deployment (Regression Coefficients and p-values)

	Teen Report					
	Baseline Social Support		Socialization with Military Children during Deployment		Frequency of Communication with Deployed Parent	
	Mean	p-value	Mean	p-value	Mean	p-value
Spouse Report						
SDQ Total Difficulties	−0.39	0.63	−0.45	0.50	0.35	0.51
SDQ Subscale: Emotional Problems	0.25	0.55	0.04	0.89	−0.02	0.92
SDQ Subscale: Conduct Problems	0.06	0.76	−0.36	0.14	−0.03	0.87
SDQ Subscale: Hyperactivity	0.01	0.97	0.16	0.56	0.23	0.33
SDQ Subscale: Peer Problems	−0.23	0.45	−0.41	0.14	0.32	0.19
SDQ Subscale: Prosocial Behavior	−0.80	0.10	0.62	0.15	−0.55*	0.04
Anxiety	1.24*	0.03	−0.22	0.67	0.73*	0.02
Depressive Symptoms	0.25	0.58	0.27	0.50	0.57	0.20
Pediatric Quality of Life	−0.03	0.88	−0.19	0.54	−0.15	0.51
Need for Mental Health Services (%)	2.46	0.14	−0.18	0.19	−1.32	0.22
Teen Self-Report						
SDQ Total Difficulties	−0.43	0.72	**−2.70****	**0.00**	−0.30	0.68
SDQ Subscale: Emotional Problems	0.74	0.09	−0.89*	0.01	−0.09	0.78
SDQ Subscale: Conduct Problems	0.09	0.77	−0.49*	0.03	−0.23	0.19
SDQ Subscale: Hyperactivity	−0.26	0.60	−0.72	0.08	0.20	0.53
SDQ Subscale: Peer Problems	0.00	0.99	**−1.05*****	**0.00**	−0.21	0.33
SDQ Subscale: Prosocial Behavior	−0.16	0.79	0.82*	0.03	−0.06	0.80
Anxiety	0.74	0.19	**−1.00****	**0.01**	0.10	0.76
Depressive Symptoms	−0.76	0.40	**−1.49****	**0.01**	0.05	0.91
Need for Mental Health Services (%)	0.52	0.63	**−2.95****	**0.00**	−0.20	0.13
Overall Health Functioning	0.44	0.08	0.24	0.19	−0.07	0.65
Risky Behaviors						
Physical Aggression	−0.09	0.35	0.05	0.39	0.08*	0.03
Nonphysical Aggression	0.144	0.26	0.02	0.81	0.03	0.63
Relational Aggression	0.40*	0.05	−0.03	0.78	0.09*	0.03
Drug Use	−0.25	0.33	0.23	0.08	0.02	0.86
Life Satisfaction	−0.09	0.77	**0.56*****	**0.00**	0.00	0.99
Academic Disengagement	0.20	0.18	−0.16	0.18	0.09	0.25
Family Cohesion	−0.03	0.75	**0.19****	**0.01**	−0.09	0.13
Relationship Quality with Service Member	0.05	0.78	0.16	0.42	0.01	0.96
Relationship Quality with Spouse	0.06	0.83	0.03	0.86	−0.24	0.06

NOTE: Significant associations p<0.01 shown in bold. Models control for study child age and gender; an indicator of whether the service member had a deployment prior to the start of the study; service member branch, pay grade, and baseline combat trauma scale; and the baseline measure of the outcome in question.

line over the deployment cycle. That is, for many outcomes, we did not find evidence of much change over the course a deployment cycle (using trajectory models), and those that did change might reflect maturational changes rather than changes related to deployment. There were a few significant exceptions, however. Among the ten child outcomes reported by spouses, three showed change over the deployment cycle: total difficulties, and more specifically, emotional problems, as well as depression screener scores. Emotional problems and the depression screener scores show in post-hoc testing that these outcomes differ across the three time periods (before, during, and after deployment), such that spouses reported elevated symptoms in their children during deployment. In contrast, none of the ten spouse-reported teen outcomes showed any changes across the deployment cycle. Finally, teens reported on 19 outcomes for themselves; two of these showed changes across the deployment cycle. Teen reports of drug use were very low before and during deployment (hovering around "never"), but increased afterward (to just slightly more than "never" on average). In addition, teens reported higher-quality relationships with their parent who deployed before and during deployment, with lower quality upon return.

Causal modeling comparing families that experienced a study deployment with matched families that did not showed that the children and teens were generally very similar—again, with some notable exceptions. Spouses in families that experienced a study deployment reported elevated child difficulties at the end of the study (specifically, emotional conduct and peer problems) as well as a higher need for child mental health services compared with spouses in families that did not experience a study deployment. In contrast, there was no difference observed in spouse reports of teen outcomes between the two groups. Teens' own reports of their functioning showed some trends toward differences in family relationships, but no significant differences between the groups. Thus, we see evidence of spouse concerns about their children younger than age 11 following a study deployment, but little evidence in relation to teens that those who experienced a study deployment differ from those who did not.

We also examined three sets of risk and resilience factors within families that experienced a study deployment. Parent deployment factors (i.e., deployment trauma, length of deployment, and separation from the military) show that, for children, longer deployment during the study period was related to spouse reports of elevated child emotional problems, but the other factors were unrelated. For teens, these factors were not related to spouse report of teen outcomes or for most of the teen self-reported outcomes. However, there was a pattern of relationships between the service member's experience of traumas during the study deployment and teen reports of their own adjustment and family relationships (particularly teen behavioral aggression, teen depressive symptoms, family cohesion, and the quality of the relationship with the service member). Interestingly, service member experience of combat trauma during the study deployment was related to teen ratings of poorer adjustment and relationships, whereas experience of psychological trauma (without combat exposure or injury) was related to better adjustment and relationships.

The second set of factors we examined involved child or teen adjustment during deployment. These factors were expected to be highly related to outcomes at the end of the study, and we did find many significant associations. In particular, when the same informant reported on adjustment and outcomes, there were many significant associations and trends. That is, when teens self-reported on adjustment during deployment and postdeployment outcomes, many significant associations were observed. The same was true when parents reported on teen adjustment during deployment and teen outcomes postdeployment. However, when informants were mixed—for example, when we examined parent reports of teen adjustment during deployment and teen self-reports on postdeployment outcomes, these associations were less robust. Thus, perceptions of problems during deployment are highly related to perceptions of problems post-deployment, especially when the informant is the same. Finally, we examined three types of social support for teens. We found no significant association between baseline social support or frequency of communication with the deployed parent while deployed. However, we found a set of strong associations between socializing with other military children during deployment, with this factor being protective and associated with more positive outcomes for teens at the end of the study.

Discussion

This study is the first to examine children and teens in military families over time as they experience parental deployments. The study collected longitudinal data over a three-year period and used advanced statistical methods to account for differences between those who experience a deployment and those who do not, as well as to examine the longitudinal trajectories and risk and resilience within the sample of those who experienced a deployment.

We examined a broad array of child and teen outcomes, including emotional, behavioral, social, and academic functioning, and used two informants (nondeployed parent, or "spouse," and teen self-report) as well as data related to the deployments for the service member. As described in the introduction to this chapter, the literature to date regarding the impact of deployment on children in military families has been very limited; therefore, we planned this study to be exploratory in nature. With a total of ten outcomes for children (by spouse report), and 29 outcomes for teens (by a mix of spouse and teen report), there are a large number of analyses that can provide insight and avenues for future research. Here, we discuss the most robust findings.

First, baseline analyses show that the children and teens in the study were functioning well when recruited into the study, with low levels of emotional or behavioral problems, and high levels of family cohesion and good relationships. Thus, it is a relatively healthy sample at the beginning of the study, and there were few apparent differences between the children and teens who subsequently experienced a study deployment and those who did not. By and large, this health was maintained throughout the study, regardless of deployment experience. That is, we observed this group of children and teens to be resilient to parental deployment for most outcomes measured. Of course, as discussed in Chapter One, the timing of this study was such that parental deployments may have been less stressful than earlier in the Operation Iraqi Freedom/Operation Enduring Freedom (OIF/OEF) conflicts for U.S. service members and their families. With the conflicts winding down, the deployments during our study period were generally less dangerous than those that came earlier in the conflicts.

Examination of trajectories over the deployment cycle shows that for the few outcomes that did change, deployment worsened outcomes, as expected. However, there were also a few outcomes that showed some worsening during deployment that then returned to baseline after deployment. By and large, the outcomes under study were stable, with either some trends in maturational changes over time, or no changes at all across the deployment cycle.

We found a strong association between deployment and the spouse report of emotional problems in children younger than 11 years old—both in the causal modeling comparing families that experienced a deployment and a matched comparison group of families that did not, and in the trajectories within the deployed sample that show changes across the deployment cycle. This finding is consistent with the extant research (e.g., Chandra, Lara-Cinisomo, et al., 2010), as well as with our finding of more depressive symptoms (as reported by the spouse) during deployment scores. Indeed, we also found that length of deployment was related to spouse report of emotional problems and depressive symptoms among children. This finding is based solely on parent report, without any confirming information from the child, and thus could in part reflect parental concern. We do not, however, see a similar finding in the teens ages 11 and older. The research to date on age differences has numerous limitations (e.g., small age ranges, cross-sectional designs), but generally suggests the opposite, that older children have more problems.

Among teens, we find some evidence of disruption in family relationships and in risky behaviors—specifically, a deterioration in the relationship with the deployed parent upon return, and an increase in drug use in the older teens. In terms of the drug use, the rates of use were very low, with averages just above "never" at the end of the study. For both outcomes, there were no differences observed in the causal modeling. That is, it appears that older teens may be suppressing the initiation of drug use during parental deployment, and then catching up with their peers who have begun to use drugs during a similar period of time, ending up similar at the end of the study. This finding is somewhat contrary to recent information from a cross-sectional study of teens in military and nonmilitary families in California, which showed higher rates of drug use among the military-affiliated teens (Sullivan et al., 2015). It is possible that our short time frame partly explains this difference. Longer-term longitudinal studies would be needed to reconcile these findings. Similar to our finding on drug use, some deterioration in relationships between teens and their parents might be expected during the teen years, but delayed or warded off a bit when a deployment occurs. This is, of course, conjecture based on the patterns seen across these two methodologies; we do not have trajectories for the nondeployed sample because there is no deployment cycle to examine.

Looking at risk and resilience factors within the deployed group, we see some interesting patterns of results emerging related to the types of parental deployment traumas. It appears possible that different types of traumatic events experienced by the parent during deployment are related to different outcomes for their children. Specifically, the pattern of results suggests that parental exposure to combat trauma during deployment may be related to poorer teen outcomes, whereas parental exposure to psychological traumas during deployment (without combat traumas) may be related to better outcomes. This intriguing finding deserves further exploration to see if parental deployment experiences may promote different mindsets, behaviors, and interactional styles with family members postdeployment.

This study used two informants for teen outcomes, which makes the picture of teen functioning rich and complex. Indeed, teens' and parents' reports on similar measures showed only modest correlations, indicating that they hold different perspectives on the same constructs. In the examination of the relationship between adjustment during deployment and end-of-study outcomes for teens, we found the relationships over time to be much more robust when the same informant reported on both adjustment and outcomes. Thus, the associations reflect consistency in assessment of a problem over time by an informant. We do observe some cross-informant associations as well.

Teen reports of socialization with military children during deployment was highly associated with teen self-reports of their functioning, such that those who socialized with other military children reported better functioning on several measures. This relationship is not necessarily causal, however. It is possible that those who are doing better during deployment socialize more and thus the association can be explained by their general health and well-being that is consistent over time. Moreover, we did not ask about socialization with nonmilitary children, so we do not know if this is uniquely about having the support of other children who understand deployments, or if it is a reflection of more-general social support. However, we did not find similar associations with the other indices of social support, and thus this is another intriguing finding worthy of further exploration.

Strengths and Limitations

The findings described in this chapter must be interpreted within the context of the study's strengths and limitations. In terms of strengths, this study collected longitudinal data to examine the impact of deployment on children and teens in a representative sample of military families. The use of both parent and teen self-reports for teens ages 11 and older is also a notable strength, as they offer different perspectives on the same outcomes that help clarify the implications of the findings. In addition, the advanced statistical techniques used here enable us to examine the impact of deployment on children across all service branches and components, as well as to examine trajectories across the deployment cycle with data gathered prospectively. Further, this is the first study to date that has followed the same families before, during, and after deployment.

Limitations must also be taken into consideration. First, for children younger than age 11, we rely on parent report of child functioning. Although this is relatively standard practice, self-report on some constructs would help validate that the problems go beyond parental worry or concern. Second, the use of surveys brings biases inherent to self-reports, such as forgetting or social desirability biases (i.e., trying to present oneself in a more positive light, or under or overreporting symptoms of psychological stress or distress). Third, selection bias and retention bias could affect our results, although our use of weighting attempts to correct for those. Finally, the timing of our study makes it an examination of the impact of a particular type of deployment within a particular historical context. Most families had experienced a deployment before, and the deployments were during a time that offered less danger and more predictability than was true earlier in the OEF/OIF conflicts. These experiences no doubt were associated with how families addressed the study deployment that we observed. We did not have a large enough sample of first-time deployers to examine them separately, but future work should seek to address how these families adapt to their first deployment experience. These strengths and limitations will be further discussed in Chapter Eight.

Policy Implications

We draw from these findings several policy implications.

1. Programs targeting anxiety and depressive symptoms for children whose parents deploy should be supported and evaluated. Despite much resilience to deployment among military children, this study replicates earlier research indicating that parents are concerned about their children's mental health and perceive a need for mental health services. Child outcomes change considerably across the deployment cycle, so their need for mental health services should be continuously monitored for signs of decline or improvement. Multiple perspectives on these outcomes are encouraged, as they offer different and complementary information.

2. Reintegration support to improve relationships among service members, spouses, and their children and teens could be expanded. Programs should focus on preventing declines in relationship quality and family cohesion after the service member returns. This may be particularly important for families whose service member experienced combat trauma while deployed.

3. Teen socialization with other military children should be encouraged and supported. This may be particularly important for those without ready access to other military families, such as those in the Reserve and National Guard.

4. Postdeployment drug use prevention programs for teens could be considered. Although older teens' initiation of drug use may not differ from their same-aged peers who did not experience a study deployment, it appears that deployment could delay it. Exploration of ways to continue this healthy trajectory could be fruitful.

5. The intriguing findings related to service member trauma exposure during deployment, and subsequent teen impressions of themselves and their family relationships, warrants further exploration. It is possible that different types of deployment traumas produce different mindsets in returning service members that then affect the way they interact with their families upon return. Understanding the way in which the deployment experience relates to subsequent family relations could help inform future reintegration support efforts.

Appendix 6A: Balance Tables and Plots

Tables 6A.1, 6A.2, and 6A.3 present balance statistics for children, spouse-report teens, and teen self-reports, respectively. Each table compares standardized mean differences (SMDs) across a number of key study variables for service members and spouses who did and did not experience a study deployment. SMDs are presented before and after applying propensity score weights. Generally, SMDs between 0.20 and −0.20 indicate good balance across groups.

Figures 6A.1, 6A.2, and 6A.3 present the balance plots for spouse report of children, spouse report of teens, and teen self-report, respectively, who did and did not experience a study deployment. Each dot on the plot represents a variable in Tables 6A.1, 6A.2, and 6A.3, respectively. The left side of each plot depicts absolute standard mean differences (ASMDs) before applying the propensity score weights, while the right side of each plot depicts ASMDs after applying the propensity score weights. As the figures demonstrate, once the weights are applied, most ASMDs between children, spouse-report teens, and teen self-reports who did and did not experience a study deployment fall below the cutoff of 0.20 ASMDs.

Table 6A.1
Weighted Balance Table: Spouse Report of Children (Study Deployment Versus No Study Deployment)

	Unweighted					Weighted				
	Study Deployment		No Study Deployment		SMD	Study Deployment		No Study Deployment		SMD
	Mean	SD	Mean	SD		Mean	SD	Mean	SD	
CHILD VARIABLES										
Age	5.77	2.10	6.13	2.31	−0.17	5.77	2.10	5.83	2.20	−0.03
Male	0.47	0.50	0.57	0.50	−0.20	0.47	0.50	0.56	0.50	−0.19
SDQ Total Difficulties	7.64	4.67	8.51	5.37	−0.19	7.64	4.67	7.67	5.00	−0.01
SDQ Subscale: Emotional Problems	1.54	1.65	1.87	1.88	−0.20	1.54	1.65	1.58	1.65	−0.02
SDQ Subscale: Conduct Problems	0.90	1.11	1.12	1.30	−0.20	0.90	1.11	1.03	1.27	−0.11
SDQ Subscale: Hyperactivity	3.56	2.54	3.95	2.52	−0.16	3.56	2.54	3.59	2.47	−0.01
SDQ Subscale: Peer Problems	1.64	1.60	1.57	1.61	0.05	1.64	1.60	1.48	1.59	0.10
SDQ Subscale: Prosocial Behavior	8.60	1.57	8.57	1.42	0.02	8.60	1.57	8.69	1.46	−0.06
Anxiety	1.71	1.75	1.76	1.63	−0.02	1.71	1.75	1.57	1.62	0.08
Depressive Symptoms	2.15	2.34	2.21	2.62	−0.03	2.15	2.34	2.15	2.68	0.00
Medication for Mental Health Problem	0.03	0.18	0.04	0.20	−0.06	0.03	0.18	0.04	0.20	−0.05
Need for Mental Health Services	0.09	0.28	0.08	0.28	0.01	0.09	0.28	0.07	0.26	0.06
PedsQL	4.51	0.59	4.34	0.66	0.29	4.51	0.59	4.48	0.56	0.05
SPOUSE VARIABLES										
Marital Satisfaction Scale	3.90	0.57	3.79	0.58	0.19	3.90	0.57	3.89	0.52	0.01
Employment: Other	0.02	0.14	0.04	0.20	−0.14	0.02	0.14	0.04	0.20	−0.15
Employment: Employed	0.22	0.41	0.35	0.48	−0.31	0.22	0.41	0.28	0.45	−0.14
Employment: Homemaker	0.49	0.50	0.51	0.50	−0.05	0.49	0.50	0.47	0.50	0.03
Employment: Student	0.07	0.26	0.05	0.21	0.09	0.07	0.26	0.07	0.25	0.02
Employment: Not Employed	0.21	0.41	0.06	0.24	0.37	0.21	0.41	0.15	0.35	0.15
Education: Less than High School	0.01	0.08	0.02	0.13	−0.15	0.01	0.08	0.02	0.13	−0.15
Education: High School	0.21	0.41	0.18	0.38	0.08	0.21	0.41	0.18	0.38	0.09
Education: Some College	0.28	0.45	0.25	0.43	0.07	0.28	0.45	0.28	0.45	0.00
Education: Associate/Vocational/Technical Degree	0.20	0.40	0.20	0.40	0.01	0.20	0.40	0.18	0.38	0.05
Education: Bachelor's Degree	0.24	0.43	0.29	0.45	−0.11	0.24	0.43	0.27	0.45	−0.07

Table 6.A1—Continued

	Unweighted					Weighted				
	Study Deployment		No Study Deployment			Study Deployment		No Study Deployment		
	Mean	SD	Mean	SD	SMD	Mean	SD	Mean	SD	SMD
Education: Graduate or Professional Degree	0.06	0.24	0.07	0.25	-0.03	0.06	0.24	0.07	0.26	-0.05
Depression (Patient Health Questionnaire)	2.63	3.51	2.65	3.17	-0.01	2.63	3.51	2.66	3.15	-0.01
Posttraumatic Stress Disorder (PTSD)	0.46	0.92	0.56	0.97	-0.11	0.46	0.92	0.43	0.92	0.04
Anxiety	1.94	0.85	2.09	0.89	-0.17	1.94	0.85	1.98	0.89	-0.04
Binge Drinking	0.12	0.33	0.10	0.30	0.06	0.12	0.33	0.11	0.32	0.03
SERVICE MEMBER VARIABLES										
Marital Satisfaction Scale	3.95	0.43	3.93	0.49	0.05	3.95	0.43	3.95	0.46	-0.01
Pay Grade: Junior Enlisted	0.02	0.13	0.04	0.19	-0.14	0.02	0.13	0.02	0.14	-0.01
Pay Grade: Junior Officer	0.08	0.27	0.09	0.28	-0.03	0.08	0.27	0.10	0.31	-0.09
Pay Grade: Mid and Senior Enlisted	0.79	0.41	0.70	0.46	0.22	0.79	0.41	0.73	0.44	0.14
Pay Grade: Mid and Senior Officer	0.10	0.30	0.15	0.35	-0.15	0.10	0.30	0.12	0.32	-0.05
Pay Grade: Warrant Officer	0.01	0.11	0.03	0.17	-0.17	0.01	0.11	0.03	0.16	-0.14
Army	0.45	0.50	0.48	0.50	-0.06	0.45	0.50	0.49	0.50	-0.09
Air Force	0.16	0.36	0.21	0.41	-0.15	0.16	0.36	0.16	0.36	0.00
Navy	0.24	0.42	0.18	0.38	0.13	0.24	0.42	0.27	0.44	-0.07
Marine Corps	0.16	0.37	0.14	0.34	0.07	**0.16**	**0.37**	**0.09**	**0.29**	**0.20**
Reserve Component	0.11	0.31	0.29	0.45	-0.60	0.11	0.31	0.16	0.36	-0.17
Total Number of Prior Deployments	2.15	1.24	1.64	1.26	0.41	**2.15**	**1.24**	**1.90**	**1.16**	**0.20**
Years of Service	11.21	5.10	12.36	6.51	-0.23	11.21	5.10	11.73	5.54	-0.10
Hoge CES	5.50	4.75	4.21	4.36	0.27	5.50	4.75	4.70	4.44	0.17
Deployment Trauma Exposure	2.58	2.63	1.94	2.56	0.24	2.58	2.63	2.22	2.53	0.14
Depression (PHQ)	2.81	3.38	3.02	3.66	-0.06	2.81	3.38	2.85	3.52	-0.01
PTSD	22.84	9.51	23.22	11.17	-0.04	22.84	9.51	22.19	9.65	0.07
Anxiety	2.17	1.02	2.09	1.02	0.09	2.17	1.02	2.08	1.01	0.09
Binge Drinking	0.30	0.46	0.22	0.41	0.18	0.30	0.46	0.24	0.43	0.13
Traumatic Brain Injury (TBI)	0.17	0.38	0.16	0.37	0.04	0.17	0.38	0.13	0.34	0.10

Table 6A.2
Weighted Balance Table: Spouse Report of Teens (Study Deployment Versus No Study Deployment)

	Unweighted					Weighted				
	Study Deployment		No Study Deployment		SMD	Study Deployment		No Study Deployment		SMD
	Mean	SD	Mean	SD		Mean	SD	Mean	SD	
SPOUSE REPORT TEEN VARIABLES										
Age	13.84	1.95	13.15	1.89	0.36	13.84	1.95	13.58	1.95	0.13
Male	0.47	0.50	0.36	0.48	0.21	0.47	0.50	0.47	0.50	0.00
SDQ Total Difficulties	6.95	5.89	7.64	5.03	-0.12	6.95	5.89	6.94	5.40	0.00
SDQ Subscale: Emotional Problems	1.65	2.12	1.66	1.62	-0.01	1.65	2.12	1.52	1.71	0.06
SDQ Subscale: Conduct Problems	1.13	1.69	0.96	1.33	0.11	1.13	1.69	0.96	1.54	0.10
SDQ Subscale: Hyperactivity	2.44	2.14	2.86	2.17	-0.19	2.44	2.14	2.70	2.40	-0.12
SDQ Subscale: Peer Problems	1.72	1.83	2.16	1.90	-0.24	1.72	1.83	1.76	1.78	-0.02
SDQ Subscale: Prosocial Behavior	8.39	1.79	8.16	1.55	0.13	8.39	1.79	8.46	1.69	-0.04
Anxiety	1.69	2.40	1.33	1.32	0.15	1.69	2.40	1.24	1.48	0.19
Depressive Symptoms	1.03	1.92	1.04	1.79	-0.01	1.03	1.92	0.95	1.73	0.04
Medication for Mental Health Problem	0.11	0.32	0.08	0.27	0.12	0.11	0.32	0.09	0.28	0.08
Need for Mental Health Services	0.12	0.33	0.10	0.30	0.06	0.12	0.33	0.14	0.35	-0.05
PedsQL	4.07	0.82	3.95	0.81	0.14	4.07	0.82	4.18	0.76	-0.14
SPOUSE VARIABLES										
Marital Satisfaction Scale	3.92	0.53	3.52	0.80	0.75	3.92	0.53	3.81	0.65	0.20
Employment: Other	0.01	0.09	0.02	0.13	-0.10	0.01	0.09	0.01	0.11	-0.03
Employment: Employed	0.45	0.50	0.62	0.49	-0.35	0.45	0.50	0.51	0.50	-0.14
Employment: Homemaker	0.35	0.48	0.27	0.44	0.17	0.35	0.48	0.34	0.47	0.02
Employment: Student	0.08	0.27	0.04	0.19	0.16	0.08	0.27	0.05	0.21	0.13
Employment: Not Employed	0.12	0.32	0.06	0.24	0.17	0.12	0.32	0.09	0.29	0.08
Education: Less than High School	0.01	0.10	0.01	0.09	0.02	0.01	0.10	0.02	0.12	-0.05
Education: High School	0.21	0.41	0.16	0.37	0.12	0.21	0.41	0.17	0.38	0.09
Education: Some College	0.22	0.41	0.29	0.45	-0.18	0.22	0.41	0.25	0.43	-0.09
Education: Associate/Vocational/Technical Degree	0.19	0.40	0.16	0.36	0.09	0.19	0.40	0.21	0.41	-0.04
Education: Bachelor's Degree	0.24	0.43	0.18	0.39	0.14	0.24	0.43	0.25	0.43	-0.02

Table 6.A2—Continued

	Unweighted					Weighted				
	Study Deployment		No Study Deployment			Study Deployment		No Study Deployment		
	Mean	SD	Mean	SD	SMD	Mean	SD	Mean	SD	SMD
Education: Graduate or Professional Degree	0.13	0.34	0.20	0.40	-0.21	0.13	0.34	0.10	0.30	0.08
Depression (PHQ)	2.09	3.29	2.96	3.27	-0.26	2.09	3.29	2.34	3.20	-0.08
PTSD	0.23	0.74	0.45	0.93	-0.30	0.23	0.74	0.35	0.85	-0.17
Anxiety	2.08	0.91	1.99	0.83	0.10	**2.08**	**0.91**	**1.90**	**0.88**	**0.20**
Binge Drinking	0.06	0.23	0.04	0.19	0.09	0.06	0.23	0.07	0.26	-0.06
SERVICE MEMBER VARIABLES										
Marital Satisfaction Scale	4.05	0.40	3.71	0.68	0.85	4.05	0.40	4.00	0.51	0.15
Pay Grade: Junior Enlisted	0.01	0.09	0.02	0.14	-0.12	0.01	0.09	0.02	0.12	-0.07
Pay Grade: Junior Officer	0.07	0.26	0.04	0.19	0.13	0.07	0.26	0.05	0.21	0.09
Pay Grade: Mid and Senior Enlisted	0.70	0.46	0.75	0.43	-0.11	0.70	0.46	0.70	0.46	-0.01
Pay Grade: Mid and Senior Officer	0.17	0.37	0.17	0.38	-0.01	0.17	0.37	0.19	0.39	-0.06
Pay Grade: Warrant Officer	0.05	0.23	0.02	0.14	0.15	0.05	0.23	0.04	0.20	0.04
Army	0.44	0.50	0.47	0.50	-0.07	0.44	0.50	0.50	0.50	-0.12
Air Force	0.31	0.46	0.33	0.47	-0.04	**0.31**	**0.46**	**0.20**	**0.40**	**0.23**
Navy	0.22	0.42	0.18	0.38	0.10	0.22	0.42	0.27	0.44	-0.11
Marine Corps	0.04	0.18	0.02	0.15	0.06	0.04	0.18	0.04	0.19	-0.01
Reserve Component	0.33	0.47	0.50	0.50	-0.37	0.33	0.47	0.36	0.48	-0.07
Total Number of Prior Deployments	2.04	1.22	1.16	1.19	0.72	2.04	1.22	1.86	1.28	0.15
Years of Service	17.59	7.50	19.29	8.42	-0.23	17.59	7.50	18.41	7.45	-0.11
Hoge CES	4.05	4.06	3.52	3.86	0.13	4.05	4.06	4.10	3.86	-0.01
Deployment Trauma Exposure	1.65	2.06	1.76	2.44	-0.05	**1.65**	**2.06**	**2.11**	**2.36**	**-0.23**
Depression (PHQ)	1.84	2.38	2.64	3.85	-0.34	1.84	2.38	2.15	3.20	-0.13
PTSD	20.07	6.43	23.22	10.71	-0.49	20.07	6.43	21.06	8.14	-0.16
Anxiety	1.73	0.78	2.09	0.98	-0.46	**1.73**	**0.78**	**1.91**	**0.92**	**-0.23**
Binge Drinking	0.18	0.38	0.30	0.46	-0.33	0.18	0.38	0.19	0.39	-0.03
TBI	0.05	0.21	0.07	0.25	-0.11	0.05	0.21	0.06	0.24	-0.07

Table 6A.3
Weighted Balance Table: Teen Self-Report (Study Deployment Versus No Study Deployment)

	Unweighted					Weighted				
	Study Deployment		No Study Deployment			Study Deployment		No Study Deployment		
	Mean	SD	Mean	SD	SMD	Mean	SD	Mean	SD	SMD
TEEN SELF-REPORT VARIABLES										
Age	13.78	1.92	13.66	1.83	0.07	13.78	1.92	13.66	1.99	0.06
Male	0.51	0.50	0.50	0.50	0.02	0.50	0.50	0.43	0.50	0.14
Social Support										
Enough People	0.88	0.33	0.91	0.28	-0.10	0.88	0.33	0.91	0.28	-0.10
Not Enough People	0.11	0.32	0.07	0.26	0.13	0.11	0.32	0.08	0.27	0.11
No One	0.01	0.08	0.02	0.13	-0.10	0.01	0.08	0.01	0.11	-0.05
Overall Health Functioning	4.04	0.83	4.05	0.93	-0.02	4.04	0.83	3.99	0.84	0.05
Plan Career in the Military	0.20	0.40	0.38	0.49	-0.46	0.20	0.40	0.26	0.44	-0.17
Socialize with Other Military Children	0.67	0.47	0.70	0.46	-0.06	0.67	0.47	0.73	0.45	-0.11
Retention Intentions	3.80	1.18	3.99	1.21	-0.16	3.79	1.18	3.76	1.22	0.02
Military Commitment	4.10	0.71	4.24	0.66	-0.20	4.10	0.71	4.19	0.63	-0.12
Relationship Quality with Service Member	4.21	0.52	4.16	0.58	0.11	4.21	0.52	4.19	0.55	0.04
Relationship Quality with Spouse	4.24	0.67	4.12	0.69	0.17	4.23	0.68	4.17	0.71	0.08
Positive Affect Following Communication	4.22	0.53	4.11	0.63	0.22	4.22	0.53	4.16	0.59	0.12
Negative Affect Following Communication	2.01	0.54	1.92	0.54	0.18	2.01	0.54	1.96	0.57	0.09
SDQ Total Difficulties	7.89	5.40	8.53	5.13	-0.12	7.91	5.43	7.80	5.05	QQ
SDQ Subscale: Emotional Problems	1.81	1.93	1.91	1.95	-0.05	1.82	1.93	1.81	1.97	0.01
SDQ Subscale: Conduct Problems	1.25	1.27	1.39	1.40	-0.11	1.26	1.29	1.24	1.39	0.02
SDQ Subscale: Hyperactivity	3.05	2.33	3.32	1.98	-0.12	3.06	2.35	2.98	2.06	0.03
SDQ Subscale: Peer Problems	1.78	1.58	1.91	1.54	-0.08	1.78	1.58	1.78	1.52	0.00
SDQ Subscale: Prosocial Behavior	8.28	1.60	8.54	1.51	-0.16	8.28	1.60	8.43	1.57	-0.09
Anxiety	1.26	1.24	1.37	1.57	-0.09	1.26	1.24	1.48	1.48	-0.17
Depressive Symptoms	0.88	1.52	0.83	1.69	0.03	0.88	1.52	0.73	1.61	0.09
Medication for Mental Health Problem	0.10	0.30	0.07	0.26	0.09	0.10	0.30	0.09	0.29	0.02
Need for Mental Health Services	0.14	0.35	0.06	0.25	0.22	0.14	0.35	0.08	0.27	0.18

Table 6.A3—Continued

	Unweighted					Weighted				
	Study Deployment		No Study Deployment			Study Deployment		No Study Deployment		
	Mean	SD	Mean	SD	SMD	Mean	SD	Mean	SD	SMD
Family Cohesion	2.70	0.32	2.73	0.30	-0.09	2.69	0.33	2.70	0.31	-0.02
Risky Behaviors										
Physical Aggression	1.14	0.36	1.20	0.34	-0.17	1.14	0.37	1.14	0.27	0.00
Physical Aggression: N/A	0.16	0.37	0.15	0.36	0.04	0.16	0.37	0.17	0.38	-0.02
Drug Use	1.08	0.27	1.05	0.23	0.10	1.08	0.27	1.07	0.25	0.03
Drug Use: N/A	0.16	0.37	0.15	0.36	0.04	0.16	0.37	0.17	0.38	-0.02
Nonphysical Aggression	1.24	0.67	1.50	0.97	-0.40	1.24	0.67	1.33	0.72	-0.14
Nonphysical Aggression: N/A	0.16	0.37	0.15	0.36	0.04	0.16	0.37	0.17	0.38	-0.02
Relational Aggression	1.08	0.40	1.14	0.38	-0.18	1.08	0.41	1.09	0.32	-0.03
Relational Aggression: N/A	0.16	0.37	0.15	0.36	0.04	0.16	0.37	0.17	0.38	-0.02
Academic Disengagement	1.77	0.87	1.78	0.82	-0.01	1.77	0.87	1.87	0.77	-0.11
Life Satisfaction	4.53	0.85	4.47	0.73	0.07	4.52	0.86	4.50	0.77	0.03
SPOUSE VARIABLES										
Marital Satisfaction Scale	3.88	0.58	3.76	0.60	0.21	3.87	0.58	3.85	0.60	0.04
Employment: Other	0.01	0.11	0.01	0.07	0.07	0.01	0.11	0.01	0.11	0.01
Employment: Employed	0.38	0.49	0.52	0.50	-0.28	0.38	0.49	0.43	0.49	-0.09
Employment: Homemaker	0.40	0.49	0.34	0.47	0.13	0.40	0.49	0.40	0.49	-0.01
Employment: Student	0.08	0.27	0.03	0.18	0.18	0.08	0.27	0.06	0.24	0.08
Employment: Not Employed	0.12	0.33	0.11	0.31	0.05	0.12	0.33	0.10	0.30	0.07
Education: Less Than High School	0.01	0.09	0.02	0.12	-0.09	0.01	0.09	0.02	0.13	-0.11
Education: High School	0.22	0.41	0.15	0.35	0.18	0.22	0.41	0.16	0.37	0.14
Education: Some College	0.24	0.43	0.24	0.43	0.00	0.24	0.43	0.22	0.42	0.05
Education: Associate/Vocational/Technical Degree	0.20	0.40	0.28	0.45	-0.21	0.20	0.40	0.23	0.42	-0.09
Education: Bachelor's Degree	0.28	0.45	0.25	0.43	0.08	0.28	0.45	0.29	0.46	-0.04
Education: Graduate or Professional Degree	0.05	0.23	0.08	0.26	-0.09	0.06	0.23	0.07	0.26	-0.08
Teen PedsQL	4.24	0.70	4.34	0.66	-0.14	4.24	0.71	4.28	0.68	-0.06

Table 6.A3—Continued

	Unweighted					Weighted				
	Study Deployment		No Study Deployment			Study Deployment		No Study Deployment		
	Mean	SD	Mean	SD	SMD	Mean	SD	Mean	SD	SMD
Teen PedsQL: N/A	0.05	0.21	0.19	0.39	-0.51	0.05	0.22	0.09	0.28	-0.11
Depression (PHQ)	2.84	3.84	3.01	3.94	-0.04	2.86	3.85	3.11	4.29	-0.07
PTSD	0.29	0.83	0.34	0.85	-0.06	0.29	0.83	0.39	0.90	-0.12
Anxiety	2.09	0.99	1.92	0.79	0.17	2.09	0.99	1.96	0.93	0.13
Binge Drinking	0.06	0.23	0.03	0.17	0.12	0.06	0.24	0.04	0.19	0.10
SERVICE MEMBER VARIABLES										
Marital Satisfaction Scale	3.94	0.49	3.98	0.45	-0.08	3.94	0.49	3.99	0.43	-0.09
Pay Grade: Junior Enlisted	0.00	0.00	0.01	0.10	NA	0.00	0.00	0.01	0.10	NA
Pay Grade: Junior Officer	0.08	0.27	0.04	0.19	0.15	0.08	0.27	0.07	0.26	0.03
Pay Grade: Mid and Senior Enlisted	0.76	0.43	0.73	0.44	0.06	0.76	0.43	0.72	0.45	0.09
Pay Grade: Mid and Senior Officer	0.12	0.33	0.20	0.40	-0.25	0.12	0.33	0.18	0.38	-0.18
Pay Grade: Warrant Officer	0.04	0.20	0.02	0.12	0.14	0.04	0.20	0.02	0.15	0.11
Army	0.64	0.48	0.45	0.50	0.41	0.64	0.48	0.63	0.48	0.03
Air Force	0.26	0.44	0.28	0.45	-0.03	0.26	0.44	0.17	0.38	0.20
Navy	0.08	0.28	0.25	0.44	-0.61	0.09	0.28	0.18	0.38	-0.33
Marine Corps	0.01	0.11	0.03	0.16	-0.13	0.01	0.11	0.02	0.13	-0.05
Reserve Component	0.35	0.48	0.54	0.50	-0.39	0.35	0.48	0.41	0.49	-0.14
Total Number of Prior Deployments	1.97	1.32	1.68	1.05	0.23	1.98	1.33	1.70	1.19	0.21
Years of Service	17.43	8.11	17.75	8.21	-0.04	17.40	8.14	17.94	7.77	-0.07
Hoge CES	4.56	4.05	4.03	3.65	0.13	4.56	4.06	4.66	3.76	-0.03
Deployment Trauma Exposure	2.03	2.25	1.86	2.30	0.08	2.04	2.26	2.31	2.40	-0.12
Depression (PHQ)	1.76	2.56	3.38	3.87	-0.63	1.77	2.57	2.33	3.15	-0.22
PTSD	20.80	7.23	25.37	12.31	-0.63	20.78	7.21	21.56	8.26	-0.11
Anxiety	1.80	0.91	2.08	1.08	-0.31	1.79	0.91	1.84	0.89	-0.05
Binge Drinking	0.16	0.36	0.14	0.35	0.05	0.16	0.37	0.15	0.35	0.03
TBI	0.07	0.26	0.15	0.36	-0.30	0.07	0.26	0.07	0.26	0.00

Figure 6A.1
Balance Plot for Spouse Report of Children Sample

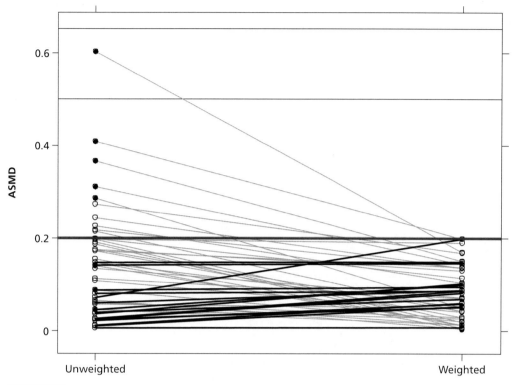

Figure 6A.2
Balance Plot for Spouse Report of Teens Sample

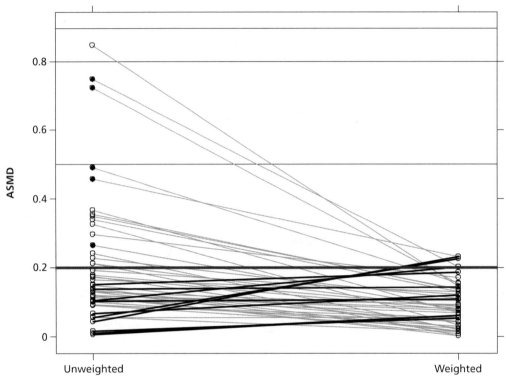

RAND *RR1388-6A.2*

Figure 6A.3
Balance Plot for Teen Self-Report Sample

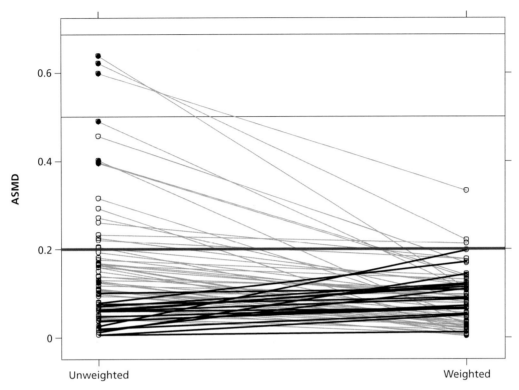

Appendix 6B: Additional Child and Teen Trajectory Models

Additional Child Trajectory Results

Figure 6B.1
Trajectory Model for Spouse Report of Child SDQ Conduct Problems Scores

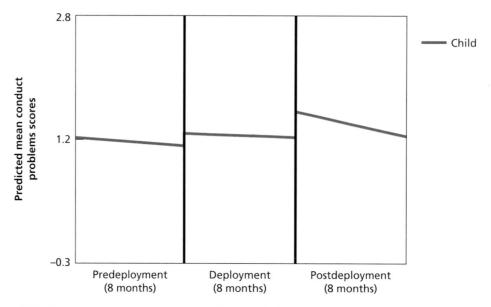

NOTE: The trajectory does not show significant variation over the deployment cycle ($p=0.64$) and is not significantly different from a constant trend over time ($p=0.80$).
RAND RR1388-6B.1

Figure 6B.2
Trajectory Model for Spouse Report of Child SDQ Hyperactivity Scores

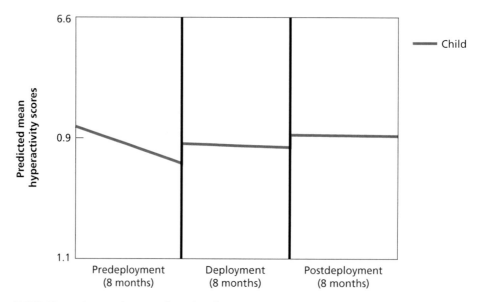

NOTE: The trajectory does not show significant variation over the deployment cycle ($p=0.32$) and is not significantly different from a constant trend over time ($p=0.47$).
RAND RR1388-6B.2

Figure 6B.3
Trajectory Model for Spouse Report of Child SDQ Peer Problems Scores

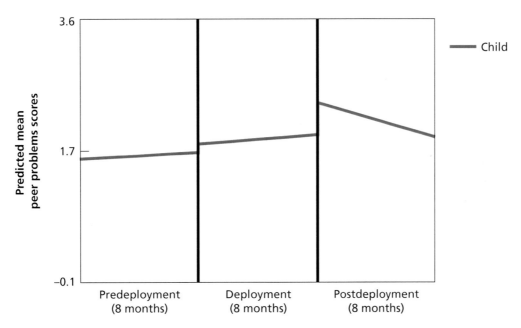

NOTE: The trajectory shows significant variation over the deployment cycle ($p=0.006$) but was not significantly different from a constant trend over time ($p=0.12$).
RAND *RR1388-6B.3*

Figure 6B.4
Trajectory Model for Spouse Report of Child SDQ Prosocial Behavior Scores

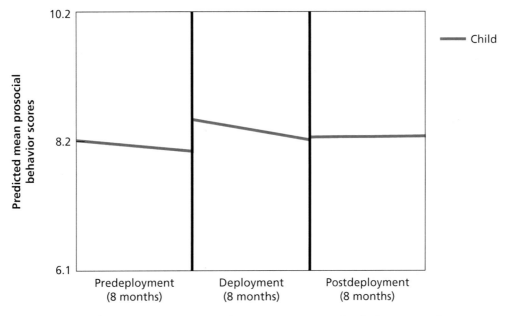

NOTE: The trajectory does not show significant variation over the deployment cycle ($p=0.33$) and is not significantly different from a constant trend over time ($p=0.33$).
RAND *RR1388-6B.4*

Figure 6B.5
Trajectory Model for Spouse Report of Child Anxiety Scores

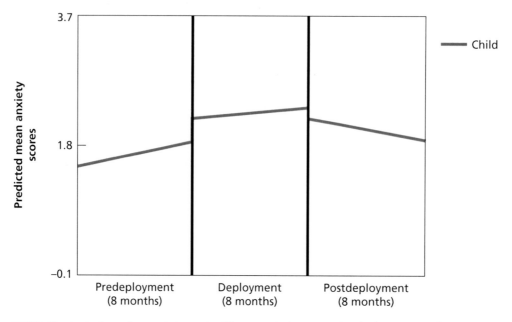

NOTE: The trajectory does not show significant variation over the deployment cycle ($p=0.06$) and is not significantly different from a constant trend over time ($p=0.06$).
RAND *RR1388-6B.5*

Figure 6B.6
Trajectory Model for Spouse Report of Child Pediatric Quality of Life

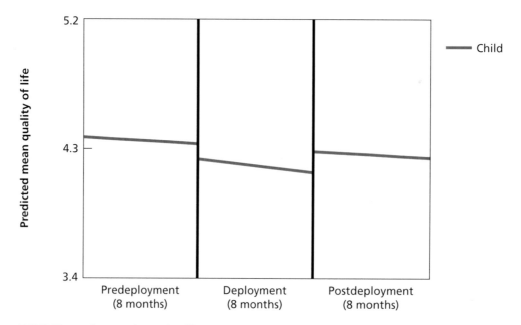

NOTE: The trajectory shows significant variation over the deployment cycle ($p=0.006$) but is not significantly different from a constant trend over time ($p=0.07$).
RAND *RR1388-6B.6*

Additional Spouse Reports of Teens Trajectory Results

Figure 6B.7
Trajectory Model for Spouse Report of Teen SDQ Total Difficulties Scores

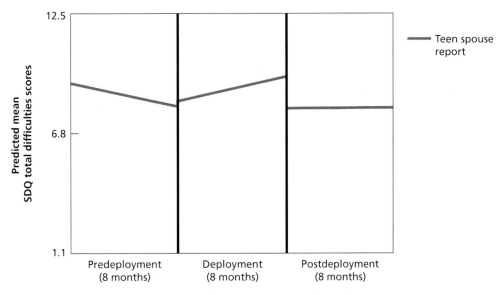

NOTE: The trajectory does not show significant variation over the deployment cycle (p=0.41) and is not significantly different from a constant trend over time (p=0.36).
RAND RR1388-6B.7

Figure 6B.8
Trajectory Model for Spouse Report of Teen SDQ Emotional Problems Scores

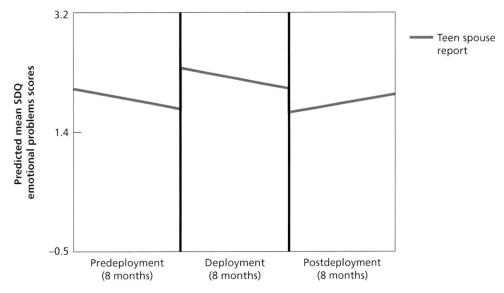

NOTE: The trajectory does not show significant variation over the deployment cycle (p=0.09) and is not significantly different from a constant trend over time (p=0.08).
RAND RR1388-6B.8

Figure 6B.9
Trajectory Model for Spouse Report of Teen SDQ Conduct Problems Scores

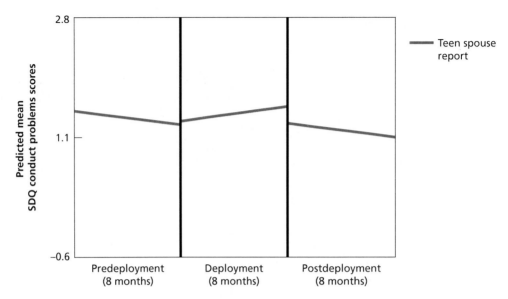

NOTE: The trajectory does not show significant variation over the deployment cycle (*p*=0.35) and is not significantly different from a constant trend over time (*p*=0.36).
RAND *RR1388-6B.9*

Figure 6B.10
Trajectory Model for Spouse Report of Teen SDQ Hyperactivity Scores

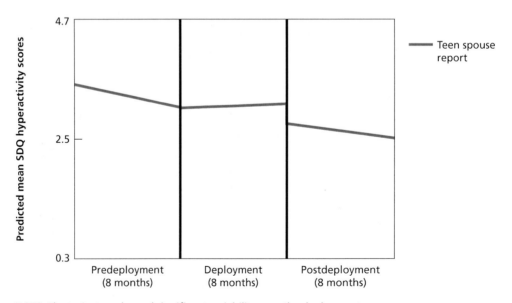

NOTE: The trajectory showed significant variability over the deployment cycle (*p*<0.001) but is not significantly different from a constant trend over time (*p*=0.17).
RAND *RR1388-6B.10*

Figure 6B.11
Trajectory Model for Spouse Report of Teen SDQ Peer Problems Scores

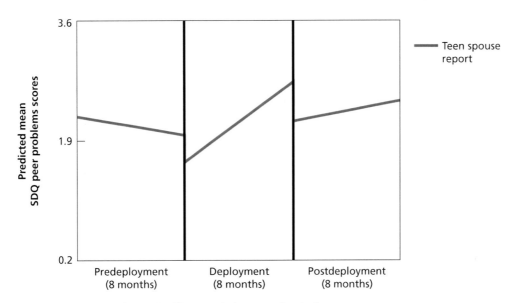

NOTE: The trajectory shows significant variation over the deployment
cycle (*p*=0.02) but is not significantly different from a constant trend over time (*p*=0.43).
RAND *RR1388-6B.11*

Figure 6B.12
Trajectory Model for Spouse Report of Teen SDQ Prosocial Behavior Scores

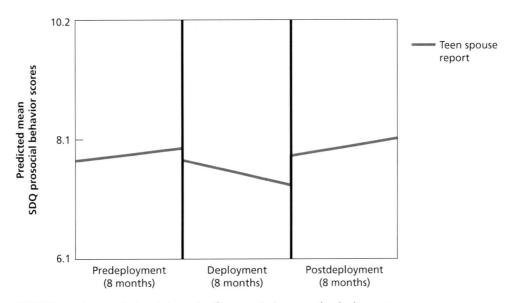

NOTE: The trajectory does not show significant variation over the deployment
cycle (*p*=0.23) and is not significantly different from a constant trend over time (*p*=0.25).
RAND *RR1388-6B.12*

Figure 6B.13
Trajectory Model for Spouse Report of Teen Anxiety

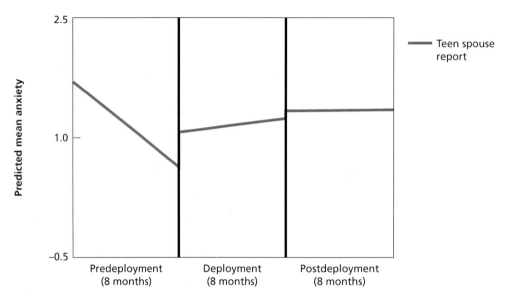

NOTE: The trajectory does not show significant variation over the deployment cycle ($p=0.06$) but is significantly different from a constant trend over time ($p=0.004$).

RAND *RR1388-6B.13*

Figure 6B.14
Trajectory Model for Spouse Report of Teen Depressive Symptoms

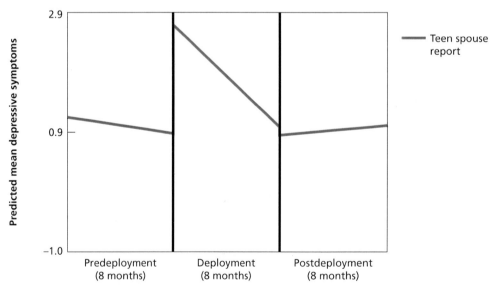

NOTE: The trajectory does not show significant variation over the deployment cycle ($p=0.06$) but is significantly different from a constant trend over time ($p=0.02$).

RAND *RR1388-6B.14*

Figure 6B.15
Trajectory Model for Spouse Report of Teen Pediatric Quality of Life Scores

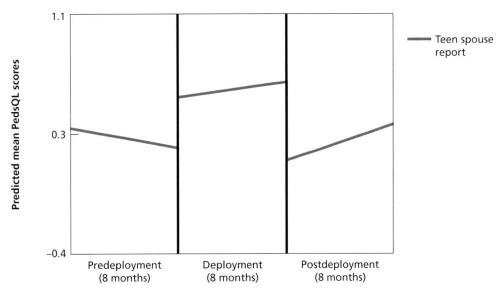

NOTE: The trajectory does not show significant variation over the
deployment cycle (p=0.05) and is not significantly different from a constant trend
over time (p=0.09).
RAND RR1388-6B.15

Figure 6B.16
Trajectory Model for Spouse Report of Teen Need for Mental Health Services

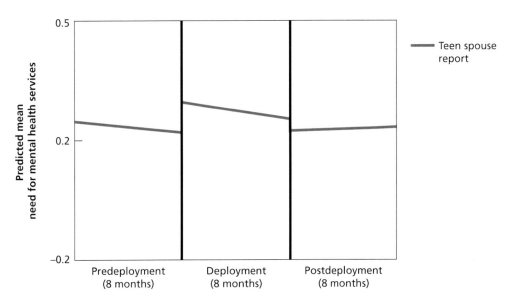

NOTE: The trajectory does not show significant variation over the deployment
cycle (p=0.58) and is not significantly different from a constant trend over
time (p=0.35).
RAND RR1388-6B.16

Additional Teen Self-Reported Trajectory Results

Figure 6B.17
Trajectory Model for Teen Self-Reported SDQ Total Difficulties

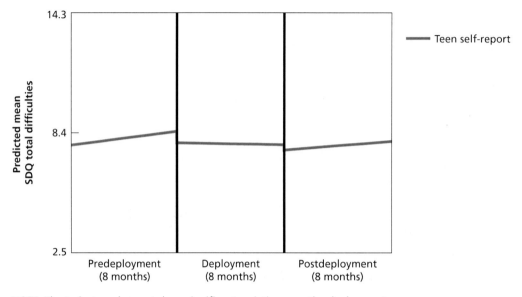

NOTE: The trajectory does not show significant variation over the deployment
cycle (p=0.92) and is not significantly different from a constant trend over time (p=0.92).
RAND *RR1388-6B.17*

Figure 6B.18
Trajectory Model for Teen Self-Reported SDQ Emotional Problems

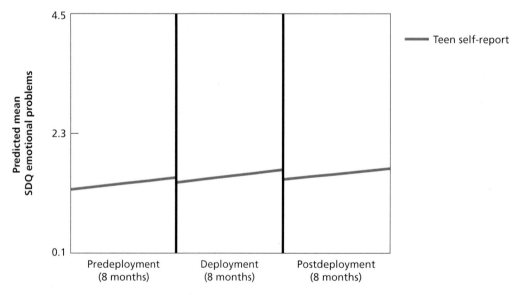

NOTE: The trajectory does not show significant variation over the deployment cycle
(p=0.95) and is not significantly different from a constant trend over time (p=0.99).
RAND *RR1388-6B.18*

Figure 6B.19
Trajectory Model for Teen Self-Reported SDQ Conduct Problems

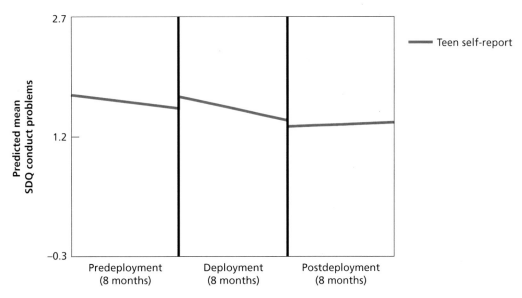

NOTE: The trajectory does not show significant variation over the deployment cycle (p=0.26) and is not significantly different from a constant trend over time (p=0.73).
RAND RR1388-6B.19

Figure 6B.20
Trajectory Model for Teen Self-Reported SDQ Hyperactivity

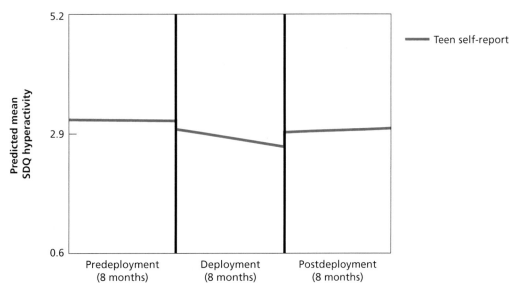

NOTE: The trajectory does not show significant variation over the deployment cycle (p=0.18) and is not significantly different from a constant trend over time (p=0.10).
RAND RR1388-6B.20

Figure 6B.21
Trajectory Model for Teen Self-Reported SDQ Peer Problems

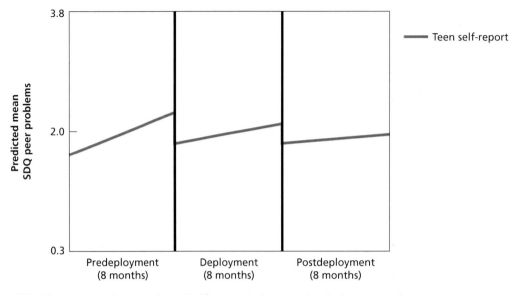

NOTE: Thetrajectory does not show significant variation over the deployment cycle (*p*=0.39) and is not significantly different from a constant trend over time (*p*=0.17).
RAND *RR1388-6B.21*

Figure 6B.22
Trajectory Model for Teen Self-Reported SDQ Prosocial Behavior

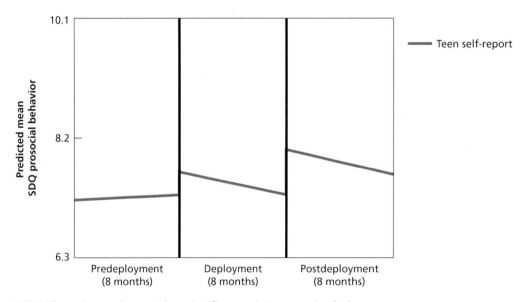

NOTE: The trajectory does not show significant variation over the deployment cycle (*p*=0.10) and is not significantly different from a constant trend over time (*p*=0.14).
RAND *RR1388-6B.22*

Figure 6B.23
Trajectory Model for Teen Self-Reported Depressive Symptoms

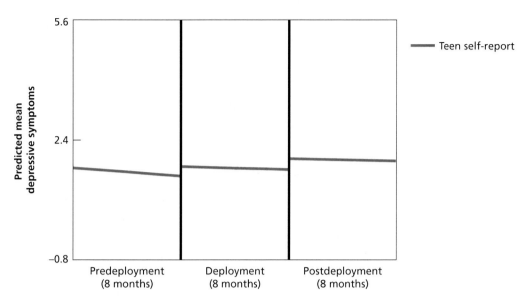

NOTE: The trajectory does not show significant variation over the deployment cycle ($p=0.27$) and is not significantly different from a constant trend over time ($p=0.20$).

RAND *RR1388-6B.23*

Figure 6B.24
Trajectory Model for Teen Self-Reported Need for Mental Health Services

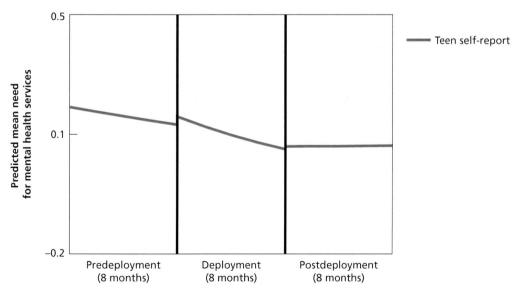

NOTE: The trajectory does not show significant variation over the deployment cycle ($p=0.28$) and is not significantly different from a constant trend over time ($p=0.60$).

RAND *RR1388-6B.24*

Figure 6B.25
Trajectory Model for Teen Self-Reported Overall Health Functioning

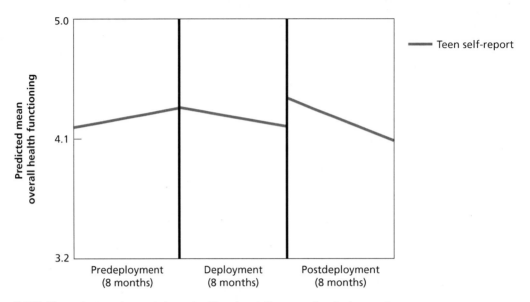

NOTE: The trajectory does not show significant variation over the deployment
cycle ($p=0.15$) and is not significantly different from a constant trend over time ($p=0.26$).
RAND *RR1388-6B.25*

Figure 6B.26
Trajectory Model for Teen Self-Reported Physical Aggression

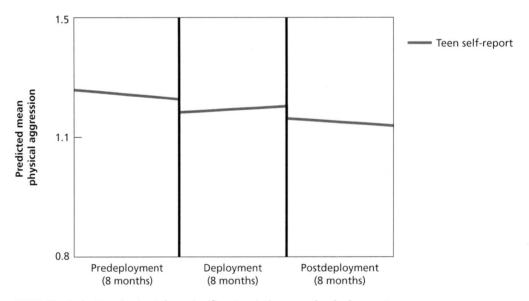

NOTE: The trajectory does not show significant variation over the deployment
cycle ($p=0.47$) and is not significantly different from a constant trend over time ($p=0.70$).
RAND *RR1388-6B.26*

Figure 6B.27
Trajectory Model for Teen Self-Reported Nonphysical Aggression

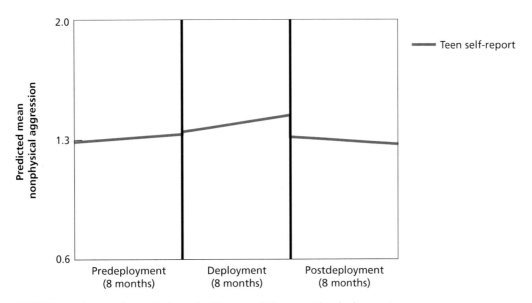

NOTE: The trajectory does not show significant variation over the deployment
cycle ($p=0.34$) and is not significantly different from a constant trend over time ($p=0.43$).
RAND RR1388-6B.27

Figure 6B.28
Trajectory Model for Teen Self-Reported Relational Aggression

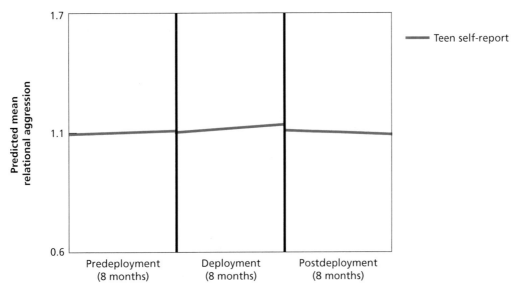

NOTE: The trajectory does not show significant variation over the deployment
cycle ($p=0.74$) and is not significantly different from a constant trend over time ($p=0.81$).
RAND RR1388-6B.28

Figure 6B.29
Trajectory Model for Teen Self-Reported Life Satisfaction

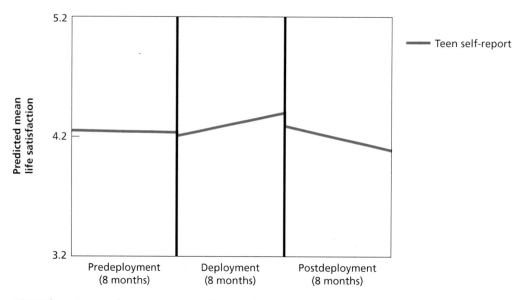

NOTE: The trajectory does not show significant variation over the deployment
cycle ($p=0.12$) and is not significantly different from a constant trend over time ($p=0.52$).
RAND RR1388-6B.29

Figure 6B.30
Trajectory Model for Teen Self-Reported Academic Disengagement

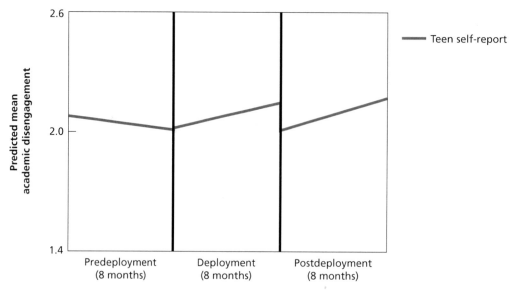

NOTE: The trajectory does not show significant variation over the deployment
cycle ($p=0.42$) and is not significantly different from a constant trend over time ($p=0.40$).
RAND RR1388-6B.30

Figure 6B.31
Trajectory Model for Teen Self-Reported Family Cohesion

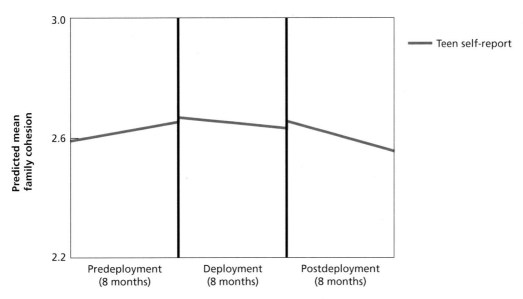

NOTE: The trajectory does not show significant variation over the deployment cycle (p=0.33) and is not significantly different from a constant trend over time (p=0.64).
RAND *RR1388-6B.31*

Figure 6B.32
Trajectory Model for Teen Self-Reported Relationship Quality with Spouse

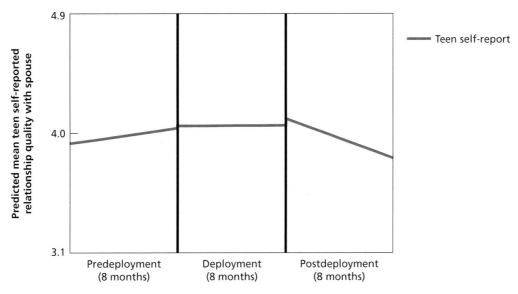

NOTE: The trajectory showed significant variation over the deployment cycle (p=0.049) but it is not significantly different from a constant trend over time (p=0.23).
RAND *RR1388-6B.32*

References

American Academy of Pediatrics, *Addressing Mental Health Concerns in Primary Care: A Clinician's Toolkit*, Washington, D.C.: American Academy of Pediatrics, 2010.

Aranda, M. C., L. S. Middleton, E. Flake, and B. E. Davis, "Psychosocial Screening in Children with Wartime-Deployed Parents," *Military Medicine*, Vol. 176, No. 4, 2011, pp. 402–407.

Barker, L. H., and K. D. Berry, "Developmental Issues Impacting Military Families with Young Children During Single and Multiple Deployments," *Military Medicine*, Vol. 174, No. 10, 2009, pp. 1033–1040.

Barnes, V. A., H. Davis, and F. A. Treiber, "Perceived Stress, Heart Rate, and Blood Pressure Among Adolescents with Family Members Deployed in Operation Iraqi Freedom," *Military Medicine*, Vol. 172, No. 1, 2007, pp. 40–43.

Birmaher, B., D. A. Brent, L. Chiappetta, J. Bridge, S. Monga, and M. Baugher, "Psychometric Properties of the Screen for Child Anxiety Related Emotional Disorders (SCARED): A Replication Study," *Journal of the American Academy of Child and Adolescent Psychiatry*, Vol. 38, No. 10, 1999, pp. 1230–1236.

Birmaher, B., S. Khetarpal, D. Brent, M. Cully, L. Balach, J. Kaufman, and S. M. Neer, "The Screen for Child Anxiety Related Emotional Disorders (SCARED): Scale Construction and Psychometric Characteristics," *Journal of the American Academy of Child and Adolescent Psychiatry*, Vol. 36, No. 4, 1997, pp. 545–553.

Chandra, A., S. Lara-Cinisomo, R. M. Burns, B. A. Griffin, *Assessing Operation Purple: A Program Evaluation of a Summer Camp for Military Youth*, Santa Monica, Calif.: RAND Corporation, TR-1234-NMFA, 2013.

Chandra, A., S. Lara-Cinisomo, L. H. Jaycox, T. Tanielian, R. M. Burns, T. Ruder, and B. Han, "Children on the Homefront: The Experience of Children from Military Families," *Pediatrics*, Vol. 125, No. 1, 2010, pp. 16–25.

Chandra, A., L. T. Martin, S. A. Hawkins, and A. Richardson, "The Impact of Parental Deployment on Child Social and Emotional Functioning: Perspectives of School Staff," *Journal of Adolescent Health*, Vol. 46, No. 3, 2010, pp. 218–223.

Chartrand, M. M., D. A. Frank, L. F. White, and T. R. Shope, "Effect of Parents' Wartime Deployment on the Behavior of Young Children in Military Families," *Archives of Pediatric Adolescent Medicine*, Vol. 162, No. 11, 2008, pp. 1009–1014.

Diener, E. D., R. A. Emmons, R. J. Larsen, and S. Griffin, "The Satisfaction with Life Scale," *Journal of Personality Assessment*, Vol. 49, No. 1, 1985, pp. 71–75.

Engel, C. C., K. C. Hyams, and K. Scott, "Managing Future Gulf War Syndromes: International Lessons and New Models of Care," *Philosophical Transactions of the Royal Society of London B: Biological Sciences*, Vol. 361, No. 1468, 2006, pp. 707–720.

Farrell, A. D., E. M. Kung, K. S. White, and R. F. Valois, "The Structure of Self-Reported Aggression, Drug Use, and Delinquent Behaviors During Early Adolescence," *Journal of Clinical Child Psychology*, Vol. 29, No. 2, 2000, pp. 282–292.

Gewirtz, A. H., M. A. Polusny, D. S. DeGarmo, A. Khaylis, and C. R. Erbes, "Posttraumatic Stress Symptoms Among National Guard Soldiers Deployed to Iraq: Associations with Parenting Behaviors and Couple Adjustment," *Journal of Consulting in Clinical Psychology*, Vol. 78, No. 5, 2010, pp. 599–610.

Gibbs, D. A., S. L. Martin, L. L. Kupper, and R. E. Johnson, "Child Maltreatment in Enlisted Soldiers' Families During Combat-Related Deployments," *Journal of the American Medical Association*, Vol. 298, No. 5, 2007, pp. 528–535.

Goodman, R., "The Strengths and Difficulties Questionnaire: A Research Note," *Journal of Child Psychology and Psychiatry*, Vol. 38, No. 5, 1997, pp. 581–586.

Gorman, G. H., M. Eide, and E. Hisle-Gorman, "Wartime Military Deployment and Increased Pediatric Mental and Behavioral Health Complaints," *Pediatrics*, Vol. 126, No. 6, 2010, pp. 1058–1066.

Hoge, C. W., C. A. Castro, S. C. Messer, D. McGurk, D. I. Cotting, and R. L. Koffman, "Combat Duty in Iraq and Afghanistan, Mental Health Problems, and Barriers to Care," *New England Journal of Medicine*, Vol. 351, No. 1, 2004, pp. 13–22.

Jaycox, L. H., B. D. Stein, S. Paddock, J. Miles, A. Chandra, L. Meredith, and M. A. Burnam, "Impact of Teen Depression on Academic, Social, and Physical Functioning," *Pediatrics*, Vol. 124, No. 4, 2009, pp. e596–e605.

Lester, P., K. Peterson, J. Reeves, L. Knauss, D. Glover, C. Mogil, and W. Beardslee, "The Long War and Parental Combat Deployment: Effects on Military Children and At-Home Spouses," *Journal of the American Academy of Child Adolescent Psychiatry*, Vol. 49, No. 4, 2010, pp. 310–320.

Loeber, R., D. P. Farrington, M. Stouthamer-Loeber, and W. B. Van Kammen, "Multiple Risk Factors for Multiproblem Boys: Co-Occurrence of Delinquency, Substance Use, Attention Deficit, Conduct Problems, Physical Aggression, Covert Behavior, Depressed Mood, and Shy/Withdrawn Behavior," in R. Jessor, ed., *New Perspectives on Adolescent Risk Behavior*, New York: Cambridge University Press, 1998, pp. 90–149.

Lorig, K., A. Stewart, P. Ritter, and V. González, *Outcome Measures for Health Education and Other Health Care Interventions*, Thousand Oaks, Calif.: Sage, 1996.

Moos, R. H., and B. S. Moos, *Family Environment Scale Manual*, Menlo Park, Calif.: Consulting Psychologists Press, 1994.

Palmer, C., "A Theory of Risk and Resilience Factors in Military Families," *Military Psychology*, Vol. 20, No. 3, 2008, p. 205.

Reichman, N. E., J. O. Teitler, I. Garfinkel, and S. S. McLanahan, "Fragile Families: Sample and Design," *Children and Youth Services Review*, Vol. 23, 2001, pp. 303–326.

Repetti, R. L., S. E. Taylor, and T. E. Seeman, "Risky Families: Family Social Environments and the Mental and Physical Health of Offspring," *Psychological Bulletin*, Vol. 128, No. 2, 2002, pp. 330–366.

Rosenthal, D. A., and S. S. Feldman, "The Influence of Perceived Family and Personal Factors on Self-Reported School Performance of Chinese and Western High School Students," *Journal of Research on Adolescence*, Vol. 1, No. 2, 1991, pp. 135–154.

Sheppard, S. C., J. W. Malatras, and A. C. Israel, "The Impact of Deployment on U.S. Military Families," *American Psychologist*, Vol. 65, No. 6, 2010, pp. 599–609.

Sullivan, K., G. Capp, T. D. Gilreath, R. Benbenishty, I. Roziner, R. Astor, "Substance Abuse and Other Adverse Outcomes for Military-Connected Youth in California: Results From a Large-Scale Normative Population Survey," *JAMA Pediatrics*, Vol. 169, No. 10, 2015, pp. 922–928.

Tanielian, T., and L. H. Jaycox, *Invisible Wounds of War: Psychological and Cognitive Injuries, Their Consequences, and Services to Assist Recovery*, Santa Monica, Calif.: RAND Corporation, MG-720-CCF, 2008. As of November 21, 2015:
http://www.rand.org/pubs/monographs/MG720.html

Tanielian, T., B. R. Karney, A. Chandra, and S. O. Meadows, *The Deployment Life Study: Methodological Overview and Baseline Sample Description*, Santa Monica, Calif.: RAND Corporation, RR-209-A, 2014. As of November 21, 2015:
http://www.rand.org/pubs/research_reports/RR209.html

Trautmann, J., J. Alhusen, and D. Gross, "Impact of Deployment on Military Families with Young Children: A Systematic Review," *Nursing Outlook*, Vol. 63, No. 6, 2015.

Varni, J. W., M. Seid, and C. A. Rode, "The PedsQL™: Measurement Model for the Pediatric Quality of Life Inventory," *Medical Care*, Vol. 37, No. 2, 1999, pp. 126–139.

White, C. J., H. T. de Burgh, N. T. Fear, and A. C. Iversen, "The Impact of Deployment to Iraq or Afghanistan on Military Children: A Review of the Literature," *International Review of Psychiatry*, Vol. 23, No. 2, 2011, pp. 210–217.

CHAPTER SEVEN

Military Integration

Natalie D. Hengstebeck, Sarah O. Meadows, Beth Ann Griffin, Esther M. Friedman, and Robin Beckman

Introduction

Serving in the military is a special type of work that includes travel and family separation, non-normative physical and mental health risks, nonstandard work hours, frequent (mandatory) relocation, and regular role renegotiations. Together with military culture, this combination of characteristics makes for not only a unique work environment for service members, but also a central context affecting all members of military families. With the transition to an all-volunteer force (AVF), rapid growth in the female labor force, and increased demands for men's involvement in family life, there is more potential than in the past for conflict between the "greedy institutions" of military and family (Segal, 1986). Although the link between individuals' work experiences and their own and other family members' well-being is well-established among civilian populations (e.g., Perry-Jenkins and Wadsworth, 2013), the work experiences that compose military service are likely to be even more salient among military families.[1] This chapter focuses on how families' *military integration,* or *perceived connectedness to the institution of the military*, changes over the deployment cycle, the impact of deployment on those who experience it relative to those who do not, and factors that may alter the association between deployment and family outcomes.

Given previous research suggesting that deployment is the most stressful aspect of military service (e.g., Rosen, Durand, and Martin, 2000), it is likely that family members' reports of military integration will change over the deployment cycle. Further, the toll of deployment on specific family members' military integration is likely to vary based on a number of individual and contextual characteristics. Because family members' (especially spouses') experiences influence decisions about continued military service, it is important to examine individual variation across the deployment cycle, but also matches and mismatches among family members' military integration across the cycle (Bourg and Segal, 1999). Previous research has yet to examine family members' military integration over the deployment cycle. In addition, research has been limited by the use of cross-sectional data, often gathered from single reporters, that are not linked to deployment; focus on a single aspect of military integration; use of samples made up of previous generations of military families; and a lack of understanding about military children's experiences (e.g., Bourg and Segal, 1999; Faris, 1981; Griffith, Rakoff, and Helms, 1992; Miller et al., 2011). Addressing these limitations is important not only to facilitate understanding about the experiences of military families during deployment, but also understanding of whether specific types

---

[1] Although there is some literature examining other occupations similar in some dimensions to military careers (e.g., police officers, oil rig workers), none have all of the nuances of a military career.

of respondents are more vulnerable than others, in general or at particular time points. To the extent that family members' reports of military integration are interdependent and implicated in families' decisionmaking about retention behavior, it is important that multiple family members' experiences be examined.

This chapter addresses the limitations of the existing literature in four ways. First, this study uses recently collected longitudinal data, which capture several aspects of family members' military integration over time. Second, this chapter examines data from multiple reporters to examine within-family variability in military integration. Third, this study is the first to use a matched comparison approach (i.e., matching families on key characteristics that may influence outcomes) to compare families that do and do not deploy. Finally, this study is the first to examine children's military integration, particularly their aspirations for their own military careers. *The goals of this study are to examine (a) how military integration changes within and between family members across the deployment cycle, (b) how study deployments affect family members' postdeployment military integration, and (c) how specific risk and resilience factors may account for differences in family members' postdeployment military integration.*

Background

Military integration is important to consider in planning for the present and future success of the military. Since 1973, the U.S. military has been an AVF, which is important for two key reasons. First, relative to conscription, an AVF requires more resources to recruit and retain service members, thus warranting the need to understand how to best maximize military resources. The military spends an average of $115,000 annually per service member on personnel costs, which consist of recruitment and retention incentives, training, education subsidies, retirement packages, and other benefits (Korb, Rothman, and Hoffman, 2012). Despite this considerable investment in the human and social capital of military personnel and their families, the average military career lasts for less than ten years (Blaisure et al., 2012). Given that the retention of career service members is particularly important (because of higher military investment and presumably greater expertise), it is worthwhile to examine how to retain committed, qualified service members over time. Second, given that younger generations are less willing to serve in the military than previous generations, have fewer ties to the military, and have been exposed to longer and more frequent deployments than in the past (Ender, Rohall, and Matthews, 2013; Pew Research Center, 2011), it is important to consider factors that predict *future* recruitment and retention of service members. In particular, given that about half of the current generation of service members grew up in military families (Elbogen et al., 2013), children in military families are likely to make up a significant proportion of the pool of future service members. To the extent that children pursue careers similar to their parents (Egerton, 1997; Trice et al., 1995) and that parents' satisfaction with their jobs increases children's likelihood of pursuing a similar profession (Trice and Tillapaugh, 1991), it is important to understand how deployment predicts the likelihood of intergenerational military careers. Taken together, in the high-stakes military context, it is important to develop a more-comprehensive understanding of the factors related to the current retention and future recruitment of service members.

Previous empirical and theoretical work supports our hypothesized link between deployment and military integration. Broadly, this study is situated within a larger Family Stress Process perspective—for example, the ABC-X model (Hill, 1949)—which suggests that families' responses to a stressful event (e.g., deployment, trauma exposure during deployment, duration of deployment, frequent relocation) are shaped by the combination of the severity of the stressful situation, the resources available to cope with the stress, and how family members evaluate and interpret the stress (see Chapters Three and Four in this report). Deployments are major life events that operate as a significant source of stress for military families (Rosen, Durand, and Martin, 2000). Although military integration is probably stable over time, the substantial disruption of families' status quo during deployment is likely to trigger family members to reevaluate their military integration attitudes (Lee and Mitchell, 1994). Change in military integration is likely to depend on families' ability to cope with the new circumstances. However, families' balance of vulnerabilities and resources is predictive of their abilities to adapt (Karney and Bradbury, 1995). Whereas the benefits of the substantial income boost associated with combat deployment may be enough to protect one family's military integration, it may not be enough for another family with more vulnerabilities. Deployment also could have mixed effects within families. To the extent that family members' reports match those of other family members, entire families' military integration is likely to be higher at subsequent points in time. Thus, when deployment narrows the gap between family members' military integration, higher military integration is expected at subsequent time points. Conversely, when deployment widens the gap between family members, military integration is expected to be lower at subsequent time points. In the next section, we discuss a model designed to contextualize the myriad factors that may influence the link between deployment and military integration.

The Family Military Integration Model

This chapter is framed by the Family Military Integration Model (FMIM) (see Figure 7.1), which is informed by previous work (e.g., Orthner, 1990; Weiss et al., 2002; Wood, 1991) and builds on Hill's (1949) model. Families' responses to deployment will depend on objective characteristics of the deployment (e.g., danger of the location, length of deployment). We understand families' resources and vulnerabilities to fall into four categories: (a) social and psychological, (b) military, (c) economic, and (d) community. These factors shape family members' interpretations of the deployment, which then shapes their military integration. Military integration is operationalized as individuals' military satisfaction, commitment, and retention intentions (i.e., desire [for the service member] to stay on active duty). These key aspects of military integration are shown in the center of the model. Given the importance of retaining quality military personnel, it is worthwhile to examine these military integration factors, which have been linked with actual retention behavior (Guthrie, 1992; Hom and Hulin, 1981; Motowidlo and Lawton, 1984).

According to the model there are four key types of factors that shape family members' military integration: psychosocial, military, economic, and community factors. *Psychosocial factors* include demographics (e.g., age, education, minority status), family life cycle (e.g., years married), family history (e.g., parent in the military), expectations (e.g., how frequently the service member will be deployed), family support, family functioning and relationship satisfaction, and child factors (e.g., presence of children). *Military factors* include deployment history and characteristics, rank and years of service, occupation, programs and support (e.g., support from leadership), and work environment. *Economic factors* include compensation (e.g., pay, selective bonuses), civilian employment alternatives, investment in military life, spousal (under)employment, and financial stress. *Community factors* include support for military, eco-

Figure 7.1
The Family Military Integration Model

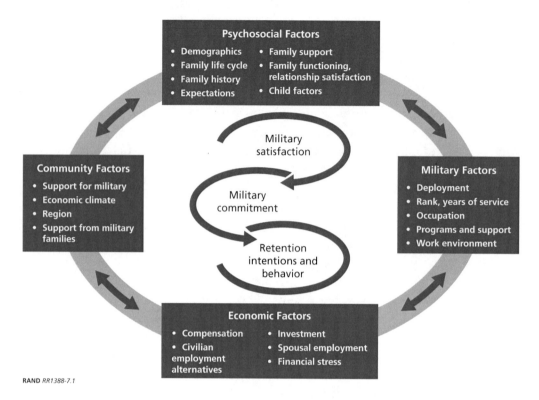

RAND *RR1388-7.1*

nomic climate, region, and support from military families (e.g., communication with other military families).

The application of this model to the study of military integration is useful for four reasons. First, it examines multiple contextual layers of interdependent factors that may shape military integration in complex ways over time. Individuals' attitudes change over time as a function of evolving interactions between psychosocial, military, economic, and community factors. For example, family members' military integration is likely to change based on how reality matches with their expectations, perceived alternatives, and (significant) others' attitudes (Davis and Rusbult, 2001). Second, it allows different aspects of military integration (and predictors of retention behavior) to be examined within the same framework. Although previous research suggests that these aspects are interrelated (e.g., Bourg and Segal, 1999; Vernez and Zellman, 1987), no existing research has examined whether the processes underlying these constructs operate similarly over time. Third, the contextual approach inherently acknowledges that family members' experiences are interdependent, but unique. Thus, it is important to include multiple perspectives to understand how military integration operates within a family. Fourth, it enables deductive selection of critical intervening factors and covariates to be included in the models. The factors expected to be the most salient intervening mechanisms in the link between deployment and military integration are trauma exposure during study deployment, duration of study deployment, military separation, civilian spouses' underemployment, and communication with other military families. These factors were selected because it may be possible to design programs and policies that target these factors with the aim of helping families navigate the challenges of deployment.

Risk and Resilience Factors

Service members' *trauma exposure during study deployment*, a psychosocial factor, is likely to influence families' military integration by undermining mental health and family relationships. Specifically, combat exposure and trauma have been linked to increased risk of posttraumatic stress disorder (PTSD), anxiety, and depression (Adler et al., 2005; Hoge et al., 2004; Tanielian and Jaycox, 2008). In addition, service members who have experienced trauma are less likely to stay in the military (Hosek, Kavanagh, and Miller, 2006), and thus, are likely to have lower military integration as well. Taken together, trauma exposure is likely to represent an important risk factor for families' military integration during the postdeployment period.

Duration of study deployment, a military factor, is also likely to shape families' adaptation during deployment and subsequent evaluations of military integration. Previous research suggests that longer deployments are detrimental to family members' military integration (e.g., Hosek and Wadsworth, 2013). Longer (and presumably more stressful) deployments have been shown to be detrimental to family members, manifesting indirectly through psychological and marital problems for service members and spouses (e.g., Adler et al., 2005; de Burgh et al., 2011; Karney and Trail, forthcoming), and academic problems for children (Engel, Gallagher, and Lyle, 2010). In addition, longer deployments have been linked with service members' and spouses' greater desire to leave the military and lower perceived military support (Werber et al., 2008). Therefore, longer deployments are likely to challenge family members' military integration by taxing families' psychological and interpersonal coping resources.

We also include *military separation*, including retirement, as a military-related potential risk factor for postdeployment military integration outcomes. One could hypothesize that individuals who eventually leave the military are in fact less satisfied, less committed, and have lower retention intentions than those who do not leave, even *before* separation has occurred. Separation also could be considered a risk factor for other individual- and family-level problems following a deployment. For example, as shown in Chapter Five, service members who left the military subsequent to an observed study deployment have worse psychological and behavioral health than their peers who did not separate.

Civilian spouses' underemployment, an economic factor, is likely to shape family members' connectedness to the military. A number of studies have highlighted the costs of military life for spouses' careers. Specifically, these studies suggest that relative to their civilian counterparts, military spouses earn less, are more vulnerable to unemployment or underemployment, and are more likely to be overqualified in their current position (Harrell et al., 2004; Kniskern and Segal, 2010; Lim and Schulker, 2010). One recent study using the Deployment Life Data suggests that military spouses work as much as their civilian peers, but earn less (Meadows et al., 2015). These experiences are likely to be particularly salient for spouses, whose careers may suffer because of adaptation to the deployments, relocations, and poor civilian labor market opportunities that are inherent in military life (Maury and Stone, 2014). Spouses' career frustration and reduced income potential are likely to spill over to affect all family members' military integration attitudes.

Communication with other military families, a community factor, may buffer families from the stress of deployment. Specifically, qualitative (Nichols et al., 2014) and quantitative (Rosen and Moghadam, 1990) research suggest that engaging with other military families was beneficial for spouses during deployment. Interacting with other families experiencing the unique strains of deployment is likely to be protective of all family members' military integration.

Military Integration Outcomes

As indicated, military satisfaction, military commitment, and retention intentions are established predictors of retention behavior (Guthrie, 1992; Hom and Hulin, 1981; Motowidlo and Lawton, 1984). The study variables were selected for two critical reasons. First, each assesses an important aspect of military integration. *Military satisfaction* refers to cognitive evaluations of fulfillment in their enactment of their roles as military service members or spouses. *Military commitment* is dedication to and support of the military institution. *Retention intentions* refer to expectations (for service members) to continue on active duty. In this chapter, we also include teens' *military career aspirations*, which we define as the preference for pursuing a military career in the future. The combination of these measures of families' satisfaction with, commitment to, and desire for continued military service, and teens' desire for their own military career, represent a more holistic understanding of connectedness with the institution of the military than would be possible from an examination of only a single construct. Second, for military commitment and retention intentions, our data used the same items for service members, spouses, and teens. A comparable item about military satisfaction was asked of both service members and spouses (but not teens). Thus, we were able to compare at least two family members across three outcomes. Of course, the item for military career aspirations was only asked of teens.

Research Questions

This study examines family members' military integration before, during, and after deployment. Informed by the literature, three research questions were addressed:

- **Research Question (RQ)1:** How does military integration change over the deployment cycle (i.e., before, during, and after deployment) and how do family members' trajectories converge or diverge over the deployment cycle?
  - **RQ1a:** Is the trajectory a flat line (i.e., zero slope or no change) over the deployment cycle?
    - **Hypothesis:** We do not expect trajectories to be flat across the deployment cycle, as we expect changes in military integration to occur during the study deployment.
  - **RQ1b:** Is the trajectory significantly different from a straight line (i.e., linear slope or constant trend), over the deployment cycle?
    - **Hypothesis:** We do not expect trajectories to be linear across the deployment cycle; instead, we expect there to be periods of constant change within a given stage (before, during, and after deployment) that vary between periods (e.g., a trajectory may decline immediately prior to a deployment and then improve/recover during the postdeployment period).
  - **RQ1c:** How do trajectories of different family members compare? For example, are trajectories for service members and spouses parallel?
    - **Hypothesis:** We expect trajectories between service members and spouses to differ significantly across the deployment cycle, especially during the study deployment, given their different experiences.
- **RQ2:** How does deployment affect postdeployment military integration?
  - **Hypothesis:** Given the prior military experience of our sample, we do not expect long-term decreases in military integration.
- **RQ3:** What risk and resilience factors from the FMIM (i.e., communication with other military families, spouses' underemployment, length of deployment, trauma exposure

during study deployment, military separation) account for differences in postdeployment military integration outcomes among deployed families?

- ○ **Hypothesis:** We expect that communication with other military families during deployment will serve as a protective factor in the postdeployment period (i.e., there will be higher levels of integration). In contrast, we expect that experiencing longer deployments, trauma during deployment, military separation, and spouses' underemployment will act as risk factors and be associated with lower military integration during the postdeployment period.

Method

Data

The Deployment Life Study is uniquely suited to address these research questions and expand previous research in this area. First, the study sample is representative of married U.S. Army, Air Force, Navy, and Marine Corps families in the military between 2012 and 2013; deployed families in the study are weighted to be representative of families that deployed between 2012 and 2013. Families were assessed at four-month intervals over a three-year period for a total of nine waves for Army, Air Force, and Marine Corps families and seven waves for Navy families.[2] Second, whereas several previous studies have included some combination of service members, spouses, and children (e.g., Mazur, 2011; Andres and Moelker, 2011), the Deployment Life Study is one of the few studies to integrate reports from service members, spouses, and teens (within the same families) to allow a more complete perspective of the associations between deployment and families' military integration. Third, the data include both standard, comparable measures of military integration used in other studies (e.g., the Defense Manpower Data Center's [DMDC's] Status of Forces Survey), but also an item that is far less commonly used, which assesses teens' military career aspirations. In addition, our study measures are well suited to capture individuals' subjective experiences (e.g., attitudes, satisfaction), thus enabling a better understanding of the underlying mechanisms that motivate retention behavior. Finally, this sample is uniquely qualified for studying families that have been affiliated with the military for an average of ten years and may be at the point of choosing whether to continue until retirement or to pursue a civilian career. Details about the Deployment Life Study can be found in Tanielian, et al. (2014).

Analytic Sample

Of the 2,724 families that participated in the study, the sample for service members and spouses in this chapter was restricted to families in which (a) service members were in the active component (i.e., not a member of the reserve component) and (b) service members and spouses did *not* divorce during the study period. The sample of teens is similarly limited to active component families that remain intact over the study period. In total, the analyses in this chapter are based on reports of 1,509 service members, 1,625 spouses, and 240 teens.[3] See Chapter Two and Tanielian et al. (2014) for additional details of the baseline sample.

---

[2]   Data collection in the Navy was delayed and resulted in a condensed data collection period.

[3]   Limiting the sample to matched pairs in families that experienced a study deployment results in a sample of 110 for spouse-teen models and 104 for service member–teen models due to missing service member data in the matched pair.

Measures

Dependent Variables

The four primary outcomes of interest in this chapter include: military satisfaction, military commitment, retention intentions, and military career aspirations among teens. *Military satisfaction*, or satisfaction with military life, was assessed using a single item from the DMDC Status of Forces Survey (DMDC, 2012). Using a 5-point scale ranging from "very dissatisfied" to "very satisfied," service members and spouses indicated their response to a single question: "Generally, on a day-to-day basis, how satisfied are you with the military way of life?" This question was not asked of teens. Higher scores on this item indicated more satisfaction with the military way of life.

Military commitment was measured via three items used previously in the DMDC Status of Forces Survey (adapted from O'Reilly and Chatman, 1996). Respondents reported on the extent to which being a service member or being married to a service member inspired them to do the best job possible, affected their willingness to make sacrifices to help the military or help the service member serve in the military, and made them glad to be in the military or married to someone in the military. Teens responded to similar questions, which asked the extent to which being a child in a military family inspired them to do the best job possible, whether they were willing to make sacrifices so that family can contribute to the military, and whether they were glad to be in a military family. All participants used a 5-point scale ranging from "strongly disagree" to "strongly agree" to indicate their response to each of the three items. Across respondents, higher scores on this scale indicated stronger commitment to the military. Scores were calculated for each family member by taking the average across the three items at each wave. Averaged across waves, alphas for service members, spouses, and teens were 0.85, 0.79, and 0.81, respectively.

Based on items from the DMDC Status of Forces Survey, service members, spouses, and teens reported on *retention intentions*. Service members were asked, "Assuming you have a choice to stay on active duty or not, how likely is it that you would choose to stay on active duty?" and asked to respond using a 5-point scale ranging from "very unlikely" to "very likely." Spouses were asked to use a 5-point scale ranging from "strongly favor leaving" to "strongly favor staying" to answer whether they believed that their partner should stay or leave the military after completing service obligations. Teens were asked to indicate using a 5-point scale the extent to which they favor their service member parent leaving or staying in the military. Across respondents, higher scores indicated stronger retention intentions (i.e., greater preference for continued military service).

A single item, created specifically for use in the Deployment Life Study, addressed teens' *military career aspirations*. At baseline, teens were asked whether they planned to have a career in the military, with the response options of "yes" or "no." At consecutive waves, teens were asked how *likely* they were to join the military, with response options of "not at all likely," "somewhat likely," or "very likely." Responses were reverse-coded such that a higher score indicated a greater likelihood of joining the military. To minimize the potential for an artificial difference between waves, the baseline item was used to balance families and as a control in the analyses; however, the three-response format was used for the main analyses.

Table 7.1 shows the means and standard deviations (SDs) for each outcome at baseline by whether families experienced a study deployment. Overall, service members, spouses, and teens reported very high military commitment, and moderately high satisfaction and retention intentions. Approximately one-third of teens indicated aspirations for a future military career.

Table 7.1
Means and Standard Deviations (SDs) of Military Integration Outcomes at Baseline

	Overall Sample			Service Members			Spouses			Teens		
	Service Members (n=1509)	Spouses (n=1625)	Teens (n=240)	Study Deployment (n=688)	No Study Deployment (n=821)	p-value	Study Deployment (n=727)	No Study Deployment (n=898)	p-value	Study Deployment (n=110)	No Study Deployment (n=130)	p-value
Military Satisfaction[a]	3.73 (0.06)	4.02 (0.06)	—	**3.93** **(0.07)**	**3.65** **(0.08)**	**0.01**	4.1 (0.07)	3.98 (0.07)	0.24	—	—	—
Military Commitment[b]	4.34 (0.04)	4.42 (0.04)	4.09 (0.06)	4.39 (0.04)	4.32 (0.05)	0.31	4.49 (0.04)	4.39 (0.05)	0.10	4.13 (0.08)	4.05 (0.09)	0.51
Retention Intentions[c]	4.16 (0.07)	3.90 (0.08)	3.63 (0.11)	4.23 (0.07)	4.13 (0.09)	0.42	**4.12** **(0.06)**	**3.81** **(0.11)**	**0.01**	3.54 (0.14)	3.69 (0.17)	0.48
Military Career Aspirations[d]	—	—	24.24% (3.28)	—	—	—	—	—	—	18.40% (3.96)	28.56% (4.86)	0.11

NOTE: Results are weighted. Missing data are imputed. Bold indicates a statistically significant difference between the study deployment and no study deployment groups based on a weighted t-test.

[a] Higher scores=more satisfaction. Range: 1–5.

[b] Higher scores=more commitment. Range: 1–5.

[c] Higher scores=stronger preference for continued military service. Range: 1–5.

[d] Higher scores=interest in future military career. Range: 0–1.

At baseline, there are two significant differences to note. First, service members who eventually experienced a study deployment reported significantly higher military satisfaction than those who did not (M=3.93 versus 3.65, p=0.01). Second, spouses who eventually experienced a study deployment reported significantly higher retention intentions than those who did not (M=4.12 versus 3.81, p=0.01).

Table 7.2 shows the correlation between outcomes for service members, spouses, and teens. The shaded boxes indicate dyadic (i.e., between-person) correlations on the dependent variables. For military satisfaction, service members' and spouses' reports were correlated at 0.20. For military commitment, service members' reports were correlated with spouses' and teens' at 0.28 and 0.31, respectively. Spouses' and teens' military commitment were correlated at 0.33. For retention intentions, service members' reports were correlated with spouses' and teens' reports at 0.43 and 0.25, respectively. Spouses' and teens' retention intentions were correlated at 0.10. Teens' military career aspirations were negatively related to service members' military commitment (r=−0.16), and positively related to teens' military commitment (r=0.20), and teens' retention intentions (r=0.16).

Covariates

Models for this chapter include covariates that may be associated with the military integration outcomes described above (see Table 7.3). The bulk of these covariates are related to individual service member, spouse, and teen demographic and military characteristics. In the models for service members and spouses, we include age, gender, minority status, presence of children younger than age six in the household, and length of marriage. To capture spouses' socio-economic statuses, models also include information on spouse educational attainment and employment status.

For service members, spouses, and teens, we control for branch of service (i.e., Army, Air Force, Navy, Marine Corps) and pay grade. For service members and spouses, we include the number of prior combat deployments experienced by the service member (including all deployments as part of Operation Iraqi Freedom/Operation Enduring Freedom/Operation New Dawn [OIF/OEF/OND]), whereas for teens, we only include whether service members had any prior deployment.

In addition, we include two historical measures of deployment experiences and combat trauma exposure that occurred prior to the baseline survey. The first, preexisting deployment trauma, is an 11-item checklist of possible traumatic experiences during deployment and has been used in prior work (Tanielian and Jaycox, 2008). Preexisting deployment trauma was used in models for service members, spouses, and teens. It includes items such as, "During any prior deployment, did you witness an accident that resulted in serious injury or death?" Endorsed items are summed to create an index score. The second is a modified version of the Hoge et al., (2004) Combat Experiences Scale (CES). The original CES contains 18 items that assess the occurrence of different potentially traumatic events in combat (e.g., being attacked or ambushed, participating in demining operations.) Three items were eliminated to minimize the sensitivity of the questions and the time it takes to complete the measure (see Tanielian and Jaycox, 2008). Endorsed items are summed to create an index score. The CES was used in service member and spouse models only.

Table 7.3 presents means, percentages, and standard errors for all the covariates at baseline for the overall sample of service members and spouses (i.e., the deployed and nondeployed

Table 7.2
Correlation Between Military Integration Outcomes at Baseline

		Service Members			Spouses			Teens		
		Military Satisfaction	Military Commitment	Retention Intentions	Military Satisfaction	Military Commitment	Retention Intentions	Military Commitment	Retention Intentions	Military Career Aspirations
Service Members	Military Satisfaction	—								
	Military Commitment	0.52	—							
	Retention Intentions	0.44	0.51	—						
Spouses	Military Satisfaction	0.20	0.22	0.16	—					
	Military Commitment	0.24	0.28	0.22	0.48	—				
	Retention Intentions	0.26	0.32	0.43	0.37	0.43	—			
Teens	Military Commitment	0.37	0.31	0.28	0.09	0.33	0.03	—		
	Retention Intentions	0.38	0.36	0.25	0.09	0.17	0.10	0.28	—	
	Military Career Aspirations	−0.09	−0.16	−0.03	0.11	0.03	−0.01	0.20	0.16	—

NOTE: Results are weighted. Highlighted values indicate dyadic correlations. Service member and spouse correlations above the absolute value of 0.10 and teen correlations above the absolute value of 0.12 are significant at $p<0.05$.

Table 7.3
Means, Percentages, and Standard Errors of Study Variables at Baseline

	Overall Sample			Service Members			Spouses			Teens		
	Service Members	Spouses	Teens	Study Deployment Mean (SE)	No Study Deployment Mean (SE)	p-value	Study Deployment Mean (SE)	No Study Deployment Mean (SE)	p-value	Study Deployment Mean (SE)	No Study Deployment Mean (SE)	p-value
Age[a]	32.47 (0.41)	31.58 (0.29)	13.49 (0.16)	**31.46 (0.31)**	**32.86 (0.55)**	**0.03**	30.90 (0.36)	31.85 (0.39)	0.07	13.66 (0.21)	13.37 (0.22)	0.34
Length of Marriage[b]	89.87 (4.64)	87.33 (3.02)	—	85.86 (3.03)	91.42 (6.32)	0.43	85.07 (3.39)	88.22 (4.01)	0.55	—	—	—
Number of Prior Combat Deployments[c]	1.60 (0.11)	1.68 (0.09)	—	**2.11 (0.10)**	**1.40 (0.14)**	**0.00**	**2.12 (0.08)**	**1.51 (0.11)**	**0.00**	—	—	—
Preexisting Deployment Trauma[d]	1.86 (0.16)	1.96 (0.13)	2.58 (0.20)	**2.24 (0.18)**	**1.71 (0.20)**	**0.05**	2.36 (0.20)	1.80 (0.16)	0.03	2.43 (0.25)	2.69 (0.28)	0.53
Combat Experiences Scale[e]	4.30 (0.26)	4.19 (0.20)	—	4.78 (0.38)	4.11 (0.32)	0.18	4.79 (0.34)	3.95 (0.23)	0.04	—	—	—
Male	88.06% (3.03)	11.71% (2.99)	40.87% (3.88)	92.48% (1.55)	86.35% (4.13)	0.10	6.44% (1.37)	13.8% (4.06)	0.03	50.27% (5.70)	33.92% (5.02)	0.03
Minority Race/Ethnicity	36.40% (3.41)	34.94% (2.90)	—	33.75% (2.95)	37.43% (4.59)	0.50	31.01% (2.88)	36.49% (3.85)	0.25	—	—	—
Children Younger Than Age 6 in Household	50.57% (3.63)	48.86% (2.81)	—	55.00% (3.21)	48.85% (4.89)	0.29	52.04% (3.03)	47.59% (3.72)	0.35	—	—	—
Parent in the Military	50.13% (3.64)	45.63% (2.93)	—	51.05% (3.35)	49.78% (4.88)	0.83	37.91% (2.94)	48.69% (3.8)	0.02	—	—	—
Any Prior Deployment[f]	—	—	88.90% (2.97)	—	—	—	—	—	—	91.93% (2.71)	86.66% (4.70)	0.29

Table 7.3—Continued

	Overall Sample			Service Members			Spouses			Teens		
	Service Members	Spouses	Teens	Study Deployment Mean (SE)	No Study Deployment Mean (SE)	p-value	Study Deployment Mean (SE)	No Study Deployment Mean (SE)	p-value	Study Deployment Mean (SE)	No Study Deployment Mean (SE)	p-value
Branch of Service												
Army	39.50% (3.12)	38.53% (2.43)	53.75% (4.10)	41.16% (3.07)	38.86% (4.12)	0.93	40.87% (2.80)	37.60% (3.17)	0.94	61.07% (5.78)	48.34% (5.68)	0.29
Air Force	25.84% (2.13)	25.56 (1.75)	19.21% (2.35)	24.29% (2.26)	26.44% (2.86)		24.69% (2.21)	25.91% (2.3)		13.48% (2.73)	23.44% (3.63)	
Navy	23.77% (4.86)	24.37% (3.52)	23.54% (4.22)	22.31% (2.45)	24.33% (6.62)		23.04% (2.43)	24.9% (4.8)		23.59% (5.87)	23.51% (5.93)	
Marine Corps	10.89% (2.11)	11.54% (1.88)	3.50% (1.72)	12.23% (4.40)	10.37% (2.34)		11.40% (3.63)	11.6% (2.2)		1.85% (1.83)	4.71% (2.66)	
Pay Grade												
E1 to E3	4.35% (1.08)	3.74% (0.78)	0.67% (0.41)	4.63% (1.38)	4.25% (1.40)	0.12	4.93% (1.60)	3.27% (0.87)	0.55	—	0.49% (0.49)	n/a
E4 to E9	72.61% (2.85)	72.82% (2.43)	73.83% (4.40)	68.09% (3.12)	74.36% (3.72)		70.16% (2.60)	73.88% (3.24)		73.35% (4.51)	81.29% (3.67)	
O1 to O3	11.04% (1.92)	11.29% (1.77)	5.20% (1.10)	12.02% (1.58)	10.66% (2.59)		11.78% (1.52)	11.10% (2.4)		8.50% (2.42)	5.78% (1.99)	
O4 +	8.58% (1.74)	9.44% (1.72)	17.90% (4.31)	8.36% (1.36)	8.66% (2.36)		9.05% (1.52)	9.59% (2.33)		12.06% (3.58)	10.37% (2.69)	
Warrant Officer	3.42% (0.97)	2.7% (0.60)	2.40% (0.69)	6.91% (2.65)	2.07% (0.82)		4.07% (0.96)	2.16% (0.74)		6.09% (1.89)	2.06% (1.62)	
Spouse Education												
Less Than High School	0.65% (0.20)	1.23% (0.36)	—	0.65% (0.28)	0.64% (0.25)	0.79	0.78% (0.31)	1.41% (0.49)	0.66	—	—	n/a
High School	17.69% (3.00)	18.68% (2.87)	—	19.44% (2.34)	17.01% (4.06)		18.30% (2.08)	18.83% (3.92)		—	—	
Some College	35.09% (3.99)	30.73% (2.63)	—	32.85% (3.86)	35.95% (5.31)		29.25% (2.92)	31.31% (3.48)		—	—	

Table 7.3—Continued

	Overall Sample			Service Members			Spouses			Teens		
	Service Members	Spouses	Teens	Study Deployment Mean (SE)	No Study Deployment Mean (SE)	p-value	Study Deployment Mean (SE)	No Study Deployment Mean (SE)	p-value	Study Deployment Mean (SE)	No Study Deployment Mean (SE)	p-value
Associate/ Vocational/ Technical Degree	14.22% (1.59)	15.78% (1.59)	—	16.63% (1.89)	13.29% (2.05)	—	19.35% (2.85)	14.36% (1.86)	—	—	—	n/a
Bachelor's Degree	26.76% (2.70)	27.18% (2.37)	—	24.08% (2.39)	27.79% (3.66)		25.50% (2.47)	27.85% (3.16)		—	—	
Graduate Degree	5.60% (0.75)	6.39% (0.75)	—	6.36% (1.11)	5.30% (0.93)		6.81% (1.15)	6.23% (0.94)		—	—	
Spouse Employment Status												
Military Spouse	8.91% (2.98)	8.86% (2.94)	—	6.59% (1.41)	9.81% (4.07)	0.06	5.65% (1.20)	10.14% (4.03)	0.13	—	—	
Employed	32.33% (3.91)	29.75% (2.50)	—	25.38% (2.43)	35.02% (5.23)		25.76% (2.33)	31.33% (3.37)		—	—	
Homemaker	37.26% (3.15)	39.07% (2.59)	—	46.02% (3.50)	33.87% (3.95)		44.46% (3.06)	36.93% (3.35)		—	—	
Student	9.76% (1.84)	9.43% (1.60)	—	8.04% (1.37)	10.43% (2.51)		8.24% (1.36)	9.91% (2.17)		—	—	
Unemployed	11.74% (1.35)	12.88% (1.38)	—	13.96% (1.81)	10.88% (1.70)		15.88% (2.82)	11.69% (1.51)		—	—	

NOTE: Results are weighted. Missing data are imputed. Bold indicates a statistically significant difference between the study deployment and no study deployment groups.

[a] Service member range: 20–56; spouse range: 19–63; teen range: 11–17.

[b] In months. Service member range: 0–528; spouse range: 0–405.

[c] Includes deployments as part of OIF/OEF/OND. Service member range: 0–5.

[d] See Tanielian and Jaycox (2008, p.91). These items are taken from the first follow-up survey (Wave 2). Service member range: 0–10.

[e] See Hoge et al. (2004). Service member range: 0–15.

[f] Includes all deployments outside the continental United States (OCONUS) of 30 days or more.

sample combined),[4] as well as the sample used in the analyses contained in this chapter. Means are reported separately for service members, spouses, and teens who do and do not experience a study deployment. All means are weighted and baseline data are imputed, as detailed in Chapter Two. Both service members and spouses are in their early 30s and teens are approximately 14 years old. Service members who eventually experienced a study deployment are younger than those who do not (31.46 versus 32.86, $p=0.03$). The vast majority of service members are male (approximately 90 percent), and the majority of spouses are female. Forty-one percent of teens are male. Relative to teens in deployed families, teens in nondeployed families are less likely to be male (33.92 percent versus 50.27 percent, $p=0.03$). Roughly one-third of service members and spouses are of a minority race or ethnicity (i.e., nonwhite or Hispanic). About half of families have a child younger than age six in the home.

All analyses for service members, spouses, and teens are based on active component families. The largest portion of service members comes from the Army (39 percent), followed by the Air Force (26 percent) and Navy (24 percent), and the Marine Corps (11 percent). Almost three-quarters of the sample of service members is in the mid to senior enlisted group (E4 to E9), followed by mid to senior officers (O4 and above), junior officers (O1 to O3), warrant officers, and junior enlisted (E1 to E3). For service members and spouses, differences were found between the distributions of service member branch and pay grade between those who experience a study deployment and those who do not. At the time of the baseline survey, more than two-thirds of service members had experienced at least one OCONUS deployment of at least 30 days, with an average of 1.60 combat deployments.

Finally, given the prior experience with deployment in the sample, it is not surprising that service members also have experience with combat, and in some cases, related trauma. Average scores on preexisting deployment trauma are roughly two out of 11, and four to five on the CES. With one exception (the CES for service members) service members and spouses who eventually experienced a study deployment differed significantly on these measures of pre-baseline combat and trauma exposure.

Taken together, the descriptive results reviewed here show that there are differences in how families that experience deployment compare with those that do not on baseline characteristics. Because service members, spouses, and teens who experience a study deployment differ in numerous ways from those who do not, we employ propensity score methods to match service members (and their families) who deploy with those who do not in the results below.

Risk and Resilience Factors

As described earlier, we also hypothesized that a number of risk and resilience factors might mitigate (or exacerbate) the influence of deployment on families' military integration (Table 7.4). At each wave, all respondents reported on their *communication with other military families/ children*. Service members and spouses were asked, "Do you and/or other members of your immediate family socialize or communicate with other military families?" They responded "no" or "yes," which were coded as 0 and 1, respectively. In response to the question, "Do you know, socialize, or communicate regularly with other kids from military families?" teens indicated "no" or "yes," which were coded as 0 and 1, respectively. *Spouses' underemployment* responses of "not employed but looking for work" were coded as 1; all other employment sta-

---

[4]   Preexisting deployment trauma is actually measured at Wave 2, not baseline.

Table 7.4
Means, Percentages, and Standard Errors of Risk and Resilience Factors (Study Deployment Sample Only)

	Service Members	Spouses	Teens
Communication with Other Military Families[a]	51.44% (3.91)	68.74% (2.43)	62.04% (5.69)
Spouses' Underemployment[b]	5.44% (1.54)	5.77% (1.76)	—
Length of Study Deployment[c]	7.91 (0.13)	7.89 (0.13)	7.77 (0.25)
Military Separation[d]	6.99% (1.50)	6.22% (1.58)	10.87% (3.79)
Trauma Exposure During Study Deployment			
Physical	19.01% (2.50)	16.99% (2.54)	16.29% (4.80)
Psychological	33.93% (2.73)	37.21% (3.56)	36.63% (5.98)
Combat	5.95% (1.25)	5.55% (1.22)	5.19% (2.36)

NOTES: Standard errors are in parentheses. Results are weighted.

[a] Range: 0–1.

[b] Spouse range: 0 (not looking for work) or 1 (unemployed, looking for work).

[c] In months.

[d] Includes both separation (involuntary and voluntary) and retirement.

tuses were coded as 0. For both of these measures, if multiple assessments were obtained during one study deployment, we took the average across all assessments.

In addition, we examined three military factors based on service members' reports. First, to assess *trauma exposure during study deployment*, we used three dichotomous variables to indicate whether the service members experienced any physical trauma (e.g., received an injury requiring hospitalization), psychological trauma (e.g., having a friend who was seriously wounded or killed), or combat trauma (e.g., engaging in hand-to-hand combat) during the deployment (see Chapter Two of this report for more details). These measures were created from 11 items from Tanielian and Jaycox (2008, p. 91). These measures are cumulative across the study deployment. Thus, if a service member indicates "yes" to any items in the three categories, she or he receives a score of "1". During study deployments, 19 percent of service members experienced physical trauma, 34 percent experienced psychological trauma, and 6 percent experienced combat trauma. Overall, the percentage of service members who experienced one or more types of trauma is 45 percent. Second, we measured the *length of the study deployment* in months. The average study deployment for service members in this chapter was 8.0 months. Third, we measured whether service members' *military separation*, or whether the service member leaves—either through separation (voluntary or involuntary) or retirement during any of the follow-up waves.[5] Seven percent of service members reported leaving the military during the study, 6 percent of spouses were married to service members who left the military during the study, and 11 percent of teens had a parent who left the military during the study.

---

[5] Respondents are not asked military satisfaction, military commitment, or retention intention items (i.e., the outcomes) if they indicate in the survey that the service member has separated. To be included in this analysis, a service member had to have (a) experienced a study deployment, (b) reported a valid response to at least one of the military integration outcomes, and (c) left the military after experiencing a deployment and providing the response to the outcome(s). Given the time dimension involved (i.e., that separation occurred prior to the measure of retention intentions), the results for separation should not in any way be viewed as causal; rather, they represent the partial correlation between separation and retention intentions.

Analysis Plan

A detailed analysis plan is described in Chapter Two. *To address RQ1, descriptive trajectory models* are used to illustrate the outcomes of interest before, during, and after a study deployment. Given that predeployment, deployment, and postdeployment durations averaged eight months in our sample, the predicted means of service members, spouses, and teens are plotted in three eight-month increments. Outcomes are modeled jointly for each dyad (i.e., service member/spouse) controlling for respondent gender, age, racial/ethnic minority status, length of marriage, spouse education, spouse employment status, presence of children younger than age six in the household, rank and officer/enlisted status, number of prior combat deployments, years of service, branch, preexisting deployment trauma, and random effects at the dyad and respondent level. Teen models control for age, gender, service member's pay grade and branch, whether service members ever deployed previously, preexisting deployment trauma, and random effects at the respondent level. Survey mode (phone or web) is included as a time-varying covariate at each wave. Wald tests are used to determine the outcome of hypothesis tests. Results are presented in graphical form.

RQ2 is addressed via doubly robust propensity score–matching models with the aim of testing the "causal" impact of deployment on military integration outcomes. These models match service members, spouses, and teens who experienced a study deployment across a number of demographic and military characteristics with counterparts who did not experience a study deployment (see Appendix 7A for service members and spouses and Appendix 6A for teens). In addition to matching across these characteristics, these models also control for the characteristics shown in Table 7.3, thus making the model "doubly robust." Models are estimated separately for each type of respondent. Here, random effects models are fit separately to the service member and spouse data, which appropriately adjusted for repeated measures within each respondent using a random effect at the respondent level. Predicted mean differences in outcomes are compared across the deployed versus nondeployed groups and reported in the next section.

To address RQ3, we used random effects regression models, adjusted for repeated measures within each respondent (i.e., allowing for a random effects for each respondent), to estimate the association between the risk and resilience factors noted above and outcomes among only those service members, spouses, and teens who have experienced a study deployment. We examined communication with other military families, spouses' underemployment, length of study deployment, trauma exposure during study deployment, and separation from the military. All outcomes stem from the final three postdeployment assessments of the study for each respondent (thus necessitating a control for repeated measures). Each risk and resilience factor was added to the multivariate models one at a time, in separate models and controls for the extensive set of characteristics shown in Table 7.3.

All analyses presented in this chapter use the poststratification weights for the service member and spouse and the attrition weights for the teens, which are described in detail in Chapter Two.

Results

Research Question 1: Trajectories over the Deployment Cycle

RQ1 asks how family members' military integration changes over the deployment cycle. Figures 7.2 through 7.7 present the results of the trajectory analysis for service members, spouses, and teens for the four military integration outcomes examined in this chapter: military satisfaction, commitment, retention intentions, and military career aspirations. For each figure, we also test three global hypotheses: (1) whether the military integration outcome in question follows a flat line (i.e., no slope or no change) over the deployment cycle (RQ1a); (2) whether the trajectory is a straight line (i.e., linear slope) over the deployment cycle, and if not, whether the deployment period was significantly different from the pre- and postdeployment periods (RQ1b); and (3) whether the trajectories of different family members (i.e., service members and spouses, service members and teens, and spouses and teens) are parallel to one another over the deployment cycle (RQ1c).

Each figure depicts trajectories of the outcome in question for an eight-month period immediately prior to a deployment, eight months during a deployment, and eight months after deployment on the x-axis. As noted in Chapter Two, these are the average periods this sample of deployed families spent in each phase of deployment.

Figure 7.2 shows the trajectory for *military satisfaction* for service members and spouses. The blue lines represent the trajectories for service members and the green lines represent the trajectories for the spouses. The null hypothesis for the first test (i.e., that the line is flat over the deployment cycle) was rejected for service members (χ^2, 8 df=21.23, p=0.007), but could not be rejected for spouses (χ^2, 8 df=10.71, p=0.218). In other words, whereas there is evidence that service members' military satisfaction changes over time, there is no evidence that spouses' military satisfaction changes across the deployment cycle.

The null hypothesis for the second test is that the trajectory does not significantly differ from a straight line. The second test establishes whether a trajectory is linear or straight across

Figure 7.2
Military Satisfaction over the Deployment Cycle, Service Members and Spouses

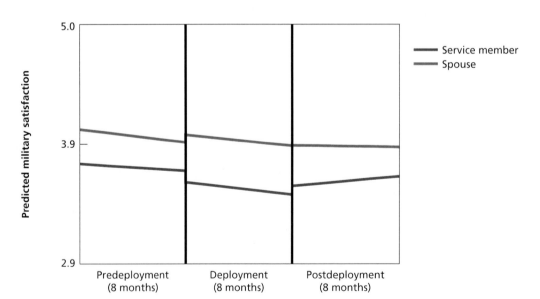

NOTES: Statistical tests show service member trajectories are significantly different from no change over time (p=0.0066); spouse trajectory is not (p=0.2184). Statistical tests also show that the service member trajectory is significantly different from a constant trend over time (p=0.0012); the spouse trajectory is not (p=0.5007). Finally, statistical tests show that the service member trajectory is not significantly different from the spouse trajectory (p=0.4989).
RAND RR1388-7.2

time periods. Again, for service members, the null hypothesis of a straight, linear slope over the deployment cycle can be rejected (χ^2, 8 df=25.63, p=0.001). For service members, post-hoc tests confirm that mean military satisfaction differs during the deployment phase relative to the pre- and postdeployment phases (χ^2, 1 df=4.21, p=0.04). It appears that service members' military satisfaction is lower during the deployment phase relative to the other phases and returns to predeployment levels after the deployment period. However, for spouses, the null cannot be rejected (χ^2, 8 df=7.34, p=0.501), reinforcing the earlier finding that we have no evidence that spouses' military satisfaction changes over the deployment cycle.

The third test examines the null hypothesis that trajectories of service members and spouses are parallel over the deployment cycle. Despite differences above, the null cannot be rejected (χ^2, 8 df=7.35, p=0.499) for RQ3; thus, there is no evidence of a significant difference in the way in which service members' and spouses' trajectories change over the deployment cycle.

Figure 7.3 shows the trajectory for *military commitment* for service members and spouses over the deployment cycle. For Figure 7.3, statistical tests indicated that the trajectory slope is not a flat line across the deployment cycle for service members (χ^2, 8 df=37.07, p=0.000) or spouses (χ^2, 8 df=40.17, p=0.000). In addition, whereas we have no significant evidence that the spouse trajectory does not differ from a straight or linear line across time periods (χ^2, 8 df=11.64, p=0.168), the service member trajectory does differ (χ^2, 8 df=23.15, p=0.003), indicating that the slope of service members' military commitment changes across periods in the deployment cycle. The lack of statistical significance for spouses on this test suggests that, although there is evidence that military commitment changes significantly over time for

Figure 7.3
Military Commitment over the Deployment Cycle, Service Members and Spouses

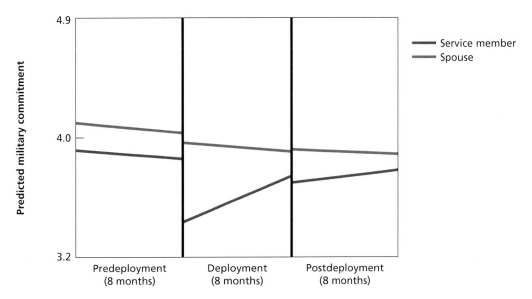

NOTES: Statistical tests show that the service member and spouse trajectories are significantly different from no change over time (p=0.0000 for both). Statistical tests also show that the service member trajectory is significantly different from a constant trend over time (p=0.0032); the spouse trajectory is not (p=0.1679). Finally, statistical tests show that the service member trajectory is not significantly different from spouse trajectory (p=0.3909).
RAND RR1388-7.3

spouses, there is no significant evidence that these changes are tied to the deployment cycle, as opposed to just a constant trend over time. Post-hoc tests suggest that the mean during the deployment period is only marginally different from the mean during the other, non-deployment periods for service members (χ^2, 1 *df*=3.05, *p*=0.081). Moreover, despite the slight differences noted above, we failed to reject the null hypothesis that the trajectories for service members and spouses are parallel (χ^2, 8 *df*=8.45, *p*=0.391), indicating no significant difference in the way in which service members' and spouses' trajectories change over the deployment cycle.

Figure 7.4 shows the military commitment trajectories for teens. Statistical tests indicated that there is no evidence of significant changes across the deployment cycle for teens (χ^2, 8 *df*=11.36, *p*=0.182). In addition, the teen trajectory does not differ significantly from a straight line (χ^2, 8 *df*=7.32, *p*=0.503), reiterating that we have no evidence that military commitment changes across phases of the deployment cycle for teens in our sample.

Figure 7.5 shows trajectories for retention intentions for service members and spouses over the deployment cycle.[6] Statistical tests indicated that we can reject the null hypothesis that the trajectory is a flat line, with zero slope for service members (χ^2, 8 *df*=37.32, *p*=0.000) and spouses (χ^2, 8 *df*=44.04, *p*=0.000). In addition, both the service member (χ^2, 8 *df*=25.98, *p*=0.01) and spouse (χ^2, 8 *df*=28.36, *p*=0.001) trajectories differ from a straight (or linear) line, indicating that both slopes differ across periods in the deployment cycle. Post-hoc tests confirm that mean retention intentions differ during the deployment phase relative to the other phases for both service members (χ^2, 1 *df*=5.89, *p*=0.02) and spouses (χ^2, 1 *df*=6.14, *p*=0.01). From

Figure 7.4
Military Commitment over the Deployment Cycle, Teens

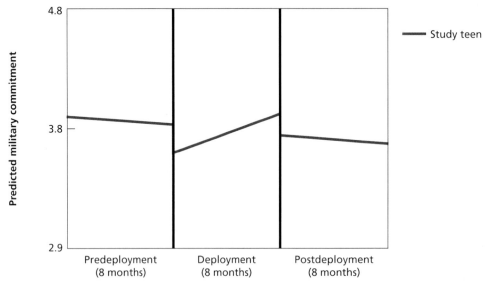

NOTES: Statistical tests show that the trajectory is not significantly different from no change over time (*p*=0.1821). Statistical tests also show that the trajectory is not significantly different from a constant trend over time (*p*=0.5030).
RAND RR1388-7.4

---

[6]   To verify the robustness of the test, we also tested a logged version of retention intentions. The results did not change, so we proceeded to interpret the standard results.

Figure 7.5
Retention Intentions over the Deployment Cycle, Service Members and Spouses

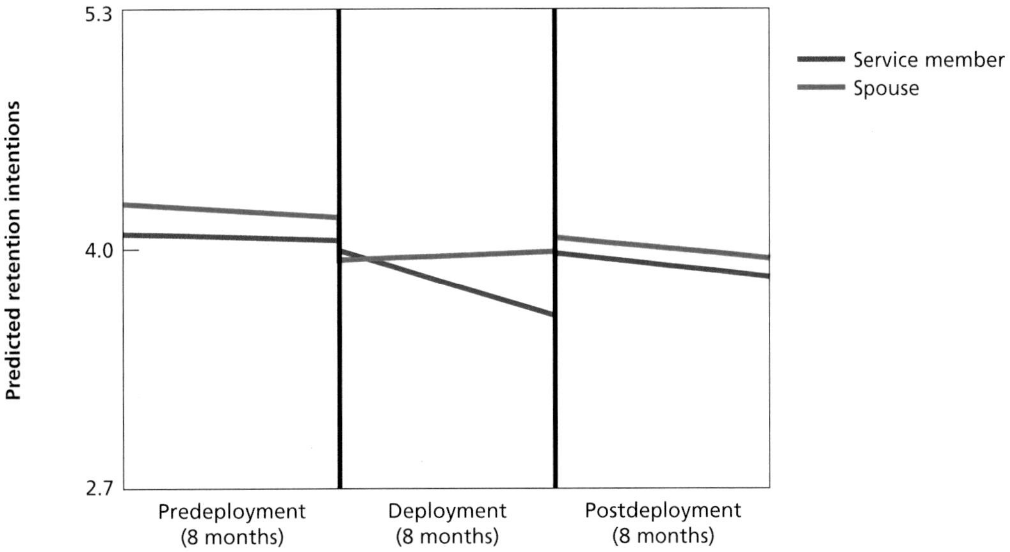

NOTES: Statistical tests show that the service member and spouse trajectories are significantly different from no change over time (p=0.0000 for both). Statistical tests also show that the service member (p=0.0011) and spouse (p=0.0004) trajectories are significantly different from a constant trend over time. Finally, statistical tests show that the service member trajectory is not significantly different from the spouse trajectory (p=0.4608).
RAND RR1388-7.5

the figure, it appears that retention intentions are significantly lower during the deployment phase, relative to the other phases, for both service members and spouses but appear to return to predeployment levels upon return from deployment. For the final hypothesis test, we cannot reject the null that service member and spouse trajectories are parallel (χ^2, 8 df=7.72, p=0.461), indicating no significant difference in the way in which service member and spouse trajectories change over the deployment cycle.

Figure 7.6 shows the retention intentions trajectories for teens. Statistical tests indicated no evidence that the trajectory changes across the deployment cycle for teens (χ^2, 8 df=9.21, p=0.325). In addition, teen trajectories do not differ from a straight (or linear) line, indicating that slopes are not different across phases of the deployment cycle (χ^2, 8 df=8.82, p=0.358). Thus, we have no evidence that retention intentions change across phases of the deployment cycle for teens in our sample.

Figure 7.7 shows the trajectory for teen military career aspirations over the deployment cycle. Statistical tests indicated that the trajectory shows no evidence of a significant change across the deployment cycle for teens (χ^2, 8 df=12.08, p=0.148). In addition, the teen trajectory does not differ from a straight (or linear) line (χ^2, 8 df=11.65, p=0.167). Thus, we have no evidence suggesting that teen military career aspirations change over the course of the deployment cycle.

Research Question 2: Impact of Deployment

RQ2 explores whether deployment affects family members' postdeployment military integration outcomes using a doubly robust matched comparison approach. Table 7.5 presents the

Figure 7.6
Retention Intentions over the Deployment Cycle, Teens

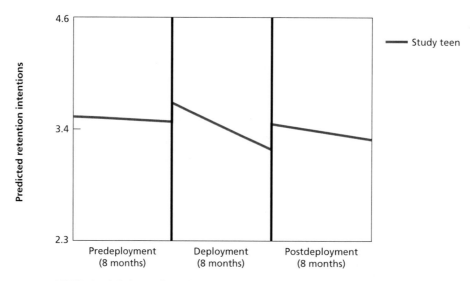

NOTES: Statistical tests show that the trajectory is not significantly different from no change over time ($p=0.3251$). Statistical tests also show that the trajectory is not significantly different from a constant trend over time ($p=0.3575$).
RAND *RR1388-7.6*

Figure 7.7
Military Career Aspirations over the Deployment Cycle, Teens

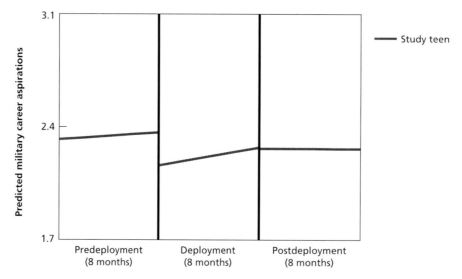

NOTES: Statistical tests show that the teen trajectory is not significantly different from no change over time ($p=0.1475$). Statistical tests also show that the teen trajectory is not significantly different from a constant trend over time ($p=0.1674$).
RAND *RR1388-7.7*

Table 7.5
Predicted Mean Differences and Standard Errors of Military Integration Outcomes by Study Deployment Status

	Service Members		Spouses		Teens	
	Study Deployment	No Study Deployment	Study Deployment	No Study Deployment	Study Deployment	No Study Deployment
Military Satisfaction	3.80 (0.05)	3.84 (0.05)	3.97 (0.05)	4.06 (0.03)	—	—
Military Commitment	3.95 (0.04)	3.98 (0.04)	3.98 (0.04)	4.06 (0.03)	3.73 (0.08)	3.69 (0.10)
Retention Intentions	3.87 (0.06)	3.80 (0.06)	3.93 (0.05)	3.98 (0.04)	3.33 (0.11)	3.06 (0.11)
Military Career Intentions	—	—	—	—	2.43 (0.07)	2.56 (0.06)

NOTE: Standard errors are presented in parentheses.

* $p<0.05$; ** $p<0.01$; *** $p<0.001$ when comparing means of study deployment versus no study deployment groups.

predicted means for each of the military integration outcomes we examined among service members, spouses, and teens.[7] As shown, the predicted military integration means do not differ between families in which service members deployed during the study and those who did not.[8] Thus, study deployments do not appear to have negatively or positively affected post-deployment military integration in this sample of active component, nondivorced families.

One explanation for the lack of differences may be that the families who do not deploy are experiencing different stressors at home that deployed families are not experiencing. For example, we found that family relocation was significantly negatively associated with the military integration outcomes for service members, marginally associated for two outcomes for spouses, and not significant for teens. Specifically, relocation predicted lower military satisfaction ($\beta=-0.34$, $p=0.00$), military commitment ($\beta=-0.51$, $p=0.02$), and retention intentions ($\beta=-0.54$, $p=0.04$) for service members and marginally lower military satisfaction ($\beta=-0.16$, $p=0.06$) and commitment ($\beta=-0.13$, $p=0.06$) for spouses. Given that 71.2 percent of nondeployed families relocated during the study, the nondeployment stress of uprooting relationships with friends and family, spouses' employment, and children's academic curriculum may mask group differences.

Research Question 3: Risk and Resilience Factors

RQ3 examines a set of random effects regression models, adjusted for repeated measures within each respondent (i.e., allowing for a random effects for each respondent), to estimate the association between the risk and resilience factors and outcomes among only those service members and spouses who have experienced a study deployment. We examine communication with other military families, spouses' underemployment, length of study deployment, and trauma

---

[7]   Here, the sample size for teens is 240 (130 without a study deployment and 110 with a study deployment).

[8]   To test the robustness of the results, the data were re-analyzed excluding the families in which service members separated from the military. Spouses' military satisfaction and retention intentions became significant with p-values of 0.030 and 0.049, respectively, such that spouses reported lower levels of retention intentions and job satisfaction when service members were deployed. However, given the marginal significance and that none of the other factors were sensitive to the change, we are hesitant to interpret these findings.

exposure during study deployment. Table 7.6 presents the results of a series of multivariate models run separately for service members, spouses, and teens for each outcome.

Several of the factors examined in Table 7.6 show a significant association with post-deployment family functioning. It is important to interpret these results cautiously, given the number of statistical tests examined in the analyses. First, service members who report that their families engaged in communication with other military families report higher retention intentions ($\beta=0.30$, $p=0.046$) than those who report no communication with other military families. In addition, spouses ($\beta=0.28$, $p=0.00$) and teens ($\beta=0.48$, $p=0.01$) who report that their families engaged in communication with other military families report higher military commitment than those who report no communication with other military families. Second, as expected, service members who experienced more physical ($\beta=-0.43$) or psychological ($\beta=-0.30$) trauma during the study deployment reported significantly lower military satisfaction than those who report less trauma ($p=0.00$). Further, service members who experienced more collective trauma during the study deployment reported significantly lower retention intentions ($p=0.01$) relative to those who report less collective trauma. Surprisingly, service members' combat trauma was associated with teens' higher military commitment ($\beta=0.97$, $p=0.03$). In contrast, and consistent with our expectations, service members' psychological trauma predicted lower retention intentions for teens ($\beta=-0.62$, $p=0.05$). Third, and perhaps not surprisingly, service members who eventually separate from the military after a study deployment reported significantly lower military satisfaction ($\beta=-0.39$, $p=0.01$), military commitment ($\beta=-0.29$, $p=0.03$), and retention intentions ($\beta=-1.55$, $p=0.00$) prior to separation than those who did not separate. Likewise, spouses of service members who eventually separated reported significantly lower military commitment ($\beta=-0.54$, $p=0.00$) and retention intentions ($\beta=-0.47$, $p=0.02$) prior to the separation event. However, we caution that these results should not in any way be interpreted as causal, given that separation occurred prior to the outcomes (i.e., future separation does not predict past retention intentions). The results presented here reflect partial correlations between separation and military commitment.

Discussion

This chapter expands previous research on families' military integration through the use of longitudinal data following multiple reporters, matched comparisons inferring the causal effect of deployment on family members' military integration, and an examination of teens' military integration. Results highlight variability within and between family members over time. For example, the results of the trajectory models revealed significant variability in service members' military integration over the deployment cycle, and notably more variability than in the trajectories for spouses' and teens' military integration. There was no evidence of significant changes over time for teens. When there were changes in aspects of military integration during deployment, families appeared to adapt well and return to predeployment levels in the post-deployment period. None of the dyadic comparisons between spouses and service members showed significant differences between family members.

The lack of findings for deployment on family members' military integration provides additional support for the remarkable resilience of military families over the deployment cycle. It may be the case that deployment is not as challenging for families as previous studies have suggested, or it may be that the experienced families—those that have been in the military

Table 7.6
Regression Coefficients (p-values) of Risk and Resilience Factors (Study Deployment Sample Only)

		Service Members			Spouses			Teens		
		Military Satisfaction	Military Commitment	Retention Intentions	Military Satisfaction	Military Commitment	Retention Intentions	Military Commitment	Retention Intentions	Military Career Aspirations
Communication with Other Military Families[a]	Coefficient	0.21	0.07	0.30*	0.22	0.28***	0.19	0.48*	0.26	-0.17
	p-value	0.11	0.42	0.05	0.06	0.00	0.13	0.01	0.35	0.33
Spouses' Underemployment[b]	Coefficient	-0.09	-0.01	-0.28	-0.12	-0.39	0.13	0.62	-1.19	-0.36
	p-value	0.99	0.94	0.37	0.69	0.24	0.61	0.08	0.10	0.45
Length of Study Deployment[c]	Coefficient	-0.02	-0.01	-0.01	-0.03	-0.02	-0.02	0.01	0.03	-0.03
	p-value	0.31	0.35	0.72	0.05	0.20	0.31	0.80	0.47	0.20
Military Separation[d]	Coefficient	-0.39**	-0.29*	-1.55***	0.03	-0.54**	-0.47*	-0.18	-0.07	0.08
	p-value	0.01	0.03	0.00	0.84	0.00	0.02	0.47	0.83	0.64
Trauma Exposure During Study Deployment (%)										
Physical	Coefficient	-0.43*	-0.24	-0.32	-0.21	-0.27	-0.24	0.20	-0.3	-0.11
Psychological	Coefficient	-0.30*	0.06	-0.24	-0.11	0.03	0.02	-0.24	-0.62*	0.18
Combat	Coefficient	-0.09	-0.05	-0.18	-0.14	-0.07	-0.02	0.97*	0.70	0.17
	Joint F-Test p-value	0.00	0.29	0.01	0.20	0.12	0.58	0.03	0.05	0.50

NOTE: For trauma exposure during study deployment, a joint f-test p-value is presented; For individual coefficients, significance is shown only when the joint test has p-value<0.05.

[a] Range: 0 (no communication with other military families) or 1 (communication with other military families).

[b] Spouse range: 0 (not looking for work) or 1 (unemployed, looking for work).

[c] In months.

[d] Includes both separation (involuntary and voluntary) and retirement.

* p<0.05; ** p<0.01; *** p<0.001 when comparing means of study deployment versus no study deployment groups.

for ten years—are more adept at navigating the stresses of deployment than would have been the case in a less-experienced sample. Another explanation suggests that because nondeployed families are much more likely to relocate, it may be that the stress of relocation masks differences between deployed and nondeployed families. Although relocation may be beneficial in some cases, frequent relocation may undermine family members' communication with other military families, spouses' employment prospects, and children's academic curriculum (Segal, Lane, and Fisher, 2015). Alternatively, had our sample experienced deployments more typical of those earlier in Iraq or Afghanistan (12+ months), we might have seen more-negative effects of deployment.

Among families in which service members deployed, we examined factors anticipated to predict more or less resilience in military integration over the deployment cycle. Identifying intervening factors associated with military integration is essential to inform programs and policies aimed at promoting long-term retention behavior. First, we found that communication with other military families was positively associated with service members' retention intentions and spouses' and teens' military commitment. Our findings support previous research that found that communication with other military families is particularly beneficial for spouses (Nichols et al., 2014; Rosen and Moghadam, 1990), although neither this research nor ours is able to address the issue of reverse causality (i.e., families that function better communicate more). However, to our knowledge, this study is the first to examine this communication with other military families among military children and service members. The protective effect of this factor for all family members highlights an important avenue for intervention and that it may be worthwhile to expand support groups for all family members. Second, with the exception of one test, trauma experienced during the study deployment was a risk factor for service members' military satisfaction and service members' and teens' retention intentions. The contradictory test found that service members' combat trauma during deployment predicted higher military commitment for teens. However, as discussed previously, without corrections for the number of tests, single findings that contradict the rest of results may be due to chance and should not be overinterpreted. Thus, despite one contradictory finding, the overall results suggest that making service members more resilient to trauma or reducing their exposure is important for protecting family members' military integration.

Taken together, the results demonstrate that family members (especially service members) experience changes over the deployment cycle, highlighting the importance of including multiple family members. In addition, Deployment Life Study families appear remarkably resilient to the stress of deployment, but also may benefit from programs that promote communication with other military families and trauma prevention (and coping) services.

Strengths and Limitations

Strengths of this study include the longitudinal examination over the deployment cycle (before, during, and after deployment), reports from (a representative sample of) multiple reporters within families (i.e., service members, spouses, teens), and the advanced statistical techniques that enable the examination of the causal (or quasicausal) impact of deployment on families' military integration. Despite these strengths, several methodological and design limitations should also be taken into consideration. First, the use of survey methodology for all study constructs introduces several biases inherent to self-reports, such as forgetfulness or social desirability biases (i.e., trying to present oneself in a more positive light, or under- or over-reporting of symptoms of psychological stress or distress). Second, selective attrition, both among families that experienced a study deployment and those that did not, could have affected our results, especially if those families that cease participation are worse off on the outcomes examined in this chapter. We found some evidence that families that leave the military during the study period have lower levels of commitment postdeployment, but preseparation. Thus, it is not unreasonable to think that families that attrit from the study also have lower levels of military integration. Third, that same sort of selectivity potentially affected the beginning of the survey: Clearly, we had an experienced sample of military families in our study; most had experienced a deployment before. In addition, we included only active component and nondivorced families in these analyses. These experiences no doubt were associated with how families addressed the study deployment that we observed. We did not have a large enough sample of first-time deployers to examine them separately, but future work should seek to address how these families adapt to their first deployment experience. Finally, although we agree with previous work highlighting the importance of examining the intersections of military career (e.g., deployment, promotion, relocation) and family life (e.g., birth of a child) at specific points in time (Segal, Lane, and Fisher, 2015), we were not able to examine the interaction of these events in our data. These strengths and limitations will be discussed further in Chapter Eight.

Policy Implications

Because it is much easier to target families' military integration than to change their actual retention behavior, it is worthwhile to establish a deeper understanding of the factors underlying retention behavior. Based on the results of this chapter, families' connectedness to the military is higher when families engage with other military families. These relationships are likely to help family members share important emotional, instrumental, and informational resources and to develop strong ties within the military community. Indeed, *programs that facilitate communication between (and social events for) members of military families* are likely to promote not only greater military integration, but also better outcomes across the domains highlighted in this report. In addition, given the negative association between relocation and family members' military integration, frequent relocation may also be considered a risk factor for military integration and potentially military separation, although it was not the primary objective of our analysis to tease out the impact of this specific stressor. *Efforts to minimize the number of relocations families experience, and perhaps the costs on family members' relationships with other military families and spouses' employment,* are likely to be beneficial for families' military integration. Finally, as discussed in earlier chapters, *efforts to help service members (and their family members) access targeted prevention and coping programs that help deal with trauma* are likely to be very important for families' military integration.

Although beyond the scope of the current study's data, future research should examine whether military integration is related to service members' long-term retention decisions and teens' future enlistment decisions. Future research also should examine how aspects of military integration are related and provide support for the directions of the associations (e.g., whether commitment predicts higher retention intentions over time). In addition, despite some variability in military integration, the construct was relatively stable over time. Future research should examine whether military integration at the point of enlistment predicts mid- or late-career military integration. If this is the case, it could be worthwhile early on to target the recruitment and retention of those individuals likely to maintain high military integration over time. Finally, research should examine how interactions between military and family life events shape families' military integration both during deployment and throughout a family's military life course (see Segal, Lane, and Fisher, 2015).

Appendix 7A: Balance Tables and Plots

Tables 7A.1 and 7A.2 present balance statistics for service members and spouses, respectively.[9] Each table compares standardized mean differences (SMDs) across a number of key study variables for service members and spouses who do and do not experience a study deployment. SMDs are presented before and after applying propensity score weights. Generally, SMDs under 0.20 (or above −0.20) indicate good balance across groups.

Figures 7A.1 and 7A.2 present the balance plots for service members and spouses, respectively, who did and did not experience a study deployment.[10] Each dot on the plot represents a variable in Tables 7A.1 and 7A.2. The left side of each plot depicts absolute standard mean differences (ASMDs) before applying propensity score weights, while the right side of each plot depicts ASMDs after applying the propensity score weights. As can be seen in both figures, once the weights are applied, ASMDs between service members and spouses who do and do not experience a study deployment fall below the cutoff of 0.20 ASMDs.

---

[9] A balance table for teens can be found in Chapter Six (see Table 6A.3).

[10] A balance plot for teens can be found in Chapter 6 (see Figure 6A.3).

Table 7A.1
Weighted Balance Table: Service Members (Study Deployment Versus No Study Deployment)

| | Unweighted | | | | | Weighted | | | | |
| | Study Deployment | | No Study Deployment | | | Study Deployment | | No Study Deployment | | |
SERVICE MEMBER VARIABLES	Mean	SD	Mean	SD	SMD	Mean	SD	Mean	SD	SMD
Female	0.08	0.26	0.14	0.34	-0.23	0.08	0.26	0.08	0.27	-0.01
Age	31.46	6.15	32.85	6.72	-0.23	31.46	6.15	32.20	6.44	-0.12
Minority Race/Ethnicity	0.34	0.47	0.37	0.48	-0.08	0.34	0.47	0.30	0.46	0.09
Children Younger Than Age 6	0.55	0.50	0.49	0.50	0.12	0.55	0.50	0.50	0.50	0.09
Paygrade: Junior Enlisted	0.05	0.21	0.04	0.20	0.02	0.05	0.21	0.04	0.20	0.03
Paygrade: Junior Officer	0.12	0.33	0.11	0.31	0.04	0.12	0.33	0.13	0.34	-0.04
Paygrade: Mid and Senior Enlisted	0.68	0.47	0.74	0.44	-0.14	0.68	0.47	0.70	0.46	-0.05
Paygrade: Mid and Senior Officer	0.08	0.28	0.09	0.28	-0.01	0.08	0.28	0.10	0.30	-0.06
Paygrade: Warrant Officer	0.07	0.25	0.02	0.14	0.19	0.07	0.25	0.02	0.15	0.18
Length of Marriage (Months)	85.91	64.75	91.16	70.73	-0.08	85.91	64.75	88.58	66.41	-0.04
Parents in the Military	0.51	0.50	0.50	0.50	0.03	0.51	0.50	0.48	0.50	0.07
Total Number of Prior Deployments	2.11	1.32	1.40	1.32	0.54	2.11	1.32	1.96	1.26	0.12
Years of Service	10.80	6.22	11.59	7.08	-0.13	10.80	6.22	11.28	6.55	-0.08
Army	0.41	0.49	0.39	0.49	0.05	0.41	0.49	0.44	0.50	-0.06
Navy	0.24	0.43	0.26	0.44	-0.05	0.24	0.43	0.32	0.47	-0.18
Air Force	0.22	0.42	0.24	0.43	-0.05	0.22	0.42	0.18	0.38	0.11
Marine Corps	0.12	0.33	0.10	0.31	0.06	0.12	0.33	0.06	0.24	0.18
Reserve Component	—	—	—	—	—	—	—	—	—	—
Hoge CES	4.79	4.49	4.11	4.20	0.15	4.79	4.49	4.35	4.15	0.10
Preexisting Deployment Trauma	2.25	2.43	1.72	2.57	0.22	2.25	2.43	2.04	2.46	0.09
Marital Satisfaction Scale	4.02	0.42	3.91	0.49	0.27	4.02	0.42	4.01	0.42	0.04
Positive and Negative Affect Schedule (PANAS): Positive	4.28	0.61	4.15	0.68	0.20	4.28	0.61	4.25	0.59	0.05
PANAS: Negative	1.90	0.50	2.07	0.62	-0.32	1.90	0.50	1.94	0.52	-0.07

Table 7.A1—Continued

	Unweighted					Weighted				
	Study Deployment		No Study Deployment			Study Deployment		No Study Deployment		
	Mean	SD	Mean	SD	SMD	Mean	SD	Mean	SD	SMD
Conflict Tactics Scale: Prevalence of Physical Aggression Toward Partner	0.02	0.13	0.02	0.13	0.01	0.02	0.13	0.02	0.13	0.00
Conflict Tactics Scale: Chronicity of Psychological Aggression Toward Partner	0.63	0.87	0.82	0.94	-0.22	0.63	0.87	0.65	0.86	-0.02
Conflict Tactics Scale: Prevalence of Physical Aggression Toward You	0.05	0.22	0.05	0.23	-0.02	0.05	0.22	0.05	0.21	0.01
Conflict Tactics Scale: Chronicity of Psychological Aggression Toward You	0.69	0.99	0.94	1.06	-0.25	0.69	0.99	0.70	0.96	-0.01
Depressive Symptoms	2.42	2.95	3.13	3.89	-0.24	2.42	2.95	2.52	3.25	-0.03
Anxiety	2.02	1.00	2.25	1.06	-0.23	2.02	1.00	2.07	1.00	-0.05
PTSD	4.41	8.06	5.71	10.32	-0.16	4.41	8.06	4.44	8.54	0.00
Traumatic Brain Injury (TBI)	0.13	0.33	0.11	0.32	0.05	0.13	0.33	0.10	0.30	0.08
Binge Drinking	0.27	0.45	0.32	0.47	-0.11	0.27	0.45	0.28	0.45	-0.01
Problematic Substance Use Scale	0.14	0.49	0.19	0.64	-0.11	0.14	0.49	0.16	0.56	-0.05
Medication for Mental Health Problem	0.03	0.17	0.06	0.24	-0.18	0.03	0.17	0.03	0.18	-0.02
Received Mental Health Care	0.08	0.26	0.18	0.39	-0.41	0.08	0.26	0.11	0.31	-0.11
Financial Distress Scale	1.74	0.60	1.93	0.70	-0.32	1.74	0.60	1.78	0.62	-0.07
Family Environment Scale (FES)	2.82	0.23	2.73	0.32	0.38	2.82	0.23	2.82	0.24	-0.02
Parenting Satisfaction	3.35	0.36	3.31	0.44	0.09	3.35	0.36	3.32	0.38	0.07
Military Commitment	4.39	0.64	4.32	0.71	0.10	4.39	0.64	4.33	0.66	0.09
Job Satisfaction	3.93	0.96	3.65	1.03	0.29	3.93	0.96	3.81	0.99	0.12
Retention Intentions	4.23	1.22	4.13	1.35	0.08	4.23	1.22	4.13	1.32	0.08
SPOUSE VARIABLES										
Marital Satisfaction Scale	4.01	0.49	3.85	0.54	0.33	4.01	0.49	3.95	0.49	0.12
PANAS: Positive	4.27	0.65	4.15	0.72	0.19	4.27	0.65	4.21	0.63	0.09
PANAS: Negative	1.98	0.59	2.09	0.60	-0.18	1.98	0.59	2.04	0.59	-0.10
Conflict Tactics Scale: Prevalence of Physical Aggression Toward Partner	0.05	0.21	0.07	0.25	-0.09	0.05	0.21	0.05	0.23	-0.03

Table 7.A1—Continued

	Unweighted					Weighted				
	Study Deployment		No Study Deployment			Study Deployment		No Study Deployment		
	Mean	SD	Mean	SD	SMD	Mean	SD	Mean	SD	SMD
Conflict Tactics Scale: Chronicity of Psychological Aggression Toward Partner	0.71	0.88	0.74	0.94	-0.03	0.71	0.88	0.72	0.91	-0.01
Conflict Tactics Scale: Prevalence of Physical Aggression Toward You	0.01	0.12	0.02	0.14	-0.05	0.01	0.12	0.02	0.13	-0.02
Conflict Tactics Scale: Chronicity of Psychological Aggression Toward You	0.59	0.85	0.73	0.95	-0.17	0.59	0.85	0.64	0.90	-0.06
Depressive Symptoms	2.74	3.74	2.91	3.51	-0.05	2.74	3.74	2.99	3.62	-0.07
Anxiety	2.05	0.95	1.96	0.89	0.10	2.05	0.95	2.10	0.99	-0.05
PTSD	0.49	1.00	0.56	0.99	-0.07	0.49	1.00	0.49	0.99	0.01
Binge Drinking	0.15	0.36	0.12	0.33	0.07	0.15	0.36	0.14	0.34	0.04
Problematic Substance Use Scale	0.08	0.44	0.07	0.43	0.03	0.08	0.44	0.08	0.45	0.01
Medication for Mental Health Problem	0.11	0.31	0.11	0.31	0.00	0.11	0.31	0.13	0.34	-0.08
Received Mental Health Care	0.14	0.34	0.13	0.34	0.02	0.14	0.34	0.15	0.36	-0.05
Financial Distress Scale	1.83	0.65	1.93	0.69	-0.16	1.83	0.65	1.84	0.68	-0.02
FES	2.86	0.22	2.81	0.23	0.21	2.86	0.22	2.85	0.22	0.05
Parenting Stress Scale	3.24	0.34	3.27	0.38	-0.09	3.24	0.34	3.23	0.38	0.02
Military Commitment	4.50	0.58	4.44	0.58	0.10	4.50	0.58	4.49	0.56	0.01
Satisfaction as Military Spouse	4.13	1.00	3.93	1.00	0.20	4.13	1.00	4.18	0.90	-0.05
Retention Intentions	4.09	1.19	3.90	1.35	0.16	4.09	1.19	4.06	1.28	0.03
TEEN VARIABLES										
Strengths and Difficulties Questionnaire (SDQ): Total	7.07	5.11	7.96	5.39	-0.18	7.07	5.11	7.53	5.29	-0.09
SDQ Subscale: Emotional Problems	1.55	1.73	1.63	1.74	-0.05	1.55	1.73	1.57	1.75	-0.01
SDQ Subscale: Conduct Problems	0.94	1.29	1.09	1.30	-0.11	0.94	1.29	0.94	1.29	0.00
SDQ Subscale: Hyperactivity	3.17	2.60	3.43	2.50	-0.10	3.17	2.60	3.42	2.55	-0.10
SDQ Subscale: Peer Relationships	1.66	1.58	1.82	1.81	-0.10	1.66	1.58	1.60	1.60	0.04
SDQ Subscale: Prosocial Behavior	8.54	1.63	8.46	1.53	0.05	8.54	1.63	8.71	1.53	-0.10
Depressive Symptoms	0.97	1.81	1.26	1.95	-0.16	0.97	1.81	1.26	1.95	-0.16
Anxiety (Screen for Child Anxiety Related Emotional Disorders [SCARED])	1.65	1.95	1.34	1.46	0.16	1.65	1.95	1.49	1.74	0.08

Table 7A.2
Weighted Balance Table: Spouses (Study Deployment Versus No Study Deployment)

	Unweighted					Weighted				
	Study Deployment		No Study Deployment			Study Deployment		No Study Deployment		
	Mean	SD	Mean	SD	SMD	Mean	SD	Mean	SD	SMD
SERVICE MEMBER VARIABLES										
Pay Grade: Junior Enlisted	0.05	0.22	0.03	0.18	0.08	0.05	0.22	0.03	0.16	0.10
Pay Grade: Junior Officer	0.12	0.32	0.11	0.31	0.02	0.12	0.32	0.11	0.32	0.01
Pay Grade: Mid and Senior Enlisted	0.70	0.46	0.74	0.44	-0.08	0.70	0.46	0.74	0.44	-0.09
Pay Grade: Mid and Senior Officer	0.09	0.29	0.10	0.29	-0.02	0.09	0.29	0.10	0.30	-0.03
Pay Grade: Warrant Officer	0.04	0.20	0.02	0.15	0.10	0.04	0.20	0.02	0.14	0.10
Length of Marriage (Months)	84.39	65.17	88.90	68.72	-0.07	84.39	65.17	88.45	66.94	-0.06
Total Number of Prior Deployments	2.11	1.24	1.51	1.29	0.49	2.11	1.24	1.95	1.22	0.14
Years of Service	10.68	6.21	11.26	6.99	-0.09	10.68	6.21	11.32	6.68	-0.10
Army	0.41	0.49	0.38	0.48	0.07	0.41	0.49	0.43	0.50	-0.04
Navy	0.25	0.43	0.26	0.44	-0.03	0.25	0.43	0.30	0.46	-0.12
Air Force	0.23	0.42	0.25	0.43	-0.04	0.23	0.42	0.20	0.40	0.07
Marine Corps	0.11	0.32	0.12	0.32	-0.01	0.11	0.32	0.07	0.26	0.14
Reserve Component	—	—	—	—	—	—	—	—	—	—
Hoge CES	4.79	4.53	3.94	4.14	0.19	4.79	4.53	4.42	4.23	0.08
Preexisting Deployment Trauma	2.36	2.54	1.79	2.53	0.22	2.36	2.54	2.09	2.48	0.11
Marital Satisfaction Scale	4.01	0.43	3.94	0.49	0.18	4.01	0.43	4.01	0.44	0.00
PANAS: Positive	4.29	0.61	4.16	0.67	0.23	4.29	0.61	4.24	0.60	0.09
PANAS: Negative	1.92	0.54	2.02	0.60	-0.18	1.92	0.54	1.94	0.53	-0.03
Conflict Tactics Scale: Prevalence of Physical Aggression Toward Partner	0.02	0.15	0.02	0.14	0.03	0.02	0.15	0.02	0.13	0.04
Conflict Tactics Scale: Chronicity of Psychological Aggression Toward Partner	0.66	0.88	0.80	0.92	-0.16	0.66	0.88	0.64	0.87	0.02
Conflict Tactics Scale: Prevalence of Physical Aggression Toward You	0.05	0.22	0.06	0.23	-0.03	0.05	0.22	0.05	0.22	0.00
Conflict Tactics Scale: Chronicity of Psychological Aggression Toward You	0.71	1.00	0.90	1.06	-0.19	0.71	1.00	0.70	0.99	0.01

Table 7.A2—Continued

	Unweighted					Weighted				
	Study Deployment		No Study Deployment		SMD	Study Deployment		No Study Deployment		SMD
	Mean	SD	Mean	SD		Mean	SD	Mean	SD	
Depressive Symptoms	2.40	2.98	2.95	3.69	−0.19	2.40	2.98	2.47	3.26	−0.02
Anxiety	2.02	1.02	2.21	1.04	−0.18	2.02	1.02	2.05	0.98	−0.02
PTSD	4.38	7.83	5.57	10.17	−0.15	4.38	7.83	4.48	8.37	−0.01
TBI	0.15	0.36	0.11	0.31	0.12	0.15	0.36	0.11	0.31	0.11
Binge Drinking	0.31	0.46	0.28	0.45	0.06	0.31	0.46	0.25	0.43	0.12
Problematic Substance Use Scale	0.19	0.65	0.18	0.62	0.01	0.19	0.65	0.15	0.57	0.06
Medication for Mental Health Problem	0.04	0.20	0.06	0.24	−0.11	0.04	0.20	0.04	0.20	0.01
Received Mental Health Care	0.08	0.27	0.17	0.38	−0.35	0.08	0.27	0.11	0.31	−0.10
Financial Distress Scale	1.79	0.64	1.90	0.70	−0.16	1.79	0.64	1.81	0.64	−0.04
FES	2.79	0.25	2.75	0.29	0.15	2.79	0.25	2.81	0.25	−0.09
Parenting Satisfaction	3.33	0.37	3.33	0.41	−0.01	3.33	0.37	3.32	0.38	0.00
Military Commitment	4.40	0.62	4.30	0.68	0.15	4.40	0.62	4.35	0.65	0.09
Job Satisfaction	3.96	0.93	3.66	1.02	0.32	3.96	0.93	3.83	0.97	0.14
Retention Intentions	4.14	1.28	4.04	1.39	0.07	4.14	1.28	4.13	1.32	0.00
SPOUSE VARIABLES										
Female	0.94	0.25	0.86	0.35	0.30	0.94	0.25	0.93	0.26	0.04
Age	30.89	6.80	31.84	6.92	−0.14	30.89	6.80	31.53	6.81	−0.09
Minority Race/Ethnicity	0.31	0.46	0.37	0.48	−0.12	0.31	0.46	0.31	0.46	0.00
Children Younger Than Age 6	0.52	0.50	0.48	0.50	0.09	0.52	0.50	0.51	0.50	0.02
Education: Less than High School	0.01	0.09	0.01	0.12	−0.07	0.01	0.09	0.02	0.12	−0.09
Education: High School	0.18	0.39	0.19	0.39	−0.01	0.18	0.39	0.18	0.39	0.01
Education: Some College	0.29	0.46	0.31	0.46	−0.04	0.29	0.46	0.28	0.45	0.03
Education: Degree	0.19	0.40	0.15	0.35	0.12	0.19	0.40	0.17	0.38	0.06
Education: Bachelor's Degree	0.25	0.44	0.28	0.45	−0.06	0.25	0.44	0.28	0.45	−0.05
Education: Graduate School or Professional Degree	0.07	0.25	0.06	0.24	0.02	0.07	0.25	0.08	0.27	−0.04

Table 7.A2—Continued

| | Unweighted | | | | | Weighted | | | | |
| | Study Deployment | | No Study Deployment | | SMD | Study Deployment | | No Study Deployment | | SMD |
	Mean	SD	Mean	SD		Mean	SD	Mean	SD	
Employment: Other	0.06	0.23	0.10	0.30	-0.20	0.06	0.23	0.06	0.24	-0.02
Employment: Employed	0.26	0.44	0.31	0.46	-0.12	0.26	0.44	0.30	0.46	-0.09
Employment: Homemaker	0.45	0.50	0.37	0.48	0.15	0.45	0.50	0.42	0.49	0.06
Employment: Student	0.08	0.27	0.10	0.30	-0.06	0.08	0.27	0.08	0.28	-0.01
Employment: Not Employed	0.16	0.37	0.12	0.32	0.11	0.16	0.37	0.14	0.35	0.05
Marital Satisfaction Scale	3.97	0.52	3.86	0.54	0.20	3.97	0.52	3.93	0.50	0.07
PANAS: Positive	4.21	0.65	4.11	0.71	0.17	4.21	0.65	4.19	0.64	0.04
PANAS: Negative	2.07	0.61	2.10	0.60	-0.04	2.07	0.61	2.05	0.59	0.04
Conflict Tactics Scale: Prevalence of Physical Aggression Toward Partner	0.07	0.25	0.06	0.25	0.01	0.07	0.25	0.05	0.22	0.05
Conflict Tactics Scale: Chronicity of Psychological Aggression Toward Partner	0.72	0.89	0.70	0.94	0.02	0.72	0.89	0.68	0.90	0.05
Conflict Tactics Scale: Prevalence of Physical Aggression Toward You	0.02	0.13	0.03	0.16	-0.09	0.02	0.13	0.02	0.15	-0.07
Conflict Tactics Scale: Chronicity of Psychological Aggression Toward You	0.58	0.87	0.74	0.94	-0.18	0.58	0.87	0.62	0.89	-0.04
Depressive Symptoms	2.94	3.76	2.91	3.54	0.01	2.94	3.76	2.95	3.61	0.00
Anxiety	2.08	0.92	2.01	0.93	0.07	2.08	0.92	2.07	0.97	0.01
PTSD	0.51	1.02	0.50	0.96	0.01	0.51	1.02	0.47	0.99	0.04
Binge Drinking	0.15	0.36	0.11	0.31	0.11	0.15	0.36	0.12	0.32	0.09
Problematic Substance Use Scale	0.11	0.57	0.06	0.41	0.09	0.11	0.57	0.07	0.40	0.08
Medication for Mental Health Problem	0.11	0.31	0.12	0.33	-0.04	0.11	0.31	0.14	0.35	-0.09
Received Mental Health Care	0.13	0.34	0.14	0.34	-0.01	0.13	0.34	0.16	0.36	-0.07
Financial Distress Scale	1.86	0.68	1.90	0.68	-0.05	1.86	0.68	1.89	0.68	-0.04
FES	2.84	0.25	2.82	0.23	0.07	2.84	0.25	2.84	0.23	-0.02
Parenting Stress Scale	3.23	0.35	3.26	0.38	-0.06	3.23	0.35	3.24	0.37	-0.01

Table 7.A2—Continued

| | Unweighted | | | | | | Weighted | | | | | |
| | Study Deployment | | No Study Deployment | | | | Study Deployment | | No Study Deployment | | | |
	Mean	SD	Mean	SD	SMD		Mean	SD	Mean	SD	SMD	
Parent(s) in the Military	0.38	0.49	0.49	0.50	−0.22		0.38	0.49	0.44	0.50	−0.12	
Military Commitment	4.49	0.60	4.39	0.62	0.17		4.49	0.60	4.48	0.57	0.03	
Satisfaction as Military Spouse	4.10	1.03	3.98	0.99	0.12		4.10	1.03	4.14	0.91	−0.04	
Retention Intentions	4.13	1.14	3.81	1.39	0.27		4.13	1.14	4.05	1.26	0.07	
TEEN VARIABLES												
SDQ: Total	7.02	4.85	7.92	5.60	−0.19		7.02	4.85	7.58	5.35	−0.12	
SDQ Subscale: Emotional Problems	1.45	1.70	1.66	1.80	−0.12		1.45	1.70	1.61	1.76	−0.10	
SDQ Subscale: Conduct Problems	0.90	1.23	1.10	1.41	−0.16		0.90	1.23	1.00	1.38	−0.08	
SDQ Subscale: Hyperactivity	3.10	2.51	3.47	2.60	−0.15		3.10	2.51	3.39	2.56	−0.12	
SDQ Subscale: Peer Relationships	1.68	1.56	1.69	1.78	−0.01		1.68	1.56	1.59	1.62	0.05	
SDQ Subscale: Prosocial Behavior	8.58	1.61	8.45	1.58	0.08		8.58	1.61	8.64	1.56	−0.03	
Depressive Symptoms	0.93	1.68	1.16	1.95	−0.13		0.93	1.68	0.86	1.72	0.04	
Anxiety (SCARED)	1.74	2.00	1.44	1.51	0.15		1.74	2.00	1.56	1.71	0.09	

Figure 7A.1
Balance Plot for Service Members

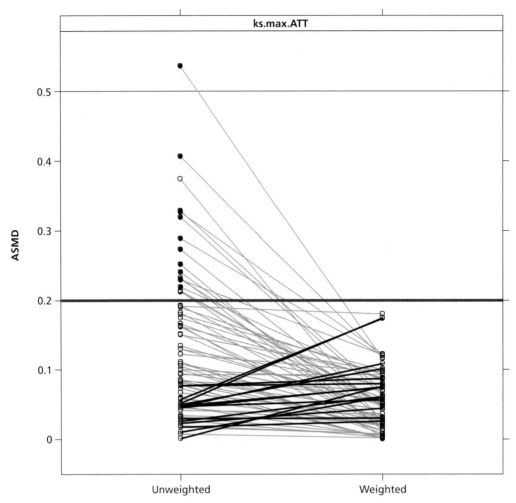

Figure 7A.2
Balance Plot for Spouses

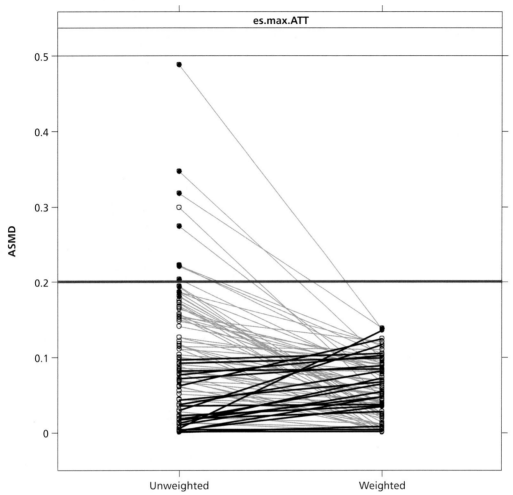

References

Adler, A. B., A. H. Huffman, P. D. Bliese, and C. A. Castro, "The Impact of Deployment Length and Experience on the Well-Being of Male and Female Soldiers," *Journal of Occupational Health Psychology*, Vol. 10, No. 2, 2005, pp. 121–137.

Andres, M. D., and R. Moelker, "There and Back Again: How Parental Experiences Affect Children's Adjustments in the Course of Military Deployments," *Armed Forces & Society*, Vol. 37, No. 3, 2011, pp. 418–447.

Blaisure, K. R., T. Saathoff-Wells, A. Pereira, S. M. Wadsworth, and A. L. Dombro, *Serving Military Families in the 21st Century*, New York: Taylor & Francis, 2012.

Bourg, C., and M. W. Segal, "The Impact of Family Supportive Policies and Practices on Organizational Commitment to the Army," *Armed Forces & Society*, Vol. 25, No. 4, 1999, pp. 633–652.

Davis, J. L., and C. E. Rusbult, "Attitude Alignment in Close Relationships," *Journal of Personality and Social Psychology*, Vol. 81, No. 1, 2001, p. 65.

de Burgh, H. T., C. J. White, N. T. Fear, and A. C. Iversen, "The Impact of Deployment to Iraq or Afghanistan on Partners and Wives of Military Personnel," *International Review of Psychiatry*, Vol. 23, No. 2, 2011, pp. 192–200.

Defense Manpower Data Center, *February 2012 Status of Forces Survey of Active-Duty Members: Tabulations of Responses*, Alexandria, Va., 2012. As of September 30, 2015:
http://mldc.whs.mil/public/docs/report/qol/DMDC_Status-of-Forces-Survey-of-Active-Duty-Members_Feb2012.pdf

DMDC—*See* Defense Manpower Data Center.

Egerton, M., "Occupational Inheritance: The Role of Cultural Capital and Gender," *Work, Employment and Society*, Vol. 11, No. 2, 1997, pp. 263–282.

Elbogen, E. B., H. R. Wagner, S. C. Johnson, P. M. Kinneer, H. K. Kang, J. J. Vasterling, C. Timko, and J. C. Beckham, "Are Iraq and Afghanistan Veterans Using Mental Health Services? New Data from a National Random-Sample Survey," *Psychiatric Services*, Vol. 64, No. 2, February 2013, pp. 134–141.

Ender, M. G., D. E. Rohall, and M. D. Matthews, *The Millennial Generation and National Defense: Attitudes of Future Military and Civilian Leaders*, London: Palgrave Macmillan, 2013.

Engel, R. C., L. B. Gallagher, and D. S. Lyle, "Military Deployments and Children's Academic Achievement: Evidence from Department of Defense Education Activity Schools," *Economics of Education Review*, Vol. 29, No. 1, 2010, pp. 73–82.

Faris, J. H., "The All-Volunteer Force: Recruitment from Military Families," *Armed Forces & Society*, Vol. 7, No. 4, 1981, pp. 545–559.

Griffith, J., S. H. Rakoff, and R. F. Helms, *Family and Other Impacts on Retention*, Alexandria, Va.: U.S. Army Research Institute for the Behavioral and Social Sciences, Technical Report 951, 1992.

Guthrie, T. J., *Career Intentions and Behavior of Army Officers: A Model Testing Approach*, U.S. Army Research Institute for the Behavioral and Social Sciences, Technical Report 946, 1992.

Harrell, M. C., N. Lim, L. Werber, and D. Golinelli, *Working Around the Military: Challenges to Military Spouse Employment and Education*, Santa Monica, Calif.: RAND Corporation, MG-196-OSD, 2004. As of November 22, 2015:
http://www.rand.org/pubs/monographs/MG196.html

Hill, R., *Families Under Stress*, New York: Harper & Row, 1949.

Hoge, C. W., C. A. Castro, S. C. Messer, D. McGurk, D. I. Cotting, and R. L. Koffman, "Combat Duty in Iraq and Afghanistan, Mental Health Problems, and Barriers to Care," *New England Journal of Medicine*, Vol. 351, No. 1, 2004, pp. 13–22.

Hom, P. W., and C. L. Hulin, "A Competitive Test of the Prediction of Reenlistment by Several Models," *Journal of Applied Psychology*, Vol. 66, No. 1, 1981, p. 23.

Hosek, J., J. E. Kavanagh, and L. L. Miller, *How Deployments Affect Service Members*, Santa Monica, Calif.: RAND Corporation, MG-432-RC, 2006. As of November 21, 2015: http://www.rand.org/pubs/monographs/MG432.html

Hosek, J., and S. M. Wadsworth, "Economic Conditions of Military Families," *The Future of Children*, Vol. 23, No. 2, 2013, pp. 41–59.

Karney, B. R., and T. N. Bradbury, "The Longitudinal Course of Marital Quality and Stability: A Review of Theory, Methods, and Research," *Psychological Bulletin*, Vol. 118, No. 1, 1995, p. 3.

Karney, B. R., and T. E. Trail, "Associations Between Prior Deployments and Marital Satisfaction in the Deployment Life Study," *Journal of Marriage and Family*, forthcoming.

Kniskern, M. K., and D. R. Segal, *Mean Wage Differences between Civilian and Military Wives*, College Park, Md.: University of Maryland Center for Research on Military Organizations, 2010.

Korb, L. J., A. Rothman, and M. Hoffman, *Reforming Military Compensation: Addressing Runaway Military Personnel Costs is a National Imperative*, Washington, D.C.: Center for American Progress, 2012.

Lee, T. W., and T. R. Mitchell, "An Alternative Approach: The Unfolding Model of Voluntary Employee Turnover," *Academy of Management Review*, Vol. 19, No. 1, 1994, pp. 51–89.

Lim, N., and D. Schulker, *Measuring Underemployment among Military Spouses,* Santa Monica, Calif.: RAND Corporation, MG-918-OSD, 2010. As of November 21, 2015: http://www.rand.org/pubs/monographs/MG918.html

Maury, R., and B. Stone, *Military Spouse Employment Report*, Syracuse, N.Y.: Institute for Veterans and Military Families, Syracuse University, 2014. As of October 30, 2015: http://vets.syr.edu/wp-content/uploads/2014/02/MilitarySpouseEmploymentReport_2013.pdf

Mazur, E., "Parent and Adolescent Positive and Negative Disability-Related Events and Their Relation to Adjustment," in S. M. Wadsworth and D. S. Riggs, eds., *Risk and Resilience in U.S. Military Families,* New York: Springer, 2011, pp. 235–257.

Meadows, S. O., B. A. Griffin, B. R. Karney, and J. Pollak, "Employment Gaps Between Military Spouses and Matched Civilians," *Armed Forces & Society*, 2015, advance online publication.

Miller, L. L., S. O. Meadows, L. M. Hanser, and S. L. Taylor, *Year of the Air Force Family: 2009 Survey of Active-Duty Spouses*, Santa Monica, Calif.: RAND Corporation, TR-879-AF, 2011. As of November 21, 2015: http://www.rand.org/pubs/technical_reports/TR879.html

Motowidlo, S. J., and G. W. Lawton, "Affective and Cognitive Factors in Soldiers' Reenlistment Decisions," *Journal of Applied Psychology*, Vol. 69, No. 1, 1984, p. 157.

Nichols, L. O., J. Martindale-Adams, M. J. Graney, J. Zuber, P. E. Miller, and D. V. Brown, "Feasibility of Telephone Support Groups for Spouses of Returning Iraq and Afghanistan Service Members," in S. M. Wadsworth and D. S. Riggs, eds., *Military Deployment and its Consequences for Families*, New York: Springer, 2014, pp. 61–78.

O'Reilly, C. A., and J. A. Chatman, "Culture as Social Control: Corporations, Cults, and Commitment," *Research in Organizational Behavior*, Vol. 18, 1996, pp. 157–200. As of October 30, 2015: http://faculty.haas.berkeley.edu/chatman/papers/30_cultureassocialcontrol.pdf

Orthner, D. K., *Family Impacts on the Retention of Military Personnel*, Alexandria, Va.: U.S. Army Research Institute for the Behavioral and Social Sciences, Research Report 1556, 1990.

Perry-Jenkins, M., and S. M. Wadsworth, "Work and Family Through Time and Space: Revisiting Old Themes and Charting New Directions," in G. W. Peterson and K. R. Bush, eds., *Handbook of Marriage and the Family*, Boston: Springer U.S., 2013, pp. 549–572.

Pew Research Center, *The Military-Civilian Gap: War and Sacrifice in the Post-9/11 Era*, Washington, D.C.: Social & Demographic Trends, Pew Research Center, 2011.

Rosen, L. N., D. B. Durand, and J. A. Martin, "Wartime Stress and Family Adaptation," in J. A. Martin, L. N. Rosen, and L. R. Sparachino, eds., *The Military Family: A Practice Guide for Human Service Providers*, Westport, Conn.: Praeger, 2000, pp. 123–138.

Rosen, L. N., and L. Z. Moghadam, "Matching the Support to the Stressor: Implications for the Buffering Hypothesis," *Military Psychology*, Vol. 2, 1990, pp. 193–204.

Segal, M. W., "The Military and the Family as Greedy Institutions," *Armed Forces & Society*, Vol. 13, No. 1, 1986, pp. 9–38.

Segal, M. W., M. D. Lane, and A. G. Fisher, "Conceptual Model of Military Career and Family Life Course Events, Intersections, and Effects on Well-Being," *Military Behavioral Health*, Vol. 3, No. 2, 2015, pp. 95-107.

Tanielian, T., and L. H. Jaycox, *Invisible Wounds of War: Psychological and Cognitive Injuries, Their Consequences, and Services to Assist Recovery*, Santa Monica, Calif.: RAND Corporation, MG-720-CCF, 2008. As of November 21, 2015:
http://www.rand.org/pubs/monographs/MG720.html

Tanielian, T., B. Karney, A. Chandra, and S. O. Meadows, *The Deployment Life Study: Methodological Overview and Baseline Sample Description*, Santa Monica, Calif.: RAND Corporation, RR-209-A/OSD, 2014. As of November 22, 2015:
http://www.rand.org/pubs/research_reports/RR209.html

Trice, A. D., M. A. Hughes, C. Odom, K. Woods, and N. C. McClellan, "The Origins of Children's Career Aspirations: IV. Testing Hypotheses from Four Theories," *The Career Development Quarterly*, Vol. 43, No. 4, 1995, pp. 307–322.

Trice, A. D., and P. Tillapaugh, "Children's Estimates of their Parents' Job Satisfaction," *Psychological Reports*, Vol. 69, No. 1, 1991, pp. 63–66.

Vernez, G., and G. L. Zellman, *Families and Mission: A Review of the Effects of Family Factors on Army Attrition, Retention, and Readiness*, Santa Monica, Calif.: RAND Corporation, N-264-A, 1987. As of November 22, 2015:
http://www.rand.org/pubs/notes/N2624.html

Weiss, H. M., S. M. MacDermid, R. Strauss, K. E. Kurek, B. Le, and D. Robbins, *Retention in the Armed Forces: Past Approaches and New Research Directions*, West Lafayette, Ind.: Purdue University, Military Family Research Institute, 2002.

Werber, L., M. C. Harrell, D. M. Varda, K. C. Hall, M. K. Beckett, and S. Howard, *Deployment Experiences of Guard and Reserve Families: Implications for Support and Retention*, Santa Monica, Calif.: RAND Corporation, MG-645-OSD, 2008. As of November 21, 2015:
http://www.rand.org/pubs/monographs/MG645.html

Wood, L. L., "Family Factors and the Reenlistment Intentions of Army Enlisted Personnel," *Interfaces*, Vol. 21, No. 4, 1991, pp. 92–110.

CHAPTER EIGHT

Discussion, Policy Implications, and Conclusion

Sarah O. Meadows, Benjamin R. Karney, Terri Tanielian, and Terry L. Schell

The goal of the Deployment Life Study was to describe and evaluate the effects of deployment on service members, spouses, and their children. To that end, this report has described the results of analyses designed to address the following questions:

- How do military families fare on a set of outcomes over the course of a deployment cycle?
- How do the changes experienced by families from predeployment to postdeployment compare with the changes experienced by matched families that did not deploy over the same period?
- Which characteristics of deployment are associated with better or worse postdeployment outcomes?
- Which characteristics of families are associated with better or worse postdeployment outcomes?
- Which coping strategies predeployment and during deployment are associated with better or worse postdeployment outcomes?

To address these questions, the analyses presented here draw upon repeated, longitudinal assessments of more than 2,700 married military families across all services and components. The multi-informant format allows for assessment of service members, spouses, and their children across all phases of the deployment cycle. Using descriptive and quasi-experimental methods, the analyses described in this report aimed to document the initial results of the Deployment Life Study with respect to understanding the impact of deployments on marital relationships, family relationships, psychological and behavioral health, child and teen well-being, and military integration among military families.

Summary of Findings

Chapters Three through Seven of this report present detailed findings across a number of important domains. Here, we summarize high-level findings from each chapter.

Marital Relationships

Chapter Three examined marital satisfaction, positive and negative affect, and psychological and physical aggression as reported by service members and spouses. Key findings include the following:

- Across the entire deployment cycle, couples, on average, become significantly less satisfied with their marriages and engaged in less psychological and physical aggression than they reported prior to the deployment.
- These changes in marital outcomes across the deployment cycle do not differ significantly from the changes experienced during the same period by matched couples that did not deploy.
- For spouses, more-frequent communication with the service member during deployment predicts greater marital satisfaction postdeployment, controlling for baseline characteristics of the couple.
- Service members' exposure to physical and psychological trauma during deployment predicts spouses' reports of *higher* levels of psychological and physical aggression postdeployment while service members' exposure to combat trauma during deployment predicts *lower* levels of partner and own psychological aggression postdeployment, as reported by the spouse.
- For spouses, separating from the military during the postdeployment period is associated with lower marital satisfaction, and lower positive affect and higher negative affect after communicating with the service member, during the postdeployment period.

Family Relationships

Chapter Four examined the family environment, satisfaction with parenting, and financial distress as reported by service members and spouses. Key findings include:

- Family outcomes change over the deployment cycle, but these changes occur primarily during the deployment itself and are not always the same for all family members.
- Service members report *better* family environments during deployments than before or after deployments, possibly because they are removed from the day-to-day challenges associated with family life. Spouses, in contrast, report no significant changes in family environment across the deployment cycle.
- Service members' and spouses' reports of parenting satisfaction both change over a deployment cycle, but service members report *higher* parenting satisfaction during the deployment while spouses report *lower* parenting satisfaction over the entire deployment cycle.
- Financial distress, as felt by both service members and spouses, declined during deployment.
- Service members who report engaging in more predeployment preparation activities report higher satisfaction with parenting postdeployment. Similarly, spouses who report more preparation activities and greater satisfaction with the frequency of communication with the service member during deployment reported higher parenting satisfaction postdeployment.
- The negative psychological consequences of deployment, including psychological trauma and stress reported by the service member, are associated with increased risk for negative family outcomes for both service members and spouses postdeployment.

Psychological and Behavioral Health

Chapter Five examined several psychological and behavioral health outcomes, including posttraumatic stress disorder (PTSD), depression, binge drinking and perceived need for counseling or therapy as reported by service members and spouses. Key findings include the following:

- We found no overall significant effect of deployment on persistent psychological or behavioral health outcomes for service members or spouses. This is consistent with the fact that we studied a relatively experienced population, serving during a period of the conflict with comparatively low levels of reported deployment trauma.
- However, those deployed service members who did experience deployment trauma during the study showed a persistent increase in their depression, PTSD, and anxiety symptoms relative to their predeployment levels. When the service member experienced physical trauma (i.e., injury) during the study deployment, their spouses also showed persistent increases in those symptoms, as well as in binge drinking.
- Mean levels of psychological symptoms showed substantial variation across the deployment cycle. For service members, depressive symptoms were heightened during the deployment; by contrast, spouses showed elevated depression, PTSD, and anxiety symptoms during the deployment period. In contrast, service members showed significantly less binge drinking during deployments, perhaps because of limited access to alcohol.
- Those deployed members who subsequently separated or retired from the military showed increased levels of psychological symptoms.

Child and Teen Well-Being

Chapter Six examined the emotional, behavioral, social, and academic functioning of children (as reported by spouses) and teens, across some 40 outcomes as reported by spouses (for children) and teens. Key findings include the following:

- Based on trajectory models of outcomes over the deployment cycle, most outcomes did not change over the course of a deployment cycle. Those that did change might reflect maturational changes among children and teens rather than changes related to deployment.
- There were a few significant exceptions, however:
  - Three child outcomes (reported by spouses) showed significant changes over the deployment cycle: Total difficulties (and more specifically, emotional problems), as well as depression screener scores. Spouses reported elevated symptoms in their children during deployment.
  - Two self-reported teen outcomes showed significant changes across the deployment cycle. Teen reports of drug use were very low before and during deployment (hovering around "never"), but increased afterward (to just slightly more than "never" on average). In addition, teens reported higher-quality relationships with their parent who deployed before and during deployment, with lower quality upon return.
- We generally found no significant effect of deployment on child and teen outcomes, which is consistent with the fact that we studied a relatively experienced population, serving during a period of the conflict with comparatively low levels of reported deployment trauma. However, there were some notable exceptions.
  - Spouses in families that experienced a study deployment reported elevated child difficulties at the end of the study (specifically, emotional conduct and peer problems), as well as a higher need for child mental health services, compared with spouses in matched families that did not experience a study deployment. Interestingly, this was only found for spouse concerns about their children (younger than age 11) following a

study deployment; there was no such evidence of an effect for spouse concerns on teens or in teen self-reports.

- We also examined three sets of risk and resilience factors within families that experienced a study deployment.
    - The first set included parent deployment factors (e.g., deployment trauma, length of deployment, and separation from the military). Based on spouses' reports, the longer the study deployment, the more emotional problems and depressive symptoms children had. For teens, these factors were not related to spouses' reports of teen outcomes or for most of the teen self-reported outcomes. However, there were two exceptions: Parental experience of trauma during the study deployment was associated with teen reports of their functioning and family relationships. The pattern of findings indicates that combat traumas were related to poorer functioning and relationships, whereas psychological traumas (in the absence of injury or combat trauma) were related to better functioning and relationships.
    - The second set of factors examined several measures of child or teen adjustment during the study deployment. When the same informant reported on adjustment and outcomes, there were many significant associations and also many trends. That is, when teens self-reported on both adjustment during deployment and postdeployment outcomes, many significant associations were observed. The same was true when parents reported on both teen adjustment during deployment and teen outcomes during postdeployment. However, when informants were mixed—for example when we examined parent report of teen adjustment during deployment and teen self-report on post-deployment outcomes, these associations were less robust. Thus, perceptions of problems during deployment are highly related to perceptions of problems postdeployment, especially when the informant is the same.
    - Finally, we examined three types of social support for teens. We found a set of strong associations between socializing with other military children during deployment, with this factor being protective and associated with more-positive outcomes for teens at the end of the study.

Military Integration

Chapter Seven examined the military satisfaction, military commitment, retention intentions, and teen military career aspirations as reported by service members, spouses, and teens in non-divorced, active component families. Key findings include the following:

- Across the phases of the deployment cycle, measures of military integration varied more for service members than for spouses and teens. In fact, teen trajectories revealed no evidence of change over time. When there were changes in aspects of military integration during deployment, family members appeared to adapt well and return to predeployment levels in the postdeployment period.
- Any communication with other military families during deployment was associated with higher service member retention intentions and greater spouse and teen military commitment postdeployment.
- Trauma experienced during the study deployment, especially physical and psychological trauma, was associated with decreased military satisfaction among service members post-

deployment, as well as decreased retention intentions by service members themselves and by teens of service members postdeployment.

- Experiences of nondeployed families may also be stressful, which may minimize the gap between deployed and nondeployed families. For example, among nondeployed families, relocation was related to decreased military satisfaction, commitment, and retention intentions among service members.

Common Themes

Although each of the chapters assembled in this report examined a separate set of outcomes, several common themes emerged across multiple chapters.

First, and most notably, the most significant changes experienced by military families across the deployment cycle occur during the deployment itself. With respect to many of the outcomes examined in this study, the participants' status during the study deployment was significantly different from their status reported before and after the deployment. The dominant pattern over the deployment cycle was a change or adaptation during the deployment period, followed by a return to near predeployment levels of functioning.

Second, significant variation exists across family members with respect to how they experience deployment. For example, although service members rated the family environment higher and reported higher parenting satisfaction during deployment, spouses showed little change in these outcomes across the deployment cycle. It is plausible that service members are spared from day-to-day difficulties that families experience during their absences, although we have no direct evidence from our study to support this hypothesis. Given the physical absence of a service member during deployment, some of the differences we observed across family members (e.g., declines in binge drinking, as well as psychological and physical aggression) were expected. However, absence may not fully explain all the variation in outcomes across service members, spouses, children, and teens. And for children and teens in particular, it may be important to ask them directly about how well they are coping with a deployment, as we found that for some outcomes (e.g., total difficulties and anxiety) parent and teen reports about teen well-being had little association with one another.

Third, the analyses reported here revealed a set of risk and readiness factors that appear to be associated reliably with multiple domains of postdeployment outcomes. With respect to factors associated with more-successful adaptation to deployment, several chapters report that families that engaged in predeployment readiness activities experienced more-favorable outcomes postdeployment than families that did not. Given the correlational design of this study, it is not possible to know whether these activities protect or enhance family functioning across the deployment experience, or whether the most-resilient families are the ones most likely to engage in these activities. Several of our analyses also found that more-frequent communication with the service member during deployment, and higher satisfaction with the amount of that communication, was associated with more-favorable outcomes postdeployment. Here, too, it is not possible to know whether communication plays a causal role in effective coping or if the most-resilient families were the ones taking the time to communicate with each other regularly. Until further research attempts to tease apart these alternatives, the fact that these associations emerge even after controlling for family characteristics at baseline is consistent with the view that more-frequent communication during deployment has incremental benefits for families after the deployment.

Finally, with respect to risk factors, multiple chapters identified the experience of traumatic events during the deployment as a risk factor for worse outcomes postdeployment. These findings join an emerging body of research suggesting that it may be the traumatic experience that service members are exposed to during deployment, rather than separation from family itself, that carries any negative effects associated with the deployment experience. Indeed, in most analyses, the length of the deployment itself showed little association with the postdeployment status of service members, spouses, or children—even when we did not control for deployment trauma.

However, the relationship between deployment experiences and postdeployment outcomes was far more complex than the current literature suggests. The measure of deployment experiences used in the study was designed to assess psychological trauma, included a range of descriptively different experiences that were all hypothesized to be psychologically traumatic, and were all shown to be associated with posttraumatic psychopathology (Schell and Marshall, 2008). As expected, we found evidence that the members' physical trauma (i.e., being injured), combat trauma (i.e., hand-to-hand combat or experiencing explosions), and psychological trauma (i.e., witnessing trauma or vicarious exposure to trauma) were each positively associated with postdeployment symptoms of PTSD and depression. However, these different types of service member experiences did not have homogeneous effects when looking at other service member outcomes, or when looking at outcomes for spouses or children/teens. This may suggest that the deployment experiences may have direct effects on the family that are not mediated through service member psychopathology. For example, being directly engaged in violence against the enemy during deployment may affect a service member's interactions with his or her family even in the absence of PTSD or depression. This intriguing finding deserves further exploration to see if parental deployment experiences may promote different mindsets, behaviors, and interactional styles with family members postdeployment. Unfortunately, this study (along with most others designed to look at the effects of deployment) has focused narrowly on assessing deployment events hypothesized to be traumatic. And most prior studies analyze these experiences as functionally interchangeable. New theory, measures, and analyses may be needed to better understand which deployment experiences have persistent effects on service members and their families, as well as how those effects are produced. Viewing all deployment events through the narrow lens of psychological trauma may lead us to miss, or misrepresent, the long-term effects of deployment.

Limitations

A number of strengths in the methods and design of the Deployment Life Study—anchoring on the predeployment period, shorter intervals between surveys, data from multiple family informants—strengthen our confidence in the results presented in this report. Despite these strengths, however, the Deployment Life Study is limited in several ways that constrain the conclusions that these results can support. First, the baseline sample of the Deployment Life Study consisted of a selective sample of older, more-experienced family members who not only have remained in the military but also stayed married long enough to be included in our sample. This selectivity may have increased our odds of finding resilient families. We cannot speculate about what the results would look like for first-time deployers or newlyweds, given our sample. Nor can we speak to what deployment looks like for other types of families, including single-parent families or unmarried service members without dependents. These family types could be among those most likely to experience negative outcomes associated with deployment so their omission from our study, although purposeful, suggests a key area for future research.

Second, some families that participated in the baseline assessment dropped out during the course of the study. This is typical of most longitudinal studies. If those families that left the survey are somehow different on unmeasured characteristics, and those unmeasured characteristics are associated with our outcomes of interest, we may have biased estimates. However, it is not entirely clear which direction the bias is in. Most likely, these families are worse on our outcomes, which would upwardly bias our estimates. We also lost some families between the time we received our sampling data and the start of the survey because they were no longer eligible (i.e., separated, divorced, or left the military). It is worth noting, however, that because the Deployment Life Study uses multiple informants per family, even if one member of the family opts not to participate, we still may have some information about that family from other members.

Third, as we noted in Chapter One, during the field period of this study, deployments were shorter and arguably less dangerous (because the combat zones were less volatile) than they had been earlier in the decade. In particular, the number and rates of injury and death among American troops were much lower than in prior years, and significantly less than during the peak of combat operations (Fischer, 2015). This historical context limits our ability to generalize the findings beyond any other periods in which the demands on military families may have been greater.

Fourth, as we noted in Chapter Two, our analyses include a large number of statistical tests. Although we opted not to perform statistical corrections that account for multiple tests (for the reasons noted in Chapter Two), we do caution readers that the results presented in this report should be viewed in terms of patterns, rather than select, individually significant associations. This is especially true for our analysis of risk and resilience factors.

Fifth, as with any survey that attempts to measure phenomena that cannot be observed directly, measurement error is a potential problem. To the extent possible, our surveys used well-validated measures that have been used in other studies of both civilians and service members and their families. Many of these measures are described in detail in each chapter, but more details can be found in Tanielian et al. (2014).

Sixth, self-report data, even if it is collected outside of direct human contact (i.e., over the phone) may be subject to social response bias. That is, service members, spouses, and teens may have overestimated the positive aspects of their lives and underestimated the negative aspects.

Finally, although we have done a significant amount of work to minimize bias from observed differences between the deployed and nondeployed samples in our doubly robust analyses, a limitation of doubly robust methods is that they cannot guard against bias from unobserved factors whose effect on an outcome is not captured via the included confounders. That said, we believe that our particular selection of variables is likely to cover almost all the important factors. First, in our longitudinal model, we control for each individual's pre-exposure value of the outcome when looking at the postexposure value of the same outcome. Second, we attempted to include measures of all major risk factors for these outcomes in the baseline assessment. That is, covariates were purposely selected for inclusion as the most important covariates to control for based on the available literature. Although omitted variable bias may exist, we have tried to include all of the known risk factors, as well as the outcomes themselves assessed prior to the study deployments to ensure we have as robust results as possible with these data.

Taken together, these potential limitations should not overshadow the uniqueness of the Deployment Life Study or the contribution it makes to understanding the consequences of deployment for military families. Rather, they should be viewed simply as a caution for how broadly the results apply to the overall population of military families.

Policy Implications

Improving the Well-Being of Military Families

Our findings have a number of implications for programs and policies aimed at improving the well-being and quality of life of service members, spouses, and their children across the deployment cycle.

Programs, services, and policies should target families that experience deployment trauma, especially during the postdeployment phase. To the extent that traumatic experiences during deployment are associated with a host of negative consequences in the postdeployment period, these experiences, when documented during deployments, can be used to target families for extra support upon the return of the service member. Programs that target families based on documented experiences, regardless of self-reported symptoms, might help mitigate problems before they are exacerbated, or at least before they have time to affect multiple family members. The challenge for providing the programs, services, and supports to these families, of course, is identifying the families *before* problems occur. While the military employs several screening tools to identify service members at risk for postdeployment health-related consequences at the population level (e.g., the Post-Deployment Health Assessment and the Post-Deployment Health Re-Assessment), we are not aware of any evidence-based or evidence-informed screening tools to identify military families who may be in need of assistance at various time points across the deployment cycle. While our study was partially motivated by an interest in helping to identify risk factors that could be assessed by screening tools, our findings indicate the only consistent risk factor linked to our outcomes of interest was combat exposure. As such, information available to line leaders with respect to a unit's level of trauma exposure (e.g., the event-based traumatic brain injury screening program) could help identify units whose members have traumatic exposures and perhaps help garrison commanders to mobilize postdeployment support for their families upon return. It is beyond the scope of this report to make recommendations about which of the many existing screeners of traumatic exposure should be used, but we note that there are several that have been used extensively in the existing literature.[1] We also acknowledge that, because not all service members will be exposed to the various types of deployment trauma, identifying families based on this criterion is not a panacea for identifying families that may experience problems in the postdeployment period.

Addressing psychological problems around the time of separation may be important for avoiding the longer-term impairments caused by these problems, such as increased morbidity, homelessness, unemployment, or substance abuse among veterans. Our results indicate that service members who have separated from service postdeployment have significantly elevated psychological

---

[1] For a list of trauma screener examples, see the Department of Veterans Affairs National Center for PTSD website (2016).

symptoms. Regardless of whether psychological problems predate separation, the separation period appears to be a high-risk time for individuals who leave the military.

Attention to the challenges associated with deployment should not detract from supporting services that address other challenges of military life. Although they are perhaps the most salient stressor in the lives of military families, deployments are far from the only challenges that military families face. The fact that characteristics of military families measured prior to the deployment accounted for outcomes after the deployment highlights the importance of programs that support families in other ways; e.g., by reducing financial stress, addressing mental health issues, and reducing or adjusting to relocation.

Programs that facilitate communication both between and within military families during a deployment may promote not only greater military integration, but also better outcomes across the domains highlighted in this report. Family connectedness to the military is higher when families engage with other military families. In addition, interacting with other military children was protective among teens in our study across a number of outcomes. These relationships with peers are likely to help family members share important emotional, instrumental, and informational resources that can be used to cope with a deployment and to develop strong ties within the military community. Our finding that relocation is a risk factor for families' military integration suggests that families may benefit from reducing the frequency of relocations or developing strategies to help families maintain and build new relationships after moving. Similarly, communication among family members, and satisfaction with that communication, were associated with improved marital and parenting relationships. However, this study was not designed to evaluate family support programs. Thus, the actual impact of programs to improve communication and support within and between military families remains to be seen. Nonetheless, these are areas that our results show could have great promise for family support programs.

Support to improve relationships among service members, spouses, and their teen children during the postdeployment reintegration period may improve family functioning. Our results indicate that both postdeployment family cohesion and the quality of the relationship with spouse parents were worse among teens with deployed service member parents than for teens with nondeployed service member parents, and that relationship quality with the service member parents declined during the deployment period. Programs should focus on preventing declines in relationship quality and family cohesion after the service member returns, as opposed to waiting for families to seek help once the relationship(s) disintegrate.

Future Research on Military Families

Informed policy is derived from high-quality, timely inputs. Our findings also highlight several areas where changes to research strategies could result in improved data—both in terms of timeliness and quality—for making policy decisions. Thus, we offer several areas for future research regarding military families that ultimately could have important implications for policy.

Future work on military families should explore ways in which data can be collected from multiple family members at the same time. Across the chapters of this report, results based on spouses' data were more frequently significant than results based on data from service members. Spouses' reports may be more sensitive to conditions within the family and thus may be promising sources of data on military families when data from service members are unavailable. For some outcomes, such as the family environment and anxiety, family members' (i.e., service members and spouses) reports of outcomes differed during the same period of the deployment cycle. Collecting data from multiple members of the same families can capture these differences and help tailor support for individual family members based on their relation to the service member (e.g., spouse, child, teen).

As funding resources become scarcer, future work on military families should prioritize longitudinal studies. As we noted in Chapter One, many existing studies of military families rely on retrospective or cross-sectional reports. Unfortunately, this means that much of the existing body of work on the impact of deployment on families does not allow for anchoring of family function prior to the deployment, potentially leading to an exaggeration of any deployment effect. Longitudinal study designs offer the most methodologically robust way to assess the impact of deployment on families. Without following the same families over time, we would not have been able to observe changes in functioning of family members (and families) during the deployment period, and we would not have been able to report that those changes do not usually lead to sustained problems in the postdeployment period.

Procedures for collecting real-time data from military families should be explored. Throughout these chapters, we have been sensitive to the unique historical climate in which the data collection for the Deployment Life Study took place. Had we conducted the same study in 2006 or 2007, when deployments to Iraq and Afghanistan were longer and more frequent, our results may have painted a different picture of how well military families adapt to deployment. Longitudinal data have a lot to offer researchers, but they are time-consuming to collect and results are often not known until several months or even years after the respondents have provided their data. Future research may be strengthened by continuing efforts to use smartphone applications with military families (for a review, see Shore et al., 2014). Having a real-time source of data that is capable of tracking changes in the historical, political, and social climates would provide a huge benefit to researchers and policymakers who seek to help families navigate the stress associated with military life.

Looking to the future, identifying families before problems occur remains a considerable challenge. As we have noted in this report, doing so is perhaps key to circumventing later problems. Part of the difficulty in pre-identifying families that may have problems following a deployment is having appropriate measures; however, another difficulty is having appropriate measures at the right time. Future research targeted on identifying measures that are appropriate and available at the right time could have considerable payoff in determining how to allocate help to families.

There is no single type of type of real-time data that would be able to address all the relevant research and policy questions that could be asked. The costs and benefits associated with different types of data should also be considered when deciding what type of real-time data collection methods to invest in. Some combination of administrative data for service members (e.g., medical records, personnel data) as well as ongoing data from a representative panel of military family members could prove to be a very useful, cost-effective solution.

Develop new theories, measures, and analyses of deployment experiences that can account for apparent complexities of the relationship between deployment and postdeployment outcomes. The complex pattern of findings relating service member deployment experiences and the outcomes across the family deserves further study. It is possible, for instance, that the experience of combat during deployment produces a set of psychological and behavioral factors that make reintegration with the family more difficult. On the other hand, witnessing of wartime traumas without being in combat or being injured may produce a very different set of psychological and behavioral reactions that make service members more eager or able to engage with their families. Further research is needed to investigate the persistent effects of deployment, both good and bad. The existing theory (focused almost exclusively on factors leading to post-traumatic psychopathology), the existing measures (focused on traumatic events and often geared toward the experiences of infantry) and the standard analyses (focused on using these measures as forming a homogeneous scale with consistent effects) may obscure the full effects of deployment on members and their families. Such research is necessary to develop policies or interventions that can effectively minimize the harms—and maximize the benefits—from military deployments.

Examine the intersections and relative timing of military and family events. Contemporary service members are more likely than previous generations to have families. When examining outcomes, including those detailed in this report, it is worthwhile for future research to examine interactions between the relative timing of military (e.g., deployment, promotion, relocation) and family (e.g., birth of a child) events. Such research would facilitate a deeper understanding of when families might be most vulnerable or resilient in the face of deployment.

Conclusion

Across the chapters contained in this report, comparisons between families that experienced a deployment and matched families that did not experience a deployment revealed few significant differences in outcomes that occurred after a service member returned from a deployment. Yet, the Deployment Life Study data revealed that life during the deployment itself was stressful in a number of ways, albeit differently for different family members. Given the unquestionable stresses of the deployment period and the well-established negative associations between stress and family outcomes among civilians, it is remarkable that most families are able to adjust. On one hand, this apparent resilience might reveal the noteworthy success of the support programs in place for military families. On the other hand, the findings presented here may reflect the natural ability of many military families to thrive, even in the face of severe challenges. In reality, both stories are probably true—existing programs help military families cope, and families have natural coping abilities. However, it is important to remember that not all military families are the same. Although the sample of families in the Deployment Life Study is generally more experienced—with deployments and with military life in general—some are not. Likewise, for some families, military life is a struggle. What we can learn from these more-experienced, resilient families can then be used to help those that may be less successful at adapting and adjusting to the unique demands associated with military life.

Finally, we would be remiss if we did not acknowledge the vast amount of data collected from military families during the course of the Deployment Life Study that was not included in these analyses. Given a number of resource constraints, many important research questions were not included. It is our goal to continue to use the data for analyses that create and promote readiness and resilience among military families.

References

Fischer, H., *A Guide to U.S. Military Casualty Statistics: Operation Freedom's Sentinel, Operation Inherent Resolve, Operation New Dawn, Operation Iraqi Freedom, and Operation Enduring Freedom*, Washington, D.C.: Congressional Research Service, 2015.

Schell, T. L., and G. N. Marshall, "Survey of Individuals Previously Deployed for OEF/OIF," in T. Tanielian and L. H. Jaycox, eds., *Invisible Wounds of War: Psychological and Cognitive Injuries, Their Consequences, and Services to Assist Recovery*, Santa Monica, Calif.: RAND Corporation, MG-720-CCF, 2008, pp. 887–115. As of November 20, 2015:
http://www.rand.org/pubs/monographs/MG720.html

Shore, J. H., M. Aldag, F. L. McVeigh, R. L. Hoover, R. Ciulla, and A. Fisher, "Review of Mobile Health Technology for Military Mental Health," *Military Medicine*, Vol. 179, No. 8, August 2014, pp. 865–878.

Tanielian, T., B. R. Karney, A. Chandra, and S. O. Meadows, *The Deployment Life Study: Methodological Overview and Baseline Sample Description*, Santa Monica, Calif.: RAND Corporation, RR-209-A/OSD, 2014. As of November 20, 2015:
http://www.rand.org/pubs/research_reports/RR209.html

U.S. Department of Veterans Affairs, PTSD: National Center for PTSD, web page, last updated February 2016. As of March 11, 2016:
http://www.ptsd.va.gov/professional/assessment/all_measures.asp

Additional Tables

This final set of appendixes to the report provides means of key outcomes for service members and spouses by wave and by study deployment status (Appendix A1 tables), by wave and by gender (Appendix A2 tables), by wave and by component (i.e., active versus reserve/guard; Appendix A3 tables), and by wave and by service branch (i.e., Army, Air Force, Navy, Marine Corps; Appendix A4 tables). A final table presents means for teens by wave (Appendix A5 table). Lowercase table letters indicate: (a) family outcomes; (b) marital outcomes; (c) psychological and behavioral health outcomes; and (d) military integration outcomes.

Table A.1a
Family Outcome Means by Study Wave and Study Deployment Status

			Family Environment Scale[a]		Satisfaction with Parenting[b]		Financial Distress Scale[c]	
			Mean	SE	Mean	SE	Mean	SE
Baseline	Overall Sample	SMs	2.68	−0.03	3.22	−0.06	1.97	−0.06
		SPs	2.63	−0.07	3.08	−0.04	2.05	−0.06
	Study Deployment	SMs	2.81	−0.01	3.36	−0.02	1.80	−0.05
		SPs	2.81	−0.02	3.23	−0.02	1.90	−0.03
	No Study Deployment	SMs	2.73	−0.04	3.34	−0.05	2.02	−0.06
		SPs	2.73	−0.05	3.20	−0.03	2.10	−0.05
Wave 2	Overall Sample	SMs	2.68	−0.03	3.22	−0.06	1.97	−0.06
		SPs	2.63	−0.07	3.08	−0.04	2.05	−0.06
	Study Deployment	SMs	2.76	−0.02	3.29	−0.03	1.82	−0.05
		SPs	2.75	−0.02	3.12	−0.04	1.86	−0.06
	No Study Deployment	SMs	2.72	−0.02	3.19	−0.05	1.99	−0.06
		SPs	2.72	−0.02	3.16	−0.03	2.00	−0.05
Wave 3	Overall Sample	SMs	2.68	−0.03	3.22	−0.06	1.97	−0.06
		SPs	2.63	−0.07	3.08	−0.04	2.05	−0.06
	Study Deployment	SMs	2.80	−0.02	3.37	−0.04	1.69	−0.04
		SPs	2.72	−0.03	3.02	−0.04	1.91	−0.04
	No Study Deployment	SMs	2.71	−0.03	3.22	−0.04	2.06	−0.07
		SPs	2.64	−0.07	3.13	−0.04	1.96	−0.05
Wave 4	Overall Sample	SMs	2.68	−0.03	3.22	−0.06	1.97	−0.06
		SPs	2.63	−0.07	3.08	−0.04	2.05	−0.06
	Study Deployment	SMs	2.75	−0.03	3.32	−0.03	1.73	−0.04
		SPs	2.74	−0.02	3.08	−0.03	1.83	−0.04
	No Study Deployment	SMs	2.71	−0.03	3.17	−0.05	2.03	−0.06
		SPs	2.63	−0.07	3.16	−0.04	1.99	−0.06
Wave 5	Overall Sample	SMs	2.68	−0.03	3.22	−0.06	1.97	−0.06
		SPs	2.63	−0.07	3.08	−0.04	2.05	−0.06
	Study Deployment	SMs	2.78	−0.02	3.29	−0.04	1.69	−0.04
		SPs	2.74	−0.02	3.03	−0.03	1.80	−0.04
	No Study Deployment	SMs	2.72	−0.03	3.12	−0.05	1.99	−0.06
		SPs	2.65	−0.07	3.16	−0.03	1.98	−0.05
Wave 6	Overall Sample	SMs	2.68	−0.03	3.22	−0.06	1.97	−0.06
		SPs	2.63	−0.07	3.08	−0.04	2.05	−0.06
	Study Deployment	SMs	2.73	−0.03	3.27	−0.04	1.82	−0.04
		SPs	2.68	−0.03	3.06	−0.03	1.91	−0.05
	No Study Deployment	SMs	2.76	−0.03	3.18	−0.05	2.05	−0.08
		SPs	2.68	−0.06	3.09	−0.04	2.11	−0.06

Table A.1a—Continued

			Family Environment Scale[a]		Satisfaction with Parenting[b]		Financial Distress Scale[c]	
			Mean	SE	Mean	SE	Mean	SE
Wave 7	Overall Sample	SMs	2.68	−0.03	3.22	−0.06	1.97	−0.06
		SPs	2.63	−0.07	3.08	−0.04	2.05	−0.06
	Study Deployment	SMs	2.70	−0.02	3.26	−0.06	1.84	−0.04
		SPs	2.71	−0.03	3.05	−0.03	1.89	−0.04
	No Study Deployment	SMs	2.69	−0.03	3.20	−0.04	2.05	−0.07
		SPs	2.64	−0.06	3.13	−0.03	2.10	−0.08
Wave 8[d]	Overall Sample	SMs	2.68	−0.03	3.22	−0.06	1.97	−0.06
		SPs	2.63	−0.07	3.08	−0.04	2.05	−0.06
	Study Deployment	SMs	2.75	−0.03	3.24	−0.04	1.77	−0.06
		SPs	2.74	−0.03	3.07	−0.05	1.88	−0.06
	No Study Deployment	SMs	2.65	−0.06	3.22	−0.08	2.04	−0.07
		SPs	2.60	−0.10	3.13	−0.04	2.10	−0.08
Wave 9[d]	Overall Sample	SMs	2.68	−0.03	3.22	−0.06	1.97	−0.06
		SPs	2.63	−0.07	3.08	−0.04	2.05	−0.06
	Study Deployment	SMs	2.75	−0.03	3.28	−0.07	1.88	−0.05
		SPs	2.71	−0.03	3.04	−0.04	1.91	−0.06
	No Study Deployment	SMs	2.67	−0.04	3.20	−0.07	1.99	−0.07
		SPs	2.61	−0.08	3.09	−0.05	2.08	−0.08

NOTES: Data are weighted. SM=service member; SP=spouse.

[a] Higher scores=more positive environment. Range: 1–3.

[b] Higher scores=more satisfaction. Range: 1–4.

[c] Higher scores=more distress. Range: 1–4.

[d] The Navy sample does not have data at this wave by design.

Table A.1b
Marital Relationship Outcome Means by Study Wave and Study Deployment Status

		Marital Satisfaction[a]		PANAS: Positive[b]		PANAS: Negative[c]		Physical Aggression: Prevalence Against You[d]		Physical Aggression: Prevalence Against Partner[e]		Psychological Aggression: Frequency Against You[f]		Psychological Aggression: Frequency Against Partner[g]	
		Mean	SE	Mean	SE	Mean	SE	Mean	SE	Mean	SE	Mean	SE	Mean	SE
Baseline	Overall Sample	SMs	3.53	−0.06	3.70	−0.05	2.26	−0.05	0.74	−0.09	0.03	−0.01	0.07	−0.02	0.60	−0.08
		SPs	3.47	−0.09	3.68	−0.12	2.36	−0.11	0.70	−0.08	0.04	−0.01	0.03	−0.01	0.62	−0.05
	Study Deployment	SMs	4.01	−0.03	4.24	−0.04	1.92	−0.03	0.67	−0.05	0.01	0.00	0.05	−0.01	0.62	−0.04
		SPs	3.95	−0.03	4.19	−0.03	2.07	−0.03	0.60	−0.04	0.06	−0.02	0.02	−0.01	0.71	−0.04
	No Study Deployment	SMs	3.90	−0.04	4.10	−0.05	2.07	−0.05	0.89	−0.07	0.02	−0.01	0.05	−0.01	0.77	−0.07
		SPs	3.70	−0.06	3.95	−0.09	2.27	−0.07	0.87	−0.08	0.06	−0.01	0.05	−0.02	0.78	−0.06
Wave 2	Overall Sample	SMs	3.53	−0.06	3.70	−0.05	2.26	−0.05	0.74	−0.09	0.03	−0.01	0.07	−0.02	0.60	−0.08
		SPs	3.47	−0.09	3.68	−0.12	2.36	−0.11	0.70	−0.08	0.04	−0.01	0.03	−0.01	0.62	−0.05
	Study Deployment	SMs	3.88	−0.03	4.07	−0.05	1.99	−0.04	0.82	−0.07	0.05	−0.01	0.09	−0.02	0.68	−0.06
		SPs	3.78	−0.03	4.03	−0.04	2.17	−0.04	0.69	−0.05	0.04	−0.01	0.03	−0.01	0.71	−0.05
	No Study Deployment	SMs	3.74	−0.04	3.91	−0.05	2.15	−0.04	0.84	−0.07	0.05	−0.02	0.09	−0.02	0.71	−0.06
		SPs	3.60	−0.04	3.84	−0.05	2.32	−0.04	0.80	−0.07	0.07	−0.02	0.06	−0.01	0.75	−0.06
Wave 3	Overall Sample	SMs	3.53	−0.06	3.70	−0.05	2.26	−0.05	0.74	−0.09	0.03	−0.01	0.07	−0.02	0.60	−0.08
		SPs	3.47	−0.09	3.68	−0.12	2.36	−0.11	0.70	−0.08	0.04	−0.01	0.03	−0.01	0.62	−0.05
	Study Deployment	SMs	3.90	−0.04	4.14	−0.04	1.97	−0.04	0.58	−0.05	0.02	−0.01	0.04	−0.01	0.49	−0.05
		SPs	3.69	−0.04	4.03	−0.05	2.17	−0.04	0.54	−0.05	0.03	−0.01	0.02	−0.01	0.55	−0.04
	No Study Deployment	SMs	3.74	−0.04	3.89	−0.05	2.15	−0.04	0.75	−0.07	0.03	−0.01	0.07	−0.02	0.61	−0.05
		SPs	3.39	−0.12	3.62	−0.14	2.41	−0.13	0.81	−0.08	0.05	−0.01	0.05	−0.01	0.75	−0.07
Wave 4	Overall Sample	SMs	3.53	−0.06	3.70	−0.05	2.26	−0.05	0.74	−0.09	0.03	−0.01	0.07	−0.02	0.60	−0.08
		SPs	3.47	−0.09	3.68	−0.12	2.36	−0.11	0.70	−0.08	0.04	−0.01	0.03	−0.01	0.62	−0.05
	Study Deployment	SMs	3.78	−0.04	4.05	−0.05	2.08	−0.05	0.65	−0.07	0.02	−0.01	0.05	−0.01	0.52	−0.05
		SPs	3.68	−0.03	4.02	−0.04	2.22	−0.03	0.44	−0.04	0.03	−0.01	0.02	−0.01	0.45	−0.04
	No Study Deployment	SMs	3.62	−0.04	3.80	−0.05	2.21	−0.05	0.80	−0.07	0.02	−0.01	0.08	−0.02	0.60	−0.05
		SPs	3.42	−0.12	3.59	−0.14	2.41	−0.12	0.80	−0.10	0.05	−0.01	0.04	−0.01	0.65	−0.08

Table A.1b—Continued

		Marital Satisfaction[a]		PANAS: Positive[b]		PANAS: Negative[c]		Physical Aggression: Prevalence Against You[d]		Physical Aggression: Prevalence Against Partner[e]		Psychological Aggression: Frequency Against You[f]		Psychological Aggression: Frequency Against Partner[g]	
		Mean	SE	Mean	SE	Mean	SE	Mean	SE	Mean	SE	Mean	SE	Mean	SE
Wave 5	Overall Sample														
	SMs	3.53	−0.06	3.70	−0.05	2.26	−0.05	0.74	−0.09	0.03	−0.01	0.07	−0.02	0.60	−0.08
	SPs	3.47	−0.09	3.68	−0.12	2.36	−0.11	0.70	−0.08	0.04	−0.01	0.03	−0.01	0.62	−0.05
	Study Deployment														
	SMs	3.85	−0.04	4.01	−0.04	2.01	−0.04	0.58	−0.06	0.02	−0.01	0.03	−0.01	0.46	−0.05
	SPs	3.69	−0.04	3.97	−0.05	2.18	−0.04	0.47	−0.05	0.03	−0.01	0.01	−0.01	0.47	−0.05
	No Study Deployment														
	SMs	3.65	−0.05	3.82	−0.05	2.14	−0.05	0.79	−0.09	0.06	−0.02	0.13	−0.03	0.61	−0.06
	SPs	3.47	−0.13	3.68	−0.14	2.37	−0.14	0.70	−0.07	0.05	−0.01	0.05	−0.02	0.63	−0.06
Wave 6	Overall Sample														
	SMs	3.53	−0.06	3.70	−0.05	2.26	−0.05	0.74	−0.09	0.03	−0.01	0.07	−0.02	0.60	−0.08
	SPs	3.47	−0.09	3.68	−0.12	2.36	−0.11	0.70	−0.08	0.04	−0.01	0.03	−0.01	0.62	−0.05
	Study Deployment														
	SMs	3.80	−0.04	3.95	−0.05	2.06	−0.05	0.61	−0.05	0.01	0.00	0.03	−0.01	0.50	−0.05
	SPs	3.68	−0.04	3.90	−0.05	2.20	−0.04	0.54	−0.06	0.02	−0.01	0.02	−0.01	0.53	−0.04
	No Study Deployment														
	SMs	3.63	−0.05	3.83	−0.05	2.18	−0.05	0.67	−0.07	0.03	−0.01	0.06	−0.01	0.60	−0.06
	SPs	3.42	−0.13	3.62	−0.15	2.40	−0.14	0.74	−0.13	0.03	−0.01	0.04	−0.01	0.59	−0.08
Wave 7	Overall Sample														
	SMs	3.53	−0.06	3.70	−0.05	2.26	−0.05	0.74	−0.09	0.03	−0.01	0.07	−0.02	0.60	−0.08
	SPs	3.47	−0.09	3.68	−0.12	2.36	−0.11	0.70	−0.08	0.04	−0.01	0.03	−0.01	0.62	−0.05
	Study Deployment														
	SMs	3.78	−0.03	3.98	−0.04	2.02	−0.04	0.65	−0.08	0.02	−0.01	0.04	−0.01	0.51	−0.05
	SPs	3.62	−0.05	3.85	−0.05	2.20	−0.04	0.55	−0.05	0.05	−0.02	0.03	−0.01	0.53	−0.04
	No Study Deployment														
	SMs	3.60	−0.05	3.81	−0.07	2.23	−0.06	0.77	−0.07	0.03	−0.01	0.11	−0.02	0.63	−0.06
	SPs	3.40	−0.10	3.61	−0.14	2.41	−0.13	0.76	−0.08	0.02	−0.01	0.07	−0.04	0.57	−0.06
Wave 8[h]	Overall Sample														
	SMs	3.53	−0.06	3.70	−0.05	2.26	−0.05	0.74	−0.09	0.03	−0.01	0.07	−0.02	0.60	−0.08
	SPs	3.47	−0.09	3.68	−0.12	2.36	−0.11	0.70	−0.08	0.04	−0.01	0.03	−0.01	0.62	−0.05
	Study Deployment														
	SMs	3.77	−0.04	4.03	−0.06	2.00	−0.04	0.59	−0.07	0.03	−0.01	0.06	−0.02	0.47	−0.06
	SPs	3.67	−0.05	3.89	−0.06	2.19	−0.04	0.48	−0.07	0.02	−0.01	0.02	−0.01	0.46	−0.06
	No Study Deployment														
	SMs	3.48	−0.11	3.68	−0.10	2.34	−0.12	0.90	−0.15	0.02	−0.01	0.15	−0.05	0.67	−0.10
	SPs	3.40	−0.12	3.58	−0.16	2.44	−0.15	0.77	−0.08	0.03	−0.01	0.04	−0.01	0.57	−0.07

Table A.1b—Continued

		Marital Satisfaction[a]		PANAS: Positive[b]		PANAS: Negative[c]		Physical Aggression: Prevalence Against You[d]		Physical Aggression: Prevalence Against Partner[e]		Psychological Aggression: Frequency Against You[f]		Psychological Aggression: Frequency Against Partner[g]	
		Mean	SE	Mean	SE	Mean	SE	Mean	SE	Mean	SE	Mean	SE	Mean	SE
Wave 9[h] Overall Sample	SMs	3.53	−0.06	3.70	−0.05	2.26	−0.05	0.74	−0.09	0.03	−0.01	0.07	−0.02	0.60	−0.08
	SPs	3.47	−0.09	3.68	−0.12	2.36	−0.11	0.70	−0.08	0.04	−0.01	0.03	−0.01	0.62	−0.05
Study Deployment	SMs	3.66	−0.08	3.88	−0.06	2.05	−0.05	0.63	−0.07	0.03	−0.01	0.06	−0.02	0.46	−0.06
	SPs	3.62	−0.06	3.83	−0.07	2.19	−0.06	0.57	−0.07	0.03	−0.01	0.02	−0.01	0.45	−0.04
No Study Deployment	SMs	3.49	−0.07	3.65	−0.06	2.31	−0.06	0.77	−0.11	0.03	−0.01	0.08	−0.02	0.64	−0.10
	SPs	3.43	−0.12	3.63	−0.16	2.40	−0.14	0.74	−0.09	0.04	−0.01	0.03	−0.01	0.66	−0.06

NOTES: Data are weighted.

[a] Higher scores=greater satisfaction. Range: 1.63–4.63.

[b] Higher scores=more positive affect following communication. Range: 1-5.

[c] Higher scores=more negative affect following communication. Range: 1-5.

[d] Higher scores=increased presence of physical aggression against respondent (yes=1, no=0).

[e] Higher scores=increased presence of physical aggression against partner (yes=1, no=0).

[f] Higher scores=more psychological aggression against respondent. Range: 0–6.

[g] Higher scores=more psychological aggression against partner. Range: 0–6.

[h] The Navy sample does not have data at this wave by design.

Table A.1c
Psychological and Behavioral Health Outcome Means by Study Wave and Study Deployment Status

Wave	Group		Depression[a] Mean	SE	Anxiety[b] Mean	SE	PTSD[c] Mean	SE	Binge Drinking[d] Mean	SE	Problematic Substance Use[e] Mean	SE	Medication Use[f] Mean	SE	Needed Counseling[g] Mean	SE
Baseline	Overall Sample	SMs	5.16	-0.39	2.43	-0.10	26.47	-1.16	0.23	-0.03	0.21	-0.03	0.10	-0.01	0.24	-0.04
		SPs	3.98	-0.21	2.36	-0.05	0.46	-0.06	0.17	-0.02	0.13	-0.04	0.15	-0.02	0.25	-0.04
	Study Deployment	SMs	2.39	-0.16	2.02	-0.05	21.33	-0.41	0.25	-0.03	0.14	-0.02	0.03	-0.01	0.07	-0.01
		SPs	2.84	-0.17	2.08	-0.04	0.48	-0.05	0.15	-0.02	0.10	-0.03	0.11	-0.01	0.13	-0.01
	No Study Deployment	SMs	3.11	-0.21	2.13	-0.06	22.69	-0.55	0.24	-0.03	0.17	-0.03	0.06	-0.01	0.18	-0.02
		SPs	3.25	-0.19	2.18	-0.05	0.49	-0.05	0.09	-0.01	0.05	-0.01	0.13	-0.02	0.14	-0.02
Wave 2	Overall Sample	SMs	5.16	-0.39	2.43	-0.10	26.47	-1.16	0.23	-0.03	0.21	-0.03	0.10	-0.01	0.24	-0.04
		SPs	3.98	-0.21	2.36	-0.05	0.46	-0.06	0.17	-0.02	0.13	-0.04	0.15	-0.02	0.25	-0.04
	Study Deployment	SMs	2.87	-0.26	2.14	-0.07	20.60	-0.37	0.23	-0.02	0.15	-0.03	0.05	-0.01	0.11	-0.02
		SPs	3.99	-0.23	2.55	-0.07	0.39	-0.05	0.19	-0.03	0.06	-0.01	0.11	-0.01	0.16	-0.02
	No Study Deployment	SMs	4.48	-0.33	2.35	-0.07	24.58	-0.89	0.28	-0.03	0.24	-0.06	0.11	-0.02	0.23	-0.03
		SPs	3.83	-0.19	2.44	-0.06	0.42	-0.05	0.11	-0.02	0.07	-0.02	0.15	-0.02	0.19	-0.02
Wave 3	Overall Sample	SMs	5.16	-0.39	2.43	-0.10	26.47	-1.16	0.23	-0.03	0.21	-0.03	0.10	-0.01	0.24	-0.04
		SPs	3.98	-0.21	2.36	-0.05	0.46	-0.06	0.17	-0.02	0.13	-0.04	0.15	-0.02	0.25	-0.04
	Study Deployment	SMs	3.07	-0.21	2.08	-0.05	21.58	-0.48	0.19	-0.02	0.13	-0.02	0.04	-0.01	0.09	-0.02
		SPs	4.25	-0.22	2.60	-0.05	0.44	-0.05	0.19	-0.02	0.13	-0.03	0.14	-0.02	0.19	-0.02
	No Study Deployment	SMs	4.31	-0.33	2.24	-0.07	24.33	-0.73	0.23	-0.03	0.17	-0.03	0.09	-0.02	0.20	-0.02
		SPs	3.93	-0.21	2.41	-0.07	0.46	-0.07	0.12	-0.02	0.07	-0.01	0.12	-0.02	0.19	-0.02
Wave 4	Overall Sample	SMs	5.16	-0.39	2.43	-0.10	26.47	-1.16	0.23	-0.03	0.21	-0.03	0.10	-0.01	0.24	-0.04
		SPs	3.98	-0.21	2.36	-0.05	0.46	-0.06	0.17	-0.02	0.13	-0.04	0.15	-0.02	0.25	-0.04
	Study Deployment	SMs	3.51	-0.25	2.25	-0.07	21.15	-0.42	0.19	-0.02	0.12	-0.02	0.04	-0.01	0.11	-0.02
		SPs	4.04	-0.23	2.51	-0.06	0.42	-0.05	0.16	-0.02	0.12	-0.03	0.13	-0.02	0.18	-0.02
	No Study Deployment	SMs	4.47	-0.30	2.34	-0.07	25.00	-0.81	0.24	-0.03	0.17	-0.03	0.08	-0.02	0.19	-0.02
		SPs	3.83	-0.26	2.37	-0.07	0.43	-0.08	0.13	-0.02	0.11	-0.03	0.12	-0.02	0.18	-0.02

Table A.1c—Continued

		Depression[a]		Anxiety[b]		PTSD[c]		Binge Drinking[d]		Problematic Substance Use[e]		Medication Use[f]		Needed Counseling[g]	
		Mean	SE	Mean	SE	Mean	SE	Mean	SE	Mean	SE	Mean	SE	Mean	SE
Wave 5	Overall Sample SMs	5.16	−0.39	2.43	−0.10	26.47	−1.16	0.23	−0.03	0.21	−0.03	0.10	−0.01	0.24	−0.04
	Overall Sample SPs	3.98	−0.21	2.36	−0.05	0.46	−0.06	0.17	−0.02	0.13	−0.04	0.15	−0.02	0.25	−0.04
	Study Deployment SMs	3.02	−0.21	2.14	−0.06	21.53	−0.46	0.23	−0.03	0.12	−0.02	0.05	−0.01	0.10	−0.01
	Study Deployment SPs	3.86	−0.23	2.45	−0.06	0.28	−0.04	0.17	−0.03	0.14	−0.03	0.13	−0.02	0.14	−0.02
	No Study Deployment SMs	4.30	−0.33	2.28	−0.08	23.62	−0.81	0.23	−0.03	0.18	−0.03	0.09	−0.02	0.21	−0.03
	No Study Deployment SPs	3.68	−0.28	2.28	−0.07	0.41	−0.08	0.12	−0.02	0.10	−0.02	0.11	−0.01	0.21	−0.03
Wave 6	Overall Sample SMs	5.16	−0.39	2.43	−0.10	26.47	−1.16	0.23	−0.03	0.21	−0.03	0.10	−0.01	0.24	−0.04
	Overall Sample SPs	3.98	−0.21	2.36	−0.05	0.46	−0.06	0.17	−0.02	0.13	−0.04	0.15	−0.02	0.25	−0.04
	Study Deployment SMs	3.51	−0.21	2.19	−0.07	22.12	−0.51	0.26	−0.03	0.17	−0.04	0.07	−0.01	0.14	−0.02
	Study Deployment SPs	3.88	−0.24	2.44	−0.07	0.33	−0.04	0.21	−0.03	0.14	−0.03	0.13	−0.01	0.16	−0.02
	No Study Deployment SMs	4.40	−0.35	2.30	−0.07	24.22	−0.86	0.23	−0.03	0.19	−0.03	0.11	−0.02	0.22	−0.03
	No Study Deployment SPs	3.99	−0.26	2.36	−0.07	0.48	−0.09	0.16	−0.02	0.12	−0.02	0.10	−0.01	0.24	−0.04
Wave 7	Overall Sample SMs	5.16	−0.39	2.43	−0.10	26.47	−1.16	0.23	−0.03	0.21	−0.03	0.10	−0.01	0.24	−0.04
	Overall Sample SPs	3.98	−0.21	2.36	−0.05	0.46	−0.06	0.17	−0.02	0.13	−0.04	0.15	−0.02	0.25	−0.04
	Study Deployment SMs	3.39	−0.21	2.08	−0.06	22.57	−0.62	0.29	−0.03	0.19	−0.04	0.07	−0.01	0.16	−0.02
	Study Deployment SPs	3.82	−0.24	2.32	−0.05	0.32	−0.04	0.19	−0.03	0.13	−0.03	0.13	−0.02	0.17	−0.02
	No Study Deployment SMs	4.56	−0.35	2.31	−0.08	25.07	−0.84	0.20	−0.02	0.17	−0.03	0.10	−0.02	0.21	−0.02
	No Study Deployment SPs	4.27	−0.26	2.37	−0.07	0.46	−0.06	0.13	−0.02	0.11	−0.02	0.12	−0.02	0.20	−0.03
Wave 8[h]	Overall Sample SMs	5.16	−0.39	2.43	−0.10	26.47	−1.16	0.23	−0.03	0.21	−0.03	0.10	−0.01	0.24	−0.04
	Overall Sample SPs	3.98	−0.21	2.36	−0.05	0.46	−0.06	0.17	−0.02	0.13	−0.04	0.15	−0.02	0.25	−0.04
	Study Deployment SMs	3.46	−0.30	2.04	−0.06	23.32	−0.59	0.22	−0.04	0.23	−0.05	0.10	−0.02	0.16	−0.02
	Study Deployment SPs	3.65	−0.27	2.28	−0.07	0.36	−0.05	0.16	−0.02	0.14	−0.03	0.13	−0.02	0.17	−0.02
	No Study Deployment SMs	4.67	−0.35	2.23	−0.10	25.34	−1.00	0.27	−0.05	0.23	−0.05	0.12	−0.02	0.26	−0.05
	No Study Deployment SPs	4.15	−0.28	2.40	−0.08	0.46	−0.08	0.15	−0.03	0.08	−0.02	0.14	−0.03	0.22	−0.04

Table A.1c—Continued

		Depression[a]		Anxiety[b]		PTSD[c]		Binge Drinking[d]		Problematic Substance Use[e]		Medication Use[f]		Needed Counseling[g]	
		Mean	SE	Mean	SE	Mean	SE	Mean	SE	Mean	SE	Mean	SE	Mean	SE
Wave 9[h] Overall Sample	SMs	5.16	−0.39	2.43	−0.10	26.47	−1.16	0.23	−0.03	0.21	−0.03	0.10	−0.01	0.24	−0.04
	SPs	3.98	−0.21	2.36	−0.05	0.46	−0.06	0.17	−0.02	0.13	−0.04	0.15	−0.02	0.25	−0.04
Study Deployment	SMs	3.79	−0.30	2.13	−0.08	24.14	−0.71	0.23	−0.03	0.24	−0.05	0.10	−0.02	0.18	−0.02
	SPs	3.61	−0.22	2.32	−0.07	0.37	−0.05	0.21	−0.03	0.16	−0.04	0.13	−0.02	0.14	−0.02
No Study Deployment	SMs	5.54	−0.49	2.51	−0.12	27.11	−1.44	0.23	−0.04	0.20	−0.04	0.10	−0.02	0.26	−0.05
	SPs	4.08	−0.26	2.37	−0.06	0.49	−0.07	0.16	−0.03	0.12	−0.04	0.15	−0.03	0.28	−0.05

NOTES: Data are weighted.

[a] Higher scores=more depressive symptoms. Range: 0–24.

[b] Higher scores=more anxiety. Mean subscale score range: 1–6.

[c] Higher scores=more PTSD symptoms. Range: 17–85 for service member, 0–4 for spouse.

[d] Percentage reporting binge drinking (5+ drinks for men; 4+ drinks for women).

[e] Higher scores=more problematic substance use. Range: 0–7.

[f] Percentage reporting use of medication for a mental health problem.

[g] Percentage reporting need for treatment for mental health treatment.

[h] The Navy sample does not have data at this wave by design.

Table A.1d
Military Integration Outcome Means by Study Wave and Study Deployment Status (Active Component Only)

			Job Satisfaction Scale[a]		Military Commitment Scale[b]		Retention Intentions[c]	
			Mean	SE	Mean	SE	Mean	SE
Baseline	Overall Sample	SMs	3.85	−0.09	3.79	−0.12	3.66	−0.17
		SPs	4.07	−0.05	4.03	−0.05	3.78	−0.10
	Study Deployment	SMs	3.93	−0.07	4.39	−0.04	4.23	−0.07
		SPs	4.10	−0.07	4.49	−0.04	4.12	−0.06
	No Study Deployment	SMs	3.65	−0.08	4.32	−0.05	4.13	−0.09
		SPs	3.98	−0.07	4.39	−0.05	3.81	−0.11
Wave 2	Overall Sample	SMs	3.85	−0.09	3.79	−0.12	3.66	−0.17
		SPs	4.07	−0.05	4.03	−0.05	3.78	−0.10
	Study Deployment	SMs	3.75	−0.06	4.04	−0.06	4.00	−0.08
		SPs	3.96	−0.06	4.11	−0.06	4.00	−0.09
	No Study Deployment	SMs	3.54	−0.08	3.96	−0.06	3.72	−0.11
		SPs	4.01	−0.06	4.03	−0.05	3.82	−0.08
Wave 3	Overall Sample	SMs	3.85	−0.09	3.79	−0.12	3.66	−0.17
		SPs	4.07	−0.05	4.03	−0.05	3.78	−0.10
	Study Deployment	SMs	3.70	−0.10	3.85	−0.17	3.96	−0.10
		SPs	4.08	−0.05	4.08	−0.05	4.03	−0.07
	No Study Deployment	SMs	3.61	−0.08	3.83	−0.07	3.68	−0.10
		SPs	4.00	−0.06	4.12	−0.07	3.80	−0.09
Wave 4	Overall Sample	SMs	3.85	−0.09	3.79	−0.12	3.66	−0.17
		SPs	4.07	−0.05	4.03	−0.05	3.78	−0.10
	Study Deployment	SMs	3.61	−0.08	3.87	−0.07	3.92	−0.08
		SPs	4.01	−0.06	4.07	−0.04	3.97	−0.07
	No Study Deployment	SMs	3.64	−0.08	3.98	−0.06	3.82	−0.10
		SPs	4.13	−0.07	4.12	−0.06	3.93	−0.07
Wave 5	Overall Sample	SMs	3.85	−0.09	3.79	−0.12	3.66	−0.17
		SPs	4.07	−0.05	4.03	−0.05	3.78	−0.10
	Study Deployment	SMs	3.76	−0.06	3.97	−0.05	4.02	−0.08
		SPs	4.00	−0.06	4.06	−0.05	4.02	−0.07
	No Study Deployment	SMs	3.69	−0.08	3.89	−0.06	3.69	−0.11
		SPs	4.08	−0.08	4.06	−0.06	3.80	−0.10
Wave 6	Overall Sample	SMs	3.85	−0.09	3.79	−0.12	3.66	−0.17
		SPs	4.07	−0.05	4.03	−0.05	3.78	−0.10
	Study Deployment	SMs	3.77	−0.06	3.97	−0.08	4.01	−0.09
		SPs	3.99	−0.05	4.01	−0.05	3.99	−0.07
	No Study Deployment	SMs	3.74	−0.09	3.86	−0.07	3.64	−0.12
		SPs	4.16	−0.08	4.12	−0.08	3.97	−0.08

Table A.1d—Continued

			Job Satisfaction Scale[a]		Military Commitment Scale[b]		Retention Intentions[c]	
			Mean	SE	Mean	SE	Mean	SE
Wave 7	Overall Sample	SMs	3.85	−0.09	3.79	−0.12	3.66	−0.17
		SPs	4.07	−0.05	4.03	−0.05	3.78	−0.10
	Study Deployment	SMs	3.85	−0.09	3.97	−0.07	3.94	−0.10
		SPs	4.00	−0.07	4.02	−0.05	3.98	−0.08
	No Study Deployment	SMs	3.82	−0.12	3.96	−0.09	3.71	−0.13
		SPs	4.02	−0.08	4.04	−0.05	3.81	−0.09
Wave 8[d]	Overall Sample	SMs	3.85	−0.09	3.79	−0.12	3.66	−0.17
		SPs	4.07	−0.05	4.03	−0.05	3.78	−0.10
	Study Deployment	SMs	3.80	−0.10	4.02	−0.08	3.86	−0.11
		SPs	3.89	−0.09	3.97	−0.06	3.86	−0.09
	No Study Deployment	SMs	3.81	−0.09	4.00	−0.13	3.84	−0.17
		SPs	4.05	−0.08	3.98	−0.07	3.85	−0.11
Wave 9[d]	Overall Sample	SMs	3.85	−0.09	3.79	−0.12	3.66	−0.17
		SPs	4.07	−0.05	4.03	−0.05	3.78	−0.10
	Study Deployment	SMs	3.84	−0.10	3.89	−0.08	3.85	−0.12
		SPs	4.03	−0.07	3.95	−0.07	3.93	−0.08
	No Study Deployment	SMs	3.85	−0.12	3.74	−0.17	3.57	−0.25
		SPs	4.09	−0.07	4.06	−0.06	3.71	−0.15

NOTE: Data are weighted.

[a] Higher scores=more satisfaction. Range: 1–5.

[b] Higher scores=more commitment. Range: 1–5.

[c] Higher scores=strong preference for continued military service. Range: 1–5.

[d] The Navy sample does not have data at this wave by design.

Table A.2a
Family Outcome Means by Study Wave and Gender

			Family Environment Scale[a]		Satisfaction with Parenting[b]		Financial Distress Scale[c]	
			Mean	SE	Mean	SE	Mean	SE
Baseline	Male	SMs	2.76	−0.04	3.34	−0.04	1.96	−0.05
		SPs	2.75	−0.04	3.20	−0.02	2.07	−0.04
	Female	SMs	2.65	−0.07	3.42	−0.07	2.13	−0.18
		SPs	2.70	−0.07	3.25	−0.06	1.91	−0.20
Wave 2	Male	SMs	2.74	−0.02	3.22	−0.04	1.95	−0.05
		SPs	2.74	−0.02	3.14	−0.03	1.99	−0.04
	Female	SMs	2.66	−0.06	3.15	−0.11	1.96	−0.16
		SPs	2.62	−0.08	3.22	−0.09	1.73	−0.11
Wave 3	Male	SMs	2.76	−0.02	3.26	−0.04	1.94	−0.05
		SPs	2.66	−0.06	3.11	−0.03	1.96	−0.04
	Female	SMs	2.53	−0.09	3.17	−0.13	2.25	−0.22
		SPs	2.65	−0.12	3.06	−0.12	1.78	−0.17
Wave 4	Male	SMs	2.72	−0.02	3.20	−0.04	1.95	−0.04
		SPs	2.68	−0.06	3.15	−0.03	1.94	−0.04
	Female	SMs	2.69	−0.08	3.22	−0.12	2.18	−0.28
		SPs	2.47	−0.16	3.11	−0.13	2.04	−0.31
Wave 5	Male	SMs	2.74	−0.02	3.15	−0.04	1.91	−0.05
		SPs	2.69	−0.06	3.14	−0.02	1.94	−0.04
	Female	SMs	2.72	−0.07	3.29	−0.12	2.06	−0.27
		SPs	2.47	−0.15	3.04	−0.14	1.93	−0.26
Wave 6	Male	SMs	2.75	−0.02	3.20	−0.04	1.97	−0.06
		SPs	2.69	−0.05	3.09	−0.03	2.06	−0.05
	Female	SMs	2.77	−0.06	3.24	−0.13	2.12	−0.24
		SPs	2.52	−0.12	3.04	−0.15	2.02	−0.29
Wave 7	Male	SMs	2.70	−0.02	3.22	−0.04	1.97	−0.05
		SPs	2.67	−0.05	3.11	−0.03	2.06	−0.07
	Female	SMs	2.62	−0.07	3.12	−0.14	2.22	−0.20
		SPs	2.51	−0.10	3.11	−0.13	1.92	−0.26
Wave 8[d]	Male	SMs	2.67	−0.05	3.23	−0.07	1.94	−0.06
		SPs	2.65	−0.09	3.12	−0.04	2.06	−0.07
	Female	SMs	2.72	−0.07	3.14	−0.10	2.28	−0.26
		SPs	2.45	−0.11	3.04	−0.14	2.03	−0.30
Wave 9[d]	Male	SMs	2.68	−0.03	3.21	−0.06	1.92	−0.05
		SPs	2.64	−0.07	3.09	−0.05	2.05	−0.07
	Female	SMs	2.70	−0.07	3.31	−0.15	2.38	−0.26
		SPs	2.51	−0.11	2.92	−0.13	2.06	−0.27

NOTE: Data are weighted.

[a] Higher scores=more positive environment. Range: 1–3.

[b] Higher scores=more satisfaction. Range: 1–4.

[c] Higher scores=more distress. Range: 1–4.

[d] The Navy sample does not have data at this wave by design.

Table A.2b
Marital Relationship Outcome Means by Study Wave and Gender

			Marital Satisfaction[a]		PANAS: Positive[b]		PANAS: Negative[c]		Physical Aggression: Prevalence Against You[d]		Physical Aggression: Prevalence Against Partner[e]		Psychological Aggression: Frequency Against You[f]		Psychological Aggression: Frequency Against Partner[g]	
			Mean	SE	Mean	SE	Mean	SE	Mean	SE	Mean	SE	Mean	SE	Mean	SE
Baseline	Male	SMs	3.97	-0.03	4.18	-0.04	1.98	-0.03	0.80	-0.06	0.02	0.00	0.05	-0.01	0.67	-0.06
		SPs	3.78	-0.06	4.05	-0.08	2.23	-0.06	0.75	-0.06	0.06	-0.01	0.02	-0.01	0.79	-0.04
	Female	SMs	3.59	-0.08	3.83	-0.11	2.43	-0.10	1.19	-0.16	0.04	-0.02	0.04	-0.03	1.24	-0.17
		SPs	3.62	-0.10	3.70	-0.13	2.20	-0.08	1.17	-0.21	0.02	-0.02	0.16	-0.08	0.60	-0.16
Wave 2	Male	SMs	3.79	-0.04	3.96	-0.04	2.09	-0.04	0.80	-0.06	0.04	-0.01	0.09	-0.02	0.65	-0.05
		SPs	3.67	-0.04	3.89	-0.04	2.28	-0.04	0.75	-0.06	0.06	-0.02	0.05	-0.01	0.75	-0.05
	Female	SMs	3.60	-0.10	3.87	-0.14	2.29	-0.11	1.10	-0.20	0.10	-0.05	0.08	-0.05	1.15	-0.15
		SPs	3.47	-0.11	3.80	-0.14	2.29	-0.13	0.99	-0.24	0.03	-0.03	0.10	-0.04	0.67	-0.19
Wave 3	Male	SMs	3.82	-0.04	3.98	-0.05	2.06	-0.03	0.70	-0.06	0.02	-0.01	0.07	-0.01	0.54	-0.04
		SPs	3.50	-0.10	3.77	-0.12	2.35	-0.12	0.68	-0.06	0.04	-0.01	0.04	-0.01	0.70	-0.06
	Female	SMs	3.44	-0.08	3.69	-0.12	2.44	-0.11	0.80	-0.14	0.03	-0.02	0.02	-0.02	0.85	-0.15
		SPs	3.15	-0.19	3.32	-0.17	2.40	-0.12	1.25	-0.25	0.04	-0.03	0.10	-0.05	0.72	-0.16
Wave 4	Male	SMs	3.69	-0.04	3.88	-0.04	2.15	-0.04	0.76	-0.06	0.02	-0.01	0.08	-0.02	0.55	-0.04
		SPs	3.50	-0.10	3.73	-0.12	2.36	-0.10	0.71	-0.08	0.04	-0.01	0.03	-0.01	0.65	-0.07
	Female	SMs	3.39	-0.11	3.64	-0.15	2.44	-0.09	0.84	-0.14	0.01	-0.01	0.01	0.00	0.80	-0.17
		SPs	3.35	-0.26	3.36	-0.26	2.41	-0.19	0.72	-0.27	0.03	-0.02	0.06	-0.03	0.25	-0.09
Wave 5	Male	SMs	3.73	-0.04	3.87	-0.04	2.08	-0.04	0.75	-0.08	0.04	-0.01	0.11	-0.02	0.54	-0.05
		SPs	3.52	-0.11	3.76	-0.12	2.34	-0.12	0.62	-0.06	0.05	-0.01	0.04	-0.02	0.61	-0.05
	Female	SMs	3.42	-0.11	3.82	-0.11	2.31	-0.10	0.67	-0.18	0.09	-0.05	0.06	-0.04	0.82	-0.19
		SPs	3.53	-0.21	3.64	-0.26	2.20	-0.19	0.79	-0.23	0.03	-0.03	0.03	-0.03	0.44	-0.14
Wave 6	Male	SMs	3.71	-0.05	3.87	-0.04	2.12	-0.04	0.65	-0.06	0.02	0.00	0.05	-0.01	0.54	-0.05
		SPs	3.46	-0.11	3.68	-0.12	2.38	-0.12	0.68	-0.11	0.03	-0.01	0.03	-0.01	0.59	-0.06
	Female	SMs	3.46	-0.12	3.78	-0.13	2.34	-0.12	0.69	-0.15	0.06	-0.03	0.04	-0.02	0.80	-0.17
		SPs	3.65	-0.21	3.72	-0.28	2.12	-0.17	0.78	-0.25	0.00	0.00	0.05	-0.04	0.47	-0.14

Table A.2b—Continued

		Marital Satisfaction[a]		PANAS: Positive[b]		PANAS: Negative[c]		Physical Aggression: Prevalence Against You[d]		Physical Aggression: Prevalence Against Partner[e]		Psychological Aggression: Frequency Against You[f]		Psychological Aggression: Frequency Against Partner[g]	
		Mean	SE	Mean	SE	Mean	SE	Mean	SE	Mean	SE	Mean	SE	Mean	SE
Wave 7	Male SMs	3.67	−0.04	3.85	−0.05	2.13	−0.04	0.73	−0.06	0.02	−0.01	0.10	−0.02	0.55	−0.04
	SPs	3.45	−0.09	3.69	−0.12	2.37	−0.12	0.67	−0.07	0.03	−0.01	0.06	−0.04	0.57	−0.05
	Female SMs	3.46	−0.17	3.82	−0.24	2.45	−0.25	0.83	−0.21	0.05	−0.03	0.06	−0.04	0.87	−0.21
	SPs	3.44	−0.14	3.50	−0.22	2.31	−0.20	0.98	−0.26	0.02	−0.02	0.06	−0.03	0.49	−0.17
Wave 8[h]	Male SMs	3.58	−0.10	3.78	−0.09	2.22	−0.10	0.80	−0.13	0.02	−0.01	0.13	−0.05	0.57	−0.09
	SPs	3.47	−0.10	3.67	−0.14	2.37	−0.13	0.65	−0.06	0.03	−0.01	0.03	−0.01	0.53	−0.06
	Female SMs	3.24	−0.15	3.55	−0.15	2.64	−0.12	1.14	−0.21	0.07	−0.03	0.11	−0.06	1.08	−0.23
	SPs	3.41	−0.16	3.46	−0.20	2.50	−0.23	1.22	−0.22	0.03	−0.03	0.09	−0.05	0.74	−0.21
Wave 9[h]	Male SMs	3.56	−0.06	3.72	−0.06	2.21	−0.05	0.70	−0.09	0.02	−0.01	0.07	−0.02	0.57	−0.09
	SPs	3.48	−0.10	3.71	−0.14	2.34	−0.12	0.66	−0.08	0.04	−0.01	0.02	−0.01	0.60	−0.05
	Female SMs	3.23	−0.13	3.49	−0.14	2.62	−0.13	1.09	−0.28	0.11	−0.05	0.14	−0.07	0.89	−0.20
	SPs	3.29	−0.17	3.31	−0.16	2.47	−0.16	1.09	−0.27	0.04	−0.04	0.08	−0.05	0.79	−0.21

NOTE: Data are weighted.

[a] Higher scores=greater satisfaction. Range: 1.63–4.63.

[b] Higher scores=more positive affect following communication. Range: 1–5.

[c] Higher scores=more negative affect following communication. Range: 1–5.

[d] Higher scores=increased presence of physical aggression against respondent (yes=1, no=0).

[e] Higher scores=increased presence of physical aggression against partner (yes=1, no=0).

[f] Higher scores=more psychological aggression against respondent. Range: 0–6.

[g] Higher scores=more psychological aggression against partner. Range: 0–6.

[h] The Navy sample does not have data at this wave by design.

Table A.2c
Psychological and Behavioral Health Outcome Means by Study Wave and Gender

		Depression[a] Mean	SE	Anxiety[b] Mean	SE	PTSD[c] Mean	SE	Binge Drinking[d] Mean	SE	Problematic Substance Use[e] Mean	SE	Medication Use[f] Mean	SE	Needed Counseling[g] Mean	SE
Baseline	Male														
	SMs	2.72	−0.16	2.04	−0.05	22.10	−0.42	0.26	−0.03	0.18	−0.03	0.05	−0.01	0.14	−0.02
	SPs	3.28	−0.16	2.19	−0.04	0.50	−0.05	0.09	−0.01	0.05	−0.01	0.14	−0.02	0.14	−0.01
	Female														
	SMs	4.60	−0.66	2.53	−0.12	24.41	−1.82	0.11	−0.03	0.06	−0.03	0.05	−0.02	0.30	−0.08
	SPs	2.33	−0.34	1.92	−0.14	0.43	−0.12	0.15	−0.04	0.16	−0.07	0.03	−0.02	0.10	−0.03
Wave 2	Male														
	SMs	4.03	−0.28	2.29	−0.06	23.30	−0.67	0.29	−0.03	0.24	−0.06	0.09	−0.02	0.18	−0.02
	SPs	3.86	−0.17	2.49	−0.05	0.40	−0.04	0.13	−0.01	0.05	−0.01	0.15	−0.02	0.18	−0.02
	Female														
	SMs	4.87	−0.84	2.43	−0.17	26.79	−3.05	0.12	−0.03	0.02	−0.01	0.10	−0.05	0.34	−0.09
	SPs	3.92	−0.51	2.25	−0.13	0.56	−0.17	0.11	−0.04	0.19	−0.11	0.06	−0.03	0.22	−0.09
Wave 3	Male														
	SMs	3.76	−0.28	2.15	−0.06	23.24	−0.56	0.24	−0.02	0.18	−0.02	0.08	−0.01	0.15	−0.02
	SPs	4.00	−0.16	2.50	−0.04	0.43	−0.05	0.14	−0.02	0.07	−0.01	0.14	−0.02	0.20	−0.02
	Female														
	SMs	5.93	−0.68	2.56	−0.16	27.06	−2.15	0.09	−0.03	0.04	−0.03	0.11	−0.04	0.35	−0.08
	SPs	3.98	−0.74	2.08	−0.24	0.68	−0.31	0.14	−0.05	0.20	−0.08	0.03	−0.02	0.17	−0.08
Wave 4	Male														
	SMs	4.10	−0.24	2.29	−0.06	23.81	−0.68	0.25	−0.02	0.17	−0.03	0.07	−0.01	0.15	−0.02
	SPs	3.87	−0.20	2.46	−0.04	0.44	−0.07	0.14	−0.02	0.11	−0.03	0.14	−0.02	0.19	−0.02
	Female														
	SMs	5.43	−0.74	2.51	−0.14	26.51	−1.76	0.10	−0.03	0.08	−0.04	0.12	−0.05	0.33	−0.08
	SPs	3.93	−0.99	1.99	−0.21	0.30	−0.10	0.16	−0.05	0.10	−0.04	0.05	−0.02	0.13	−0.04
Wave 5	Male														
	SMs	3.87	−0.26	2.20	−0.06	22.80	−0.59	0.25	−0.02	0.18	−0.03	0.07	−0.01	0.16	−0.02
	SPs	3.69	−0.19	2.35	−0.05	0.33	−0.04	0.13	−0.02	0.09	−0.02	0.13	−0.01	0.19	−0.02
	Female														
	SMs	5.03	−0.81	2.58	−0.24	25.51	−2.74	0.10	−0.03	0.07	−0.04	0.09	−0.03	0.36	−0.08
	SPs	3.96	−1.16	2.13	−0.31	0.69	−0.37	0.14	−0.04	0.26	−0.11	0.06	−0.02	0.24	−0.11
Wave 6	Male														
	SMs	3.97	−0.27	2.23	−0.05	23.15	−0.63	0.25	−0.02	0.19	−0.03	0.09	−0.01	0.18	−0.02
	SPs	3.95	−0.17	2.42	−0.05	0.40	−0.05	0.17	−0.02	0.11	−0.02	0.12	−0.01	0.23	−0.04
	Female														
	SMs	5.59	−0.88	2.59	−0.17	27.27	−2.49	0.10	−0.04	0.15	−0.07	0.15	−0.07	0.31	−0.08
	SPs	4.05	−1.16	2.15	−0.29	0.74	−0.37	0.22	−0.08	0.24	−0.11	0.06	−0.03	0.19	−0.10

330   The Deployment Life Study: Longitudinal Analysis of Military Families Across the Deployment Cycle

Table A.2c—Continued

		Depression[a]		Anxiety[b]		PTSD[c]		Binge Drinking[d]		Problematic Substance Use[e]		Medication Use[f]		Needed Counseling[g]	
		Mean	SE	Mean	SE	Mean	SE	Mean	SE	Mean	SE	Mean	SE	Mean	SE
Wave 7	Male SMs	4.15	-0.25	2.26	-0.06	24.02	-0.60	0.25	-0.02	0.20	-0.02	0.09	-0.01	0.18	-0.02
	SPs	4.17	-0.20	2.38	-0.05	0.39	-0.04	0.14	-0.02	0.09	-0.01	0.13	-0.01	0.19	-0.02
	Female SMs	5.09	-1.23	2.26	-0.27	27.21	-2.92	0.06	-0.02	0.04	-0.02	0.13	-0.06	0.26	-0.08
	SPs	4.13	-0.93	2.21	-0.26	0.70	-0.28	0.14	-0.05	0.32	-0.14	0.07	-0.03	0.23	-0.10
Wave 8[h]	Male SMs	4.17	-0.28	2.12	-0.08	24.30	-0.78	0.28	-0.04	0.24	-0.04	0.10	-0.01	0.21	-0.04
	SPs	3.97	-0.24	2.37	-0.07	0.40	-0.06	0.15	-0.03	0.07	-0.01	0.13	-0.02	0.20	-0.03
	Female SMs	6.34	-0.82	2.77	-0.19	29.87	-2.52	0.07	-0.03	0.12	-0.08	0.21	-0.08	0.44	-0.09
	SPs	4.67	-0.69	2.40	-0.32	0.78	-0.35	0.16	-0.05	0.30	-0.11	0.21	-0.12	0.25	-0.12
Wave 9[h]	Male SMs	4.97	-0.42	2.41	-0.11	26.10	-1.26	0.25	-0.03	0.21	-0.04	0.09	-0.01	0.23	-0.05
	SPs	3.97	-0.22	2.36	-0.05	0.44	-0.06	0.17	-0.02	0.11	-0.04	0.14	-0.02	0.25	-0.04
	Female SMs	6.81	-1.11	2.58	-0.25	29.52	-2.73	0.13	-0.04	0.16	-0.07	0.16	-0.05	0.33	-0.08
	SPs	4.07	-0.55	2.42	-0.20	0.64	-0.23	0.17	-0.05	0.23	-0.09	0.21	-0.11	0.23	-0.11

NOTE: Data are weighted.

[a] Higher scores=more depressive symptoms. Range: 0–24.

[b] Higher scores=more anxiety. Mean subscale score range: 1–6.

[c] Higher scores=more PTSD symptoms. Range: 17–85 for service member, 0–4 for spouse.

[d] Percentage reporting binge drinking (5+ drinks for men; 4+ drinks for women).

[e] Higher scores=more problematic substance use. Range: 0–7.

[f] Percentage reporting use of medication for a mental health problem.

[g] Percentage reporting need for treatment for mental health treatment.

[h] The Navy sample does not have data at this wave by design.

Table A.2d
Military Integration Outcome Means by Study Wave and Gender (Active Component Only)

			Job Satisfaction Scale[a]		Military Commitment Scale[b]		Retention Intentions[c]	
			Mean	SE	Mean	SE	Mean	SE
Baseline	Male	SMs	4.17	−0.07	3.77	−0.07	4.37	−0.04
		SPs	4.00	−0.06	4.09	−0.05	4.46	−0.03
	Female	SMs	4.08	−0.27	3.44	−0.16	4.12	−0.11
		SPs	3.17	−0.33	3.49	−0.18	4.09	−0.14
Wave 2	Male	SMs	3.85	−0.08	3.65	−0.06	4.01	−0.05
		SPs	3.95	−0.06	4.01	−0.05	4.07	−0.04
	Female	SMs	3.43	−0.31	3.28	−0.20	3.80	−0.15
		SPs	3.11	−0.27	3.77	−0.21	3.87	−0.16
Wave 3	Male	SMs	3.76	−0.08	3.66	−0.07	3.87	−0.08
		SPs	3.95	−0.06	4.05	−0.05	4.10	−0.04
	Female	SMs	3.77	−0.23	3.44	−0.15	3.60	−0.15
		SPs	3.19	−0.20	3.84	−0.13	4.20	−0.30
Wave 4	Male	SMs	3.90	−0.08	3.65	−0.06	3.97	−0.05
		SPs	3.96	−0.06	4.06	−0.05	4.08	−0.04
	Female	SMs	3.49	−0.27	3.46	−0.18	3.79	−0.12
		SPs	3.84	−0.14	4.36	−0.26	4.27	−0.16
Wave 5	Male	SMs	3.83	−0.08	3.74	−0.06	3.93	−0.05
		SPs	3.95	−0.07	4.04	−0.04	4.06	−0.04
	Female	SMs	3.47	−0.30	3.52	−0.19	3.75	−0.15
		SPs	3.24	−0.19	4.18	−0.29	4.04	−0.24
Wave 6	Male	SMs	3.81	−0.09	3.76	−0.07	3.91	−0.06
		SPs	4.00	−0.06	4.07	−0.05	4.06	−0.04
	Female	SMs	3.43	−0.32	3.67	−0.15	3.77	−0.14
		SPs	3.79	−0.18	4.31	−0.27	4.26	−0.28
Wave 7	Male	SMs	3.78	−0.08	3.79	−0.08	3.94	−0.05
		SPs	3.90	−0.06	3.96	−0.04	4.03	−0.03
	Female	SMs	3.75	−0.46	4.07	−0.35	4.10	−0.30
		SPs	3.61	−0.23	4.41	−0.23	4.04	−0.16
Wave 8[d]	Male	SMs	3.90	−0.13	3.82	−0.07	4.04	−0.10
		SPs	3.89	−0.08	4.03	−0.06	4.00	−0.05
	Female	SMs	3.21	−0.26	3.69	−0.22	3.63	−0.14
		SPs	3.30	−0.23	3.70	−0.22	3.72	−0.11
Wave 9[d]	Male	SMs	3.68	−0.19	3.89	−0.09	3.80	−0.13
		SPs	3.80	−0.11	4.09	−0.05	4.06	−0.05
	Female	SMs	3.39	−0.32	3.31	−0.27	3.69	−0.18
		SPs	3.46	−0.26	3.85	−0.18	3.63	−0.12

NOTE: Data are weighted.

[a] Higher scores=more satisfaction. Range: 1–5.

[b] Higher scores=more commitment. Range: 1–5.

[c] Higher scores=strong preference for continued military service. Range: 1–5.

[d] The Navy sample does not have data at this wave by design.

Table A.3a
Family Outcome Means by Study Wave and Component

			Family Environment Scale[a]		Satisfaction with Parenting[b]		Financial Distress Scale[c]	
			Mean	SE	Mean	SE	Mean	SE
Baseline	Active	SMs	2.76	−0.05	3.33	−0.05	1.87	−0.04
		SPs	2.83	−0.01	3.24	−0.02	1.96	−0.04
	Reserve	SMs	2.73	−0.03	3.38	−0.04	2.19	−0.12
		SPs	2.60	−0.08	3.13	−0.05	2.24	−0.08
Wave 2	Active	SMs	2.73	−0.02	3.19	−0.04	1.88	−0.05
		SPs	2.76	−0.02	3.12	−0.03	1.89	−0.04
	Reserve	SMs	2.73	−0.04	3.25	−0.07	2.09	−0.10
		SPs	2.66	−0.04	3.21	−0.05	2.12	−0.07
Wave 3	Active	SMs	2.75	−0.02	3.22	−0.04	1.86	−0.04
		SPs	2.75	−0.02	3.07	−0.03	1.93	−0.04
	Reserve	SMs	2.69	−0.05	3.30	−0.06	2.19	−0.11
		SPs	2.52	−0.11	3.17	−0.06	1.97	−0.09
Wave 4	Active	SMs	2.72	−0.02	3.18	−0.04	1.90	−0.04
		SPs	2.75	−0.02	3.15	−0.03	1.90	−0.04
	Reserve	SMs	2.71	−0.04	3.24	−0.07	2.09	−0.11
		SPs	2.50	−0.12	3.12	−0.08	2.03	−0.10
Wave 5	Active	SMs	2.73	−0.03	3.16	−0.05	1.85	−0.04
		SPs	2.75	−0.02	3.14	−0.02	1.92	−0.04
	Reserve	SMs	2.73	−0.04	3.17	−0.08	2.05	−0.12
		SPs	2.54	−0.12	3.12	−0.05	1.97	−0.09
Wave 6	Active	SMs	2.74	−0.02	3.21	−0.05	1.89	−0.05
		SPs	2.74	−0.02	3.10	−0.03	1.96	−0.05
	Reserve	SMs	2.76	−0.04	3.19	−0.07	2.20	−0.14
		SPs	2.57	−0.10	3.05	−0.06	2.22	−0.10
Wave 7	Active	SMs	2.68	−0.02	3.23	−0.04	1.93	−0.04
		SPs	2.72	−0.02	3.11	−0.03	1.93	−0.04
	Reserve	SMs	2.70	−0.04	3.17	−0.06	2.13	−0.13
		SPs	2.54	−0.11	3.11	−0.06	2.24	−0.14
Wave 8[d]	Active	SMs	2.64	−0.06	3.22	−0.09	1.91	−0.07
		SPs	2.72	−0.03	3.14	−0.03	1.88	−0.06
	Reserve	SMs	2.73	−0.04	3.22	−0.06	2.07	−0.11
		SPs	2.51	−0.16	3.09	−0.07	2.27	−0.11
Wave 9[d]	Active	SMs	2.67	−0.05	3.23	−0.09	1.90	−0.06
		SPs	2.73	−0.03	3.12	−0.04	1.90	−0.06
	Reserve	SMs	2.71	−0.04	3.20	−0.06	2.06	−0.10
		SPs	2.49	−0.13	3.03	−0.08	2.23	−0.10

NOTE: Data are weighted.

[a] Higher scores=more positive environment. Range: 1–3.

[b] Higher scores=more satisfaction. Range: 1–4.

[c] Higher scores=more distress. Range: 1–4.

[d] The Navy sample does not have data at this wave by design.

Table A.3b
Marital Relationship Outcome Means by Study Wave and Component

		Marital Satisfaction[a]		PANAS: Positive[b]		PANAS: Negative[c]		Physical Aggression: Prevalence Against You[d]		Physical Aggression: Prevalence Against Partner[e]		Psychological Aggression: Frequency Against You[f]		Psychological Aggression: Frequency Against Partner[g]	
		Mean	SE	Mean	SE	Mean	SE	Mean	SE	Mean	SE	Mean	SE	Mean	SE
Baseline	Active SMs	3.94	-0.04	4.17	-0.06	2.03	-0.05	0.87	-0.07	0.02	0.00	0.05	-0.01	0.78	-0.07
	SPs	3.87	-0.02	4.12	-0.04	2.11	-0.03	0.74	-0.06	0.07	-0.02	0.03	-0.01	0.75	-0.05
	Reserve SMs	3.90	-0.05	4.06	-0.06	2.06	-0.06	0.79	-0.09	0.02	-0.01	0.05	-0.02	0.67	-0.08
	SPs	3.55	-0.12	3.80	-0.17	2.44	-0.13	0.93	-0.13	0.04	-0.02	0.06	-0.03	0.79	-0.09
Wave 2	Active SMs	3.78	-0.03	4.01	-0.04	2.10	-0.03	0.89	-0.06	0.05	-0.01	0.08	-0.02	0.81	-0.06
	SPs	3.70	-0.03	3.94	-0.04	2.24	-0.04	0.80	-0.07	0.08	-0.02	0.06	-0.02	0.77	-0.05
	Reserve SMs	3.77	-0.07	3.87	-0.09	2.13	-0.07	0.75	-0.10	0.05	-0.03	0.10	-0.04	0.55	-0.08
	SPs	3.54	-0.08	3.77	-0.08	2.36	-0.07	0.73	-0.11	0.02	-0.01	0.04	-0.01	0.68	-0.10
Wave 3	Active SMs	3.81	-0.03	3.98	-0.04	2.14	-0.03	0.74	-0.06	0.03	-0.01	0.06	-0.01	0.64	-0.05
	SPs	3.59	-0.05	3.88	-0.05	2.22	-0.04	0.80	-0.07	0.06	-0.02	0.06	-0.02	0.75	-0.05
	Reserve SMs	3.72	-0.07	3.89	-0.09	2.07	-0.07	0.67	-0.10	0.01	-0.01	0.06	-0.03	0.50	-0.08
	SPs	3.23	-0.21	3.44	-0.26	2.57	-0.25	0.67	-0.12	0.02	-0.01	0.03	-0.01	0.63	-0.11
Wave 4	Active SMs	3.71	-0.04	3.89	-0.04	2.18	-0.04	0.80	-0.06	0.03	-0.01	0.08	-0.02	0.65	-0.05
	SPs	3.66	-0.04	3.93	-0.04	2.19	-0.04	0.66	-0.07	0.05	-0.01	0.05	-0.01	0.60	-0.05
	Reserve SMs	3.58	-0.07	3.79	-0.09	2.18	-0.08	0.71	-0.10	0.01	0.00	0.06	-0.03	0.46	-0.08
	SPs	3.17	-0.21	3.29	-0.24	2.66	-0.21	0.80	-0.16	0.03	-0.01	0.02	-0.01	0.61	-0.15
Wave 5	Active SMs	3.73	-0.04	3.93	-0.04	2.12	-0.04	0.81	-0.09	0.08	-0.02	0.12	-0.02	0.67	-0.06
	SPs	3.67	-0.04	3.93	-0.05	2.16	-0.04	0.66	-0.05	0.05	-0.01	0.03	-0.01	0.62	-0.05
	Reserve SMs	3.63	-0.08	3.77	-0.08	2.09	-0.09	0.64	-0.12	0.00	0.00	0.09	-0.03	0.43	-0.07
	SPs	3.25	-0.25	3.41	-0.26	2.63	-0.26	0.61	-0.12	0.03	-0.02	0.06	-0.04	0.55	-0.11
Wave 6	Active SMs	3.74	-0.04	3.91	-0.04	2.12	-0.05	0.68	-0.05	0.03	-0.01	0.05	-0.01	0.62	-0.05
	SPs	3.67	-0.04	3.92	-0.05	2.16	-0.04	0.61	-0.05	0.03	-0.01	0.04	-0.01	0.58	-0.04
	Reserve SMs	3.57	-0.09	3.78	-0.08	2.20	-0.07	0.61	-0.13	0.01	0.00	0.05	-0.02	0.49	-0.10
	SPs	3.15	-0.22	3.29	-0.25	2.68	-0.25	0.82	-0.24	0.02	-0.01	0.02	-0.01	0.55	-0.14

Table A.3b—Continued

			Marital Satisfaction[a]		PANAS: Positive[b]		PANAS: Negative[c]		Physical Aggression: Prevalence Against You[d]		Physical Aggression: Prevalence Against Partner[e]		Psychological Aggression: Frequency Against You[f]		Psychological Aggression: Frequency Against Partner[g]	
			Mean	SE	Mean	SE	Mean	SE	Mean	SE	Mean	SE	Mean	SE	Mean	SE
Wave 7	Active	SMs	3.69	-0.04	3.91	-0.06	2.13	-0.06	0.77	-0.07	0.03	-0.01	0.08	-0.02	0.65	-0.05
		SPs	3.58	-0.03	3.82	-0.04	2.20	-0.04	0.64	-0.05	0.04	-0.01	0.03	-0.01	0.60	-0.04
	Reserve	SMs	3.55	-0.08	3.74	-0.10	2.27	-0.07	0.69	-0.11	0.03	-0.02	0.12	-0.04	0.51	-0.09
		SPs	3.22	-0.20	3.39	-0.26	2.65	-0.25	0.82	-0.14	0.01	-0.01	0.12	-0.09	0.50	-0.09
Wave 8[h]	Active	SMs	3.49	-0.13	3.74	-0.13	2.31	-0.14	0.97	-0.17	0.04	-0.01	0.16	-0.07	0.77	-0.11
		SPs	3.59	-0.04	3.83	-0.05	2.22	-0.04	0.66	-0.08	0.03	-0.01	0.03	-0.01	0.62	-0.07
	Reserve	SMs	3.62	-0.08	3.78	-0.10	2.20	-0.10	0.65	-0.13	0.01	-0.01	0.08	-0.03	0.44	-0.08
		SPs	3.30	-0.20	3.42	-0.26	2.59	-0.26	0.75	-0.10	0.03	-0.02	0.03	-0.02	0.46	-0.08
Wave 9[h]	Active	SMs	3.54	-0.09	3.75	-0.06	2.21	-0.05	0.85	-0.12	0.03	-0.01	0.08	-0.02	0.72	-0.12
		SPs	3.63	-0.04	3.90	-0.05	2.17	-0.05	0.62	-0.05	0.05	-0.01	0.02	-0.01	0.59	-0.05
	Reserve	SMs	3.51	-0.07	3.64	-0.09	2.32	-0.08	0.61	-0.11	0.02	-0.01	0.07	-0.03	0.44	-0.09
		SPs	3.25	-0.19	3.37	-0.25	2.60	-0.23	0.81	-0.16	0.03	-0.01	0.03	-0.02	0.65	-0.09

NOTE: Data are weighted.

[a] Higher scores=greater satisfaction. Range: 1.63–4.63.

[b] Higher scores=more positive affect following communication. Range: 1–5.

[c] Higher scores=more negative affect following communication. Range: 1–5.

[d] Higher scores=increased presence of physical aggression against respondent (yes=1, no=0).

[e] Higher scores=increased presence of physical aggression against partner (yes=1, no=0).

[f] Higher scores=more psychological aggression against respondent. Range: 0–6.

[g] Higher scores=more psychological aggression against partner. Range: 0–6.

[h] The Navy sample does not have data at this wave by design.

Table A.3c
Psychological and Behavioral Health Outcome Means by Study Wave and Component

Wave	Component		Depression[a] Mean	SE	Anxiety[b] Mean	SE	PTSD[c] Mean	SE	Binge Drinking[d] Mean	SE	Problematic Substance Use[e] Mean	SE	Medication Use[f] Mean	SE	Needed Counseling[g] Mean	SE
Baseline	Active	SMs	2.96	-0.19	2.19	-0.06	22.47	-0.52	0.30	-0.04	0.17	-0.03	0.05	-0.01	0.15	-0.02
		SPs	3.05	-0.15	2.07	-0.05	0.53	-0.05	0.12	-0.01	0.09	-0.02	0.13	-0.01	0.15	-0.01
	Reserve	SMs	2.93	-0.32	1.93	-0.09	22.22	-0.76	0.12	-0.02	0.15	-0.05	0.05	-0.01	0.17	-0.04
		SPs	3.38	-0.33	2.32	-0.08	0.42	-0.08	0.06	-0.01	0.02	-0.01	0.12	-0.03	0.11	-0.03
Wave 2	Active	SMs	4.32	-0.30	2.37	-0.06	23.92	-0.76	0.30	-0.03	0.30	-0.08	0.09	-0.02	0.21	-0.03
		SPs	3.91	-0.19	2.43	-0.05	0.43	-0.04	0.15	-0.02	0.08	-0.02	0.14	-0.02	0.19	-0.02
	Reserve	SMs	3.82	-0.49	2.20	-0.11	23.36	-1.33	0.21	-0.05	0.09	-0.02	0.09	-0.03	0.18	-0.05
		SPs	3.79	-0.29	2.54	-0.10	0.40	-0.07	0.08	-0.02	0.04	-0.01	0.13	-0.03	0.17	-0.04
Wave 3	Active	SMs	4.52	-0.33	2.38	-0.06	24.16	-0.66	0.28	-0.02	0.19	-0.03	0.10	-0.02	0.21	-0.02
		SPs	4.14	-0.21	2.45	-0.07	0.42	-0.04	0.17	-0.02	0.11	-0.02	0.14	-0.02	0.20	-0.02
	Reserve	SMs	3.29	-0.41	1.93	-0.09	23.05	-1.04	0.14	-0.04	0.12	-0.03	0.06	-0.01	0.13	-0.03
		SPs	3.76	-0.29	2.45	-0.08	0.51	-0.13	0.09	-0.02	0.05	-0.02	0.11	-0.03	0.19	-0.04
Wave 4	Active	SMs	4.52	-0.26	2.42	-0.06	24.17	-0.67	0.26	-0.02	0.21	-0.04	0.09	-0.02	0.21	-0.02
		SPs	3.84	-0.22	2.33	-0.07	0.43	-0.05	0.15	-0.02	0.14	-0.04	0.13	-0.01	0.20	-0.02
	Reserve	SMs	3.84	-0.44	2.15	-0.10	24.06	-1.27	0.18	-0.04	0.08	-0.02	0.04	-0.01	0.12	-0.03
		SPs	3.95	-0.43	2.52	-0.07	0.42	-0.14	0.12	-0.03	0.06	-0.02	0.12	-0.03	0.16	-0.04
Wave 5	Active	SMs	4.20	-0.28	2.35	-0.07	23.07	-0.56	0.28	-0.03	0.20	-0.03	0.09	-0.02	0.19	-0.02
		SPs	3.72	-0.22	2.31	-0.07	0.32	-0.03	0.15	-0.02	0.13	-0.03	0.12	-0.01	0.17	-0.02
	Reserve	SMs	3.71	-0.49	2.08	-0.12	23.25	-1.40	0.16	-0.04	0.11	-0.03	0.05	-0.01	0.18	-0.04
		SPs	3.72	-0.48	2.33	-0.11	0.50	-0.15	0.11	-0.03	0.07	-0.03	0.11	-0.03	0.24	-0.06
Wave 6	Active	SMs	4.36	-0.30	2.38	-0.06	23.69	-0.64	0.27	-0.02	0.19	-0.03	0.10	-0.02	0.21	-0.02
		SPs	3.75	-0.22	2.35	-0.07	0.34	-0.04	0.19	-0.02	0.14	-0.03	0.11	-0.01	0.18	-0.02
	Reserve	SMs	3.88	-0.51	2.10	-0.10	23.72	-1.43	0.18	-0.04	0.18	-0.04	0.11	-0.03	0.19	-0.04
		SPs	4.32	-0.41	2.44	-0.09	0.62	-0.17	0.14	-0.04	0.09	-0.03	0.11	-0.02	0.30	-0.08

Table A.3c—Continued

		Depression[a]		Anxiety[b]		PTSD[c]		Binge Drinking[d]		Problematic Substance Use[e]		Medication Use[f]		Needed Counseling[g]	
		Mean	SE	Mean	SE	Mean	SE	Mean	SE	Mean	SE	Mean	SE	Mean	SE
Wave 7	Active SMs	4.36	-0.33	2.29	-0.08	24.38	-0.69	0.25	-0.02	0.20	-0.03	0.09	-0.01	0.21	-0.02
	SPs	3.94	-0.23	2.31	-0.07	0.41	-0.04	0.17	-0.02	0.16	-0.03	0.12	-0.01	0.20	-0.02
	Reserve SMs	4.17	-0.49	2.20	-0.12	24.71	-1.36	0.18	-0.04	0.13	-0.03	0.11	-0.03	0.16	-0.04
	SPs	4.56	-0.39	2.45	-0.09	0.45	-0.12	0.10	-0.03	0.04	-0.02	0.12	-0.03	0.19	-0.04
Wave 8[h]	Active SMs	4.69	-0.33	2.23	-0.12	25.56	-0.99	0.35	-0.06	0.31	-0.07	0.13	-0.02	0.33	-0.06
	SPs	3.79	-0.26	2.30	-0.07	0.43	-0.07	0.18	-0.03	0.12	-0.02	0.15	-0.03	0.23	-0.03
	Reserve SMs	4.01	-0.47	2.14	-0.10	23.96	-1.27	0.13	-0.03	0.12	-0.03	0.10	-0.03	0.12	-0.03
	SPs	4.37	-0.40	2.47	-0.12	0.45	-0.12	0.10	-0.03	0.05	-0.01	0.13	-0.04	0.18	-0.04
Wave 9[h]	Active SMs	5.07	-0.35	2.46	-0.10	26.60	-1.12	0.30	-0.05	0.29	-0.05	0.12	-0.02	0.27	-0.06
	SPs	4.00	-0.21	2.36	-0.06	0.42	-0.05	0.19	-0.02	0.13	-0.02	0.14	-0.03	0.21	-0.03
	Reserve SMs	5.29	-0.77	2.39	-0.19	26.31	-2.22	0.15	-0.03	0.10	-0.02	0.07	-0.02	0.20	-0.06
	SPs	3.94	-0.40	2.36	-0.08	0.52	-0.12	0.15	-0.04	0.13	-0.08	0.16	-0.04	0.30	-0.08

NOTE: Data are weighted.

[a] Higher scores=more depressive symptoms. Range: 0–24.

[b] Higher scores=more anxiety. Mean subscale score range: 1–6.

[c] Higher scores=more PTSD symptoms. Range: 17–85 for service member, 0–4 for spouse.

[d] Percentage reporting binge drinking (5+ drinks for men; 4+ drinks for women).

[e] Higher scores=more problematic substance use. Range: 0–7.

[f] Percentage reporting use of medication for a mental health problem.

[g] Percentage reporting need for treatment for mental health treatment.

[h] The Navy sample does not have data at this wave by design.

Table A.3d
Military Integration Outcome Means by Study Wave and Component

			Job Satisfaction Scale[a]		Military Commitment Scale[b]		Retention Intentions[c]	
			Mean	SE	Mean	SE	Mean	SE
Wave 1	Active	SMs	3.74	0.06	4.34	0.04	4.15	0.07
		SPs	3.98	0.06	4.40	0.04	3.89	0.08
	Reserve	SMs	4.16	0.10	4.48	0.05	0.86	5.14
		SPs	3.96	0.12	4.30	0.08	0.67	5.37
Wave 2	Active	SMs	3.59	0.06	3.98	0.04	3.80	0.08
		SPs	3.95	0.05	4.03	0.04	3.86	0.06
	Reserve	SMs	4.10	0.10	4.00	0.13	0.58	5.44
		SPs	3.99	0.09	4.06	0.09	0.51	6.29
Wave 3	Active	SMs	3.63	0.07	3.84	0.07	3.76	0.07
		SPs	3.99	0.05	4.06	0.06	3.87	0.07
	Reserve	SMs	3.87	0.13	3.82	0.17	0.61	5.47
		SPs	4.10	0.07	4.16	0.06	0.65	5.50
Wave 4	Active	SMs	3.61	0.06	3.95	0.05	3.84	0.08
		SPs	4.05	0.06	4.07	0.05	3.95	0.05
	Reserve	SMs	3.90	0.13	3.70	0.16	0.59	5.45
		SPs	3.73	0.14	3.96	0.10	0.56	6.02
Wave 5	Active	SMs	3.72	0.06	3.91	0.05	3.78	0.08
		SPs	4.03	0.06	4.02	0.05	3.88	0.07
	Reserve	SMs	3.89	0.14	3.78	0.17	0.60	5.41
		SPs	3.90	0.10	3.94	0.08	0.63	5.52
Wave 6	Active	SMs	3.73	0.06	3.89	0.05	3.75	0.08
		SPs	4.08	0.06	4.05	0.06	3.98	0.06
	Reserve	SMs	3.92	0.12	3.85	0.17	0.49	5.20
		SPs	3.80	0.15	3.95	0.08	0.51	6.28
Wave 7	Active	SMs	3.82	0.09	3.97	0.06	3.75	0.09
		SPs	4.00	0.06	4.03	0.04	3.88	0.06
	Reserve	SMs	3.74	0.16	4.04	0.12	0.52	5.34
		SPs	3.93	0.10	4.02	0.09	0.61	5.70
Wave 8[d]	Active	SMs	3.80	0.07	3.99	0.09	3.84	0.12
		SPs	4.00	0.06	3.98	0.05	3.87	0.08
	Reserve	SMs	3.90	0.12	4.03	0.10	0.56	5.42
		SPs	3.98	0.10	3.94	0.08	0.63	5.46
Wave 9[d]	Active	SMs	3.84	0.09	3.79	0.12	3.66	0.17
		SPs	4.06	0.05	4.02	0.05	3.79	0.10
	Reserve	SMs	3.98	0.09	3.89	0.14	0.53	5.37
		SPs	3.83	0.13	3.94	0.07	0.53	6.11

NOTES: Data are weighted.

[a] Higher scores=more satisfaction. Range: 1–5.

[b] Higher scores=more commitment. Range: 1–5.

[c] For the active component, this variable ranges from 1–5, with higher scores indicating stronger preference for continued military service. For the reserve component, this variable indicates the percentage of service members (or spouses) who plan to stay beyond their (the service member's) current obligation.

[d] The Navy sample does not have data at this wave by design.

Table A.4a
Family Outcome Means by Study Wave and Service

			Family Environment Scale[a]		Satisfaction with Parenting[b]		Financial Distress Scale[c]	
			Mean	SE	Mean	SE	Mean	SE
Baseline	Army	SMs	2.74	−0.02	3.35	−0.02	2.18	−0.07
		SPs	2.74	−0.02	3.20	−0.03	2.27	−0.05
	Air Force	SMs	2.68	−0.12	3.36	−0.13	1.76	−0.10
		SPs	2.65	−0.13	3.19	−0.06	1.79	−0.14
	Navy	SMs	2.82	−0.01	3.31	−0.03	1.85	−0.04
		SPs	2.81	−0.02	3.22	−0.03	1.96	−0.04
	Marine Corps	SMs	2.88	−0.03	3.34	−0.09	1.66	−0.15
		SPs	2.90	−0.02	3.26	−0.05	1.86	−0.09
Wave 2	Army	SMs	2.67	−0.02	3.22	−0.04	2.05	−0.05
		SPs	2.68	−0.03	3.14	−0.03	2.12	−0.05
	Air Force	SMs	2.86	−0.04	3.16	−0.11	1.91	−0.15
		SPs	2.75	−0.06	3.16	−0.08	1.68	−0.12
	Navy	SMs	2.73	−0.03	3.26	−0.04	1.73	−0.04
		SPs	2.76	−0.02	3.10	−0.04	1.84	−0.05
	Marine Corps	SMs	2.92	−0.04	3.23	−0.12	2.06	−0.24
		SPs	2.85	−0.05	3.27	−0.09	1.97	−0.17
Wave 3	Army	SMs	2.68	−0.03	3.23	−0.03	2.11	−0.06
		SPs	2.66	−0.03	3.15	−0.04	2.09	−0.05
	Air Force	SMs	2.79	−0.06	3.25	−0.13	1.90	−0.17
		SPs	2.52	−0.17	3.07	−0.09	1.74	−0.11
	Navy	SMs	2.75	−0.03	3.26	−0.04	1.80	−0.06
		SPs	2.74	−0.03	3.04	−0.04	1.89	−0.05
	Marine Corps	SMs	2.90	−0.04	3.40	−0.13	1.64	−0.14
		SPs	2.89	−0.04	3.15	−0.09	1.83	−0.13
Wave 4	Army	SMs	2.68	−0.03	3.21	−0.04	2.10	−0.07
		SPs	2.65	−0.04	3.07	−0.05	2.13	−0.06
	Air Force	SMs	2.79	−0.05	3.17	−0.12	1.78	−0.13
		SPs	2.55	−0.19	3.25	−0.06	1.70	−0.08
	Navy	SMs	2.70	−0.03	3.24	−0.04	1.85	−0.06
		SPs	2.74	−0.02	3.14	−0.04	1.82	−0.04
	Marine Corps	SMs	2.77	−0.07	3.18	−0.15	2.05	−0.18
		SPs	2.86	−0.06	3.28	−0.10	1.93	−0.18
Wave 5	Army	SMs	2.65	−0.04	3.18	−0.05	2.06	−0.07
		SPs	2.68	−0.04	3.13	−0.04	2.06	−0.06
	Air Force	SMs	2.83	−0.05	2.98	−0.13	1.76	−0.12
		SPs	2.51	−0.17	3.13	−0.06	1.70	−0.06
	Navy	SMs	2.75	−0.03	3.25	−0.04	1.82	−0.06
		SPs	2.75	−0.02	3.07	−0.04	1.87	−0.05
	Marine Corps	SMs	2.91	−0.05	3.26	−0.13	1.91	−0.22
		SPs	2.83	−0.06	3.26	−0.07	2.05	−0.16

Table A.4a—Continued

			Family Environment Scale[a]		Satisfaction with Parenting[b]		Financial Distress Scale[c]	
			Mean	SE	Mean	SE	Mean	SE
Wave 6	Army	SMs	2.70	−0.03	3.21	−0.04	2.21	−0.09
		SPs	2.69	−0.03	3.08	−0.04	2.20	−0.07
	Air Force	SMs	2.87	−0.04	3.03	−0.14	1.65	−0.09
		SPs	2.57	−0.15	3.04	−0.08	1.91	−0.16
	Navy	SMs	2.73	−0.03	3.26	−0.04	1.95	−0.07
		SPs	2.71	−0.03	3.11	−0.04	1.99	−0.08
	Marine Corps	SMs	2.84	−0.06	3.42	−0.14	1.73	−0.12
		SPs	2.80	−0.08	3.19	−0.07	1.90	−0.13
Wave 7	Army	SMs	2.65	−0.03	3.21	−0.03	2.14	−0.08
		SPs	2.69	−0.03	3.14	−0.04	2.15	−0.06
	Air Force	SMs	2.77	−0.05	3.11	−0.14	1.86	−0.13
		SPs	2.50	−0.16	3.02	−0.06	2.01	−0.25
	Navy	SMs	2.68	−0.03	3.19	−0.04	1.87	−0.05
		SPs	2.68	−0.03	3.10	−0.04	1.91	−0.06
	Marine Corps	SMs	2.83	−0.07	3.48	−0.16	1.78	−0.14
		SPs	2.84	−0.04	3.22	−0.08	1.88	−0.17
Wave 8[d]	Army	SMs	2.66	−0.03	3.21	−0.04	2.10	−0.06
		SPs	2.69	−0.03	3.13	−0.04	2.14	−0.07
	Air Force	SMs	2.66	−0.13	3.22	−0.19	1.82	−0.16
		SPs	2.45	−0.21	3.07	−0.07	1.94	−0.18
	Navy	SMs	2.68	−0.03	3.19	−0.04	1.87	−0.05
		SPs	2.68	−0.03	3.10	−0.04	1.91	−0.06
	Marine Corps	SMs	2.78	−0.07	3.29	−0.14	1.72	−0.11
		SPs	2.83	−0.06	3.16	−0.10	1.93	−0.18
Wave 9[d]	Army	SMs	2.66	−0.03	3.15	−0.04	2.18	−0.07
		SPs	2.66	−0.03	3.07	−0.04	2.17	−0.06
	Air Force	SMs	2.67	−0.09	3.29	−0.18	1.61	−0.06
		SPs	2.55	−0.19	3.09	−0.11	1.86	−0.18
	Navy	SMs	na	na	na	na	na	na
		SPs	na	na	na	na	na	na
	Marine Corps	SMs	2.85	−0.05	3.42	−0.14	1.79	−0.13
		SPs	2.68	−0.12	3.10	−0.10	1.95	−0.19

NOTE: Data are weighted.

[a] Higher scores=more positive environment. Range: 1–3.

[b] Higher scores=more satisfaction. Range: 1–4.

[c] Higher scores=more distress. Range: 1–4.

[d] The Navy sample does not have data at this wave by design (na=not applicable).

Table A.4b
Marital Relationship Outcome Means by Study Wave and Service

		Marital Satisfaction[a]		PANAS: Positive[b]		PANAS: Negative[c]		Physical Aggression: Prevalence Against You[d]		Physical Aggression: Prevalence Against Partner[e]		Psychological Aggression: Frequency Against You[f]		Psychological Aggression: Frequency Against Partner[g]	
		Mean	SE	Mean	SE	Mean	SE	Mean	SE	Mean	SE	Mean	SE	Mean	SE
Baseline	Army SMs	3.86	-0.03	4.07	-0.04	2.05	-0.05	0.90	-0.07	0.03	-0.01	0.09	-0.02	0.75	-0.06
	Army SPs	3.68	-0.04	3.97	-0.04	2.29	-0.03	0.86	-0.07	0.08	-0.02	0.07	-0.02	0.84	-0.06
	Air Force SMs	3.96	-0.08	4.18	-0.13	2.03	-0.10	0.81	-0.18	0.00	0.00	0.01	0.00	0.75	-0.19
	Air Force SPs	3.72	-0.18	3.87	-0.25	2.25	-0.19	0.89	-0.18	0.03	-0.02	0.01	-0.01	0.67	-0.13
	Navy SMs	4.00	-0.03	4.22	-0.04	1.98	-0.03	0.71	-0.05	0.01	0.00	0.03	-0.01	0.66	-0.05
	Navy SPs	3.88	-0.03	4.17	-0.04	2.07	-0.03	0.61	-0.06	0.03	-0.01	0.02	-0.01	0.68	-0.05
	Marine Corps SMs	4.01	-0.09	4.18	-0.12	2.10	-0.09	0.90	-0.16	0.00	0.00	0.01	-0.01	0.82	-0.14
	Marine Corps SPs	4.04	-0.06	4.29	-0.09	2.07	-0.08	0.66	-0.13	0.09	-0.06	0.04	-0.04	0.76	-0.14
Wave 2	Army SMs	3.70	-0.05	3.85	-0.06	2.18	-0.05	1.01	-0.08	0.05	-0.02	0.10	-0.02	0.80	-0.06
	Army SPs	3.61	-0.05	3.82	-0.04	2.34	-0.04	0.85	-0.09	0.07	-0.02	0.06	-0.01	0.80	-0.06
	Air Force SMs	3.94	-0.07	4.15	-0.08	1.90	-0.06	0.57	-0.12	0.02	-0.01	0.09	-0.05	0.43	-0.10
	Air Force SPs	3.65	-0.11	3.98	-0.15	2.18	-0.12	0.49	-0.12	0.06	-0.04	0.06	-0.04	0.53	-0.12
	Navy SMs	3.85	-0.05	4.09	-0.06	2.08	-0.05	0.68	-0.06	0.03	-0.01	0.04	-0.01	0.71	-0.06
	Navy SPs	3.67	-0.05	3.92	-0.06	2.17	-0.05	0.69	-0.09	0.04	-0.01	0.04	-0.01	0.63	-0.08
	Marine Corps SMs	3.66	-0.15	3.74	-0.20	2.35	-0.20	0.75	-0.26	0.19	-0.13	0.19	-0.13	0.80	-0.26
	Marine Corps SPs	3.80	-0.13	3.93	-0.13	2.38	-0.10	1.13	-0.22	0.06	-0.05	0.06	-0.05	1.05	-0.17
Wave 3	Army SMs	3.67	-0.05	3.85	-0.06	2.19	-0.05	0.82	-0.07	0.03	-0.01	0.07	-0.02	0.71	-0.06
	Army SPs	3.47	-0.07	3.71	-0.07	2.32	-0.05	0.84	-0.08	0.04	-0.01	0.06	-0.02	0.75	-0.06
	Air Force SMs	3.97	-0.07	4.08	-0.08	1.95	-0.07	0.50	-0.12	0.00	0.00	0.01	-0.01	0.29	-0.08
	Air Force SPs	3.22	-0.30	3.48	-0.37	2.59	-0.36	0.64	-0.18	0.04	-0.03	0.03	-0.03	0.64	-0.15
	Navy SMs	3.83	-0.05	4.00	-0.06	2.08	-0.05	0.60	-0.07	0.03	-0.01	0.06	-0.02	0.54	-0.06
	Navy SPs	3.65	-0.05	3.92	-0.05	2.19	-0.05	0.53	-0.08	0.02	-0.01	0.03	-0.02	0.52	-0.08
	Marine Corps SMs	3.82	-0.19	4.05	-0.17	2.09	-0.10	0.78	-0.20	0.01	-0.02	0.14	-0.11	0.64	-0.13
	Marine Corps SPs	3.74	-0.12	4.04	-0.11	2.13	-0.08	1.03	-0.19	0.14	-0.08	0.01	-0.01	1.01	-0.16

Table A.4b—Continued

		Marital Satisfaction[a]		PANAS: Positive[b]		PANAS: Negative[c]		Physical Aggression: Prevalence Against You[d]		Physical Aggression: Prevalence Against Partner[e]		Psychological Aggression: Frequency Against You[f]		Psychological Aggression: Frequency Against Partner[g]	
		Mean	SE	Mean	SE	Mean	SE	Mean	SE	Mean	SE	Mean	SE	Mean	SE
Wave 4	Army SMs	3.58	-0.05	3.76	-0.07	2.22	-0.06	0.91	-0.07	0.02	-0.01	0.09	-0.02	0.65	-0.06
	SPs	3.39	-0.07	3.56	-0.08	2.43	-0.05	0.78	-0.09	0.04	-0.01	0.04	-0.01	0.61	-0.05
	Air Force SMs	3.76	-0.07	3.97	-0.08	2.09	-0.08	0.56	-0.13	0.01	0.00	0.05	-0.03	0.33	-0.09
	SPs	3.43	-0.33	3.63	-0.39	2.45	-0.35	0.67	-0.23	0.03	-0.02	0.01	-0.01	0.63	-0.22
	Navy SMs	3.74	-0.05	3.93	-0.07	2.18	-0.05	0.70	-0.08	0.03	-0.01	0.05	-0.01	0.66	-0.08
	SPs	3.70	-0.04	3.92	-0.05	2.15	-0.05	0.57	-0.05	0.04	-0.01	0.05	-0.02	0.55	-0.05
	Marine Corps SMs	3.64	-0.16	3.87	-0.18	2.24	-0.14	0.67	-0.12	0.09	-0.08	0.10	-0.08	0.67	-0.13
	SPs	3.77	-0.12	4.24	-0.10	2.15	-0.10	0.78	-0.21	0.07	-0.06	0.07	-0.06	0.65	-0.19
Wave 5	Army SMs	3.60	-0.06	3.71	-0.06	2.16	-0.07	0.88	-0.10	0.04	-0.01	0.12	-0.03	0.66	-0.07
	SPs	3.53	-0.06	3.68	-0.05	2.34	-0.04	0.79	-0.08	0.04	-0.01	0.06	-0.03	0.70	-0.06
	Air Force SMs	3.82	-0.08	4.01	-0.08	2.00	-0.09	0.47	-0.15	0.04	-0.03	0.05	-0.03	0.37	-0.10
	SPs	3.37	-0.35	3.66	-0.40	2.47	-0.38	0.30	-0.07	0.05	-0.03	0.01	-0.01	0.34	-0.09
	Navy SMs	3.75	-0.05	3.99	-0.05	2.16	-0.05	0.73	-0.06	0.05	-0.02	0.05	-0.01	0.65	-0.06
	SPs	3.63	-0.05	3.86	-0.05	2.16	-0.05	0.62	-0.06	0.04	-0.01	0.02	-0.01	0.60	-0.06
	Marine Corps SMs	3.71	-0.15	4.07	-0.16	2.05	-0.12	0.81	-0.35	0.10	-0.09	0.29	-0.12	0.56	-0.19
	SPs	3.70	-0.13	4.11	-0.10	2.14	-0.10	0.92	-0.25	0.06	-0.06	0.06	-0.06	0.80	-0.25
Wave 6	Army SMs	3.55	-0.07	3.72	-0.06	2.24	-0.06	0.79	-0.09	0.03	-0.01	0.08	-0.02	0.58	-0.06
	SPs	3.41	-0.05	3.62	-0.06	2.38	-0.04	0.74	-0.07	0.04	-0.01	0.04	-0.01	0.74	-0.10
	Air Force SMs	3.81	-0.07	4.03	-0.06	1.99	-0.09	0.30	-0.09	0.01	0.00	0.01	0.00	0.44	-0.12
	SPs	3.42	-0.35	3.63	-0.40	2.46	-0.38	0.72	-0.33	0.02	-0.01	0.01	-0.01	0.36	-0.09
	Navy SMs	3.76	-0.05	3.90	-0.06	2.15	-0.05	0.64	-0.08	0.05	-0.02	0.04	-0.01	0.58	-0.07
	SPs	3.60	-0.07	3.81	-0.07	2.26	-0.07	0.52	-0.05	0.03	-0.01	0.03	-0.01	0.53	-0.05
	Marine Corps SMs	3.85	-0.14	4.15	-0.09	2.00	-0.12	0.81	-0.18	0.00	0.00	0.00	0.00	0.85	-0.18
	SPs	3.76	-0.11	3.97	-0.12	2.06	-0.08	0.70	-0.22	0.01	-0.01	0.06	-0.05	0.44	-0.12

Table A.4b—Continued

		Marital Satisfaction[a]		PANAS: Positive[b]		PANAS: Negative[c]		Physical Aggression: Prevalence Against You[d]		Physical Aggression: Prevalence Against Partner[e]		Psychological Aggression: Frequency Against You[f]		Psychological Aggression: Frequency Against Partner[g]	
		Mean	SE	Mean	SE	Mean	SE	Mean	SE	Mean	SE	Mean	SE	Mean	SE
Wave 7 Army	SMs	3.55	-0.05	3.73	-0.06	2.30	-0.06	0.91	-0.08	0.04	-0.01	0.11	-0.02	0.74	-0.06
	SPs	3.46	-0.05	3.68	-0.06	2.35	-0.05	0.71	-0.06	0.03	-0.01	0.03	-0.01	0.66	-0.05
Air Force	SMs	3.77	-0.10	4.07	-0.15	2.00	-0.13	0.36	-0.11	0.00	0.00	0.07	-0.04	0.28	-0.09
	SPs	3.30	-0.27	3.52	-0.37	2.53	-0.36	0.68	-0.21	0.01	-0.01	0.14	-0.12	0.35	-0.10
Navy	SMs	3.70	-0.05	3.88	-0.05	2.14	-0.05	0.70	-0.07	0.03	-0.01	0.05	-0.01	0.59	-0.05
	SPs	3.57	-0.05	3.71	-0.07	2.26	-0.07	0.73	-0.10	0.03	-0.01	0.04	-0.02	0.59	-0.07
Marine Corps	SMs	3.68	-0.11	3.88	-0.17	2.06	-0.14	0.93	-0.24	0.00	0.00	0.13	-0.10	0.73	-0.19
	SPs	3.66	-0.12	3.96	-0.12	2.14	-0.10	0.72	-0.14	0.06	-0.05	0.00	0.00	0.64	-0.14
Wave 8[h] Army	SMs	3.56	-0.05	3.74	-0.07	2.25	-0.06	0.89	-0.10	0.04	-0.01	0.11	-0.02	0.67	-0.07
	SPs	3.47	-0.04	3.68	-0.05	2.31	-0.05	0.76	-0.07	0.03	-0.01	0.04	-0.01	0.60	-0.05
Air Force	SMs	3.49	-0.26	3.71	-0.24	2.33	-0.27	0.74	-0.35	0.00	0.00	0.17	-0.13	0.53	-0.23
	SPs	3.37	-0.28	3.51	-0.37	2.61	-0.35	0.63	-0.14	0.02	-0.01	0.01	-0.01	0.42	-0.14
Navy	SMs	3.70	-0.05	3.88	-0.05	2.14	-0.05	0.70	-0.07	0.03	-0.01	0.05	-0.01	0.59	-0.05
	SPs	3.57	-0.05	3.71	-0.07	2.26	-0.07	0.73	-0.10	0.03	-0.01	0.04	-0.02	0.59	-0.07
Marine Corps	SMs	3.64	-0.13	3.93	-0.18	2.18	-0.15	0.78	-0.18	0.00	0.00	0.10	-0.08	0.67	-0.16
	SPs	3.69	-0.09	3.93	-0.11	2.14	-0.09	0.64	-0.14	0.06	-0.05	0.05	-0.05	0.66	-0.14

Table A.4b—Continued

| | | Marital Satisfaction[a] | | PANAS: Positive[b] | | PANAS: Negative[c] | | Physical Aggression: Prevalence Against You[d] | | Physical Aggression: Prevalence Against Partner[e] | | Psychological Aggression: Frequency Against You[f] | | Psychological Aggression: Frequency Against Partner[g] | |
		Mean	SE	Mean	SE	Mean	SE	Mean	SE	Mean	SE	Mean	SE	Mean	SE
Wave 9[h] Army	SMs	3.50	-0.05	3.63	-0.06	2.31	-0.06	0.79	-0.09	0.04	-0.01	0.08	-0.02	0.57	-0.06
	SPs	3.45	-0.05	3.70	-0.06	2.32	-0.05	0.73	-0.07	0.04	-0.01	0.03	-0.01	0.70	-0.06
Air Force	SMs	3.58	-0.17	3.80	-0.11	2.19	-0.08	0.63	-0.23	0.02	-0.01	0.05	-0.03	0.57	-0.23
	SPs	3.44	-0.29	3.57	-0.37	2.48	-0.33	0.69	-0.20	0.02	-0.01	0.02	-0.01	0.50	-0.10
Navy	SMs	na	na	na	na	na	na	na	na	na	na	na	na	na	na
	SPs	na	na	na	na	na	na	na	na	na	na	na	na	na	na
Marine Corps	SMs	3.49	-0.16	3.76	-0.15	2.17	-0.14	0.78	-0.18	0.01	-0.01	0.09	-0.07	0.81	-0.18
	SPs	3.63	-0.13	3.85	-0.17	2.20	-0.14	0.57	-0.20	0.07	-0.05	0.06	-0.05	0.51	-0.17

NOTE: Data are weighted.

[a] Higher scores=greater satisfaction. Range: 1.63–4.63.

[b] Higher scores=more positive affect following communication. Range: 1–5.

[c] Higher scores=more negative affect following communication. Range: 1–5.

[d] Higher scores=increased presence of physical aggression against respondent (yes=1, no=0).

[e] Higher scores=increased presence of physical aggression against partner (yes=1, no=0).

[f] Higher scores=more psychological aggression against respondent. Range: 0–6.

[g] Higher scores=more psychological aggression against partner. Range: 0–6.

[h] The Navy sample does not have data at this wave by design (na=not applicable).

Table A.4c
Psychological and Behavioral Health Outcome Means by Study Wave and Service

		Depression[a]		Anxiety[b]		PTSD[c]		Binge Drinking[d]		Problematic Substance Use[e]		Medication Use[f]		Needed Counseling[g]	
		Mean	SE	Mean	SE	Mean	SE	Mean	SE	Mean	SE	Mean	SE	Mean	SE
Baseline	Army SMs	3.54	−0.27	2.14	−0.07	24.70	−0.69	0.21	−0.02	0.19	−0.04	0.08	−0.01	0.21	−0.02
	SPs	3.61	−0.18	2.30	−0.05	0.60	−0.06	0.10	−0.01	0.08	−0.02	0.16	−0.02	0.17	−0.02
	Air Force SMs	1.85	−0.23	1.83	−0.10	19.11	−0.55	0.20	−0.10	0.04	−0.02	0.01	0.00	0.09	−0.04
	SPs	2.95	−0.45	2.03	−0.12	0.41	−0.12	0.05	−0.01	0.02	−0.01	0.10	−0.03	0.09	−0.03
	Navy SMs	2.90	−0.18	2.22	−0.06	19.82	−0.39	0.30	−0.03	0.17	−0.03	0.03	−0.01	0.11	−0.02
	SPs	2.54	−0.14	1.97	−0.05	0.37	−0.04	0.12	−0.02	0.09	−0.02	0.10	−0.02	0.14	−0.02
	Marine Corps SMs	2.91	−0.55	2.42	−0.20	23.94	−1.65	0.44	−0.10	0.34	−0.15	0.06	−0.04	0.18	−0.08
	SPs	2.49	−0.47	2.07	−0.13	0.36	−0.11	0.21	−0.07	0.08	−0.05	0.09	−0.05	0.05	−0.02
Wave 2	Army SMs	4.53	−0.34	2.35	−0.07	26.06	−0.96	0.25	−0.03	0.21	−0.04	0.13	−0.02	0.21	−0.03
	SPs	4.06	−0.19	2.54	−0.05	0.52	−0.05	0.12	−0.02	0.06	−0.02	0.16	−0.02	0.21	−0.02
	Air Force SMs	2.61	−0.55	1.96	−0.14	19.52	−0.87	0.22	−0.06	0.03	−0.01	0.07	−0.04	0.21	−0.07
	SPs	2.96	−0.43	2.16	−0.13	0.26	−0.08	0.07	−0.02	0.01	−0.01	0.08	−0.02	0.17	−0.06
	Navy SMs	4.33	−0.35	2.50	−0.07	21.13	−0.79	0.32	−0.04	0.20	−0.04	0.06	−0.01	0.17	−0.03
	SPs	4.27	−0.34	2.48	−0.09	0.33	−0.07	0.15	−0.02	0.08	−0.02	0.12	−0.02	0.16	−0.02
	Marine Corps SMs	5.52	−1.24	2.57	−0.24	27.02	−3.90	0.36	−0.11	0.77	−0.43	0.02	−0.02	0.20	−0.10
	SPs	3.71	−0.63	2.60	−0.22	0.37	−0.16	0.25	−0.08	0.15	−0.10	0.16	−0.08	0.12	−0.06
Wave 3	Army SMs	4.52	−0.31	2.30	−0.08	25.77	−0.89	0.21	−0.02	0.19	−0.03	0.11	−0.02	0.23	−0.03
	SPs	4.43	−0.20	2.53	−0.05	0.64	−0.09	0.14	−0.02	0.11	−0.02	0.18	−0.02	0.23	−0.02
	Air Force SMs	2.58	−0.73	1.75	−0.11	19.59	−0.69	0.17	−0.06	0.08	−0.04	0.05	−0.04	0.10	−0.04
	SPs	3.22	−0.41	2.23	−0.16	0.21	−0.07	0.10	−0.03	0.02	−0.01	0.08	−0.02	0.16	−0.05
	Navy SMs	4.36	−0.32	2.40	−0.07	20.92	−0.60	0.28	−0.03	0.19	−0.03	0.06	−0.01	0.12	−0.02
	SPs	3.98	−0.23	2.47	−0.07	0.34	−0.05	0.15	−0.02	0.10	−0.02	0.09	−0.01	0.16	−0.02
	Marine Corps SMs	4.20	−1.14	2.41	−0.22	27.33	−2.26	0.39	−0.12	0.10	−0.07	0.04	−0.03	0.18	−0.09
	SPs	3.81	−0.56	2.63	−0.13	0.36	−0.19	0.25	−0.07	0.10	−0.04	0.02	−0.01	0.15	−0.07

Table A.4c—Continued

		Depression[a]		Anxiety[b]		PTSD[c]		Binge Drinking[d]		Problematic Substance Use[e]		Medication Use[f]		Needed Counseling[g]	
		Mean	SE	Mean	SE	Mean	SE	Mean	SE	Mean	SE	Mean	SE	Mean	SE
Wave 4															
Army	SMs	4.94	-0.37	2.40	-0.08	26.12	-0.91	0.19	-0.02	0.12	-0.02	0.11	-0.02	0.22	-0.03
	SPs	4.53	-0.22	2.49	-0.05	0.52	-0.10	0.15	-0.02	0.09	-0.02	0.17	-0.02	0.19	-0.02
Air Force	SMs	3.02	-0.46	1.96	-0.12	20.94	-1.01	0.09	-0.04	0.06	-0.02	0.04	-0.03	0.12	-0.04
	SPs	2.61	-0.46	2.23	-0.16	0.19	-0.06	0.09	-0.03	0.07	-0.03	0.07	-0.02	0.17	-0.05
Navy	SMs	4.13	-0.30	2.41	-0.07	20.94	-0.60	0.34	-0.03	0.26	-0.04	0.05	-0.01	0.15	-0.02
	SPs	4.03	-0.25	2.38	-0.08	0.40	-0.07	0.15	-0.02	0.10	-0.03	0.10	-0.01	0.20	-0.03
Marine Corps	SMs	4.15	-0.85	2.62	-0.21	28.12	-3.33	0.57	-0.10	0.43	-0.20	0.04	-0.02	0.14	-0.08
	SPs	3.47	-0.67	2.42	-0.19	0.65	-0.27	0.18	-0.06	0.41	-0.27	0.08	-0.06	0.19	-0.08
Wave 5															
Army	SMs	4.69	-0.39	2.35	-0.10	25.65	-1.10	0.23	-0.03	0.15	-0.03	0.12	-0.02	0.25	-0.03
	SPs	4.50	-0.30	2.46	-0.07	0.55	-0.11	0.13	-0.02	0.10	-0.02	0.16	-0.02	0.24	-0.03
Air Force	SMs	2.79	-0.55	1.92	-0.13	20.26	-1.06	0.10	-0.04	0.03	-0.01	0.04	-0.03	0.13	-0.05
	SPs	2.22	-0.36	2.03	-0.13	0.21	-0.07	0.07	-0.02	0.03	-0.01	0.07	-0.02	0.18	-0.06
Navy	SMs	3.80	-0.27	2.40	-0.07	20.56	-0.52	0.29	-0.03	0.27	-0.04	0.06	-0.01	0.13	-0.02
	SPs	3.88	-0.29	2.32	-0.08	0.30	-0.04	0.17	-0.02	0.11	-0.03	0.09	-0.01	0.17	-0.02
Marine Corps	SMs	4.18	-1.04	2.26	-0.24	23.48	-2.02	0.51	-0.12	0.37	-0.19	0.02	-0.02	0.08	-0.05
	SPs	3.63	-0.55	2.43	-0.17	0.11	-0.05	0.29	-0.09	0.36	-0.15	0.06	-0.05	0.02	-0.01
Wave 6															
Army	SMs	4.92	-0.41	2.33	-0.08	26.87	-1.14	0.21	-0.02	0.20	-0.04	0.15	-0.02	0.29	-0.03
	SPs	4.54	-0.28	2.46	-0.07	0.64	-0.12	0.19	-0.03	0.14	-0.03	0.16	-0.02	0.23	-0.03
Air Force	SMs	3.15	-0.70	2.07	-0.12	19.69	-0.84	0.13	-0.04	0.10	-0.05	0.08	-0.04	0.10	-0.04
	SPs	3.04	-0.44	2.14	-0.13	0.28	-0.09	0.12	-0.04	0.07	-0.04	0.07	-0.02	0.29	-0.11
Navy	SMs	3.87	-0.28	2.46	-0.08	20.48	-0.59	0.31	-0.03	0.22	-0.04	0.04	-0.01	0.11	-0.02
	SPs	4.00	-0.27	2.42	-0.09	0.31	-0.04	0.16	-0.02	0.11	-0.02	0.09	-0.01	0.19	-0.02
Marine Corps	SMs	3.46	-0.58	2.12	-0.14	23.16	-1.98	0.45	-0.12	0.23	-0.11	0.03	-0.02	0.17	-0.09
	SPs	3.51	-0.60	2.61	-0.20	0.14	-0.10	0.30	-0.09	0.19	-0.08	0.01	-0.01	0.02	-0.01

Table A.4c—Continued

		Depression[a]		Anxiety[b]		PTSD[c]		Binge Drinking[d]		Problematic Substance Use[e]		Medication Use[f]		Needed Counseling[g]	
		Mean	SE	Mean	SE	Mean	SE	Mean	SE	Mean	SE	Mean	SE	Mean	SE
Wave 7	Army SMs	4.93	-0.37	2.40	-0.08	26.81	-1.06	0.24	-0.02	0.21	-0.03	0.15	-0.02	0.27	-0.03
	Army SPs	4.54	-0.27	2.46	-0.06	0.55	-0.08	0.16	-0.02	0.14	-0.04	0.17	-0.02	0.24	-0.03
	Air Force SMs	3.24	-0.77	1.92	-0.17	21.08	-1.09	0.18	-0.05	0.08	-0.04	0.04	-0.02	0.11	-0.04
	Air Force SPs	3.94	-0.55	2.24	-0.15	0.37	-0.10	0.07	-0.02	0.05	-0.02	0.06	-0.02	0.15	-0.05
	Navy SMs	4.26	-0.29	2.28	-0.06	22.15	-0.75	0.26	-0.02	0.24	-0.03	0.05	-0.01	0.14	-0.02
	Navy SPs	4.05	-0.32	2.35	-0.09	0.33	-0.04	0.17	-0.02	0.11	-0.02	0.13	-0.02	0.20	-0.02
	Marine Corps SMs	3.45	-0.55	2.29	-0.28	25.47	-2.09	0.18	-0.07	0.10	-0.06	0.02	-0.02	0.11	-0.06
	Marine Corps SPs	2.93	-0.55	2.16	-0.14	0.13	-0.07	0.22	-0.07	0.18	-0.07	0.02	-0.01	0.09	-0.05
Wave 8[h]	Army SMs	4.96	-0.38	2.37	-0.08	26.33	-0.99	0.23	-0.03	0.28	-0.05	0.18	-0.02	0.26	-0.03
	Army SPs	4.25	-0.22	2.43	-0.09	0.50	-0.08	0.15	-0.02	0.10	-0.02	0.17	-0.03	0.23	-0.03
	Air Force SMs	3.14	-0.35	1.79	-0.16	21.05	-1.01	0.27	-0.12	0.03	-0.01	0.03	-0.01	0.23	-0.12
	Air Force SPs	3.83	-0.54	2.33	-0.14	0.42	-0.14	0.15	-0.06	0.06	-0.03	0.14	-0.06	0.23	-0.07
	Navy SMs	4.26	-0.29	2.28	-0.06	22.15	-0.75	0.26	-0.02	0.24	-0.03	0.05	-0.01	0.14	-0.02
	Navy SPs	4.05	-0.32	2.35	-0.09	0.33	-0.04	0.17	-0.02	0.11	-0.02	0.13	-0.02	0.20	-0.02
	Marine Corps SMs	4.78	-1.02	2.29	-0.17	27.35	-2.91	0.41	-0.11	0.52	-0.19	0.04	-0.02	0.17	-0.08
	Marine Corps SPs	3.51	-0.77	2.19	-0.13	0.19	-0.07	0.13	-0.04	0.13	-0.05	0.00	0.00	0.03	-0.02

Table A.4c—Continued

		Depression[a]		Anxiety[b]		PTSD[c]		Binge Drinking[d]		Problematic Substance Use[e]		Medication Use[f]		Needed Counseling[g]	
		Mean	SE	Mean	SE	Mean	SE	Mean	SE	Mean	SE	Mean	SE	Mean	SE
Wave 9[h] Army	SMs	6.14	−0.55	2.66	−0.13	28.52	−1.58	0.22	−0.02	0.20	−0.03	0.16	−0.02	0.28	−0.04
	SPs	4.28	−0.20	2.43	−0.06	0.58	−0.07	0.18	−0.03	0.13	−0.02	0.18	−0.03	0.23	−0.03
Air Force	SMs	3.95	−0.61	2.19	−0.19	23.34	−2.11	0.21	−0.08	0.15	−0.08	0.02	−0.01	0.23	−0.12
	SPs	3.48	−0.43	2.25	−0.11	0.37	−0.12	0.11	−0.03	0.03	−0.02	0.12	−0.06	0.35	−0.11
Navy	SMs	na	na	na	na	na	na	na	na	na	na	na	na	na	na
	SPs	na	na	na	na	na	na	na	na	na	na	na	na	na	na
Marine Corps	SMs	3.07	−0.66	1.85	−0.16	23.46	−1.97	0.38	−0.11	0.37	−0.12	0.00	0.00	0.05	−0.03
	SPs	3.66	−0.99	2.28	−0.15	0.05	−0.03	0.31	−0.09	0.37	−0.29	0.06	−0.05	0.06	−0.05

NOTE: Data are weighted.

[a] Higher scores=more depressive symptoms. Range: 0–24.

[b] Higher scores=more anxiety. Mean subscale score range: 1–6.

[c] Higher scores=more PTSD symptoms. Range: 17–85 for service member, 0–4 for spouse.

[d] Percentage reporting binge drinking (5+ drinks for men; 4+ drinks for women).

[e] Higher scores=more problematic substance use. Range: 0–7.

[f] Percentage reporting use of medication for a mental health problem.

[g] Percentage reporting need for treatment for mental health treatment.

[h] The Navy sample does not have data at this wave by design (na=not applicable).

Table A.4d
Military Integration Outcome Means by Study Wave and Service (Active Component Only)

			Job Satisfaction Scale[a]		Military Commitment Scale[b]		Retention Intentions[c]	
			Mean	SE	Mean	SE	Mean	SE
Baseline	Army	SMs	3.84	−0.10	3.60	−0.07	4.24	−0.06
		SPs	3.84	−0.08	3.98	−0.06	4.38	−0.04
	Air Force	SMs	4.59	−0.12	3.82	−0.23	4.45	−0.09
		SPs	3.82	−0.30	4.02	−0.18	4.42	−0.12
	Navy	SMs	4.13	−0.07	3.66	−0.06	4.26	−0.04
		SPs	3.99	−0.06	3.94	−0.07	4.43	−0.04
	Marine Corps	SMs	4.44	−0.15	4.21	−0.12	4.64	−0.07
		SPs	4.07	−0.17	4.30	−0.14	4.50	−0.13
Wave 2	Army	SMs	3.58	−0.12	3.33	−0.09	3.84	−0.07
		SPs	3.74	−0.09	3.81	−0.06	4.04	−0.04
	Air Force	SMs	4.04	−0.26	3.90	−0.15	4.20	−0.09
		SPs	4.05	−0.17	4.28	−0.11	4.08	−0.10
	Navy	SMs	3.81	−0.10	3.59	−0.08	3.92	−0.07
		SPs	3.94	−0.09	4.02	−0.06	3.99	−0.06
	Marine Corps	SMs	4.22	−0.17	4.16	−0.15	4.30	−0.12
		SPs	3.93	−0.24	4.14	−0.19	4.15	−0.16
Wave 3	Army	SMs	3.49	−0.12	3.36	−0.09	3.72	−0.09
		SPs	3.78	−0.09	3.90	−0.06	4.04	−0.05
	Air Force	SMs	4.01	−0.15	3.92	−0.14	4.11	−0.10
		SPs	3.83	−0.22	4.18	−0.12	4.26	−0.16
	Navy	SMs	3.86	−0.09	3.68	−0.07	3.86	−0.07
		SPs	3.98	−0.07	3.99	−0.06	3.99	−0.06
	Marine Corps	SMs	4.35	−0.21	4.37	−0.17	3.86	−0.50
		SPs	3.97	−0.28	4.25	−0.18	4.37	−0.13
Wave 4	Army	SMs	3.47	−0.12	3.38	−0.10	3.80	−0.08
		SPs	3.65	−0.09	3.94	−0.06	3.99	−0.05
	Air Force	SMs	4.09	−0.19	3.89	−0.07	4.00	−0.09
		SPs	4.18	−0.12	4.33	−0.14	4.26	−0.11
	Navy	SMs	3.94	−0.09	3.66	−0.08	3.94	−0.06
		SPs	4.02	−0.06	3.99	−0.05	4.02	−0.05
	Marine Corps	SMs	4.49	−0.18	3.95	−0.19	4.35	−0.15
		SPs	4.31	−0.17	4.38	−0.16	4.33	−0.11
Wave 5	Army	SMs	3.43	−0.14	3.50	−0.11	3.72	−0.09
		SPs	3.76	−0.10	3.95	−0.06	3.99	−0.05
	Air Force	SMs	4.02	−0.25	3.98	−0.14	4.08	−0.08
		SPs	3.70	−0.22	4.21	−0.17	4.14	−0.12
	Navy	SMs	3.93	−0.08	3.69	−0.07	3.96	−0.05
		SPs	4.00	−0.07	4.00	−0.06	4.00	−0.06
	Marine Corps	SMs	4.32	−0.19	4.09	−0.14	4.21	−0.12
		SPs	4.15	−0.23	4.19	−0.16	4.23	−0.13

Table A.4d—Continued

			Job Satisfaction Scale[a]		Military Commitment Scale[b]		Retention Intentions[c]	
			Mean	SE	Mean	SE	Mean	SE
Wave 6	Army	SMs	3.45	−0.12	3.48	−0.09	3.65	−0.08
		SPs	3.84	−0.10	3.93	−0.06	3.97	−0.05
	Air Force	SMs	4.00	−0.26	4.17	−0.18	4.14	−0.11
		SPs	4.13	−0.12	4.41	−0.13	4.28	−0.15
	Navy	SMs	3.78	−0.09	3.76	−0.07	3.91	−0.06
		SPs	3.95	−0.07	3.94	−0.06	4.02	−0.05
	Marine Corps	SMs	4.38	−0.22	3.92	−0.15	4.28	−0.17
		SPs	4.12	−0.18	4.34	−0.13	4.18	−0.15
Wave 7	Army	SMs	3.43	−0.14	3.65	−0.11	3.72	−0.07
		SPs	3.78	−0.08	3.89	−0.06	4.00	−0.05
	Air Force	SMs	4.31	−0.20	4.31	−0.21	4.31	−0.19
		SPs	3.75	−0.19	4.12	−0.19	3.93	−0.08
	Navy	SMs	3.89	−0.09	3.90	−0.06	3.96	−0.06
		SPs	3.98	−0.08	4.02	−0.06	4.04	−0.06
	Marine Corps	SMs	3.93	−0.26	3.55	−0.37	4.36	−0.15
		SPs	4.08	−0.19	4.18	−0.17	4.29	−0.13
Wave 8[d]	Army	SMs	3.56	−0.11	3.65	−0.10	3.82	−0.06
		SPs	3.77	−0.09	3.89	−0.05	3.92	−0.05
	Air Force	SMs	4.28	−0.23	3.96	−0.06	4.34	−0.19
		SPs	3.93	−0.19	4.12	−0.13	3.93	−0.13
	Navy	SMs	3.89	−0.09	3.90	−0.06	3.96	−0.06
		SPs	3.98	−0.08	4.02	−0.06	4.04	−0.06
	Marine Corps	SMs	4.05	−0.21	4.00	−0.18	4.06	−0.18
		SPs	3.94	−0.17	4.11	−0.18	4.21	−0.12
Wave 9[d]	Army	SMs	3.35	−0.11	3.63	−0.09	3.76	−0.07
		SPs	3.71	−0.09	3.97	−0.06	4.00	−0.05
	Air Force	SMs	3.84	−0.50	4.12	−0.15	3.53	−0.35
		SPs	3.90	−0.26	4.18	−0.11	3.99	−0.10
	Navy	SMs	na	na	na	na	na	na
		SPs	na	na	na	na	na	na
	Marine Corps	SMs	4.25	−0.20	3.91	−0.22	4.34	−0.12
		SPs	3.75	−0.25	4.17	−0.14	4.16	−0.15

NOTE: Data are weighted.

[a] Higher scores=more satisfaction. Range: 1–5.

[b] Higher scores=more commitment. Range: 1–5.

[c] Higher scores=strong preference for continued military service. Range: 1–5.

[d] The Navy sample does not have data at this wave by design (na=not applicable).

Table A.5a
Child Well-Being Outcomes by Study Wave and Child Age

		Item/Scale Range	Anxiety[a] Mean	SE	Depression Screener[b] Mean	SE	SDQ Emotional Problems[c] Mean	SE	SDQ Conduct Problems[d] Mean	SE	SDQ Hyperactivity[e] Mean	SE	SDQ Peer Problems[f] Mean	SE	SDQ Prosocial Behavior[g] Mean	SE	SDQ Total Difficulties[h] Mean	SE	Medication Use[i] Mean	SE	Needed Counseling[j] Mean	SE
Baseline	Overall Sample	Teen	1.89	-0.20	0.60	-0.10	2.51	-0.24	1.01	-0.11	3.01	-0.23	2.33	-0.22	8.09	-0.23	8.84	-0.67	0.08	-0.02	0.14	-0.03
		Child	1.85	-0.35	0.27	-0.05	1.74	-0.24	1.10	-0.11	3.17	-0.16	1.86	-0.22	8.05	-0.46	7.87	-0.43	0.08	-0.02	0.20	-0.07
	Study Deployment	Teen	1.26	-0.12	0.41	-0.08	1.81	-0.21	1.25	-0.13	3.05	-0.26	1.78	-0.19	8.29	-0.21	7.89	-0.61	0.10	-0.04	0.14	-0.04
		Child	1.71	-0.14	0.21	-0.04	1.58	-0.13	0.98	-0.10	3.18	-0.15	1.67	-0.12	8.53	-0.11	7.41	-0.32	0.06	-0.01	0.10	-0.02
	No Study Deployment	Teen	1.36	-0.19	0.41	-0.08	1.90	-0.24	1.39	-0.18	3.31	-0.22	1.90	-0.21	8.54	-0.22	8.51	-0.73	0.08	-0.02	0.06	-0.02
		Child	1.53	-0.14	0.26	-0.04	1.76	-0.14	1.03	-0.11	3.38	-0.17	1.88	-0.16	8.35	-0.14	8.06	-0.33	0.06	-0.01	0.09	-0.02
Wave 2	Overall Sample	Teen	1.89	-0.20	0.60	-0.10	2.51	-0.24	1.01	-0.11	3.01	-0.23	2.33	-0.22	8.09	-0.23	8.84	-0.67	0.08	-0.02	0.14	-0.03
		Child	1.85	-0.35	0.27	-0.05	1.74	-0.24	1.10	-0.11	3.17	-0.16	1.86	-0.22	8.05	-0.46	7.87	-0.43	0.08	-0.02	0.20	-0.07
	Study Deployment	Teen	1.86	-0.29	0.65	-0.12	2.40	-0.31	1.62	-0.20	3.22	-0.28	2.07	-0.20	7.98	-0.27	9.31	-0.75	0.15	-0.05	0.22	-0.06
		Child	1.53	-0.12	0.34	-0.08	1.41	-0.18	1.13	-0.17	3.08	-0.22	1.70	-0.13	8.05	-0.17	7.30	-0.54	0.10	-0.02	0.13	-0.03
	No Study Deployment	Teen	1.43	-0.24	0.62	-0.20	1.88	-0.30	1.23	-0.34	3.42	-0.49	2.07	-0.41	8.39	-0.26	8.60	-1.37	0.05	-0.02	0.04	-0.02
		Child	1.42	-0.12	0.28	-0.06	1.45	-0.12	1.14	-0.10	3.21	-0.17	1.49	-0.13	8.24	-0.14	7.29	-0.39	0.09	-0.02	0.11	-0.02
Wave 3	Overall Sample	Teen	1.89	-0.20	0.60	-0.10	2.51	-0.24	1.01	-0.11	3.01	-0.23	2.33	-0.22	8.09	-0.23	8.84	-0.67	0.08	-0.02	0.14	-0.03
		Child	1.85	-0.35	0.27	-0.05	1.74	-0.24	1.10	-0.11	3.17	-0.16	1.86	-0.22	8.05	-0.46	7.87	-0.43	0.08	-0.02	0.20	-0.07
	Study Deployment	Teen	1.77	-0.17	0.67	-0.12	2.43	-0.19	1.29	-0.13	3.09	-0.25	2.09	-0.17	7.94	-0.20	8.90	-0.50	0.16	-0.05	0.21	-0.05
		Child	1.63	-0.12	0.45	-0.08	1.99	-0.17	1.22	-0.15	3.49	-0.22	1.87	-0.14	7.90	-0.19	8.56	-0.52	0.07	-0.02	0.16	-0.03
	No Study Deployment	Teen	1.30	-0.23	0.29	-0.07	1.55	-0.29	1.28	-0.22	2.97	-0.29	2.25	-0.44	8.12	-0.29	8.05	-0.74	0.06	-0.02	0.06	-0.02
		Child	1.48	-0.18	0.33	-0.08	1.54	-0.19	1.38	-0.15	3.47	-0.21	1.68	-0.16	7.69	-0.25	8.05	-0.38	0.06	-0.01	0.14	-0.03
Wave 4	Overall Sample	Teen	1.89	-0.20	0.60	-0.10	2.51	-0.24	1.01	-0.11	3.01	-0.23	2.33	-0.22	8.09	-0.23	8.84	-0.67	0.08	-0.02	0.14	-0.03
		Child	1.85	-0.35	0.27	-0.05	1.74	-0.24	1.10	-0.11	3.17	-0.16	1.86	-0.22	8.05	-0.46	7.87	-0.43	0.08	-0.02	0.20	-0.07
	Study Deployment	Teen	1.47	-0.18	0.63	-0.12	2.05	-0.21	1.19	-0.15	2.93	-0.27	1.90	-0.21	8.08	-0.21	8.06	-0.62	0.17	-0.05	0.15	-0.04
		Child	1.68	-0.24	0.39	-0.10	1.82	-0.25	1.17	-0.18	3.48	-0.30	2.01	-0.20	8.32	-0.21	8.45	-0.73	0.11	-0.03	0.15	-0.04
	No Study Deployment	Teen	1.38	-0.22	0.47	-0.09	1.81	-0.30	1.22	-0.22	3.22	-0.35	1.99	-0.16	8.43	-0.20	8.23	-0.71	0.07	-0.02	0.07	-0.02
		Child	1.25	-0.17	0.25	-0.06	1.19	-0.17	1.39	-0.23	3.17	-0.40	1.95	-0.23	7.90	-0.25	7.71	-0.78	0.05	-0.02	0.14	-0.05

Table A.5a—Continued

Wave	Group	Item/Scale Range	Anxiety[a] Mean	Anxiety[a] SE	Depression Screener[b] Mean	Depression Screener[b] SE	SDQ Emotional Problems[c] Mean	SDQ Emotional Problems[c] SE	SDQ Conduct Problems[d] Mean	SDQ Conduct Problems[d] SE	SDQ Hyperactivity[e] Mean	SDQ Hyperactivity[e] SE	SDQ Peer Problems[f] Mean	SDQ Peer Problems[f] SE	SDQ Prosocial Behavior[g] Mean	SDQ Prosocial Behavior[g] SE	SDQ Total Difficulties[h] Mean	SDQ Total Difficulties[h] SE	Medication Use[i] Mean	Medication Use[i] SE	Needed Counseling[j] Mean	Needed Counseling[j] SE
Wave 5	Overall Sample	Teen	1.89	-0.20	0.60	-0.10	2.51	-0.24	1.01	-0.11	3.01	-0.23	2.33	-0.22	8.09	-0.23	8.84	-0.67	0.08	-0.02	0.14	-0.03
		Child	1.85	-0.35	0.27	-0.05	1.74	-0.24	1.10	-0.11	3.17	-0.16	1.86	-0.22	8.05	-0.46	7.87	-0.43	0.08	-0.02	0.20	-0.07
	Study Deployment	Teen	1.69	-0.21	0.46	-0.10	2.35	-0.24	1.33	-0.15	3.03	-0.31	2.00	-0.19	8.29	-0.21	8.68	-0.63	0.11	-0.04	0.12	-0.04
		Child	1.45	-0.18	0.24	-0.07	1.48	-0.18	1.45	-0.19	3.46	-0.28	1.92	-0.17	8.06	-0.24	8.08	-0.64	0.10	-0.03	0.17	-0.04
	No Study Deployment	Teen	1.26	-0.24	0.37	-0.08	2.43	-0.41	1.13	-0.17	3.24	-0.31	1.88	-0.33	8.09	-0.43	8.69	-0.91	0.07	-0.02	0.06	-0.02
		Child	1.23	-0.16	0.37	-0.09	1.44	-0.20	1.44	-0.27	3.26	-0.27	2.11	-0.25	7.82	-0.25	8.25	-0.78	0.06	-0.02	0.09	-0.03
Wave 6	Overall Sample	Teen	1.89	-0.20	0.60	-0.10	2.51	-0.24	1.01	-0.11	3.01	-0.23	2.33	-0.22	8.09	-0.23	8.84	-0.67	0.08	-0.02	0.14	-0.03
		Child	1.85	-0.35	0.27	-0.05	1.74	-0.24	1.10	-0.11	3.17	-0.16	1.86	-0.22	8.05	-0.46	7.87	-0.43	0.08	-0.02	0.20	-0.07
	Study Deployment	Teen	1.49	-0.24	0.53	-0.15	2.16	-0.27	1.31	-0.15	2.91	-0.28	2.21	-0.18	7.60	-0.36	8.59	-0.58	0.14	-0.04	0.16	-0.06
		Child	1.52	-0.16	0.22	-0.04	1.48	-0.16	1.23	-0.14	3.41	-0.22	1.76	-0.13	8.08	-0.16	7.84	-0.52	0.07	-0.02	0.16	-0.03
	No Study Deployment	Teen	1.61	-0.18	0.56	-0.11	2.20	-0.28	1.16	-0.15	3.68	-0.25	2.82	-0.48	7.28	-0.76	9.86	-0.87	0.15	-0.09	0.06	-0.02
		Child	1.32	-0.12	0.24	-0.04	1.47	-0.15	1.17	-0.12	3.03	-0.17	1.89	-0.13	7.99	-0.15	7.57	-0.45	0.08	-0.02	0.12	-0.02
Wave 7	Overall Sample	Teen	1.89	-0.20	0.60	-0.10	2.51	-0.24	1.01	-0.11	3.01	-0.23	2.33	-0.22	8.09	-0.23	8.84	-0.67	0.08	-0.02	0.14	-0.03
		Child	1.85	-0.35	0.27	-0.05	1.74	-0.24	1.10	-0.11	3.17	-0.16	1.86	-0.22	8.05	-0.46	7.87	-0.43	0.08	-0.02	0.20	-0.07
	Study Deployment	Teen	1.78	-0.22	0.48	-0.09	2.51	-0.29	1.20	-0.25	3.07	-0.31	2.52	-0.24	7.85	-0.27	9.29	-0.87	0.15	-0.04	0.15	-0.04
		Child	1.79	-0.18	0.27	-0.05	1.82	-0.14	1.15	-0.16	3.12	-0.27	1.97	-0.17	8.20	-0.19	8.06	-0.56	0.13	-0.03	0.13	-0.02
	No Study Deployment	Teen	1.67	-0.27	0.46	-0.11	2.12	-0.32	1.21	-0.24	3.14	-0.37	2.37	-0.26	8.02	-0.20	8.84	-0.85	0.06	-0.02	0.08	-0.03
		Child	1.33	-0.14	0.43	-0.16	1.84	-0.43	1.17	-0.13	3.20	-0.16	2.08	-0.17	7.96	-0.34	8.33	-0.61	0.07	-0.02	0.09	-0.02
Wave 8[h]	Overall Sample	Teen	1.89	-0.20	0.60	-0.10	2.51	-0.24	1.01	-0.11	3.01	-0.23	2.33	-0.22	8.09	-0.23	8.84	-0.67	0.08	-0.02	0.14	-0.03
		Child	1.85	-0.35	0.27	-0.05	1.74	-0.24	1.10	-0.11	3.17	-0.16	1.86	-0.22	8.05	-0.46	7.87	-0.43	0.08	-0.02	0.20	-0.07
	Study Deployment	Teen	1.75	-0.26	0.43	-0.10	2.45	-0.33	1.33	-0.15	2.92	-0.38	2.08	-0.24	8.14	-0.29	8.78	-0.91	0.12	-0.04	0.14	-0.05
		Child	1.45	-0.14	0.31	-0.11	1.75	-0.22	1.06	-0.17	3.15	-0.27	2.26	-0.19	8.30	-0.22	8.20	-0.62	0.09	-0.02	0.16	-0.04
	No Study Deployment	Teen	1.74	-0.32	0.65	-0.16	2.51	-0.44	0.99	-0.16	3.28	-0.37	2.22	-0.28	8.56	-0.25	9.00	-1.07	0.11	-0.04	0.20	-0.06
		Child	1.51	-0.20	0.26	-0.06	1.65	-0.18	1.24	-0.16	2.86	-0.22	1.77	-0.21	8.05	-0.37	7.52	-0.44	0.06	-0.02	0.09	-0.02

Table A.5a—Continued

	Item/Scale Range	Anxiety[a]		Depression Screener[b]		SDQ Emotional Problems[c]		SDQ Conduct Problems[d]		SDQ Hyperactivity[e]		SDQ Peer Problems[f]		SDQ Prosocial Behavior[g]		SDQ Total Difficulties[h]		Medication Use[i]		Needed Counseling[j]	
		Mean	SE	Mean	SE	Mean	SE	Mean	SE	Mean	SE	Mean	SE	Mean	SE	Mean	SE	Mean	SE	Mean	SE
Wave 9[h]																					
Overall Sample	Teen	1.89	−0.20	0.60	−0.10	2.51	−0.24	1.01	−0.11	3.01	−0.23	2.33	−0.22	8.09	−0.23	8.84	−0.67	0.08	−0.02	0.14	−0.03
	Child	1.85	−0.35	0.27	−0.05	1.74	−0.24	1.10	−0.11	3.17	−0.16	1.86	−0.22	8.05	−0.46	7.87	−0.43	0.08	−0.02	0.20	−0.07
Study Deployment	Teen	1.80	−0.29	0.72	−0.13	2.30	−0.24	1.12	−0.15	2.80	−0.27	2.27	−0.21	7.68	−0.50	8.49	−0.52	0.12	−0.04	0.11	−0.04
	Child	1.53	−0.16	0.23	−0.05	1.69	−0.17	1.07	−0.17	3.19	−0.23	2.11	−0.21	8.46	−0.18	8.06	−0.61	0.11	−0.03	0.13	−0.03
No Study Deployment	Teen	1.93	−0.28	0.54	−0.14	2.63	−0.35	0.94	−0.14	3.13	−0.33	2.37	−0.33	8.32	−0.20	9.04	−1.01	0.06	−0.02	0.16	−0.05
	Child	1.92	−0.42	0.27	−0.07	1.76	−0.29	1.10	−0.13	3.17	−0.20	1.80	−0.27	7.96	−0.55	7.83	−0.51	0.07	−0.02	0.22	−0.09

NOTE: Data are weighted. Child=children ages 11 and older for whom the spouse reports. Teen=children ages 11 and older who complete their own survey.

[a] Higher score=greater anxiety symptoms. Range 0–10.

[b] Higher scores=more depression symptoms. Range 0–3.

[c] Higher scores=more emotional problems. Range 0–9.

[d] Higher scores=more conduct problems. Range 0–9.

[e] Higher scores=greater hyperactivity. Range: 0–10.

[f] Higher scores=more peer problems. Range: 0–8.

[g] Higher scores=more prosocial behavior. Range: 0–10.

[h] Higher scores=more difficulties. Range: 0–32.

[i] Percentage reporting use of medication for a mental health problem.

[j] Percentage reporting need for treatment for mental health treatment.

[k] The Navy sample does not have data at this wave by design.